SOURCEBOOK OF SOCIAL SUPPORT AND PERSONALITY

THE PLENUM SERIES IN SOCIAL/CLINICAL PSYCHOLOGY

Series Editors: C. R. Snyder

University of Kansas
Lawrence, Kansas

Current Volumes in the Series:

AGGRESSION
Biological, Developmental, and Social Perspectives
Edited by Seymour Feshbach and Jolanta Zagrodzka

AGGRESSIVE BEHAVIOR
Current Perspectives
Edited by L. Rowell Huesmann

COERCION AND AGGRESSIVE COMMUNITY TREATMENT
A New Frontier in Mental Health Law
Edited by Deborah L. Dennis and John Monahan

THE ECOLOGY OF AGGRESSION
Arnold P. Goldstein

EFFICACY, AGENCY, AND SELF-ESTEEM
Edited by Michael H. Kernis

HUMAN LEARNED HELPLESSNESS
A Coping Perspective
Mario Mikulincer

PATHOLOGICAL SELF-CRITICISM
Assessment and Treatment
Raymond M. Bergner

PROCRASTINATION AND TASK AVOIDANCE
Theory, Research, and Treatment
Joseph R. Ferrari, Judith L. Johnson, and William G. McCown

THE PSYCHOLOGY OF VANDALISM
Arnold P. Goldstein

SELF-EFFICACY, ADAPTATION, AND ADJUSTMENT
Theory, Research, and Application
Edited by James E. Maddux

SOCIAL COGNITIVE PSYCHOLOGY
History and Current Domains
David F. Barone, James E. Maddux, and C. R. Snyder

SOURCEBOOK OF SOCIAL SUPPORT AND PERSONALITY
Edited by Gregory R. Pierce, Brian Lakey, Irwin G. Sarason, and Barbara R. Sarason

A Continuation Order Plan is available for this series. A continuation order will bring delivery of each new volume immediately upon publication. Volumes are billed only upon actual shipment. For further information please contact the publisher.

SOURCEBOOK OF SOCIAL SUPPORT AND PERSONALITY

EDITED BY

GREGORY R. PIERCE
Hamilton College
Clinton, New York

BRIAN LAKEY
Wayne State University
Detroit, Michigan

AND

IRWIN G. SARASON AND
BARBARA R. SARASON
University of Washington
Seattle, Washington

PLENUM PRESS • NEW YORK AND LONDON

Library of Congress Cataloging-in-Publication Data

Sourcebook of social support and personality / edited by Gregory R.
 Pierce ... [et al.].
      p.   cm. -- (The Plenum series in social/clinical psychology)
   Includes bibliographical references and index.
   ISBN 0-306-45535-8
    1. Social networks--Psychological aspects. 2. Social interaction-
 -Psychological aspects. 3. Personality and social intelligence.
 4. Personality and emotions.   I. Pierce, Gregory R. II. Series.
 HM131.S61869 1997
 302--dc21   97-17811
                                                                 CIP

ISBN 0-306-45535-8

© 1997 Plenum Press, New York
A Division of Plenum Publishing Corporation
233 Spring Street, New York, N. Y. 10013

http://www.plenum.com

All rights reserved

10 9 8 7 6 5 4 3 2 1

Printed in the United States of America

CONTRIBUTORS

MARK W. BALDWIN, Department of Psychology, University of Winnipeg, Winnipeg, Manitoba, Canada R3B 2E9

KIM BARTHOLOMEW, Department of Psychology, Simon Fraser University, Burnaby, British Columbia, Canada V5A 1S6

STEVEN R. H. BEACH, Department of Psychology, University of Georgia, Athens, Georgia 30602-3013

LIZA BONIN, Department of Psychology, University of Texas at Austin, Austin, Texas 78712

THOMAS N. BRADBURY, Department of Psychology, University of California at Los Angeles, Los Angeles, California 90024-1563

REBECCA J. COBB, Department of Psychology, Simon Fraser University, Burnaby, British Columbia, Canada V5A 1S6

LAWRENCE H. COHEN, Psychology Department, University of Delaware, Newark, Delaware 19716

PATRICIA M. COLBY, Department of Psychology, University of California at Davis, Davis, California 95616

REBECCA COLLINS RAND, 1700 Main Street, P.O. Box 2138, Santa Monica, California 90407-2138

ADAM DI PAULA, Department of Psychology, University of British Columbia, Vancouver, British Columbia, Canada V6T 1Z4

JANNA BRITTAIN DREW, Department of Psychology, Wayne State University, Detroit, Michigan 48202

ROBERT A. EMMONS, Department of Psychology, University of California at Davis, Davis, California 95616

IAN H. GOTLIB, Department of Psychology, Stanford University, Stanford, California 94305

IGOR GRANT, Department of Psychiatry, University of California at San Diego, La Jolla, California 92093-0622

SHEILA GROSS, Department of Psychology, Bucknell University, Lewisburg, Pennsylvania 17837

TANYA A. HETTLER, Psychology Department, University of Delaware, Newark, Delaware 19716

CHARLES J. HOLAHAN, Department of Psychology, University of Texas at Austin, Austin, Texas 78712

HELENE J. JOSEPH, Department of Psychology, Hamilton College, Clinton, New York 13323

ROBERT M. KAPLAN, Division of Health Care Sciences 0622, Department of Family and Preventive Medicine, University of California at San Diego, La Jolla, California 92093-0622

JENNIFER KATZ, Department of Psychology, University of Georgia, Athens, Georgia 30602-3013

KEUNHO KEEFE, Reiss-Davis Child Study Center, Los Angeles, California 90034

GIORA KEINAN, Department of Psychology, Tel-Aviv University, Tel Aviv 69978, Israel

DAVID KERNER, SDSU/UCSD Joint Doctoral Program in Clinical Psychology, University of California at San Diego, La Jolla, California 92093-0622

NEAL KRAUSE, Department of Health Behavior and Health Education, School of Public Health, University of Michigan, 1420 Washington Heights, Ann Arbor, Michigan 48109-2029

BRIAN LAKEY, Department of Psychology, Wayne State University, Detroit, Michigan 48202

JOHN E. LYDON, Department of Psychology, McGill University, Montreal, Quebec, Canada H3A 1B1

ERIC S. MANKOWSKI, The Center for Health Care Evaluation, Veterans Affairs Health Care System and Stanford University, School of Medicine, Palo Alto, California 94025

RUDOLF H. MOOS, Center for Health Care Evaluation, Veterans Affairs Health Care System and Stanford University Medical Center, Palo Alto, California 94025

LISA B. MYERS, Department of Psychology, Ohio State University, Columbus, Ohio 43210-1222

ARIE NADLER, Department of Psychology, Tel-Aviv University, Tel-Aviv 69978, Israel

MICHAEL D. NEWCOMB, Division of Counseling Psychology, University of Southern California, Los Angeles, California 90089-0031

CRYSTAL L. PARK, Department of Psychology, Miami University, Oxford, Ohio 45056

LAURI A. PASCH, Department of Pediatrics, University of California at San Francisco, San Francisco, California 94143-0844

THOMAS L. PATTERSON, Department of Psychiatry, University of California at San Diego, La Jolla, California 92093-0622

GREGORY R. PIERCE, Department of Psychology, Hamilton College, Clinton, New York 13323

TAMARHA PIERCE, Department of Psychology, McGill University, Montreal, Quebec, Canada H3A 1B1

JENNIFER A. POOLE, Department of Psychology, Simon Fraser University, Burnaby, British Columbia, Canada V5A 1S6

MARY E. PROCIDANO, Department of Psychology, Fordham University, Bronx, New York 10458

J. T. PTACEK, Department of Psychology, Bucknell University, Lewisburg, Pennsylvania 17837

JOHN E. ROBERTS, Department of Psychology, State University of New York, Buffalo, New York 14260-4110

RICHARD M. RYAN, Department of Psychology, University of Rochester, Rochester, New York 14627

BARBARA R. SARASON, Department of Psychology, University of Washington, Seattle, Washington 98195

IRWIN G. SARASON, Department of Psychology, University of Washington, Seattle, Washington 98195

DAVID A. SMITH, Department of Psychology, Ohio State University, Columbus, Ohio 43210-1222

WALANDA WALKER SMITH, Department of Psychology, Fordham University, Bronx, New York 10458

JESSICA SOLKY BUTZEL, Department of Psychology, University of Rochester, Rochester, New York 14627

KIERAN T. SULLIVAN, Department of Psychology, University of California at Los Angeles, Los Angeles, California 90024-1563

ROBERT S. WYER JR., Department of Psychology, University of Illinois at Urbana–Champaign, Champaign, Illinois 61820

PREFACE

The impetus for this book grew out of the need to take stock of the accomplishments and challenges of research and theory on social support, especially that which has focused on personality and social support. The accomplishments are numerous, as attested by the chapters that make up this volume. A substantial literature has accumulated indicating that personality may influence the course of support-related transactions, how these transactions are encoded and remembered, as well as the impact that such processes may have on outcomes. Acknowledgement of these accomplishments must be tempered by the recognition that several conceptual and methodological issues must be addressed before further advancement is likely. The chapters in this book present an impressively diverse discussion of the role of personality in social support processes and represent an important step in tackling these challenges.

The sourcebook is divided into three parts. The first addresses the conceptualization of social support, its theoretical links to related constructs, and methodological issues. The chapters in this part reflect two critical needs in theory development on social support. First is recognition of the fact that the construct of social support is multifaceted and complex; attempts to define the support construct, therefore, must not only distinguish among the several components that comprise the more general construct of support, but also specify the links among these elements. Second, social support research has been pursued largely independently of other topics within psychology and related disciplines. Thus, social support theories are needed that embed the construct in broader theoretical frameworks that incorporate observations established by researchers in other domains.

In the second part, personality processes linking that social support construct to mental and physical health are explored. Social support researchers have been criticized for adopting a largely atheoretical approach to the study of social support phenomena. By specifying mechanisms to account for observed associations between social support on the one hand, and physical health and well-being on the other, the scholars represented in this section take an important step in advancing social support theory by addressing the psychological processes underlying these connections. Several of the authors report findings from new studies to illustrate empirical approaches to explore proposed mechanism.

The third part of the volume focuses on connections between social support and social behavior. For nearly a decade, researchers have noted that the links between perceptions of social support and transactions among network members are modest and are not well understood. The chapters in this part underscore the point that potentially supportive transactions represent interactions between relationship participants' personal dispositions and the situational contexts in which they respond to each other.

Our confidence in the ability of science to advance our understanding of important topics has been greatly strengthened as a consequence of our interactions with the numerous scholars who have contributed to this volume. Their efforts to organize and synthesize much of what is currently known about the topic of social support, and to chart new paths for further work in the field, reflect a substantial achicvement. Our own appreciation for the topic of social support has been greatly enhanced by the thoughtful and stimulating analyses offered by the contributing authors. We hope readers of this volume will share this experience as well.

ACKNOWLEDGMENTS

We wish to thank several individuals and institutions for making this sourcebook a reality. Hamilton College generously provided sabbatical leave to Gregory Pierce, which greatly facilitated the development of the book. In addition, several former Hamilton students, two of whom are currently in graduate school, collaborated in writing chapters for the book: Helene Joseph and Jessica Solky Butzel. Their contributions serve to illustrate the active role of young — as well as estabished — scholars in the social support field. Tracy Hildebrand, a current Hamilton student, invested considerable energy and time in helping to complete the indexes.

We also wish to thank Eliot Werner, Executive Editor at Plenum, for encouraging the pursuit of this volume; his support and assistance aided greatly in its production.

CONTENTS

CONCEPTUAL AND METHODOLOGICAL ISSUES IN RESEARCH ON SOCIAL SUPPORT AND PERSONALITY

CHAPTER 1

PERSONALITY AND
SOCIAL SUPPORT PROCESSES
A CONCEPTUAL OVERVIEW

GREGORY R. PIERCE, BRIAN LAKEY, IRWIN G. SARASON,
BARBARA R. SARASON, AND HELENE J. JOSEPH

Investigators at the intersection of personality and social support research have developed a number of theoretical models to account for the role of a broad range of individual differences variables in social support processes. Such efforts have met with considerable success and underscore the notion that personality serves as an important influence on social behavior. Because other chapters in the present volume provide excellent summaries of these models, our goal in the present chapter is to take a broad view of how social support and personality research fit together, as well as to identify some of the key conceptual and methodological issues that need to be addressed in order to make continued progress.

Our chapter is organized into three parts. In the first, we identify the major ways in which personality factors may be important in social support. For example, two issues that have received considerable attention by social support researchers are whether social support is a property of the individual or of the environment, and whether personality characteristics can account for the relation between social support, health, and well-being. In the second part, we discuss how social support and personality research can contribute to each other. Until recently, social support research has

GREGORY R. PIERCE AND HELENE J. JOSEPH • Department of Psychology, Hamilton College, Clinton, New York 13323.   BRIAN LAKEY • Department of Psychology, Wayne State University, Detroit, Michigan 48202. IRWIN G. SARASON AND BARBARA R. SARASON • Department of Psychology, University of Washington, Seattle, Washington 98195.

Sourcebook of Social Support and Personality, edited by Gregory R. Pierce, Brian Lakey, Irwin G. Sarason, and Barbara R. Sarason. Plenum Press, New York, 1997.

tended to develop in a vacuum, making few direct references to pertinent disciplines such as psychology, psychiatry, sociology, and communications studies. Likewise, social support research has not been integrated into a more comprehensive knowledge of human behavior. However, we believe that the field of social support can gain substantially from drawing more heavily on relevant theory and findings from these areas, and that what we have learned about social support can benefit these disciplines. In the final part, we identify several theoretical and methodological needs for further research and suggest several lines of research that might make important contributions in the future.

THE ROLE OF PERSONALITY IN SOCIAL SUPPORT PROCESSES: A BLESSING OR A CURSE?

In thinking about the relationship between social support and personality research, it is helpful to review the historical development of the social support construct. The concept of social support grew out of early epidemiological studies suggesting that the presence of others was positively related to health and well-being (e.g., Caplan, 1974; Cobb, 1976; Dean & Lin, 1977). Most of the investigators who contributed to this work conceptualized social support as a property of the social environment. To them, social support was a promising new environmental construct. Many of these scholars who contributed to the explosion of social support research in the late 1970s and early 1980s were associated with community psychology (e.g., Barrera, Heller, Hirsch, Sandler, Swindle), and many important early studies were published in the *American Journal of Community Psychology*. Understandably, then, much of this early social support research reflected the major focus of community psychology: the investigation of environmental and social influences on behavior. Thus, early efforts to define social support focused on the exchange of social provisions—a feature of the social environment. Even though virtually all of the new social support measures relied upon self-report, researchers initially assumed that these measures reflected the objective provision of a variety of social resources, including assistance, guidance, and emotional sustenance. But as research on such self-report measures of social support proliferated, investigators noted that instruments focusing on respondents' subjective appraisals of their social environment (i.e., perceived support) were more consistently related to outcome variables than were more objectively oriented measures of social interaction (e.g., received/enacted support and network indices; Barrera, 1986; Wetherington & Kessler, 1986). In addition, measures of enacted support were less highly correlated with perceived support than expected (Barrera, 1986; Heller & Lakey, 1985; Sarason, Shearin, Pierce, & Sarason, 1987). These findings ultimately gave rise to the hypothesis that perceived support might reflect primarily the personality of the perceiver.

The fact that personality might play a role in social support processes has posed a number of conceptual and methodological challenges. Many of these issues are variations of the general hypothesis that personality, rather than the social environment, may be the major contributor to health and well-being. As such, personality characteristics may serve as a threat to the construct validity of measures of social support. Early on, Heller (1979) called attention to two important issues: whether social support was merely a reflection of social competence and whether competence had the actual effect on health. Cutrona (1989) has addressed the question of whether individual differences in appraisals of the social environment reflected only response bias. Others have addressed whether social support was confounded with chronic (Henderson, Byrne, & Duncan-Jones, 1981; Monroe & Steiner, 1986) or momentary (Cohen, Flowbes, & Tocco, 1988) increases in psychological distress.

Other scholars went beyond viewing personality as a potential rival hypothesis for social support effects and advanced models that conceptualized social support as an individual difference variable itself (Lakey & Cassady, 1990; Sarason, Pierce, & Sarason, 1990; Sarason, Sarason, & Shearin, 1986). One line of evidence indicated considerable discrepancies in network members' perceptions of support exchanged between relationship participants as well as their judgments about each other's inclusion in their support networks (Alexander & Campbell, 1964; Antonnuci & Israel, 1986; Coleman, Katz, & Menzel, 1957; Laumann, 1973; Shulman, 1976). Other research demonstrated that perceptions of support were stable across time, even when network composition changed dramatically (Sarason, Levine, Basham, & Sarason, 1983; Solomon, Mikulincer, & Avitzur, 1988). A third group of studies yielded patterns of association between measures of social support and a range of personality characteristics, including extraversion, neuroticism, self-esteem, trait anxiety, and Type A personality (Krause, Liang, & Keith, 1990; Lakey & Cassady, 1990; Nakano, 1992; Procidano & Heller, 1983; Sarason et al., 1983; Watkins, Ward, Southard, & Fisher, 1992). A fourth set of evidence comes from studies that have demonstrated a relation between perceived support and retrospective accounts of the quality of parental care (Sarason et al., 1986, 1987). A fifth paradigm has shown that individuals who differ in perceived social support also differ in their interpretation of and memory for novel supportive stimuli (Lakey & Cassady, 1990; Lakey & Dickinson, 1994; Lakey, Moineau, & Drew, 1992; Mallinckrodt, 1991; Pierce, Sarason, & Sarason, 1992; Rudolph, Hammen, & Burge, 1995; Sarason et al., 1991). Thus, there is substantial evidence that perceived support has some personality-like qualities.

Unfortunately, these competing models have sometimes led researchers to pit the role of personality and of the social environment against each other. Although it has been useful to social support research to have personality models to contrast with purely environmental models, we believe that the field needs to develop more complex models that explain how both types of variables work together to produce social support and its effects. For example, Vinokur, Schul, and Caplan (1987) showed that recipients' reports of support were a function of both objective properties of interpersonal transactions and personality characteristics. Barrera and Baca (1990) also found that perceptions of support were uniquely predicted by properties of the environment and the respondent. Lakey (1989) found that support developed in a new social environment was predicted by prior levels of personality and aspects of the environment. These studies are important because they illustrate the need to develop theoretical models of social support that seek to account for both personal and environmental influences.

More recent investigations have indicated that perceived social support, as experienced by the respondent, reflects a unique matching between the respondent and the person to which he or she is responding (Lakey, McCabe, Fisicaro, & Drew, 1996; Pierce, et al., 1992). For example, Lakey et al. (1996) found that although respondents' appraisals of the supportiveness of a target individual were determined by both the objective features of the target and individual differences between perceivers, the largest portion of variance was accounted for by the interaction between perceivers and targets; that is, different targets were reliably seen as differentially supportive by different perceivers. These findings make it clear that social support is not simply a product of either personality or the social environment; instead, it reflects a unique matching between objective properties of social interaction and the personalities of the relationship participants. Efforts to determine which factor (i.e., personality or the social environment) is the key ingredient in social support appear to be missing this critical feature of the construct.

MECHANISMS BY WHICH PERSONALITY MAY INFLUENCE SOCIAL SUPPORT PROCESSES

Our own thinking about the role of personality in social support processes has been strongly influenced by models of personality–environment interactions proposed by Sandra Scarr and her colleagues (Scarr & McCartney, 1983). Although Scarr's conceptualization deals primarily with temperament in childhood, the basic concepts of personality–environment interaction can apply to a wide range of personality characteristics across the life span. The following is a summary of some of the major concepts put forth by Scarr and her colleagues, with descriptions of how they apply to social support.

REACTIVE INTERACTION

Reactive interaction refers to the observation that individuals differ in the manner in which they respond to the same social stimulus. As applied to social support, we would expect that the same supportive behavior would be responded to differently by different persons. There are a wide range of mechanisms by which this could occur. For example, enduring characteristics of the person could lead to whether a particular behavior was seen as supportive. Pierce et al. (1992) conducted a study in which college students and their mothers participated together in a stressful situation. Students were asked to prepare and give a speech arguing for the value of a college education. The mothers were taken to another room and asked to copy two standardized notes in their own handwriting. While preparing and giving their speech, the students received and read these standardized notes; in other words, all students received the same supportive stimulus. We found considerable individual differences in students' appraisals of the supportiveness of their mothers' notes. Students' support judgments were associated with measures of the students' working models regarding general perceived support, their perceptions of the supportiveness and conflictualness of their relationship with their mother, but not their relationship with their father or best same-sex friend or the experimentally manipulated level of stress associated with the task. Findings from this and other studies parallel growing interest in the cognitive aspects of social support processes, especially those focusing on the mechanisms accounting for individuals' construals of potentially supportive transactions.

Beyond the interpretation of supportive persons or behaviors, recipients may vary in their ability to utilize the assistance that has been given them. Keinan, Ezer, and Feigin (1992) found that women whose husbands were present during childbirth and who were high in trait anxiety reported less state anxiety during delivery than did high-trait-anxiety women whose husbands were not present; low-trait-anxiety women did not appear to benefit from their husbands' presence. Sarason and Sarason (1986) found that subjects low in perceived support performed better on an intellective task when the experimenter emphasized his or her availability to help if needed (none of the subjects ever sought the experimenter's assistance); the performance of high-perceived-support subjects did not differ as a function of the experimenter's offer of help. Lefcourt, Martin, and Saleh (1984) and Sandler and Lakey (1982) found that internals benefited more than externals from the provision of social support. Elliott and Gramling (1990) demonstrated that perceived social support was more helpful for assertive than unassertive individuals in buffering the strains of daily hassles and depressive symptomatology. Results from these and other studies therefore suggest that personality influences the manner in which individuals appraise important features of the social environment, both in terms of the supportive relationships they develop with others and the potentially supportive transactions that take place in the context of these relationships.

EVOCATIVE INTERACTION

Evocative interaction refers to the tendency of individuals to differ in the reactions they evoke from others. Thus, our personalities appear to influence the way in which others respond to us. Sarason, Sarason, Hacker, and Basham (1985) provided support for such a process in an observational study of college students. They found that, compared with students low in general perceived available support, those high in available support were rated by an interaction partner as more enjoyable and likable, and less tense. High-perceived-support subjects were also rated by their partners as being more effective at an experimental task in which the subject and partner had to resolve a hypothetical conflict between themselves and a roommate. These findings indicate that those who perceive the social environment as supportive and positive are, in turn, perceived by others in more positive terms.

Individuals' personality characteristics may also influence their ability to elicit support. In a recent experimental study of social support, Pierce, Ptacek, Contey, and Pollack (1996) examined the roles of support provider's behavior, recipients' support appraisals, and situational factors on recipients' task performance. In this study, the situational context and the support provider's behavior were experimentally manipulated. The situational context was manipulated by either informing the participant about the topic of his or her speech prior to preparing to give it, or by asking that the participant prepare to give an impromptu speech for which the topic would be provided just prior to the participant actually giving the speech. To manipulate the provider's behavior, a confederate enacted either emotional or instrumental support. Several assessments were obtained to measure the amount and type of supportive behavior enacted by the provider, both as a manipulation check and to investigate participants' appraisals of the supportive behavior. One interesting finding to emerge was that, despite considerable efforts on the part of the confederates, the amount of support they provided—as measured by trained raters' frequency counts of the number of instrumental and emotional support acts provided to the participant—were systematically related to participants' general perceived social support scores. When confederates interacted with a low-perceived-support participant, they provided fewer acts of instrumental and emotional support than they did when interacting with a high-perceived-support participant—and the confederates were blind to the participants' perceived support scores. This finding could reasonably be interpreted as a confound in the study in that the "treatment conditions" were not "randomly assigned." However, we believe a more conceptually promising interpretation is that it is extremely difficult to prevent individuals from shaping the nature and outcomes of their social interactions, particularly with respect to potentially supportive interactions.

One implication of this observation is that the support individuals perceive to be available to them partly reflects their skills in eliciting support as well as building and sustaining relationships. It is ironic that many individuals who need social support lack the skills to have developed close relationships that could be a source of support or the skills to elicit it. In a study of 107 Israeli mothers of young children being seen for possible health problems, Hobfoll and Lerman (1988) found that mothers who reported discomfort in seeking support received less support in response to their children's potential illness. Interestingly, the mothers' reports of their discomfort in seeking support across a 1-year period were quite stable ($r = .69$), suggesting the possible role of personality characteristics in seeking social support. Similarly, Lakey (1989) and Lakey and Dickinson (1994) found that more distressed individuals developed less support in a new social setting than did their less symptomatic counterparts. Ironically, the persons needing support the most (i.e., distressed individuals) were the least able to obtain it.

PROACTIVE INTERACTION

Proactive interaction refers to the tendency of individuals to play an active role in the social environments they experience; that is, individuals actively construct their support networks. People select certain types of social environments, and these may have implications for the development of social support. For example, research by Swann and his colleagues suggests that people choose relationship partners that confirm their own self-views, even if these views are negative. For those with positive self-views, self-verification may be supportive; but for those with negative views, self-verification may amount to criticism. Swann has acknowledged that it is certainly painful to maintain a negative self-concept, but argues that the confusion that would occur without the maintenance of one's self-concepts is yet more painful. Research findings suggest that as people strive to have their self-concepts confirmed, they create a social world that reflects those self-concepts (e.g., Swann, Stein-Seroussi, & Giesler, 1992a; Swann, Wenzlaff, Krull, & Pelham, 1992b).

For example, Swann, et al. (1992b) studied the role of self-verification among dysphoric persons, a group known to have comparatively negative self-concepts. They found evidence in two studies that, compared to nondysphorics, dysphoric individuals preferred to interact with people, including friends and dating partners, who evaluated them unfavorably. A third study suggested that dysphorics, compared to nondysphorics, were more inclined to seek negative feedback from their roommates. Finally a fourth study found that, compared to people with positive self-views, people with negative self-views preferred negative feedback, even though such feedback made them unhappy.

Our discussion of potential mechanisms linking personality and social support is by no means meant to be exhaustive. Instead, our intention has been to illustrate some ways in which individual-difference variables might influence the development of supportive relationships, the enactment and receipt of support within these relationships, and the interpretations individuals give to supportive transactions.

INTEGRATING PERSONALITY AND SOCIAL SUPPORT RESEARCH

A major goal in editing this book was to facilitate the integration of research in personality and social support. An important problem in social support research is that it has developed in relative isolation from specific disciplines. In reading classic social support papers, it is rare to find any well-developed discussions of other psychological processes. This is unfortunate, because basic research in other areas of psychology, especially personality psychology, as well as related disciplines, can help us solve key problems in social support research. In turn, social support research can contribute to these disciplines as well.

One problem in social support research has been the rather weak link between perceptions of support and the actual supportive behaviors provided. Although social support scholars have suffered substantial confusion over this issue, researchers on social perceptions have made substantial progress toward an understanding of this general issue. For example, they have recognized since the mid-1980s that thought about others is dominated by trait judgments, but that these judgments and memory for targets' actual behaviors are not linked in a straightforward fashion (e.g., Hastie & Park, 1986). When making judgments of others, people do not typically recall specific behaviors at all. Rather, they appear to recall the most accessible summary judgment of the targets' personal qualities (Hastie & Park, 1986; Kihlstrom & Klein, 1994). Thus, it would be a strikingly discrepant finding if judgments of supportiveness and recall of supportive behavior received were closely linked.

Research on the person–situation debate is also relevant to social support research. In the late 1960s, personality research was rocked by the finding that at the situational level of analysis, there is practically no consistency in behavior from one situation to another (Mischel, 1968). For example, a person's level of extraversion in one situation was practically unrelated to levels of extraversion in another context. This finding was important because it appeared to undercut the very rationale for the concept of personality. In the late 1970s and early 1980s, it became clear that behavior was impressively cross-situationally consistent at the aggregate level (Epstein, 1979; Epstein & O'Brien, 1985). All one had to do to find consistency in behavior was to average estimates of behavior across multiple settings.

Social support research has generally ignored such basic principles of behavior. Support research has been dominated by highly aggregated measures of support, as indicated by the observation that standard measures of perceived support aggregate across different behaviors, situations, and support providers. However, the lessons from the consistency debate tell us not to expect constructs measured at the aggregate level to be closely related to situation-specific processes. Unfortunately, many models of social support (e.g., stress-buffering models) primarily deal with situation-specific processes. Thus, researchers who are primarily interested in such processes may need to take more situation-specific approaches. For example, rather than relying on global measures of support and stress that have dominated the literature, investigators may need to study specific supportive transactions, such as the provision of cognitive guidance for a specific stressor.

Perhaps the most important potential contribution of personality to social support is that it provides a link to processes within the person. A major goal of social support research has been to understand individual differences in psychological symptoms. However, at some point, any model of social support must show how social processes have an effect on intrapsychic processes. This statement is based on our assumption that the final common pathway for emotional distress occurs within the person (e.g., disrupted serotonin regulation). Even a very accurate, complete, and situation-specific account of how emotional support assists an individual in a specific situation will have to include a description of how emotional support is represented cognitively, and how this information interacts with existing cognitive structures about the self, as well as how such structures interact with negative emotion. Of course, for some time, there has been a growing literature on such cognitive processes in personality and psychopathology research (Kihlstrom & Klein, 1994; Williams, Mathews, & McCleod, 1996). Social support research could benefit from drawing more heavily from this literature.

Although social support researchers can benefit by looking to advances in personality psychology, we believe that social support research can contribute to personality research as well. It would be a bad disappointment for support researchers if our scholarship ultimately had nothing to contribute to more generally to the field of psychology and allied disciplines. Fortunately, we believe that this will not be the case.

One of the most important potential contributions of social support research to personality is that it provides new ways of conceptualizing situations (Bem & Funder, 1978; Forgas, 1982; Magnussen, 1981; Martha, Kanfer, & Ackerman, 1996). Although behavior is highly consistent at the aggregate level, it is not at all consistent at the situation-specific level. However, many research questions lie between these levels. For example, we want to predict what types of employees will do well at certain jobs, or whether a person will develop symptoms following a certain type of event. There have been several attempts to develop taxonomies of situations, but none have become dominant. Social-support-related constructs may be useful in these efforts. One could conceptualize situations in terms of the extent to which they involve interactions with supportive others. For example, there has been recent interest in state-like fluctuations in self-esteem and in how individuals who display high levels of fluctuations may be at greater risk for depression following life events (Roberts & Munroe, 1992). Ultimately, this research will need to determine what situations are associated with more or less self-esteem (cf. Larson & Csikszentmihalyi, 1983). Given that self-esteem is related both to perceived support and interpersonal stress, it may be that self-esteem is high when in the presence of some supportive persons, and low when in the presence of unsupportive others. Such an approach may allow for much greater prediction of situational variation in self-esteem as well as other constructs than is currently available.

Social support research also provides new types of person variables that are explicitly rooted in a social context. Most traditional personality variables make no reference to social context. In fact, personality constructs have been criticized for focusing only on the individual, as though the social context did not exist. However, concepts such as perceived social support offer a construct that is defined explicitly in terms of person × situation interactions. Because it reflects one person's subjective appraisal, it is a property of the individual. Moreover, perceived support has several important properties shared with traditional personality constructs: It is stable over time, is associated in meaningful ways with numerous other personality constructs, and is associated with individual differences in cognition regarding social behavior. Yet, at the same time that support perceptions are the property of the person, they make specific reference to particular types of social contexts. In fact, the bulk of their variance reflects the perceiver's unique relationships with others. Traditionally, the interactional approach to personality has relied upon paradigms in which personality characteristics are used to predict reactions in one type of situation but not in another. In this paradigm, personality and situations are two distinct constructs. Constructs such as perceived support represent the blending of person and situational constructs. Rather than talking in terms of personality and situations, we would talk in terms of persons-in-situations. In this regard, the construct of perceived support is similar to Rotter's construct of interpersonal trust (1967) and the diagnostic category of Social Phobia (Barlow, 1988). These constructs represent implicit interactionist views as they reflect the reactions of the individual within a specific set of social contexts.

Social cognition research has also been criticized for ignoring the social world. Most social cognition research deals with semantic trait concepts and makes little reference to specific social contexts. In addition, the traits that are studied in much person-perception research are not chosen because they are particularly important to understand. Researchers appear to take the stance that any trait will do. The consequence of this is that although these researchers are amassing impressive knowledge about the general cognitive processes important in person memory and judgment, these processes are not tied to any particular socially important social judgment. Many more applied researchers, and perhaps funding agencies, have difficulty seeing how research on such judgments are socially important. A similar situation may have had a very negative effect on research on implicit personality theory. Although work progressed, demonstrating that people had different concepts, progress in this field appeared to abruptly stop around 1970. One reason may have been that there was no compelling reason to understand how people combined certain traits to arrive at inferences for other traits. Incorporating social support constructs into social cognition research would have at least two advantages. First, because perceived support judgments have well-documented relevance to important health outcomes, studies of cognitive processes in making these judgments have clear applied value. Second, every basic research study that happens to include support judgments as dependent variables not only adds knowledge about basic processes, but also informs us of how support judgments are made.

Social support research can also provide insight into factorial models of personality (Goldberg, 1993). These models have been criticized as potentially overlooking important components of personality (Block, 1995). We wonder whether interpersonal constructs have been well represented in the descriptions of personality that are actually subjected to factor analysis. For example, many of these studies involve ratings of peers. If peers were rated in terms of their relationship with the respondent (e.g., supportive, critical), as well as what is traditionally thought of as personality, would the traditional five-factor model emerge? Would supportiveness and conflict emerge as separate factors? Given that the construct of agreeableness involves such traits as "sympathetic" and "understanding," we wonder how similar the concept of supportiveness is with agreeableness. Could it be that social support researchers have been studying people who differ primarily in whether their friends and families are high or low in agreeableness? On the other hand, if support-related qualities emerge as distinct factors, it would broaden the five-factor model considerably. One could argue that such support-related characteristics would not represent "true" personality. Rather, as we discussed earlier in this chapter, they would reflect person-in-situation constructs. But personality psychology may benefit by including constructs that explicitly conceptualize individual differences in terms of person × situation interactions.

DIRECTIONS FOR FUTURE RESEARCH

Research on social support has made substantial progress over the past several decades, but much remains to be done. Theoretical developments are needed that focus on the conceptualization of the construct of personality as it relates to social support processes. Our own thinking has been influenced by the concept of working models or schemes, but other features of personality are undoubtedly important. In addition, researchers need to emphasize interactional models that account for the roles of personality and the social environment in social support processes. It is no longer meaningful to speak of a definition of social support that will narrow investigators' focus to either features of the person (e.g., his or her general tendency to construe transactions with network members as supportive) or the environment (e.g., objectively defined behaviors that will, for nearly everyone, facilitate their coping with specific stressors).

Methodological issues also need to be addressed. Assessment strategies are needed that take into account both relationship participants' views regarding their potentially supportive interactions and behavioral observations to assess objective features of supportive interactions. This will facilitate an understanding of the manner in which individuals engage in, interpret, and respond to supportive interactions. Studies are needed that employ experimental/observational designs involving social interaction; we need to conduct increasingly stringent tests of interactional theories that emphasize links between personality and situational factors. Longitudinal studies are needed to examine the development of supportive relationships. These studies would permit us to explore the mechanisms by which individuals initiate, maintain, and dissolve supportive relationships. Efforts to determine whether personality characteristics or social support serve as the antecedent of one another are likely to be unproductive. We believe that a more fruitful path of inquiry focuses on questions aimed at the interplay between personality and social support across the life span. In this regard, we concur with Newcomb's (1990) assertion that "a social support network is constructed throughout life in a reciprocal developmental manner between personal characteristics and social contacts" (p. 54).

Another point we wish to raise concerns the tendency of social support researchers—ourselves included—to frame our thinking in terms of the roles assumed by support providers and recipients. Understandably, our theoretical analyses often involve assigning to one person the role of provider, while ascribing to the other person the role of recipient. Although such an approach undoubtedly has merit (see, e.g., Dunkel-Schetter & Skokan, 1990), it fails to capture a fundamental feature of supportive transactions: They occur in the context of relationships in which each participant is, across time, both a support provider and a support recipient. In fact, some scholars have asserted that the act of rendering support to another person serves a supportive function for the person providing the assistance (Weiss, 1974). Thus, while theoretical and empirical analyses may, when examining coping transactions with respect to a specific life event, yield useful information about social support processes, a more comprehensive understanding of psychological mechanisms underlying such processes will require attending to the multiple roles that relationship participants play in each other's lives as they confront a range of situations requiring coping efforts.

One consequence of this focus has been that although we know a fair amount about the characteristics of individuals who have high social support, we know very little about the characteristics of people with whom the perceivers have relationships. For example, Lakey, Ross, Butler, and Bentley (1996) have shown that perceived support judgments are derived, in part, from the network member's similarity to the perceiver and level of conscientiousness. These findings suggest that the more global characteristics of network members are important in determining whether they will be seen as supportive. Moreover, how a given supportive behavior is viewed may depend on the perceived personality characteristics of the provider. For example, advice may be viewed completely differently depending upon whether the provider is viewed as warm or cold (Asch, 1946). Thus, another important role for personality in social support research is to help understand the personal characteristics of supportive people.

Understanding the personal characteristics of support providers and how they influence perceptions of support opens a new area of investigation. One characteristic that may be important is the level of skill in providing enacted support. Persons who are equally well intentioned will not be equally capable of saying helpful things (Lehman, Ellard, & Wortman, 1986; Wortman & Silver, 1983). Such supportiveness skills may largely overlap with general social skills, although there may be abilities specific to saying helpful things during times of duress. These skills may overlap largely with psychotherapeutic skills. An understanding of supportive skills may be important in developing new preventive and therapeutic interventions. For example, some investigators have attempted to teach supportive skills to the social networks of persons who were under high stress, with the aim of increasing the support available to the stressed individuals.

Another point to consider is that conceptual and empirical analyses of social support typically begin at the point at which a person has become actively engaged in coping with a life stress; however, considerable activity pertinent to confronting the life event occurs prior to this point in the process. Some individuals, for a variety of reasons, seem to be more prone to experiencing particular life events than others. Consider two individuals who differ in their attachment styles: Scott has a working model of self and others that reflects secure attachment, whereas George's working model reflects insecure/ambivalent attachment. Thus, Scott believes that he is worthy of the attention and help he is confident will be forthcoming from others should he need it; George worries that those with whom he has tried to be close will in some manner fail him when he needs their help. Research on the consequences of attachment styles for adult relationship formation suggests that George is likely to experience more interpersonal difficulties with network members than is Scott; in other words, George is likely to have higher levels of life stress associated with relational problems. In this sense, relative to Scott's personality, George's personal characteristics render him more vulnerable to experiencing events requiring coping efforts. In addition, because George is less likely to have developed an effective network of supportive relationships, his risk for distress is increased, because the interpersonal resources he may need to cope with problems in his relationships are less likely to be available should he need such assistance. In a sense, then, George is doubly cursed; not only is he more likely to have troubles in his relationships with others, but also the personality characteristics that contribute to his interpersonal distress are likely to undermine his ability to develop a support network capable of meetings his needs for help in coping with such stressors.

The observation that personality characteristics influence social network formation is certainly not new. And social support researchers have documented links between early caregiver experiences and supportive relationships in adulthood. Such studies typically follow the general conceptual premise established by Bowlby (1980), in which he postulated that early attachment bonds serve to influence subsequent social behavior. However, the bulk of these studies has focused on family and romantic relationships; little attention has been given to the development of friendships, despite the fact that social support researchers have marshaled considerable evidence indicating that friendships, above and beyond other central network members (e.g., family members and romantic partners), contribute to psychological well-being. Our own view is that we need to go beyond the identification of cross-sectional associations between early and later relationships, and instead pursue studies that identify specific mechanisms by which personality characteristics—which presumably have their roots in early developmental periods—shape the formation of supportive relationships in adulthood. Understandably, such studies are likely to be daunting, since they will require not only the specification of hypotheses but also the implementation of paradigms (e.g., longitudinal) that require considerable time and energy to conduct.

CONCLUSION

From an initial focus on interpersonal behaviors to an emphasis on the unique appraisals individuals attach to their transactions, social support researchers now view social support as a complex interaction among personal and environmental variables. Our understanding of the role social support plays in health and well-being is increasingly recognizing the interplay between both environment and personality in determining the costs and benefits associated with the provision and receipt of social support. Identification of these interconnections has emerged from numerous studies employing diverse methodologies to examine widely different populations, confronting stressors ranging from daily hassles to major life events. We are confident that the creativity, enthusiasm, and perseverance of social support researchers, which have contributed importantly to our understanding of the nature and impact of social support, will continue to illuminate our understanding of social support processes in the decades to come.

REFERENCES

Alexander, C. N., & Campbell, E. Q. (1964). Peer influences on adolescent aspirations and attainments. *American Sociological Review, 29*, 568-575.

Antonucci, T. C., & Israel, B. A. (1986). Veridicality of social support: A comparison of principal and network members' responses. *Journal of Consulting and Clinical Psychology, 54*, 432-437.

Asch, S. E. (1946). Forming impressions of personality. *Journal of Abnormal and Social Psychology, 41*, 1230-1240.

Barlow, D. H. (1988). *Anxiety and its disorders: The nature and treatment of anxiety and panic.* New York: Guilford.

Barrera, M. Jr. (1986). Distinctions between social support concepts, measures and models. *American Journal of Community Psychology, 14*, 413-455.

Barrera, M. Jr., & Baca, L. M. (1990). Recipient reactions to social support: Contributions of enacted support, conflicted support and network orientation. *Journal of Social and Personal Relationships, 7*, 541-551.

Bem, D. J., & Funder, D. C. (1978). Predicting more of the people more of the time: Assessing the personality of situations. *Psychological Review, 85*, 485-501.

Block, J. (1995). A contrarian view of the five-factor approach to personality description. *Psychological Bulletin, 117*, 187-215.

Bowlby, J. (1980). *Attachment and loss, Vol. 3, Loss: Sadness and depression.* New York: Basic Books.

Caplan, G. (1974). *Support systems and community mental health: Lectures on concept development.* New York: Behavioral Publications.

Cobb, S. (1976). Social support as a moderator of life stress. *Psychosomatic Medicine, 38*, 300-314.

Cohen, L. H., Towbes, L. C., & Flocco, R. (1988). Effects of induced mood on self-reported life events and perceived and received social support. *Journal of Personality and Social Psychology, 55*, 669-674.

Coleman, J., Katz, E., & Menzel, H. (1957). The diffusion of an innovation among physicians. *Sociometry, 20*, 253-270.

Coyne, J. C., Ellard, J. H., & Smith, D. A. F. (1990). Social support, interdependence, and the dilemmas of helping. In B. R. Sarason, I. G. Sarason, & G. R. Pierce (Eds.), *Social support: An interactional view* (pp. 129-149). New York: Wiley.

Cutrona, C. E. (1986). Objective determinants of perceived social support. *Journal of Personality and Social Psychology, 50*, 349-355.

Cutrona, C. E. (1989). Ratings of social support by adolescents and adult informants: Degree of correspondence and prediction of depressive symptoms. *Journal of Personality and Social Psychology, 57*, 723-730.

Cutrona, C. E., Cohen, B. B., & Igram, S. (1990). Contextual determinants of the perceived supportiveness of helping behaviors. *Journal of Social and Personal Relationships, 7*, 553-562.

Dean, A., & Lin, N. (1977). The stress buffering role of social support: Problems and prospects for systematic investigation. *Journal of Nervous and Mental Disease, 165*, 403-417.

Dunkel-Schetter, C., & Skokan, L.A. (1990). Determinants of social support provision in personal relationships, *Journal of Social and Personal Relationships, 7*, 437-450.

Elliot, T. R., & Gramling, S. E. (1990). Personal assertiveness and the effects of social support among college students. *Journal of Counseling Psychology*, *37*, 427–436.

Epstein, S. (1979). The stability of behavior: I. On predicting most of the people much of the time. *Journal of Personality and Social Psychology*, *37*, 1097–1126.

Epstein, S., & O'Brien, E. J. (1985). The person–situation debate in historical and current perspective. *Psychological Bulletin*, *98*, 513–537.

Fincham, F. D., & Bradbury, T. N. (1990). Social support in marriage: The role of social cognition. *Journal of Social and Clinical Psychology*, *9*, 31–42.

Flaherty, J. A., & Richman, J. A. (1986). Effects of childhood relationships on the adult's capacity to form social supports. *American Journal of Psychiatry*, *143*, 851–855.

Forgas, J. P. (1982). Social skills and the perception of interaction episodes. *British Journal of Clinical Psychology*, *22*, 195–207.

Goldberg, L. R. (1993). The structure of phenotypic personality traits. *American Psychologist*, *48*, 26–33.

Hastie, R., & Park, B. (1986). The relationship between memory and judgment depends on whether the judgment task is memory-based or on-line. *Psychological Review*, *93*, 258–268.

Heller, K. (1979). The effects of social support: Prevention and treatment implications. In A. P. Goldstein & F. H. Kanfer (Eds.), *Maximizing treatment gains: Transfer enhancement in psychotherapy* (pp. 253–382). New York: Academic Press.

Heller, K., & Lakey, B. (1985). Perceived support and social interaction among friends and confidants. In I. G. Sarason & B. R. Sarason (Eds.), *Social support: Theory, research and applications* (pp. 287–300). The Hague: Martinus Nijhoff.

Heller, K., Swindle, R. W., & Dusenbury, L. (1986). Component social support processes: Comments and integration. *Journal of Consulting and Clinical Psychology*, *54*, 466–470.

Henderson, S., Byrne, D.G., & Duncan-Jones, P. (1981). *Neurosis and the social environment*. New York: Academic Press.

Hobfoll, S. E., & Lerman, M. (1988). Personal relationships, personal attributes, and stress resistance: Mothers' reactions to their child's illness. *American Journal of Community Psychology*, *16*, 565–589.

Ingersoll-Dayton, B., & Antonucci, T. C. (1983, November). *Non-reciprocal social support: Another side of intimate relationships*. Paper presented at the 36th Annual Meeting of the Gerontological Society, San Francisco, CA.

Keinan, G., Ezer, A., & Feigin, M. (1992). The influence of situational and personal variables on the effectiveness of social support during childbirth. *Anxiety Research*, *4*, 325–337.

Keinan, G., & Hobfoll, S. E. (1989). Stress, dependency, and social support: Who benefits from husband's presence in delivery? *Journal of Social and Clinical Psychology*, *8*, 32–44.

Kihlstrom, J. F., & Klein, S. B. (1994). The self as a knowledge structure. In R. S. Wyer & T. K. Srull (Eds.), *Handbook of social cognition* (Vol. 1, pp. 153–208). Hillsdale, NJ: Erlbaum.

Krause, N., Liang, J., & Keith, V. (1990). Personality, social support, and psychological distress. *Psychology and Aging*, *5*, 315–326.

Lakey, B. (1989). Personal and environmental antecedents of perceived social support. *American Journal of Community Psychology*, *59*, 337–343.

Lakey, B., & Cassady, P. B. (1990). Cognitive processes in perceived social support. *Journal of Personality and Social Psychology*, *59*, 337–343.

Lakey, B., & Dickinson, L. G. (1994). Antecedents of perceived support: Is perceived family environment generalized to new social relationships? *Cognitive Therapy and Research*, *18*, 39–53.

Lakey, B., McCabe, K. M., Fisicaro, S. A., & Drew, J. B. (1996). Environment and perceived determinants of support perceptions: Three generalizability studies. *Journal of Personality and Social Psychology*, *70*, 1270–1280.

Lakey, B., Moineau, S., & Drew, J. B. (1992). Perceived social support and individual differences in the interpretation and recall of supportive behavior. *Journal of Social and Clinical Psychology*, *11*, 336–348.

Lakey, B., Ross, L. T., Butler, C., & Bentley, K. (1996). Making social support judgments: The role of similarity and conscientiousness. *Journal of Social and Clinical Psychology*, *15*, 283–304.

Larson, R., & Csikszentmihalyi, M. (1983). The Experience Sampling Method. *New Directions for Methodology of Social and Behavioral Sciences*, *15*, 41–56.

Laumann, E. O. (1973). *Bonds of pluralism*. New York: Wiley.

Lefcourt, H. M., Martin, R. A., & Saleh, W. E. (1984). Locus of control and social support: Interactive moderators of stress. *Journal of Personality and Social Psychology, 47,* 378–389.

Lehman, D. R., Ellard, J. H., & Wortman, C. B. (1986). Social support for the bereaved: Recipients' and providers' perspectives on what is helpful. *Journal of Consulting and Clinical Psychology, 54,* 438–446.

Magnussen, D. (1981). Wanted: A psychology of situations. In D. Magnussen (Ed.), *Toward a psychology of situations: An interactional perspective* (pp. 9–32). Hillsdale, NJ: Erlbaum.

Mallinckrodt, B. (1991). Clients' representations of childhood emotional bonds with parents, social support and formation of the working alliance. *Journal of Counseling Psychology, 38,* 401–409.

Mischel, W. (1968). *Personality and assessment.* New York: Wiley.

Monroe, S. M., & Steiner, S. C. (1986). Social support and psychopathology: Interrelations with preexisting disorder, stress, and personality. *Journal of Abnormal Psychology, 95,* 29–39.

Murtha, T. C., Kanfer, R., & Ackerman, P. L. (1996). Toward an interactionist taxonomy of personality and situations: An integrative situational–dispositional representation of personality traits. *Journal of Personality and Social Psychology, 71,* 193–207.

Nakano, K. (1992). Role of personality characteristics in coping behaviors. *Psychological Reports, 71,* 687–690.

Newcomb, M. B. (1990). Social support and personal characteristics. *Journal of Social and Clinical Psychology, 9,* 54–68.

Pierce, G. R., Ptacek, J. T., Contey, C., & Pollack, K. (1996). *Supportive behavior and support appraisals: An experimental study.* Manuscript submitted for publication.

Pierce, G. R., Sarason, B. R., & Sarason, I. G. (1992). General and specific support expectations and stress as predictors of perceived supportiveness: An experimental study. *Journal of Personality and Social Psychology, 63,* 297–307.

Procidano, M. E., & Heller, K. (1983). Measures of perceived social support from friends and from family: Three validation studies. *American Journal of Community Psychology, 11,* 1–24.

Roberts, J. E., & Monroe, S. M. (1992). Vulnerable self-esteem and depressive symptoms: Prospective findings comparing three alternative conceptualizations. *Journal of Personality and Social Psychology, 62,* 804–812.

Rotter, J. B. (1967). A new scale for the measurement of interpersonal trust. *Journal of Personality, 35,* 651–665.

Rudolph, K. D., Hammen, C., & Burge, D. (1995). Cognitive representations of self, family, and peers in school-age children: Links with social competence and sociometric status. *Child Development, 66,* 1385–1402.

Sandler, I. N., & Lakey, B. (1982). Locus of control as a stress moderator: The role of control perceptions and social support. *American Journal of Community Psychology, 10,* 65–80.

Sarason, B. R., Pierce, G. R., & Sarason, I. G. (1990). Social support: The sense of acceptance and the role of relationships. In B. R. Sarason, I. G. Sarason, & G. R. Pierce (Eds.), *Social support: An interactional view* (pp. 97–128). New York: Wiley.

Sarason, B. R., Pierce, G. R., Shearin, E. N., Sarason, I. G., Waltz, J. A., & Poppe, L. (1991). Perceived social support and working models of self and actual others. *Journal of Personality and Social Psychology, 60,* 273–287.

Sarason, B. R., Sarason, I. G., Hacker, T. A., & Basham, R. B. (1985). Concomitants of social support: Social skills, physical attractiveness, and gender. *Journal of Personality and Social Psychology, 49,* 469–480.

Sarason, B. R., Shearin, E. N., Pierce, G. R., & Sarason, I. G. (1987). Interrelationships of social support measures: Theoretical and practical implications. *Journal of Personality and Social Psychology, 52,* 813–832.

Sarason, I. G., Levine, H. M., Basham, R. B., & Sarason, B. R. (1983). Assessing social support: The Social Support Questionnaire. *Journal of Personality and Social Psychology, 44,* 127–139.

Sarason, I. G., & Sarason, B. R. (1986). Experimentally provided social support. *Journal of Personality and Social Psychology, 50,* 1222–1225.

Sarason, I. G., Sarason, B. R., & Shearin, E. N. (1986). Social support as an individual difference variable: Its stability, origins, and relational aspects. *Journal of Personality and Social Psychology, 50,* 845–855.

Sarason, I. G., Smith, R. E., & Diener, E. (1975). Personality research: Components of variance attributable to the person and the situation. *Journal of Personality and Social Psychology, 3,* 199–204.

Scarr, S., & McCartney, K. (1983). How people make their own environments: A theory of genotype-environment effects. *Child Development, 54,* 424-435.

Schuster, T. L., Kessler, R. C., & Aseltine, R. H. Jr. (1990). Supportive interactions, negative interactions, and depressed mood. *American Journal of Community Psychology, 18,* 423-438.

Shulman, N. (1976). Network analysis: A new addition to an old bag of tricks. *Acta Sociologica, 19,* 307-323.

Solomon, Z., Mikulincer, M., & Avitzur, E. (1988). Coping, locus of control, social support, and combat-related posttraumatic stress disorder: A prospective study. *Journal of Personality and Social Psychology, 55,* 279-285.

Swann, W. B., Jr., Stein-Seroussi, A., & Giesler, R. B. (1992a). Why people self-verify. *Journal of Personality and Social Psychology, 62,* 392-401.

Swann, W. B. Jr., Wenzlaff, R. M., Krull, D. S., & Pelham, B. W. (1992b). Allure of negative feedback: Self-verification strivings among depressed persons. *Journal of Abnormal Psychology, 101,* 293-306.

Vinokur, A., Schul, Y., & Caplan, R.D. (1987). Determinants of perceived social support: Interpersonal transactions, personal outlook, and transient affect states. *Journal of Personality and Social Psychology, 53,* 1137-1145.

Wallace, J. L., & Vaux, A. (1993). Social support network orientation: The role of adult attachment style. *Journal of Social and Clinical Psychology, 12,* 354-365.

Watkins, P. L., Ward, C. H., Southard, D. R., & Fisher, E. B. (1992). The Type A belief system: Relationships to hostility, social support, and life stress. *Behavioral Medicine, 18,* 27-32.

Weiss, R. S. (1974). The provisions of social relationships. In Z. Rubin (Ed.), *Doing unto others.* Englewood Cliffs, NJ: Prentice-Hall.

Wetherington, E., & Kessler, R. C. (1986). Perceived support, received support, and adjustment to stressful life events. *Journal of Health and Social Behavior, 27,* 78-89.

Williams, J. M. G., Mathews, A., & McLeod, C. (1996). The emotional stroop task and psychopathology. *Psychological Bulletin, 120,* 3-24.

Wortman, C. B., & Silver, R. C. (1989). The myths of coping with loss. *Journal of Consulting and Clinical Psychology, 57,* 349-357.

CHAPTER 2

A RELATIONAL SCHEMA APPROACH TO SOCIAL SUPPORT

TAMARHA PIERCE, MARK W. BALDWIN, AND JOHN E. LYDON

Psychological Bulletin (Burman & Margolin, 1992), *Science* (House, Landis, & Umberson, 1988), and a lot of grandmothers attest to the impact that relationships have on health, illness, and subjective well-being. This apparent fact has spawned a great deal of research directed at understanding the role of social support: Database searches of just a 5-year period, using the keywords *social support*, recently yielded 2,508 citations from PsycInfo and 1,321 from Medline.

One of the unfortunate byproducts of such a voluminous research area is the development of many different interpretations of social support that, because they are often focused on specific subissues and couched in idiosyncratic labels, are difficult to compare or integrate. Research in the area has consequently been criticized for the lack of any unified theory to explain the processes by which social support affects stress and well-being, and thus we are left with interesting but often inconclusive correlational findings (Cohen, 1988; Thoits, 1986; Wallston, Alagna, DeVellis, & DeVellis, 1983).

Sarason, Sarason, and G. Pierce (1990b) advocated beginning the search for a unifying theoretical framework with an examination of people's perceptions of how supportive the world is. Recent research is showing that one of the critical factors mediating the impact of close relationships on emotional and physical well-being— perhaps even more significant than the actual receipt of support or tangible help—is the expectation that help would be there if needed. A substantial body of research has shown that the perception of availability of support from significant others is a more

TAMARHA PIERCE AND JOHN E. LYDON • Department of Psychology, McGill University, Montreal, Quebec, Canada H3A 1B1.   MARK W. BALDWIN • Department of Psychology, University of Winnipeg, Winnipeg, Manitoba, Canada R3B 2E9.

Sourcebook of Social Support and Personality, edited by Gregory R. Pierce, Brian Lakey, Irwin G. Sarason, and Barbara R. Sarason. Plenum Press, New York, 1997.

reliable predictor of adjustment and health outcomes than are measures of support actually received from others (Cohen, 1988; Cutrona, 1986; Gottlieb, 1985; Sarason, G. Pierce, & Sarason, 1994). The impact of perceived support does not seem to be mediated by received support, as both experimental and field studies have shown weak or nonexistent correlations between the perception of available support (or expectations of support) and actual support received (see Dunkel-Schetter & Bennett, 1990 for a review; Cutrona, 1986; Lakey & Cassady, 1990, Study 1; Lakey & Heller, 1988; Lakey, Tardiff, & Drew, 1994).

We agree that the issue of perceived support is a good place to start the search for an integrated model. The social perception literature presents a smorgasbord of models, however, and some approaches may be better suited than others to the specific topic of perceived support. We see a promising paradigm emerging from work focusing on the role of mental representations in close relationships (Baldwin, 1992), particularly in the attachment (e.g., Ainsworth, 1982; Baldwin & Fehr, 1995; Baldwin, Fehr, Keedian, Seidel, & Thomson, 1993; Bretherton, 1990; Collins & Read, 1994; Main, Kaplan, & Cassidy, 1985) and, recently, social support literatures (e.g., Lakey & Cassady, 1990; Sarason, G. Pierce, & Sarason, 1990a, 1990c, 1994). This work examines cognitive processes but focuses specifically on cognitions about interpersonal dynamics, thus facilitating research into the link between interpersonal and intrapsychic factors. Drawing heavily from these sources and other research findings, we will first sketch out a social-cognitive framework for interpreting perceived social support, and then apply it to some of the issues in the social support literature. Within this framework, we will address questions of whether perceived social support is a global personality style or a differentiated set of expectations; whether it consists of positive or negative expectations; and whether it is a stable construct or should be expected to vary in meaningful ways. As shall become apparent, we believe most of these either–or questions fall away once one begins examining the structure and dynamics of relational cognition.

RELATIONAL COGNITION

In principle, people's beliefs about the availability of social support could relate to the provision of all manner of resources, such as advice, reassurance, or tangible assistance (e.g., Weiss, 1974). Much research has led to the conclusion that what is primarily supportive in interpersonal exchanges, however, may be what is communicated about the relationship to the recipient, rather than what is actually performed in a supportive transaction. The central communication appears to involve the message that one is "loved, valued, and unconditionally accepted" (Sarason, G. Pierce, & Sarason, 1994, p. 110; see also Cobb, 1976; Coyne, Ellard, & Smith, 1990). In contrast, relationships based on only limited acceptance, or involving rejection and conflict, can undermine people's sense of social support, increase their perception of stress, and reduce their well-being in response to stress (e.g., Coyne et al., 1990; Rook, 1992). We will focus on issues of acceptance and rejection, therefore, while touching on more instrumental forms of support when relevant.

Social-cognitive formulations suggest that perceived support derives from people's mental representations of self and others, and from their expectancies about the nature of interpersonal acceptance. There have been a variety of terms used in general theories about positive and negative relationship cognition. Many writers use the attachment theory concept of *working models* (Bowlby, 1969, 1973), which includes models of self and significant others (see, e.g., Collins & Read, 1994; Sarason et al., 1991). Others use conceptualizations derived from object relations, symbolic inter-actionist, anthropological or social learning theories (e.g., Cantor & Kihlstrom, 1987; Fiske, 1992; Horowitz, 1988; Planalp, 1985; Safran, 1990).

After surveying a number of perspectives, Baldwin (1992) developed the notion of *relational schemas*, or *cognitive structures representing regularities in patterns of interpersonal relatedness*. A relational schema is assumed to comprise, as an inte-grated unit, three major components of social knowledge: a self-schema, an other-schema, and, importantly, an interpersonal script for typical or overlearned interaction patterns between self and other.

Research into social support has demonstrated the influence of people's views of self and other. A relational schema approach emphasizes that self and other schemas likely are not isolated, independent representations. Rather, they are associated with each other in self-other units, linked by an interpersonal script for typical patterns of interaction. This interrelation is in fact implicit in many trait adjectives, such as when self is seen as "dependent" and a significant other is seen as "dependable"—underlying both is obviously the assumption of an interaction in which self successfully depends on other. Similarly, the perception that "even if I fail, my significant others will love me" implies a view of others as "loving" and a view of self as "worthy of love." Presumably this association is to some degree bidirectional, as anyone basking in the warm glow of an affectionate relationship can tell us: Feeling loved makes one feel lovable, and feeling lovable leads one to expect that others will be loving.

A person's expectations about interactions with significant others, particularly when the person is under stress or in need of help, is precisely what is assessed in most measures of perceived support such as the Social Support Questionnaire (Sarason, Levine, Basham, & Sarason, 1983), the Interpersonal Support Evaluation List (Cohen & Hoberman, 1983), the Social Provisions Scale (Cutrona & Russell, 1987) or the measure of Perceived Social Support from Family and Friends (Procidano & Heller, 1983). Research is documenting the links between these interpersonal expectations and images of self and other. Recent studies of self-esteem (e.g., Leary, Tambor, Terdal, & Downs, 1995), for example, have supported the symbolic interactionist tenet that feelings about the self are closely associated with beliefs about how others would see self. Evidence in the support literature is also consistent with this relational schema view: Perceiving support as generally available has been associated with expecting positive interactions with significant others (G. Pierce, Sarason, & Sarason, 1991; Sarason et al., 1991; Sarason, Pierce, Bannerman, & Sarason, 1993), possessing a positive view of self (Lakey & Cassady, 1990; Major et al., 1990; Sarason et al., 1991), and believing that others see the self positively (Sarason et al., 1991; Sarason, G. Pierce, & Sarason, 1983). Finally, in a recent sample of 533 undergraduates (Baldwin, 1996), perceived available support (measured by the Social Support Questionnaire, Sarason et al., 1983) correlated .45 with self-esteem (Rosenberg, 1965) and .31 with attachment security (Hazan & Shaver, 1987), demonstrating the links between support, self-esteem, and attachment.

INFORMATION-PROCESSING EFFECTS

As Lakey and Drew (Chapter 6, this volume) and others have stated, the major reason for developing a social-cognitive view of perceived support is to integrate this topic more fully with the vast literature on the information-processing effects of knowledge structures such as schemas, prototypes, and scripts. The simple message of this research is that people do not approach social experiences as a *tabula rasa*. Their expectancies and understandings, usually based on past interpersonal experience, affect the way they perceive and interpret new events.

In work on self-schemas, for example, researchers have shown that firmly held self-views can facilitate the processing of schema-relevant information, typically resulting in a schema-congruency bias in interpretation and memory (see Markus & Wurf, 1987). Similarly, schemas for significant others can serve as guides when learning about a new person. Andersen and Cole (1990) described to subjects a target person who shared a number of features with one of the subject's significant others. In a subsequent memory task, recall errors suggested that subjects tended to assume the target person also possessed additional features of the significant other—features that had not been presented—implying that a schema relevant to the significant other was generalized to the novel person.

The same principle applies to interpersonal expectancies: A number of studies have shown that perceptions of available social support can be generalized to novel contexts, influencing the perception of support available from new acquaintances. In a study of students moving away to college, for example, Lakey and Dickinson (1994) found that students' perceptions of their family environment predicted their perception of support available from campus friends after the first semester at college. This effect was not accounted for by psychological distress, social competence, agreeableness, or extraversion, but rather seemed to result, in large part, from the generalization of relational expectations.

It is useful to examine in detail the cognitive structures and processes that underlie such generalization effects. Theoretically, a key mechanism in the generalization of expectancies is thought to be spreading activation (Collins & Loftus, 1975), whereby once one element or node of a cognitive network is activated, this triggers other nodes that are closely associated. In the Andersen and Cole (1990) paradigm just reviewed, for example, hearing that a novel person smokes a cigar might activate a schema representing one's cigar-smoking uncle, and spreading activation would automatically lead one to anticipate that the new person has a wry sense of humor much like the uncle has.

The principle of spreading activation, which is the basis of the conjoint priming of schema elements (Baldwin, 1992), can also be studied in more direct ways than by generalization effects. For example, Segal (Segal, Hood, Shaw, & Higgins, 1988; Segal & Vella, 1990) used a modified Stroop test to examine the structure of depressed patients' self-schemas. They found that priming subjects with one of their negative self-conceptions (e.g., stupid) produced increased reaction-time interference on other negative self-conception targets (e.g., ugly), indicating the spread of activation through the self-schema from one negative trait to the other.

Recent research shows that it is possible to study the structure of interpersonal expectations in a similar way. To do so, it is theoretically and empirically useful to conceptualize interpersonal expectations as constituted of *if-then* contingency statements, of the form *If I do X, then the other person will do Y* (Baldwin, 1992; Mischel, 1973). The if-then format forces the researcher to go beyond the notion that interpersonal expectations are generally positive or negative, to try to identify the specific expectancies that automatically shape a person's view of the social world. This formulation also lends itself well to social cognitive research, which can be used to examine the automatic spread of activation from the thought of a specific context or behavior (e.g., If I am in need, If I seek help) to the expected outcome (e.g., Then I will be supported, rejected, or abandoned) that is associated with it in cognitive structure.

For example, recent studies using a modified lexical decision task (Meyer & Schvanlveldt, 1971) have revealed some of the if-then contingencies underlying people's self-esteem and attachment security. In one study of attachment styles (Baldwin et al., 1993, Study 2), participants were presented with a series of letter strings and asked to decide whether each string represented a word or a nonword. Subjects were able to respond more quickly when the target words, which described interpersonal behavior, were placed in a meaningful relational context that was consistent with their attachment expectations. For example, on trials when they first read the context sentence *If I trust my partner, then my partner will* ..., chronically avoidant subjects subsequently showed more reaction-time facilitation than secure subjects for the target word *hurt*. A parallel series of studies (Baldwin & Sinclair, 1996) into the if-then contingencies related to self-esteem has shown that low-self-esteem individuals were quicker than high-self-esteem individuals to recognize words such as *rejection* or *abandoned* when given a context word such as *lose* or *failure*.

Thus, if-then expectations of contingent and precarious acceptance have been implicated in low self-esteem and insecure attachment. Research is currently in progress to identify specific expectations underlying perceptions of social support. Cognitive paradigms such as these may at times seem somewhat artificial, if not inconsequential, but in the depression and anxiety literatures, they are proving quite useful in sorting out the specific information-processing mechanisms underlying various disorders (Williams, Watts, MacLeod, & Mathews, 1988). They should prove useful to social support researchers as well, as a complement to the various self-report approaches being used in the social support literature.

WORKING MODELS AND ASSOCIATIVE NETWORKS OF RELATIONAL KNOWLEDGE

The focus in the support literature on intrapsychic factors is being driven in part by the finding that perceptions of available support tend to be fairly stable across time, and so might reasonably be considered to function like a personality variable (Sarason et al., 1994). This would be an unsatisfying hypothesis if all it implied were that there is some kind of "trait" that different people have different amounts of. Numerous researchers (e.g., Sarason et al., 1990; Cutrona, Cole, Colangelo, Assouline, & Russell, 1994), however, are taking a more interpersonal and cognitive approach, drawing on Bowlby's (1969) notion of working models and the impact they have on personal attachments and the sense of self. Retrospective studies have shown, for example, that perceived support is correlated with the quality of childhood relationships with the parent (e.g., Sarason & Sarason, 1986; Sarason et al., 1991).

While this is an important step in the right direction, theorists often do not take the social-cognitive analysis far enough. An important implication of social-cognitive approaches to personality (e.g., Cantor & Kihlstrom, 1987; Mischel, 1973) is the emphasis on the multiplicity of working models or relational schemas available to most people (Baldwin, 1992). For example, in the adult attachment literature, it is often tacitly assumed that people have a single attachment "style," deriving from stable mental models of self and other that were learned in childhood. In one recent study, however, it was found that when people characterized their significant relationships, the vast majority (88% of the sample) endorsed different attachment orientations in different relationships (Baldwin, Keelan, Fehr, Enns, & Koh-Rangarajoo, 1996). Because of these and similar findings, the study of working models of attachment is undergoing a shift away from an individual-difference approach, toward mapping out how people store in memory a wide range of interpersonal experiences, and how this social knowledge influences their behavior in close relationships (Baldwin, 1995; Baldwin & Fehr, 1995).

In the social support literature, a related question arises with respect to the influence of general versus relationship-specific models of available support (Sarason et al., 1991, 1994). We find it is helpful to conceptualize both general and specific models as embedded in, and arising from, an associative network of relational knowledge. Presumably, people derive their expectations of support largely from a pool of episodic memories about past interactions with significant others. Over time, experiences with similar features or contexts become associated in generalized or prototypical event representations, such as "dependent self relying on dependable other" or "angrily demanding self being rejected by aloof other" (see, e.g., Lalljee, Lamb, & Abelson, 1992; Mayer, Rapp, & Williams, 1993; Trafimow & Wyer, 1993, for recent analyses of the development of event schemas). These relational schemas may then function more or less autonomously from the episodic memories from which they were derived. People also develop organized relational schemas for particular relationships, such as representations of one's nurturant grandmother or authoritarian father. Finally, specific relational schemas should also be connected to relevant contexts, affects, goals, and needs, as well as specific strategies in order to achieve goals and satisfy needs (Baldwin, 1992; Collins & Read, 1994). For example, a person might link feelings of sadness with *If I sigh and express my feelings, someone will cheer me up*.

Beyond the notion that people develop an associative network of relational knowledge, there is little agreement about how this knowledge is organized. Many writers postulate that people have a small number of central, or default, models of relationships, that exert a strong influence on social perception. These models presumably are highly elaborated and derived from the person's most common or significant experiences—perhaps deriving first and foremost from early relationships with caregivers, as attachment theorists suggest (Collins & Read, 1994). These central models may share some common themes and dynamics, but they also may be clearly differentiated from one another. For example, self-with-mother and self-with-spouse schemas should differ somewhat in content because of the different roles and expectations within parent–child and romantic relationships (Collins & Read, 1994; Hazan & Shaver, 1994). Nonetheless, these central models are assumed to be instrumental in shaping social perception across a range of interactions, as indicated by the finding that students' view of the quality of the relationship with their parents predicts their reports of support available more generally (Sarason et al., 1993).

It is less clear how much variability is to be expected within types of relationships, and how a person's knowledge about intimate relationships is related to knowledge about less significant acquaintances. Some writers (e.g., Collins & Read, 1994) postulate a fairly well-organized hierarchical structure, with integrated, central working models being superordinate to, or even independent of, memories and expectations about specific relationships and contexts. Others (e.g., Baldwin et al., 1996) lean more toward exemplar formulations (e.g., Smith & Zarate, 1992) in which the associative network is more of a tangled web than an organized hierarchy. In this view, relational expectations are produced more or less ad hoc by the massed influence of relevant memories. Reasonably stable expectations arise when there is a large amount of information available in memory that is consistent with a given pattern, or if a certain pattern has been identified often enough that strong associative links among the constituent elements have been formed. Such expectations may also be influential to the extent that they are associated with important goals or predominant affects. In any case, they are assumed to be closely tied to specific interpersonal experiences and memories.

ACCESSIBILITY AND ACTIVATION OF RELATIONAL SCHEMAS

Irrespective of how the network of relational knowledge is organized, an important corollary of the notion of multiple models is the principle of knowledge activation and accessibility (Higgins & King, 1981; Higgins, King, & Mavin, 1982; Sedikides & Skowronski, 1991; Srull & Wyer, 1979). Simply put, a knowledge structure is *activated* when it is influencing information processing, and *accessible* if it can be activated easily by relevant information. Almost by definition, a person's default working model is that which is chronically accessible, and so is activated most frequently in perceiving ongoing relationships. This may be the model that carries the most weight when people respond to measures of perceived social support, chronic attachment style, or chronic self-esteem (Baldwin & Fehr, 1995).

Once one considers the possibility of multiple relational schemas, however, one recognizes the importance of *temporary* sources of accessibility, determining which relational schemas tend to be activated at which times and in which contexts. For example, although the relational schemas reflecting a person's general attachment style are chronically accessible, those that reflect other attachment styles are also available and may be activated by recent interpersonal events, social contexts, or transient affect states (Baldwin & Fehr, 1995; Baldwin et al., 1996; Pierce & Lydon, 1995). Accordingly, in studying perceived social support, it is important to look beyond a person's relatively stable personality "traits" to examine meaningful variability in his or her perceptions from one moment to the next (see, e.g., Mischel & Shoda, 1995).

First, as a result of spreading activation, situational or person cues can activate specific relational models. Usually this will involve the activation of directly relevant information: A child's initial interactions with an elderly neighbor, for example, might be guided by a self-with-elderly-stranger schema, or perhaps by a self-with-grandmother schema, as a result of appearance and demeanor cues (Andersen & Cole,

1990). This type of schema-transference does not always occur in such a sensible manner, however. If the elderly neighbor wears jasmine perfume, and the child has come to associate the smell of jasmine perfume with the ruthless evaluative style of a hypercritical piano teacher, a mere whiff of the kindly neighbor's scent might send the child running for his or her security blanket (see, e.g., Lewicki, 1985, for evidence of such transference effects in adults).

Based on research findings in the social-cognitive literature on person perception (e.g., Bargh & Pietromonaco, 1982; Higgins, Rholes, & Jones, 1977; Srull & Wyer, 1979, 1980), we should also expect that it is possible to experimentally activate, or prime, specific relational schemas with resulting effects on the perception of self and social support. This kind of experimental finding would provide strong evidence for the value of a relational schema view of support perceptions. In a study by Sarason and Sarason (1986), for example, some subjects were led to believe that an experimenter would be available to help them if they had trouble with an experimental task. Even though they never actually sought help from the experimenter, these subjects felt less anxious and performed better on the task than subjects who were not offered the social support. Interestingly, this effect was not observed for subjects who came to the study with already chronically high levels of perceived available support; the manipulation of temporary accessibility was influential only for people without such a schema chronically accessible to them.

Other research has shown that it is not even necessary that there be real people on hand to offer assistance, providing further evidence of the influence of intrapsychic structures. Simply leading subjects to think momentarily about supportive or nonsupportive relationships can affect people's subsequent feelings and social perceptions in unrelated situations. This phenomenon has been demonstrated using a variety of cognitive priming techniques, including guided visualizations or subliminal presentations of interpersonal stimuli (e.g., Baldwin, 1994; Baldwin, Carrell, & Lopez, 1990; Baldwin & Holmes, 1987; T. Pierce & Lydon, 1995).

In one recent study (Baldwin & Sinclair, 1996), for example, people spent a few moments visualizing a person who made them feel criticized, and then performed the lexical decision task described earlier. Their reaction times to various interpersonal words were similar to those of chronically low-self-esteem individuals. For example, subjects who had visualized a critical person were quicker (compared with control subjects) to identify words representing *rejection* after they had been exposed to words representing *failure*.

Other priming studies in the domain of self-evaluation have examined links between self-perception and other-representations, showing that relational primes can influence how people perceive themselves in stressful performance situations. Baldwin and Holmes (1987; also Baldwin, 1994, Study 2) found that people were more self-critical when evaluating their performance on a difficult task if they had previously visualized a person whose acceptance of them was highly conditional on achievement and success, than if they had visualized a person who accepted them unconditionally.

In other studies (e.g., Baldwin et al., 1990; Baldwin, 1994, Study 1), subliminal presentations of significant others' pictures or names were used to activate the relational schemas associated with those individuals. Baldwin et al. (1990, Study 1), for example, found that graduate students evaluated their own research ideas more severely when the evaluation phase was preceded by subliminal presentations of a scowling picture of their demanding department chair, compared to when the picture was of a smiling, accepting postdoctoral student. In a second experiment, when undergraduate Catholic women were given a sexual passage to read, they reported more negative self-concepts if they were shown subliminal presentations of a picture of the Pope than if they were shown a picture of an unfamiliar other or a blank screen. These effects were most pronounced for practicing Catholic subjects, for whom the Pope was presumably a significant authority figure.

These and other priming studies demonstrate that specific relational schemas can be activated experimentally to mimic the more naturalistic activations caused by spreading activation from ongoing relationships or momentary social contexts. This illustrates the heuristic value of the relational schema approach in generating novel social-cognitive paradigms to study perceived support. Priming and lexical decision methodologies can be combined with other like techniques to develop a comprehensive, testable model of the self-schemas, other-schemas, and if–then interpersonal expectations involved in social support.

THE ROLE OF RELATIONAL SCHEMAS IN STRESS AND COPING

Having sketched out a general model of relational cognition, we now turn our attention more directly to issues relevant to social support in particular, to explore in more detail the impact relational schemas can have on the experience of stress. We consider hypotheses relevant to the appraisal process, the interpretation of support attempts, and the interpersonal consequences of relational schemas.

In their theory of stress and coping, Lazarus and Folkman identified the coping process as initiated by a cognitive appraisal of the situation. Cognitive appraisal

> includes an evaluation of the personal significance of the encounter (primary appraisal) and an evaluation of the options for coping (secondary appraisal). In primary appraisal the person asks: "What do I have at stake in this encounter?" and in secondary appraisal the question is "What can I do?" (Folkman, 1992, p. 34)

Primary appraisal consists of an evaluation of the situation, which determines the extent to which it is perceived as stressful. In secondary appraisal, the person takes stock of resources available in the situation and devises strategies to deal with the stressor. We theorize that relational schemas may influence both primary and secondary appraisal.

PRIMARY APPRAISAL: RELATIONAL SCHEMAS AND THE EXPERIENCE OF STRESS

Relational schemas can affect the appraisal of stress in positive or negative ways both chronically, as the result of chronically accessible schemas, or temporarily, as the result of schemas that have recently been activated. First, relational schemas that afford high perceived available support can have a dampening effect on the appraised stressfulness of a situation. Lakey and Heller (1988) measured subjects' overall perceived social support from friends (using the Perceived Social Support from Friends; Procidano & Heller, 1983). They found that the subjects who perceived a high level of support available from friends rated a difficult social problem-solving task as less stressful than did their low-perceived-support counterparts. They also found that when friends actually provided supportive comments during a practice trial, subjects were able to perform better on the test, although they did not rate it as less stressful. Other studies of testing situations have yielded positive results on performance and/or stressfulness measures as a result of the availability of a supportive experimenter (e.g., Sarason & Sarason, 1986), a recent discussion with a supportive group (e.g., Sarason, 1981) or the subliminal priming of a supportive versus unsupportive relationship (Baldwin, 1994).

Conversely, negative interpersonal expectations can increase the perception of threat. Rook (1984, 1990, 1992) has demonstrated the impact of negative social exchanges on well-being, conceptualizing these interactions as significant stressors in themselves. Lakey et al. (1994) demonstrated that negative and positive social interactions contributed independently to the prediction of subjective distress. By extension, merely anticipating negative interpersonal exchanges, or expecting others to be unavailable in times of stress, may heighten the stressfulness of an already negative event. Indeed, there is some evidence that negative relational schemas are even more impactful than positive ones in determining the support–stress relationship. A number of studies have shown, for example, that the negative views held by significant others are more potent predictors of low perceived support and distress than positive views are of high perceived support and well-being (see, e.g., Coyne & Bolger, 1990; Coyne et al., 1990). Sarason et al. (1993) found that parents' negative views of students were better than their positive views as predictors of the students' judgments of how accepting their parents were.

Explanations for the impact of working models can focus on both interpersonal expectations and the self-concept. In a testing situation, for example, having the expectation that help is directly available (e.g., Lakey & Heller, 1988; Sarason & Sarason, 1986) can decrease the stressfulness of the task itself, as subjects are aware that if the task is too difficult, they can always get assistance. From an attachment perspective, perceived support activates a sense of "felt security" (Sroufe & Waters, 1977) that serves as a secure base from which the person can approach the world with confidence. This phenomenon can be quite obvious in the behavior of a toddler at a family picnic, periodically checking back with his mother while he explores the strange environs; it is no less important in adulthood in the development and maintenance of intimate and community relationships that characterize a supportive social network.

Having the expectation that others will react with scorn to one's failures and weaknesses, on the other hand, would add an additional threat on top of the possibility of failing at a task. Indeed, Thoits (1983) has reported that stressors that threaten a person's self-image or self-esteem are generally more distressing than stressors that do not affect self-concepts. From a relational schema perspective, of course, interpersonal- and self-oriented cognitions are highly interdependent and probably should not be considered separately, because perceptions about the availability of support and acceptance can influence the self-concept. The feeling of being loved and cared for can enhance a person's feelings of self-worth and self-efficacy, promoting self-confidence and facilitating more benign appraisals of threats in the environment (Sarason et al., 1994); the anticipation of rejection can do quite the opposite.

To go beyond merely observing correlations between globally positive or negative views of others and of self, we need to try to study the cognitive mechanisms of how relational schemas influence the sense of self. Baldwin (1994) argued that activated relational schemas define inference procedures for drawing conclusions from information about the self. For example, a person with a demanding piano teacher might develop the reaction that *If I do not practice hard without complaining, I am a lazy shirker who does not deserve anyone's attention*; and this inference procedure might be activated automatically when in a difficult situation or as a result of cues that activate the schema for that relationship.

Priming research has offered some clues as to how the sense of self-esteem is socially constructed, particularly with respect to negative self-views. Baldwin and Holmes (1987, Study 2), for example, found that people who were primed with a relationship in which they were accepted only conditionally were particularly likely to evaluate themselves according to the kinds of problematic inference procedures that have been identified in the self-esteem and depression literatures. After failing on a difficult task, they attributed their failure to something about themselves, expected that others would have done better, and showed a tendency toward overgeneralizing, or drawing global negative conclusions about themselves on the basis of single negative behaviors.

The influence of relational schemas need not stop at single inferences about isolated events, but rather can have ripple effects throughout the relational schema network. In interpersonally oriented models of social support, various authors (e.g., Coyne & Bolger, 1990; Rook, 1990) have argued that stressful experiences can lead to support seeking from a close relationship partner, putting a strain on the relationship, further increasing stress and the need for support, eventually leading to a gradual deterioration of the relationship. A parallel phenomenon may occur intrapsychically as a result of spreading activation between different schemas and their associated affect. A situation that threatens persons' self-view, the view others have of them, and/or the quality of their relationships and interpersonal exchanges, may diminish their sense of self-esteem and self-efficacy (e.g., Lakey & Edmunson, 1993; Lakey et al., 1994), as we have seen. It may induce a negative mood, leading to the increased accessibility of all manner of negative cognitions (Bower, 1981), including negative expectancies about the availability of social support (e.g., Cohen, Towbes, & Flocco, 1988). This might result in their viewing the event as more stressful and possibly discourage them from seeking social support as a coping strategy. This type of "downward spiral" is well recognized in the depression literature; the task remains of specifying the most common routes of activation among self-representations, interpersonal expectancies, affects, social goals, and strategies in stressful contexts. Considerable research is also required into mechanisms having a more salutary effect, whereby positive relational expectations lead to positive self-views and positive reactions to stress.

Together, then, positive and negative interpersonal expectations—both chronic and temporarily activated—can influence the perceived stressfulness of a situation. This effect may be mediated by specific expectations of others' behaviors, or else more indirectly via effects on the perceiver's feelings of self-esteem and self-efficacy.

Secondary Appraisal: Relational Schemas
and the Selection of Coping Strategies

Once the primary appraisal of a situation has yielded an evaluation of what is at stake and how stressful the situation is, the person engages in secondary appraisal, which involves an evaluation of coping options (Folkman, 1992). Possible coping strategies range from self-reliance and emotional control to seeking instrumental and emotional support from others (e.g., Hobfoll, Freedy, Lane, & Geller, 1990; Thoits, 1986; Weiss, 1974).

When engaging in secondary appraisal, the assumption is that people adopt strategies that maximize the likelihood of positive outcomes as well as optimally preserving coping resources (Cutrona & Russell, 1987; Hobfoll et al., 1990). The extent to which social support is chosen as a coping option, therefore, is determined in part by expectations of whether others will be helpful and responsive. The perception that social support is available should increase the likelihood of turning to others for support when needed in highly stressful situations, and may also prompt the person to adopt various other adaptive coping strategies. Manne and Zautra (1989) found that rheumatoid arthritis patients who perceived their spouse as supportive were most likely to engage in adaptive coping behaviors such as information seeking and cognitive restructuring. Similarly, in studies of both depressed and nondepressed individuals, the perception of family members as supportive was negatively related to the use of avoidant coping strategies when facing stress, and, for depressed subjects at least, positively related to engaging in active behavioral coping strategies, including seeking social support (Holahan & Moos, 1987).

Not surprisingly, the converse is true as well: Negative interpersonal expectations can lead to dysfunctional coping responses. For example, Manne and Zautra (1989) found that patients' expectations of spousal criticism were associated with maladaptive coping strategies (e.g., wishful thinking) and poorer psychological outcomes. In a study of depression, Pietromonaco and Rook (1987) found that depressed subjects were particularly likely to perceive that initiating social contact with a significant other in order to discuss a personal problem entailed more risks of rejection or conflict, and fewer benefits such as feeling respected or liked by the other person. Such expectations that others will react negatively can lead people to avoid social contact (e.g., Thoits, 1986). For instance, cancer patients who expected that others would be overly upset, worried, or bored if they disclosed their feelings, chose to cope by "keeping their thoughts and feelings to themselves" (Dunkel-Schetter, 1984, p. 87).

General Expectations

One can examine the influence of both general perceptions of support and specific models of specific relationships. Just as general models of self-esteem and acceptance from others influence the primary appraisal of stress, they also influence the choice of coping strategies. This is most apparent in situations when the sense of self-esteem is threatened: In such situations, seeking support may be seen as distressing, as it may cause embarrassment (Fisher, Goff, Nadler, & Chinsky, 1988) and could open oneself to the negative effects of others viewing one as weak and incompetent at solving problems on one's own (Nadler, 1990; Sarason et al., 1990a). Indeed, even the self-perception that one requires help is a potent threat to self-esteem (Coyne et al., 1990). As a result, research shows that stressful situations that are appraised as threats to self-esteem tend to be associated with a reduced likelihood of seeking and receiving social support, including aid, informational and emotional support (Dunkel-Schetter, Folkman, & Lazarus, 1987; Folkman, Lazarus, Dunkel-Schetter, DeLongis & Gruen, 1986). It is when people do not perceive themselves as responsible for the problem, and so do not blame themselves for their predicament, that they seem to be most likely to seek social support (Karuza, Zevon, Gleason, Karuza, & Nash, 1990).

These findings demonstrate that in self-esteem-threatening situations, people are less likely to disclose their problem to others and more likely to cope with the situation on their own. The choice to rely on individualistic coping strategies certainly is not all bad—in fact, it might be the most adaptive choice when these strategies promise the best outcomes. For example, relying on oneself might actually be a functional way to restore damaged self-esteem and the view of self as a competent person, assuming one can successfully resolve the situation alone. This might explain the finding that high-self-esteem individuals are less likely than low-self-esteem individuals to seek support on ego-central tasks (Nadler, 1991).

Whereas not seeking support may result in a performance that is not quite as good as it would have been had help been sought, it does maintain or even bolster self-esteem and feelings of self-efficacy, which are what are actually at stake in such tasks (Nadler, 1991). Those high in self-esteem can be seen as optimally maximizing their personally relevant outcome (performance or self-view), while minimizing the negative consequences of stress on their personal and social resources (Hobfoll et al., 1990). This strategy is likely to be more effective with respect to both outcomes and preservation of coping resources than the indiscriminating dependency demonstrated by persons low in self-esteem.

Differentiated Expectations

General expectations of social acceptance and rejection, then, and the implications for self-esteem seem to be central determinants of whether a person seeks social support when under stress. Following the notion of multiple models, however, it is also important to look more closely: Although people might have a general perception of the availability of support, they also have distinct expectations about what is available or helpful within particular relationships and situations (Cutrona, Cohen, & Igram, 1990; Dakof & Taylor, 1990; G. Pierce et al., 1991, 1992; Procidano & Heller, 1983; Sarason et al., 1990c, 1994). Based on the idea that people have multiple self- and other schemas, and corresponding interpersonal scripts, we tend to agree with theoretical perspectives hypothesizing that people choose whom to turn to on the basis of relationship-specific expectations.

The evaluation of a significant other's supportiveness is likely influenced by a host of factors, including characteristics of the person and features of the situation. Researchers have examined the support provider's role, interpersonal skills, ability to empathize, attitudinal similarity, and the level of intimacy of the relationship (e.g., Dunkel-Schetter, 1984). Especially important may be the particular "support style" believed to be preferred by the significant other. For example, Folkman et al. (1986) classified coping strategies as either problem-focused or emotion-focused, and significant others may be seen as preferentially offering one form of support or the other (see Lakey & Drew, Chapter 6, this volume, for relevant data).

Matching coping needs with appropriate strategies is an important aspect of secondary appraisal, as a poor fit between the appraisal of stress, coping options, and the actual coping that occurs can itself be upsetting, adding to the stressfulness of the situation (e.g., Folkman, 1992). It would not be surprising, therefore, to find that people attend to any systematic variability in the behavior of potential support providers. The responses of significant others may be perceived as constant across situations, for example, or they may vary according to situational characteristics. For example, although a certain significant other might be generally expected to provide helpful, emotion-focused support, in a situation that is very threatening to their beliefs, they may be expected to react negatively. In that particular situation, that person would likely be avoided (Fisher et al., 1988).

Similarly, how much expertise the person has with the specific type of stressor may also play a role in the choice of support providers and the extent to which their support is perceived as helpful. For example, cancer patients report that they viewed receiving information and advice on how to cope with the illness as helpful when provided by physicians and health professionals, but as unhelpful when coming from family and friends, who were perceived as nonexperts (Dunkel-Schetter, 1984; Taylor & Dakof, 1988).

Although it is cumbersome to try to specify all the situational and interpersonal factors that go into perceived support, we believe that much is to be gained by examining specific if–then contingencies rather than only global or averaged perceptions (cf. Cantor & Kihlstrom, 1987; Mischel & Shoda, 1995). Consider a young woman who has failed an exam. She may expect her parents to be caring and emotionally supportive, her best friend to be critical but instrumentally helpful, her boyfriend uninterested, and her competitive acquaintances somewhat gleeful. In contrast, if she unexpectedly becomes pregnant, she might expect her parents to be critical and judgmental, her best friend to be caring and supportive, her boyfriend distant and angry, and her acquaintances mildly anxious or indifferent. If the strategy is to optimize the likelihood of positive outcomes by seeking support from significant others who are expected to be the most helpful in meeting the needs of the moment and avoiding those who may be expected to exacerbate the problem, words of encouragement might be sought from a parent in one situation, and a helping hand from a friend might be sought in a different situation (e.g., Cutrona et al., 1990; Dakof & Taylor, 1990).

Making things even more perplexing is that a single exchange can activate both positive and negative interpersonal understandings, and this can complicate decisions about seeking support from others (see, e.g., Horowitz, 1988). Many young people who have considered borrowing significant amounts of money from their parents, for example, can attest to difficulty of deciding whether receiving much-needed instrumental support is worth the price of activating *Greedy-child-bailed-out-by-resentful-parent*, or *Dependent-child-taken-care-of-by-altruistic-caregiver* scripts (e.g., Dunkel-Schetter & Bennett, 1990).

Thus, while we recognize the difficulties inherent in developing a fully articulated model of perceived support, we suggest that whereas global or aggregate measures of perceived support might identify central, default dispositions toward seeking social support, much increased specificity in behavioral prediction will come from studying people's specific if–then expectations (Mischel, 1973). Ultimately, of course, the goal should be to map out the nature of cognitive structures encompassing both general and specific models.

Activation of Relational Schemas

Because of the possibility of multiple models, different schemas can be activated in many different ways: by situational cues (e.g., piano recitals), interpersonal cues (e.g., physical resemblance), or mood states (e.g., sadness), for example. Activated relational schemas should define the extent to which seeking support is seen as primarily beneficial or as involving risks of rejection.

It should be possible to demonstrate the effects of activated relational schemas on primary and secondary appraisals of a stressful situation by experimentally priming either positive or negative interpersonal concepts. This idea was tested in a study by T. Pierce and Lydon (1995) in which female university students were asked to imagine themselves in a scenario that described a young woman facing an unplanned pregnancy, and then to indicate what their affective state and likely coping strategies would be in that situation. Before allowing subjects to listen to the scenario, positive or negative interpersonal expectations were primed in the two experimental groups. Subjects were shown subliminal presentations of positive or negative interactional words (e.g., *caring, supportive* vs. *critical, rejecting*) during a bogus "attention facilitating" exercise on a computer. Control-group subjects were presented with strings of consonants that looked similar to the experimental primes. Subjects then listened to the pregnancy scenario and completed affect and coping scales.

Subjects in the negative-prime condition reported significantly less positive affect following the scenario than did positive-prime and control subjects (see Table 2.1). Also, consistent with the idea that secondary appraisal can be shaped by activated relational structures, subjects in the positive-prime condition reported that they would

TABLE 2.1. Positive Affect and the Likelihood
of Seeking Emotional Support as a Function
of Priming Condition (Pierce & Lydon, 1995)

	Priming condition		
	Negative	Control	Positive
Positive affect[a]	1.12	1.67	1.81
SD	.23	.82	.81
Seek emotional support[b]	2.91	2.69	3.20
SD	.61	.69	.70

Note. Means adjusted for covariates.
[a]Negative versus Control/Positive contrast is significant ($p < .003$)
[b]Positive versus Control/Negative contrast is significant ($p < .03$)

be more likely to seek emotional support (from parents, partner, and friends) as a coping strategy than did subjects in the two other conditions, when controlling for self-esteem, optimism, and two factors from the Collins and Read (1990) attachment measure. These results demonstrate that a person's choice of strategies can be influenced by relational schemas rendered accessible by temporary factors, over and above those that are chronically accessible. A fully elaborated theory of secondary appraisal, therefore, will need to include a consideration of how different cues can activate different relational models.

RELATIONAL SCHEMAS AND THE INTERPRETATION OF RECEIVED SUPPORT

Relational schemas can also influence the interpretation of significant others' potentially supportive behaviors after they have been received (Lakey et al., 1994; G. Pierce et al., 1992). A person with positive interpersonal expectations, for example, might tend to perceive others' behaviors as supportive, regardless of whether they were intended to be so. Alternatively, a person anticipating negative responses might perceive a significant other, intending to be supportive and helpful, as manipulative, deceitful, or self-interested.

Evidence of this assimilation bias, in which people interpret behavior in ways consistent with their expectations, has been extensive in both the general social-cognitive literature and the social support literature. For example, in one study (Lakey, Moineau, & Drew, 1992), subjects considered a hypothetical stressful event and then observed videotaped presentations of other people's neutral responses to them. It was found that those with high perceived available support (on the Interpersonal Support Evaluation List; Cohen & Hoberman, 1983) rated these fairly neutral responses as more helpful than those who had low perceived support scores. In other studies, a negative outlook, as indicated by low perceived available support, resentment, low self-esteem, or a negative view of parental support, has been found to reduce the perceived supportiveness of others' attempts at helping (Lakey & Cassady, 1990, Study 2; Vinokur, Schul, & Caplan, 1987). Depending on the circumstances, these findings seem to apply to both strangers and significant others, and both general and relationship-specific expectations. G. Pierce et al. (1992), for example, had undergraduate students perform a stress-inducing public speaking task. Subjects then received a supportive note from their mothers, who had supposedly been watching from another room. Subjects' interpretations of their mother's message were strongly influenced by preexisting views of the relationship with the mother: Those with positive expectations rated the feedback (which was predetermined by the experimenter and identical for all subjects) as reflecting more understanding and a more positive evaluation of the speech.

It is likely that relational expectancies are maintained, in part, through attributional patterns. Various researchers (e.g., Bradbury & Fincham, 1989, 1990; Fletcher & Fincham, 1991; Murray & Holmes, 1993, 1996) have studied attributions in close relationships, and their findings suggest that if a person expects that support is generally available from a significant other, any positive behavior from the other is likely to be attributed to internal, global, and stable factors, and seen as helpful and supportive. On the other hand, if the person does not expect the other to be supportive, attempts at helpfulness might be discredited by attributions to external, unstable, and specific factors (e.g., "He says everything will be all right because that's what you say in this kind of situation. He really doesn't care."). Murray and Holmes (1996) review evidence demonstrating the power of this kind of attributional bias: Positive assumptions about one's romantic partner, even if based largely in fantasy and illusion, can function as interpretive filters to skew one's perceptions considerably to sustain the positive view of one's partner. For example, they suggest that a partner's obstinate stubbornness can be interpreted as a sign of integrity, or an inexpressive partner can be cast as the "strong, silent type."

These attribution models can be extended by examining attributions about all aspects of the relational schema conjointly. In any interpersonal interaction, attributions can be made for one's own behavior, for the other's behavior, as well as for positive and negative interpersonal outcomes. Consider, for example, persons with a "preoccupied" attachment orientation (Bartholomew & Horowitz, 1991), who presumably see themselves as weak, inadequate, and dependent on some strong but unresponsive other. These individuals might develop an attributional style that maintains this negative view of self and positive view of other. When negative events occur within the relationship, they might attribute blame to themselves and not to their partner. In contrast, when positive events occur within the relationship, they might tend to see their partner as the one worthy of praise for the events, while not taking credit themselves. If the partner tries to offer support during a time of stress, the preoccupied person might assimilate this to a "charity" or "performing obligations" script. As a consequence of this self-deprecating and partner-enhancing attributional style, the existing chronic relational schemas of negative-self and positive-other would be maintained, even strengthened. This would also promote the interpersonal pattern of dependency on the partner, as he or she is perceived as responsible for positive events in the relationship. Thus, relational expectations can engender an attributional style that confirms and strengthens all facets of the relational schema.

Contrast Effects

Although assimilation and confirmatory effects have been a major focus of social-cognitive research, there is a growing awareness in the literature of circumstances in which contrast effects can occur instead (e.g., Herr, Sherman, & Fazio, 1983; Martin, 1986; Newman & Uleman, 1990; Strack, Schwarz, Bless, Kubler, & Wanke, 1993). Studies of the self-evaluative effects of primed relational schemas (Baldwin, 1994; Baldwin et al., 1990; Baldwin & Holmes, 1987) have demonstrated the importance of focus of attention. When people are not attending to a primed relational model, either because they are self-focused, or because the prime was subtle or subliminal, their self-evaluations tend to be influenced by the evaluative style associated with the primed relationship—demonstrating an assimilation effect. When people can focus their attention on a primed relationship, however, they seem to override their automatic responses and give self-evaluative responses that adjust for the influence of the prime. It seems that if people can attribute their negative self-feelings to having recently thought about a critical other, they are able to dismiss those feelings and access a more positive self-schema (Baldwin, 1994).

We recently have observed similar phenomena in some experimental studies of social support. In one study (T. Pierce, Lydon, & Leroux, 1995a), we had subjects respond to the pregnancy scenario (described earlier; T. Pierce & Lydon, 1995) after either a subliminal prime or a supraliminal prime. The supraliminal prime consisted of having subjects describe in detail a recent supportive or nonsupportive social inter-action with a significant other, as part of a supposed "second study" for a different experimenter. Results showed a significant interaction effect, with mood ratings showing assimilation to the prime only in the subliminal condition.

Other factors, in addition to prime-awareness, have been shown to produce even stronger contrast effects. In a study of person perception, Herr (1986) showed that if a prime sets an extreme or exaggerated standard, novel information can be seen as quite different from it, rather than assimilated to the prime and seen as somewhat similar to it. He found, for example, that when people were primed with a moderate exemplar of a category (e.g., Joe Frazier as an example of hostility), their subsequent judgments of a target person showed the usual assimilation effects, such that ambiguously aggressive behaviors were judged as fairly hostile. When subjects were primed with an extreme exemplar of a category (e.g., Adolph Hitler as an example of hostility), however, their subsequent judgments showed contrast effects, such that behaviors were judged as not particularly hostile.

Accordingly, the extremity of an activated relational schema might similarly be expected to determine whether people exhibit assimilation or contrast effects. For example, idealistic interpersonal expectations can define standards by which the behavior of others is evaluated. Behavior that is discrepant from the expectancy can then attract increased attention, trigger increased thought and more pronounced evaluations, and produce stronger memory traces to affect later judgments (see, e.g., Hamilton & Sherman, 1994; Mankowski & Wyer, Chapter 7, this volume).

Related to contrast effects is the finding of enhanced recall for schema-inconsistent information, especially in the case of clear, extreme schemas (Hastie & Kumar, 1979; Higgins & Bargh, 1987). In a study of memory for supportive behaviors, Lakey et al. (1992) have reported that social support schematics tend to show better recall for unhelpful or negative support attempts than support aschematics. These and other studies conducted by Lakey and his colleagues (Lakey et al., 1992; also Lakey & Cassady, 1990) suggest that when people have highly positive expectations, their memory for negative information is either just as good as or even better than that of people with negative expectations. However, the converse—an enhanced recall of positive infor-mation by subjects with negative expectations—has not been found. This asymmetry is not too surprising, given that negative information generally elicits more attention, more causal attribution activity, and more complex cognitive representations than positive information (Taylor, 1991).

Also, the focus on negative information is perhaps especially reasonable in the context of stress and social support. In highly stressful situations, when a person needs and expects to be able to count on another's support, a negative response from the other might be quite harmful to the person as well as to the relationship. In fact, a negative behavior from a significant other in a highly stressful situation might be more harmful to a person who confidently expected others to be supportive than to a person who expected others to react negatively. The negative-expectation person, anticipat-ing unsupportive reactions from his or her network, would most likely have initially appraised the situation as more stressful and would have opted for coping strategies other than seeking support. Conversely, the person who perceived support as available would not anticipate a negative response from significant others, so might have appraised the situation as less stressful than it actually is, and might have relied on social support as a coping strategy. He or she now faces unexpected social strain, in addition to the stressful situation itself, and is unlikely to have adopted adequate coping strategies to face the current situation.

A Diary Study

The notion of contrast effects might help explain the nonsignificant or counter-intuitive findings sometimes observed when people are asked to report their satisfaction with the social support received from others. A study was recently conducted with women who were undergoing pregnancy tests for what would be an unplanned pregnancy (T. Pierce & Lydon, 1993). Women's initial expectations about how supportive significant others would be of their decision regarding an unplanned pregnancy were measured at Time 1, before receiving test results. This measure of perceived support significantly predicted changes in affective state 2 to 7 days after receiving the test result (Time 2). This correlation between expectations and subsequent affect was not mediated by the amount of satisfaction with support actually received from significant others since finding out about the pregnancy.

From this finding, we might be tempted to conclude that satisfaction with social support does not play a distinctive role in adjusting to stressful life events. However, an alternative explanation is that initial interpersonal expectations might have altered the perception that the woman had of others' supportive attempts; that is, satisfaction with support might be evaluated in terms of a discrepancy between what was expected and what was actually received. A woman with highly positive expectations as a reference point might have perceived the level of support she received as less satisfactory than would a woman who had more moderate expectations and received the same level of support.

This possibility is currently under investigation in a study in which subjects are keeping records of their social interactions for a period of 7 days (T. Pierce, Lydon, & Sugar, 1995b). Perception of the availability of social support is assessed on the day before the recording begins, using a short version of the Interpersonal Support Evaluation List (Cohen & Hoberman, 1983). On the day following the end of the diary records, a retrospective rating is obtained of the extent to which they felt that the people they interacted with during the week were helpful or supportive of them, along with a rating of how satisfied they were with how helpful or supportive others had been during the week.

We have conducted preliminary analyses on an initial sample of 29 subjects, categorized by median splits as either high or low on initial perceived availability of support (hereafter referred to as high or low perceived, although low perceived actually reflects moderately positive support expectations), and also as high or low in retrospectively reported received support (high or low received). There were a number of main effects: Subjects with high initial levels of perceived support had significantly more interactions during the week, spent more time interacting with others, and tended to have more interactions that they rated as helpful or supportive than subjects in the low perceived group (regardless of their received support classification). Subjects in the high-received group rated others, on average, as significantly more supportive across their daily interactions than those in the low-received group (regardless of their initial level of perceived support).

However, the findings also indicate an interaction effect, such that subjects who were both high in perceived and low in received rated their satisfaction with the supportiveness of others more harshly than those in the other three groups (see Table 2.2). We compared this high-perceived but low-received group with their counterparts who had low initial expectations. Although the subjects with higher initially perceived support had somewhat more interactions, spent significantly more time interacting with others, and rated their level of support received similarly to those in the low-perceived–low-received group, they were significantly less satisfied with how supportive others had been. Objectively, the experience of subjects in the high-perceived–low-received group seemed quite similar to that of subjects in the low-perceived–low-received group, if not somewhat better. Yet, their satisfaction ratings were substantially lower than those of all other groups in the study. In comparison, the low-perceived–low-received group seemed just as satisfied with their interactions as those in the high-received groups.

These data support the idea of a contrast effect, particularly involving negative information: People who had highly positive expectations of support that were not met were more dissatisfied with their interactions than those who had more moderate expectations. No indications were found that receiving support beyond one's expectations inflated people's sense of satisfaction.

Viewed together with the assimilation results described earlier, these findings suggest that it may be more beneficial to have moderate relational expectations about support than to have highly positive ones. Having highly positive interpersonal expectations can be problematic, as they seem to place persons at risk for experiencing disappointment and lead them to appraise moderate levels of support more harshly and recall unhelpful interactions with greater ease. Yet, much of the research on social support suggests that highly positive expectations are associated with positive mental

TABLE 2.2. Satisfaction with Support
Received over the Course of the Week
(T. Pierce, Lydon, & Sugar, 1995b)

Support received (Time 2)	Perceived availability of support (Time 1)	
	Low	High
Low	M = 5.63	M = 4.29
	SD = .52	SD = .23
	n = 8	n = 7
High	M = 5.86	M = 6.14
	SD = .90	SD = .69
	n = 7	n = 7

Note. Satisfaction ratings were made on a scale of 1 to 7.

health outcomes (Cohen, 1988; Murray & Holmes, 1996; T. Pierce & Lydon, 1993; Thoits, 1986; Wallston et al., 1983). How might we resolve this apparent contradiction to anticipate when positive expectations will produce contrast rather than assimilation effects?

We suggest that relational expectations can be formed primarily in a bottom-up fashion, based on interpersonal experiences, or else primarily in a top-down fashion, based on implicit theories about relationships and idealized relationship illusions. For example, a person's schema of how close-relationship partners react in stressful situations may arise from past relationships, or from the internalization of relationship ideals conveyed in movies and romance novels. Excessively positive schemas drawn in a top-down fashion from illusory beliefs may be largely divorced from the hard reality of typical relationship dynamics, and so should be more fragile and more vulnerable to disconfirming evidence. Those schemas grounded in interpersonal experience, in contrast, should be more resilient in the face of negative or schema-inconsistent interactions. The bottom-up approach still allows for poetic license in the positively biased interpretations of the partner's behavior and motives, but there is a realistic foundation set in actual interpersonal experience. This type of relational schema may be best conceptualized as having a prototype structure, with a generally positive model emerging from numerous exemplars of imperfect but nevertheless positive experiences. Thus, disconfirming evidence can be more easily integrated into an experience-based relational schema or prototype, as its fuzzy boundaries allow for a reinterpretation of negative interpersonal events within a positive context (see, e.g., Hamilton & Sherman, 1994). The study of contrast effects could lead to significant advances in our understanding of how interpersonal knowledge is aggregated and organized in relational schemas, and how these structures influence the processing of social information.

RELATIONAL SCHEMAS AND THE INTERPERSONAL CONSEQUENCES OF EXPECTATIONS

Lest we risk leaving social support all in the perceiver's head, we will finish with a brief discussion of the links between relational schemas and interpersonal behavior. As numerous authors (e.g., Lazarus, Coyne, & Folkman, 1982; Safran, 1990; Wachtel 1977) have pointed out, cognition about relationships is only one part of a cognitive-interpersonal cycle, wherein cognition affects social interaction, which in turn activates and shapes cognitive structures. The task, then, is to discover the interrelations of social support cognitions and behaviors.

As previously noted, because people often interpret others' behavior in a way that is consistent with chronically accessible relational schemas, interpersonal experiences might tend to confirm expectations and maintain existing schemas. Researchers interested in a cognitive view of social support have suggested that this confirmatory bias may be further bolstered by its behavioral counterpart, the self-fulfilling prophecy. Numerous studies have shown that when perceivers behave in accordance with their expectations, they often elicit schema-congruent responses from others (see, e.g., Miller & Turnbull, 1986, and Snyder, 1984, for reviews). This cycle maintains the perceiver's schema and also influences the other person's script for future interactions—all leading to continued confirmation of the original expectation.

Although substantial experimental evidence supports the general phenomenon of self-fulfilling prophecies, the application of this interpretation to the support domain seems limited somewhat by the finding that expectations of support available from others does not tend to correlate with support actually received when stressors arise. On the other hand, actively seeking support generally does lead others to provide more support (Dunkel-Schetter et al., 1987; Dunkel-Schetter & Skokan, 1990), confirming the self-fulfilling-prophecy dynamic. One resolution of this incongruity involves the notion that people may or may not seek support in times of stress (Coyne & Bolger, 1990). People who perceive support as readily available may not need to seek it out, for example, because their sense of security provides intrapsychic resources to allow them to cope on their own. If they do elect to seek support, however, it is generally provided. Thus, the expectancy is unchallenged—either because of behavioral confirmation, or because the person never put the expectancy to the test. People who do not perceive support as available, in contrast, may avoid social contact entirely, thus never testing their negative assumptions.

More interestingly perhaps, relationship-specific if–then expectations might determine the circumstances under which a person will or will not seek support from certain others, and, as a result, self-fulfilling effects might be observed at the level of specific relationships. For example, seeking support from a person who is expected to respond positively in a particular situation, and receiving helpful responses from that person, confirms the belief that this person is indeed supportive in this type of situation. Avoiding negatively perceived others, on the other hand, prevents disconfirmation from occurring and maintains the expectation that they would not have been understanding or helpful—again strengthening existing relational schemas.

Finally, although social support is generally considered positive, some researchers (e.g., Coyne & Bolger, 1990; Coyne et al., 1990; Rook 1992) have explored some of the negative interpersonal effects of support seeking. In and of itself, support seeking has an ironic twist: Because close relationship partners are expected to be responsive to one another's needs (Clark & Mills, 1979), if significant others are not instinctively responsive to a person's needs, and the person is forced to expressly request support, this may be interpreted as meaning that significant others are not really interested in providing support (e.g., Dunkel-Schetter et al., 1987). Indeed, support provided spontaneously is perceived as more helpful than support given in response to a direct request (Cutrona et al., 1990). Also, situations that entail the explicit expression of the need for support can expose weaknesses or problems in a relationship (Coyne & Bolger, 1990). Even in relatively secure relationships, chronic dependence can lead others to progressively distance themselves because of the burden of providing support and the perception of inequity in the relationship (Rook 1990).

The contribution of a relational schema approach to this kind of analysis is to make the simple point that what people think about their relationships plays a critical role in how they behave toward each other and can bias the perception and development of new relationships, resulting in the re-creation of patterns similar to those that had developed in a different social network. Once the importance of relational cognition is considered, this raises many questions about how the representation and activation of relational knowledge shapes people's interactions and experiences of social support in different relationships. A man might find, for example, that he seems to have many warm, supportive relationships with gray-haired women, who resemble his grandmother, but mostly conflictual, mutually hostile relationships with red-haired women, who resemble his first piano teacher (e.g., Andersen & Cole, 1990). Or, a woman might find that soon after her emotionally unavailable father dies, her husband also begins to withdraw, complaining about her incessant demands for attention. These kinds of interpersonal phenomena can be fully understood only by considering issues of knowledge representation and activation.

SOME CAVEATS AND CONCLUDING REMARKS

We realize that, apart from the preceding section, we have focused almost entirely on the cognitions of the individual and how he or she experiences stress and social support. It is important to acknowledge that the development of any relationship obviously is based on the interactions that occur between the partners, which are influenced not just by one person's schemas and behaviors, but also by the other person's schemas and behaviors (G. Pierce et al., 1991). Research approaches that emphasize relationship characteristics emerging from a combination of the individuals' traits and cognitions (e.g., Kenny & Albright, 1987) will help to map out how individuals' understandings of stress and social support can work together to produce supportive or nonsupportive relationships.

An important first step, though, is to recognize the integrative possibilities in adopting a social-cognitive approach and exploring the information-processing dynamics of perceived support. It should not seem a radical proposition that the structures and mechanisms relevant to social support share much in common with those relevant to attachment, self-esteem, and relationship success, or that these cognitive factors are primarily concerned with interpersonal information. We need to identify the specific if–then expectations that are most influential in determining the perception and generation of social support, and the perception and generation of rejection and conflict. This will involve an examination of how interpersonal knowledge is represented in memory, as exemplars, prototypes, scripts, or hierarchies, for example. It also will involve exploring the interrelations between general and relationship-specific models of support availability. And, it will require developing a clearer understanding of factors determining whether relational schemas will produce assimilation or contrast effects in the perception of interpersonal experience.

Perhaps one of the most intriguing and promising issues raised by this approach is that of knowledge accessibility. We need to understand better how specific models become activated as a result of situational, interpersonal, or affective cues, and how the activation of different schemas can lead to very different interpersonal outcomes. Then we may realize a more fully elaborated, integrated model of when and how relationships influence responses to stress.

REFERENCES

Ainsworth, M. D. S. (1982). Attachment: Retrospect and prospect. In C. M. Parkes & J. Stevenson-Hinde (Eds.), *The place of attachment in human behavior* (pp. 3–30). New York: Basic Books.

Andersen, S. M., & Cole, S. W. (1990). "Do I know you?": The role of significant others in general social perception. *Journal of Personality and Social Psychology*, *59*, 384–399.

Baldwin, M. W. (1992). Relational schemas and the processing of social information. *Psychological Bulletin*, *112*, 461–484.

Baldwin, M. W. (1994). Primed relational schemas as a source of self-evaluative procedures. *Journal of Social and Clinical Psychology*, 380–403.

Baldwin, M. W. (1995). Relational schemas and cognition in close relationships. *Journal of Social and Personal Relationships*, *12*, 547–552.

Baldwin, M. W. (1996). *Relational schemas underlying the sense of acceptance*. Unpublished raw data.

Baldwin, M. W., Carrell, S. E, & Lopez, D. F. (1990). Priming relationship schemas: My advisor and the pope are watching me from the back of my mind. *Journal of Experimental Social Psychology*, *26*, 435–454.

Baldwin, M. W., & Fehr, B. (1995). On the instability of attachment style ratings. *Personal Relationships*, *2*, 247–261.

Baldwin, M. W., Fehr, B., Keedian, E., Seidel, M., & Thomson, D. W. (1993). An exploration of the relational schemas underlying attachment styles: Self-report and lexical decision approaches. *Personality and Social Psychology Bulletin*, *19*, 748–754.

Baldwin, M. W., & Holmes, J. G. (1987). Salient private audiences and awareness of the self. *Journal of Personality and Social Psychology*, *53*, 1087–1098.

Baldwin, M. W., Keelan, J. P. R., Fehr, B., Enns, V. & Koh-Rangarajoo, E. (1996). Social cognitive conceptualization of attachment working models: Availability and accessibility effects. *Journal of Personality and Social Psychology*, *71*, 94–109.

Baldwin, M. W., & Sinclair, L. (1996). Self-esteem and "if ... then" contingencies of interpersonal acceptance. *Journal of Personality and Social Psychology*, *71*, 1130–1141.

Bargh, J. A., & Pietromonaco, P. (1982). Automatic information processing and social perception: The influence of trait information presented outside conscious awareness on impression formation. *Journal of Personality and Social Psychology*, *43*, 437–449.

Bartholomew, K., & Horowitz, L. M. (1991). Attachment styles among young adults: A test of a four category model. *Journal of Personality and Social Psychology*, *61*, 226–244.

Bower, G. H. (1981). Emotional mood and memory. *American Psychologist*, *36*, 129–148.

Bowlby, J. (1969). *Attachment and Loss: Vol. 1. Attachment*. New York: Basic Books.

Bowlby, J. (1973). *Attachment and Loss: Vol. 2. Separation*. New York: Basic Books.

Bradbury, T. N., & Fincham, F. D. (1989). Behavior and satisfaction in marriage: Prospective mediating processes. In C. Hendrick (Ed.), *Close relationships* (pp. 119–143). Newbury Park, CA: Sage Publications.

Bradbury, T. N., & Fincham, F. D. (1990). Attribution in marriage: Review and critique. *Psychological Bulletin*, *107*, 3–33.

Bretherton, I. (1990). Communication patterns, internal working models, and the intergenerational transmission of attachment relationships. *Infant Mental Health Journal*, *11*, 237–252.

Burman B., & Margolin G. (1992). Analysis of the association between marital relationships and health problems: An interactional perspective. *Psychological Bulletin*, *112*, 39–63.

Cantor, N., & Kihlstrom, J. F. (1987). *Personality and social intelligence*. Englewood Cliffs, NJ: Prentice-Hall

Clark, M. S., & Mills, J. (1979). Interpersonal attraction in exchange and communal relationships. *Journal of Personality and Social Psychology*, *51*, 333–338.

Cobb, S. (1976). Social support as a moderator of life stress. *Psychosomatic Medicine*, *38*, 300–314.

Cohen, L. H., Towbes, L. C., & Flocco, R. (1988). Effects of induced mood on self-reported life events and perceived and received social support. *Journal of Personality and Social Psychology*, *55*, 669–674.

Cohen, S. (1988). Psychosocial models of the role of social support in the etiology of physical disease. *Health Psychology*, *7*, 269–297.

Cohen, S., & Hoberman, H. M. (1983). Positive events and social supports as buffers of life change stress. *Journal of Applied Social Psychology*, *13*, 99–125.

Cohen, S., Sherrod, D. R., & Clark, M. S. (1986). Social skills and the stress-protective role of social support. *Journal of Personality and Social Psychology*, *50*, 963–973.

Collins, A. M., & Loftus, E. F. (1975). A spreading-activation theory of semantic processing. *Psychological Review*, *82*, 407–428.

Collins, N. L., & Read, S. J. (1990). Adult attachment, working models, and relationship quality in dating couples. *Journal of Personality and Social Psychology*, *58*, 644–663.

Collins, N. L., & Read, S. J. (1994). Cognitive representations of attachment: The structure and function of working models. In K. Bartholomew & D. Perlman (Eds.), *Attachment process in adulthood. Advances in personal relationships* (pp. 53–90). London: Jessica Kingsley Publishers.

Coyne, J. C., & Bolger, N. (1990). Doing without social support as an explanatory concept. *Journal of Social and Clinical Psychology, 9,* 148-158.

Coyne, J. C., Ellard, J. H., & Smith, D. A. F. (1990). Social support, interdependence, and the dilemmas of helping. In B. R. Sarason, I. G. Sarason, & G. R. Pierce (Eds.), *Social support: An interactional view* (pp. 129-149). New York: Wiley.

Cutrona, C. (1986). Behavioral manifestations of social support: A microanalytic investigation. *Journal of Personality and Social Psychology, 51,* 201-208.

Cutrona, C. E., Cohen, B. B., & Igram, S. (1990). Contextual determinants of the perceived supportiveness of helping behaviors. *Journal of Social and Personal Relationships, 7,* 553-562.

Cutrona, C. E., Cole, V., Colangelo, N., Assouline, S. G., & Russell, D. W. (1994). Perceived parental support and academic achievement: An attachment theory perspective. *Journal of Personality and Social Psychology, 66,* 369-378.

Cutrona, C. E., & Russell, D. (1987). The provisions of social relationships and adaptation to stress. In W. H. Jones & D. Perlman (Eds.), *Advances in personal relationships* (Vol. 1, pp. 37-68). Greenwich, CT: JAI Press.

Dakof, G. A, & Taylor, S. E. (1990). Victims' perceptions of social support: What is helpful from whom? *Journal of Personality and Social Psychology, 58,* 80-89.

Dunkel-Schetter, C. (1984). Social support and cancer: Findings based on patient interviews and their implications. *Journal of Social Issues, 40,* 77-98.

Dunkel-Schetter, C., & Bennett, T. L. (1990). Differentiating the cognitive and behavioral aspects of social support. In B. R. Sarason, I. G. Sarason, & G. R. Pierce (Eds.), *Social support: An interactional view* (pp. 267-296). New York: Wiley.

Dunkel-Schetter, C., Folkman, S., & Lazarus, R. S. (1987). Correlates of social support receipt. *Journal of Personality and Social Psychology, 53,* 71-80.

Dunkel-Schetter, C., & Skokan, L. A. (1990). Determinants of social support provision in personal relationships. *Journal of Social and Personal Relationships, 7,* 437-450.

Fisher, J. D., Goff, B. D., Nadler, A., & Chinsky, J. M. (1988). Social psychological influences on help seeking and support from peers. In B. H. Gottlieb (Ed.), *Marshaling social support* (pp. 267-304). Newbury Park, CA: Sage Publications.

Fiske, A. (1992). The four elementary forms of sociality: Framework for a unified theory of social relations. *Psychological Review, 99,* 689-723.

Fletcher, G., & Fincham, F. (1991). Attribution processes in close relationships. In G. Fletcher & F. Fincham (Eds.), *Cognition in close relationships* (pp. 7-35). Hillsdale, NJ: Erlbaum.

Folkman, S. (1992). Making the case for coping. In B. N. Carpenter (Ed.), *Personal coping: Theory, research, and application* (pp. 31-46). Westport, CT: Praeger.

Folkman, S., Lazarus, R. S., Dunkel-Schetter, C., DeLongis, A., & Gruen, R. J. (1986). Dynamics of a stressful encounter: Cognitive appraisal, coping, and encounter outcomes. *Journal of Personality and Social Psychology, 50,* 92-103.

Gottlieb, B. H. (1985). Social support and the study of personal relationships. *Journal of Social and Personal Relationships, 2,* 351-375.

Hamilton, D. L., & Sherman, J. W. (1994). Stereotypes. In R. S. Wyer & T. K. Srull (Eds.), *Handbook of social cognition* (Vol. 2, pp. 1-68). Hillsdale, NJ: Erlbaum.

Hastie, R., & Kumar, P. A. (1979). Person memory: Personality traits as organizing principles in memory for behaviors. *Journal of Personality and Social Psychology, 37,* 23-38.

Hazan, C., & Shaver, P. (1987). Romantic love conceptualized as an attachment process. *Journal of Personality and Social Psychology, 52,* 511-524.

Hazan, C., & Shaver, P. R. (1994). Attachment as an organizational framework for research on close relationships. *Psychological Inquiry, 5,* 1-22.

Herr, P. M. (1986). Consequences of priming: Judgment and behavior. *Journal of Personality and Social Psychology, 51,* 1106-1115.

Herr, P. M., Sherman, S. J., & Fazio, R. H. (1983). On the consequences of priming: Assimilation and contrast effects. *Journal of Experimental Social Psychology, 19,* 323-340.

Higgins, E. T., & Bargh, J. A. (1987). Social cognition and social perception. *Annual Review of Psychology, 38,* 369-425.

Higgins, E. T., & King, G. (1981). Accessibility of social contracts: Information-processing consequences of individual and contextual variability. In N. Cantor & J. F. Kihlstrom (Eds.), *Personality, cognition, and social interaction* (pp. 69-121). Hillsdale, NJ: Erlbaum.

Higgins, E. T., King, G. A., & Mavin, G. H. (1982). Individual construct accessibility and subjective impressions and recall. *Journal of Personality and Social Psychology, 43*, 35-47.

Higgins, E. T., Rholes, W. S., & Jones, C. R. (1977). Category accessibility and impression formation. *Journal of Experimental Social Psychology, 13*, 141-154.

Hobfoll, S. E., Freedy, J., Lane, C., & Geller, P. (1990). Conservation of social resources: Social support resource theory. *Journal of Social and Personal Relationships, 7*, 465-478.

Holahan, C. J., & Moos, R. H. (1987). Personal and contextual determinants of coping strategies. *Journal of Personality and Social Psychology, 52*, 946-955.

Horowitz, M. J. (1988). *Introduction to psychodynamics*. New York: Basic Books.

House, J., Landis, K., & Umberson, D. (1988). Social relationships and health. *Science, 241*, 540-545.

Karuza, J., Zevon, M. A., Gleason, T. A., Karuza, C. M., & Nash, L. (1990). Models of helping and coping, responsibility attributions and well-being in community elderly and their helpers. *Psychology and Aging, 5*, 194-208.

Kenny, D. A., & Albright, L. (1987). Accuracy in interpersonal perception: A social relations analysis. *Psychological Bulletin, 102*, 390-402.

King, K. B., Reis, H. T., Porter, L. A., & Norsen, L. H. (1993). Social support and long-term recovery from coronary artery surgery: Effects on patients spouses. *Health Psychology, 12*, 56-63.

Lakey, B., & Cassady, P. (1990). Cognitive processes in perceived social support. *Journal of Personality and Social Psychology, 59*, 337-343.

Lakey, B., & Dickinson, L. G. (1994). Antecedents of perceived support: Is perceived family environment generalized to new social relationships? *Cognitive Therapy and Research, 18*, 39-53.

Lakey, B., & Edmunson, D. D. (1993). Role evaluations and stressful life events: Aggregate versus domain-specific predictors. *Cognitive Therapy and Research, 17*, 249-267.

Lakey, B., & Heller, K. (1988). Social support from a friend, perceived support, and social problem solving. *American Journal of Community Psychology, 16*, 811-824.

Lakey, B., Moineau, S., & Drew, J. B. (1992). Perceived social support and individual differences in the interpretation and recall of supportive behaviors. *Journal of Social and Clinical Psychology, 11*, 336-348.

Lakey, B., Tardiff, T. A., & Drew, J. B. (1994). Negative social interactions: Assessment and relations to social support, cognition, and psychological distress. *Journal of Social and Clinical Psychology, 13*, 42-62.

Lalljee, M., Lamb, R., & Abelson, R. P. (1992). The role of event prototypes in categorization and explanation. In W. Stroebe & M. Hewstone (Eds.) *European review of social psychology* (Vol 3, pp. 153-181). London: Wiley.

Lazarus, R. S., Coyne, J. C., & Folkman, S. (1982). Cognition, emotion, and motivation: The doctoring of Humpty-Dumpty. In R. W. J. Neufeld (Ed.), *Psychological stress and psychopathology* (pp. 218-239). New York: McGraw-Hill.

Leary, M. R., Tambor, E. S., Terdal, S. K., & Downs, D. L. (1995). Self-esteem as an interpersonal monitor: The sociometer hypothesis. *Journal of Personality and Social Psychology, 68*, 518-530.

Lewicki, P. (1985). Nonconscious biasing effects of single instances on subsequent judgments. *Journal of Personality and Social Psychology, 48*, 563-574.

Main, M., Kaplan, N., & Cassidy, J. (1985). Security in infancy, childhood, and adulthood: A move to the level of representation. *Monographs of the Society for Research in Child Development, 50*, 67-104.

Major, B., Cozzarelli, C., Sciacchitano, A. M., Cooper, M. L., Testa, M. & Mueller P. M. (1990). Perceived social support, self-efficacy, and adjustment to abortion. *Journal of Personality and Social Psychology, 59*, 452-463.

Manne, S. L., & Zautra, A. J. (1989). Spouse criticism and support: Their association with coping and psychological adjustment among women with rheumatoid arthritis. *Journal of Personality and Social Psychology, 56*, 608-617.

Markus, H. R., & Wurf, E. (1987). The dynamic self-concept: A social psychological perspective. *Annual Review of Psychology, 38*, 299-337.

Martin, L. L. (1986). Set/reset: Use and disuse of concepts in impression formation. *Journal of Personality and Social Psychology, 51*, 493-504.

Mayer, J. D., Rapp, H. C. III, & Williams, L. (1993). Individual differences in behavioral prediction: The acquisition of personal-action schemata. *Personality and Social Psychology Bulletin, 19*, 443–451.

Meyer, D., & Schvaneveldt, R. W. (1971). Facilitation in recognizing pairs of words: Evidence of a dependence between retrieval operations. *Journal of Experimental Psychology, 90*, 227–234.

Miller, D. T., & Turnbull, W. (1986). Expectancies and interpersonal processes. *Annual Review of Psychology, 37*, 233–256.

Mischel, W. (1973). Toward a cognitive social learning reconceptualization of personality. *Psychological Review, 80*, 252–283.

Mischel, W., & Shoda, Y. (1995). A cognitive–affective system theory of personality: Reconceptualizing situations, dispositions, dynamics, and invariance in personality structure. *Psychological Review, 102*, 246–268.

Murray, S. L., & Holmes, J. G. (1993). Seeing virtues in faults: Negativity and the transformation of interpersonal narratives in close relationships. *Journal of Personality and Social Psychology, 65*, 707–722.

Murray, S. L., & Holmes, J. G. (1996). The construction of relationship realities. In G. Fletcher & J. Fitness (Eds.), *Knowledge structures and interaction in close relationships: A social psychological approach*. Hillsdale, NJ: Erlbaum.

Nadler, A. (1987). Determinants of help seeking behaviour: The effects of helper's similarity, task centrality and recipient's self-esteem. *European Journal of Social Psychology, 17*, 57–67.

Nadler, A. (1990). Help-seeking behavior as a coping resource. In M. Rosenbaum (Ed.), *Learned resourcefulness on coping skills. self-control, and adaptive behavior* (pp. 127–162) New York: Springer.

Nadler, A. (1991). Help-seeking behavior, psychological costs and instrumental benefits. In M. S. Clark (Ed.), *Prosocial behavior* (pp. 290–311). Newbury Park, CA: Sage Publications.

Newman, L. S., & Uleman, J. S. (1990). Assimilation and contrast effects in spontaneous trait inference. *Personality and Social Psychology Bulletin, 16*, 224–240.

Pagel, M., & Becker, J. (1987). Depressive thinking and depression: Relations with personality and social resources. *Journal of Personality and Social Psychology, 52*, 1043–1052.

Pierce, G. R., Sarason, B. R., & Sarason, I. G. (1992). General and specific support expectations and stress as predictors of perceived supportiveness: An experimental study. *Journal of Personality and Social Psychology, 63*, 297–307.

Pierce, G. R., Sarason, I. G., & Sarason, B. R. (1991). General and relationship-based perceptions of social support: Are two constructs better than one? *Journal of Personality and Social Psychology, 61*, 1028–1039.

Pierce, T., & Lydon, J. E. (May 1993). *A longitudinal study of social support and coping with an unplanned pregnancy*. Poster presented at the annual conference of the Canadian Psychological Association, Montreal.

Pierce, T., & Lydon, J. E. (1995). *Subliminal priming of interpersonal expectations and coping with an unplanned pregnancy*. Unpublished raw data.

Pierce, T., Lydon, J. E., & Leroux, M. J. (1995a). *Contextual versus subliminal priming and responses to a stressful life event*. Unpublished raw data.

Pierce T., Lydon, J. E., & Sugar, L. (1995b). *Relational schemas and daily interactions*. Unpublished raw data.

Pietromonaco, P. R, & Rook, K. S. (1987). Decision style in depression: The contribution of perceived risks versus benefits. *Journal of Personality and Social Psychology, 52*, 399–408.

Planalp, S. (1985). Relational schemata: A test of alternative forms of relational knowledge as guides to communication. *Human Communications Research, 12*, 3–29.

Procidano, M. E., & Heller, K. (1983). Measures of perceived social support from friends and from family: Three validation studies. *American Journal of Community Psychology, 11*, 1–24.

Rook, K. S. (1984). The negative side of social interaction: Impact on psychological well-being. *Journal of Personality and Social Psychology, 46*, 1097–1108.

Rook, K. S. (1990). Parallels in the study of social support and social strain. *Journal of Social and Clinical Psychology, 9*, 118–132.

Rook, K. S. (1992). Detrimental aspects of social relationships: Taking stock of an emerging literature. In H. O. F. Veiel & U. Baumann (Eds.), *The meaning and measurement of social support* (pp. 157–169). New York: Hemisphere.

Rosenberg, M. (1965). *Society and the adolescent self-image*. Princeton, NJ: Princeton University Press.

Safran, J. D. (1990). Toward a refinement of cognitive therapy in light of interpersonal theory: I. Theory. *Clinical Psychology Review, 10*, 87-105.

Sarason, B. R., Pierce, G. R., Bannerman, A., & Sarason, I. G. (1993). Investigating the antecedents of perceived social support: Parents' views of and behavior toward their children. *Journal of Personality and Social Psychology, 65*, 1071-1085.

Sarason, B. R., Pierce, G. R., & Sarason, I. G. (1990a). Social support: The sense of acceptance and the role of relationships. In B. R. Sarason, I. G. Sarason, & G. R. Pierce (Eds.), *Social support: An interactional view* (pp. 97-128). New York: Wiley.

Sarason, B. R., Pierce, G. R., Shearin, E. N., Sarason, I. G., Waltz, A., Poppe L. (1991). Perceived social support and working models of self and actual others. *Journal of Personality and Social Psychology, 60*, 273-287.

Sarason, B. R., Sarason, I. G., & Pierce, G. R. (1990b). Traditional views of social support and their assessment. In B. R. Sarason, I. G. Sarason, & G. R. Pierce (Eds.), *Social support: An interactional view* (pp. 9-25). New York: Wiley.

Sarason, I. G. (1981). Test anxiety, stress, and social support. *Journal of Personality, 49*, 101-114.

Sarason, I. G., Levine, H. M., Basham, R. B., & Sarason, B. R. (1983). Assessing social support: The social support questionnaire. *Journal of Personality and Social Psychology, 44*, 127-139.

Sarason, I. G., Pierce, G. P., & Sarason, B. R. (1990c). Social support and interactional processes: A triadic hypothesis. *Journal of Social and Personal Relationships, 7*, 495-506.

Sarason, I. G., Pierce, G. P., & Sarason, B. R. (1994). General and specific perceptions of social support. In W. R. Avison & I. H. Gotlib (Eds.), *Stress and mental health* (pp. 151-177). New York: Plenum Press.

Sarason, I. G., & Sarason, B. R. (1986). Experimentally provided social support. *Journal of Personality and Social Psychology, 50*, 1222-1225.

Sarason, I. G., Sarason, B. R, & Pierce, G. R. (1992). Three contexts of social support. In H. O. F. Veiel & U. Baumann (Eds.), *The meaning and measurement of social support* (pp. 143-154). New York: Hemisphere.

Sedikides, C., & Skowronski, J. J. (1991). The law of cognitive structure activation. *Psychological Inquiry, 2*, 169-184.

Segal, Z. V., Hood, J. E., Shaw, B. F., & Higgins, E. T. (1988). A structural analysis of the self-schema construct in major depression. *Cognitive Therapy and Research, 12*, 471-485.

Segal, Z. V., & Vella, D. D. (1990). Self-schema in major depression: Replication and extension of a priming methodology. *Cognitive Therapy and Research, 14*, 161-176.

Smith, E. R., & Zarate, M. A. (1992). Exemplar-based model of social judgment. *Psychological Review, 99*, 3-21.

Snyder, M. (1984). When belief creases reality. In L. Berkowitz (Ed.), *Advances in experimental social psychology* (Vol. 18, pp. 247-305). Orlando, FL: Academic Press.

Sroufe, L. A., & Waters, E. (1977). Attachment as an organizational construct. *Child Development, 48*, 1184-1199.

Srull, T. K., & Wyer, R. S. (1979). The role of category accessibility in the interpretation of information about persons: Some determinants and implications. *Journal of Personality and Social Psychology, 37*, 1660-1672.

Srull, T. K., & Wyer, R. S. (1980). Category accessibility and social perception: Some implications for the study of person memory and interpersonal judgements. *Journal of Personality and Social Psychology, 38*, 841-856.

Strack, F., Schwarz, N., Bless, H., Kubler, A., & Wanke, M. (1993). Awareness of the influence as a determination of assimilation versus contrast. *European Journal of Social Psychology, 23*, 53-62.

Taylor, S. (1991). Asymmetrical effects of positive and negative events: The mobilization-minimization hypothesis. *Psychological Bulletin, 110*, 67-85.

Taylor, S., & Dakof, G. A. (1988). Social support and the cancer patient. In S. Spacapan & S. Oskamp (Eds.), *The social psychology of health* (pp. 95-116). Newbury Park, CA: Sage.

Thoits, P. A. (1983). Dimensions of life events that influence psychological distress: An evaluation and synthesis of the literature. In H. B. Kaplan (Ed.), *Psychological stress: Trends in theory and research* (pp. 33-103). New-York: Academic Press.

Thoits, P. A. (1986). Social support as coping assistance. *Journal of Consulting and Clinical Psychology, 54*, 416-423.

Trafimow, D., & Wyer, R. S. (1993). Cognitive representation of mundane social events. *Journal of Personality and Social Psychology, 64*, 365–376.

Vinokur, A., Schul, Y., & Caplan, R. D. (1987). Determinants of perceived social support: Interpersonal transactions, personal outlook, and transient affective states. *Journal of Personality and Social Psychology, 53*, 1137–1145.

Wachtel, P. (1977). *Psychoanalysis and behavior therapy: Toward an integration.* New York: Basic Books.

Wallston, B. R., Alagna, S. W., DeVellis, B. M., & DeVellis, R. F. (1983). Social support and physical health. *Health Psychology, 2*, 367–391.

Weiss, R. S. (1974). The provisions of social relationships. In Z. Rubin (Ed.), *Doing unto others* (pp. 17–26). Englewood Cliffs. NJ: Prentice-Hall.

Williams, J. M. G., Watts, F. N., MacLeod, C., & Mathews, A. (1988). *Cognitive psychology and emotional disorders.* New York: Wiley.

CHAPTER 3

THE DYNAMICS OF VOLITIONAL RELIANCE
A MOTIVATIONAL PERSPECTIVE ON DEPENDENCE, INDEPENDENCE, AND SOCIAL SUPPORT

JESSICA SOLKY BUTZEL AND RICHARD M. RYAN

The idea of self-reliance can evoke quite disparate images in the minds of people from different backgrounds and cultures. For some, self-reliance implies competence, independence, resourcefulness, and strength of character. Self-reliant persons are those who "keep their chins up," "pull themselves up by their own bootstraps," and "stand on their own two feet." This vision of the self-reliant person as stoic, self-empowered, and purposive is prominent in individualistic cultural ideologies; it is associated with the ideals of self-efficacy, personal determination, and progress (Bellah, Madsen, Sullivan, Swidler, & Tipton, 1985; May, 1991, Triandis, 1989). The converse of this idealized image is a view of non-self-reliance (dependence) as weakness, immaturity, or incompetence.

For several decades, however, there has been growing recognition that self-reliance is not necessarily a positive attribute. First, there is considerable evidence, much of it from the literature on social support, pointing to the substantial benefits derived from being socially interreliant—benefits such as greater well-being, increased ability to buffer stress, and higher quality interpersonal relationships (see, e.g., Pierce, Sarason, & Sarason, 1996). Furthermore, it has been argued that persons who are

JESSICA SOLKY BUTZEL AND RICHARD M. RYAN • Department of Psychology, University of Rochester, Rochester, New York 14627.

Sourcebook of Social Support and Personality, edited by Gregory R. Pierce, Brian Lakey, Irwin G. Sarason, and Barbara R. Sarason. Plenum Press, New York, 1997.

unwilling or unable to turn to others for support are often not so much "self-reliant" as self-contained, detached, or alienated (Ryan & Lynch, 1989). When self-reliance is recast as isolation and detachment, we see the less attractive side of this Janus-faced construct.

Extending this point, it is clear that self-reliance and independence are not values that are equally shared across or even within cultures. Many cultures, specifically those labeled collectivistic, emphasize or encourage interdependence over independence (Rhee, Uleman, Lee, & Roman, 1995; Triandis, 1989). Additionally, significant between- and within-gender differences with regard to the willingness to rely (and be relied upon) have been reported, further suggesting how socialization factors may play a role in the formation of attitudes regarding dependencies and self-reliance (e.g., Aube, Krane, & Koestner, 1995; Shumaker & Hill, 1991).

Given these conflicting theoretical, cultural, and gender-related views of self-reliance, it should come as no surprise that many individuals have highly ambivalent feelings about relying on others. But it is not ideologies *per se* that exert, perhaps, the most direct influence upon one's willingness to rely on others. Rather, the source of intrapsychic ambivalence concerning reliance on others is most likely to be found in one's personal experiences of having been in a dependent position. If relying on significant others (e.g., one's parents) has historically been associated with feeling humiliated or incompetent, then, expectably, here-and-now relations of dependency may feel threatening to self-esteem and a sense of competence. Similarly, if one has felt that one's dependencies were used by those on whom one was dependent as an instrument of control, then being supported may, in the present, continue to feel threatening to one's autonomy. By contrast, if in receiving aid from significant others one has generally felt neither shamed nor controlled, but rather respected and responded to, then one will likely experience more openness to the idea of turning to others for support or aid. Such examples illustrate how relationships of dependence on past caregivers may shape one's current receptivity toward receiving social support.

In this chapter, we focus specifically on the dynamic factors that are associated with people's *willingness to rely* on others. We shall examine not only the beneficial aspects of reliance on others, but also the threatening and conflictual sides of "being supported." Using an approach derived from *self-determination theory* (Deci & Ryan, 1985; Ryan, 1995), in which social support processes are evaluated with respect to their impact on psychological needs, we describe how support providers can foster negative reactions in those whom they intend to help, and, alternatively, how caregivers can facilitate the satisfaction of significant psychological needs in a dependent person while providing tangible and/or emotional support. Following this analysis of the motivational dynamics underlying the acceptance of social support, we shall present some recent research on a construct we label *volitional reliance* (Solky & Ryan, 1996), defined as one's willingness to turn to others in emotional situations. Individual differences in volitional reliance are related both to one's perceptions of prior relationships and to current outcomes associated with well-being. Finally, we discuss some of the personal and cultural factors associated with values for interdependence versus self-reliance and, ultimately, with the differential experiences of individuals within relationships of dependence.

A SELF-DETERMINATION THEORY APPROACH
TO THE ISSUE OF DEPENDENCY

Clearly, for both the cultural and familial reasons cited earlier, people can vary greatly in terms of whether they feel comfortable turning to others for help, support, or emotional aid. Knowing specifically what factors make interpersonal reliance psychologically threatening versus inviting is therefore critical to understanding how individuals reach out to, or can be reached by, potentially supportive others.

Self-determination theory (Deci & Ryan, 1985, 1995) provides one set of principles through which the complex dynamics of support and dependence may be understood. The theory most centrally concerns the idea of basic *psychological needs* and the impact of social contexts upon their expression and satisfaction. In brief, the theory posits three central, innate psychological needs for *autonomy, competence, and relatedness*. These three needs are viewed as basic insofar as their satisfaction is regarded as essential to psychological growth and integrity (Ryan, 1995). According to the theory, although we may have many forms of goals, desires, and wants, it is only the attainment of satisfaction with regard to the three basic needs that optimizes psychological development and well-being.

The proposition that there are a limited number of basic psychological needs provides a critical tool for analyzing the dynamic impact of social events and influences on personal growth. People's intentions, goals, and strivings can, for example, be analyzed for their relation to basic needs. Goals that yield satisfactions with regard to these needs are thus predicted to enhance well-being and be associated with growth and integrity, whereas goals unrelated to them generally do not—even when they are successfully attained (see, e.g., Kasser & Ryan, 1993, 1996; Ryan, Sheldon, Kasser, & Deci, 1996). Furthermore, we argue that relationships and social contexts that facilitate the satisfaction of needs for autonomy, competence, and relatedness are ones in which people feel more at home, that engender more inner motivation and elicit more vitality and engagement (Deci & Ryan, 1991). By contrast, settings and persons that fail to support the satisfaction of one or more of these basic needs are likely to produce feelings of alienation, amotivation, and disaffection, and tend to contribute negatively to the well-being of participants.

A great deal of research has accumulated that is consistent with the view that supports for autonomy, relatedness, and competence are critical to both motivation and well-being in diverse settings and developmental epochs (Ryan, 1995; Ryan, Deci, & Grolnick, 1995). In terms of developmental processes, the presence of supports for autonomy, competence, and relatedness has been repeatedly shown to be essential to both intrinsic motivation and internalization (e.g., Ryan & Stiller, 1991; Deci & Ryan, 1991). Applied work has also shown that whether people are in school (Grolnick & Ryan, 1989), at work (Ilardi et al., 1993), in medical treatments (Williams, Grow, Freedman, Ryan, & Deci, 1996), at worship (Strahan, 1995), or even at leisure (Frederick & Ryan, 1995), issues of autonomy and relatedness are salient predictors of both active involvement and positive experience. Furthermore, meeting needs for autonomy, competence, and relatedness is a lifelong issue, spanning developmental periods rather than being stage-specific (Grow & Ryan, 1997; Ryan et al. 1995).

According to self-determination theory, social support–related interactions, like any other social event, can have various meanings with regard to the psychological needs of the recipient. Whether social supports are willingly received or avoided is therefore in large part expected to be a function of the recipient's interpretation of the support in terms of its impact on feelings of autonomy, competence, and relatedness. Because social support evokes concerns with dependence and independence, as well as other issues, potential meanings are manifold.

On the surface, the very concept of social "support" would seem to suggest that such interactions are positively helpful and need-fulfilling. It would seem to be noncontroversial that one is being supported, for example, if fed when hungry, given water when thirsty, or provided a coat when cold, because, in these instances, others are helping one fulfill essential physical needs. In addition, being given to would, in itself, seem to be a sign of caring and connectedness—suggesting support for feelings of relatedness as well. Accordingly, theorists have been prone to view interactions involving social support as generally psychologically positive.

However, we suggest that it is not unusual for social supports, even of the tangible variety, to be troublesome with respect to the recipient's psychological needs. For example, being given food may contribute to feelings of *incompetence*, since one might interpret such a transaction as meaning that one cannot adequately care for oneself. Or one might feel that food is given contingently—it may have "strings attached"—in which case, even such tangible support may feel *controlling* or coercive. Or one may be provided for resentfully, or in a disrespectful way, which may promote feelings of *disconnectedness*. In all of these examples, the impact of others' supportive efforts on the satisfaction of psychological needs in every way depends upon the perceived meaning of these events with respect to one's basic psychological needs.

Therefore an important thrust of the self-determination theory approach to social support involves the dynamic motivational analysis of support-related behaviors with regard to perceptions of competence, autonomy, or relatedness (Ryan & Solky, 1996). Specifically, we argue that socially supportive interactions have a specific meaning, or what we call a *functional significance* (Deci & Ryan, 1985, 1991; Ryan & Grolnick, 1986) that is determined by the perceived relation between the offering of support and one's psychological needs. Social supports that are perceived as threatening with regard to basic psychological needs for autonomy, competence, and relatedness tend to evoke inner conflict or distress, and may even be avoided or refused; those that facilitate (or at least do not diminish) feelings of autonomy, competence, and relatedness are engaged in more willingly and, we suggest, carry positive effects beyond those predictable by the tangible benefits they afford. This dynamic model of the mediation of supportive events by their psychological meaning or functional significance with regard to psychological needs is illustrated in Figure 3.1.

RELATING SOCIAL SUPPORT TO BASIC PSYCHOLOGICAL NEEDS

These preceding comments illustrate the fact that accepting social support is neither dynamically simple nor an invariantly positive experience. Specifically, relying

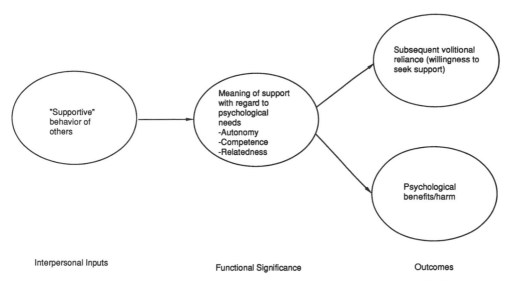

FIGURE 3.1. Theoretical model of social support effects as mediated by functional significance.

on others involves risk and vulnerability with respect to one's sense of autonomy, competence, and/or relatedness. Because being in a position of dependence can pose conflicts with respect to psychological needs, individuals may at times resist or avoid opportunities to be supported, even those that could be of clear benefit.

It follows from this view that people might be more willing to rely on others who convey, along with their help, sensitivity for these psychological needs. In the self-determination view, we specifically expect that the willingness to rely on an other will, in large part, be a function of whether one expects that person to respect one's autonomy, support one's confidence, and/or communicate a sense of connection when presented with a concern (Ryan & Solky, 1996). Although such interpersonal factors have been widely recognized within the literature of psychotherapy (e.g., Rogers, 1957; Stiver, 1986; Storr, 1992), they have been less extensively studied with regard to naturally occurring social interactions. Let us consider each of these three needs and its dynamic relation to social support–related events in turn.

RELIANCE AND THE NEED FOR AUTONOMY

Social support can easily pose a threat to the need for autonomy. For example, a man seeking support from a friend concerning romantic troubles may feel more alienated than supported if his friend "helps" by immediately taking sides, offering advice, or giving directives. In the face of emotional concerns, such "solutions" often feel not only unresponsive and unempathic, but they also feel like an external pressure toward specific outcomes. Such directive help, even if well intentioned, may lead the receiver of support to feel controlled (or reactive), with his or her sense autonomy undermined.

In contrast, someone who listens empathically to concerns and helps one to reflectively consider possible solutions and make one's own choices is more likely to be experienced as a true support. Not only is this type of interaction likely to feel better with regard to autonomy (since it facilitates self-regulation and choice), it is also likely to enhance feelings of competence (ability to work through one's problem) and relatedness (feeling connected to the supporter). As we have previously argued, it is typically the case that autonomy-supportive interactions tend to fulfill multiple psychological needs (see, e.g., Ryan, 1991, 1993; Ryan & Solky, 1996).

What does it mean, then, to support another's autonomy? According to self-determination theory, autonomous actions are those that are regulated and endorsed by the self (Deci & Ryan, 1985), and are therefore accompanied by a sense of freedom and volition. DeCharms' (1968, 1976) described autonomy in terms of experiencing an "internal perceived locus of causality" or the sense of oneself as the "origin" of one's actions, rather than as a "pawn." When people feel that their actions originate from the self, they have the experience of authenticity, creativity, and vitality. The opposite of autonomy, referred to as "heteronomy," is the experience of feeling controlled and manipulated. When controlled, a person experiences his or her actions as being induced or coerced by forces external to the self—be it others or internalized "introjects." When controlled, whether by internal or external demands, the attributes of inauthenticity, lack of vitality, and decreased quality of performance are often in evidence (Ryan, 1995).

Relationships that support autonomy are those that foster self-regulation. The starting point of all self-regulation, however, is clarity concerning one's feelings, needs, and goals—or what Kuhl and his colleagues refer to as access to holistic self-feelings and representations (Kuhl & Fuhrmann, in press; Kuhl & Kazen, 1994). Thus, a central feature of autonomy-supportive relationships is the opportunity to express and clarify one's real feelings, motives, and perceptions of the social context. In the language of self-determination theory, autonomy-supportive others openly receive and acknowledge the actor's *internal frame of reference* and thereby facilitate access to his or her feelings and motives, and reflective appraisal processes. If successful, the recipient not only feels accepted and understood but also has attained greater awareness of his or her own emotional preferences.

A second feature of autonomy-supportive interactions is the encouragement of choice with regard to both expression and action (Deci & Ryan, 1987; Ryan, Mims, & Koestner, 1983). It is critical that there be an absence of pressure toward specific behavioral outcomes and instead a fostering of reflective decision making. In an autonomy-supportive context, people feel free not only to say what they experience, but also to entertain various choices and formulate actions free of surplus evaluation, pressure, or control.

Although autonomy support involves openness to a variety of outcomes, it does not preclude supporters from stating opinions, insights, or personal beliefs. Such inputs are often helpful in fostering self-regulation, particularly when they are *effectance-relevant* inputs (Deci, 1975; Deci & Ryan, 1985)—in other words, when they provide information pertinent to making choices and acting effectively. However, when one offers inputs in a manner that is, in fact, an attempt to externally sway, pressure, or shape another's behavior, then the recipient's experience may be one of being controlled rather than one of being supported.

Similarly, autonomy support does not necessarily entail permissiveness or a laissez-faire attitude on the part of authority figures such as parents, teachers, or employers (Ryan et al., 1995; Grolnick, Deci, & Ryan, in press). Rules, limits, or guiding regulations can be conveyed either in a way that acknowledges the perspective and feelings of the other, or they may be set in extremely controlling ways. It has been experimentally shown, for example, that autonomy-supportive styles of setting limits maintain intrinsic motivation relative to no-limits conditions, whereas limits implemented with a controlling, directive style undermine intrinsic motivation (Koestner, Ryan, Bernieri, & Holt, 1984).

In summary, autonomy support entails relating in a way that maximally supports self-reflection and volitional action. It is absent to the degree that others use evaluations, contingent approval, rewards, or other forms of control to pressure one toward specified outcomes. Autonomy support, which is a central feature of healthy, intimate relationships at all ages (Reis & Franks, 1994; Ryan, 1993), thus supplies a primary aliment for the organismic tendency toward self-regulation across the life span.

AUTONOMY VERSUS INDEPENDENCE

There is frequent confusion within the theoretical literature of psychology between the concept of autonomy and that of *independence* (e.g., Murray, 1938; Steinberg & Silverberg, 1986). Although the dictionary definitions of autonomy and independence overlap, we suggest that they *can* refer to vastly different psychological attributes, and they ought to be differentiated. Whereas autonomy, as we define it, refers to the *intra*personal experience of volition, independence typically refers to the *inter*personal issue of not relying on others. The opposite of independence is not heteronomy but rather being provided for or cared for by others — that is, *dependence* (Memmi, 1984; Ryan & Lynch, 1989). The opposite of autonomy is not dependence but being controlled (heteronomy).

In situations of social support, one's dependence can either be experienced as volitional or controlled. One may feel particularly nonautonomous when receiving help from providers who attempt to use their provisions as a vehicle of control. Teenagers, for example, may wish they did not have to depend on their parents, who seem to always offer help in ways that "have strings attached." Or one may be reluctant to receive support from a "well-intentioned" friend whose support inevitably is accompanied by unsolicited advice or external pressures toward certain outcomes. On the other hand, one may quite freely and happily accept help from a parent whose tangible aid is freely given; or one can, with true volition, look forward to hearing a friend's nonintrusive perspective on a difficult problem.

Ryan and Lynch (1989) attempted to disentangle the concepts of independence and autonomy in an investigation of adolescent–parent relationships. They argued that adolescents who indicated a low willingness to rely on parents would not be characterized by autonomy (as had been suggested by Steinberg & Silverberg, 1986), but rather by *detachment*. Whereas autonomy is associated with positive attributes, detachment, argued Ryan and Lynch, should be associated with a number of maladaptive outcomes. Results in three samples of adolescents of varied ages confirmed this reasoning. Detached ("independent") teens had lower self-esteem and perceived loveability, as well as greater susceptibility to peer conformity. In other words, independence and autonomy were in this instance more negatively than positively related.

Ryan and Lynch (1989) also investigated the links between parental acceptance and empathy (i.e., autonomy support) and adolescents' self-reports of utilizing parents for support in times of need. They found that, indeed, those who experienced their parents as more accepting were more likely to turn to their parents when distressed. It is clear that if a relationship affords rather than stifles autonomy, a person will more likely view that relation as an attractive option for obtaining emotional support.

Similarly, Koestner and Loiser (1996) used self-determination theory to distinguish between what they labeled *reactive autonomy* (the tendency to prefer acting without, or against, the influence of others) and *reflective autonomy* (the tendency to experience choice and volition in acting). They showed that the former trait was associated with numerous negative outcomes, whereas the latter predicted positive experience and adjustment. Hodgins, Koestner, and Duncan (1996) further applied this distinction in studies of relational supports and patterns of self-disclosure. They found that reflective autonomy was associated with more flexible and honest interaction patterns, whereas reactive autonomy was associated with more defensive interactions and inappropriate disclosures.

Such research underscores the fact that the issues of volition and dependence are separable, and they can interact in volatile ways. At times, people forego supports to preserve a sense of autonomy; more often, people lean on others with full volition. That being supported *can* threaten autonomy is clear; that it *must* is straightforwardly false.

RELIANCE AND THE NEED FOR COMPETENCE

Not only does relying on others have implications for one's sense of autonomy, it can also influence feelings of *competence*. Competence has been a long-recognized psychological need (Deci & Ryan, 1980; Koestner & McClelland, 1990; White, 1959). People have a need to feel able and effective at life tasks, to feel an internal sense of mastery and be able to have an impact on their world. This sense of mastery is best obtained under conditions that are optimally challenging for the individual—that is, a task should be neither too difficult nor too easy (Csikszentmihalyi, 1975; Deci, 1975). The experience of competence not only enhances one's self-esteem, but it is also a basis for intrinsic motivation that facilitates learning and development (Elkind, 1971; Grolnick, et al., in press).

The manner in which social support is offered can either enhance another's sense of competence or leave a person feeling as if he or she is ineffective or inadequate. Consider a 5-year-old girl who is learning to tie her shoe. Her well-intentioned mother leans down to assist her, only to find that the young novice pushes her mother's hands away, defiantly refusing to be helped. The little girl is struggling for a sense of competence. She needs to demonstrate to herself (and perhaps to her mother) that she can tie her own shoe. The mother's act of helping her daughter was experienced as intrusive. In this case, a more supportive action might be for the mother to sit beside her daughter and watch with admiration and respect for the child's effort and accomplishment. Here, support may mean not helping, thus furthering a sense of competence, or helping only in response to bidding.

Such dynamics are not limited to childhood. One can imagine analogous examples at all ages of development, in all domains of life: an executive who feels demeaned by the boss's "suggestions"; a budding cook who finds a friend's helpful "tips" condescending; a Boy Scout trying to help an unwilling, indignant, elderly person to cross the street.

Because relying on others can have such salient implications for one's sense of competence, certain individuals may have developed a strong reluctance to rely on others, viewing support seeking as a compromise to their sense of efficacy and self-esteem. In such instances, receiving help can become a "narcissistic injury," causing psychological hurt rather than relief. This is particularly true when help is unrequested, intrusive, condescending, or otherwise conveys inferiority upon the recipient.

This idea is interestingly demonstrated in a study by Schneider, Major, Luhtanen, and Crocker (1996), who investigated a process they labeled *assumptive help*. Assumptive help was defined as unsolicited help, provided without evidence of personal need on the part of the recipient. Schneider et al. found that when a white peer offered assumptive help to a black student, negative effects on self-esteem occurred relative to receiving no assumptive help. Here, for black students, help from a white peer carried within it a functional significance that detracted from their sense of competence.

One way in which a supporter can ensure that he or she does not intrude upon a person's sense of mastery is to lend support when it seems needed, or when it is bid for, not when the supporter needs to feel helpful. In the literature on attachment, such responsivity rather than intrusiveness is referred to as *sensitivity* (Bretherton, 1987). The issue of sensitivity, like that of the competence need itself, is not restricted to infancy but continues throughout the life span (Ryan et al., 1995). Sensitivity in later stages of development may differ in surface characteristics, but it still concerns knowing when help is wanted, and when it is intrusive.

Similarly, theorists from the object relations school of psychoanalytic psychology have proposed that empathic and sensitive mothering (i.e., autonomy support) is an important part of the mother–child connection and includes knowing when and when not to become involved in a child's affairs (Greenberg & Mitchell, 1983; Ryan et al., 1995). For example, Winnicott (1958) poignantly argued that one of the most powerful ways in which a mother can support her infant is to facilitate in him or her the capacity to be alone. He suggested that too much coddling and attending to the child, when it occurs as a satisfaction of the mother's rather than the child's needs, may be experienced as intrusive and actually impede rather than foster development.

Although we have focused on the potential for social supports to undermine one's sense of competence, it is equally important to recognize that frequently people use supportive others to enhance their feelings of success and effectance. Thus, it is easy to imagine a young man who has just learned that he was passed over for a job promotion turning to others for emotional support. However, he may be equally eager to turn to others when he gets the promotion—hoping for them to share his enthusiasm, mirror his success, and thereby enhance his self-related feelings as they partake in his excitement, pride, and joy.

In a recent study, Harlow (1995) examined people's utilization of social supports following positive events in their lives. Harlow found that those participants who were more socially self-competent were those who were more likely to obtain a "listening ear" on days following a *positive* social event. Furthermore, those who obtained a listening ear following successes showed increases in subsequent initiation of social interactions over prior levels.

Harlow (1995), drawing from self-determination theory, also hypothesized that those who felt warmth and autonomy support from support providers would much more frequently obtain a listening ear following positive social events than those who did not. Results confirmed this idea; that is, subjects were more willing to express their positive experiences to friends and relatives who were perceived to be autonomy supportive, and to reap the enhanced sense of competence that such confirmed self-expression affords.

Our discussion of competence can be summarized as follows: Although helping would seem generally to benefit a person's efficacy and competence, there is a difference between the direct benefits of help and the self-evaluative consequences of being helped. Often the latter issue is so salient—namely, being helped threatens one's sense of competence—that help itself can be wounding and may be less willingly received as a result.

RELIANCE AND THE NEED FOR RELATEDNESS

The third psychological need proposed in self-determination theory is the *need for relatedness* (Deci & Ryan, 1985). Developmentalists have long posited a fundamental human need to be connected with others (Ainsworth, Blehar, Waters, & Wall, 1978; Bowlby, 1969) and a natural tendency to form lasting, positive, and meaningful interpersonal relationships (Baumeister & Leary, 1995). Furthermore, like other basic needs, relatedness has been demonstrated to be central to well-being and healthy development (Grolnick, et al., in press; Reis, & Shaver, 1988).

Social supports afford one potential means of satisfying the need for interpersonal relatedness. Supportive relationships give rise to warmth and good feelings beyond those associated with any tangible help received, insofar as attempts at support convey an investment in or valuing of oneself by the supporter.

However, behaviors of support do not invariantly enhance feelings of relatedness. Supports that are offered resentfully or imply that the giving is a burden to the provider may actually detract from, rather than foster, a sense of secure relatedness. In addition, any sense of inauthenticity in the provider may leave the supported person feeling disconnected or distant. The college student who needs to beg for a tuition check, the child whose parents sigh heavily when asked for help on homework, the friend who "waits in line" to get the ear of a helper, may all come away from their "supportive" interactions feeling less connection to those to whom they have turned.

Reciprocally, people typically do not want to rely on persons to whom they do not feel securely or closely related. Ryan, Stiller, and Lynch (1994), for example, examined the willingness of early adolescents to rely on parents, teachers, friends, or "no one" in emotionally charged situations, or when they came across difficult experiences in school. They found that ratings of willingness to rely were highly related to the adolescents' felt security with that person. Adolescents who felt less secure with parents were less likely, for example, to turn to them with troubles. Interestingly, adolescents who felt connected with their parents, and who were willing to rely on them, also showed a willingness to rely on teachers—suggesting some generalizability of feelings of connectedness across adults. Students indicating greater willingness to rely on parents and teachers generally showed higher motivation, more positive coping, and fuller identity integration than those who showed lower willingness to rely. By contrast, adolescents who were unwilling to turn to others for support showed poorer adjustment on a number of outcome variables related to both school and self. Here, we see not only the downsides of "independence" but also the negative impact of poor relatedness on the receptivity of adolescents to social supports.

It should be recalled that models of human attachment are premised upon the idea of social support (e.g., Bowlby, 1969). The securely attached person sees his or her caregiver or partner as a secure base that can be returned to for protection, aid, soothing, or other forms of renewal. The ease of turning to another for support is, then, integrally intertwined with one's sense of attachment and connectedness from infancy through adulthood. Dynamic issues within either the provider or receiver of support that disrupt the security of attachment will therefore negatively impact upon one's willingness to enter into a position of dependence. Furthermore, experiences within support-related interactions in turn have the power to impact upon the security and strength of one's attachment to a supportive (or supported) other.

INDIVIDUAL DIFFERENCES IN THE WILLINGNESS TO RELY: TOWARD A THEORY AND MEASURE OF VOLITIONAL RELIANCE

The preceding discussion of the dynamic relations between basic psychological needs and social support interactions suggest that there are good reasons for the variation in people's attitudes toward reliance. Clearly, relationships involving reliance are dynamically complex and often involve conflict with basic psychological needs. Accordingly, one's history with others in relationships involving dependence will undoubtedly lead to the development of significant individual differences in the tendency toward *volitional reliance*, or the willingness to utilize others for support in times of need.

We have recently begun to investigate volitional reliance in a series of studies. To assess volitional reliance, we developed a survey called the *Volitional Reliance Questionnaire* (VRQ) The VRQ consists of items pertaining to the degree to which the respondent would be willing to turn to specific others for support in a series of both positively and negatively valenced situations, such as a personal tragedy (e.g., the loss of a loved one), feeling depressed or unhappy, feeling angry or frustrated, feeling proud of one's accomplishments, or hearing some good news. Both pleasant and unpleasant circumstances are included in the measure, because it has been established that turning to others for support can be valuable when things go well, as well as when they do not (Harlow, 1995; Harlow & Cantor, 1995).

The construct of volitional reliance underlying the VRQ differs from previous approaches to the understanding of social support. Much of the literature on social support has been devoted to exploring perceptions of the "availability" and/or "enactment" of social supports, issues that concern the individual's perception of his or her environment (Cohen & Hoberman, 1983; Cohen, Mermelstein, Kamarck, & Hoberman, 1985; Sandler & Barrera, 1984; Sarason, Levine, Basham, & Sarason, 1983; Vaux & Harrison, 1985). However, the issue of volitional reliance focuses less on environmental affordances and more on one's inner attitude toward receiving support.

In an initial study using the VRQ, Solky and Ryan (1996) examined the extent to which young adults' volitional reliance on parents and peers would be related to their mental health. Subjects completed the VRQ, rating their willingness to turn to mother, father, best friend, roommate, or to "no one" in various emotionally charged scenarios. Participants also completed assessments of well-being (e.g., depression, vitality, anxiety). Results showed that, in general, greater volitional reliance (i.e., openness to receiving support from others) was associated with enhanced well-being and better mental health.

Assuming that early support experiences would have a lasting impact on personal well-being, we also predicted that, among the available targets of support for college subjects, willingness to rely on parents for emotional support would most strongly predict well-being. However, results revealed not only that students' willingness to rely on parents was important, but also that volitional reliance on "best friends" was a robust influence on well-being—especially their sense of energy, as indexed by measures of depression and vitality. Willingness to rely on "roommates" was, by contrast, only weakly linked to well-being compared to parents or best friends. This suggests that it is not openness to just anybody that predicts well-being, but rather openness with regard to receiving support from intimate others. People's reluctance to utilize their most significant relationships may thus be more indicative of psychological difficulties than is an unwillingness to rely on less intimate others (see also Hodgins et al., 1996).

Clearly, reaching out to specific others for guidance and nurturance in times of need is beneficial. What, then, becomes of the person who is *unwilling* to rely on others? Given past research (e.g., Ryan & Lynch, 1989; Ryan et al., 1994) that has demonstrated that an unwillingness to turn to others for support bodes poorly for mental health, we examined the relations between one's self-reported desire to rely on "no one" and well-being outcomes. As expected, a willingness to rely on "no one" was positively related to depressive symptoms, and negatively linked to subjective vitality. Those who balk at social supports clearly fare worse than their more volitionally reliant peers.

Participants in this initial study also rated their own experiences of parental autonomy support and control when they were growing up. For example, they rated the degree to which their parents tried to take their perspective on important matters (autonomy support), and how much their parents tried to tell them directly what to do (control) versus encourage reflective choice. Results showed that the degree to which these young adults were willing to rely on their parents relative to other targets was a positive function of the perceived autonomy support of parents. Conversely, those who experienced their parents as more controlling were more likely to rely upon their peers or "no one" for emotional support rather than on their parents. These findings support our earlier speculations that people *selectively* seek social support from those whom they view as sensitive to their psychological needs. Likewise, they avoid relying on those whom they perceive as more controlling.

We extended this examination of volitional reliance in two other samples of college students (Solky & Ryan, 1996). These later studies assessed students' willingness to rely on parents, romantic partners, or "no one" (unwillingness to rely).

Findings from these later studies again demonstrated that young adults were highly willing to rely on parents whom they perceived to be supportive of their autonomy. Those who viewed their parents as controlling were, conversely, less willing to rely on them. Similar results were obtained from subjects in one of these samples, who also rated parental styles using measures based on Baumrind's (1977) distinction between authoritarian and authoritative approaches to discipline. *Authoritarian* parents value obedience and compliance, and they exert power and place demands on the child without considering the child's perspective or desires (i.e., they are controlling). *Authoritative* parents, by contrast, set limits and convey expectations but do so in a way that involves more communication and emotional support (i.e., they are more autonomy supportive). While young adults' ratings of their parents' authoritarian style were unrelated to volitional reliance, ratings of authoritative parenting were associated not only with a greater willingness to rely on parents in times of emotional need, but also on romantic partners. Again, these findings suggest both that (1) a person's willingness to rely on a specific person is, in part, a function of that persons perceived autonomy supportiveness, and (2) having had relationships with early caregivers that are characterized by autonomy support results in a greater subsequent openness to sharing emotional concerns with other important people in one's life.

In yet another facet of this research, we examined other personality attributes associated with volitional reliance. We found that those young adults who were willing to rely on others reported feeling more self-determined (i.e., choiceful, volitional) in their day-to-day actions. This finding highlights an important theoretical fact that not only is autonomy not inversely related to interdependence as some claim, but rather, typically, is positively associated with a willingness to lean on available supports.

Another individual difference associated with volitional reliance was participants' style of adult attachment. Young adults reporting a secure attachment style were more likely to be willing to rely on others when emotionally challenged. By contrast, those reporting an avoidant attachment style were less likely to be willing to rely on others such as parents or romantic partners. These findings, like those of Ryan and Lynch (1989), suggest that a safe, close relationship with significant caregivers can facilitate greater subsequent openness to receiving support. Furthermore, subjects who were high on volitional reliance were also likely to describe their parents as more affectionate and physically demonstrative of their love (e.g., giving hugs, kissing in public), and they reported greater personal comfort in showing affection in demonstrative ways within their own romantic relationships.

Finally, drawing from the theoretical work of recent cultural theorists, we examined how internalized attitudes or ideology toward collectivism versus individualism may be associated with individual differences in volitional reliance. Triandis, Bontempo, Villareal, and Lucca (1988), for example, distinguish between *individualistic* cultural attitudes that regard the individual as the central focus and deemphasize connectedness among these individuals, and *collectivistic* cultural attitudes that focus on group membership and harmonious interdependence. According to Triandis and others (e.g., Markus & Kitayama, 1991), Western cultures have been predominantly individualistically oriented, whereas Eastern cultures are more collectivistic in orientation.

In our research on volitional reliance, however, our interest was on the "within-culture" attitudes of American students along the collectivist–individualistic dimension. In other words, we reasoned that the ideological attitudes toward individualism versus collectivism are not equally shared by all members of a culture, and that within-cultural differences regarding such ideology will be related to volitional reliance patterns. Supporting this view, we found that our more individualistically oriented American subjects were lower on volitional reliance, whereas those espousing more collectivistic attitudes were more willing to rely on others, as indexed by the VRQ. Moreover, individualistically oriented persons were more likely to report having been raised in controlling home environments, and to feel less autonomy supported by their parents; that is, the same factors that are predictive of being willing to rely on others are those associated with the development of a more collectivist ideology.

Together, our work on the construct of volitional reliance supports a number of hypotheses derived from the self-determination model of social supports. First, it seems that a willingness to rely on others is a positive contributor to mental health and well-being. Second, one is most willing to rely on those who are sensitive to ones needs, and especially those that are autonomy supportive. Third, early caregivers who have been controlling rather than autonomy-supportive may lessen one's desire to depend on others and contribute to lower willingness to rely on others in subsequent life. Those who are most "independent"—who report a tendency to rely on no one—tend to be more detached, less adjusted, and less autonomous in daily life. Finally, persons low in volitional reliance espouse a more individualistic cultural viewpoint, whereas those who are willing to rely on others express a more collectivistic ideology.

CONCLUSIONS

In the psychological literature, social support has been primarily regarded as an extremely beneficial aspect of personal relationships that can facilitate the psychological health of recipients. With this point we do not disagree. We, too, from the standpoint of organismic psychological theory, believe that interdependence is typically better for the growth and integrity of a person than is self-reliance (Angyal, 1941; Ryan, 1995).

However, in this chapter we focus on the potential "downside" of social support—arguing that the reception (and provision) of social support is dynamically complex and can even sometimes yield negative psychological effects. Allowing oneself to be supported, in particular, can engender conflict and exact heavy costs with regard to one's psychological needs for autonomy, competence, or relatedness.

Accordingly, we introduce a dynamic model, derived from self-determination theory (Deci & Ryan, 1985, Ryan, 1995) that specifies that it is the functional significance, or meaning, of offered supports with regard to the needs for autonomy, competence, and relatedness that predicts both the psychological benefits derived from social supports and the supported individual's subsequent willingness to rely on the provider. Within this model, characteristics of both the supporter and of the receiver of support are viewed as important elements in the determination of the functional significance of social support processes.

With regard to providers of social support, the theory suggests that an intent to control or pressure the recipient, however conveyed, both increases the conflict associated with dependence and leads to a lessened subsequent willingness to rely on the provider. Similarly, support offered in ways that convey inadequacy or disconnectedness increases the threat to satisfaction of psychological needs for competence and relatedness, respectively, and thereby exacerbates the dynamic concerns of the person receiving support. Conversely, the model suggests that people are most likely to be willing to rely upon those whose offerings of support are made in ways that maintain or enhance the recipient's sense of self-determination, connection, and effectiveness.

With regard to recipients of support, we examined factors that determine one's inner willingness to rely on others. We argued, and reviewed preliminary support for the notion, that persons whose parents or caregivers were more controlling are both more distrustful of supportive others and less likely to seek help in times of stress or need; that is, potential recipients of support often attempt to protect themselves from psychological harm by avoiding supportive others insofar as past supports have been insensitive to their basic psychological needs for autonomy support, competence, and relatedness. We also found that low levels of volitional reliance are associated with a number of negative adjustment outcomes, poorer perceived childrearing backgrounds, and greater adoption of individualistic ideologies.

It appears from this initial work on volitional reliance that the path of "independence" is far more treacherous than an alternative route that entails a willingness to be supported by others. As has often been said, humans are social animals—beings who more fully flourish when embedded in caring relationships with others on whom they can volitionally rely. However, we also underscore that developing a willingness to rely on others is intimately intertwined with the issue of psychological needs and their dynamics within relations of dependence and support.

It is our hope that future research on the issue of volitional reliance will further clarify the inner processes associated with being supported and the nature of how social contexts affect such processes. Toward that end, we are currently engaged in longitudinal work that examines how persons with different sets toward volitional reliance may interact over time. In addition, because our work has mainly focused on adolescents (Ryan et al., 1994) and young adults (Solky & Ryan, 1996), research examining volitional reliance in other developmental periods is needed. Particularly important would be the exploration of volitional reliance in the elderly, in whom it undoubtedly represents an important strategy in adapting to the challenges of aging (Baltes & Baltes, 1990).

Another direction for future work is the examination of individual differences in *volitional supportiveness*. We expect that there are significant individual differences in persons' willingness to support others that, like the issue of volitional reliance, are a function of both past experiences within supportive relationships and characteristics of the persons who present themselves as needing support. Providing support, like receiving it, is complex with respect to psychological needs, being potentially both taxing and fulfilling. Being a supporter, that is, can sometimes satisfy and other times threaten one's sense of autonomy, competence, or relatedness.

Finally, the processes and factors that iterate between culture and individual in the formation of attitudes and ideologies regarding interpersonal reliance deserve increased empirical attention. While, clearly, there may be main effects of culture on attitudes toward dependencies, there are also large differences within cultures regarding such ideologies whose determinants warrant equal attention. For example, we have recently found that adolescents who come from more nurturing home environments, where basic psychological needs are being met, place stronger value on giving to others, whereas offspring from nonnurturing homes are more prone to materialism and other self-oriented values (Kasser, Ryan, Zax, & Sameroff, 1995; Ryan et al., 1995). Such findings suggest some of the mechanisms through which cultures may transmit so-called collectivistic versus individualistic styles, as well as differences in attitudes toward volitional reliance and volitional supportiveness. Insofar as we wish to create social contexts that nurture development, motivation, and well-being, then the economic arrangements, cultural teachings, and familial dynamics associated with the volitional providing and receiving of social supports will need to become focal concerns.

REFERENCES

Ainsworth, M. D. S., Blehar, M. C., Waters, E., & Wall, S. (1978). *Patterns of attachment*. Hillsdale, NJ: Erlbaum.

Angyal, A. (1941). *Foundations for a science of personality*. New York: Commonwealth Fund.

Aube, J., Krane, E., & Koestner, R. (1995). Sex differences in social interactions: Does gender socialization play a role? Unpublished manuscript, University of Ottawa, Ottawa, Canada.

Baltes, P. B., & Baltes, M. M. (Eds.). (1990). *Successful aging: Perspectives from the behavioral sciences*. New York: Cambridge University Press.

Baumeister, R., & Leary, M. R. (1995). The need to belong: Desire for interpersonal attachments as a fundamental human motivation. *Psychological Bulletin, 117*, 497–529.

Baumrind, D. (1977, April). *Socialization determinants of personal agency*. Paper presented at the biennial meeting of the Society for Research in Child Development, New Orleans, LA.

Bellah, R. N., Madsen, R., Sullivan, W. M., Swidler, A., & Tipton, S. M. (1985). *Habits of the heart: Individualism and commitment in American life*. New York: Harper & Row.

Bowlby, J. (1969). *Attachment*. New York: Basic Books.

Bretherton, I. (1987). New perspectives on attachment relations: Security, communication and internal working models. In J. Osofsky (Ed.), *Handbook of infant development* (pp. 1061–1100). New York: Wiley.

Cohen, S., & Hoberman, H. M. (1983). Positive events and social supports as buffers of life change stress. *Journal of Applied Social Psychology, 13*, 99–125.

Cohen, S., Mermelstein, R., Kamarck, T., & Hoberman, H. (1985). Measuring the functional componenents of social support. In I. G. Sarason & B. R. Sarason (Eds.), *Social support: Theory, research, and applications* (pp. 73–94). The Hague, The Netherlands: Martinus Nijhoff.

Csikszentmihalyi, M. (1975). *Beyond boredom and anxiety*. San Francisco: Jossey-Bass.

deCharms, R. (1968). *Personal causation: The internal affective determinants of behavior*. New York: Academic Press.

deCharms, R. (1976). *Enhancing motivation: Change in the classroom*. New York: Irvington.

Deci, E. L. (1975). *Intrinsic motivation*. New York: Plenum.

Deci, E. L., & Ryan, R. M. (1980). The empirical exploration of intrinsic motivational processes. In L. Berkowitz (Ed.), *Advances in experimental social psychology* (Vol. 13, pp. 39–80). New York: Academic Press.

Deci, E. L., & Ryan, R. M. (1985). *Intrinsic motivation and self-determination in human behavior*. New York: Plenum.

Deci, E. L., & Ryan, R. M. (1987). The support of autonomy and the control of behavior. *Journal of Personality and Social Psychology, 53*, 1024–1037.

Deci, E. L., & Ryan, R. M. (1991). A motivational approach to self: Integration in personality. In R. Dienstbier (Ed.), *Nebraska Symposium on Motivation: Vol. 38. Perspectives on motivation* (pp. 237–288). Lincoln: University of Nebraska Press.

Deci, E. L., & Ryan, R. M. (1995). Human autonomy: The basis for true self-esteem. In M. Kernis (Ed.), *Efficacy, agency, and self-esteem* (pp. 31–49). New York: Plenum.

Elkind, D. (1971). Cognitive growth cycles in mental development. In J. K. Cole (Ed.), *Nebraska Symposium on Motivation* (Vol. 19, pp. 1–31). Lincoln: University of Nebraska Press.

Frederick, C. M., & Ryan, R. M. (1995). Self-determination in sport: A review using cognitive evaluation theory. *International Journal of Sport Psychology, 26*, 5–23.

Greenberg, J. R., & Mitchell, S. A. (1983). *Object relations in psychoanalytic theory*. Cambridge, MA: Harvard University Press.

Grolnick, W. S., Deci, E. L., & Ryan, R. M. (in press). Internalization within the family: The self-determination theory perspective. In J. E. Grusec & L. Kuczynski (Eds.), *Parenting strategies and children's internalization of values: A handbook of theoretical and research perspectives*. New York: Wiley.

Grolnick, W. S., & Ryan, R. M. (1989). Parent styles associated with children's self-regulation and competence in school. *Journal of Educational Psychology, 81*, 143–154.

Grow, V. M., & Ryan, R. M. (1997). *Autonomy and relatedness as predictors of health, vitality, and psychological well-being for elderly individuals in a nursing home facility*. Unpublished manuscript, University of Rochester, Rochester, NY.

Harlow, R. E. (1995). Self-competence and sharing positive events with others: A daily life process analysis. Unpublished manuscript, Princeton University, Princeton, NJ.

Harlow, R. E., & Cantor N. (1995). To whom do people turn when things go poorly? Task orientation and functional social contacts. *Journal of Personality and Social Psychology, 69*, 329–340.

Hodgins, H. S., Koestner, R., & Duncan, N. (1996). On the compatibility of autonomy and relatedness. *Personality and Social Psychology Bulletin, 22*, 227–237.

Ilardi, B. C., Leone, D., Kasser, T., & Ryan, R. M. (1993). Employee and supervisor ratings of motivation: Main effects and discrepancies associated with job satisfaction and adjustment in a factory setting. *Journal of Applied Social Psychology, 23*, 1789–1805.

Kasser, T., & Ryan, R. M. (1993). A dark side of the American dream: Correlates of financial success as a central life aspiration. *Journal of Personality and Social Psychology, 65*, 410–422.

Kasser, T., & Ryan, R. M. (1996). Further examining the American dream: Differential correlates of intrinsic and extrinsic goals. *Personality and Social Psychology Bulletin, 22*, 80–87.

Kasser, T., Ryan, R. M., Zax, M., & Sameroff, A. J. (1995). The relations of maternal and social environments to late adolescents' materialistic and prosocial values. *Developmental Psychology, 31*, 907–914.

Koestner, R., & Loiser, G. F. (1996). Distinguishing reactive and reflective forms of autonomy. *Journal of Personality, 64*, 465–494.

Koestner, R., & McClelland, D. C. (1990). Perspectives on competence motivation. In L. A. Pervin (Ed.), *Handbook of personality: Theory and research* (pp. 527–548). New York: Guilford.

Koestner, R., Ryan, R. M., Bernieri, F., & Holt, K. (1984). Setting limits on children's behavior: The differential effects of controlling versus informational styles on intrinsic motivation and creativity. *Journal of Personality, 52*, 233–248.

Kuhl, J., & Fuhrmann, A. (in press). Decomposing self-regulation and self-control: The theoretical and empirical basis of the Volitional Components Checklist. In J. Heckhausen & C. Dweck (Eds.), *Motivation and control across the life-span*.

Kuhl, J., & Kazen, M. (1994). Self-discrimination and memory: State orientation and false self-ascription of assigned activities. *Journal of Personality and Social Psychology, 66*, 1103–1115.

Markus, H. R., & Kitayama, S. (1991). Culture and the self: Implications for cognition, emotion, and motivation. *Psychological Review, 92*, 224–253.

May, R. (1991). *The cry for myth*. New York: Dell.

Memmi, A. (1984). *Dependence*. Boston: Beacon Press.

Murray, H. A. (1938). *Explorations in personality*. New York: Oxford University Press.

Pierce, G. R., Sarason, B. R., & Sarason, I. G. (Eds.). (1996). *Handbook of social support and the family*. New York: Plenum.

Reis, H. T., & Franks, P. (1994). The role of intimacy and social support in health outcomes: Two processes or one? *Personal Relationships, 1*, 185–197.

Reis, H. T., & Shaver, P. (1988). Intimacy as an interpersonal process. In S. Duck (Ed.), *Handbook of personal relationships* (pp. 367–389). Chichester, UK: Wiley.

Rhee, E., Uleman, J. S., Lee, H. K., & Roman, R. J. (1995). Spontaneous self-descriptions and ethnic identities in individualistic and collectivistic cultures. *Journal of Personality and Social Psychology, 69*, 142–152.

Rogers, C. (1957). The necessary and sufficient conditions of therapeutic personality change. *Journal of Consulting Psychology, 21*, 95–103.

Ryan, R. M. (1991). The nature of the self in autonomy and relatedness. In J. Strauss & G. R. Goethals (Eds.). *The self: Interdisciplinary approaches* (pp. 208–238). New York: Springer-Verlag.

Ryan, R. M. (1993). Agency and organization: Intrinsic motivation, autonomy and the self in psychological development. In J. Jacobs (Ed.), *Nebraska Symposium on Motivation: Developmental perspectives on motivation* (Vol. 40, pp. 1–56). Lincoln: University of Nebraska Press.

Ryan, R. M. (1995). Psychological needs and the facilitation of integrative processes. *Journal of Personality, 63*, 397–427.

Ryan, R. M., Deci, E. L., & Grolnick, W. S. (1995). Autonomy, relatedness, and the self: Their relation to development and psychopathology. In D. Cicchetti & D. J. Cohen (Eds.), *Developmental psychopathology: Vol. 1. Theory and methods* (pp. 618–655). New York: Wiley.

Ryan, R. M., & Grolnick, W. S. (1986). Origins and pawns in the classroom: Self-report and projective assessments of individual differences in children's perceptions. *Journal of Personality and Social Psychology, 50*, 550–558.

Ryan, R. M., & Lynch, J. (1989). Emotional autonomy versus detachment: Revisiting the vicissitudes of adolescence and young adulthood. *Child Development, 60*, 340–356.

Ryan, R. M., Mims, V., & Koestner, R. (1983). Relation of reward contingency and interpersonal context to intrinsic motivation: A review and test using cognitive evaluation theory. *Journal of Personality and Social Psychology, 45*, 736–750.

Ryan, R. M., Sheldon, K. M., Kasser, T., & Deci, E. L. (1996). All goals are not created equal: An organismic perspective on the nature of goals and their regulation. In P. M. Gollwitzer & J. A. Bargh (Eds.), *The psychology of action: Linking motivation and cognition to behavior* (pp. 7–26). New York: Guilford.

Ryan, R. M., & Solky, J. A. (1996). What is supportive about social support? On the psychological needs for autonomy and relatedness. In G. R. Pierce, B. R. Sarason, & I. G. Sarason (Eds.), *Handbook of social support and the family* (pp. 249–267) New York: Plenum.

Ryan, R. M., & Stiller, J. (1991). The social contexts of internalization: Parent and teacher influences on autonomy, motivation and learning. In P. R. Pintrich & M. L. Maehr (Eds.), *Advances in motivation and achievement: Vol. 7. Goals and self-regulatory processes* (pp. 115–149). Greenwich, CT: JAI Press.

Ryan, R. M., Stiller, J., & Lynch, J. H. (1994). Representations of relationships to teachers, parents, and friends as predictors of academic motivation and self-esteem. *Journal of Early Adolescence, 14*, 226–249.

Sandler, I. N., & Barrera, M. Jr. (1984). Toward a multimethod approach to assessing the effects of social support. *American Journal of Community Psychology, 12*, 37–52.

Sarason, I. G., Levine, H. M., Basham, R. B., & Sarason, B. R. (1983). Assessing social support: The Social Support Questionnaire. *Journal of Personality and Social Psychology, 44*, 127–139.

Schneider, M. E., Major, B., Luhtanen, R., & Crocker, J. (1996). Social stigma and the potential costs of assumptive help. *Personality and Social Psychology Bulletin, 22*, 201–209.

Shumaker, S. A., & Hill, D. R. (1991). Gender differences in social support and physical health. *Health Psychology, 10*(2), 102–111.

Solky, J. A., & Ryan, R. M. (1996). *Volitional reliance: A motivational perspective on social dependencies*. Unpublished manuscript, University of Rochester, Rochester, NY.

Steinberg, L., & Silverberg, S. (1986). The vicissitudes of autonomy in adolescence. *Child Development, 57*, 841–851.

Stiver, I. P. (1986). The meaning of care: Reframing treatment models for women. *Psychotherapy*, *23*, 221-226.

Storr, A. (1992). *The integrity of the personality*. New York: Ballantine Books.

Strahan, B. J. (1995). *Marriage, family, and religion*. Sydney, Australia: Adventist Institute of Family Relations.

Triandis, H. C. (1989). Cross-cultural studies of individualism and collectivism. In J. Berman (Ed.), *Nebraska symposium on motivation: Cross-cultural perspectives* (pp. 41-133). Lincoln: University of Nebraska Press.

Triandis, H. C., Bontempo, M. J., Villareal, M. A., & Lucca, N. (1988). Individualism and collectivism: Cross-cultural perspectives on self-ingroup relationships. *Journal of Personality Review*, *96*(3), 506-520.

Triandis, H. C., McCusker, C., & Hui, C. H. (1990). Multimethod probes of individualism and collectivism. *Journal of Personality and Social Psychology*, *59*(5), 1006-1020.

Vaux, A., & Harrison, D. (1985). Support network characteristics associated with support satisfaction and perceived support. *American Journal of Community Psychology*, *13*, 245-267.

White, R. W. (1959). Motivation reconsidered: The concept of competence. *Psychological Review*, *66*, 297-333.

Williams, G. C., Grow, V. M., Freedman, Z., Ryan, R. M., & Deci, E. L. (1996). Motivational predictors of weight loss and weight-loss maintenance. *Journal of Personality and Social Psychology*, *70*, 115-126.

Winnicott, D. W. (1958). The capacity to be alone. *International Journal of Psychoanalysis*, *39*, 416-420.

CHAPTER 4

COPING AS AN INDIVIDUAL DIFFERENCE VARIABLE

J. T. PTACEK AND SHEILA GROSS

Bill, a 20-year-old psychology major at Bucknell University, is experiencing numerous life stresses. In addition to the expected academically related events, Bill is also "stressed" about his transition from college to the real world. Questions about what he can do with a psychology degree, what he should do about a long-standing romantic relationship, and where he will live after graduation are each associated with substantial psychological and emotional discomfort. Understanding how Bill deals with these stresses, why he uses the strategies he uses, and what impact these efforts have on his adjustment have long been of interest to coping researchers. In obtaining answers to these three issues, coping researchers have, over the preceding 15 years, taken a decidedly situation-specific view. Of paramount concern has been understanding how characteristics of the situation itself and one's view of that situation influence coping strategy use. While providing us with a wealth of detailed information about what individuals do when confronted with particular life circumstances, the situation-specific view has to some extent neglected the role played by stable aspects of the individual.

Although researchers have accounted for significant variance in coping strategy use by examining transient aspects of stressful situations and cognitions (e.g., perceived control), we may be able to account for substantially more coping variance, and perhaps adjustment variance, by also considering dispositional factors. Moreover, by failing to include these person variables, researchers have limited themselves to examining main effects and have missed the opportunity to explore potentially interesting and important stable person × situation interactions.

J. T. PTACEK AND SHEILA GROSS • Department of Psychology, Bucknell University, Lewisburg, Pennsylvania 17837.

Sourcebook of Social Support and Personality, edited by Gregory R. Pierce, Brian Lakey, Irwin G. Sarason, and Barbara R. Sarason. Plenum Press, New York, 1997.

Our primary goal in writing the present chapter is to argue that coping itself can be considered an individual difference variable. Although we intend our discussion to relate to coping more generally, in keeping with the theme of this volume, we will focus most specifically on coping by seeking the support of others. In attempting to accomplish our goal, we have structured this chapter in three sections, each of which will address a primary issue or question. First, we will explore the types of evidence upon which researchers might rely to determine that a construct has dispositional qualities. We will argue that the most important evidence—evidence that is consistent both with transactional, situation-based coping conceptualizations and methodologies, and with dispositional conceptualizations—is whether coping is cross-temporally and cross-situationally stable. Second, does the coping literature provide evidence for the dispositional qualities of coping? To answer this question, we will address several other issues, most notably: Is consistency in coping most appropriately assessed at the strategy level or with respect to the pattern of strategy use across all possible strategies? Finally, from a theoretical perspective, why might we expect coping to be personality-like?

DEFINITIONS OF SUPPORT AND COPING

Before addressing the issues of primary importance to this chapter, we will take a moment for construct definition. Regarding social support, our focus is on the active seeking of tangible or emotional aid from others. Although, as we will discuss in the later sections of the chapter, definitions of social support that rely upon characteristics of the person's environment (network measures such as number and density; House & Kahn, 1985) and characteristics of the person's perceptions (perceived support; Sarason, Levine, Basham, & Sarason, 1983) may influence the use and stability of support seeking as a coping strategy, we will not be considering these operational definitions of support directly. For us, then, social support is one strategy individuals may use when they encounter life's stresses. This being said, we next endeavor to place seeking support into the broader coping literature and in so doing establish the foundation for our consideration of dispositional coping in general and, where possible, seeking support as an individual difference variable.

HISTORICAL PERSPECTIVES ON COPING

Coping Dispositions

Historically, coping theory and research have been dominated by two paradigms. The first, with its historical roots in the Freudian concept of defense mechanisms, views coping in dispositional terms. From this perspective, coping strategies are applied relatively consistently over time and across different life stresses. Examples of the effort to understand these coping styles have included the constructs of repression–sensitization (Krohne & Rogner, 1982) and blunting and monitoring (Hoffner, 1993: Miller, 1987; Muris & Schouten, 1994; Muris et al., 1994).

Specific to support seeking, theorists have long speculated that individuals habitually and differentially relate to others in attempts to cope with anxiety. The early work of Karen Horney (1945) is theoretically important in this regard. She postulated that persons differ in their tendencies to move toward, away, and against others. These trends can be viewed in terms of one's willingness to engage others when anxiety arises, and one's style in doing so.

One of the main criticisms of the dispositional approach to coping is that it largely fails to predict behavior in discrete, stressful transactions (Lazarus & Folkman, 1984). As Lazarus and Folkman have stated, "These attempts grossly simplify complex patterns of coping into unidimensional schemes such as repression–sensitization which have little explanatory and predictive value for what the person actually does in particular contexts" (p. 178). Our reading of these authors suggests that they are not critical of the notion of coping styles or dispositional coping *per se*, but rather they are critical of the way in which such styles have typically been measured. First, and perhaps most important, coping is clearly multidimensional. At the time Lazarus and Folkman were explicating their theoretical perspective, most dispositional measures included only one dimension (e.g., blunting vs. monitoring). Although the number of coping dimensions necessary to adequately describe the construct is still debated (Carver, Scheier, & Weintraub, 1989) and the statistical independence of the numerous possible coping dimensions is still questioned (Amirkhan, 1990), nearly all current researchers, regardless of whether they conceptualize coping dispositionally, transactionally, or both, would agree that coping is not unidimensional. Second, nearly all dispositional measures—past and present—rely upon a self-report methodology. With the exception of the work by Sidle, Moos, Adams, and Cody (1969), which asks respondents how they would typically cope with each of several hypothetical situations, most dispositional measures ask about a person's use of specific thoughts and behaviors to deal with stressful events generally.

Coping Transactions

Regardless of their beliefs about the existence of coping styles or in the viability of measuring coping styles, Lazarus's work (Lazarus, 1966, 1993; Lazarus & Folkman, 1984) has altered dramatically how coping is viewed and, concomitantly, assessed. His approach, which takes a decidedly transactional view, has clearly been the dominant coping model for the past 15 years. Proponents of this perspective postulate that coping is best understood and studied as an ongoing interaction between a person and a particular situation that unfolds over time. The goal of this approach is not to understand what a person typically does but rather to understand what a person did (or is currently doing) to deal with a stressful event. Researchers relying on this theoretical perspective have focused their empirical attention on describing the coping strategies people use, explicating the causal antecedents of coping strategy use, and demonstrating links between coping strategy use and physical and psychological outcomes. Of these three lines of inquiry, the second is most germane to the present work. In looking for the causes of coping strategy use, researchers have focused on the objective characteristics of the stressful event (e.g., the life category from which the event comes), the coper's personal characteristics, skills, and resources (e.g., neuroticism, social competence, social network), and the coper's subjective appraisals of these internal and external characteristics. It is in these potential causes that, even with its focus on specific stressful transactions, this perspective contributes to our understanding of why individuals should be expected to cope consistently over time. Specifically, to the extent that situations, resources, and appraisals are consistent over time, so, too, should coping be consistent. It is thus possible for coping to be transactional (unfolding) at the level of a specific situation but be relatively stable across situations; the same transaction may be repeated time and again.

Returning to the multidimensional nature of coping, a sizable literature indicates that people use numerous coping strategies to deal with stressful events (Folkman & Lazarus, 1980; Pearlin & Schooler, 1978) and that these discrete efforts are part of higher order clusters (e.g., problem solving, avoidance, and seeking support; Amirkhan, 1990; Folkman & Lazarus, 1980). It has often been conceptually and empirically advantageous to rely upon lower order clusterings within such higher order factors. Specific to social support, people may seek support for instrumental or emotional reasons. The fact that people can and do use multiple coping methods to deal with stressful events, and that a specific strategic domain (e.g., support seeking) can be used to obtain different outcomes (e.g., make myself feel better vs. solving the source of the problem) raises important issues about how coping consistency should be conceptualized. As we will shortly explore in some detail, consistency may be observed with one operational definition of consistency but not with others. Moreover, where seeking support is concerned, individuals may be quite consistent in their seeking of tangible aid but be less consistent in their seeking of emotional aid.

In summary, the dispositional paradigm, which dominated coping research through the 1970s, was supplanted by the transactional paradigm in the 1980s. Researchers appear only now to be recognizing the utility of both approaches and using both approaches in the context of empirical investigations (e.g., Carver & Scheier, 1994; Terry, 1991). Presently, the primary difference between the approaches as it relates to the issue of consistency in coping is methodological in nature. Traditional dispositional approaches seek to quantify coping by asking respondents to indicate how they generally or typically deal with stress. By repeatedly assessing situation-specific coping transactions, reliance on a transactional perspective and the use of statistical aggregation will also provide information about coping dispositions. We believe that by combining the approaches, we may more fully explore issues related to dispositional coping.

OPERATIONAL DEFINITIONS OF COPING AS PERSONALITY

We begin this section with a brief consideration of what conditions are necessary for determining whether a given psychological construct is a personality attribute. From a measurement perspective, it has long been recognized that a personality trait may be inferred when a given construct demonstrates both temporal and cross-situational consistency (Mischel, 1968). Moreover, we may be more likely to discover evidence of trait-like constructs when measurement is based both on multiple observations made by multiple people who know the person well and on publicly observable behavior that is directly relevant to the construct (Kendrik & Funder, 1988). Formulating a definition of personality and exploring in depth the issue of what level of stability is necessary for a construct to be considered personality is beyond the scope of this chapter. However, for those interested in this topic, we recommend the excellent edited volume by Heatherton and Weinberger (1994). For our purposes, we will place the most weight on evidence of stability over time and across events.

As in the more distant past, researchers currently interested in dispositional coping have tended to operationally define coping styles in terms of scores on coping questionnaires that direct respondents to report about how they "typically" or "usually" deal with stressful events. However, rather than focusing on unidimensional constructs such as repression–sensitization, researchers are now using reworded versions of situation-specific coping measures (e.g., Amirkhan, 1990; Carver et al., 1989). For instance, "I sought or found emotional support from friends or loved ones" becomes "I seek or find emotional support from friends or loved ones." By asking respondents about their typical coping behaviors, researchers require respondents to cognitively aggregate their coping efforts across time and events. The primary advantage of these new dispositional measures is that they allow researchers to assess more thoroughly the multidimensional nature of coping. An alternative method of examining coping styles is to summarize an individual's coping strategy use across numerous stressful events. In this case, respondents provide coping reports multiple times in reference to specific stresses, and the researcher performs a statistical aggregation. We believe that the latter approach to dispositional coping, consistency in responses to stressful events across time, is the more valid approach and should be used as the criterion against which the more traditional dispositional measures are to be judged. The validity of using repeated, situation-specific assessment, particularly when reports are made in reference to events with which respondents are currently coping, is the fact that it is based on behavioral, cognitive, and emotional referents.

EVIDENCE OF COPING AS PERSONALITY

There has for some time been an awareness of the utility in obtaining information about both situational and dispositional aspects of coping. For instance, over a decade ago, Menaghan (1983) speculated that coping can be conceptualized in terms of either disposition-like styles or situation-specific responses, while the importance of the issue has been highlighted by Folkman and Lazarus (1985), who stated that "individual differences in coping stability–variability may be an important factor in coping effectiveness, and in short- and long-term adaptational outcomes in stressful encounters" (p. 169).

There thus seems to be theoretical import to understanding coping consistency, and we now examine research that speaks to the issue. As noted earlier, evidence for dispositional properties of a construct can be obtained from authors holding different theoretical perspectives and from researchers relying upon distinct research methodologies. With regard to the latter, both cross-sectional and longitudinal methodologies can be used to garner support for the proposition that coping is in part dispositional. In examining the research literature, we will focus on three sources of evidence and address three central questions. First, do coping reports covary with other aspects of individuals assumed to be stable? Second, are coping reports cross-temporally and cross-situationally consistent? Third, are self-reports and peer reports correlated? To the extent that coping has dispositional qualities, we should expect affirmative answers to one or more of these questions.

COPING AND OTHER INDIVIDUAL DIFFERENCE VARIABLES

Attempts to link personality constructs to coping are diverse but not nearly as extensive as one would imagine, given the size of the coping literature. Notable in these attempts are the following constructs: optimism (Scheier, Weintraub, & Carver, 1986), sex-role orientation (Hobfoll, Dunahoo, Ben-Porath, & Monnier, 1994; Nezu & Nezu, 1987), locus of control and self-efficacy (Brown & Nicassio, 1987; Terry, 1991), extraversion (Parkes, 1986), neuroticism (Bolger, 1990; Parkes, 1986; Terry, 1991, 1994), self-confidence and easygoing disposition (Holahan & Moos, 1987), and self-esteem (Causey & Dubow, 1992). Looking for trends in this literature is difficult because of the number of constructs assessed and coping measures employed. Examining support seeking is even more problematic, because several authors relied upon measures that either did not include a support scale, or they included support-seeking strategies in a higher order scale.

Those researchers who did include support seeking as a distinct scale reported mixed findings. For instance, Scheier et al. (1986) found a significant positive correlation between optimism and support in only one of the two studies. Bolger (1990) found no group differences in support seeking between those with low, moderate, or high levels of neuroticism, whereas Terry (1991) found that higher neuroticism scores were associated with less reported use of seeking emotional support. In this same study, Terry reported a similar pattern for internal control beliefs. Terry (1994) found that as a group control, self-esteem, neuroticism, social support, denial, and Type A personality accounted for significant variance in support seeking. However, not one of these constructs accounted for unique support-seeking variance. Hobfoll et al. (1994) found no significant association between seeking support and sex-role orientation.

The associations between personality constructs and coping may be more complex than can be captured with relatively simple correlational analyses. For instance, Parkes's (1984) work, suggests that the association between internal locus of control and coping is mediated by situational factors. A similar conclusion can be reached from the work of Causey and Dubow (1992), who found that seeking support and self-esteem in children were significantly correlated for coping with a poor grade but not for coping with a peer argument.

Overall, our reading of the work linking personality to coping leads us to the same conclusion reached by Amirkhan (1994b). The associations appear to lack consistency across studies, and when significant associations do emerge, they seldom eclipse the .30 "personality coefficient" discussed by Mischel (1968).

One explanation for this discouraging pattern of findings is that the research has typically mixed units of analysis. We should be reminded that it is difficult to predict any one behavioral response from any other single report (Kendrick & Funder, 1988), and that this task becomes even more challenging as the level of specificity at which the construct is measured differs markedly across assessments (e.g., global personality trait predicting a specific coping report). Unfortunately, the strength and consistency of the findings have not depended on whether dispositional or transactional coping measures have been used; researchers have been equally unsuccessful at showing consistently strong correlations when dispositional measures are employed. Typical here are the findings of Carver et al. (1989), who found nearly no association between a host of personality constructs (including optimism, control, self-esteem, Type A personality, and others) and emotional and instrumental support scores on the dispositional form of the COPE.

A somewhat different methodology used by researchers has been to examine whether dispositional coping itself predicts specific coping responses. Here, the unit of analysis is still mixed, but there is consistency in the construct being measured. These studies, however, move us somewhat closer to the heart of the matter, namely, can dispositional coping predict coping during a particular coping transaction? Here, too, the evidence of associations remains equivocal. Across dimensions, Carver et al. (1989) reported that their dispositional coping measure predicted situation-specific coping responses for some but not all coping strategies. Even across support dimensions (instrumental vs. emotional), disparate patterns emerged, with statistically significant correlations emerging for emotional support but not for instrumental support.

COPING AND REPEATED MEASURES

Before turning our attention to repeated measures studies of coping, we would like to address briefly the issue of which aspects of the repeated measures data provide evidence for stability. Here, we are interested in contrasting stability, as measured by mean levels, with stability, as measured by the relative maintenance of individuals' positions in the distribution of a particular coping dimension across assessments (see Costa & McCrae, 1994). The need to distinguish these approaches is important, because various authors have reached different conclusions about the stability of coping by examining different aspects of the data.

In several of the studies exploring changes in coping across phases of academic examinations, authors have concluded, based on mean-level changes, that coping is not stable. So changeable was coping across three distinct stages of a college examination that Folkman and Lazarus (1985) concluded in their title that "If It Changes, It Must Be a Process." In this study, one of the more substantial shifts occurred for seeking support; mean levels of support seeking changed from Time 1 (preparation) to Time 2 (waiting), and from Time 2 to Time 3 (postgrade). Regarding the specific types of support sought, students reported decreases in the seeking of informational support from Time 1 to Time 2, while reporting increases in the seeking of emotional support across the same two time periods. Thus, seeking support changed not only in its overall level but also in what form of support was sought. Bolger (1990) conducted a similar study using students who were preparing to take the Medical College Admissions Test (MCAT). Comparing pre-MCAT coping to post-MCAT coping, Bolger found significant changes; the most notable changes involved the use of problem-focused coping, distancing, seeking social support, wishful thinking, and self-blame. Regarding the seeking of support, students reported using less of this strategy during the post-MCAT period than during the pre-MCAT period. Bolger had anticipated that coping reports would differ across these two periods due to the specific nature of the demands at each phase of the stressor.

These studies, although providing valuable information about the consistency of stress and coping processes, tell us little about the stability of coping within persons relative to others. This information is better captured by examining the correlations between responses made across time. For instance, using an intensive daily-assessment procedure in the week preceding the first examination of the semester, we have found significant changes in many of the coping strategies reported, while at the same time finding substantial correlations between the coping reports made over time. In one of our weeklong studies, the average correlation between the use of a particular coping strategy during the first half of the week and the same strategy during the second half of the week was .66, for support seeking, $r = .63$ (Ptacek, Smith, & Chun, 1992).

Assessments within the Same Questionnaire

Sidle et al. (1969) presented some of the first data regarding the issue of coping stability, although, because of the statistical procedures they used, it is not possible to say anything about seeking support *per se*. In their work, these authors asked respondents to indicate the extent to which they would use each of 10 coping strategies to deal with each of three stressful events (choosing a college, early marriage, and a college examination). The findings revealed that some people had a preference for certain methods of coping across the three situations, while others employed coping strategies more variably. Interestingly, these authors went on to discuss the implications of having a dominant style of coping on the efficacy of certain coping efforts in specific contexts. They reasoned that those people who use coping strategies in a less flexible fashion (i.e., have greater coping consistency) have a greater likelihood of low coping efficacy. Such a result stems from the greater likelihood of a mismatch between what coping strategies are maximally effective, given the parameters of the situation, and what coping strategies the person has available for that situation. From this perspective, then, the person who has the greatest number of strategies available for use should exhibit the best psychological and emotional adjustment.

A similar approach was taken by Causey and Dubow (1992), who asked children how they normally respond when they get a bad grade and when they get in a fight or argument with a friend. These authors found a significant correlation ($r = .64$) for the reported use of seeking social support across the two events. Returning to a point we made earlier, it is interesting to note that these authors also report significant differences in the mean level of use for these two classes of events, with seeking support being higher for receiving a poor grade than for having an argument. Thus, if one were to focus on the mean level of the coping strategy, he or she would conclude that coping is changeable, while the correlational evidence suggests otherwise. In our own work, we have asked mothers of second, fourth, and sixth graders to indicate how their children cope with both school-related and medically related stressful events (Taylor, Ptacek, & Swanston, 1995). Unlike Causey and Dubow, we found no evidence of differences in use across situations, but we did find a statistically significant correlation ($r = .47$) between reports of support seeking in the two situations. Our preference for conceptualizing stability is to rely upon correlational data.

Assessments across Time

A number of studies have relied upon repeated assessment of coping to make statements about consistency in coping. Across these investigations, researchers have made use of several different operational definitions of consistency and have relied upon several different statistical procedures. Given this diversity, it should not come as a surprise that here, too, we will uncover divergent findings and conflicting conclusions regarding stability.

Several investigations have addressed the issue of coping consistency by assessing coping on two occasions. For instance, Amirkhan (1994a) presented findings suggesting that the reported use of coping strategies correlated across time even for events from different life areas. The correlation between reports of support seeking across a 4- to 8-week period was impressively high, $r = .60$. Unfortunately, the apparent consistency in coping suggested by Amirkhan's use of zero order correlations may be falsely high because of the methodology he employed. In an attempt to provide validity data for the Coping Strategy Indicator (specifically, test–retest reliability), Amirkhan asked participants to recall how they had coped with a previously experienced and previously recalled event just prior to reporting about how they had coped with a different stressful event. Thus, because of sequencing, participants may have been primed to respond in ways that would heighten the appearance of consistency. This potential confound was avoided by McCrae (1989), who, across a 7-year period, assessed coping with two events classified as either a loss, threat, or challenge. Although he found no consistent maturational effects for coping strategy use, he did find some evidence for stability of coping reports within event categories. Seeking support was associated with a stability coefficient of .20.

Like McCrae (1989), Holahan and Moos (1987) made use of repeated assessment, this time made 1 year apart. Despite the fact that these authors did not direct respondents to recall events from similar life domains across the two assessments, they found impressively high stability coefficients for both control and patient (diagnosed with depression) samples, ranging from $r = .38$ (active-cognitive coping for controls) to $r = .54$ (avoidance coping for controls). Terry (1994) found that the use of seeking support at Time 1 accounted for significant variance in the use of the same strategy 4 weeks later, even after having statistically controlled for a host of resource variables. We note here that Terry also found significant effects for situation type on the seeking of support; that is, after controlling for both resource variables and previous use of seeking support, situation type accounted for a significant increment to R^2. However, Terry found no evidence suggesting that the association between reports of support seeking was a function of the degree of similarity between the events reported to two measurement times.

Amirkhan (1994b) has taken a somewhat different and creative approach to the issue of stability. His laboratory-based approach asked the question of whether one's responses on a coping questionnaire would predict his or her choice of coping strategy use in a subsequent laboratory situation. After completing the Coping Strategy Indicator (CSI), students were given the choice of one of three coping options while they participated in a stress (threat of electric shock) and academic achievement task. Thirty-six percent of the sample selected the social support option. T-tests revealed that the group that selected this option had support scores that were significantly higher than were their problem-solving or avoidance scores. One should note that this is particularly strong evidence of consistency in coping. Not only was coping assessed with two different stressful events (which for at least some of the participants was likely not to have been academically related—information about the category of event subjects completed the CSI in reference to was not provided) but also with different measures of coping. Thus, both situation and method variance were controlled to some extent.

Combining a dispositional measure with repeated assessment, Glyshaw, Cohen, and Towbes (1989) found significant correlations between coping reports made 5 months apart. Seeking support from two sources, family and peers, were examined. Glyshaw et al. found correlations of $r = .54$ for peer support and $r = .50$ for parent support in a junior high sample. Similar values were found at the senior high level, $r = .52$ and $r = .64$ for peer and family support, respectively. This work is important because, from a developmental perspective, stability in coping (including the seeking of support from parents) appears to develop relatively early.

The studies just described each made use of only two assessments. Although the findings from these investigations are largely consistent with the idea that coping does include a stable component, we should recognize that stability cannot be adequately addressed with only two data points (Epstein, 1979; Kendrick & Funder, 1988). Only a handful of studies have assessed coping more than twice and analyzed the data in ways that allow conclusions to be drawn about consistency in coping. Folkman and Lazarus (1980) examined consistency by focusing on *patterns* of coping across problem-focused and emotion-focused methods across time, namely, the ratio of the use of the two methods. By examining the distributions of use across subjects, these authors were able to identify people as using a high, medium, or low amount of each of the coping methods, resulting in nine patterns. These authors then examined for each subject the percentage of coping reports (the mean number of reports per subject was 13.3) for which the same pattern (e.g., Low, Medium; Medium, High; High, High) of coping emerged. With a mean consistency score of .265, Folkman and Lazarus argued that coping is more variable than it is consistent for most people. However, these authors were able to identify a group of highly consistent copers (i.e., used the same coping pattern on more than 71% of the occasions). Regarding these consistent copers, it is important to note that consistency emerged despite substantial diversity in the life areas from which the stresses emerged. Folkman and Lazarus concluded that when high levels of consistency are observed, they arise "as a function of a personality factor or trait rather than the result of the person experiencing the same situation over and over again" (p. 229).

The results of this study raise two questions related to coping consistency. First, is consistency more appropriately examined in relation to a given strategy (e.g., seeking support) or to a pattern of use across strategies? Folkman and Lazarus (1980) suggest that consistency in coping is evidenced by a stable pattern of coping across domains of coping strategies. What this approach misses, however, is that persons could be highly consistent in their use of seeking support but vary in their use of avoidance. Given evidence suggesting that some coping dimensions are not highly interrelated (Amirkhan, 1990), and that coping dimensions differentially relate to other important variables (e.g., adjustment; Ptacek, Ptacek, & Dodge, 1994), we believe that examining consistency at the strategy level may be most appropriate. Thus, we would prefer to speak about consistency in the use of seeking support or counting blessings or avoidance rather than consistency in the use of seeking support and counting blessings and avoidance. Practically speaking, it becomes nearly impossible to find evidence for consistency at the pattern level when using coping questionnaires that examine more than two dimensions. Second, to what extent do researchers agree on what level of consistency is needed to conclude that the construct in question is consistent? In speaking to the issue of stability in personality constructs generally, Pervin (1994) was "struck with how much subjectivity is involved in characterizing something as having substantial stability or reasonable stability, or in characterizing a correlation as very high or moderately high" (pp. 318–319). The literature on coping consistency is not immune from this observation.

Using a structured interview, Ilfeld (1980) examined the issue of coping styles by asking participants to provide coping information from several life areas (e.g., finance, parenting, work, marriage). Consistency in coping was examined by determining the percentage of the sample who used the two most dominant strategies (action and avoidance) across life areas. Only 25% of the sample demonstrated the action coping style for two or more life areas, while 28% demonstrated the avoidance coping style for two or more life areas. Unfortunately, Ilfeld elected to define the existence of a style as having a score on a particular coping dimension that fell in the upper one-third of that distribution. Such an operational definition ignores the fact that persons can be consistent in their use of a strategy regardless of the magnitude of their score. For instance, a husband who turns to his wife each time he experiences stress is just as consistent in his use of support seeking as a husband who never turns to his wife.

We agree with Compas, Forsythe, and Wagner's (1988) appraisal of this literature that many of the studies considering stability in coping have failed to adequately distinguish between temporal stability and cross-situational consistency. Based on clear evidence that situational factors influence coping strategy use, we expect higher degrees of consistency when the same event is coped with on more than one occasion than when one copes with different events. Even the level of consistency in coping within a class of events may be more variable than one might expect due to differential outcomes associated with the previous coping efforts within that class of events. Within a given class of events, the most compelling evidence of consistency would be to demonstrate that people are consistent from one occasion to the next, even after they failed to successfully cope (from either an objective or subjective perspective) with the same class of events the last time they dealt with it. To the extent that learning is involved in the development of coping styles, we should expect that individuals will alter their coping efforts, thus contributing to inconsistency. We recognize, however, that failure to alter coping strategy use in the face of *repeated* failures may reflect psychopathology. This pattern could be examined either in a classroom setting or in a laboratory setting. The former has the advantage of occurring naturally in the lives of students. The downside of examining coping repeatedly with such a task is that students, at least by the time they reach college, likely have a stable set of coping strategies in their academic repertoire. We thus may expect little change in the face of failure. In a laboratory task, alternatively, a researcher could conceivably concoct a situation that was stressful and more or less unique. As with a projective personality test, such a laboratory approach may provide fewer external coping cues and may be less strongly associated with a routinized, situation-specific coping script.

In an attempt to tease apart the temporal and cross-situational components of stability, Compas et al. (1988) asked college-age students to provide coping reports four times in reference to an interpersonal and an academically related event. The results support only the idea of temporal stability in coping within a class of stressors. On the one hand, the temporal correlations (e.g., the average correlation between coping reports made at across time) for support seeking were statistically significant ($r = .32$ and $r = .28$ for academic and interpersonal events, respectively). On the other hand, the cross-situational correlations failed to reach statistical significance. These authors also examined individual differences in stability by examining the number of strategies used consistently (for at least three of the four coping occasions). They found that over 70% of students were consistent in their use of between one and four coping strategies for each event type, but that evidence for stability was much worse when examined across events.

In one of the more ambitious longitudinal studies on coping yet performed, Stone and Neale (1984) also addressed the issue of stability in a way that did not confound temporal and cross-situational stability. Looking across days on which nearly identical stressful situations were reported, these authors found that the predominant coping style (the one that was used most often) was used on average 70% of the time. These authors concluded that "when the same problem is coped with on several occasions, subjects tend to be consistent." (p. 902).

Adopting the reasoning of Bem and Allen (1974), Amirkhan (1994b) hypothesized that not only are people differentially consistent in their coping but also that other individual difference variables will differentially relate to coping for those who are and are not consistent. This work is important, because Amirkhan raises some interesting possibilities about how best to conceptualize consistency. As have others, he elected to focus on patterns of use across multiple methods of coping (cf. Folkman & Lazarus, 1980; Ilfeld, 1980). Unlike these other researchers, Amirkhan argues that consistency can be assessed with a single event. To be labeled a consistent coper, participants needed to use one domain of coping to a great extent while using the others to a small extent. This pattern of use is thought to represent consistency, in that to obtain a high score on one strategy necessitates the use of multiple, related strategies that comprise the higher order factor. Amirkhan found a different pattern of associations between coping and other stable characteristics of the individual for consistent and nonconsistent copers.

Although we believe that coping needs to be assessed more than once to assess consistency, Amirkhan's work raises in our minds the idea that coping stability may be multidimensional in nature. Work on coping assessment indicates that how we choose to define a given coping effort can alter the results we obtain. Multidimensional approaches that have explored operational definitions, including whether a strategy was or was not used, the extent to which it was used, its relative use, and when in a sequence of coping behaviors it was used, have found that the relations between coping and other constructs vary as a function of which operational definition one adopts (Ptacek et al., 1992; Vitaliano, Maiuro, Russo, & Becker, 1987).

At a minimum, we might find that the degree to which we appear consistent varies with how consistency is defined. We may also find that the extent to which people are consistent will vary as a function of which coping strategy we examine. Finally, we may find that different operational definitions of consistency will relate differentially to outcomes, as may consistency in the use of different coping strategies. With these possibilities in mind, we have recently analyzed daily coping stress and mood data (21 consecutive days) provided by college students (Bostic & Ptacek, 1996). We focused on three operational definitions of consistency: number of times each strategy was used, each subject's standard deviation of use for each strategy across the assessment period, and the average number of strategies used per day. Several interesting findings have emerged. First, regarding the standard deviation in use, students were less consistent in their use of support seeking (when they used it, they tended to vary the extent to which it was used) than they were in their use of counting blessings, wishful thinking, avoidance, and blaming. This suggests that it may be most fruitful to examine consistency in reference to specific coping strategies rather than in reference to a pattern of strategy use across strategies. Second, across coping methods, the different operational definitions of consistency tended to be moderately to strongly positively correlated. Interestingly, the only strategy to substantially deviate from this pattern was seeking support. The correlation between the number of times it was used and the standard deviation in use was $r = -.33$, and the correlation between the standard deviation in use and average number of strategies used per day was $r = -.53$. Overall, the magnitude and direction of these correlations have given us reason to believe that there may be some utility in examining these different definitions of consistency separately. Finally, the pattern of correlations between our three definitions of coping consistency and the outcomes of mood and psychological adjustment was not entirely consistent. The number of times seeking support was used positively correlated with only well-being scores on the MHI, whereas the standard deviation in use correlated negatively with negative mood, positively with well-being, and negatively with distress scores on the MHI. Based on these findings and those reviewed earlier, it appears to us that it may indeed be fruitful to adopt a mutidimensional approach to coping consistency.

Self–Other Correlations

Another way to examine consistency indirectly is to examine the correlations between self-reports and the reports of others who know the person well. Given that it is unlikely that two people (self and other, or two informants reporting about a target subject) base their coping reports on the same set of stressful occurrences, significant levels of covariation across these reports may well suggest a coping disposition. If the same event or events are not being called to mind when these coping reports are made, then it is unlikely that situational factors can account for the correlations that emerge. Moreover, if the informants do not know each other or come from different areas of a target person's life, then communication about the target's coping strategy use is not a compelling explanation for the emergence of significant correlations (Kendrick & Funder, 1988).

Glyshaw et al. (1989) found that self-reports of seeking support correlated significantly with mothers' reports for female students ($r = .46$ and $r = .32$ for peer support and parental support, respectively). Ignoring sex, mothers' and students' reports were significantly correlated for senior high students ($r = .45$ and $r = .33$ for the two support types, respectively). Finally, ignoring grade and sex of student, mothers' and students' reports significantly correlated for peer support ($r = .35$). Although modest in magnitude, these correlations suggest that there is convergence between the reports of children and their parents about the extent to which the children typically seek support as a means of coping. Students' peers also appear to agree to some extent with students' own coping reports (Causey & Dubow, 1992). These authors found small to moderate correlations involving support seeking, regardless of the type of situation to which students and peers responded. We have found similar levels of association in adults (Ptacek, Ptacek, & Dodge, 1994). In a sample of breast cancer couples, we asked each couple member to provide a self-report about how he or she coped with cancer-related stress and a report about how her or his partner coped. The average correlation across coping strategies and couple member was $r = .39$. For seeking support, the values were $r = .39$ (wive's self-report with husband's report about spouse) and $r = .54$ (husband's self-report with wive's report about spouse). In our work, it is not clear whether we were assessing event-specific coping or coping dispositions. Although we directed participants to report on how they coped with cancer, we asked them to summarize their coping across an entire treatment period and across the numerous specific stresses associated with the cancer experiences. This is potentially important, because we might expect higher levels of agreement when recalling specific events than when reporting general dispositions.

In summary, across the three sources of data we examined, it appears that coping does have a stable component. Although coping reports do not correlate highly with other self-reported constructs, data from repeated measures studies reveal some consistency over time, particularly when information is obtained repeatedly in relation to the same event. Additionally, in the few studies that have examined self–other agreement, statistically significant correlations have emerged, particularly for seeking social support.

MECHANISMS FOR CONSISTENCY IN COPING

If people do cope relatively consistently across time, if coping can to some extent be considered a dimension of personality, we should then ask, "Why?" Why should we expect consistency in coping? In answering this question, Patterson and McCubbin (1987) recognized that in dealing with life's multiple stresses we employ methods of coping that are not necessarily sensitive to the situation. These authors suggest that coping is learned in part from previous experiences, vicarious experiences, and social persuasion. Implicit in their argument is the assumption that once learned, coping strategies are applied in a stylistic fashion. Thus, one's coping style may change only in times of rapid change in one's experiences, times during which existing coping skills and resources are stretched so thin or taxed so severely that new modes of coping must be initiated. As we will see, however, there is more to suggest coping consistency than merely learning; genetic, environmental, and cognitive mechanisms also contribute to consistency. Moreover, at a more abstract, distal level, attachment theory provides one theoretical account for why coping should be stable.

Specific Factors

Recently, a sizable literature has developed specific to the topic of help seeking. This literature considers at some length the factors that may influence one's decision to seek help or accept help for a given event. These factors include demographic characteristics, the personality of the help seeker, the type of support needed, the nature of potential support providers (formal vs. informal), and the perceived costs and benefits of seeking help (Fisher, Goff, Nadler, & Chinsky, 1988; Nadler, 1986; Nadler, Mayseless, Peri, & Chemerinski, 1985; Wills, 1987). We find it interesting that this work has not been integrated more thoroughly with coping literature *per se*. We note that many of the variables the help-seeking literature has examined fall under the rubric of cognitive appraisal within the transactional coping perspective. Although we will not explicitly discuss this literature further, it is clearly one worthy of careful consideration by coping researchers.

Genetics

Work has now begun that examines whether genetic makeup contributes to coping strategy use. Relying on a twin study methodology, Kendler and his colleagues (Kendler, Kessler, Heath, Neale, & Eaves, 1991) have estimated the heritability of coping. These authors used a modified version of the Ways of Coping Checklist (Folkman & Lazarus, 1980), one that included only the two highest loading items on each of the seven factors and a response format that allowed for the assessment of dispositional coping. Results indicated that the use of seeking support could be accounted for largely by genetic factors, associated with an estimated heritability of 30%.

Environment

Stable aspects of the environment should also lead to apparent consistency in coping. One of the fundamental tenets of the transactional perspective to stress and coping is that the situation has a sizable effect on coping strategy use (Folkman & Lazarus, 1980; Pearlin & Schooler, 1978). Thus, persons who report experiencing stress in only one life area may appear more consistent in their coping than persons reporting stress across a variety of role areas. Consistency within a class of events can of course be expected only as long as the individual is satisfied with the coping outcome and thus has no incentive to employ a different strategy or set of strategies. We recognize that the cross-temporal consistency we would observe if one repeatedly examined coping with the same class of events may be construed as evidence of situational rather than dispositional effects. However, because of the effects of strategy-specific efficacy beliefs on coping strategy choice (Jensen, Turner, & Romano, 1991), we imagine that repeated success in coping with one class of events will carry over to other types of events.

Because of the hypothesized role played by social resources on coping processes, stability in social network variables may also be associated with stability in coping (Fondacaro & Moos, 1987; Holahan & Moos, 1987; Parkes, 1986). Knowing that others are available to help if needed can change perceptions of the event and thus alter coping indirectly. Alternatively, to the extent that one perceives a useful and available social network, he or she may be more likely to rely upon these resources to cope. Stability in network variables have been observed in both adolescent and adult samples (Antonucci & Akiyama, 1987a; 1987b; Antonucci, Kahn, & Akiyama, 1989; Sarason, Sarason, & Shearin, 1986) and is postulated to include stability in network size, network composition, and support type.

Cognitions

One explanation for why people will be consistent in their coping efforts is because they view the world in consistent ways. As noted, cognitive appraisals play a critical role in coping processes, as described by Lazarus and his colleagues. Specifically, coping efforts are thought to be under the direct control of appraisal processes. We act in reference to a particular event only after having appraised the event and the resources we have available to deal with the event. Put most simply, if people view situations and themselves in a consistent fashion, then they should cope in a consistent manner. Of greatest importance may be how people view their characteristics, skills, and resources. If, for example, a woman believes that she has persons to whom she can turn and believes that she is capable of eliciting the support she needs, then she is likely to rely more consistently upon that coping strategy than would others who do not hold such perceptions.

A THEORETICAL EXPLANATION: ATTACHMENT

From our previous discussion, it should be clear that the development of a coping style is a product of the individual and his or her environment. People have certain biological predispositions to experience different levels of stress and, as we have seen, may be biologically predisposed to cope in certain ways. It is clear that coping behaviors are learned, and it seems that mothers may be particularly important in transmitting coping information to their children (Miller, Kliewer, Hepworth, & Sandler, 1994). It is also clear, at the level of the coping transaction, that cognitive processes play a large role in determining what people do. Also of import is what resources people have available to them prior to and during the coping transaction (Gore, 1985; Hobfoll et al., 1994). Given these multiple determinants, the question becomes whether there is a general theoretical perspective that can point us to the underlying factors that will contribute to stability in coping. We believe that the answer is "yes," and that attachment theory has tremendous explanatory power in this regard.

Several aspects of attachment theory, as outlined by Bowlby (1969, 1973, 1980) and Ainsworth (1967, 1989), speak to the issue of coping development and coping consistency. First among these is the notion of a secure base. A secure base (marked by a positive, supportive, warm relationship between a child and his primary caregiver) functions like a magnet, the strength of whose pull varies depending on the anxiety experienced by the child as he explores the world. As such, this base operates in a homeostatic manner, allowing the child to leave his mother, returning when experiences with the world result in uncomfortable levels of anxiety. A child with a secure base develops the belief that he can return to the base and will be "welcomed when he gets there, nourished physically and emotionally, comforted if distressed, reassured if frightened" (Bowlby, 1988, p. 11). The quality of the caregiver–child relationship is typically quantified by the infant's behavioral response to caregiver absence (Ainsworth, Blehar, Waters, & Wall, 1978). The theory involves three attachment types: secure attachment, avoidant attachment, and anxious attachment. Securely attached infants respond with distress and concern to caregiver absence, and with relief and happiness to caregiver return. In contrast, avoidantly attached infants appear not to notice, or at least show little reaction to, caregiver absence and return. Finally, anxiously attached infants are distressed at caregiver absence but show a combination of anger and relief at caregiver return.

Ainsworth (1967) has argued that, armed with the knowledge that mother is there if needed, the child has more freedom to explore his or her world. The more experiences children have with the world, the greater the likelihood that they will develop a diverse set of coping strategies. An additional function of the secure base is to teach the child to deal with the anxiety-provoking event. Thus, frequent and diverse experiences with the world and a caregiver who takes an active role in teaching the child to deal with the world are each ways that attachment relationships contribute to the development of coping strategies. Consistent with these theoretical functions is empirical evidence suggesting that coping styles are indeed transmitted from parents to children (Miller et al., 1994). These authors found that maternal socialization of coping was stable across time, related to mothers' reports of their children's coping, and related to mothers' reports of their own coping. Thus, mothers apparently do serve the teaching role hypothesized by Ainsworth (1967).

Specific to seeking social support, if, in the past, a child has encountered a stressor and has returned to a parental figure for guidance, protection, and support, and has received it, then he or she has learned the adaptiveness of that behavioral pattern. In addition to being directly taught by his or her parents — gaining an understanding of stress and the environment — the child has gained experience as well as confidence in his or her ability to ask for and receive help. Also, somewhat parodoxically, the child will gain greater self-reliance and self-confidence and may thus experience less need to turn to others when distressed. Furthermore, the child's impressions of others may be changed as he or she begins to perceive others as helpful and supportive, and perceive him- or herself as worthy of help. If an infant experiences its caregiver as responsive, interacting in a healthy manner, as is the case in secure attachment, the infant will grow to expect a response to its cries of distress, eventually becoming an adult who will seek support when necessary. As Kenny explains, "Secure attachment fosters feelings of confidence in expressing one's needs and feelings with the expectation that one will influence and be accepted by others" (1987, p. 19). Similarly, people with an avoidant attachment style will have experienced little, if any, response to their requests for assistance and/or support throughout their lives and so will come to reject their own needs as inappropriate and eventually cease to express them. As a result, they become less trusting, less communicative, and so less likely to engage in support-seeking behavior. Finally, variability in maternal responsiveness and inconsistency in support are typical of the environment that fosters the development of an anxious attachment style. Anxiously attached individuals can become accustomed to the occasional positive responses to their requests for aid and support, but they typically lack any confidence in its actual occurrence. Therefore, such people may become quite demanding, compulsively trying to guarantee the support they feel they need, but not believing that they will obtain.

These beliefs about self and others are termed *working models* (Bowlby, 1980) and represent the second way that attachment relationships influence coping. Recall, here, that cognitive processes (appraisals) are an integral part of the transactional theory of stress and coping. How people deal with a given stressful event has been shown to relate to how they appraise themselves, their resources, and the situation. People who report a secure attachment history tend to have positive self-images and higher self-esteem, viewing themselves as outgoing, well-liked, and socially competent. At the same time, such people tend to view others as responsive, available, trustworthy, and well-meaning. In contrast, anxiously attached people tend to have lower social self-confidence and poor communication skills, and tend to view others as inconsistent and unreliable. Finally, those with an avoidant attachment style perceive themselves as somewhat distant, guarded, or aloof, and view others as overcommitted and intrusive (e.g., Collins & Read, 1990; Feeney & Noller, 1990; Simpson, 1990). These perceptions are predictable based on each person's past relationship experiences, and in turn, these perceptions affect present behavior.

To the extent that these cognitions are consistent over time, they should exert a similar effect on our coping efforts across a variety of stressful encounters. Bowlby (1988) has speculated that working models are relatively resistant to change. Moreover, as related to the stability of the secure base, Antonucci (1991) suggests that adult attachment relationships are parallel to those of infants to primary caregivers, and that the secure, anxious, and avoidant characteristics observed in infants are observable in adults. This speaks to the continuity of the attachment bond and its influence on subsequent relationships. It thus seems reasonable to expect that coping will be somewhat stable because stress-specific working models are stable, and that those who are more comfortable returning to their secure base as infants will be more comfortable doing so as adults. This comfort may manifest itself as consistency in seeking support, and, perhaps, the efficacy in doing so.

Successfully using support seeking to cope with stress depends upon not only one's beliefs in one's abilities to successfully elicit desired support and in others' ability and willingness to provide it, but also the social skills necessary to obtain the desired responses. Again, securely attached people appear to have an advantage. Bell, Avery, Jenkins, Feld, and Schoenrock (1985) found a positive relation between positive family relations and later social competence, whereas a study by Pastor (1981) demonstrated that securely attached toddlers were rated as more sociable on scales of overall sociability, orientation to peers, and purposeful activity than their anxiously attached peers. Studies by Main and Weston (1981) have indicated that securely attached 12-month-old infants demonstrated greater responsiveness and fewer "conflict behaviors" (abnormal or disordered behaviors in response to stress) than anxious or avoidant subjects.

Attachment has also been linked to the later development of social competencies. In a study by Waters, Wippman, and Sroufe (1979), preschoolers who had been classified as securely attached at 15 months of age were rated significantly higher on social competencies with peers, such as likelihood to engage others and participate in activities, than anxiously attached infants. Similarly, studies by La Freniere and Sroufe (1985) also obtained significantly higher scores on several social competency scales for preschoolers who had been classified as securely attached as infants than for infants who had been considered anxiously attached. Secure attachment histories have also been linked to greater emotional health, positive affect, lower levels of dependency (Sroufe, 1983), better conflict resolution skills, more accurate social perceptions, and lower occurrence of problem behaviors (Suess, 1987, as cited by Elicker, Englund, & Sroufe, 1992). Meanwhile, the poor communication skills, low self-esteem, and defensive natures of anxious and avoidant people may leave them at a disadvantage when attempting to elicit social support.

Finally, research conducted on adult attachment styles has provided additional support for the possible links between attachment and the issue of seeking social support. Kenny (1987) found that within a sample of securely attached undergraduates, a majority reported frequent requests for and reliance upon parental support and reassurance. Similarly, Simpson (1992) examined support-seeking behaviors within romantic couples as a function of attachment style. By placing the couple in a situation that evoked anxiety in the female member of the couple, while allowing the male member of the couple to respond, both support-seeking and support-giving behaviors could be examined. The results indicated that women with secure attachments more frequently sought support than women with avoidant histories, whereas anxiously attached subjects tended not to exhibit any clearly discriminating or significant behaviors.

In summary, attachment theory suggests several avenues through which coping styles may develop and provides a relatively clear rationale for why coping should have a stable component. The attachment relationship appears to be associated with a host of working models of self, others, and the environment that remain consistent across time. Individual differences in attachment history are associated with stable differences in personal characteristics and attributes that may relate to the ability to successfully elicit the support of others. Finally, differences in the security of one's base is associated with differences in exploration and the ability of parents to teach their children effective coping strategies.

CONCLUSIONS AND FUTURE DIRECTIONS

Our goal in writing this chapter was to explore issues related to dispositional coping in general and to the seeking of social support in particular. Despite the dominance of the transactional theory of coping, many authors have recognized the importance of operationally defining coping in terms of dispositions. We, like others (Carver & Scheier, 1994), recognize that a construct can have process qualities at one level and dispositional qualities at another. Specifically, it is possible for the process to be relatively invariant across occasions. One justification for studying coping styles is that the style one adopts and the consistency with which that style is applied appear to have implications both for what persons do to cope in specific instances and for the efficacy of these coping efforts.

In many ways, our understanding of coping stability has been hampered by methodological shortcomings and differences across studies in the statistical methods used. Too few studies have assessed coping frequently enough to meaningfully examine stability, and researchers have not been sensitive enough to the psychometric properties of the instruments they have employed (Amirkhan, 1994b). Those researchers who have assessed coping more than once have relied upon examinations of either mean-level differences or correlations. As we have seen, the conclusion one reaches about stability is a function of which of these approaches he or she takes (Caspi & Bem, 1990). Although the evidence for the existence of coping styles remains mixed, we believe that the literature is sufficiently suggestive to warrant additional investigation. Most intriguing, we think, is the notion that coping stability may itself be an individual difference variable (Amirkhan 1994b), and the possibility that stability can be examined from a multivariate perspective.

Finally, despite mixed findings, we believe that there is ample theoretical justification for believing in the existence of relatively pervasive coping styles. Specifically, attachment theory provides a rich account of how coping skills develop and of why they should take on dispositional qualities.

REFERENCES

Ainsworth, M. D. S. (1967). *Infancy in Uganda: Infant care and the growth of love*. Baltimore: Johns Hopkins University Press.

Ainsworth, M. D. S. (1989). Attachments beyond infancy. *American Psychologist, 44*, 709–716.

Ainsworth, M. S. D., Blehar, M.C., Waters, E., & Wall, S. (1978). Patterns of attachment: A psychological study of the strange situation. Hillsdale, NJ: Erlbaum.

Amirkhan, J. M. (1990). A factor analytically derived measure of coping: The coping strategy indicator. *Journal of Personality and Social Psychology, 59*, 1066–1074.

Amirkhan, J. M. (1994a). Criterion validity of a coping measure. *Journal of Personality Assessment, 62*, 242–261.

Amirkhan, J. M. (1994b). Seeking person-related predictors of coping: Exploratory analysis. *European Journal of Personality, 8*, 13–30.

Antonucci, T. C. (1991). Attachment, social support, and coping with negative life events in mature adulthood. In E. M. Cummings, A. L. Greene, & K. H. Karraker, (Eds.), *Life Span Developmental Psychology: Perspectives on Stress and Coping*, Hillsdale, NJ: Erlbaum.

Antonucci, T. C., & Akiyama, H. (1987a). An examination of sex differences in social support in older men and women. *Sex Roles, 17*, 737–749.

Antonucci, T. C., & Akiyama, H. (1987b). Social networks in adult life and a preliminary examination of the convoy model. *Journal of Gerontology, 42*, 519–527.

Antonucci, T. C., Kahn, R. L., & Akiyama, H. (1989). Psychosocial factors and the response to cancer symptoms. In R. Yancik & J. Yates (Eds.), *Cancer in the elderly: Approaches to early detection and treatment* (pp. 40–52). New York: Springer.

Bell, N. J., Avery, A. W., Jenkins, D., Feld, J., & Schoenrock, C. J. (1985). Family relationships and social competence during late adolescence. *Journal of Youth and Adolescence, 14*, 109–119.

Bem, D. J., & Allen, A. (1974). On predicting some of the people some of the time: The search for cross-situational consistencies in behavior. *Psychological Review, 81*, 506–520.

Bolger, N. (1990). Coping as a personality process: A prospective study. *Journal of Personality and Social Psychology, 59*, 525–537.

Bostic, T. J., & Ptacek, J. T. (1996). *Individual differences in the stability of coping.* Paper presented at the meeting of the Eastern Psychological Association, Philadelphia, PA.

Bowlby, J. (1969). *Attachment and loss: Vol. 1. Attachment.* New York: Basic Books.

Bowlby, J. (1973). *Attachment and loss: Vol.2. Separation: Anxiety and anger.* New York: Basic Books.

Bowlby, J. (1980). *Attachment and loss: Vol. 3. Sadness and depression.* New York: Basic Books.

Bowlby, J. (1988). *A secure base: Parent–child attachment and health human development.* New York: Basic Books.

Brown, G. K., & Nicassio, P. M. (1987). Development of a questionnaire for the assessment of active and passive coping strategies in chronic pain patients. *Pain, 31,* 53–64.

Carver, C. S., & Scheier, M. F. (1994). Situational coping and coping dispositions in a stressful transaction. *Journal of Personality and Social Psychology, 66,* 184–195.

Carver, C. S., Scheier, M. F., & Weintraub, J. K. (1989). Assessing coping strategies: A theoretically based approach. *Journal of Personality and Social Psychology, 56,* 267–283.

Caspi, A., & Bem, D. J. (1990). Personality continuity and chance across the life course. In L. A Pervin (Ed.), *Handbook of personality theory and research* (pp. 549–575). New York: Guilford.

Causey, D. L., & Dubow, E. F. (1992). Development of a self-report coping measure for elementary school children. *Journal of Clinical Child Psychology, 21,* 47–59.

Collins, N.J, & Read, S. J. (1990). Working models and relationship quality in dating couples. *Journal of Personality and Social Psychology, 58,* 644–663.

Compas, B. E., Forsythe, C. J., & Wagner, B. M. (1988). Consistency and variability in causal attributions and coping with stress. *Cognitive Therapy and Research, 12,* 305–320.

Costa, P. T., & McCrae, R. R. (1994). Set like plaster? Evidence for the stability of adult personality. In T. Heatherton & J. Weinberger (Eds.), *Can personality change?* Washington, DC: American Psychological Association.

Elicker, J., Englund, M., & Sroufe, L. A. (1992). Predicting peer competence and peer relations in childhood from early parent–child relationships. In R. Parke & G. Ladd (Eds.), *Family–Peer Relations: Modes of Linkage* (pp. 77–106). Hillsdale, NJ: Erlbaum.

Epstein, S. (1979). The stability of behavior: I. On predicting most of the people much of the time. *Journal of Personality and Social Psychology, 37,* 1097–1126.

Feeney, J. A., & Noller, P. (1990). Attachment style as a predictor of adult romantic relationships. *Journal of Personality and Social Psychology, 58,* 281–291.

Fisher, J. D., Goff, B. A., Nadler, A., & Chinsky, J. M. (1988). Social psychological influences on help-seeking and support from peers. In B. H. Gottlieb, (Ed.), *Marshaling social support: Formats, processes and effects* (pp. 267–304). Newbury Park, CA: Sage Publications.

Folkman, S., & Lazarus, R. S. (1980). An analysis of coping in a middle-aged community sample. *Journal of Health and Social Behavior, 21,* 219–239.

Folkman, S., & Lazarus, R. S. (1985). If it changes it must be a process: Study of emotion and coping during three stages of a college examination. *Journal of Personality and Social Psychology, 48,* 150–170.

Fondacaro, M. R., & Moos, R. H. (1987). Social support and coping: A longitudinal analysis. *American Journal of Community Psychology, 15* 653–673.

Glyshaw, K., Cohen, L. H., & Towbes, L. C. (1989). Coping strategies and psychological distress: Prospective analyses of early and middle adolescents. *American Journal of Community Psychology, 17,* 607–623.

Gore, S. (1985). Social support and styles of coping with stress. In S. Cohen & S. L. Syme (Eds.), *Social support and health* (pp. 263–276). Orlando, FL: Academic Press.

Heatherton, T., & Weinberger, J. (Eds.). (1994). *Can personality change?* Washington, DC: American Psychological Association.

Hobfoll, S. E., Dunahoo, C. L., Ben-Porath, Y., & Monnier, J. (1994). Gender and coping: The dual-axis model of coping. *American Journal of Community Psychology, 22,* 49–82.

Hoffner, C. (1993). Children's strategies for coping with stress: Blunting and monitoring. *Motivation and Emotion, 17,* 91–106.

Holahan, C. J., & Moos, R. H. (1987). Personal and contextual determinants of coping strategies. *Journal of Personality and Social Psychology, 52,* 946–955.

Horney, K. (1945). *Our inner conflicts.* New York: W. W. Horton.

House, J. S., & Kahn, R. L. (1985). Measuring concepts of social support. In S. Cohen & S. L. Syme (Eds.), *Social support and health* (pp. 83–108). New York: Academic Press.

Ilfeld, F. W. (1980). Coping styles of Chicago adults: Description. *Journal of Human Stress, 6,* 2-10.

Jensen, M. P., Turner, J. A., & Romano, J. M. (1991). Self-efficacy and outcome expectancies: Relationship to chronic pain coping strategies and adjustment. *Pain, 44,* 263-269.

Kendler, K. S., Kessler, R. C., Heath, A. C., Neale, M. C., & Eaves, L. J. (1991). Coping: A genetic epidemiological investigation. *Psychological Medicine, 2,* 337-346.

Kendrick, D. T., & Funder, D.C. (1988). Profiting from controversy: Lessons from the person-situation debate. *American Psychologist, 43,* 23-34.

Kenny, M. (1987). Extent and function of parental attachment among first year college students. *Journal of Youth and Adolescence, 16,* 17-29.

Krohne, H. W., & Rogner, J. (1982). Repression-sensitization as a central construct in coping research. In H. W. Krohne & L. Laux (Eds.), *Achievement, stress, and anxiety.* Washington, DC: Hemisphere.

LaFreniere, P., & Sroufe, L. A. (1985). Profiles of peer competence in the preschool: Interrelations between measures, influence of social ecology, and relation to attachment history. *Developmental Psychology, 21,* 56-69.

Lazarus, R. S. (1966). *Psychological stress and the coping process.* New York: McGraw-Hill.

Lazarus, R. S. (1993). Coping theory and research: Past, present, and future. *Psychosomatic Medicine, 55,* 234-247.

Lazarus, R. S., & Folkman, S. (1984). *Stress, appraisal, and coping.* New York: Springer.

Main, M., & Weston, D. R. (1981). The quality of the toddler's relationship to mother and father: Related to conflict behavior and the readiness to establish new relationships. *Child Development, 52,* 932-940.

McCrae, R. R. (1989). Age differences and changes in the use of coping mechanisms. *Journal of Gerontology, 44,* 161-169.

Menaghan, E. G. (1983). Individual coping efforts and family studies: Conceptual and methodological issues. *Marriage and Family Review, 6,* 113-135.

Miller, P. A., Kliewer, W., Hepworth, J. T., & Sandler, I. N. (1994). Maternal socialization of children's post-divorce coping: Development of a measurement model. *Journal of Applied Developmental Psychology, 15,* 457-487.

Miller, S. M. (1987). Monitoring and blunting: Validation of a questionnaire to assess styles of information seeking under threat. *Journal of Personality and Social Psychology, 52,* 345-353.

Mischel, W. (1968). *Personality assessment.* New York: Wiley.

Muris, P., & Schouten, E. (1994). Monitoring and blunting: A factor analysis of the Miller Behavioral Style Scale. *Personality and Individual Differences, 17,* 285-287.

Muris, P., van Zuuren, F. J., De Jong, P. J., DeDeurs, E., et al. (1994). Monitoring and blunting coping styles: The Miller Behavioral Style Scale and its correlates, and the development of an alternative questionnaire. *Personality and Individual Differences, 17,* 9-19.

Nadler, A. (1986). Self-esteem and the seeking and receiving of help: Theoretical and empirical perspectives. In B. Maher (Ed.), *Progress in experimental personality research* (Vol. 14). Orlando, FL: Academic Press.

Nadler, A., Mayseless, O., Peri, N., & Chemerinski, A. (1985). Effects of opportunity to reciprocate and self-esteem on help-seeking behavior. *Journal of Personality, 53,* 23-35.

Nezu, A. M., & Nezu, C. M. (1987). Psychological distress, problem solving and coping reactions: Sex role differences. *Sex Roles, 16,* 205-214.

Parkes, K. R. (1984). Locus of control, cognitive appraisal, and coping in stressful episodes. *Journal of Personality and Social Psychology, 46,* 655-668.

Parkes, K. R. (1986). Coping in stressful episodes: The role of individual differences, environmental factors, and situational characteristics. *Journal of Personality and Social Psychology, 51,* 1277-1292.

Pastor, D. L. (1981). The quality of mother-infant attachment and its relationship to toddlers' sociability with peers. *Developmental Psychology, 17*(3), 326-335.

Patterson, J. M., & McCubbin, H. I. (1987). Adolescent coping style and behaviors: conceptualization and measurement. *Journal of Adolescence, 10,* 163-186.

Pearlin, L. I., & Schooler, C. (1978). The structure of coping. *Journal of Health and Social Behavior, 19,* 2-21.

Pervin, L. A. (1994). Personality stability, personality change, and the question of process. In T. F. Heatherton & J. L. Weinberger, (Eds.), *Can Personality Change?* Washington, DC: American Psychological Association.

Ptacek, J. T., Ptacek, J. J., & Dodge, K. L. (1994). Coping with cancer from the perspective of husbands and wives. *Journal of Psychosocial Oncology*, *12*, 47–72.

Ptacek, J. T., Smith, R. E., & Chun, D. (1992). *Appraisal, emotion, and coping: The process dealing with stress*. Unpublished manuscript, Bucknell University, Lewisburg, PA.

Sarason, I. G., Levine, H. M., Basham, R. B., & Sarason, B. R. (1983). Assessing social support: The Social Support Questionnaire. *Journal of Personality and Social Psychology*, *44*, 127–139.

Sarason, I. G., Sarason, B. R., & Shearin, E. N. (1986). Social support as an individual difference variable: Its stability, origins, and relational aspects. *Journal of Personality and Social Psychology*, *50*, 845–855.

Scheier, M. F., Weintraub, J. K., & Carver, C. S. (1986). Coping with stress: Divergent strategies of optimists and pessimists. *Journal of Personality and Social Psychology*, *51*, 1257–1264.

Sidle, A., Moos, R., Adams, J., & Cady, P. (1969). Development of a coping scale. *Archives of General Psychiatry*, *20*, 226–232.

Simpson, J. A. (1990). Influence of attachment styles on romantic relationships. *Journal of Personality and Social Psychology*, *59*, 971–980.

Simpson, J. A., Rholes, W. S., & Nelligan, J. S. (1992). Support seeking and support giving within couples in an anxiety-provoking situation: The role of attachment styles. *Journal of Personality and Social Psychology*, *62*, 434–446.

Sroufe, L. A. (1983). Infant–caregiver attachment and patterns of adaptation in preschool: The roots of maladaptation and competence. In M. Perlmutter (Ed.), *Minnesota Symposia on Child Psychology*, (Vol. 16, pp. 41–81). Hillsdale, NJ: Erbaum.

Stone, A. A., & Neale, J. M. (1984). New measure of daily coping: Development and preliminary results. *Journal of Personality and Social Psychology*, *46*, 892–906.

Taylor, C., Ptacek, J. T., & Swanston, S. (1995). *Mothers' reports of their childrens' coping*. Manuscript in preparation. Bucknell University, Lewisburg, PA.

Terry, D. J. (1991). Coping resources and situational appraisals as predictors of coping behavior. *Personality and Individual Differences*, *12*, 1031–1047.

Terry, D. J. (1994). Determinants of coping: The role of stable and situational factors. *Journal of Personality and Social Psychology*, *66*, 895–910.

Vitaliano, P. P., Maiuro, R. D., Russo, J., & Becker, J. (1987). Raw versus relative scores in the assessment of coping strategies. *Journal of Behavioral Medicine*, *10*, 1–18.

Waters, E., Wippman, J., & Sroufe, L. A. (1979). Attachment, positive affect, and competence in the peer group: Two studies in construct validation. *Child Development*, *50*, 821–829.

Wills, T. A. (1987). Help-seeking as a coping mechanism. In C. R. Snyder & C. E. Ford (Eds.), *Coping with negative life events: Clinical and social psychological perspectives* (pp. 19–50). New York: Plenum.

CHAPTER 5

ASSESSING PERCEIVED
SOCIAL SUPPORT
THE IMPORTANCE OF CONTEXT

MARY E. PROCIDANO AND WALANDA WALKER SMITH

In this chapter, we discuss assessment of perceived social support with respect to three inseparable issues: defining perceived support, selecting particular approaches to assess it, and systematically organizing hypotheses regarding its origins, nature, and effects. Based on a brief history of social support research, we explain our focus on *perceived* social support. We observe that our understanding of perceived support is still hampered by vague definitions and urge that, because of its importance for theory and intervention, perceived support research must develop beyond tests of its direct, moderating, and mediating effects in different populations. Toward that end, we make three recommendations. First, the perceived support construct should be clarified through hypothesis testing in the context of contemporary psychological paradigms. Cognitive and attachment-theory approaches appear particularly promising in this regard. Second, investigators who construct and use perceived support assessments should be aware of the implicit assumptions and consequences associated with different assessment approaches. Finally, we suggest a conceptual framework to articulate hypotheses regarding perceived support's origins, nature, and effects. The framework consists of culture, development, personality, social settings, and activities.

MARY E. PROCIDANO AND WALANDA WALKER SMITH • Department of Psychology, Fordham University, Bronx, New York 10458.

Sourcebook of Social Support and Personality, edited by Gregory R. Pierce, Brian Lakey, Irwin G. Sarason, and Barbara R. Sarason. Plenum Press, New York, 1997.

A BRIEF HISTORY OF PERCEIVED SUPPORT ASSESSMENT

The call for social support assessments came approximately 20 years ago (e.g., Rabkin & Struening, 1976), due in part to researchers' disappointment regarding the low magnitude of empirical relationships between stressful life events and symptomatology. Because an environmentally directed, prevention-oriented Zeitgeist favored pursuit of empirical questions related to the pathogenic role of stress, many new assessments were constructed in an effort to increase life-events measures' predictive validity. For instance, the prevailing approach of life-events measurement itself shifted, from gauging life-change impact via previously established normative weightings, which assumed a given event's impact to be constant across persons, and which did not differentiate between desirable and undesirable events (e.g., Holmes & Rahe, 1967), to measuring each event's impact by self-reported, subjective weightings, thereby incorporating each individual's appraisal of the event's intensity and desirability (e.g., Sarason, Johnson, & Siegel, 1978). Furthermore, a substantial research impetus came in the form of the buffering hypothesis: the expectation that social support (or some other psychosocial assets, such as coping style or coping skills) might buffer, or moderate, the impact of stressful events. The many social support assessments constructed to test the buffering hypothesis later were categorized into measures of social embeddedness, enacted support, and perceived support (Barrera, 1986).

An examination of the prolific social support literature has suggested some consistent inferences. For instance, although some research has confirmed the buffering hypothesis, there has been more evidence for social support's direct contribution to well-being (positive relationship) and to symptomatology/distress (inverse relationship; see, e.g., Cohen & Wills, 1985; Procidano, 1992a); that is, social support tends to enhance self-esteem, positive mood, and favorable views of life, and to diminish or preempt feelings of distress, irrespective of stressful life events. In addition, some investigations focusing on chronically stressed groups, such as families in poverty, or persons with chronic illness, or their caregivers (see, e.g., Gersten, 1992; Procidano, 1992b), have provided evidence that social support sometimes mediates the stress–distress relationship; that is, chronic stress can isolate its victims, alienate them from persons with whom they might otherwise enjoy mutually supportive relationships, and erode their perception of being accepted and valued by others. Thus, different models linking stress, social support, and well-being–distress have been derived.

Confirmation or disconfirmation of the direct and moderating models has been found to depend in part on how social support is operationalized. (Mediating effects have been studied far less consistently.) In general, social embeddedness, as inferred from structural characteristics of peoples' social networks (e.g., number and type of relationships) generally predicts well-being but not distress, and does not buffer stress, whereas enacted support sometimes correlates with the incidence of stress but does not predict well-being or distress. Of the three approaches, perceived support most consistently contributes to well-being and distress (in the predicted directions) and buffers, or moderates, the impact of life stress (Cohen & Wills, 1985; Procidano, 1992a). Many investigators began to construe perceived support as an intermediate outcome of social relationships and enacted support that contributes to self-esteem and adjustment outcomes. This pattern of findings and tentative model provide an empirical basis for our focus on perceived support. A theoretical rationale is elaborated throughout the chapter. This is not to suggest that social network characteristics and enacted support are not important. To the contrary, as the remainder of this chapter suggests, they are essential to a full picture of the nature of social relationships and of perceived support itself.

PERCEIVED SUPPORT IN THE CONTEXT OF PSYCHOLOGICAL PARADIGMS

Construction of perceived support measures (e.g., Cutrona, 1989; Procidano & Heller, 1983; Sarason, Levine, Basham, & Sarason, 1983; Zimet, Dahlem, Zimet, & Farley, 1988) has followed widely accepted construct–validation principles (Campbell & Fiske, 1959), according to which construct refinement and test development are viewed as linked, ongoing processes that involve data collection and theory refinement. Our understanding of a construct is expected to become more specific or even change, based on an emerging pattern of correlations between a measure of that particular construct and measures of other constructs. Accordingly, our measurement approach may need revision or elaboration.

It is unfortunate, though, that we knew *so little* about perceived support before we began measuring it. Although causal models connecting social support to other variables are invaluable methodological and conceptual tools, they all too often have not embodied meaningful theories. Because perceived support has been, to an extent, a "construct without a paradigm," our assessments' validity and, correspondingly, our articulation of hypotheses and explanation for their empirical support and nonsupport have suffered. Psychological paradigms provide contexts for investigating perceived support's origins, nature, and effects. An examination of recent literature suggests that cognitive and attachment perspectives have particular potential is this regard.

A COGNITIVE PERSPECTIVE: SUPPORT SCHEMAS AND SUPPORT STATEMENTS

The relevance of a cognitive perspective is readily suggested by available consensus about the meaning of perceived support. Many investigators have been guided by Cobb's (1976) early description of social support as information that leads a person to believe that he or she "is cared for and loved ... esteemed and valued ... and belongs to a network of communication and mutual obligations" (p. 300). Support perception is generally viewed as synonymous with support appraisal (Barrera, 1986; Cohen & Wills, 1985). Sarason, Pierce, and Sarason (1990) added conceptual enrichment by defining *perceived support* as a sense of acceptance.

Some recent investigations have demonstrated that general, support-related cognitive schemas predict more specific support perceptions (Lakey & Cassady, 1990; Lakey & Dickinson, 1994; Lakey, Moineau, & Drew, 1992). Beck originally defined a schema as

> a (cognitive) structure for screening, coding, and evaluating the stimuli that impinge on the organism .... On the basis of this matrix of schemas, the individual is able to orient himself [sic] in relation to time and space and to categorize and interpret experiences in a meaningful way (1967, p. 283, as cited by Young, Beck, & Weinberger, 1993).

Somewhat in contrast to such general and relatively enduring schemas, more spontaneous and transient self-statements (e.g., "I am doing a good job" vs. "I am messing up")
are emphasized in cognitive–behavioral approaches (e.g., Meichenbaum, 1977).

We suggest that cognitive and cognitive–behavioral conceptions apply directly to
perceived support and its assessment. Like self-schemas, people simultaneously carry
both positive and negative support schemas (e.g., "I am accepted and considered
worthy" vs. "I am considered incompetent and am rejected"). A particular schema's
salience, relative to that of other schemas depends on the individual's learning history;
people's behavior can be seen as efforts to confirm positive or negative schemas (e.g.,
through striving for success or for rewarding relationships vs. through procrastination
or becoming involved in abusive relationships). A particular schema can be elicited and
strengthened by life events with which it is consistent (e.g., experiencing success vs.
being devalued). Similarly, people spontaneously make both positive and negative
support statements. Thus, support schemas influence the emergence of support
statements, which in turn, as they accumulate over time, influence both support
schemas and self-schemas (consistent with the main-effect model, which posits that
social support enhances self-esteem).

The Relevance of Attachment Theory: The Importance of Emotional Bonds

Several recent investigations have found relationships between attachment to
parents and self-models on the one hand, and perceived support on the other hand
(e.g., Blain, Thompson, & Whiffen, 1993; Lakey & Dickinson, 1994; Sarason et al., 1991).
This approach has potential to explain perceived support's origins. Attachment theory
can add validity to perceived support research through its consideration of the importance of emotional bonds. We agree with Coyne and DeLongis's (1986) counsel against
the "cognitivization of social support" (p. 457). Perceived support is undoubtedly
more than cognition, as the Sarason et al. (1990) "*sense* of acceptance" (p. 97, italics
added) definition suggests. More enduring support schemas, and more spontaneous
support statements, are interwoven with positive emotions such as contentment and
warmth, happiness and joy, as opposed to negative emotions such as anxiety, depression, and anger. This broader conception is reflected in the following definition:

> Adult attachment is the stable tendency of an individual to make substantial efforts
> to seek and maintain proximity to and contact with *one or a few specific individ-*
> *uals* who provide the subjective potential for physical and/or psychological secu-
> rity. This stable tendency is regulated by internal working models of attachment,
> which are *cognitive–affective–motivational* schemas built from the individual's
> experience in his or her interpersonal world (Berman & Sperling, 1994, p. 8, italics
> added).

The Value of an Integrated Cognitive–Attachment Conception

Cognitive and attachment perspectives, along with an examination of perceived
support assessments themselves, may provide parsimonious explanations for some
contradictory and perhaps counterintuitive empirical findings. For instance, how can

seemingly contradictory moderating effects, in which social support attenuates life-events impact, be reconciled with mediating effects, in which stress diminishes social support? Different experiential histories, including development of support and self-schemas, the characteristics of stressful events, such as their intensity and duration, and the quality and consistency of support provision, all influence peoples' support statements. "Moderating schemas" are predominantly positive (e.g., "Life can be difficult and discouraging sometimes, but I am loved and accepted for who I am, and I am a good an worthy person"). They are related to positive support statements (e.g., "My spouse does things that show his or her care for me") and to effective coping and adjustment. *Mediating schemas*, in contrast, are predominantly negative (e.g., "Life is harsh and unfair, I am all alone, and I have been cheated and have failed") and related to negative support and self-statements, and to ineffective coping and maladjustment. Again, emotional experiences that accompany particular support statements, and that are elicited along with support schemas, also contribute to the coping–adjustment process.

Why does perceived support predict adjustment better than enacted support? One explanation is cognitive in nature. Young children may say, "My brother loves me, because he gave me his cookie." Adults, however, do not encode support experiences as images of concrete, isolated behaviors *per se* (such as "My brother loaned me $25"), but in terms of their meaning in a broader, experiential context that includes the history of that and other relationships, and other characteristics of the interaction itself, which collectively initiate support-related statements (e.g., "It is easy to talk to my brother" or "My brother just doesn't get it") as well as pleasant or unpleasant emotional states. These, in turn, activate support-related schemas (e.g., "My brother/people care for me" or "My brother/people don't respect me") and associated pleasant or unpleasant emotions.

Why are cognitive schemas, perceived support, and well-being–distress related to each other but not to enacted support? Enacted support measures (e.g., Barrera, Sandler, & Ramsay, 1981) sum up instances of ostensibly supportive behaviors over some time period, such as a month, but their scores do not embody the support statements that accompany the transaction. The real salience of enacted support, though, probably resides in those statements and their congruity with people's support versus nonsupport schemas, which have developed over long periods of time, based on behavior samples far larger than enacted support measures assess. Indeed perceiving support and nonsupport in the context of one's relationship history, rather than in response to a relatively small snapshot of events, probably has adaptive value. The latter approach might contribute to some rather erratic, maladaptive behavior.

ASSESSMENT APPROACHES

Different assessment approaches carry intrinsic assumptions about the meaning of perceived support and corresponding implications for inferences that we draw from research in which they are used. In this chapter, we do not attempt to describe and review all of the available perceived support measures, but rather to indicate and discuss several dimensions along which they vary, providing relevant examples. First, perceived support measures differ in terms of the specificity of support sources to which they refer. At one pole, some measures sum support appraisals across multiple sources. Thus, support arising from different types of relationships, such as family, friends, or work associates, are not differentiated. Others, such as the Perceived Social Support from Friends and from Families measures (PSS-Fr and PSS-Fa, respectively; Procidano & Heller, 1983) specify particular support-network sources, calling for a network-specific support appraisal at the item level (e.g., "My friends/my family give(s) me the moral support I need"). Similarly, each item of the Moos Family Environment Scale (FES; Moos, 1974), of which subscales such as Cohesion and Expressiveness have been used as a perceived support index, asks respondents to render global impressions of their families. Research using measures that discriminate between different sources of support has indicated consistently that they have different natures and functions. For instance, perceived friend support (PSS-Fr) is related more consistently to social competence and extraversion and is more likely to buffer stress, while perceived family support's (PSS-Fa) inverse relation to psychological distress is stronger (Procidano, 1992a).

In contrast to both of those approaches, some measures tap relationship-specific support. Pierce, Sarason, and Sarason (1991, 1992) have highlighted the difference between general and relation-specific support, indicating that they have different patterns of relationships to adjustment, and recommending a combined assessment approach. Assessing relationship-specific support has potential for clearer understanding of support experiences in the context of different types of life transitions, such as stepfamily formation (Pruett, Calsyn, & Jensen, 1993). The Multidimensional Scale of Perceived Social Support (Zimet et al., 1988) assesses perceived support from family, friends, and significant other. The Social Provisions Scale (Cutrona, 1989) taps different support functions, namely, guidance, reliable alliance, attachment, social integration, reassurance of worth, and opportunity to provide nurturance, and can be scored to provide either total network or relationship-specific support appraisals.

Another rather subtle way that perceived support measures differ is in terms their appraisal of investigator-specified or respondent-specified support sources; that is, some measures ask specifically for perceptions of support provided by family, friends, spouse, and so on, while others first ask the respondent to select a particular number of special or most important relationships and then inquire about support perceptions. Although the two approaches have not been compared systematically, a rationale can be provided for including both when possible. Relying solely on researcher-specified sources may systematically neglect relationships that are both unique and salient, and that reflect the recipient's unique social adaptation. Research on children at elevated risk for psychopathology, for instance, suggests that the most resilient children from disorganized or neglectful home environments, such as those of children of parents with schizophrenic or substance-use disorders, may compensate by forming attachments to neighbors or teachers (Anthony, 1987). These important and potentially stress-buffering relationships typically would not be reflected in assessments based solely on researcher-specified support sources. At the same time, the high-risk literature suggests that as adults, such resilient children are still discriminable from their lower risk counterparts and may show some adverse effects of their dysfunctional primary networks (Cohler, 1987). This type of information is lost without more normative, researcher-specified support sources.

Perceived support measures also vary with respect to whether they tap subjectively positive and/or negative transactions. Most measures fall into the former category; however, investigators have increasingly attempted to assess the nature of supportive transactions in a more complete and valid way. Moos's (1974) FES also contains some subscales, such as Conflict, that tap negative family appraisals. Studies in which interpersonal conflict or hindrance are assessed along with support have found that such negative transactions add unique information to the prediction of adjustment outcomes (Coyne & DeLongis, 1986; Lackner et al., 1993; Lepore, 1992; Pierce et al., 1992). This matter clearly warrants further attention, since relationships or networks that are primarily supportive undoubtedly contribute to support schemas, coping, and adjustment more optimally than those that function in ambivalent or highly inconsistent ways, or in primarily negative ways. Conflict or nonsupport may be particularly salient in the context of attachment relationships. Stressful events, which contribute to maladaptation, also tend to increase attachment behavior, activate schemas, and increase emotional arousal. Perhaps this is why perceived family support, which may reflect conflictual attachment more than friend support, is less likely to buffer stress.

Finally, perceived support measures differ in terms of their assessment of support-related schemas versus statements. Pierce et al.'s (1992) investigation of students' perception of experimentally provided support, by virtue of its clear reference to a single support provision by a particular individual in the context of a particular task, constitutes a good example of support-related statements. In general, virtually all assessments of "real-life" support probably reflect schemas by virtue of their global wording and lack of reference to time or life context. Somewhat ironically, even explicit tests of the buffering hypothesis have typically relied solely on assessment items that ask for general support perceptions, not incorporating measures of stress-specific perceived supports. Support-related statements warrant thorough investigation because of their potential role in the development and modification of support schemas, and their relevance to change in the context of preventive and therapeutic interventions. As discussed previously, they are probably more valid reflections of support experiences than enacted support as we currently measure it. It may be that the nature and function of support statements needs to be investigated using diaries, which are often used to assess self-statements, and which may provide meaningful units of analysis.

A CONCEPTUAL FRAMEWORK

The implications of differing assessment approaches are, of course, only actualized when hypotheses are tested and inferences drawn. Accordingly, we suggest a conceptual framework consisting of five contexts within which questions about perceived support's origins, nature, and effects might be posed. The contexts include culture, development, personality, social settings, and life tasks.

CULTURE

Although psychologists are becoming more conspicuously aware of the importance of culture as a context of social experience and personality development, neither culture membership nor cultural variation has been examined systematically with respect to perceived social support. Experiences rooted in identification and participation in cultural groups, such as those associated with race, ethnicity, religion, or nontraditional lifestyles, for instance, have clear implications for perceived support from both cognitive and attachment perspectives.

Bruner recently admonished cognitive psychology in general for its lack of attention to culture as a source of cognitive structures:

> The symbolic systems that individuals used in constructing meaning were systems that were already in place, already "there," deeply entrenched in culture and language .... They constituted a very special kind of communal tool kit whose tools, once used, made the user a reflection of the community (1990, p. 11).

In a similar vein, Howard defined culture in terms of shared cognitive "narratives":

> A culture can be thought of as a community of individuals who see their world in a particular manner—who share particular interpretations as central to the meaning of their lives and actions (1991, p. 190).

The relevance to perceived support is readily apparent. People's support-related statements and schemas undoubtedly are based on their exposure to culturally derived systems of meaning, expectations, and prescriptions for interpersonal relationships and transactions. Cultural values such as familism in Hispanic groups (Rogler & Cooney, 1984) and patrilineage in Asian cultures (Ryu & Vann, 1992) are examples of salient cultural narratives that impact social–network composition, interpersonal transaction, and perceptions of support provision and mutuality.

By providing accessible and meaningful opportunities for affiliation and attachment, cultural communities probably serve to enhance continuity in support perceptions, despite social-network transition or disruption. An obvious example involves migration. A common language provides a link to compatriots despite relocation to a host society, or a common religious ritual allows meaningful participation despite unfamiliarity with the spoken language. In the case of a small-scale "migration," such as moving to college, a student's support perception is likely to be maintained by a family tradition of attendance, a high-school teacher's association, or an educational philosophy that the college shares with the high school from which the student has graduated.

DEVELOPMENT

Development is another important context in which perceived support's origins, nature, and effects should be examined more fully. In particular, normative changes in social-network composition and types of participation and transactions associated with perceived support as functions of age and/or developmental stage are not well understood. Nor do we understand sources of continuities and discontinuities of attachment, affiliation, and perceived support across the life span. In many different nonclinical and clinical groups, for instance, perceived family and friend support are interrelated, suggesting a continuity from the quality of people's early relationships to that of subsequent ones (Procidano, 1992a). Family disruption (i.e., parental divorce), however, is an apparent source of discontinuity. Saqqal and Procidano (1994), in a sample of high-school girls, found that the relationship between perceived family and friend support was somewhat higher than previously obtained norms in the subgroup whose parents were not divorced, but nonsignificant in the subgroup whose parents were divorced.

Although some findings suggest the relevance of early attachment to subsequent affiliation, Fullerton and Ursano (1994) also concluded that childhood friendships contribute to adult attachments. The attainment of social skills, such as sharing and offering assistance, can be viewed as developmental tasks that are usually achieved during the preadolescent period. Furthermore, the ability to form friendships is deemed to be a primary indicator of social competence and psychological health. Late adolescents typically show an increase in extrafamilial social supports, with family supports being more important for girls than for boys. Some components of social support decrease as adults advance (e.g., network resources and friend support), although the support–well-being relation does not vary with age (Vaux, 1985).

Theory related to stages of psychosocial development (e.g., Erikson, 1974) provide hypotheses about different sources and types of support provision important to perceived support across the life span. During Erikson's Initiative versus Guilt stage (ages 3–5), for example, it is suggested that children's opportunity to develop a sense of competence and success through exploration and action upon the environment is particularly salient. Thus, a balance of parental nurturance and particular manifestations of autonomy support may be especially important for children's perceived support, initiative, and self-efficacy. The Identity versus Role Confusion stage (ages 12–20) requires a different manifestation of autonomy support. As suggested earlier, seeming discontinuities in support experiences, or nonnormative social networks, are especially important to understanding the adjustment outcomes of persons at risk for psychological maladjustment related to family disorganization and/or stressful life events.

PERSONALITY

A growing literature, some of which is described in other chapters of this volume, demonstrates that personality traits are related to perceived support. The most fundamental questions in this context are which personality traits are particularly important to perceived support, and what models can account best for the relationships that are observed? At this point, the personality traits that have received the most empirical attention for their relevance to social support include gender-related characteristics, such as instrumentality, expressiveness, and androgyny, introversion-extraversion, and hostility. The model typically proposed suggests that individual differences in personality traits contribute to subsequent perceived support. The substantive and methodological bases for this inference deserve further consideration.

The relevance of gender-related personality traits and gender roles are indicated by some consistent findings regarding sex differences reported in the social support literature. Women report higher perceived support, have more effective support-seeking skills, are more likely to seek support openly, and tend to establish more functional support networks (e.g., Ashton & Fuehrer, 1993; Barbee et al., 1993; Flaherty & Richman, 1989; Geller & Hobfoll, 1993; Olson & Schultz, 1994). Consistent with the broader personality literature, investigations that consider the relevance of gender-role socialization and accordingly incorporate measures of gender-related personality characteristics suggest that they are more important to social support than gender *per se* (see, e.g., Ashton & Fuehrer, 1993; Maccoby & Jacklin, 1974; Vaux, 1988).

Extraversion also has been linked to support receipt and perception (Lakey & Dickinson, 1994; Procidano, 1992a), since extraverts are likely to be less aroused and more comfortable in interpersonal situations in general. On the other hand, hostility has been associated consistently with fewer positive support experiences (e.g., Hardy & Smith, 1988; Houston & Kelly, 1989; Raikkonen, Keskivaara, & Keltikangas-Jarvinen, 1992). Hostile individuals are likely to behave in ways that alienate others from providing support, and also to construe a wider variety of transactions as nonsupportive, based on their support-related schemas. It has been suggested, in fact, that the relation of hostility (or Type A behavior pattern) to poor coronary health status is mediated by diminished social support.

As evidence accumulates, it should not be surprising if personality traits are found to contribute more to support perceptions than vice versa. By definition, personality traits reflect behavior patterns that generalize across situations and time. Correspondingly, personality-trait measures have been constructed to maximize the temporal stability that their scores reflect. Somewhat in contrast, perceived support assessments reflect schemas or statements which, by definition, are somewhat tentative and vary in salience according to recent life events. Following the same rationale, it should not be surprising if perceived support mediates personality's contribution to adjustment outcomes. Just as perceived support has been found to moderate or to mediate stress, depending on whether the participants' support or stress experiences are more pervasive and consistent, scores on perceived support measures, by design, are probably more likely to change in response to environmental events than those on personality-trait assessments. Finally, it should not be surprising if personality predicts support perceptions better than enacted support, again based in part on the ways that the three respective constructs are measured. The most constructive investigations in this context probably will be those that, rather than recapitulating the now mature person–situation controversy, are designed to add specificity to the *processes* by which personality and support experiences contribute to support-related statements and schemas and, in turn, to adjustment outcomes.

A rival model, proposing that perceived support contributes to personality, remains legitimate and untested. It is, though, fundamentally a question about personality *development*, whose answer will require prospective designs in which support experiences and perceived support are assessed (possibly through the use of diaries) over long periods of time. Personality traits are assumed to be stable, and yet we do not really understand the extent to which social environments might themselves be stable in their provision of meaningful support experiences. (We have suggested, though, that cultural participation is one source of such stability.)

SOCIAL SETTINGS

Particular social settings, such as home, school, and workplace, are contexts uniquely associated with corresponding types of stress (such as child-care burden, achievement pressures, and work strain), particular sources of support and nonsupport (such as family members, teachers and classmates, supervisors, and colleagues), and particular adjustment outcomes (such as marital satisfaction, school adjustment, or occupational burnout). Discriminating among social settings provides researchers a structure for posing very specific questions about the perceived support's origins, nature, and contribution to both context-specific and general adjustment outcomes, such as life satisfaction and distress.

Context-specific support perceptions might be especially important in contributing directly to context-specific self-efficacy attributions. But what about moderating and mediating effects? In one study relevant to this question, Lepore (1992) reported evidence of cross-setting ("cross-domain") buffering effects; specifically, friend and roommate support buffered stress arising in the complementary setting. Do setting-specific, low-conflict attachment relationships have special potency? Are some settings and associated support particularly important to general adjustment outcomes? In a study of children with limb deficiencies, Varni, Setoguchi, Rappoport, and Talbot (1992) found that, of multiple perceived support domains, perceived classmate social support was the only significant predictor across depressive and anxiety symptoms and general self-esteem. Do people's personal investments in different social settings, and therefore their relevance to general adjustment, change over time as a function of their support and nonsupport experiences in them?

LIFE TASKS

Social support research has centered primarily on stress. The popular buffering hypothesis by definition demands that support be construed in relation to stress. Unfortunately, there has been a deficiency of research efforts that examine the role of perceived support in other, potentially positive life contexts, such as personal goal strivings or fulfilling roles. Within the past decade, there has been a growing interest in personal goals and how they related to psychological adjustment (Emmons, 1986; Omodei & Wearing, 1990; Ruehlman & Wolchik, 1988), but the number of studies in this area is quite limited. Emmons, for example, has specified certain attributes or dimensions, such as importance, difficulty, and commitment, by which goals can be evaluated, and found that they relate differentially to adjustment. Far less is known, however, about the relevance of perceived support in the context of personal goal strivings. Ruehlman and Wolchik (1988) studied the effects of social support and hindrance in the context of personal goal strivings ("personal projects") on well-being and distress. They found that project support was related to well-being but not distress, but that hindrance both contributed to distress and detracted from well-being; they proposed that support and encouragement from significant others communicates to the recipients that their projects are worthwhile, thereby improving motivation and increasing the likelihood of goal attainment and positive adjustment. Hindrance, in contrast, may serve as a source of stress and diminished self-esteem. Among other things, this study underscores the importance of considering negative social perceptions in an analysis of support.

Fulfillment of a parenting, spousal, professional, or other role is another life-task context in which the relevance of perceived support has been relatively neglected. Like personal goal strivings and social settings, role fulfillments undoubtedly vary in their importance to self-concept and adjustment, and therefore are contexts in which perceived support and nonsupport may be important to role-specific outcomes, such as parent–infant attachment (e.g., Spieker & Bensley, 1994) and to more general adjustment.

Incorporating multiple life tasks, such as coping with stress, personal goal striving, and role fulfillment, into the study of perceived support again implies constructing assessments to tap task-specific support and nonsupport (as in Ruehlman & Wolchik, 1988). Like social settings, life tasks may differ in their subjective importance; correspondingly, task-specific support and nonsupport may contribute uniquely to adjustment. People who perceive hindrance or nonsupport for their self-chosen roles and personal goal strivings in connection, for example, with cultural or familial norms are likely to experience distress, despite overt gestures of acceptance.

SUMMARY AND IMPLICATIONS

Perceived social support is an important psychological construct reflecting a critical aspect of human development and adaptation. Theoretical enrichment, attention to the assumptions reflected in assessment approaches, and increased specificity regarding contexts in which support perceptions arise, undoubtedly will enhance the validity of social support investigations. It is clear that more "basic" research in perceived social support is still needed, in part to help inform the design of studies in which social support is only a small part. In our laboratory at Fordham University, for example, we are currently validating newly constructed measures of relation specific perceived support and nonsupport, with slightly different forms for use in the context of stressful life events versus personal goal strivings. In particular, more prospective studies are needed to investigate the ways that personality factors and support experiences may influence each other. In turn, development of more valid and comprehensive models is important to the design of preventive and treatment interventions that seek to enhance perceived support.

REFERENCES

Anthony, E. J. (1987). Risk, vulnerability, and resilience. In E. J. Anthony & B. J. Cohler (Eds.), *The invulnerable child* (pp. 3–48). New York: Guilford.

Ashton, W. A., & Fuehrer, A. (1993). Effects of gender and gender-role identification of participant and type of social support resource on support seeking. *Sex Roles, 28*, 461–476.

Barbee, A. P., Cunningham, M. R., Winstead, B. A., Derlega, V. J., Gulley, M. R., Yankeelov, P. A., & Druen, P. B. (1993). Effects of gender-role expectations on the social support process. *Journal of Social Issues, 49*, 175–190.

Barrera, M. Jr. (1986). Distinctions between support concepts, measures and models. *American Journal of Community Psychology, 14*, 413–446.

Barrera, M. Jr., Sandler, I. N., & Ramsay, T. B. (1981). Preliminary development of a scale of social support: Studies on college students. *American Journal of Community Psychology, 9*, 435–447.

Berman, W. H., & Sperling, M. B. (1994). The structure and function of adult attachment. In M. B. Sperling & W. H. Berman (Eds.), *Attachment in adults: Clinical and developmental perspectives* (pp. 1–30). New York: Guilford.

Blain, M. D., Thompson, J. M., & Whiffen, V. E. (1993). Attachment and perceived social support in late adolescence: The interaction between working models of self and others. *Journal of Adolescent Research, 8,* 226–241.

Bruner, J. (1990). *Acts of meaning.* Cambridge, MA: Harvard University Press.

Campbell, D. T., & Fiske, D. W. (1959). Convergent and discriminant validation by the multitrait, multimethod matrix. *Psychological Bulletin, 56,* 81–105.

Cobb, S. (1976). Social support as a moderator of life stress. *Psychosomatic Medicine, 38,* 300–314.

Cohen, S., & Wills, T. A. (1985). Stress, social support, and the buffering hypothesis. *Psychological Bulletin, 98,* 310–357.

Cohler, B. J. (1987). Adversity, resilience, and the study of lives. In E. J. Anthony & B. J. Cohler (Eds.), *The invulnerable child* (pp. 363–424). New York: Guilford.

Coyne, J. C., & DeLongis, A. (1986). Going beyond social support: The role of social relationships in adaptation. *Journal of Consulting and Clinical Psychology, 54,* 454–460.

Cutrona, C. E. (1989). Ratings of social support by adolescents and adult informants: Degree of correspondence and prediction of depressive symptoms. *Journal of Personality and Social Psychology, 57,* 723–730.

Emmons, R. A. (1986). Personal strivings: An approach to personality and subjective well-being. *Journal of Personality and Social Psychology, 51,* 1058–1068.

Erikson, E. (1974). *Dimensions of a new identity.* New York: Norton.

Flaherty, J., & Richman, J. (1989). Gender differences in the perception and utilization of social support: Theoretical perspectives and an empirical test. *Social Science and Medicine, 28,* 1221–1228.

Fullerton, C. S., & Ursano, R. J. (1994). Preadolescent peer friendships: A critical contribution to adult social relatedness? *Journal of Youth and Adolescence, 23,* 43–63.

Geller, P. A., & Hobfoll, S. E. (1993). Gender differences in preference to offer social support to assertive men and women. *Sex Roles, 28,* 419–432.

Gersten, J. C. (1992). Families in poverty. In M. E. Procidano & C. B. Fisher (Eds.), *Contemporary families: A handbook for school professionals* (pp. 137–158). New York: Teachers College Press.

Hardy, J. D., & Smith, T. W. (1988). Cynical hostility and vulnerability to disease: Social support, life stress, and physiological response to conflict. *Health Psychology, 7,* 447–459.

Holmes, T. H., & Rahe, R. H. (1967). The Social Readjustment Rating Scale. *Journal of Psychosomatic Research, 11,* 213–218.

Houston, B. K., & Kelly, K. E. (1989). Hostility in employed women: Relation to work and marital experiences, social support, stress, and anger expression. *Personality and Social Psychological Bulletin, 15,* 175–182.

Howard, G. S. (1991). Culture tales: A narrative approach to thinking, cross-cultural psychology, and psychotherapy. *American Psychologist, 46,* 187–197.

Lackner, J. B., Joseph, J. G., Ostrow, D. G., Kessler, R. C., Eshleman, S., Wortman, C. B., O'Brien, K., Phair, J. P., & Chmiel, J. (1993). A longitudinal study of psychological distress is a cohort of gay men: Effects of social support and coping strategies. *Journal of Nervous and Mental Disease, 181,* 4–12.

Lakey, B., & Cassady, P. B. (1990). Cognitive processes in perceived social support. *Journal of Personality and Social Psychology, 59,* 337–343.

Lakey, B., & Dickinson, L. G. (1994). Antecedents of perceived support: Is perceived family environment generalized to new social relationships? *Cognitive Therapy and Research, 18,* 39–53.

Lakey, B., Moineau, S., & Drew, J. B. (1992). Perceived social support and individual differences in the interpretation and recall of supportive behaviors. *Journal of Social and Clinical Psychology, 11,* 336–348.

Lepore, S. J. (1992). Social conflict, social support, and psychological distress: Evidence of cross-domain buffering effects. *Journal of Personality and Social Psychology, 63,* 857–867.

Maccoby, E. E., & Jacklin, C. N. (1974). *The psychology of sex differences.* Stanford, CA: Stanford University Press.

Meichenbaum, D. (1977). *Cognitive-behavior modification: An integrative approach.* New York: Plenum.

Moos, R. H. (1974). *Family Environment Scale: Preliminary manual.* Palo Alto, CA: Consulting Psychologists Press.

Olson, D. A., & Schultz, K. S. (1994). Gender differences in the dimensionality of social support. *Journal of Applied Social Psychology, 24,* 1221–1232.

Omodei, M. M., & Wearing, A. J. (1990). Need satisfaction and involvement in personal projects: Toward an integrative model of subjective well-being. *Journal of Personality and Social Psychology, 59*, 762–769.

Pierce, G. R., Sarason, B. R., & Sarason, I. G. (1991). General and relationship-based perceptions of support: Are two constructs better than one? *Journal of Personality and Social Psychology, 61*, 1028–1039.

Pierce, G. R., Sarason, B. R., & Sarason, I. G. (1992). General and specific support expectations and stress as predictors of perceived supportiveness: An experimental study. *Journal of Personality and Social Psychology, 63*, 297–307.

Procidano, M. E. (1992a). The nature of perceived social support: Findings of meta-analytic studies. In C. D. Spielberger & J. N. Butler (Eds.), *Advances in personality assessment* (Vol. 9, pp. 1–26). Hillsdale, NJ: Erlbaum.

Procidano, M. E. (1992b). Families and schools: Social resources for students. In M. E. Procidano & C. B. Fisher (Eds.), *Contemporary families: A handbook for school professionals* (pp. 292–306). New York: Teachers College Press.

Procidano, M. E., & Heller, K. (1983). Measures of perceived social support from friends and from family: Three validation studies. *American Journal of Community Psychology, 11*, 1–24.

Pruett, C. L., Calsyn, R. J., & Jensen, F. M. (1993). Social support received by children in stepmother, stepfather, and intact families. Special issue: The stepfamily puzzle: Intergenerational influences. *Journal of Divorce and Remarriage, 19*, 165–179.

Rabkin, J. G., & Struening, E. L. (1976). Life events, stress, and illness. *Science, 194*, 1013–1020.

Raikkonen, K., Keskivaara, & Keltikangas-Jarvinen, L. (1992). Hostility and social support among Type A individuals. *Psychology and Health, 7*, 289–299.

Rogler, L. H., & Cooney, R. S. (1984). *Puerto Rican families in New York City: Intergenerational processes* (Monograph No. 11). New York: Fordham University Hispanic Research Center.

Ruehlman, L. S., & Wolchik, S. A. (1988). Personal goals and interpersonal support and hindrance as factors in psychological distress and well-being. *Journal of Personality and Social Psychology, 55*, 293–301.

Ryu, J. P., & Vann, B. H. (1992). Korean families in America. In M. E. Procidano & C. B. Fisher (Eds.). *Contemporary families: A handbook for school professionals* (pp. 117–134). New York: Teachers College Press.

Saqqal, C., & Procidano, M. (1994, July). *Adolescent daughters of divorce have higher self-esteem.* Paper presented at the annual meeting of the American Psychological Society, Washington, DC.

Sarason, B. R., Pierce, G. R., & Sarason, I. G. (1990). Social support: The sense of acceptance and the role of relationships. In B. R. Sarason, I. G. Sarason, & G. R. Pierce, (Eds.), *Social support: An interactional view* (pp. 97–128). New York: Wiley.

Sarason, B. R., Pierce, G. R., Shearin, E. N., Sarason, I. G., Waltz, J. A., & Poppe, L. (1991). Perceived social support and working models of self and actual others. *Journal of Personality and Social Psychology, 60*, 273–287.

Sarason, I. G., Johnson, J. H., & Siegel, J. M. (1978). Assessing the impact of life changes: Development of the Life Experiences Survey. *Journal of Consulting and Clinical Psychology, 46*, 932–946.

Sarason, I. G., Levine, H. M., Basham, R. B., & Sarason, B. R. (1983). Assessing social support: The Social Support Questionnaire. *Journal of Personality and Social Psychology, 44*, 127–139.

Spieker, S. J., & Bensley, L. (1994). Roles of living arrangements and grandmother social support in adolescent mothering and infant attachment. *Developmental Psychology, 30*, 102–111.

Varni, J. W., Setoguchi, Y., Rappaport, L. R., & Talbot, D. (1992). Psychological adjustment and perceived social support in children with congenital/acquired limb deficiencies. *Journal of Behavioral Medicine, 15*, 31–44.

Vaux, A. (1985). Variations in social support associated with gender, ethnicity, and age. *Journal of Social Issues, 41*, 89–110.

Vaux, A. (1988). *Social support: Theory, research, and intervention.* New York: Prager.

Young, J. E., Beck, A. T., & Weinberger. A. (1993). Depression. In D. H. Barlow (Ed.), *Clinical handbook of psychological disorders: A step-by-step treatment manual* (2d ed.) (pp. 240–277). New York: Guilford.

Zimet, G. D., Dahlem, N. W., Zimet, S. G., & Farley, G. K. (1988). The Multidimensional Scale of Perceived Social Support. *Journal of Personality Assessment, 52*, 30–41.

Chapter 6

A SOCIAL-COGNITIVE PERSPECTIVE ON SOCIAL SUPPORT

Brian Lakey and Jana Brittain Drew

Everything must be questioned ... without exception and without circumspection
— Diderot

We invite the reader to answer the following question:

My family gives me the moral support I need.   Yes   No   Don't know

We hope that you were able to answer "yes" to this question from Procidano and Heller's (1983) perceived social support scale, because "yes" answers across a number of similar items are associated with a wide range of positive outcomes. But consider for a moment how you arrived at your answer. From one perspective, you could have made your answer as a "good scientist" would. You carefully recalled and summed all the instances of emotional support that you had received and compared them to the amount that you believe most people get. If your score was a standard deviation above the mean, you answered "Yes," a standard deviation below, you answered "No," and within a standard deviation from the mean produced a "Don't know."

It seems exceedingly unlikely to us that persons respond to social support questions in this fashion. For one thing, respondents usually make their answers in a very brief period of time, much faster than required to go through the processes just described. But even if persons did attempt to answer in this way, consider some of the issues that would make answering such questions difficult. What does moral support mean? Does it mean support regarding difficult moral issues, encouragement to behave in a moral fashion, or simply general encouragement? Does "the support I need" refer to times in which moral support would be nice, but you could get by without it, or times when it is absolutely essential? What is the standard of comparison? Does the

Brian Lakey and Jana Brittain Drew • Department of Psychology, Wayne State University, Detroit, Michigan 48202.

Sourcebook of Social Support and Personality, edited by Gregory R. Pierce, Brian Lakey, Irwin G. Sarason, and Barbara R. Sarason. Plenum Press, New York, 1997.

respondent compare him or herself to what other people receive, or according to some absolute standard? If the comparison is to what other people receive, how does the respondent know what support others get? If the comparison is to an absolute standard, do subjects differ in the standard they apply? Because the question does not specify a time frame, does the respondent answer about recent support, or over the entire life span? If these issues were not daunting enough, consider the problem in recalling instances of enacted support. Are persons accurate in their memories? Do they remember all instances of support, or are some more memorable? Do individuals differ in their tendency or ability to attend to or remember support? If so, how does this influence their judgments? Of course, the "good scientist" model is not the only way to answer a support question. It is well known that persons use a variety of heuristics in making judgments (Kahneman, Slovic, & Tversky, 1982). Regarding support judgments specifically, persons may base their answers on how much they like the person, or on the target's personality traits. If so, perceived support would be quite different from what was originally imagined by social support researchers.

Such questions about how persons make perceived support judgments, and the factors that influence them, have been ignored in social support research. The implicit assumption has been that subjects provide a veridical account of the supportiveness of their social environment, without consideration of how respondents actually make these judgments. Of course, social support researchers are not alone in overlooking such vexing questions. Personality is almost always assessed through self-report, but the field of personality assessment implicitly assumes that persons know and can report personality accurately. However, there are important reasons to understand what support judgments are based on, including how situational and personal factors influence these judgments. In our view, although the robust association between perceived support and mental health clearly establishes the importance of social support, we still do not know what people are telling us when they complete social support measures. If we do not know what people are referring to when they make these judgments, it will be difficult to identify or modify the key components of social support.

The goal of this chapter is to attempt to shed light on some of these difficult questions by applying the social cognition approach to research in social support. First, we review traditional models of perceived support and critically examine the evidence for them. Next, we argue for a social-cognitive perspective of social support that draws heavily from basic research in social cognition (cf. Baldwin, 1992; Mankowski & Wyer, Chapter 7, this volume; Pierce, Baldwin, & Lydon, Chapter 2, this volume). This basic research suggests solutions for some of the most vexing empirical and theoretical problems in the social support literature. Following this, we describe research on social-cognitive processes in social support that draws directly from basic research in social cognition, and we review additional social-cognitive processes that should be particularly relevant for social support. Finally, we identify what we believe are the most crucial research issues for the future.

TRADITIONAL MODELS OF SOCIAL SUPPORT

From the very beginning of research in this area, it was assumed that perceived support reflected the actual supportive behaviors provided by others during times of stress (Sarason, Sarason, & Pierce, 1990). According to this model, high-perceived-support individuals had better mental health because they received more or better enacted support. Effective enacted support directly assisted individuals' coping efforts, and as a result of this enhanced coping, such persons were less vulnerable to stress-induced disorders (Barrera, 1986, 1988; Cohen & Wills, 1985; Cutrona & Russell, 1990; Thoits, 1986). Thus, enacted support was hypothesized to be the actual mechanism, and perceived support was related to lower symptom levels, primarily because it reflected effective enacted support. Although some scholars acknowledged that perceived support could directly reduce stress reactions by influencing appraisal processes (Cohen & Wills, 1985; Heller & Swindle, 1983), this mechanism was not emphasized (Sarason et al., 1990b).

This model has substantial intuitive appeal, and such processes immediately come to mind when thinking about "social support." Nonetheless, there are important empirical problems with this model. For example, in contrast to perceived support, enacted support is rarely associated with psychological symptoms (Barrera, 1986; Collins, Dunkel-Schetter, Lobel, & Scrimshaw, 1993; Dunkel-Schetter & Bennett, 1990; Sandler & Barrera, 1984; Sarason et al., 1990b). When it is, the effect is frequently in the direction opposite to that predicted by the traditional model (e.g., Helgeson, 1993). However, a more serious problem is the frequent observation that enacted support is only weakly related to perceived support. Studies in which subjects report both perceived and enacted support frequently show correlations below $r = .30$, with many approaching zero (Barrera, 1986; Collins et al., 1993; Dunkel-Schetter & Bennet, 1990; Newcomb, 1990; Sandler & Barrera, 1984; Sarason et al., 1990b; Sarason, Shearin, Pierce, & Sarason, 1987). Moreover, the relation between enacted and perceived support is difficult to interpret because of evidence suggesting that high-perceived-support subjects have better memory for support-relevant behavior (Drew, Lakey, & Sirl, 1995; Lakey & Cassady, 1990; Lakey, Moineau, & Drew, 1992). Thus, high-perceived-support subjects may report receiving more enacted support, because they have better memory for supportive behaviors, not because they have actually received more.

Investigators have also conducted observational studies in which high- and low-perceived-support subjects interact with social network members while their behaviors are coded by independent, blind observers. These studies were designed to identify the enacted support that discriminated between high- and low-support subjects. However, most of these studies found no relation between subjects' perceived support and levels of enacted support provided by companions (Belsher & Costello, 1991; Heller & Lakey, 1985; Lakey & Heller, 1988). The absence of effects in Heller and Lakey (1985) and Lakey and Heller (1988) are particularly noteworthy, because they showed that enacted support was related to other variables in predictable ways. For example, Heller and Lakey found that subjects' preferences for specific types of social support predicted the enacted support that they actually received from companions. Similarly, Lakey and Heller found that the enacted support provided by companions predicted subjects' later coping on a behavioral problem-solving task. Because enacted support behaved as expected on some variables, it is less likely that the absence of a relation between perceived and enacted support reflects the poor measurement of the latter. In contrast with these studies, Garung, Sarason, and Sarason (1994) recently reported that subjects' reports of their mothers' supportiveness predicted the enacted support provided by their mothers during a laboratory stressor, although this accounted for only 5% of the variance. The results of Garung et al. suggest that stronger relations between perceived and enacted support might be obtained if perceived support is assessed with regard to a specific relationship (cf. Pierce, Sarason, & Sarason, 1992). As a whole, however, these studies do not provide evidence for a strong link between perceived and enacted support.

A third group of observational studies have investigated the link between enacted support and judgments of that support within a single interaction. These studies differ from those described earlier in that subjects' characteristic levels of perceived support were not studied. Cutrona and Suhr (1992) found no relation between the enacted support provided by strangers and subjects' perceptions of the supportiveness of that interaction. However, Cutrona and Suhr (1994) found a strong relation between the constructs when wives described problems to husbands, but not when husbands described problems to wives. Similarly, Winstead, Derlega, Lewis, Sanchez-Hucles, and Clarke, (1992) found strong relations between enacted support and subjects' perceived supportiveness of the interaction, accounting for 23% of the variance in support judgments. Burleson and Sampter (1985, Study 1) had confederates describe a standardized problem to subjects, and subjects' comforting attempts were recorded and scored according to sensitivity. Confederates' ratings of the sensitivity of subjects' statements were strongly correlated with the proportion of highly sensitive statements made by subjects, as determined by independent observers. Thus, these observational studies provide much stronger evidence for a link between perceived and enacted support. However, it is not clear whether judgments of the supportiveness of specific interactions become generalized to more global perceived support judgments. The conflicting results between studies that investigate global perceived support and those that examine the supportiveness of specific interactions suggest that judgments based on specific interactions may not be generalized to enduring support perceptions.

Perceived and enacted support might be more highly related if certain methodological improvements were made. For example, enacted support may lead to perceived support only when (1) it matches the demands of the stressor (Cutrona & Russell, 1990; Cutrona & Suhr, 1992), (2) it is provided freely and without condescension, and (3) both are assessed at the same level of specificity (global vs. relationship-specific) and regarding the same period of time (e.g., during the past month). Kaul and Lakey (1996) recently conducted a study designed to assess the relation between perceived and enacted support under conditions most likely to produce strong effects. For example, subjects all experienced the same stressor, which called for substantial direct assistance (mothers whose young children suffered from congenital heart defects requiring surgery). Enacted support that matched the demands of the stressor (Cutrona & Russell, 1990), were specifically assessed by focusing on the types of support judged by experienced nurses to be most appropriate for coping with this problem. In addition, both enacted and perceived support were assessed with regard to a single, important person. To test the hypothesis that only prototypically effective instances of enacted support lead to perceived support, subjects were interviewed about times in which their supporter behaved in an especially supportive fashion. However, despite these methodological features designed to maximize the perceived–enacted support relation, only modest links between the two constructs were observed. These findings are important because they address directly the hypothesis that perceived and enacted support would be more strongly related if greater care were taken in assessment. Nonetheless, it is always possible that stronger relations would emerge if other methodological improvements were made. However, at some point the traditional enacted support model will become nonfalsifiable if negative results are always met with the response that something must be wrong with the measures.

For the time being, the best available evidence suggests that, at most, enacted support may account for about 10% of the variance in perceived support. But how strong a relation should we expect? On the one hand, effect sizes of this magnitude are perfectly respectable in psychological research, *when phenomena are assumed to be multiply determined* (Ahadi & Diener, 1989). However, traditional models of social support have emphasized enacted support and neglected the role of other variables. If perceived support is assumed to be determined by multiple causes, of which enacted support is only one, then effect sizes of this magnitude are perfectly reasonable. However, if enacted support is viewed as the primary causal agent, then these effect sizes are simply too small to support this model (Meehl, 1978).

Although perceived support does not appear to be rooted primarily in enacted support, evidence from another type of study suggests that perceived support is rooted in the social environment in important ways. These studies examine the extent to which subjects' reports of perceived support are verified by significant others, or the extent to which subjects agree on the supportiveness of the same social environment. Cutrona (1988) studied the extent to which the support perceptions of pregnant adolescents were corroborated by significant others. The average correlation between the two sources was approximately $r = .30$, although significant others corroborated the girls' perceived support from boyfriends at $r = .51$. Similarly, Vinokur, Schul, and Caplan (1987) examined the correspondence between subjects' reports of the supportiveness of a significant other, and the others' reports of their own supportiveness. Controlling for a number of individual difference variables such as general negative outlook, poor mental health, and resentment, significant others corroborated subjects' reports at beta = .35 at Time 1 and beta = .30 at Time 2. Using essentially the same design, Abbey, Andrews, and Hallman (1995) found betas in the mid-.20s in their study of fertile and infertile married couples. McCaskill and Lakey (1995) studied the correspondence between clinically disordered adolescents and their families on perceived family environment. Adolescents' and family reports of family cohesion were related at $r = .55$. Repetti (1987) examined the extent to which bank employees agreed in their assessment of the social climate of various branch offices. The intraclass correlation for intimacy, which focused on social support, was .23. Finally, Lakey, McCabe, Fisicaro, and Drew (1996) conducted three generalizability studies in which subjects all rated the same targets on supportiveness. Generalizability analyses indicated that approximately 20% of the variance could be accounted for by the actual characteristics of supporters.

Thus, unlike the laboratory and self-report investigations of enacted support, studies that use others to corroborate self-reports have been quite consistent in finding significant relations between perceptions of support and anchors in the social environment. Furthermore, some of these studies (e.g., Cutrona, 1988; Lakey et al., 1996; McCaskill & Lakey, 1995; Repetti, 1987) have found substantially stronger relations than those focusing on the relation between enacted and perceived support. But do they provide evidence that perceived support is rooted in enacted support, and do they conflict with the literature on the enacted–perceived support relation? These studies do provide good evidence that a portion of perceived support is based in the actual social environment. However, because of their correlational design, they do not indicate what aspect of the environment is related to support perceptions. The obtained agreement could be driven by a range of other factors. For example, as we will describe in more detail later in this chapter, subjects may base their support judgments on the global characteristics of supporters, unrelated to stressful transactions.

In summary, traditional views of social support have emphasized how enacted support provided by network members promotes mental health by enhancing stressed individuals' coping efforts, thereby reducing their risk for stress-related disorder. These models have been extremely useful in generating a huge volume of research on social support, mental health, and stress buffering. However, in our view, the field prematurely focused on these processes and has not considered a wider range of alternative models. This has slowed development of the field, because, as we have just seen, there are major empirical problems with traditional models that focus on enacted support. Perceived support is probably influenced by a multitude of factors, and any given one should not be expected to be the *primary* determinant. In the tradition of Goldstein, Heller, and Sechrest (1966), we argue that the field can benefit by drawing from basic research on social and cognitive processes. In fact, many of the most fundamental questions in social support research have already been addressed with great success in areas such as impression formation and person memory and judgment. In the next section of this chapter, we will outline the benefits of drawing from social cognition research in answering basic questions about social support. We begin with a brief sketch of the social cognition field and show how this research is relevant to social support processes. We then describe research on cognitive processes in social support that has drawn directly from basic research in social cognition.

ADVANTAGES OF TAKING A SOCIAL-COGNITIVE
APPROACH TO SOCIAL SUPPORT

Social cognition is a broad theoretical perspective that cuts across a wide range of content areas. Rather than referring to any particular social phenomena, social cognition refers to a group of guiding assumptions and methodological approaches (Hamilton, Devine, & Ostrom, 1994a; Sherman, Judd, & Park, 1989). As indicated by the term itself, social cognition is interested in cognitive processes in social behavior. To a large extent, this involves applying human information-processing models and methods, developed primarily in cognitive psychology, to understanding social behavior (Ostrom, 1994). Social-cognitive research investigates a wide range of processes, including how preexisting knowledge about the self or social world is represented and organized in memory, and how these structures influence attention, interpretation, memory, and efficiency of information processing. These processes are hypothesized to influence social behavior and emotion, as well as reciprocally altering the representation of the information in memory (Hamilton et al., 1994a; Sherman et al., 1989).

The advantages of social-cognitive approaches are reflected in the enormous impact they have had on content areas as diverse as social, personality, developmental and abnormal psychology (Wyer & Srull, 1994). These advantages include enhancing communication between researchers in different content areas by providing a common language and set of assumptions. In addition, the social-cognitive approach identifies a number of processes (e.g., attention and recall) likely to be important in a wide range of phenomena, and provides a number of methodological approaches to investigate these mechanisms (e.g., reaction time, clustering in free recall).

Applying social-cognitive approaches to social support research has a number of specific advantages (cf. Baldwin, 1992; Mankowksi & Wyer, Chapter 7, this volume; Pierce, Baldwin, & Lydon, Chapter 2, this volume). First, from a purely theoretical perspective, it offers a variety of processes by which social support may have its impact. Theoretical approaches that identify *processes* have many desirable qualities, including providing clues on how to modify support. An unrealized promise of social support research has been to provide a technology for the prevention and treatment of psychological problems (Heller, 1979). To do this, a theory of social support must specify *how* support leads to fewer symptoms, as well as *how* support is developed (Lakey & Lutz, 1996). Second, many of these mechanisms have solid empirical support and have already been shown to be useful in understanding other social behavior (Devine, Hamilton, & Ostrom, 1994; Wyer & Srull, 1994). Social support theory and research can be enriched by integrating these mechanisms. Third, social cognition has borrowed and developed a diverse array of well-established methods for investigating these mechanisms, and these can be applied to questions involving social support. Fourth, social-cognitive approaches create links to a wide range of other content areas. Social support research has tended to develop in isolation from other areas of psychology. However, by studying cognitive processes, direct comparisons can be drawn between social support and a wide range of other phenomena, such as the self-concept (Kihlstrom & Klein, 1994), impression formation (Leyens & Fiske, 1994), and clinical anxiety and depression (Weary & Edwards, 1994). Fifth, researchers in other content areas, using social-cognitive approaches, are making fast progress in answering some fundamental questions that are directly relevant to social support research. For example, social cognition researchers have made important advances in understanding how knowledge about others and the self are represented, and how this influences judgments (Klein & Loftus, 1990; Srull & Wyer, 1989).

BENEFITING FROM BASIC RESEARCH: HOW ARE THE PERSONAL CHARACTERISTICS OF OTHERS REPRESENTED IN MEMORY?

A fundamental question in both social support research and social cognition is "How do perceivers represent knowledge about others in memory, and how does this representation influence subsequent judgments?" This question has received substantial attention in social perception research since the 1970s (Wyer & Carlston, 1994), when research on social support was in its infancy. However, social support researchers have not shown much interest in this issue. But the question we raised at the beginning of this chapter ("How do people formulate their answers to social support questions?") cannot be resolved without knowing how social support information is represented in memory, and how this is used to make support judgments. As described earlier, traditional models emphasizing enacted support implicitly assume that perceived support is inferred by reviewing the number of supportive experiences in memory. However, basic research in social cognition suggests a different mechanism that has enormous implications for social support.

As discussed earlier, a major problem for social support theory is that perceived support is not very strongly related to enacted support. This observation is frequently met with vigorous protest. Although it conflicts with most people's informal observation, basic research on person memory and judgment actually predicts that no strong relation would be observed between perceived and enacted support under most circumstances! This is because judgments of others' personal qualities and memory for their behaviors are usually unrelated (Hastie & Park, 1986; Kilstrom & Klein, 1994; Wyer & Carlston, 1994). Hastie and Park (1986) showed that judgments and the recall of relevant behaviors will only be related when no prior judgment has been made. In this case, judgments are derived by reviewing instances of behavior in memory (*memory-based judgments*). However, because persons tend to make trait inferences soon after being exposed to behavior (Bargh, 1994; Beike & Sherman, 1994), memory-based judgments are very rare. Instead, people tend to make *on-line* judgments, in which trait inferences are formed after the first few instances of behavior. Under these circumstances, people do not usually review memories of behavior in order to make judgments. Rather, they recall their prior judgments, and thus person memory and judgment are usually unrelated.

Modern theories of person perception place great emphasis on the perceiver's tendency to construe the behavior of others in trait terms, as this tendency appears to be relatively spontaneous and occurs on the basis of very little information (Beike & Sherman, 1994; Hastie & Park, 1986; Srull & Wyer, 1989; Wyer & Carlston, 1994). For example, Park (1986) found that impressions of other persons were dominated by trait concepts rather than behavioral examples, and that this tendency increased with greater familiarity with the target. Winter and Uleman (1984) had subjects read descriptions of behaviors and then used a variety of cueing conditions in a later recall task. Trait concepts were the most effective cues for facilitating recall, suggesting that subjects had interpreted the behaviors in trait terms, even though they were unaware of doing so. Similarly, Carlston and Skowronski (1994) found in four experiments that trait descriptors of targets were learned more readily when subjects had been exposed previously to behavioral descriptions of targets consistent with these traits. This suggests that trait inferences were already derived from the behavioral descriptions. These effects occurred regardless of processing objectives (impression formation vs. memory set) and when subjects could not recognize the original behavioral examples. Furthermore, Sherman and Klein (1994; Experiment 2) demonstrated that trait inferences were formed after the presentation of only one highly diagnostic behavior.

Although it is well documented that persons think of others in trait terms, this does not directly address the question "Do people refer to behavior at all when making trait judgments?" Klein, Loftus and Burton (1989) and Klein and Loftus (1990) recently developed the *task facilitation paradigm* to address this question. They reasoned that if persons access behavioral information when making trait judgments, then a task that requires making a trait judgment should facilitate a later task involving retrieving a behavioral example. For example, if I must recall an example of supportive behavior to make a judgment of supportiveness, then making such a judgment will facilitate my performance on the subsequent task of recalling such a behavior. Similarly, recalling a behavioral exemplar should facilitate making trait judgments relevant to the behavior. If I recall behavioral examples when judging supportiveness, then having previously recalled a behavior should facilitate making a related judgment. In their experiments, subjects were presented with three types of tasks. *Define* tasks asked subjects to define a particular trait adjective. *Describe* tasks required them to determine whether the trait referred to a particular person. *Recall* tasks involved recalling an example in which that person behaved in a way suggestive of that trait. For each one of a large number of traits, subjects completed random pairs of these three tasks, and reaction times were recorded. Klein, Loftus, Trafton, and Fuhrman (1992; Study 1) studied traits that were highly, moderately, or only weakly descriptive of their mothers. They reasoned that subjects should have well-elaborated trait concepts for terms that were rated as descriptive of their mothers, but not for nondescriptive terms. When subjects thought about their mothers in terms that were not characteristic of their mothers, strong facilitation was observed when describe tasks preceded recall tasks, and when recall tasks preceded describe tasks. This was in contrast to conditions in which define tasks were presented first. This suggests that subjects referred to behavioral examples in the process of making trait judgments. However, when subjects thought about their mothers on dimensions for which they had well-developed trait concepts, there were no facilitation effects for describe tasks on recall tasks, or for recall tasks on describe tasks. This suggests that behaviors were not accessed when subjects made trait judgments on dimensions that were frequently used to think about their mothers.

Similarly, Sherman and Klein (1994; Study 1) found that when subjects had only two behavioral examples for a hypothetical other, describe tasks facilitated subsequent recall when compared with prior define tasks. However, when subjects were presented with eight exemplars, they referred only to their trait concepts of the person and did not review behaviors in memory. This conclusion was based on the fact that, compared to a define task, subjects who had been exposed to eight exemplars did not show facilitation effects in recalling exemplars when this task was preceded by a describe task. Study 2 of Sherman and Klein (1994) demonstrated that when a single behavior was highly diagnostic of a trait, subjects did not appear to refer to this behavior when making trait judgments, presumably because the presentation of such a diagnostic behavior had led to the formation of a trait concept. However, as subjects were presented with more behavioral exemplars, the accessibility of their trait concepts increased, as reflected in shorter reaction times to make trait judgments. Thus, although the behaviors themselves appeared not to be accessed in making trait judgments (as evidenced by the absence of facilitation effects), they did appear to influence the trait concept, because these concepts were more accessible as more behavioral examples were presented.

The preceding analysis suggests that people represent social support in memory as a global, highly abstracted, trait-like concept. Although specific behaviors contribute to the formation of the concept of someone as supportive, this inference and the behaviors that are associated with it, appear to be stored separately, and examples of supportive behaviors are not likely to be accessed when making support judgments.* This research makes it understandable why perceived and enacted support should not be strongly related, and it is an excellent example of how basic research in social cognition can be used to help solve research problems in social support. In fact, social-cognitive research makes a number of predictions about cognitive processes in perceived social support. In the following section, we will describe the results of research on such processes.

SOCIAL-COGNITIVE PROCESSES IN SOCIAL SUPPORT

In this section, we review the results of studies that directly test social-cognitive processes in social support. The bulk of the existing research has been on the extent to which individuals' existing beliefs about social support influence their subsequent judgments and memory for supportive behaviors and persons.

There is an extensive body of theory and research from both social cognition and psychopathology that suggests that knowledge about the self and social world is organized into cognitive structures (Beck, Rush, Shaw, & Emery, 1979; Kihlstrom & Klein, 1994; Segal, Gemar, Truchon, Guirguis, & Horowitz, 1995) that influence on-going social information processing. For example, beliefs about the self and social world are associated with a variety of individual differences in information processing, including attention (Mathews & McCloud, 1986), judgment (Devine, 1989; Gotlib, 1983) memory (Blaney, 1986; Stangor & McMillan, 1992) and efficiency (Bargh & Tota, 1988). Thus, stable beliefs about the supportiveness of others should have similar effects. Perceived support should influence the extent to which perceivers view a given person as supportive, and should influence the kinds of attributions that are made regarding failed support attempts. People with low perceived support should apply their general view of the social world to new relationships and situations. In the absence of clear information to the contrary, such persons should see other people as less supportive and enacted support as less helpful. In addition, such persons should be more likely to make correspondent inferences for failed support attempts (e.g., "My friend doesn't really care"), but make situational explanations for unexpectedly effective enacted support (e.g., "He's trying to look superior by helping"). As a result of these processes, perceived support would tend to remain relatively stable over time, as documented by Sarason, Sarason, and Shearin (1986).

---

*There are times, however, in which persons will refer to specific behavioral exemplars when making trait judgments. This occurs when persons have very little exposure to the behaviors of the target (e.g., fewer than two); (Klein et al., 1992; Sherman & Klein, 1992), when they have been only recently exposed to a salient exemplar (Carlston, 1980), or the exemplar has been recently activated (Carlston & Skowronski, 1986).

PERCEIVED SUPPORT AND THE INTERPRETATION
OF NOVEL SUPPORTIVE PERSONS AND BEHAVIORS

A number of studies have found that people with high support interpret novel supportive behaviors more favorably than do low-perceived-support individuals. For example, Lakey and Cassady (1990) presented subjects with written descriptions of six personal or academic problems and asked them to imagine that they were explaining these problems to a friend or relative. Accompanying each problem were eight responses that might be offered by the friend or relative, each of which were rated for helpfulness. The authors found that low-perceived-support subjects rated the supportive behaviors as less helpful than their high-support peers, even after statistically controlling for dysphoria. Furthermore, this interpretive effect did not appear to be driven by cognition about the self, as neither self-esteem nor dysfunctional attitudes could account for this effect.

To replicate and extend these findings, Lakey et al. (1992) asked subjects to view and rate the supportiveness of videotaped responses to problems. Videotaped behaviors were chosen to increase the ecological validity of the assessment, rather than relying on written presentation of stimuli as in Lakey and Cassady (1990). In addition, videotaped responses provided more standardized, supportive stimuli, thus eliminating the possibility that the difference between high- and low-perceived-support subjects was a reflection, not of an interpretive bias, but of who they imagined to be providing the support. For example, the interpersonal style of a low-perceived-support individual's mother really might be less helpful, making the subject's evaluation accurate and unbiased. Furthermore, Lakey et al. (1992) measured social desirability in an effort to rule out the possibility that the interpretive effects observed by Lakey and Cassady (1990) reflected response styles. As hypothesized, low-support individuals interpreted the videotaped behaviors less favorably than did high-support subjects, and this effect could not be accounted for by social desirability, dysphoria, or cognition about the self.

Pierce et al. (1992) also found evidence of such an interpretive bias in an experiment involving students and their mothers. They assessed undergraduates' perceived support specifically regarding their mothers before performing the presumably stressful task of giving a speech. All of the students were given two identically worded notes, completed in their mother's handwriting, offering support both before and after their speech. Following the task, subjects were asked to rate the quality of their mother's support. As predicted, individuals with low perceived support interpreted the notes as less supportive than individuals with high support.

Sarason et al. (1991) explored the relations between students' perceived social support and their beliefs about how supported the typical, same-sex college students felt. Subjects were asked to complete a group of measures, including a support measure, and then 1 week later were asked to complete some of these same measures as they thought a typical student of their age and sex would. Generally, compared to low-perceived-support respondents, subjects with higher perceived support saw the typical student as having higher levels of support and were more accurate in their judgments (compared to normative data).

One limitation of these studies is that they are based on college student samples with relatively low levels of psychological distress. Drew et al. (1995) studied these interpretive processes in a sample of clinically depressed, lower socioeconomic status (SES), urban residents and nondepressed controls with similar demographics. Clinically depressed subjects and nondepressed control subjects were asked to rate the supportiveness of four videotaped targets, who chatted for 5 minutes with a friend about this friend's difficulties. Thus, rather than presenting subjects with a single, isolated example of enacted support, as in most prior studies, subjects were given a range of behaviors from which to make their supportiveness judgments. Compared to the nondepressed subjects, the depressed subjects had lower perceived support and perceived the female, but not the male, targets as less supportive. The finding that depressed patients had more negative views only of female support providers is consistent with more recent research suggesting that interpretative effects associated with perceived support may not extend equally to all potential supporters (Lakey et al., 1996) and raises the question of which target factors elicit perceptions of support in some perceivers but not others. By extending the interpretative effects found in previous studies to a clinical group, this study strengthens the evidence that cognitive processes in social support may be important in clinical disorder. In addition, the use of an urban, lower-SES sample extends previous findings to a more diverse demographic group.

Mallinckrodt (1991) investigated similar processes in a clinical sample and offers evidence for interpretative effects related to social support in the therapeutic relationship. He asked therapy clients to rate their working alliance with their therapist after three sessions. The working alliance included the bond between client and therapist, as well as task and goal dimensions of the relationship. Mallinckrodt hypothesized that therapy clients' early representations of their parents and their current social support satisfaction would influence their perceived working alliance with their therapist. As expected, individuals who were more satisfied with their current levels of support, and had more favorable views of their early parent–child relationships, perceived the working alliance with their therapists more positively.

Sarason, Pierce, and Sarason (1990a) have suggested that individuals develop "working models" of the self and social relationships based upon their early attachment experiences, which influence their subsequent support perceptions. This *sense of acceptance* is hypothesized to originate in the early family environment and to be generalized, to some extent, to later relationships. To test this hypothesis and to investigate the extent to which the results of laboratory studies would generalize to naturally occurring relationships, Lakey and Dickenson (1994) studied a group of college freshmen who had moved away to college for the first time. Perceived support from family and a variety of personality characteristics were assessed within 1 week of their first semester. Perceived support from new friends met at college was assessed at the end of the students' first semester. Lakey and Dickenson observed that students with low levels of family support saw their college friendships as less supportive than did subjects from high-support families. Furthermore, these effects could not be accounted for by social desirability, psychological distress, social skills, agreeableness, or extraversion.

Sarason, et al. (1990a) have also suggested that perceived support is more closely related to general relationship qualities, such as intimacy, than to enacted support *per se*. Thus, the interpretative effects associated with perceived support may also be manifested in situations that do not involve enacted support, but more ordinary forms of interactions. Lakey, Drew, Anan, Sirl, and Butler (1995) tested this hypothesis in a community sample of adults who had recently filed for or been granted divorces. Subjects were presented with written, hypothetical, divorce-related, social situations and asked to indicate how they would most likely interpret them. In contrast to prior investigations, none of the social interactions referred to social support. Response options were written to reflect positive, neutral, negative, and very negative interpretations. This scale was modeled after Hammen and Krantz's Cognitive Bias Questionnaire (1985), in which cognitive biases are measured by presenting subjects with a range of hypothetical situations to interpret. Lakey et al. (1995) found in two independent samples that low-perceived-support subjects interpreted the social situations more negatively than high-perceived-support subjects, above and beyond the effects of social desirability. Furthermore, negative interpretations were associated with higher dysphoria levels, and these negative interpretations partially mediated the relationship between perceived support and depressive symptoms. Thus, the interpretative effects associated with perceived support appear to extend to social interactions more generally, rather than merely interactions involving enacted support.

Rudolph, Hammen, and Burge (1995) recently reported similar processes among 7-to-12-year-old children. They presented children with 30 hypothetical scenarios in which they imagined themselves being distressed (e.g., frightened at night) and attempting to elicit aid from either their mothers or peers. Children were asked to chose which of three types of outcomes they would expect in such a situation, ranging from supportive ("She might take me back to bed and sit with me for a little while"), to indifferent ("She might tell me to go back to bed, because I was just imagining things") to hostile ("She might get kind of angry at me for waking her up"). Consistent with research on adults, children with low perceived social support had more negative expectancies regarding support in these situations than did high-support children. Not only was family perceived support linked to expectancies for the mothers' supportive behaviors, but it predicted expectancies for peers' supportive behaviors as well.

Similar findings have been observed in studies of marital satisfaction, a close cousin of perceived support (Abbey et al., 1995; Acitelli & Antonucci, 1994). For example, Noller and her colleagues have conducted several studies exploring information processing in marital communication (Noller & Ruzzene, 1991). These studies have found evidence that husbands low in marital satisfaction make more negative errors in interpreting their wives' behaviors than those high in marital adjustment. In addition, individuals in less happy marriages tend to misinterpret ambiguous verbal messages coupled with nonverbal cues more frequently, and such couples are less accurate in judging the intentions of their spouses in emotionally charged situations when compared to happier couples. Furthermore, whereas happy couples tended to make smaller errors in a positive direction when judging their partners' affect, unhappy couples made larger errors in a negative direction.

Perceived support should also influence what types of attributions are made for enacted support. Extensive evidence for this hypothesis comes from research on attributions and marital satisfaction, a close correlate of perceived support (Kurdeck, 1993). Recent studies have consistently demonstrated that marital dissatisfaction is associated with a tendency to view positive partner behavior as less intentional and to infer more negative intentions for unfavorable marital events (Bradbury & Fincham, 1990). Bradbury and Fincham (1991) have proposed a contextual model of marital interaction in which negative appraisals of interactions lead to negative expectations for the future and a tendency to process one's spouse's behavior unfavorably. This, in turn, leads to a confirmation of the earlier appraisal and, ultimately, a stable belief that the marriage is unsatisfying. For example, Karney, Bradbury, Fincham, and Sullivan (1994) found that happily married individuals made more favorable attributions for their partners' behaviors. Although both marital satisfaction and attributions were related to negative affect, affect could not explain the link between dissatisfaction and attributions. In addition, Fincham and Bradbury (1987) reported that wives' positive causal and responsibility attributions regarding their marriages predicted increased relationship satisfaction a year later. Similarly, Fincham and Bradbury (1993) found that attributions for partner behavior were associated with marital satisfaction 1 year later and could not be accounted for by depression, self-esteem, or initial level of marital satisfaction. Thus, there appears to be good evidence that low marital satisfaction is associated with more negative attributions for spousal behavior, and that this cognitive style may have consequences for marital adjustment. However, further research is needed to establish the extent to which these phenomena generalize to perceived support.

Ross and Lakey (1994) and Ross, Lutz, and Lakey (1996) recently conducted two studies that tested the hypothesis that persons with high perceived support would be more likely to explain away failed support attempts as resulting from situational and unstable factors (e.g., "My friend was having a bad day"). In contrast, low-perceived-support persons were hypothesized to make more global and stable attributions (e.g., "No one cares about me"). In one study, participants were asked to recall instances in their lives in which they needed the help of others but did not receive it. They named a cause for each instance and rated each cause according to the internality, globality, and stability of the cause. Low-perceived-support persons made more stable and global attributions for these causes than did high-support individuals. In a second study, respondents completed a modified form of the Attributional Style Questionnaire (Metalsky, Halberstadt, & Abramson, 1987) that referred only to hypothetical instances of not receiving desired social support. Again, low-perceived-support individuals made more stable and global attributions for failed support attempts. Moreover, this attributional style was specific to explanations for failed support. High- and low-perceived-support subjects did not differ in their attributional style for support-irrelevant events.

Thus, a relatively large body of evidence supports the hypothesis that persons' characteristic level of perceived support is associated with individual differences in interpreting the social behaviors of others. These effects have been found in both laboratory investigations and field studies utilizing a wide range of stimuli. Furthermore, these effects have been observed among college students, psychiatric patients, community samples, children, and low-SES individuals.

Although the evidence appears strong that high- and low-perceived-support subjects interpret supportive behaviors differently, this is not the most important influence on support judgments. In addition, subsequent research has indicated that the interpretive effects depend upon characteristics of the target (Lakey et al., 1995), and Mankowski and Wyer (Chapter 7, this volume) have presented data that interpretive biases depend upon the perspective taken by the perceiver (i.e., observing support interactions between others, receiving support, and providing support). Although we initially emphasized the personality-like qualities of perceived support in our earlier work (e.g., Lakey & Cassady, 1990; Lakey et al., 1992), this now appears to have been overstated.

Lakey et al. (1996) conducted a series of three generalizability studies designed to estimate the extent to which support judgments were a function of perceivers, targets, and the Perceiver x Supporter interaction. When a group of perceivers all rate the same targets on supportiveness, generalizability theory (Shavelson & Webb, 1991) provides methods for estimating the proportion of variance accounted for by each source. Main effects due to supporters indicate the extent to which subjects agree that certain supporters are more or less supportive and reflects the extent to which supportiveness is an objective characteristic of the targets. Perceiver main effects capture the extent to which perceivers tend to see supporters similarly, regardless of their actual characteristics. Such effects capture perceptual biases of perceivers. The Perceiver x Supporter interaction reflects the extent to which different subjects reliably perceive different targets as more supportive than others, beyond the effects of random error. For example, perceiver A may see supporter A as more supportive than supporter B, but perceiver B may rate supporter B as the more supportive. Across three samples, each source of variance made significant contributions to support judgments. However, the Perceiver x Supporter interaction accounted for the greatest variance (41%), followed by the supporter main effects (20%). The perceiver main effect accounted for an average of only 8% of the variance across the three studies.

The strong effects for the Perceiver x Supporter interaction suggest the importance of idiosyncratic matching in determining supportiveness. This is consistent with ideas of other authors, who have suggested the importance of matching the type of support to the demands of the stressor (Cutrona & Russell, 1990), and the types of relationship (e.g., family, friends, or formal support providers) to types of support (Cauce & Srebnik, 1990). Alternatively, it may be that sharing similar stressors or life experiences elicits a higher level of support from certain support providers. An individual typically seen by others as cold and aloof may become uncharacteristically compassionate toward an individual who shares a similar life experience. Similarly, an individual facing a chronic illness may perceive an individual who has faced a similar illness as better able to provide support than an individual with no experience in this arena, even when the same support is offered. Another explanation is that recipients and providers may have preferred styles of support provision, and the supportiveness of a relationship depends on the match between these styles. A supporter who prefers to give advice may be seen as very supportive by recipients who prefer advice, but not by those who prefer a "good listener." However, recent research by Lakey, Ross, Butler, and Bentley (1996) has identified similarity in attitudes and values as an important component of the Perceiver x Supporter interaction. In a series of three studies employing both experimental and correlational methods, similar others were seen as more supportive. Further research is needed to explicate the mechanisms behind the strong Perceiver x Supporter interaction.

PERCEIVED SUPPORT AND THE RECALL OF SUPPORTIVE BEHAVIORS

In addition to interpretive effects, research in social cognition predicts that existing knowledge about social support will influence how support-relevant behaviors are remembered (Markus & Zajonc, 1985; Srull & Wyer, 1989). Guided by Beck's cognitive theory of depression (Beck et al., 1979) and research on mood-congruent recall (Blaney, 1986; Bower, 1981), Lakey and Cassady (1990) predicted that persons should display better memory for information consistent with their beliefs about social support. Specifically, compared to low-perceived-support individuals, high-support participants should display better memory for supportive behaviors, worse memory for unsupportive behaviors, and the groups should not differ in their recall of support-irrelevant information.

As described earlier, Lakey and Cassady (1990) asked subjects to read a series of hypothetical situations and to rate the supportiveness of other's responses to these problems. In addition, subjects were given a distractor task after the ratings were completed and then asked to recall the supportive behaviors offered for each hypothetical situation. As predicted, compared to low-perceived-support subjects, high-support individuals displayed better memory for the behaviors they rated as supportive. But they did not differ on a word-recall task, indicating that the recall effect was specific to support-relevant information. Furthermore, this did not represent a mood-congruence effect, because dysphoria was not related to recall. Contrary to predictions, perceived support was not related to the recall of unsupportive behaviors.

Rudolph et al. (1995) also found evidence among children that perceived support was associated with better memory for schema-consistent information. They developed a modified version of the Self-Referent Encoding Task (Rogers, Kuiper, & Kirker, 1977) to assess children's differential memory for the positive or negative qualities of their mothers. The children were asked to judge a number of positive and negative adjectives on whether they applied to their mothers, or whether the words had certain structural characteristics. Later, participants were asked to recall as many words as possible. Consistent with the results of Lakey and Cassady (1990), children with low perceived support recalled more negative adjectives when words were applied to their mothers.

In contrast, however, Lakey et al. (1992) found that compared to low-perceived-support subjects, high-support individuals had better recall for *unhelpful* supportive behavior. There were no differences in recall for helpful behaviors or support-irrelevant behaviors (the activities of a busy individual's day). Thus, in this study, subjects displayed better memory for behavior that was inconsistent with expectations.

Although these studies offer conflicting results for the recall of support-relevant behavior, recent research in person memory and judgment provides a basis for both types of effects (Hastie & Park, 1986; Srull & Wyer, 1989; Wyer & Carlston, 1994). For example, superior memory for expectancy-inconsistent information has been found frequently in the social cognition literature (Srull & Wyer, 1989; Wyer & Carlston, 1994). When an individual already has an impression of a person and is exposed to new behavioral information, new behaviors that are inconsistent with existing judgments are frequently remembered better than consistent information. This is thought to result from the more extensive thought devoted to inconsistent information in an attempt to reconcile it with the preexisting impression (Srull & Wyer, 1989). On the other hand, better recall for consistent information should occur in situations in which judgments are based on a review of relevant behaviors in memory (Hastie & Park, 1986).* However, because trait inferences tend to be made very quickly (Beike & Sherman, 1994; Hastie & Park, 1986), and because persons tend not to review memories of trait-relevant behaviors when making person judgments (Klein et al., 1992; Sherman & Klein, 1994), memory-based judgments should be relatively rare. Memory-based judgments should only occur when relatively little is known about the person being observed and a judgment has not yet been formed.

Schema-consistent memory for supportive behaviors may also depend on whether supportive behaviors are organized around a self-concept, or around a concept of the person providing the support. If supportive behaviors are organized around a self-schema for support, then persons should show better memory for support-relevant behaviors that are consistent with their self-concepts. However, if persons organize supportive behaviors around persons concepts, a variety of effects could occur, depending on whether the subject has already drawn an inference about the target's supportiveness.

The preceding analysis offers some understanding of the conflicting results in the recall of interpersonal behaviors reported by Lakey and Cassady (1990) and Lakey et al. (1992). First, subjects in both studies were asked to make judgments about supportive behaviors as they were presented, and recall was assessed later. Such *on-line* judgments tend to produce highly variable relations between recall and judgment (Hastie & Park, 1986). Second, the design of the two studies may have encouraged persons to store supportive behaviors differently. Lakey and Cassady (1990) presented subjects with written descriptions of supportive behaviors, and did not specify who was providing support. This may have made it difficult for subjects to store the behaviors around concepts of other persons and may have encouraged subjects to store behaviors around a self-concept as supported–unsupported. In contrast, Lakey et al. (1992) provided videotaped presentations of supportive behaviors from 60 different people. Thus, it was clear who was providing the support, perhaps making it difficult for subjects to store the behaviors as part of a self-schema. However, because 60 different persons provided the support, it would likely have been very difficult for subjects to organize the behaviors around 60 different person concepts, especially given that only one behavioral example was given for each person.

Drew et al. (1995) attempted to clarify the relation between support judgments and recall by creating conditions that would facilitate memory-based judgments and encourage subjects to store behaviors around concepts of the persons providing support, rather than around a self-schema. In this study, clinically depressed subjects and nondepressed controls viewed four, 5-minute videotaped interactions between pairs of individuals in which one person described a problem to another. Several steps were taken to encourage subjects to make memory-based judgments. First, the video-

---

*Memory for expectancy-consistent information also appears to be enhanced when it is organized around trait-behavior clusters instead of evaluative concepts (Srull & Wyer, 1989; Wyer & Gordon, 1982), and when the expectancies are very well established (Stangor & McMillan, 1992).

tapes presented persons unknown to subjects, and thus subjects could not have had well-developed impressions of these targets before observing their behaviors. Also, unlike Lakey and Cassady (1990) and Lakey et al. (1992), subjects were not asked to make support judgments until after all of the videotapes were viewed. This was done to prevent subjects from making on-line judgments about supportiveness as they viewed the filmclips. Finally, subjects were presented with multiple supportive behaviors from only 4 persons to increase the likelihood that supportive behaviors would be organized around a few, relatively well-developed person concepts.

Drew et al. (1995) found evidence for expectancy-consistent recall. As described earlier, compared to clinically depressed patients, nondepressed subjects viewed female targets as more supportive than male targets. More importantly, their recall of supportive behaviors tended to parallel their judgments. There were strong correlations between the number of helpful and unhelpful behaviors recalled and ratings of the supportiveness for female, but not male, targets. In addition, nondepressed subjects displayed better recall for the supportive behaviors of women, but the unsupportive behaviors of men, paralleling their support judgments. As expected, the groups did not differ in their recall of support-irrelevant behaviors. Thus, this study provides some evidence for expectancy-consistent recall under conditions in which no prior judgment of support has been made. However, these findings are admittedly tentative, and further research is needed on understanding how high- and low-perceived-support persons remember supportive behavior differently. For example, Mankowski and Wyer (Chapter 7, this volume) report evidence that recall biases associated with perceived support depend upon the perspective taken by the observer (i.e., an observer, support provider, or support recipient).

MAKING SOCIAL SUPPORT JUDGMENTS

As discussed earlier, the traditional assumption in social support research has been that people make perceived support judgments on the basis on the amount and quality of enacted support that they have received. However, we have also seen that the available evidence does not support this hypothesis. First, the relation between perceived and enacted support is not as strong as predicted by the traditional model. Second, recent research in social cognition suggests that conceptions of others are represented in trait terms, and that once a trait-based conception of a target is formed, people do not refer to memories of the target's behavior to form judgments of the person. If we assume that judging an individual on supportiveness involves the same types of psychological processes as judging him or her on any other personal characteristic, then the results of basic research in social cognition have important implications for understanding how support judgments are made. We believe that this is an issue of fundamental importance for social support research, because if we knew what people were referring to when they made social support judgments, we would be in a much better position to understand how social support is developed, how it is related to symptoms, and how to modify it. At present, although we know that reporting high levels of perceived support is associated with positive mental health, we do not know on what these judgments are based.

In reflecting on how people make support judgments, it is useful to consider the sequence by which people normally make judgments about supportiveness, other traits, and more general, evaluative judgments. Because persons make trait inferences very early in their acquaintance with others, we assume that persons have well-established trait concepts, as well as a global evaluation of targets (*evaluative person concepts*; Srull & Wyer, 1989) before being exposed to socially supportive behaviors. Under most circumstances, people do not begin friendships by seeking social support, or by disclosing important personal concerns. Rather, most initial social discourse begins by discussing more safe and benign topics (e.g., work, the weather, sports, current events). However, this will be enough to form trait and evaluative impressions. In addition, we assume that people seek support from others who are believed to be supportive. Why disclose a personal concern to someone who you think will respond unfavorably? But if persons already have concepts of supportiveness before having any actual supportive interactions, on what basis do they make these judgments?

When people do not already have the relevant trait judgment in memory, evidence suggests that the new judgment is inferred on the basis of other traits (Asch, 1946; Beike & Sherman, 1994; Leyens & Fiske, 1994; Schneider, 1973) or on evaluative person concepts (Srull & Wyer, 1989; Wyer & Carlston, 1994). Thus, we hypothesize that a person's initial judgment of a target's supportiveness is derived from the perceiver's already-developed conceptualization of the target's traits, as well as an evaluative concept of the target. Lakey et al. (1996) recently conducted a series of studies testing these hypotheses.

In Study 1, Lakey et al. (1996) investigated the role of evaluative person and trait concepts in judgments of persons well known to subjects (mean relationship duration = 10 years). Subjects identified a supportive person in their lives and rated them on supportiveness, the Big-5 personality traits (Goldberg, 1993), and their perceived similarity to subjects. Similarity was studied, because it is a well-established determinant of interpersonal evaluation (Byrne, 1971). Multiple regression analyses revealed that only similarity and target conscientiousness made independent contributions to the perceived supportiveness of targets, with similarity making the larger contribution. In Study 2, similarity and conscientious information were experimentally manipulated using a hypothetical other paradigm. This study was designed to investigate whether similarity and conscientiousness had a causal role in support judgments. Subjects completed an attitude scale addressing a broad range of topics. One week later, subjects were asked to form an impression of a target, based on the target's responses to conscientiousness and attitude scales. Subjects were randomly assigned to experimental conditions that manipulated levels of attitude similarity and conscientiousness. Strong effects were found for both similarity and conscientiousness on support judgments, with more similar and more conscientious targets being viewed as more supportive. Study 3 investigated the extent to which similarity and conscientiousness information were used in actual social interactions and tested the hypothesis that such inferences were made very early in the acquaintance process. Strangers were paired for 15-minute discussions about topics designed to elicit similarity and conscientiousness information. Afterward, subjects rated each other on supportiveness, similarity, and conscientiousness. In both an original and cross-validation sample, similarity emerged as the best predictor of supportiveness judgments. Target conscientiousness predicted support judgments in the original sample only.

These three studies provide evidence that similarity and conscientiousness information play a causal role in support judgments. Furthermore, the same types of processes used in making support judgments for persons well-known to subjects (Study 1) are used when evaluating relative strangers (Studies 2 and 3). Such findings are consistent with the hypothesis that trait (e.g., conscientiousness) and evaluative person concepts (stimulated by similarity information) help determine support judgments, and that such judgments can be inferred without knowledge of actual supportive behaviors. Additional evidence for the importance of similarity is provided by Suitor, Pillemer, and Keeton (1995). In two samples, women who were undergoing major life transitions (i.e., returning to college after a long absence, and becoming a caregiver for an elderly relative) perceived other women as more supportive if they were also undergoing the same transitions.

The role of enacted support may be particularly important in revising initial support judgments. However, in many cases, exposure to enacted support will result in no revision of such initial judgments. This is because enacted support that is consistent with the initial support judgment should have little influence on subsequent judgments. In these cases, the information contained in enacted support is perfectly redundant with what was already believed by the perceiver. Consequently, enacted support would make no contribution to the perceiver's view of the target's supportiveness. Rather, only enacted support that is *inconsistent* with expectations should cause substantial revisions in support judgments. This hypothesis also helps explain why the relation between perceived and enacted support has not been stronger. Enacted support should only influence perceived support under limited conditions: when the initial support judgment was favorable enough to prompt support seeking, but the enacted support differed from perceivers' expectancies.

When enacted support differs from expectation, the extent to which it leads to revised support judgments should depend upon the attributions that are made for the unexpected support. Consider the situation in which the target's enacted support is much less supportive than expected. This should only lead to a reduction in perceived support when the perceiver concludes that the behavior was a reflection of the target's personal characteristics, or his or her genuine caring for the perceiver, but not when the disappointing support is attributed to the situation. When there is a good situational explanation for the behavior (e.g., "My friend would have listened to my romantic troubles, but his mother just died"), then disappointing enacted support should not influence support judgments. Similarly, particularly effective enacted support would not be expected to have an impact if there were reasons to believe that it reflected situational factors (e.g., "Sure he helped me fix my car, but he was just trying to impress my girlfriend"). Thus, we hypothesize that any relation between perceived and enacted support is mediated by attributions for the supportive behaviors.

Schreiber (1996) recently obtained evidence that recipients' attributions for enacted support may influence how supportive the support provider is perceived. In her study, subjects were presented with hypothetical descriptions of a series of supportive or unsupportive behaviors provided by a single individual. Subsequently, participants made ratings concerning their attributions for the target's behaviors as well as the target's supportiveness as a person. Schreiber found that when participants attributed the unhelpful behaviors to stable aspects of the target's personality, participants saw the target as less supportive than when the unhelpful assistance was attributed to situational factors. Similarly, helpful behavior was more likely to be seen as a reflection of the target's supportiveness when it was attributed to stable personality factors rather than situational influences. Thus, how individuals explain the causes of enacted support appears to influence whether the aid provider will be perceived as supportive.

THE ROLE OF MOOD IN SUPPORT JUDGMENTS

Although social support research has emphasized the potential causal link between low social support and negative emotion, there is substantial evidence that negative moods cause negative judgments as well (Clore, Schwarz, & Conway, 1994). These effects have been observed on a variety of different judgments, including the evaluation of others (Forgas & Bower, 1987), satisfaction with consumer goods (Isen, Shalker, Clark, & Karp, 1978), activities (Carson & Adams, 1980), life events (Clark & Teasdale, 1982), and life satisfaction (Schwarz & Clore, 1983). One theoretical account designed to explain this phenomenon is the feelings-as-information model (Schwarz & Clore, 1983). According to this perspective, persons rely on a wide range of information to make judgments. One important type of information is their emotional experience at the time that they make the judgment. The feelings-as-information model differs from construct accessibility models (e.g., Bower, 1981) in predicting that mood effects on judgment will only occur when persons have not attributed their mood to a specific source, and that mood should have an impact on a wide range of judgments, not only those judgments most closely linked to the emotion node. For example, Schwarz and Clore (1983) found in two experiments that subjects induced to experience negative emotion reported more negative judgments of life satisfaction, but only when there was not a clear attribution available for their negative mood. Similarly, Johnson and Tversky (1983) found that exposure to information about cancer increased subjects' estimates of risk, not only for cancer, but for a wide range of negative outcomes, such as divorce and risk of accidents. Clore et al. (1994) interpreted this effect as resulting from negative emotions arising from reading about cancer and point out that construct accessibility models would predict that only events associated with a cancer node should elicit increased risk estimates.

These processes are relevant to understanding perceived support, because they suggest that negative emotion will influence perceived support judgments. For example, Lakey (1989) and Lakey and Dickinson (1994) found that chronically distressed individuals developed lower levels of perceived support in new settings. The limitation of these studies is that it is not clear whether the effect resulted from cognitive or behavioral processes (e.g., distressed individuals develop lower levels of support because they behave in ways that alienate others). However, Cohen, Towbes, and Flocco's (1988) experiment ruled out such behavioral explanations. They found that situationally induced negative emotion led subjects to report lower levels of perceived support. Although social support researchers have been aware of this possibility since the early years (Heller, 1979), it typically has been viewed as an alternative hypothesis to be ruled out rather than an interesting phenomenon of study in its own right. We suspect that perceived support and distress are reciprocally related, and that each has causal effects on the other. But our understanding of the complex interplay between affect, cognition, and the environment has been limited by only focusing on the extent to which perceived support can cause symptoms.

THE EFFECT OF CONTEXT ON SOCIAL SUPPORT JUDGMENTS

Although we have focused predominantly on how chronic accessibility of support concepts may influence support judgments, there are also a number of situational effects by which constructs are made more accessible by momentary influences from the environment. A host of studies have shown that briefly exposing individuals to information relevant to a certain person category (i.e., *priming*) influences subsequent judgments (Bargh, 1994; Wyer & Carlston, 1994). For example, Srull and Wyer (1979) primed the construct of hostility or kindness by having subjects rearrange scrambled sentences into meaningful statements (e.g., "the kicked he dog"). In an ostensibly unrelated second experiment, subjects in the hostility priming condition rated an target's ambiguous behavior as more hostile than subjects in the kindness priming condition. This experiment demonstrates assimilation, in which priming moves subjects' interpretations of ambiguous behavior toward the activated construct. However, contrast effects also occur. These involve instances in which judgments are contrasted away from the primed construct. For example, Herr (1986) primed concepts of hostility and kindness by having subjects complete word puzzles that required them to find famous persons' names. Subjects were randomly assigned to one of four priming conditions: extremely hostile (e.g., Adolf Hitler), moderately hostile (e.g., Bobby Knight), moderately kind (e.g., Robin Hood) or extremely kind (e.g., Santa Claus). In two experiments, subjects exposed to extreme primes gave ratings to others that contrasted with the prime. For example, subjects exposed to extremely hostile primes perceived a target as less hostile than subjects given moderately hostile primes. However, moderately hostile primes produced assimilation effects. Subjects exposed to moderately hostile primes rated others as more hostile than those given moderately kind primes. Experiment 2 demonstrated that these priming effects actually influenced subjects' social behavior as well. Substantial work has been conducted to understand when these two effects will occur (Martin, 1986; Petty & Wegener, 1993; Schwarz & Bless, 1992; Wegener & Petty, 1995). Contrast effects are more likely to occur when extreme primes are presented (Herr, 1986; Herr, Sherman, & Fazio, 1983), when subjects can remember the primes at the time of judgment (Lombardi, Higgins, & Bargh, 1987), and when subjects are aware of the potential influence of the prime (Strack, Schwarz, Bless, Kubler, & Wanke, 1993). Assimilation is more likely to occur when primes are presented outside subjects' awareness (Bargh & Pietromonaco, 1982; Srull & Wyer, 1979), subjects have low need for cognition (Martin, Seta, & Crelia, 1990; Experiment 3), or have concurrent memory loads (Martin et al., 1990; Experiment 2).

Applying this to perceived support, momentary exposure to situational factors should activate social support concepts and lead to assimilation or contrast effects. For example, being exposed to moderately kind behaviors of another should increase the odds that a subsequent social interaction will be seen as supportive. For example, a colleague's statements about how hard it is to publish in the top journals might be seen as a support attempt if one had previously been exposed to kind behaviors in others.

Similarly, exposure to particularly supportive behaviors might lead one to see one's own support as lacking. Hearing about a friend's remarkably supportive spouse might lead a person to view her or his own spouse as less supportive.

Lutz, Lakey, and Schreiber (1996) have recently obtained evidence for the simultaneous operation of both contrast and assimilation effects in social support. They were interested in situations in which exposure to extreme social primes may have mood effects as well. For example, participants exposed to extreme negative primes would normally be expected to show contrast effects (e.g., Herr, 1986). However, extremely negative primes may also induce negative mood, leading to mood-congruent assimilation effects (e.g., Cohen et al., 1988). Lutz et al. (1996) found that participants exposed to extreme primes of positive or negative social behavior demonstrated contrast effects in judging a videotaped supportive target. Persons exposed to the extreme negative prime (film of the atomic bombing of Hiroshima) rated the supportive target as more supportive than subjects exposed to an extreme positive prime (charming actors from a popular television sitcom). However, these primes also influenced subjects' moods, and when the source of their moods was made salient, mood-congruent assimilation occurred that counteracted contrast effects. In the high-salience conditions, subjects who experienced negative mood change rated the supportive target as less supportive than those who experienced positive mood change. This did not occur in the low-salience conditions, even though the films had equivalent effect on mood in both high- and low-salience conditions. Moreover, when subjects' moods were controlled statistically, contrast effects emerged in the high-salience conditions as well. Schreiber (1996) has also observed contrast effects in support judgments. In her study, participants who read examples of extremely supportive behaviors rated their own networks as less supportive than participants who read examples of extremely unsupportive behaviors.

The existence of priming effects in social support underscores the complexity of the processes in making social support judgments. Not only do we have to explain the role of perceivers, supporters, and their interactions (e.g., Lakey et al., 1996), we must also take into account momentary (and frequently random) exposure to situations that prime supportive stimuli and induce emotional states. Moreover, contrast effects on support judgments may complicate the design of interventions to increase perceived support. The typical social support intervention provides access to supportive others for persons who lack supportive ties (Lakey & Lutz, 1996). However, these interventions have generally not been successful in increasing participants' perceived support. Research on contrast effects suggest that providing exposure to particularly supportive others can, paradoxically, lead to reductions in an individual's own perceived support.

SUMMARY OF EVIDENCE FOR COGNITIVE
PROCESSES IN SOCIAL SUPPORT

The evidence is strong for the utility of studying cognitive process in perceived support (cf. Baldwin, 1992; Mankowski & Wyer, Chapter 7, this volume; Pierce, Baldwin, & Lydon, Chapter 2, this volume). There is strong evidence that people who differ in their chronically accessible perceived support interpret novel supportive behaviors, persons, and social situations differently. These effects have been obtained with a wide range of participants and measures, and by a range of investigators in different settings. Research on marital satisfaction, and initial studies on perceived support, suggest that high perceived support is associated with making more favorable attributions for supportive behavior, and that attributions play a role in the extent to which supportive behaviors influence perceived support. There is also consistent evidence that perceived support is associated with differential memory for support-relevant behaviors, although the exact nature of this relation remains to be clarified. Initial studies provide good evidence that initial support judgments are inferred from trait and evaluative person concepts, although more research is needed on a wider range of trait concepts. In addition to the effects of chronically accessible support constructs, social support judgments appear to be influenced by context as well. Some situational influences produce contrast effects, whereas others produce assimilation.

In the preceding sections, we described research investigating a range of cognitive processes in social support that were inspired by basic research in social cognition. However, this only skims the surface of the range of processes and paradigms that can be derived from social-cognitive theory and research. In the following paragraphs, we briefly touch upon a variety of additional social-cognitive processes that have not yet been translated into social support research, but which appear to have important implications.

We have already reviewed evidence for interpretative and memory biases associated with support perceptions (e.g., Lakey & Cassady, 1990). In addition, schema theory makes a number of predictions about information processing. For example, individuals with well-developed concepts of supportiveness will demonstrate greater attention for supportive behaviors (cf. Mathews & MacLeod, 1986; MacLeod, Mathews, & Tata, 1986) and should process this information faster and more easily than those without support schemas (cf. Fletcher, Rosanowski, & Fitness, 1994; Macrae, Milne, & Bodenhausen, 1994).

Swann and his colleagues have argued that individuals strive to verify their self-concepts, even if those self-concepts are unfavorable (Swann & Brown 1990; Swann, Stein-Seroussi, & Giesler, 1992; Swann, Wenzlaff, Krull, & Pelham, 1992). For those with positive self-views, positive statements from others would verify individuals' self-view. However, for those with negative self-views, positive statements from others would conflict with their self-views and be unwelcome. Thus, what are typically thought of as effective socially supportive behaviors may be undesired by persons who see themselves negatively. Moreover, self-verification theory predicts that low-perceived-support individuals would strive to verify this view of their social world and may act in ways to deter the provision of support (e.g., by complaining about its quality), or may gravitate toward relationships with persons who view them negatively (Swann & Predmore, 1985).

A self-fulfilling prophesy occurs when a perceiver's beliefs about a target result in perceiver behavior that elicits the expected behavior from the target (Darley & Fazio, 1980; Harris, Milich, Corbitt, Hoover, & Brady, 1992; Meichenbaum, Bowers, & Ross, 1969; Zanna, Sheras, Cooper, & Shaw, 1975). Regarding social support, one would predict a vicious circle in which low-support individuals' negative expectancies lead them to behave in a manner that ultimately elicits decreased supportive behavior (e.g., avoiding contact with others, or expressing doubt as to the sincerity of others' behaviors). Such behaviors would confirm the individual's original beliefs.

Self-discrepancy theory (Higgins, 1987) hypothesizes that discrepancies between people's view of (1) who they actually are, (2) who they believe they should ideally be, and (3) who important others believe they ought to be, are associated with negative emotional states. Discrepancies between actual selves and ideal selves are predicted to lead to depression and actual/ought discrepancies are hypothesized to lead to anxiety. In several experiments, Strauman and Higgins (1987, Experiments 1 and 2; Strauman, 1989) assessed the extent to which subjects held actual/ideal and actual/ought discrepancies. In experimental sessions occurring weeks after the initial assessment, subjects' self-discrepancies were primed by asking subjects to process trait adjectives (e.g., via sentence completion) that reflected self-discrepancies, nondiscrepant aspects of the self, and yoked control traits derived from other subjects. With few inconsistencies, the three experiments provided evidence that actual/ideal self-discrepancies were associated with increases in dysphoria compared to actual/ought discrepancies, yoked controls, and nondiscrepant controls. Actual/ought discrepancies were associated with increases in anxiety compared to actual/ideal discrepancies, yoked controls, and nondiscrepant controls. Furthermore, these effects were obtained with self-report, physiological, behavioral, and observer ratings of mood change. Subjects displayed no awareness of the nature of the primes.

Theory and research in self-discrepancy is important for social support, because it provides a rationale and methodology for experimentally testing hypotheses about causal relations between perceived support and emotional distress. If a person's appraisal of social support is discrepant from ideal or ought beliefs, then emotional distress should occur. Furthermore, experimental evidence for this hypothesis could be obtained by priming such self-discrepancies and noting subsequent emotional reactions. Baldwin (1994) appears to be the first to apply this technique to social support. He found in Study 1 that subliminally priming names of either accepting or rejecting persons influenced participants' state self-esteem. In Study 2, the same primes presented supraliminally influenced both state self-esteem and mood for participants who had been made more self-aware. These experiments by Baldwin are important in that they show how convincing experimental evidence could be obtained for a causal relation between perceived support and emotion.

RESEARCH QUESTIONS FOR THE FUTURE

In the preceding pages, we have reviewed a large amount of data on cognitive processes in social support and person perception in general. Although these findings have begun to answer some questions, they also raise a host of others. In the concluding pages, we will attempt to identify what we believe are some of the most critical research questions involving cognitive processes in social support. These include questions on the cognitive representation of social support, the mechanisms relating it to symptoms, and its determinants.

From our point of view, the most fundamental question facing perceived social support research is "What is it?" Although evidence suggests that perceived support is represented in trait-like terms, we do not know that most people think of support in the same ways that psychologists do. We need to know whether people have separate person categories for supportiveness that are distinct from other person concepts, or whether they construe social relationships in a much more global way. Although there has been extensive research on identifying the basic person concepts that are used to think about other people (Goldberg, 1993), supportiveness has not emerged as one of these basic concepts. Perhaps the closest construct that has been identified is agreeableness, which involves such qualities as "helpful" and "sympathetic." Thus, seeing another person as supportive may not differ from seeing them as agreeable. Of course, a separate person category of supportiveness may not have emerged from the factor-analytic studies, because this domain was not adequately represented in the data (Block, 1995). Nonetheless, it is important to establish perceived support's discriminant validity from other more global constructs.

Another more global construct that may subsume social support is relationship satisfaction. In Kaul and Lakey's (1996) research, these two constructs were very highly correlated, and perceived support added nothing to the prediction of emotional distress that could not be explained by global relationship satisfaction. These data need to be replicated in larger and more representative samples, but if perceived support is derived from general relationship satisfaction, it would have profound implications for intervention. For example, it would suggest that perceived support would be better improved by promoting the positive aspects of relationships generally, rather than focusing on help with coping.

Another important unanswered question is "How does low perceived support lead to emotional distress?" Although we have been very critical of traditional, enacted support models, they have at least provided a compelling theoretical account of this process. Cognitive models of perceived support need to provide a cognitive mechanism for the link between low perceived support and symptoms. Although we have tended to assume that negative thoughts about an important life domain will automatically lead to distress (Lakey & Cassady, 1990), this is not an adequate explanation. Why *should* negative thoughts about social support lead to distress? Baumeister and Leary (1995) have argued that the desire for human attachment (including social support) is a fundamental, innate, evolutionarily based human need, and that deprivation leads directly to symptoms. Thus, perceiving a lack of support may automatically lead to symptoms, because symptoms motivate an individual to repair relations with the primary social groups. In primitive societies, solitary individuals would not be expected to live very long or to have many opportunities to mate. However, as acknowledged by Baumeister and Leary, such hypotheses are difficult to test empirically.

Alternatively, perceived support may influence symptoms by leading to other cognitions that may have a more direct link to symptoms. For example, Lazarus and Folkman (1984) have argued that events are stressful insofar as they are appraised as being threatening and exceeding the individual's capacity for coping. Low-perceived-support cognitions may directly convey threat by signaling an important interpersonal loss (e.g., "She doesn't care about me"). In addition, low perceived support may negatively influence an individual's appraisal of whether he or she can cope with the situation (e.g., "How can I get out of this jam if no one will help me?"). Of course, additional work would still need to be done to explain why cognitions regarding threat and a lack of coping resources should lead to symptoms directly. Nonetheless, cognitive models of perceived support could make a larger contribution if more sustained research were directed toward understanding the potential cognitive mechanisms linking perceived support to emotional distress.

Much more research is needed in understanding how perceived support judgments are made, especially in understanding the Perceiver x Supporter interactions identified by Lakey et al. (1996). As described earlier, one of the most important determinants of support judgments is the unique matching between perceiver and supporter. For example, Lakey et al. (1996) found that supportiveness was inferred, in part, from the similarity of supporter to perceiver. But there must be a number of other variables that provide a basis for matching as well. For example, both recipients and providers may have preferred styles of enacted support, and the supportiveness of a relationship may depend upon the match between the two's styles. A provider who prefers to give advice will be seen as very supportive by some but not by others. Alternatively, support may be inferred from global liking judgments. Persons may be seen as supportive insofar as they are liked. In this case, the Perceiver x Supporter interaction reflects the fact that people differ widely on what is considered attractive. Another possibility is that people may infer supportiveness on the basis of global person characteristics, but people may differ in what qualities they use to drive these judgments. Thus, people who make light of serious situations may be seen as supportive by some people, but as insensitive to others. In this case, judging supportiveness is similar to judging art. In the same way that cubism is beautiful to some but grotesque to others, the same personal qualities that are supportive to some will seem cold to others.

SUMMARY AND CONCLUSIONS

We have argued for a social-cognitive approach to perceived social support because of the new perspectives, mechanisms, and methodologies it offers. New perspectives are urgently needed because of the deficiencies of traditional models that focus on enacted support. Although traditional models are intuitively appealing, measures of enacted support have not been very strongly related to perceived support, and have not been consistently linked to emotional well-being. Social-cognitive approaches conceptualize perceived support as primarily cognitive in nature, and thus it should be influenced by a wide range of well-established processes. For example, perceived support is probably represented in memory in very global, trait-like terms, and is probably quite distinct from memories of the behaviors that generated the original judgments. Most of the time, people do not refer to these behaviors when making support judgments. These judgments should be influenced by both the chronic accessibility of support concepts in memory (e.g., perceived support) and momentary priming from the social environment. Perceived support should be organized into cognitive structures, that have ongoing effects on social information processing. For example, support schemas should influence attention, interpretation, memory, and the efficiency of processing support-relevant information. A large body of data points to processes such as these, although research on cognitive processes in perceived support *per se* is just beginning.

One of the major advantages of a social-cognitive approach is that it permits the integration of social support research into ongoing work in social, personality, cognitive, clinical, and developmental psychology. Like many research areas, social support has developed in relative isolation, and has therefore failed to benefit from cross-fertilization. However, many fundamental questions in social support research are being addressed very successfully under other rubrics in different areas of psychology. Social support research will benefit from importing knowledge from these other areas. We hope that this chapter has been successful in describing some of the unique perspectives, processes, and methods offered by the social cognition approach. However, we do not believe that the ideas developed in this chapter represent an adequate understanding of social support. We expect that major empirical and conceptual problems will emerge here as well, once sufficient research attention has been directed toward the questions outlined in this chapter. New perspectives will then be developed that will encounter their own problems, which will give way to newer models. From our point of view, social support research will advance quickly insofar as a wide range of models are entertained and subjected to healthy skepticism and rigorous empirical tests. Only in this way can we hasten the arrival of the yet undeveloped, but more sophisticated, future perspectives on social support.

REFERENCES

Abbey, A., Andrews, F. M., & Halman, L. J. (1995). Provision and receipt of social support and disregard: What is their impact on the marital life quality of infertile and fertile couples? *Journal of Personality and Social Psychology, 68,* 455–469.

Acitelli, L. K., & Antonucci, T. C. (1994). Gender differences in the link between marital support and satisfaction in older couples. *Journal of Personality and Social Psychology, 67,* 688–698.

Ahadi, S., & Diener, E. (1989). Multiple determinants and effect size. *Journal of Personality and Social Psychology, 56,* 398–406.

Asch, S. E. (1946). Forming impressions of personality. *Journal of Abnormal and Social Psychology, 41,* 1230–1240.

Baldwin, M. W. (1992). Relational schemas and the processing of social information. *Psychological Bulletin, 112,* 461–484.

Baldwin, M. (1994). Primed relational schemas as a source of self-evaluative reactions. *Journal of Social and Clinical Psychology, 13,* 380–403.

Bargh, J. A. (1994). The four horsemen of automaticity: Awareness, intention, efficiency, and control in social cognition. In R. S. Wyer & T. K. Srull (Eds.), *Handbook of social cognition,* (Vol. 1, pp. 1–40). Hillsdale, NJ: Erlbaum.

Bargh, J. A., & Peitromonaco, P. (1982). Automatic information processing and social perception: The influence of trait information presented outside of conscious awareness on impression formation. *Journal of Personality and Social Psychology, 43,* 437–449.

Bargh, J. A., & Tota, M. E. (1988). Context-dependent automatic processing in depression: Accessibility of negative constructs with regard to self but not others. *Journal of Personality and Social Psychology, 54,* 925–939.

Barnett, P. A., & Gotlib, I. H. (1988). Psychosocial functioning and depression: Distinguishing among antecedents, concomitants, and consequences. *Psychological Bulletin, 104,* 97–126.

Barrera, M. Jr. (1986). Distinctions between social support concepts, measures and models. *American Journal of Community Psychology, 14,* 413–455.

Barrera, M. Jr. (1988). Models of social support and life stress: Beyond the buffering hypothesis. In L. H. Cohen (Ed.), *Life events and psychological functioning: Theoretical and methodological approaches* (pp. 211–236). Newbury Park, CA: Sage.

Baumeister, R. F., & Leary, M. R. (1995). The need to belong: Desire for interpersonal attachments as a fundamental human motivation. *Psychological Bulletin, 117*, 497-529.

Beach, S. R. H., Fincham, F. D., Katz, J., & Bradbury, T. N. (1996), Social support in marriage. In G. R. Pierce, B. R. Sarason, & I. G. Sarason (Eds.), *Handbook of Social Support and the Family*, (pp 43-65) New York: Plenum.

Beck, A. T., Rush, A. J., Shaw, B. F., & Emery, G. (1979). *Cognitive therapy of depression.* New York: Guilford.

Beike, D. R., & Sherman, S. J. (1994). Social inference: Inductions, deductions and analogies. In R. S. Wyer & T. K. Srull (Eds.), *Handbook of social cognition*, (Vol. 1, pp. 209-286). Hillsdale, NJ: Erlbaum.

Belsher, G., & Costello, C. G. (1991). Do confidants of depressed women provide less social support than confidants of nondepressed women? *Journal of Abnormal Psychology, 100*, 516-525.

Blaney, P. H. (1986). Affect and memory: A review. *Psychological Bulletin, 99*, 229-246.

Blazer, D. (1982). Social support and mortality in an elderly community population. *American Journal of Epidemiology, 115*, 684-694.

Block, J. (1995). A contrarian view of the five-factor approach to personality description. *Psychological Bulletin, 117*, 187-215.

Bower, G. H. (1981). Mood and memory. *American Psychologist, 36*, 129-148.

Bradbury, T. N., & Fincham, F. D. (1990). Attributions in marriage: Review and critique. *Psychological Bulletin, 107*, 3-33.

Bradbury, T. N., & Fincham, F. D., (1991). A contextual model for advancing the study of marital interaction. In G. J. O. Fletcher & F. D. Fincham (Eds.), *Cognition in close relationships* (pp. 127-147). Hillsdale, NJ: Erlbaum.

Burleson, B. R., & Samter, W. (1985). Consistencies in theoretical and naive evaluations of comforting messages. *Communication Monographs, 52*, 103-123.

Byrne, D. (1971). *The attraction paradigm.* New York: Academic Press.

Carson, T. P., & Adams, H. E. (1980). Activity valence as a function of mood change. *Journal of Abnormal Psychology, 89*, 368-377.

Carlston, D. E. (1980). The recall and use of traits and events in social inference processes. *Journal of Experimental Social Psychology, 16*, 303-328.

Carlston, D. E., & Skowronski, J. J. (1986). Trait memory and behavior memory: The effects of alternative pathways on impression judgment response times. *Journal of Personality and Social Psychology, 50*, 5-13.

Carlston, D. E., & Skowronski, J. J. (1994). Savings in the relearning of trait information as evidence for spontaneous inference generation. *Journal of Personality and Social Psychology, 66*, 840-856.

Cauce, A. M., & Srebnik, D. S. (1990). Returning to social support systems: A morphological analysis of social networks. *American Journal of Community Psychology, 18*, 609-616.

Clark, D. M., & Teasdale, J. D. (1982). Diurnal variation in clinical depression and accessibility of memories of positive and negative experiences. *Journal of Abnormal Psychology, 91*, 87-95.

Clore, G. L., Schwarz, N., & Conway, M. (1994). Affective causes and consequences of social information processing. In R. S. Wyer & T. K. Srull (Eds.), *Handbook of social cognition* (Vol. 1, pp. 323-418). Hillsdale, NJ: Erlbaum.

Cohen, L. H., Towbes, L. C., & Flocco, R. (1988). Effects of induced mood on self-reported life events and perceived and received social support. *Journal of Personality and Social Psychology, 55*, 669-674.

Cohen, S. & Wills, T. A. (1985) Stress, social support and the buffering hypothesis. *Psychological Bulletin, 98*, 310-357.

Collins, N. L., Dunkel-Schetter, C., Lobel, M., Scrimshaw, S. C. M. (1993). Social support in pregnancy: Psychosocial correlates of birth outcomes and postpartum depression. *Journal of Personality and Social Psychology, 65*, 1243-1258.

Cutrona, C. E. (1988). Ratings of social support by adolescents and adult informants: Degree of correspondence and prediction of depressive symptoms. *Journal of Personality and Social Psychology, 57*, 723-730.

Cutrona, C. E., & Russell, D. (1990). Type of social support and specific stress: Toward a theory of optimal matching. In B. R. Sarason, I. G. Sarason, & G. R. Pierce (Eds.), *Social support: An interactional view.* New York: Wiley.

Cutrona, C. E., & Suhr, J. A. (1992). Controllability of stressful events and satisfaction with spouse support behaviors. *Communication Research, 19*, 154-174.

Cutrona, C. E., & Suhr, J. A. (1994). Social support communication in the context of marriage: An analysis of couples' supportive interactions. In B. B. Burleson, T. L., Albrecht, & I. G. Sarason (Eds.), *Communication of social support: Messages, relationships and community* (pp. 113–133). Thousand Oaks, CA: Sage.

Darley, J. M., & Fazio, R. H. (1980). Expectancy confirmation processes arising in the social interaction sequence. *American Psychologist, 35*, 867–881.

Devine, P. G. (1989). Stereotypes and prejudice: Their automatic and controlled components. *Journal of Personality and Social Psychology, 56*, 5–18.

Devine, P. G., Hamilton, D. L., & Ostrom, T. M. (1994). *Social cognition: Impact on social psychology.* San Diego: Academic Press.

Drew, J. B., Lakey, B., & Sirl, K. (1995, November). *Clinical depression and cognitive processes in perceived support.* Paper presented at the annual meeting of the Association for the Advancement of Behavior Therapy, Washington, DC.

Dunkel-Schetter, C., & Bennett, T. L. (1990). Differentiating the cognitive and behavioral aspects of social support. In B. R. Sarason, I. G. Sarason, & G. R. Pierce (Eds.), *Social support: An interactional view* (pp. 267–296). New York: Wiley.

Dweck, C. S., Hong, Y., & Chiu, C. (1993). Implicit theories: Individual differences in the likelihood and meaning of dispositional inference. *Personality and Social Psychology Bulletin, 19*, 644–656.

Fincham, F. D., & Bradbury, T. N. (1987). The impact of attributions in marriage: A longitudinal analysis. *Journal of Personality and Social Psychology, 53*, 481–489.

Fincham, F. D., & Bradbury, T. N. (1991). Cognition in marriage: A program of research on attributions. *Advances in Personal Relationships, 2*, 159–203.

Fincham, F. D., & Bradbury, T. N. (1993). Marital satisfaction, depression, and attributions: A longitudinal analysis. *Journal of Personality and Social Psychology, 64*, 442–452.

Fletcher, G. J. O., Rosanowski, J., & Fitness, J. (1994). Automatic processing in intimate contexts: The role of close-relationship beliefs. *Journal of Personality and Social Psychology, 67*, 888–897.

Forgas, J. P., & Bower, G. H. (1987). Mood effects on person perception judgments. *Journal of Personality and Social Psychology, 53*, 53–60.

Gurung, R. A. R., Sarason, B. R., & Sarason, I. G. (1994, August). *Observing conflict and support: Global vs. behavioral-specific approaches.* Paper presented at the annual meeting of the American Psychological Association, Los Angeles, CA.

Gidron, D., Koehler, D. J., & Tversky, A. (1993). Implicit quantification of personality traits. *Personality and Social Psychology Bulletin, 19*, 594–604.

Goldberg, L. R. (1993). The structure of phenotypic personality traits. *American Psychologist, 48*, 26–33.

Goldstein, A. P., Heller, K., & Sechrest, L. B. (1966). *Psychotherapy and the psychology of behavior change.* New York: Wiley.

Gotlib, I. H. (1983). Perception and recall of interpersonal feedback: Negative bias in depression. *Cognitive Therapy and Research, 7*, 399–412.

Hammen, C., & Krantz, S. (1985). Measures of psychological processes in depression. In E. E. Beckham & W. R. Leber (Eds.), *Handbook of depression: Treatment assessment, and research* (pp. 408–444). Homewood IL: Dorsey.

Hamilton, D. L., Devine, P. G., & Ostrom, T. M. (1994a). Social cognition and classic issues in social psychology. In P. G. Devine, D. L. Hamilton, & T. M. Ostrom (Eds.), *Social cognition: Impact on social psychology* (pp. 1–13). San Diego: Academic Press.

Hamilton, D. L., Stroessner, S. J., & Driscoll, D. M. (1994b). Social cognition and the study of stereotyping. In P. G. Devine, D. L. Hamilton, & T. M. Ostrom (Eds.), *Social cognition: Impact on social psychology* (pp. 292–321). San Diego: Academic Press.

Harris, M. J., Milich, R., Corbitt, E. M., Hoover, D. E. W., & Brady, M. (1992). Self-fulfilling effects of stigmatizing information on children's social interactions. *Journal of Personality and Social Psychology, 63*, 41–50.

Harvey, J. H., Weary, G., & Stanley, M. A. (1985). Introduction: Attribution theory and research—still vital in the 1980s. In J. H. Harvey and G. Weary (Eds.), *Attribution: Basic issues and applications.* (pp. 1–4). Orlando, FL: Academic Press.

Hastie, R., & Park, B. (1986). The relationship between memory and judgment depends on whether the judgment task is memory-based or on-line. *Psychological Review, 93*, 258–268.

Heider, F. (1958). *The psychology of interpersonal relations*. New York: Wiley.

Helgeson, V. S. (1993). Two important distinctions in social support: Kind of support and perceived versus received. *Journal of Applied Social Psychology, 23,* 825–845.

Heller, K. (1979). The effects of social support: Prevention and treatment implications. In A. P. Goldstein & F. H. Kanfer (Eds.) *Maximizing treatment gains: Transfer enhancement in psychotherapy* (pp. 253–282). New York: Academic Press.

Heller, K., & Lakey, B. (1985). Perceived support and social interaction among friends and confidants. In I. G. Sarason & B. R. Sarason (Eds.), *Social support: Theory research and applications* (pp. 287–300). The Hague, The Netherlands: Martinus Nijhoff.

Heller, K., & Swindle, R. W. (1983). Social networks, perceived social support, and coping with stress. In R. D. Felner, L. A. Jason, J. N. Moritsugu, & S. S. Farber (Eds.), *Preventive psychology: Theory, research and practice* (pp. 87–103). New York: Pergamon.

Herr, P. M. (1986). Consequences of priming: Judgment and behavior. *Journal of Personality and Social Psychology, 51,* 1106–1115.

Herr, P. M., Sherman, S. J., & Fazio, R. H. (1983). On the consequences of priming: Assimilation and contrast effects. *Journal of Experimental Social Psychology, 19,* 323–340.

Higgins, E. T. (1987). Self-discrepancy: A theory relating self and affect. *Psychological Review, 94,* 319–340.

Isen, A. M., Shalker, T. E., Clark, M. S., & Karp, L. (1978). Affect, accessibility of material in memory, and behavior: A cognitive loop? *Journal of Personality and Social Psychology, 36,* 1–12.

Johnson, E., & Tversky, A. (1983). Affect, generalization, and the perception of risk. *Journal of Personality and Social Psychology, 45,* 20–31.

Jones, E. E., & Davis, K. E. (1965). From acts to dispositions: The attribution process in person perception. In L. Berkowitz (Ed.), *Advances in experimental social psychology* (Vol. 2, pp. 219–266). New York: Academic Press.

Kahneman, D., Slovic, P., & Tversky, A. (1982). *Judgment under uncertainty: Heuristics and biases*. New York: Cambridge University Press.

Karney, B. R., Bradbury, T. N., Fincham, F. D., & Sullivan, K. T. (1994). The role of negative affectivity in the association between attributions and marital satisfaction. *Journal of Personality and Social Psychology, 66,* 413–424.

Kaul, M., & Lakey, B. (1996). *Psychological adaptation of mothers whose children have congenital heart defects: The role of social support and social relationships*. Manuscript submitted for publication.

Kelley, H. H. (1967). Attribution theory in social psychology. In D. Levine (Ed.), *Nebraska Symposium on Motivation* (Vol. 15, pp. 192–238). Lincoln: University of Nebraska Press.

Kelley, H. H., & Michela, J. L. (1980). Attribution theory and research. *Annual Review of Psychology, 31,* 457–501.

Kihlstrom, J. F., & Klein, S. B. (1994). The self as a knowledge structure. In R. S. Wyer & T. K. Srull (Eds.), *Handbook of social cognition*, (Vol. 1, pp. 153–208). Hillsdale NJ: Erlbaum.

Klein, S. B., & Loftus, J. (1990). The role of abstract and exemplar-based knowledge in self-judgments: Implications for a cognitive model of the self. In T. K. Srull & R. S. Wyer Jr. (Eds.), *Advances in social cognition* (Vol. 3, pp. 131–139). Hillsdale, NJ: Erlbaum.

Klein, S. B., Loftus, J., & Burton, H. A. (1989). Two self-reference effects: The importance of distinguishing between self-descriptiveness judgments and autobiographical retrieval in self-referent encoding. *Journal of Personality and Social Psychology, 56,* 853–865.

Klein, S. B., Loftus, J., Trafton, J. G., & Fuhrman, R. W. (1992). Use of exemplars and abstractions in trait judgments: A model of trait knowledge about the self and others. *Journal of Personality and Social Psychology, 63,* 739–753.

Kurdek, L. A. (1993). Predicting marital dissolution: A 5-year prospective longitudinal study of newlywed couples. *Journal of Personality and Social Psychology, 64,* 221–242.

Lakey, B. (1989) Personal and environmental antecedents of perceived social support. *American Journal of Community Psychology, 17,* 503–519.

Lakey, B., & Cassady, P. B. (1990). Cognitive processes in perceived social support. *Journal of Personality and Social Psychology, 59,* 337–348.

Lakey, B., & Dickinson, L. G. (1994) Antecedents of perceived support: Is perceived family environment generalized to new social relationships? *Cognitive Therapy and Research, 18,* 39–53.

Lakey, B., Drew, J. B., Anan, R., Sirl, K., & Butler, C. (1995, November). *Social support and dysfunctional attitudes in adults' divorce adjustment.* Paper presented at the annual meeting of the Association for the Advancement of Behavior Therapy, Washington, DC.

Lakey, B., & Heller, K. (1988) Social support from a friend, perceived support, and social problem solving. *American Journal of Community Psychology, 16,* 811–824.

Lakey, B., & Lutz, C. L. (1996). Increasing social support: Preventive and therapeutic interventions. In G. R. Pierce, B. R. Sarason, & I. G. Sarason (Eds.), *Handbook of social support and the family* (pp. 435–465). New York: Plenum.

Lakey, B., McCabe, K. M., Fisicaro, S. A., & Drew, J. B. (1996). Environmental and personal determinants of support perceptions: Three generalizability studies. *Journal of Personality and Social Psychology, 70,* 1270–1280.

Lakey, B., Moineau, S., & Drew, J. B. (1992). Perceived social support and individual differences in the interpretation and recall of supportive behaviors. *Journal of Social and Clinical Psychology, 11,* 336–348.

Lakey, B., Ross, L. T., Butler, C., & Bentley, K. (1996). Making social support judgments: The role of similarity and conscientiousness. *Journal of Social and Clinical Psychology, 15,* 283–304.

Lazarus, R. S., & Folkman, S. (1984). *Stress, appraisal and coping.* New York: Springer.

Leyens, J., & Fiske, S. T. (1994). Impression formation: From recitals to *symphonie fantastique.* In P. G. Devine, D. L. Hamilton, & T. M. Ostrom (Eds.), *Social cognition: Impact on social psychology* (pp. 39–75). San Diego: Academic Press.

Lombardi, W. J., Higgins, E. T., & Bargh, J. A. (1987). The role of consciousness in priming effects on categorization: Assimilation versus contrast as a function of awareness of the priming task. *Personality and Social Psychology Bulletin, 13,* 411–429.

Lutz, C. L., Lakey, B., & Schreiber, S. N. (1996). *Contrast and assimilation in making social support judgments.* Manuscript submitted for publication.

MacLeod, C., Mathews, A., & Tata, P. (1986). Attentional bias in emotional disorders. *Journal of Abnormal Psychology, 95,* 15–20.

Macrae, C. N., Milne, A. B., & Bodenhausen, G. V. (1994). Stereotypes as energy-saving devices: A peek inside the cognitive toolbox. *Journal of Personality and Social Psychology, 66,* 37–47.

Mallinckrodt, B. (1991). Client's representations of childhood emotional bonds with parents, social support, and the formation of a working alliance. *Journal of Counseling Psychology, 38,* 401–409.

Markus, H., & Zajonc, R. B. (1985). The cognitive perspective in social psychology. In G. Lindzey & E. Aronson (Eds.), *Handbook of social psychology* (3rd ed., pp. 137–230). Reading, MA: Addison-Wesley.

Martin, L. L. (1986). Set/Reset: Use and disuse of concepts in impression formation. *Journal of Personality and Social Psychology, 51,* 493–504.

Martin, L. L., Seta, J. J., & Crelia, R. A. (1990). Assimilation and contrast as a function of people's willingness and ability to expend effort in forming an impression. *Journal of Personality and Social Psychology, 59,* 27–37.

Mathews, A., & MacLeod, C. (1986). Discrimination of threat cues without awareness in anxiety states. *Journal of Abnormal Psychology, 95,* 131–138.

McCaskill, J. W., & Lakey, B. (1995, April). *Relations between family stress, family support and psychological stress: Adolescent and family self reports.* Paper presented at biennial meeting of the Society for Research in Child Development, Indianapolis, IN.

Meehl, P. E. (1978). Theoretical risks and tabular asterisks: Sir Karl, Sir Ronald, and the slow progress of soft psychology. *Journal of Consulting and Clinical Psychology, 46,* 806–834.

Meichenbaum, D. H., Bowers, K. S., & Ross, R. R. (1969). A behavioral analysis of teacher expectancy effect. *Journal of Personality and Social Psychology, 13,* 306–313.

Metalsky, G. I., Halberstadt, L. J., & Abramson, L. Y. (1987). Vulnerability to depressive mood reactions: Toward a more powerful test of the diathesis-stress and causal mediation components of the reformulated theory of depression. *Journal of Personality and Social Psychology, 52,* 386–393.

Newcomb, M. D. (1990). What structural equation modeling can tell us about social support. In B. R. Sarason, I. G. Sarason, & G. R. Pierce (Eds.), *Social support: An interactional view* (pp. 26–63). New York: Wiley.

Noller, P., & Ruzzene, M. (1991). Communication in marriage: The influence of affect and cognition. In G. J. O. Fletcher & F. D. Fincham (Eds.), *Cognition in close relationships* (pp. 203–233). Hillsdale, NJ: Erlbaum.

Ostrom, T. M. (1981). Attribution theory: Whence and whither. In J. H. Harvey, W. Ickes, & R. F. Kidd (Eds.), *New directions in attribution research* (pp. 405–424). Hillsdale, NJ: Erlbaum.

Ostrom, T. M. (1994). Foreword. In R. S. Wyer & T. K. Srull (Eds.), *Handbook of social cognition*, (Vol. 1, pp. vii–xii). Hillsdale, NJ: Erlbaum.

Park, B. (1986). A method for studying the development of impressions of real people. *Journal of Personality and Social Psychology*, *51*, 907–917.

Petty, R. E., & Wegener, D. T. (1993). Flexible correction processes in social judgment: Correcting for context-induced contrast. *Journal of Experimental Social Psychology*, *29*, 137–165.

Pierce, G. R., Sarason, B. R., & Sarason, I. G. (1992). General an specific support expectations and stress as predictors of perceived supportiveness: An experimental study. *Journal of Personality and Social Psychology*, *63*, 297–307.

Polivy, J., & Doyle, C. (1980). Laboratory induction of mood states through the reading of self-referent mood statements: Affective changes or demand characteristics? *Journal of Abnormal Psychology*, *89*, 286–290.

Procidano, M. E., & Heller, K. (1983). Measures of perceived social support from friends and family: Three validation studies. *American Journal of Community Psychology*, *11*, 1–24.

Repetti, R. L. (1987). Individual and common components of the social environment at work and psychological well-being. *Journal of Personality and Social Psychology*, *52*, 710–720.

Rogers, T. B., Kuiper, N. A., & Kirker, W. S. (1977). Self-reference and the encoding of personal information. *Journal of Personality and Social Psychology*, *35*, 677–688.

Rosenthal, R., & Rubin, D. B. (1978). Interpersonal expectancy effects: The first 345 studies. *Behavioral and Brain Sciences*, *3*, 377–386.

Ross, L. T., & Lakey, B. (1994, May). *Social support schematic processing influences mood change and support-related appraisals*. Paper presented at the meetings of the American Psychological Society, Washington, DC.

Ross, L. T., Lutz, C., & Lakey, B. (1996). Perceived support and attributions for failed support attempts. Manuscript under review.

Rothbart, M., & Park, B. (1986). On the confirmability and disconfirmability of trait concepts. *Journal of Personality and Social Psychology*, *50*, 131–142.

Rudolph, K. D., Hammen, C., & Burge, D. (1995). Cognitive representations of self, family, and peers in school-age children: Links with social competence and sociometric status. *Child Development*, *66*, 1385–1402.

Sandler, I. N., & Barrera, M. Jr. (1984). Toward a multimethod approach to assessing the effects of social support. *American Journal of Community Psychology*, *12*, 37–52.

Sarason, B. R., Pierce, G. R., Bannerman, A., & Sarason, I. G. (1993). Investigating the antecedents of perceived social support: Parents' views of and behavior toward their children. *Journal of Personality and Social Psychology*, *65*, 1071–1085.

Sarason, B. R., Pierce, G. R., & Sarason, I. G. (1990a). Social support: The sense of acceptance and the role of relationships. In B. R. Sarason, I. G. Sarason, & G. R. Pierce (Eds.), *Social support: An interactional view*. (pp. 9–25). New York: Wiley.

Sarason, B. R., Pierce, G. R., Shearin, E. N., Sarason, I. G., Waltz, J. A., & Poppe, L. (1991). Perceived social support and working models of self and actual others. *Journal of Personality and Social Psychology*, *60*, 273–287.

Sarason, B. R., Sarason, I. G., & Pierce, G. R. (1990b). Traditional views of social support and their impact on assessment. In B. R. Sarason, I. G. Sarason, & G. R. Pierce (Eds.), *Social support: An interactional view* (pp. 9–25). New York: Wiley.

Sarason, B. R., Shearin, E. N., Pierce, G. R., & Sarason, I. G. (1987). Interrelations of social support measures: Theoretical and practical implications. *Journal of Personality and Social Psychology*, *52*, 813–832.

Sarason, I. G., Sarason, B. R., & Shearin, E. N. (1986). Social support as an individual difference variable: Its stability, origins, and relational aspects. *Journal of Personality and Social Psychology*, *50*, 845–855.

Schneider, D. J. (1973). Implicit personality theory: A review. *Psychological Bulletin*, *79*, 294–309.

Schreiber, S. M. (1996). *Processes involved in making social support judgments*. Unpublished honors thesis, Wayne State University, Detroit, MI.

Schwarz, N., & Bless, H. (1992). Constructing reality and its alternative: An inclusion/exclusion model of assimilation and contrast effects in social judgment. In L. L. Martin & A. Tesser (Eds.), *The construction of social judgments* (pp. 217–245). Hillsdale, NJ: Erlbaum.

Schwarz, N., & Clore, G. L. (1983). Mood misattribution, and judgments of well-being: Informative and directive functions of affective states. *Journal of Personality and Social Psychology, 45*, 513–523.

Segal, Z. V., Gemar, M., Truchon, C., Guirguis, M., & Horowitz, L. M. (1995). A priming methodology for studying self-representation in major depressive disorder. *Journal of Abnormal Psychology, 104*, 205–213.

Shavelson, R. J., & Webb, N. M. (1991). *Generalizability theory: A primer.* Newbury Park, CA: Sage.

Sherman, J. W., & Klein, S. B. (1994). Development and representation of personality impressions. *Journal of Personality and Social Psychology, 67*, 972–983.

Sherman, S. J., Judd, C. M., & Park, B. (1989). Social cognition. *Annual Review of Psychology, 40*, 281–326.

Srull, T. K., & Wyer, R. S. (1979). The role of category accessibility in the interpretation of information about persons: Some determinants and implications. *Journal of Personality and Social Psychology, 37*, 1660–1672.

Srull, T. K., & Wyer, R. S. (1989). Person memory and judgment. *Psychological Review, 96*, 58–83.

Stangor, C., & McMillan, D. (1992). Memory for expectancy-congruent and expectancy-incongruent information: A review of the social and social development literature. *Psychological Bulletin, 111*, 42–61.

Strack, F., Schwarz, N., Bless, H., Kubler, A., & Wanke, M. (1993). Awareness of the influence as a determinant of assimilation versus contrast. *European Journal of Social Psychology, 23*, 53–62.

Strauman, T. J. (1989). Self-discrepancies in clinical depression and social phobia: Cognitive structures that underlie emotional disorders? *Journal of Abnormal Psychology, 98*, 14–22.

Strauman, T. J., & Higgins, E. T. (1987). Automatic activation of self-discrepancies and emotional syndromes: When cognitive structures influence affect. *Journal of Personality and Social Psychology, 53*, 1004–1114.

Suitor, J. J., Pillemer, K., & Keeton, S. (1995). When experience counts: The effects of experiential and structural similarity on patterns of support and interpersonal stress. *Social Forces, 73*, 999–1014.

Swann, W. B., Jr., & Brown, J. D. (1990). From self to health: Self-verification and identity disruption. In B. R. Sarason, I. G. Sarason, & G. R. Pierce (Eds.), *Social support: An interactional view* (pp. 150–172). New York: Wiley.

Swann, W. B., & Predmore, S. C. (1985). Intimates as agents of social support: Sources of consolation or despair? *Journal of Personality and Social Psychology, 49*, 1609–1617.

Swann, W. B. Jr., Stein-Seroussi, A., & Giesler, R. B. (1992). Why people self-verify. *Journal of Personality and Social Psychology, 62*, 392–401.

Swann, W. B. Jr., Wenzlaff, R. M., Krull, D. S, & Pelham, B. W. (1992). Allure of negative feedback: Self-verification strivings among depressed persons. *Journal of Abnormal Psychology, 101*, 293–306.

Thoits, P. A. (1986). Social support as coping assistance. *Journal of Consulting and Clinical Psychology, 154*, 416–424.

Vinokur, A., Schul, Y., & Caplan, R. D. (1987). Determinants of perceived social support: Interpersonal transactions, personal outlook, and transient affective states. *Journal of Personality and Social Psychology, 53*, 1137–1145.

Weary, G., & Edwards, J. A. (1994). Social cognition and clinical psychology: Anxiety, depression and the processing of social information. In R. S. Wyer & T. K. Srull (Eds.), *Handbook of social cognition* (Vol. 2, pp. 289–338). Hillsdale, NJ: Erlbaum.

Wegener, D. T., & Petty, R. E. (1995). Flexible correction processes in social judgment: The role of naive theories in corrections for perceived bias. *Journal of Personality and Social Psychology, 68*, 36–51.

Winstead, B. A., Derlega, V. J., Lewis, R. J., Sanchez-Hucles, J., & Clarke, E. (1992). Friendship, social interaction, and coping with stress. *Communication Research, 19*, 193–211.

Winter, L., & Uleman, J. S. (1984). When are social judgments made? Evidence for the spontaneousness of trait inferences. *Journal of Personality and Social Psychology, 47*, 904–917.

Wyer, R. S., & Carlston, D. E. (1994). The cognitive representation of persons and events. In R. S. Wyer & T. K. Srull (Eds.), *Handbook of social cognition* (Vol. 1, pp. 41–98). Hillsdale, NJ: Erlbaum.

Wyer, R. S., & Gordon, S. E. (1982). The recall of information about persons and groups. *Journal of Experimental Social Psychology, 18*, 128–164.

Wyer, R. S., & Srull, T. K. (1994). *Handbook of social cognition* (Vol. 1). Hillsdale, NJ: Erlbaum.

Zanna, M. P., Sheras, P., Cooper, J., & Shaw, C. (1975). Pygmalion and Galatea: The interactive effect of teacher and student expectancies. *Journal of Experimental Social Psychology, 11*, 279–287.

CHAPTER 7

COGNITIVE CAUSES AND CONSEQUENCES OF PERCEIVED SOCIAL SUPPORT

ERIC S. MANKOWSKI AND ROBERT S. WYER JR.

People's perceptions of the social support they have available can have an important impact on their social adjustment and their ability to cope with stress. Moreover, this influence appears independent of the social support that actually exists. Indeed, there is often little relation between perceived and actual support availability. Individuals' general perceptions of the support they receive are only weakly correlated with their ratings of the supportiveness conveyed in specific events that have occurred (Dunkel-Schetter & Bennett, 1990; Lakey & Cassady, 1990; Sarason, Shearin, Pierce, & Sarason, 1987). Moreover, these perceptions are often better predictors of coping effectiveness than are either persons' own or others' ratings of the support that has actually been provided them in specific experiences they have had (Antonucci & Israel, 1986; Sandler & Barrera, 1984; Wethington & Kessler, 1986). Thus, providing persons with a supportive social environment is insufficient to ensure their ability to cope with stress and to acquire a sense of well-being. To attain these objectives, one must also understand the factors that influence people's *perceptions* of social support availability. This understanding requires an identification of not only the cognitive bases of perceived social support but also the processes that give rise to it.

The need to understand the cognitive underpinnings of social support perceptions is made particularly salient by evidence that people's expectations of receiving social support appear to remain stable despite actual changes in their social environ-

ERIC S. MANKOWSKI • The Center for Health Care Evaluation, Veterans Affairs Health Care System and Stanford University School of Medicine, Palo Alto, California 94025.   ROBERT S. WYER JR. • Department of Psychology, University of Illinois at Urbana–Champaign, Champaign, Illinois 61820.

Sourcebook of Social Support and Personality, edited by Gregory R. Pierce, Brian Lakey, Irwin G. Sarason, and Barbara R. Sarason. Plenum Press, New York, 1997.

ment (Sarason, Sarason, & Shearin, 1986). Why is this the case? An answer to this question also requires insight into the mental representations of support-related knowledge that exist in memory, the cognitive activities that underlie the retrieval and use of these representations in responding to new support-relevant experiences, and the manner in which the implications of these new experiences are integrated into the cognitions that are typically used as a basis for judgment of support availability.

In conceptualizing the cognitive determinants and effects of perceived social support availability, it is important to consider not only the different types of support-relevant information that one acquires but also the perspective from which this information is viewed. People encounter support-relevant information not only in their role as recipients of support, but also in their position as providers of support to others. Moreover, they often observe other persons interacting in situations in which they are not personally involved. Some concepts that are formed on the basis of support-relevant experiences may be similar, regardless of the persons involved in them. However, the implications that people derive from many social encounters are likely to depend on the perspective from which they consider these encounters. As a result, the prior knowledge that people bring to bear on their interpretation of new information may likewise depend on whether the information concerns themselves as support recipients, providers, or third parties. These contingencies are elaborated presently.

To provide a conceptual framework for the issues of concern in this chapter, we first identify the support-relevant knowledge that people have acquired in the course of their daily lives and the different ways that this knowledge can be represented in memory. We then discuss how different types of knowledge representations come into play in the processing of new information. In doing so, we analyze two types of situations in which people acquire support-relevant information about themselves and others, and present preliminary data that bear on the applicability of the general conceptualization we propose. In each case, we discuss the implications of our findings for the development and maintenance of perceived support availability over time.

CONCEPTUAL FRAMEWORK

MENTAL REPRESENTATIONS OF SUPPORT-RELEVANT KNOWLEDGE

Theoretical formulations of social information processing typically assume that stimulus information is processed in a number of different stages. (For a summary and evaluation of the basic assumptions underlying most social cognition theory and research, see Bodenhausen & Wyer, 1988; Wyer, 1980.) These stages often include the initial interpretation of the information, a construal of its implications with reference to previously acquired knowledge to which it is relevant, and the construction of a mental representation of the referent to which the information pertains. The implications of this representation can differ in several ways from those of the original stimulus material. Once the representation is formed, it is stored in memory. Later, it is often retrieved and used as a basis for judgments and decisions, without recourse of the original information that entered into its construction. Specific models of social information processing (Carlston, 1994; Smith, 1990; Wyer & Carlston, 1979; for a review, see Wyer & Carlston, 1994) make specific assumptions concerning the content, structure, and use of different mental representations, as well as the processes that lead to their formation.

A model of social information processing proposed by Wyer and Srull (1986, 1989) is particularly useful in the present context. This model distinguishes several different types of knowledge representations that individuals bring to bear on the information they receive, and specifies the conditions in which these representations are used. It also specifies the cognitive processes that are involved in retrieving and using the information, and when these activities are likely to occur.

MENTAL REPRESENTATION OF SUPPORT-RELEVANT KNOWLEDGE

According to Wyer and Srull's model (1986, 1989), social memory consists of a set of content-addressable "storage bins." One, *semantic* bin serves as a mental dictionary, containing noun, attribute, and action concepts that are used to interpret information at an early stage of processing, without regard to the particular persons or events to which the information refers. Other, *referent* bins are analogous to a cognitive encyclopedia. These bins, which contain knowledge about particular persons, situations, or events, are each denoted by a header, or set of features that specify the bin's referent and more generally circumscribe its contents. Several bins can pertain to the same referent in different roles or situational contexts. Thus, several "self" bins might exist, each containing information about oneself in a particular social role or type of situation.

Several types of knowledge representations are postulated to be contained in these bins.

Semantic Concepts

As noted earlier, the noun, action, and attribute concepts that are stored in the semantic bin are theoretically independent of knowledge about specific referents. They presumably include attribute concepts associated with social support (e.g., "supportive," "rejecting," etc.). These concepts are typically defined in terms of behavior-related features ("helps," "criticizes," etc.) that convey different degrees of supportiveness. Thus, specific behaviors that have these features can potentially be interpreted as instances of the concepts.

Event Schemas

A number of behaviors that occur in a situation or a series of thematically related situations may be organized into a mental representation of the sequence of events as a whole. When a number of similar sequences have occurred, a more general, prototypic event schema is likely to be constructed (Abelson, 1976, 1981; Graesser, 1981; Schank & Abelson, 1977; Wyer & Srull, 1989). Once such a schema is formed, it is stored in a referent bin and can later be used both to predict the events and to construe the implications of these events once they have occurred. For example, a schema that exemplifies the sorts of support-related interaction one has typically had in the past might be used as a standard of comparison in evaluating the support conveyed in new situations.

Some event schemas might not pertain to a single situation. Rather, they portray behavior in a series of thematically related situations involving a given group of individuals. These schemas have the form of a narrative, or "story," that is constructed from a person's encounters over a period of time. Schank (1990; see also Schank & Abelson, 1995) assumes that such narrative representations are fundamental ingredients of social knowledge that underlie our comprehension of most social experiences outside the laboratory. (For other discussions of the role of narratives in social knowing, see Wyer, 1995).

As these observations suggest, the specificity of the event representations that are used to evaluate new experiences, and the range of experiences to which they apply, can vary. On one hand, the prototypic event representations that people activate and use to evaluate a new experience could consist of features that are extracted from the entire pool of past support-relevant experiences one has had. Alternatively, they could depict a particular experience, or exemplar, that is considered to be fairly typical of those one has previously encountered (Smith, 1990; see also Hintzman, 1986, for a general exemplar-based theory of memory). Different exemplars might be retrieved and used at different times, depending on the similarity of their features to those of the experience being evaluated.

In this latter regard, different schemas could be activated and applied in construing the implications of a potentially supportive social interaction, depending on the perspective from which the situation is viewed. Thus, for example, people might use a different event schema to evaluate the supportiveness of a person's behavior toward them rather than to evaluate the same person's behavior toward another, or to evaluate their own behavior in a comparable situation. In terms of the Wyer and Srull model, these schemas might be stored in different referent bins pertaining to oneself as a support recipient, to oneself as a provider, or to support-related situations in general.

Referent-Specific Person Representations

If a number of different experiences have similar implications for the attributes of a person, a general concept is likely to be formed of the person as someone who has these attributes. Once the concept is acquired, it can provide a basis for organizing new information about the person. The representation that is constructed as a result of this latter activity could resemble those that are theoretically formed from trait and behavior information in research on person impression formation (e.g., Hastie, 1980; Srull & Wyer, 1989); that is, it might consist of a general, trait-based concept of a person to which a number of more specific behaviors are associatively linked.

One important implication of the conceptualization that underlies the postulation of these representations (Srull & Wyer, 1989; Wyer & Srull, 1989) surrounds their use in making judgments. Specifically, judgments of the person to whom a representation refers are theoretically based on the central concept of this representation, without consulting the individual behaviors that are associated with it. As a result, these judgments can often be unrelated to, or even inconsistent with, the implications of specific behaviors that one can recall about the person being judged (Hastie & Park, 1986; Lichtenstein & Srull, 1987).

This conceptualization is, of course, based on theory and research on the impressions that are formed of other persons. However, similar considerations apply in forming mental representations of oneself (Kihlstrom & Klein, 1994). In this regard, Klein and Loftus (1993) found evidence using response-time procedures that people's judgments of the traits they possessed were independent of the behaviors they could recall that exemplified these traits.* Note that if this is true, it suggests at least one reason why perceptions of social support availability might persist over time; that is, once a concept has been formed of oneself as a person who typically receives (or does not receive) support, this concept might be recalled and used as a basis for judging one's support availability independently of specific experiences that confirm or disconfirm its validity. We return to this possibility shortly.

PROCESSING ASSUMPTIONS

According to the conceptualization developed by Wyer and Srull (1989), the three types of mental representations noted earlier typically come into play at different stages of processing and can therefore have different, sometimes contradictory effects on responses to new information. A complete description of the Wyer and Srull model is beyond the scope of this chapter. We therefore restrict our attention to only those aspects that are of particular relevance to the issues at hand. First, a general overview of the processes postulated by the model will be helpful. This will be done with reference to a hypothetical example.

Suppose observers encounter a situation in which one person (either themselves or someone else) is in need of support, and another responds to this need by behaving in a certain way. For example, consider a situation in which a person conveys that she was just fired from her job after talking with a newspaper reporter about corruption in her company. Her friend responds by reminding her how unhappy she had been at the job for years. Such a response is ambiguous, in that it could convey either a sincere attempt to provide help or insensitivity to the person's feelings. Thus, it could be interpreted as either supportive or not. The observers should first encode the behavior into memory in terms of general concepts contained in the semantic bin that are relevant to its interpretation. If the behavior is ambiguous or can be interpreted in terms of more than one concept, the concept that comes to mind most quickly (e.g., one near the top of the bin) is typically applied. (For evidence that increasing a concept's accessibility in memory increases its use in interpreting behavioral information, see Bargh, Bond, Lombardi, & Tota, 1986; Higgins & King, 1981; Srull & Wyer, 1979).

---

*This finding could also be interpreted in terms of the "bin" conception of social memory proposed by Wyer and Srull (1989). As noted earlier, this theory assumes that people store self-relevant knowledge in a content-addressable storage bin whose "header" contains general attributes that have become strongly associated with oneself through learning. Self-judgments are typically based on the features of the header, and a search of the bin's contents is performed only if the header's features are insufficient to make these judgments. Thus, judgments may often be uncorrelated with the implications of the specific self-representations that are stored in the bin itself and retrieved when one is asked to recall them.

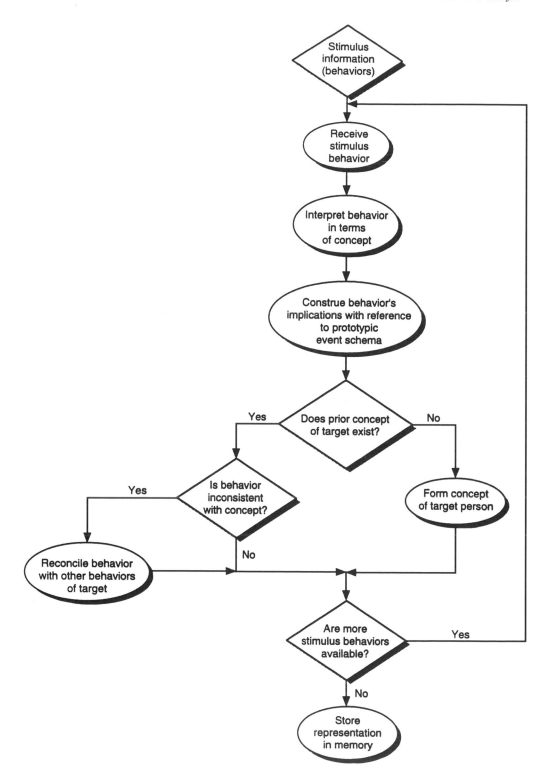

Once this initial interpretation is made, however, observers further evaluate the implications of the behavior by comparing it to a prototypic event schema of the type of situation in which the behavior has occurred. The use of this comparison standard is likely to have a *contrast* effect on judgments of the behavior's implications (Ostrom & Upshaw, 1968; Upshaw, 1969); that is, the behavior is judged as less supportive if the standard to which it is compared conveys supportiveness than if this standard conveys rejection.

Finally, once the behavior's implications are construed, observers may think about it with reference to a previously formed concept of the provider or, in some cases, the recipient. If the behavior is inconsistent with the implications of this concept, however, subjects may think about it more extensively in relation to other behaviors that are associated with the concept in an attempt to reconcile its occurrence (Hastie, 1980; Srull & Wyer, 1989). This additional cognitive activity is likely to make the behavior more easily accessible in memory and, therefore, easier to recall later than behaviors that are consistent with the concept (Srull & Wyer, 1989; for more general discussions of the effect of amount of processing on recall, see Craik & Lockhart, 1972; Wyer & Hartwick, 1980). Nevertheless, when observers are later asked to make a judgment of the provider's supportiveness, they are likely to base this judgment on the implications of the general person concept and not on the behaviors associated with it.

The sequence of processes outlined earlier is conveyed in the flow diagram shown in Figure 7.1. For example, suppose a student conveys to his roommate that he is in danger of flunking out of school, to which the roommate replies that he has also had a bad day and suggests going out for pizza. The behavior is ambiguous in that it could be interpreted either as supportive (sympathetic) or nonsupportive (concerned with one's own problems and not the other's). Acquaintances who learn about this event should theoretically interpret the roommate's behavior in terms of whichever semantic concept comes to mind more easily, and should then construe its implications with reference to a prototypic event schema (e.g., a schema pertaining to how people typically react to someone else's academic difficulties). Therefore, depending on the concepts and schemas that are applied at these two stages, the acquaintance could perceive the behavior's implications as either supportive or rejecting.

In any event, suppose, further, that the acquaintances have a previously formed concept of the roommate as supportive. They may retrieve this concept and, if they construed the behavior's implications in a way that is inconsistent with the concept, may think about it with reference to other behavior the roommate is known to have performed in order to reconcile its occurrence. As a result of this cognitive activity, they are likely to later recall the inconsistent behavior more easily than other, more consistent behaviors the roommate has performed. Nevertheless, if they are asked to judge the roommate's supportiveness, they may judge him as supportive, despite their memory for his unsupportive behavior. Note that although this example concerns the perceptions and judgments by persons who are not themselves involved in the situation described, similar considerations would theoretically apply to perceptions by the participants themselves.

FIGURE 7.1. Flow diagram of the cognitive processes assumed to mediate the use of stimulus information about a target's behavior to form a person impression.

INDIVIDUAL DIFFERENCES IN REACTIONS TO SUPPORT-RELATED INFORMATION

The cognitive processes that underlie responses to support-related information may be fairly universal under conditions in which subjects consider this information for the purpose of judging its supportiveness. However, the effects of these processes depend on the type and implications of the support-related knowledge that enters into them. Certain individual differences in this knowledge are likely to be reflected in part by differences in subjects' perceptions of their social support availability. However, the extent to which these differences have an influence on responses to new information is likely to depend on both (1) the type of information that is presented and (2) the perspective from which subjects consider the information.

Effects of Information Type

In the first regard, individual differences can exist in the semantic concepts that are chronically accessible in memory as a result of differences in the frequency with which the concepts have been used in the past (Bargh et al., 1986; see also Higgins, Bargh, & Lombardi, 1985; Srull & Wyer, 1979). However, the effects of these differences in concept accessibility on the interpretation of information are only likely to be apparent when the information is ambiguous or can be interpreted in different ways (Higgins, Rholes, & Jones, 1977; Srull & Wyer, 1979). Thus, for example, a behavior that is either clearly supportive or clearly rejecting is likely to be interpreted in terms of similar concepts, regardless of the concepts' accessibility in memory.

Individual differences may also exist in the implications of the prototypic event schemas that people have available for use as standards of comparison in construing the implications of behavior at a later stage of processing. However, such a schema is most likely to be used as a standard when the information being considered concerns a particular experience or set of thematically related experiences to which it can be applied. When several unrelated behaviors are considered, these behaviors are more likely to be thought about in relation to one another, or to a general concept of the persons involved, rather than in relation to a previously formed event schema. In this latter case, therefore, the effects of individual differences in the event schemas that people have available may be less apparent.

Effects of Perspective and Perceived Support Availability

Whether a particular semantic concept is spontaneously retrieved from the semantic bin and used to interpret support-related behavior at an early stage of processing depends in part on its chronic accessibility. Its accessibility, in turn, can be inferred from subjects' perceived support availability; that is, persons who perceive support to be generally available to them have probably applied concepts implying support more frequently in the past than persons who perceive support to be unavailable. Therefore, people with high-perceived-support availability should theoretically have concepts implying support relatively more accessible in memory, and should consequently be more likely to apply these concepts. Moreover, this should be true regardless of the particular persons involved in the behavior (Wyer & Srull, 1989).

On the other hand, people may more often form different concepts and event schemas of themselves as providers of support than of themselves as support recipients. They may also more frequently construct different event schemas pertaining to situations in which they are personally involved than in situations in which they are disinterested observers. Certain of these concepts and schemas may not vary with perceived support availability. For example, most people are motivated to believe that they personally behave in desirable ways. If this is so, they may have a concept of themselves as giving support to others, regardless of the support they believe they are likely to receive. To this extent, the self-referent person concepts and event schemas that subjects bring to bear on the processing of new, support-relevant experiences may depend on their role in these experiences. Moreover, only those concepts and schemas that subjects form of themselves as a support recipient may systematically vary with their perceptions of their own support availability.

EMPIRICAL EVIDENCE

The conceptualization outlined here has numerous implications for the processing of support-relevant information in both laboratory and nonlaboratory situations. Two studies we recently conducted (Mankowski & Wyer, 1996) bear directly on its validity in the former settings. We first describe these studies and then turn to other representative research to which their conceptualization is relevant.

In the studies by Mankowski and Wyer, people were instructed to imagine themselves as participants or observers in support-related interactions that were described to them in writing. Consequently, the generalizability of our specific results to situations in which subjects directly experience such events must, of course, be interpreted with caution. Nevertheless, the cognitive processes involved in responding to the information in these studies, and the contingency of these processes on perceived social support availability, may be similar in several respects to those that occur when people react to analogous experiences in daily life. One study examined the effect of prior knowledge on the interpretation of support-related interactions and the construal of their implications. The second study investigated the processes that underlie the organization of several different support-related episodes in memory and the effects of this processing on later recall and judgments. These studies and the implications of their findings are discussed in the following sections.

REACTIONS TO AMBIGUOUS SUPPORT-RELEVANT EXPERIENCES

Participants in the first experiment considered two 2-page scenarios, each describing thematically related interactions between two persons over the course of a day. The interactions were ones that college students might either personally experience or, alternatively, hear someone describe. In each scenario, one student was in need of social support, and the other's behavior was consistently ambiguous in terms of support it conveyed. An excerpt from one scenario, for example, was as follows:

Russell has learned he got a D on the psychology midterm. He is near tears when he gets back to his room. He tells Chris the bad news. "If I don't get good grades, I'll have to drop out of school. I can't seem to do well here."

"Wow," Chris replies. "What do you say we go out for a pizza? I haven't had a good day, either."

They go out for pizza. Russell tells Chris, "Remember that girl I met at your party? She's right over there. We were supposed to go to a movie together but she never showed up. I really thought she was interested in me. I don't know if I can eat with her sitting there."

"Oh, she won't even notice us," Chris says. "You should get fixed up with someone. Mark might have a suggestion, he seems to have no problem getting dates."

While reading one scenario, participants imagined themselves as a disinterested third party who was observing the interactions or hearing someone tell about them. While reading the other, they imagined they were personally experiencing the events from the perspective of either the potential support provider or the recipient. (The content of the two scenarios, the sex of the partners, and the order in which subjects considered the scenarios were counterbalanced over the different perspective conditions.) After reading each passage, participants generated an open-ended trait description of the provider and then rated him or her along a number of scales pertaining to social support and rejection.

The behaviors described in each scenario were ambiguous in terms of the support they conveyed. Therefore, participants' interpretation of them at the first stage of processing was expected to depend on the supportiveness of the semantic concepts that were most easily accessible in memory at the time. We expected that because participants with high-perceived-support availability (as measured by the Social Provisions Scale; see Cutrona & Russell, 1987) are likely to have used concepts implying supportiveness more frequently in the past, they should have these concepts more "chronically" accessible in memory than would participants who perceived the availability of support to be low. Therefore, the former participants should be relatively more likely to apply such concepts to the information they received; that is, they should spontaneously interpret the behaviors described as more supportive, and this should be true regardless of the perspective from which they viewed the scenarios (Wyer & Srull, 1989).

Once the behaviors were semantically encoded into memory, however, participants with the objective of evaluating the provider were expected to construe the behaviors' implications with reference to a previously formed standard of comparison. This standard may be a prototypic event schema of the behavior that typically occurs in situations of the sort described. This schema (unlike the general semantic concepts that are applied at the first stage of processing) is likely to depend on the perspective from which subjects consider the situation.

Specifically, the supportiveness of the schema applied by participants who took the recipient's role was expected to increase with their perceptions of the support they personally had available to them. However, the schema they used as a comparative standard when they took the provider's perspective was expected to convey high supportiveness, regardless of their perceived support availability. Finally, participants were not expected to have a clearly defined schema of how people respond to someone other than themselves, and the implications of this schema (like that applied by subjects with a provider's perspective) were not expected to vary consistently with their perceptions of their own support availability.*

The results of this experiment support these speculations. Mean ratings of the provider's relative supportiveness (the difference between ratings of the provider as supportive and ratings of the provider as rejecting) are shown in the top half of Table 7.1 as a function of the perspective from which participants viewed the story they read and their perceived support availability. The relative numbers of supportive versus rejecting trait adjectives that participants spontaneously used to describe the provider are summarized in the bottom half of the table. Both sets of data show a similar pattern.

Pooled over levels of perceived support availability, participants generally rated the provider as less supportive when they read the story from the recipient's perspective than they did under other conditions. This could indicate that they used a generally higher standard of comparison (i.e., a more stringent criterion) in evaluating the supportiveness of others' behavior toward them than in evaluating their own or another's behavior toward someone else.

More interesting are the effects of perceived support availability. Participants with either the perspective of a third person or that of the provider judged the provider to be more supportive when their perceived support availability was high than when it was low. These differences presumably reflect the different semantic concepts that the two groups of subjects spontaneously used to interpret the behaviors at an early stage of processing. When participants took the recipient's perspective, however, the support implied by the prototypic event schemas that they used as a comparative standard in construing the behavior's implications should also increase with their perception of support availability, and the contrast effect resulting from this comparison process should offset the effects of semantic encoding that occurred at the first stage of processing. Consistent with these speculations, the effect of perceived support availability on reactions to the provider was not apparent under recipient-perspective conditions.

There is a certain irony in the findings of this study. The fact that persons with high-perceived-support availability have semantic concepts implying supportiveness easily accessible in memory, and that they tend to use these concepts to interpret ambiguous new experiences, would seem to explain why they might maintain their perceptions of support availability over time. This tendency could also explain why persons often perceive others' support availability as similar to their own (Mankowski, Pierce, Sarason, & Sarason, 1990; Sarason, Pierce, Shearin, Sarason, Waltz, & Poppe, 1991). However, the effects of perceived support availability were only apparent when subjects imagined the situations they considered from the perspective of someone *other* than the actual support recipient. In fact, subjects who took the recipient's role actually evaluated the behaviors as nonsupportive. If this tendency generalizes to

---

*Participants who perceive themselves to have support available perceive others to do so as well (Mankowski, Pierce, Sarason, & Sarason, 1990; Sarason et al., 1991). However, this could be partly the result of interpretative differences of the sort that occur at the first stage of processing.

TABLE 7.1. Ratings and Open-Ended Trait Descriptions of
the Provider's Supportiveness as a Function of Perspective
and Perceived Social Support Availability—Experiment 1
(based on data from Mankowski and Wyer, 1996).

	Perspective		
Perceived support availability	Provider	Recipient	Third party
Relative supportiveness of ratings			
High	.81 (36)	−1.07 (34)	.26 (70)
Low	.35 (33)	−1.16 (35)	−.44 (68)
M	.59	−1.11	−.09
Relative supportiveness of trait descriptions			
High	.39	−.44	.14
Low	.18	−.26	−.26
M	.29	−.35	−.06

Note: Number of subjects in each cell is given in parentheses. Entries in the first subtable are mean differences between judgments of the provider as supportive and judgments of the provider as rejecting. Entries in the second subtable are mean differences in the numbers of supportive and rejecting trait descriptions generated.

situations outside the laboratory, why would subjects maintain their beliefs that their social environment is supportive?

One possible explanation is suggested by the results of a study by Lakey and Cassady (1990). In their study, persons imagined several hypothetical situations in which they might personally be involved and, in each case, judged the supportiveness of several alternative actions that another person might take. Participants' interpretation of these actions as supportive increased with their perceptions of support availability. In this situation, however, people were likely to compare the alternative actions they considered in each situation in relation to one another rather than in relation to their own previously formed standard (e.g., a prototypic event schema). Consequently, the effects of differences in the semantic concepts they used to interpret the behaviors at an early processing stage predominated, producing differences in judgments similar to those obtained in provider- and third-person-perspective conditions of the present study.

These considerations suggest that people with high-perceived-support availability do indeed interpret others' behavior toward them as supportive, provided they do not evaluate the behaviors in relation to a fixed standard of comparison. One such condition may arise when people consider several different behaviors in temporal proximity to one another. This condition is described in detail in the next section. An equally important consideration is implied by the information-processing model we have used as a conceptual framework for this research (Wyer & Srull, 1989); that is, the initial interpretation of information in terms of support-relevant concepts is spontaneous and may occur, regardless of any specific processing goals that exist at the time the information is received (see also Winter & Uleman, 1984). In contrast, the comparison process that leads to contrast effects occurs only when subjects have a specific objective in mind that requires them to evaluate a person's behavior (e.g., the goal of forming an impression or making a judgment, as in the present study). In many social situations in which one is personally involved, one is not required to generate an explicit estimate of the support conveyed by another's behavior, and so the comparison processes that produce contrast effects may not occur. In these situations, one's initial interpretation of the behavior, which is retained in memory, would tend to confirm one's perception of support availability.

RESPONSES TO MULTIPLE SUPPORT-RELEVANT BEHAVIORS

Rarely do people consider someone's behavior in total isolation. Rather, they evaluate it in the context of other knowledge they may have acquired about the person either in the same situation or in the past. As suggested by Srull and Wyer (1989) and noted earlier, people who have already formed a general concept of someone may think about new information about the person with reference to this concept. Moreover, when the person performs behaviors that are inconsistent with the concept's implications, people may think about the behaviors in relation to other knowledge about the person in order to reconcile their occurrence. As a result of this cognitive activity, these behaviors are more easily accessible in memory and, therefore, are more likely to be recalled than behaviors that are consistent with their general concept of the person.

This hypothesis seems surprising on first consideration; that is, people who are asked to evaluate a person are likely to base this judgment on the implications of a general concept they have formed of the person. They are nevertheless most likely to recall behaviors the person has performed that are inconsistent with this concept. One general implication of this in the present context is that people's perceptions of their general support availability are not necessarily reflected by the supportiveness of specific interactions they can recall.

Some evidence consistent with this conceptualization was obtained by Lakey, Moineau, and Drew (1992; but see Lakey & Cassady, 1990). A study we personally conducted in parallel with that described earlier confirmed Lakey et al.'s (1992) conclusions but circumscribed their applicability. Participants with each of the three perspectives we considered* were given a series of vignettes, each describing an interaction between two persons in a different situation. Some vignettes described behaviors that were unambiguously supportive. (In one, a person asked a roommate for advice on a term paper, and the roommate responded by making a few minor suggestions and saying that the paper was well written and very interesting.) Four others, however, were clearly rejecting. (For example, a person, described as having had a hard day, was seeking another's company. However, the other said that he was sick of seeing the person so bummed out and suggested not meeting.) Under provider-perspective conditions, participants imagined that the vignettes described their own behavior toward several different persons. Under recipient-perspective conditions, they imagined that the vignettes described several different persons' behavior toward

---

*This study was conducted immediately after the experiment described in the preceding section, and participants were asked to take the same perspective they had when reading the last scenario they considered in this experiment.

them. Under third-person-perspective conditions, the vignettes described the behavior of several different providers toward a single recipient of the same sex as the participants. After reading the vignettes and a short delay, participants judged the supportiveness of the provider(s) and then recalled the vignettes they had read.

We expected that people with a recipient's perspective would think about the behaviors with reference to a concept of themselves as the recipients of support, and that the supportiveness implied by this concept would increase with their perception of their general support availability. Under these conditions, therefore, we hypothesized that participants who perceived support to be generally available to them would think more about rejecting behaviors (and less about supportive ones) than would participants who perceived support to be unavailable and would consequently recall rejecting behaviors relatively better.

This difference was not expected under other perspective conditions, however. If people generally perceive that they give support to others, regardless of the support they receive, those persons with a provider's perspective should organize the behaviors around a previously formed concept of themselves as supportive. To this extent, they should have better recall of rejecting (i.e., inconsistent) behaviors, independently of their perceived support availability. Finally, if participants with a third person's perspective have no clear expectation concerning the supportiveness of the providers' behavior, they may organize the behaviors around a concept that is relatively neutral in supportiveness. To this extent, they should think about supportive and rejecting behaviors to about the same extent, and should recall them about equally well.

Results confirmed these predictions. Table 7.2 shows the proportion of supportive behaviors recalled, the proportion of rejecting behaviors recalled, and the difference between them as a function of perspective and perceived support availability. When participants took the recipient's perspective, they recalled fewer supportive behaviors, and more rejecting ones, if they perceived their available support to be high than if they perceived it to be low. When they took the provider's perspective, however, they recalled substantially more rejecting than supportive behaviors (.53 vs. .35), regardless of the support they believed was available to them personally. Finally, participants with a third person's perspective recalled about the same proportion of supportive and rejecting behaviors (.48 vs. .46), and this was also true at each level of perceived support availability. These data confirm the effects obtained by Lakey et al. (1992). However, they indicate that these effects are restricted to conditions in which subjects imagine themselves as the recipient of the behaviors they are considering.

According to the conceptualization we have proposed, however, participants' judgments of the provider's supportiveness are not based on implications of the behaviors they can recall, but rather on the central concept around which these behaviors are organized. Therefore, there should be little systematic relation between the supportiveness of the recall behaviors and their judgments of the provider. This was in fact the case; the correlation between participants' judgments under each perspective condition and the relative proportions of supportive and rejecting behaviors that they recalled was low and nonsignificant. (This finding is consistent with the results of studies in other content domains; see Hastie & Park, 1986; Lichtenstein & Srull, 1987).

Mean judgments of the providers' supportiveness, computed as in the first ex-

TABLE 7.2. Proportion of Supportive and Rejecting
Behaviors Recalled as a Function of Perspective
and Perceived Support Availability—Experiment 2
(Based on data from Mankowski & Wyer, 1996)

Perceived support availability	Perspective		
	Provider	Recipient	Third party
Supportive behaviors recalled			
High	.33 (17)	.38 (14)	.52 (39)
Low	.36 (17)	.45 (19)	.44 (32)
M	.35	.42	.48
Rejecting behaviors recalled			
High	.54	.57	.45
Low	.51	.46	.48
M	.53	.51	.46
Difference			
High	−.21	−.19	.07
Low	−.16	−.01	−.04
M	−.18	−.09	.02

Note. Number of subects in each cell is given in parentheses.

periment we described, are shown in Table 7.3. No effects of perspective and perceived support availability on these judgments were statistically reliable. With one exception, however, they were directionally consistent with expectations; that is, participants who took a third person's perspective judged the provider as only slightly more supportive than rejecting, confirming the assumption that the concept around which they organized the behaviors in this condition was fairly neutral. In contrast,

TABLE 7.3. Ratings of Provider's
Supportiveness as a Function of Perspective
and Perceived Support Availability—
Experiment 2 (based on data from
Mankowski & Wyer, 1996).

Perceived support availability	Perspective		
	Provider	Recipient	Third party
High	.57 (17)	2.38 (17)	.71 (39)
Low	−1.15 (17)	1.28 (19)	.73 (32)
M	−.29	1.75	.72

Note: Number of subjects in each cell is given in parentheses.

judgments by participants with the recipient's perspective increased with the support that they perceived was generally available to them.

Judgments by participants who took the provider's perspective are more difficult to interpret. As noted earlier, these persons recalled more rejecting than supportive behaviors, regardless of their perceived support availability (see Table 7.2), suggesting that they organized the behaviors around a concept of themselves as someone who generally gives support to others. Nevertheless, they judged the provider to be relatively unsupportive, and this was particularly true when their own perceived support availability was low. The reason for this can only be speculated. However, the rejecting behaviors that participants were asked to consider in this condition were not only unambiguous but also had rather extreme implications. When participants in this condition thought about the rejecting behaviors with reference to a concept of themselves as a support provider, they may have found it difficult to imagine themselves actually performing them. Consequently, they may have dissociated themselves from the provider despite instructions to empathize with him or her, and therefore may not have used their concept of themselves as a basis for their judgments. (Indeed, they might even have used this concept as a standard of comparison, producing a contrast effect.)

Be that as it may, the results of this study provide further insight into why persons might maintain the concepts that have formed of support availability; that is, people form a general concept of the support they are likely to receive on the basis of their past experiences in support-related situations. Once this concept is formed, they think about subsequent experiences with reference to it. They may think particularly extensively about behaviors that contradict the concept they have formed of themselves, and may in fact recall these behaviors better than those that confirm the concept's validity. Nevertheless, they base the judgments of themselves on the initial concept they have formed, thereby maintaining their self-perceptions, despite the salience of specific concept-discrepant episodes.

Several qualifications on the generality of this conclusion are in order. First, it would be incorrect to conclude that persons with high-perceived-support availability are generally more likely to recall experiences in which they have been rejected than are persons who perceive support to be unavailable. In both of our studies, participants read the information with the goal of forming an impression of the person involved in the interactions. When people do not have an implicit or explicit impression-formation objective, they may not spontaneously think about behaviors with reference to a previously formed concept of either themselves or another, and therefore, they may not attempt to reconcile behaviors that appear inconsistent with such a concept. Consequently, these latter behaviors may not be recalled any better than consistent ones. Indeed, it is conceivable that in the absence of motivation to engage in inconsistency resolution, people who are confronted with a large amount of information selectively encode this information in terms of concepts that are most easily accessible in memory, ignoring other information that can be less easily interpreted. If this is true, and if persons with high-perceived-support availability have semantic concepts implying support more easily accessible than those with low-perceived-support availability, they may be relatively more likely to encode supportive experiences into memory than rejecting ones. This could produce a bias in recall that is opposite to that which we observed.*

Second, neither our results nor the conceptualization underlying them implies that perceptions of support availability, once formed, become indelible and are never affected by new experiences. Traumatic life situations in which the support one receives is consistently greater or consistently less than expected may lead a new concept to be formed that replaces the old one as a basis for judgments. In the absence of such extreme circumstances, however, people's concepts of their support availability may be quite resilient.

Conclusions

It is perhaps somewhat hazardous to generalize the results of this research too far beyond the experimental conditions in which they were obtained. Clearly, when people encounter others' behavior in actual situations, factors arise that are not captured by the role-playing paradigm used in the studies we have reported. Moreover, people may think differently about the experiences that occur to them over a period of time than about abstract verbal descriptions of behaviors that are all conveyed in a short period of time. Despite these concerns, however, our data suggest at least two factors that can account for the stability of persons' perceptions of support availability.

First, people who have actually experienced different amounts of social support in the past may have semantic concepts implying support or rejection differentially accessible in memory. These concepts may be applied spontaneously in interpreting behaviors that occur in new support-related situations and are ambiguous in terms of the support that is actually conveyed. As a result, the behaviors are likely to be interpreted in a way that reinforces subjects' existing perceptions of the support they have available.

Second, individuals develop general concepts of themselves as persons who either typically receive or typically do not receive support on the basis of their past experiences. Once these concepts are formed, they are likely to be used as a basis for self-perceptions, even after having experiences whose implications contradict those of the concept. This can occur despite the fact that the inconsistent experiences can be easily recalled. Note that the research by Klein and Loftus (1993), in a quite different paradigm, also suggests that people's self-judgments are independent of the behaviors they can recall that have implications for these judgments. Thus, the converging conclusions drawn from these two bodies of research provide confidence in their generality.

---

*Note also that the prediction of better recall of expectancy-inconsistent than expectancy-consistent behaviors pertains to a difference in the *proportions* of behaviors of each type that are recalled and not to the absolute numbers of these behaviors. The number of behaviors of each type that are recalled is obviously a positive function of the number that are stored in memory, and therefore may increase with the number of instances that subjects have actually encountered. Therefore, if people with high-perceived-support availability have actually experienced more instances of supportiveness than people with low-perceived-support availability, they may recall a greater number of supportive behaviors, although the proportion of these behaviors (relative to the number they experienced) may be low.

FURTHER CONSIDERATIONS

IMPLICATIONS FOR OTHER RESEARCH

The research summarized in this chapter should be evaluated in relation to other recent work on the determinants and effects of perceived support availability. Two areas surrounding the generalizability of social support perceptions over situations, and developmental influences on these perceptions, are of particular interest in this context.

Generalizability of Perceived Social Support

One implication of our findings concerns the fact that the effects of perceived social support availability on responses to new information depend on the perspective from which this information is viewed. Theories of perceived social support, and the measurement instruments based on them, have tended to assume that people have a single, overall representation of social support information. The previous evidence bearing on this assumption appears to be mixed. Some researchers (e.g., Pierce, Sarason, & Sarason, 1992) have found that generalized expectations for support do not completely predict evaluations of behaviors that occur in the context of a specific ongoing relationship. Measures of relationship-specific support perceptions add predictive power (Pierce et al., 1992). These results, like Mankowski and Wyer's (1996), suggest that people have different mental representations for different relationships, and therefore categorize, interpret, and remember the behaviors in relationships differently.

In contrast, other researchers have concluded that perceptions of one's own social support *do* generalize to beliefs about the support available to similar others (Sarason et al., 1991), and that perceptions of the support available in specific relationships generalize to perceptions of relationships in general (Lakey & Dickinson, 1994; Mallinckrodt, 1991). However, these latter findings do not necessarily conflict with the implications of Pierce et al. That is, if persons with high-perceived-support availability have semantic concepts implying supportiveness easily accessible in memory, they are likely to use these concepts to interpret persons' behavior toward others as well as toward themselves. These effects of semantic encoding, which occur at an early stage of processing, could account for the findings obtained by Sarason et al., despite differences in the event schemas and person concepts that are formed of self and others, or are formed of oneself in different social roles.

In this regard, other investigators (see Jung, 1989) have also shown that support-relevant behaviors are viewed differently by providers and recipients. However, these perceptions may also depend on the nature of the role or status relationship the recipient has with the provider (Dakof & Taylor, 1990; Pierce, Sarason, & Sarason, 1991). Thus, the differences in judgments of support-related behaviors observed in our own research could be contingent on whether the persons involved in the interaction are friends, lovers, or family members, or are in subordinate–superordinate relationships, as well as whether the perceiver is the potential provider or recipient.

Developmental Determinants of Perceived Support

Perceptions of social support availability are undoubtedly influenced in part by experiences that occur at early stages of development. Several theories suggest that perceptions of support can stem from early attachment experiences that reflect the availability and quality of caregiving (see Wallace & Vaux, 1993; Sarason, Pierce, & Sarason, 1990). In this view, the experience of a consistent, caregiving relationship in infancy provides the grounds on which positive expectations for, and memories of, support are initially formed, and these expectations are carried forward to future social relationships. There is evidence that persons' perceptions of support availability are indeed related to perceptions of their family environment (Lakey & Dickinson, 1994), and to the family members' actual reactions to these persons (Sarason, Pierce, Bannerman, & Sarason, 1993). Perceptions of parental supportiveness, in turn, can predict positive behavioral outcomes such as academic achievement (Cutrona, Cole, Colangelo, Assouline, & Russell, 1994).

The theory outlined in this chapter provides a framework for interpreting such findings. For example, it suggests ways in which individual differences in the quality of mental representations of social support, formed through infancy and childhood attachment experiences, produce corresponding differences in how relevant behaviors are interpreted, whether they are attributed to situation-specific or more stable personality factors (see Fincham & Bradbury, 1990), and whether these behaviors are likely to be remembered. Ultimately, these differences in perceptions could produce differences in whether and how people solicit support and utilize available support resources. As we speculated earlier, for example, behavior based on the expectation that support will be forthcoming could actually elicit support, thereby confirming the validity of the original expectation. An understanding of the importance of early family experiences in the development of perceived social support is likely to have implications for the design of interventions that attempt to increase social support resources as a stress-preventive strategy (Brand, Lakey, & Berman, 1995). These interventions may need to adopt strategies aimed at interpreting or minimizing the ways in which negative perceptions of early family experiences are generalized to other existing and potentially useful sources of support.

ADDITIONAL DETERMINANTS AND CONSEQUENCES OF PERCEIVED SOCIAL SUPPORT

The fact that people's perceptions of support availability are often uncorrelated with the support they actually receive should not be construed as evidence that these factors are totally unrelated. Rather, the relation may be quite complex. As implied in the previous section, support-related concepts are obviously not developed in a vacuum; that is, the acquisition of such concepts is undoubtedly influenced by the actual support or rejection one receives at early stages of social development. Once these concepts are formed, they can influence behavior in a number of ways other than those we have considered.

For example, people who have received support in the past may have acquired effective, socially learned strategies for soliciting support, and their success in doing so may lead them to maintain their perceptions that support is available. On the other hand, people who perceive themselves as receiving little support may be particularly active in seeking it, and may receive substantial support as a result of their efforts. Therefore, both groups of subjects may actually receive support, resulting in little overall relation between perceived support availability and actual support received.

Behavior Confirmation Processes

A quite different set of considerations predicts a positive relation between perceived support availability and the actual receipt of support. Mark Snyder and his colleagues postulate that people with expectations for how another person will respond to them in a particular situation are likely to behave toward this person in a manner that elicits these responses, thus leading their expectations to be confirmed. Thus, for example, men who are induced to believe that their female partner in a get-acquainted telephone conversation is personally appealing (as a result of showing them an attractive photograph) tend to converse with her in ways that lead her to be actually more warm and friendly than are the partners of men who expect them to be less attractive (Snyder, Tanke, & Berscheid, 1977). Moreover, when persons expect their partners in an experiment to be antagonistic, they responded to them in ways that actually elicit more aggressive behavior (Snyder & Swann, 1978).

In the present context, it seems reasonable to suppose that persons who expect others to give them social support are more likely to seek this support than those who expect others to be rejecting. Moreover, they may adopt a general interaction style that is more likely to elicit supportiveness in others. For both reasons, their own behavior could lead them to confirm and therefore maintain their initial perceptions of support availability. These considerations raise more general questions concerning the differences in actual interpersonal behavior of persons who perceive support to be available and those who do not. The identification of these differences could provide further insight into the dynamics of perceived support availability and its effects.

Effects of Schematicity

Responses to new support-related behavior are likely to depend on a number of individual difference variables in addition to those we have personally investigated. One particularly important factor might be persons' "schematicity" with respect to social support, which reflects the extent to which perceptions of support availability are central to one's self concept (Lakey et al., 1992; for more general discussions of the effects of schematicity with respect to other attributes, see Markus & Smith, 1981). The relation of this factor to the outcome variables of interest in studies of stress and coping has yet to be evaluated. People for whom support is a meaningful, salient, and frequently applied perceptual category may have support-relevant concepts more chronically accessible in memory (Bargh, 1994), and may be more likely to bring these concepts to bear on the interpretation of support-related situations than those for whom support is a relatively rarely used or personally unimportant concept.

These issues could potentially be investigated using techniques designed to assess schematicity in other domains. For example, schematicity may be reflected by the time to evaluate potentially supportive behaviors (Markus & Smith, 1981). (That is, persons who respond quickly presumably have more well-developed support schemas, and ones that are more central to their self-concepts, than do persons who take more time to respond). The ratio of support-relevant to support-irrelevant adjectives that persons typically generate to describe target persons could be a second indicator of the importance of support-related concepts (cf. Bargh et al., 1986). Schematicity defined on the basis of such indices might mediate the relations among perceived social support, judgments, and recall that have been identified in both our own research and that of others.

METHODOLOGICAL ISSUES

Measurement of Social Support

The research discussed in this chapter suggests the desirability of modifying global measures of perceived support availability to take into account both the situations in which the support occurs and the types of persons involved in these situations. Measures of perceived social support are presumably intended to assess how much support a person believes is available in those particular situations in which this support might be needed. The evidence that enacted and perceived support indices are weakly correlated (Dunkel-Schetter & Bennett, 1990), and our own findings that perceptions of support depend on who enacts the behavior (see also Dakof & Taylor, 1990; Pierce et al., 1992), call into question the utility of simply asking people to judge supportive behaviors independently of the situational context in which the behaviors occur. The meaning of these behaviors seems clearly to depend on the nature of the personal relationship in which they occur, as well as the more general cognitive processes that underlie their interpretation.

Commonly used measures of perceived social support typically ask persons to judge the support they receive without reference to who might be providing the support. It seems reasonable to suppose that these measures would be more effective predictors of responses to new support-relevant situations if the interpersonal context to which the questionnaire items pertain were more carefully circumscribed in terms of the situations to which they apply.

An Alternative Methodology

The conceptualization we have proposed assumes the existence of several different types of mental representations of support-relevant information. However, the nature of these representations has not been directly explored. Particularly unclear are the event schemas we assume to underlie the evaluation of new support-related experiences. In conceptualizing the nature of these schemas, it may ultimately be desirable to explore more fully the implications of the conceptualization proposed by Schank and Abelson (1995; see also Schank, 1990); that is, much of the knowledge we exchange in social situations is in the form of a narrative, or story, that we tell or hear others relate. This knowledge can include personal life histories that people construct over a period of years as well as more situation-specific descriptions of experiences in particular situations. It is conceivable that narrative representations, rather than trait-based conceptions of oneself and others, are the major ingredients of self-knowledge that underlie perceptions of social support availability and provide guides for behavior in future situations. Although research on the role of narrative forms of mental representations is of relatively recent vintage (for several examples of recent work, see Wyer, 1995), it has led to important gains in conceptualizing a variety of phenomena ranging from marital conflict and its resolution (Holmes & Murray, 1995) to personal and social identity (McAdams, 1988; Mankowski & Rappaport, 1995). It seems likely that a consideration of the role of narratives in understanding social support perceptions would be equally fruitful.

One approach we are taking borrows from techniques developed by Baumeister, Stillwell, and Wotman (1990) to investigate the effects of perspective on perceptions of anger and hostility. In Baumeister et al.'s research, subjects wrote a story describing either an episode in which they made someone else angry, or an episode in which someone made them angry. A content analysis of these stories, supplemented by answers to several questions concerning the episodes described, revealed several important differences in the content of the narratives constructed from the two perspectives.

A similar approach could be taken to explore perspective differences in perceived social support and the possible contingency of these differences on the type of support exchanged (Mankowski, 1995). In this regard, Tannen (1990) postulates that men typically respond to implicit requests for support by giving advice, attempting to trivialize the problems that precipitate the need for support, and engaging in instrumental problem solving. In contrast, women are more likely to acknowledge the seriousness of the precipitating events and to provide social–emotional support. Whether a person's attempt to provide support is perceived as such by the recipient might likewise depend on the sex of the provider and recipient (see also Heller, Price, & Hogg, 1990). To examine these possibilities, male and female research participants have been asked to write narratives describing in detail (1) a situation in which they personally have given support to someone of the same or opposite sex or (2) a situation in which they received support from such a person. Content analyses of narratives may provide confirmation of Tannen's speculations, as well as insight into the dynamics of perceived support availability more generally.

FINAL COMMENTS

In this chapter, we have outlined a theoretical formulation of the cognitive dynamics underlying perceptions of social support availability, and have discussed the theory's implications for how these perceptions can affect responses to new support-relevant situations. Many assumptions we have made remain to be validated. Moreover, the research we have brought to bear on the validity of the formulation has largely been conducted in laboratory situations that differ in obvious ways from those one encounters in everyday life. Nevertheless, the theory provides a framework for conceptualizing a variety of phenomena that surround the determinants and consequences of social support perceptions and calls attention to a number of questions that have yet to be answered. To the extent that this chapter stimulates research on these questions, its primary objectives will be attained.

ACKNOWLEDGMENTS

This chapter was written with partial support of a National Science Foundation predoctoral fellowship to the first author, and grants MH 3-8585 from the National Institute of Mental Health and from the National Science Foundation to the second author.

REFERENCES

Abelson, R. P. (1976). Script processing in attitude formation and decision making. In J. S. Carroll & J. W. Payne (Eds.), *Cognitive and social behavior* (pp. 33–45). Hillsdale, NJ: Erlbaum.

Abelson, R. P. (1981). The psychological status of the script control. *American Psychologist, 36,* 715–729.

Antonucci, T. C., & Israel, B. A. (1986). Veridicality of social support: A comparison of principal and network members' responses. *Journal of Consulting and Clinical Psychology, 54,* 432–437.

Bargh, J. A. (1994). The four horsemen of automaticity: Awareness, intention, efficiency, and control in social cognition. In R. S. Wyer & T. K. Srull (Eds.), *Handbook of social cognition,* (2nd ed., Vol. 1, pp. 1–40). Hillsdale, NJ: Erlbaum.

Bargh, J. A., Bond, R. N., Lombardi, W., & Tota, M. E. (1986). The additive nature of chronic and temporary sources of construct accessibility. *Journal of Personality and Social Psychology, 50,* 869–878.

Baumeister, R. F., Stillwell, A. M., & Wotman, S. R. (1990). Victim and perpetrator accounts of interpersonal conflict: Autobiographical narratives about anger. *Journal of Personality and Social Psychology, 59,* 994–1005.

Bodenhausen, G. V., & Wyer, R. S. (1988). Social cognition and social reality information acquisition and use in the laboratory and the real world. In H. J. Hippler, N. Schwarz, & S. Sudman (Eds.), *Social information processing and survey methodology* (pp. 6–41). New York: Springer-Verlag.

Brand, E. F., Lakey, B., & Berman, S. (1995). A preventive, psychoeducational approach to perceived social support. *American Journal of Community Psychology, 23,* 117–136.

Carlston, D. E. (1994). Associated systems theory: A systematic approach to cognitive representations of persons. In R. S. Wyer, (Ed.), *Advances in social cognition* (Vol. 7, pp. 1–78). Hillsdale, NJ: Erlbaum.

Craik, F. I. M., & Lockhart, R. S. (1972). Levels of processing: A framework for memory research. *Journal of Verbal Learning and Verbal Behavior, 11,* 671–684.

Cutrona, C. E., Cole, V., Colangelo, N., Assouline, S. G., & Russell, D. (1994). Perceived parental social support and academic achievement: An attachment theory perspective. *Journal of Personality and Social Psychology, 66,* 369–378.

Cutrona, C. E., & Russell, D. (1987). The provisions of social relationships and adaptation to stress. In W. H. Jones & D. Perlman (Eds.), *Advances in personal relationships* (Vol. 1, pp. 37–67). Greenwich, CT: JAI Press.

Dakof, G. A. & Taylor, S. E. (1990). Victim's perceptions of social support: What is helpful from whom? *Journal of Personality and Social Psychology, 58,* 80–89.

Dunkel-Schetter, C., & Bennett, T. L. (1990). Differentiating the cognitive and behavioral aspects of social support. In B. R. Sarason, I. G. Sarason, & G. Pierce (Eds.), *Social support: An interfactional view* (pp. 267–296). New York: Wiley.

Fincham, F. D., & Bradbury, T. N. (1990). Social support in marriage: The role of social cognition. *Journal of Social and Clinical Psychology, 9,* 31–42.

Graesser, A. C. (1981). *Prose comprehension beyond the word.* New York: Springer-Verlag.

Hastie, R. (1980). Memory for behavioral information that confirms or contradicts a personality impression. In R. Hastie, T. Ostrom, E. Ebbesen, R. Wyer, D. Hamilton, & D. Carlston (Eds.), *Person memory: The cognitive basis of social perception* (pp. 155–177). Hillsdale, NJ: Erlbaum.

Hastie, R., & Park, B. (1986). The relationship between memory and judgment depends on whether the judgment task is memory-based or on-line. *Psychological Review, 93,* 258–268.

Heller, K., Price, R. H., & Hogg, J. R. (1990). The role of social support in community and clinical interventions. In B. R. Sarason, I. G. Sarason, & G. R. Pierce (Eds.), *Social support: An interactional view* (pp. 482–507). New York: Wiley.

Higgins, E. T., Bargh, J. A., & Lombardi, W. (1985). The nature of priming effects on categorization. *Journal of Experimental Psychology: Learning, Memory and Cognition, 11*, 59–69.

Higgins, E. T., & King, G. (1981). Accessibility of social construct: Information and contextual variability. In N. Cantor & J. F. Kihlstrom (Eds.), *Personality, cognition and social interaction*, (pp. 69–121). Hillsdale, NJ: Erlbaum.

Higgins, E. T., Rholes, W. S., & Jones, C. R. (1977). Category accessibility and impression formation. *Journal of Experimental Social Psychology, 13*, 141–154.

Hintzman, D. L. (1986). "Schema abstraction" in a multiple-trace memory model. *Psychological Review, 93*, 411–428.

Holmes, J. & Murray, S. (1995). Memory for events in close relationships: Applying Schank and Abelson's story skeleton model. In R. S. Wyer (Ed.), *Advances in social cognition* (Vol. 8, pp. 193–210). Hillsdale, NJ: Erlbaum.

Jung, J. (1989). Social support rejection and reappraisal by providers and recipients. *Journal of Applied Social Psychology, 19*, 159–173.

Kihlstrom, J. F., & Klein, S. B. (1994). The self as a knowledge structure. In R. S. Wyer & T. K. Srull (Eds.), *Handbook of social cognition* (2nd. ed., Vol. 1, pp. 153–208). Hillsdale, NJ: Erlbaum.

Klein, S. B., & Loftus, J. (1993). The mental representation of trait and autobiographical knowledge about the self. In T. K. Srull & R. S. Wyer (Eds.), *Advances in social cognition* (Vol. 5, pp. 1–49). Hillsdale, NJ: Erlbaum.

Lakey, B., & Cassady, P. B. (1990). Cognitive processes in perceived social support. *Journal of Personality and Social Psychology, 59*, 337–343.

Lakey, B., & Dickinson, L. G. (1994). Antecedents of perceived support: Is perceived family environment generalized to new social relationships? *Cognitive Therapy and Research, 18*, 39–53.

Lakey, B., Moineau, S., & Drew, J. B. (1992). Perceived social support and individual differences in the interpretation and recall of supportive behaviors. *Journal of Social and Clinical Psychology, 11*, 336–348.

Lichtenstein, M., & Srull, T. K. (1987). Processing objectives as a determinant of the relationship between recall and judgment. *Journal of Experimental Social Psychology, 23*, 93–118.

Mallinckrodt, B. (1991). Clients' representations of childhood emotional bonds with parents, social support, and formation of the working alliance. *Journal of Counseling Psychology, 38*, 401–409.

Mankowski, E. S. (1995). *Memories of supportive interactions: Gender and perspective differences in narrative accounts of helping*. Unpublished manuscript, University of Illinois at Urbana–Champaign.

Mankowski, E. S., Pierce, G. R., Sarason, B. R., & Sarason, I. G. (1990, April). *Assessing self and family support schemas: Responses to ambiguous photographs*. Paper presented at the Western Psychological Association Convention, Los Angeles, CA.

Mankowski, E. S., & Rappaport, J. (1995). Stories, identity and the psychological sense of community. In R. S. Wyer (Ed.), *Advances in social cognition* (Vol. 8., pp. 211–226). Hillsdale, NJ: Erlbaum.

Mankowski, E. S., & Wyer, R. S. (1996). Cognitive processes in perceptions of social support. *Personality and Social Psychology Bulletin, 22*, 894–905.

Markus, H., & Smith, J. (1981). The influence of self-schemas on the perception of others. In N. Cantor & J. K. Kihlstrom (Eds.), *Personality, cognition and social interaction* (pp. 233–262). Hillside, NJ: Erlbaum.

McAdams, D. P. (1988). *Power, intimacy, and the life story: Personological inquiries into identity*. New York: Guilford.

Ostrom, T. M., & Upshaw, H. S. (1968). Psychological perspectives and attitude change. In A. G. Greenwald, T. C. Brock, & T. M. Ostrom (Eds.), *Psychological foundations of attitudes* (pp. 217–242). New York: Academic Press.

Pierce, G. R., Sarason, I. G., & Sarason, B. R. (1991). General and relationship-based perceptions of social support. Are two constructs better than one? *Journal of Personality and Social Psychology, 61*, 1028–1039.

Pierce, G. R., Sarason, B. R., & Sarason, I. G. (1992). General and specific support expectations and stress as predictors of perceived supportiveness: An experimental study. *Journal of Personality and Social Psychology, 63*, 297–307.

Sandler, I. N., & Barrera, M. Jr. (1984). Toward a multimethod approach to assessing the effects of social support. *American Journal of Community Psychology, 12*, 37–52.

Sarason, B. R., Pierce, G. R., Bannerman, A., & Sarason, I. G. (1993). Investigating the antecedents of perceived social support: Parents' views of and behavior toward their children. *Journal of Personality and Social Psychology*, *65*, 1071–1085.

Sarason, B. R., Pierce, G. R., & Sarason, I. G. (1990). Social support: The sense of acceptance and the role of relationships. In B. R. Sarason, I. G. Sarason, & G. R. Pierce (Eds.), *Social support: An interactional view* (pp. 97–128). New York: Wiley.

Sarason, B. R., Pierce, G. R., Shearin, E. N., Sarason, I. G., Waltz, J. A., & Poppe, L. (1991). Perceived social support and working models of self and actual others. *Journal of Personality and Social Psychology*, *60*, 273–287.

Sarason, I. G., Sarason, B. R., & Shearin, E. N. (1986). Social support as an individual differences variable: Its stability, origins, and relational aspects. *Journal of Personality and Social Psychology*, *50*, 845–855.

Sarason, B. R., Shearin, E. N., Pierce, G. R., & Sarason, I. G. (1987). Interrelationships of social support measures: Theoretical and practical implications. *Journal of Personality and Social Psychology*, *52*, 813–832.

Schank, R. C., & Abelson, R. P. (1977). *Scripts, plans, goals and understanding*. Hillsdale, NJ: Erlbaum.

Schank, R. C. (1990). *Tell me a story: A new look at real and artificial memory*. New York: Scribner's.

Schank, R. C., & Abelson, R. P. (1995). Knowledge and memory: The real story. In R. S. Wyer (Ed.), *Advances in social cognition* (Vol. 8, pp. 1–85). Hillsdale, NJ: Erlbaum.

Smith, E. R. (1990). Content and process specificity in the effects of prior experiences. In T. K. Srull & R. S. Wyer (Eds.), *Advances in social cognition: Content and process specificity in the effects of prior experiences* (Vol. 3, pp. 1–59). Hillsdale, NJ: Erlbaum.

Snyder, M., & Swann, W. B. (1978). Behavioral confirmation in social interaction: From social perception to social reality. *Journal of Experimental Social Psychology*, *14*, 148–162.

Snyder, M., Tanke, E. D., & Berscheid, E. (1977). Social perception and interpersonal behavior: On the self-fulfilling nature of social stereotypes. *Journal of Personality and Social Psychology*, *3*, 656–666.

Srull, T. K., & Wyer, R. S. (1979). The role of category accessibility in the interpretation of information about persons: Some determinants and implications. *Journal of Personality and Social Psychology*, *37*, 1660–1672.

Srull, T. K., & Wyer, R. S. (1989). Person memory and judgment. *Psychological Review*, *96*, 58–83.

Tannen, D. (1990). *You just don't understand: Women and men in conversation*. New York: William Morrow.

Upshaw, H. S. (1969). The personal reference scale: An approach to social judgment. In L. Berkowitz (Ed.), *Advances in experimental social psychology* (Vol. 4, pp. 315–371). New York: Academic Press.

Wallace, J. L., & Vaux, A. (1993). Social support network orientation: The role of adult attachment style. *Journal of Social and Clinical Psychology*, *12*, 354–365.

Wethington, R., & Kessler, R. C. (1986). Perceived support, received support, and adjustment to stressful life events. *Journal of Health and Social Behavior*, *27*, 78–89.

Winter, L., & Uleman, J. S. (1984). When are social judgments made? Evidence for the spontaneousness of trait inferences. *Journal of Personality and Social Psychology*, *47*, 237–252.

Wyer, R. S. (1980). The acquisition and use of social knowledge: Basic postulates and representative research. *Personality and Social Psychology Bulletin*, *6*, 558–573.

Wyer, R. S. (Ed.). (1995). *Knowledge and memory: Advances in social cognition* (Vol. 8). Hillsdale, NJ: Erlbaum.

Wyer, R. S., & Carlston, D. E. (1979). *Social cognition, inference and attribution*. Hillsdale, NJ: Erlbaum.

Wyer, R. S., & Carlston, D. E. (1994). The cognitive representation of people and events. In R. S. Wyer & T. K. Srull (Eds.), *Handbook of social cognition* (2nd ed., Vol. 1, pp. 71–98). Hillsdale, NJ: Erlbaum.

Wyer, R. S., & Hartwick, J. (1980). The role of information and retrieval and conditional inference processes in belief formation and change. In L. Berkowitz (Ed.), *Advances in experimental social psychology* (Vol. 13, pp. 241–281). New York: Academic Press.

Wyer, R. S., & Srull, T. K. (1986). Human cognition in its social context. *Psychological Review*, *93*, 322–359.

Wyer, R. S., & Srull, T. K. (1989). *Memory and cognition in its social context*. Hillsdale, NJ: Erlbaum.

PART II

SOCIAL SUPPORT, PERSONALITY, AND MENTAL AND PHYSICAL HEALTH

Chapter 8

SOCIAL SUPPORT, COPING, AND PSYCHOLOGICAL ADJUSTMENT
A RESOURCES MODEL

Charles J. Holahan, Rudolf H. Moos, and Liza Bonin

The test of friendship is assistance in adversity—and that, too, unconditional assistance.

—Mohandas K. Gandhi

During the past two decades, research on social support has grown into a central domain of inquiry, informing and enriching several branches of the social sciences (see Cohen, 1992; Thoits, 1992). Today, research on social relationships is entering a new period of conceptual growth. Investigators have begun both to refine the definition of support and to uncover the mechanisms through which support operates. Our own work on the role of social support as a coping resource combines these two avenues of conceptual development in an integrative, predictive framework. We broaden the definition of social resources to include both positive and negative aspects of relationships, and we demonstrate a key mechanism through which social resources relate to adaptation.

In this chapter, we review the development of our program of research developing and testing a *resources model* of coping in which social resources relate to psychological adjustment through fostering adaptive coping strategies. We describe the conceptual rationale for the model and present supporting empirical findings from our own research as well as related work by other investigators. Next, we present more recent research refining and extending the model—work that includes social liabilities as well as social assets, and that incorporates the moderating role of stressor control-

Charles J. Holahan and Liza Bonin University of Texas at Austin • Department of Psychology, Austin, Texas 78712.   Rudolf H. Moos • Center for Health Care Evaluation, Veterans Affairs Health Care System and Stanford University Medical Center, Palo Alto, California 94305.

Sourcebook of Social Support and Personality, edited by Gregory R. Pierce, Brian Lakey, Irwin G. Sarason, and Barbara R. Sarason. Plenum Press, New York, 1997.

lability. We then consider directions for future research that can further refine our understanding of social support as a coping resource.

DEVELOPING AND TESTING THE MODEL

Our conceptualization of coping and coping responses developed inductively. The model is rooted philosophically in the *stress-resistance* perspective and is informed by a guiding respect for people's adaptive strengths in the face of adversity. A considerable body of evidence has demonstrated that both social support and adaptive coping strategies operate as protective factors during life crises. In moving toward a resources model of coping, we focused first on a new, though related, question—the role of social and personal resources in determining coping responses. We progressed next to framing and testing an integrative mediational model of coping resources, coping, and psychological health.

STRESS RESISTANCE

The last two decades have witnessed a growing societal concern with stressors and their psychological toll. Research on stress and coping with diverse population groups has shown that life change (particularly negative change) is associated with anxiety and depression as well as physical illness (Cohen & Williamson, 1991; Coyne & Downey, 1991; Thoits, 1995). At the same time, this research area has been characterized by persistent anomalies. Despite the consistency of stressor effects, the amount of variance predicted in distress is small, and individuals show highly variable reactions to stressors (Cohen & Edwards, 1989).

At first, researchers assumed that these anomalies reflected measurement error, but eventually they came to understand them as important findings in their own right. By the early 1970s, a new approach to conceptualizing and studying the process of stress and coping was beginning to emerge that has been described varyingly as "stress resistance," "resilience," and "invulnerability." The relatively poor empirical predictions of early studies of the stressor–illness relationship led researchers to focus increasingly on moderating variables, such as personal and social resources, as well as appraisal and coping processes that help individuals to maintain healthy functioning when stressors occur (see Coyne & Downey, 1991; Kessler, Price, & Wortman, 1985).

From initially placing an emphasis on people's deficits and vulnerabilities, contemporary research has evolved to placing increasing emphasis on individuals' adaptive strengths and capacity for resilience, constructive action, and personal growth in the face of challenge. Stress resistance researchers view the individual as active and resourceful. They assume that the stress and coping process is inherently complex and reflects a dynamic interplay among stressors, social and personal resources, and coping efforts (Kessler, et al., 1985; Lazarus & Folkman, 1984).

DETERMINANTS OF COPING

The conceptualization of coping processes is a central aspect of contemporary theories of stress resistance. Coping is a stabilizing factor that can help individuals maintain psychosocial adaptation during stressful periods; it encompasses cognitive and behavioral efforts to reduce or eliminate stressful conditions and associated emotional distress (Lazarus & Folkman, 1984). Although coping responses may be classified many ways, most approaches distinguish between strategies oriented toward approaching and confront the problem, and strategies oriented toward reducing tension by avoiding dealing directly with the problem (Moos & Schaefer, 1993; Roth & Cohen, 1986).

Approach coping strategies, such as problem solving and seeking information, can moderate the potential adverse influence of both negative life change and enduring role stressors on psychological functioning (Sherbourne, Hays, & Wells, 1995). In contrast, avoidance coping, such as denial and withdrawal, generally is associated with psychological distress and maladaptive behavioral outcomes—particularly when adjustment is assessed beyond the initial crisis period (Rohde, Lewinsohn, Tilson, & Seeley, 1990).

An extensive body of research also has examined the role of personality strengths and social support in stress resistance (Cohen, 1992; Cohen & Edwards, 1989; Thoits, 1992). For example, a variety of dispositional factors that relate broadly to self-confidence and personal control may protect an individual from the negative effects of stressors (Lefcourt, 1992; Wiedenfeld et al., 1990). Moreover, social support is associated with mental and physical health, with speedier recovery from illness, and with the likelihood of remaining psychologically and physically healthy when stressors occur (Cohen & Wills, 1985; House, Landis, & Umberson, 1988).

Social Support as a Coping Resource

Several investigators have speculated that social support may be linked to staying healthy under adaptive challenge in significant part, because it encourages more adaptive coping strategies. Lazarus and Folkman (1984) defined personal and social resources as what an individual "draws on in order to cope," and argued that such resources "precede and influence coping" (p. 158). Similarly, Thoits (1986, 1995) conceptualized social support as a source of coping assistance, as a "social 'fund' from which people may draw when handling stressors" (1995, p. 64). Cohen (1992) also reasoned that social relationships influence both problem-focused and emotion-focused coping efforts, and Leporte, Evans, and Schneider (1991) suggested more generally that social support is a dynamic coping resource.

Social resources can bolster coping efforts by providing emotional support that promotes feelings of self-esteem and self-confidence (Carpenter & Scott, 1992; Heller, Swindle, & Dusenbury, 1986; King, Reis, Porter, & Norsen, 1993). The sense of being supported can enable an individual to face a stressful situation that otherwise might seem overwhelming (Sarason, Sarason, & Pierce, 1990). Moreover, social resources can provide information and guidance that aid in assessing threat and in planning coping strategies (Carpenter & Scott, 1992; Cohen & McKay, 1984). Information or advice provided by a confidant may increase the likelihood that a person will rely on logical analysis, information seeking, or active problem solving under high stressors (Wills, 1985).

Empirical Evidence Relating to Coping Determinants

In a series of longitudinal studies of two community samples, we examined personal and social stress-resistance resources (Holahan & Moos, 1981, 1986, 1987b).

We began with an initial representative sample of over 500 adults, and then used a second representative sample of over 400 adults to cross-validate and extend our findings. Personality strengths such as self-confidence, family support, and less reliance on avoidance coping predicted lower levels of depression over a 1 year period, even when prior depression was controlled (Holahan & Moos, 1986, 1987b).

Turning to an examination of the interrelationships among the predictive factors, we found that individuals in supportive families engage in more active, problem-focused, and less avoidance coping than do individuals in less supportive families (Cronkite & Moos, 1984; Holahan & Moos, 1987a). For example, adults who enjoyed more social resources from their extended family and friends relied more on approach coping, such as positive reappraisal and seeking guidance and support, and less on avoidance coping, especially emotional discharge (Moos, Brennan, Fondacaro, & Moos, 1990). Similarly, increases in family support over a 1 year interval were related to increases in problem-solving coping among women and to a decline in emotional discharge among men (Fondacaro & Moos, 1987).

We also examined the associations between social resources among youth and their use of different sets of coping responses (Ebata & Moos, 1994). Youth who reported better interpersonal relationships with parents, siblings, extended family, and friends tended to favor approach coping responses such as positive reappraisal, seeking guidance, and problem solving. Youth with more positive relationships also were less likely to rely on emotional discharge.

Other investigators have obtained comparable findings. For example, Parkes (1986) reported that student nurses used more approach coping in dealing with serious work problems when support from supervisors was high. Mann and Zautra (1989) found that among women with rheumatoid arthritis, spousal support was linked to more reliance on cognitive restructuring and information seeking, and less wishful thinking.

A RESOURCES MODEL OF COPING

Based on these findings, we proposed an integrative model of the associations between personal and social resources, life stressors, coping strategies, and psychological adjustment that unified earlier work on predicting adjustment and on predicting coping responses (Holahan & Moos, 1990, 1994). In the model shown in Figure 8.1, personal and social resources relate to subsequent functioning both directly and indirectly through coping strategies. Personal resources include personality strengths such as self-confidence, self-esteem, and dispositional optimism. Social resources include emotional support as well as guidance and assistance from family members, friends, and one's broader social network.

The relative strength of the predictive associations in the model is presumed to vary with the level of life stressors. Because coping is a stabilizing factor that helps maintain psychological adjustment during stressful periods (Lazarus & Folkman, 1984), the advantage of coping efforts should be greatest under high stressors. Thus, under high stressors, we predicted that resources would relate to functioning primarily indirectly through coping strategies. Under low stressors, where coping is less neces-

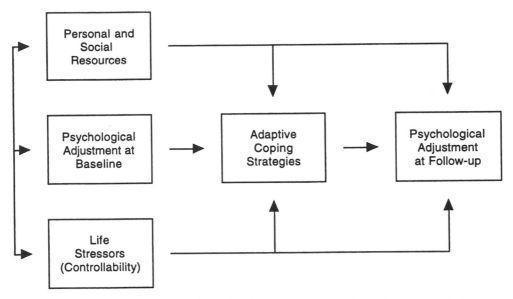

FIGURE 8.1 Integrative model of the associations between personal and social resources, life stressors, coping strategies, and psychological adjustment (adapted from Holahan & Moos, 1991, 1994).

sary (Okun, Sandler, & Baumann, 1988), we predicted that resources would relate to functioning primarily in a direct way.

An Empirical Test of the Model

We tested these hypotheses with a sample of over 400 respondents in a structural equation model (Holahan & Moos, 1991). LISREL 7 (Jöreskog & Sörbom, 1989) was used to estimate the parameters and overall goodness of fit of the model in a two-group analysis, in which respondents were divided into high and low stressor groups. The high stressor group experienced multiple (two or more) negative life events during the year prior to the follow-up assessment; the low stressor group experienced no negative life events during the year. These conservative models remove the influence of prior depression from both coping and depression at follow-up.

Personality strengths of self-confidence and an easygoing disposition and family support operated prospectively over 4 years, either directly or indirectly through coping responses, to protect individuals from becoming depressed. As hypothesized, the pattern of predictive associations differed under high and low stressors. Under high stressors, resources were related to future psychological adjustment indirectly, through their link to more approach coping strategies. Under low stressors, resources were directly related to psychological adjustment.

The findings under high stressors demonstrate the central role of coping in integrative predictive models of stress resistance. Under high stressors, adaptive personality characteristics and family support operate prospectively as coping resources; in turn, coping mediates between initial resources and later health status.

Research on the passive coping strategy of *rumination* (Nolen-Hoeksema, Parker, & Larson, 1994) also has demonstrated that maladaptive coping responses mediate between poor social support and increased depressive symptomology. Investigators who have examined the personal coping resource of dispositional optimism have obtained further support for the mediational role of coping in the stress and coping process. Among women coping with breast cancer and with breast biopsy, more active coping efforts serve as mediating routes through which optimism relates to better psychological adjustment (Carver et al., 1993; Stanton & Snider, 1993). Similarly, among first-year students adjusting to college, active coping strategies mediate the relation between optimism and subsequent adjustment (Aspinwall & Taylor, 1992).

REFINING AND EXTENDING THE MODEL

We have attempted to refine and extend the basic resources model of coping in response to recent conceptualization about the nature of social support, and about the stress and coping process more generally. For example, consistent with contemporary thinking in the social support field (Rook, 1992), we felt that the model needed to be broadened to encompass negative, as well as positive, aspects of social relationships. In addition, congruent with more refined conceptualizations of the coping process, we focused on how characteristics of life stressors may moderate the role of coping.

COPING ASSETS AND COPING LIABILITIES

Researchers traditionally have focused almost entirely on the health-promoting aspects of social support, ignoring the troublesome aspects of social ties (Coyne & DeLongis, 1986; Rook, 1992). In fact, support and conflict occur together in most relationships (Abbey, Andrews, & Halman, 1995; Coyne & Downey, 1991; Pierce, Sarason, & Sarason, 1991). In significant part, the negative aspects of social relationships involve ongoing social stressors (Coyne & Downey, 1991; Rook, 1992). As Coyne, Ellard, and Smith (1990) observed, individuals who have little or no support often need to be extricated from conflictual and stressful social ties.

Longitudinal studies that encompass both positive and negative aspects of relationships show that the negative aspects are as important as the positive ones in predicting psychological adjustment (see Abbey et al., 1995; Helgeson, 1993; Pagel, Erdly, & Becker, 1987; Vinokur & van Ryn, 1993). Especially intriguing conceptually, we speculated that negative aspects of relationships might be one key way in which social context influences reliance on less adaptive coping responses. We reasoned that social stressors may erode coping efforts just as social support enhances them (Ebata & Moos, 1994; Fondacaro & Moos, 1989). Yet, no research had systematically examined both positive and negative aspects of relationships in the context of a resources model of coping.

Coping with Cardiac Illness

Thus, we broadened our resources model of coping by examining negative as well as positive aspects of social relationships. Social relationships were indexed broadly to encompass immediate family members and the more diverse social network of friends, relatives, and coworkers. We examined this expanded model in a 4-year prospective design with 183 late-middle-aged individuals with cardiac disorders (Holahan, Moos, Holahan, & Brennan, 1997).

Cardiac illness is a major, negative life event involving multiple disruptions across physical, personal, and social domains (Bennett, 1992). Accordingly, cardiovascular disease necessitates a wide variety of cognitive and behavioral coping strategies (Ewart, 1990). Depressive symptoms are common among cardiac patients (Kaplan, 1988; Schleifer et al., 1989), and a significant subset of patients fail to achieve emotional adjustment 3 to 5 years after a heart attack (Havik & Maelands, 1990).

Confirming and broadening earlier research on the adverse side of social bonds (Abbey et al., 1995; Helgeson, 1993; Vinokur & van Ryn, 1993), the pattern of correlations showed that negative aspects of relationships were as strongly related to less adaptive coping efforts and poorer adjustment as positive aspects of relationships were related to more adaptive coping efforts and better adjustment. Moreover, social stressors added significantly to predicting adaptive coping efforts after accounting for the variance in coping predicted by social support. Also, as predicted, the link between social context and subsequent functioning reflected an indirect path through coping strategies.

A conceptually key aspect of these findings is that they broadened our resources model of coping to include psychosocial liabilities as well as psychosocial assets. We strengthened and extended current work by demonstrating a common mechanism whereby both positive and negative components of relationships are linked to psychological adjustment. Rook (1990) has argued that researchers need to identify the processes through which social stressors relate to diminished well-being.

Both social support and social stressors affect psychological adjustment, in part through their influence on coping efforts. Whereas ongoing social support enhances adaptive coping efforts, ongoing social stressors erode them. For example, in summarizing their research on couples dealing with a heart attack, Coyne et al. (1990) concluded that the feeling of support might best be construed as being freed from the social conflicts and undermining experiences that can burden coping efforts.

These findings highlight the dynamic role of ongoing stressors in the stress and coping process. Ongoing stressors increase demands while they simultaneously weaken the mechanism for managing adaptive challenge. This may be especially true of social stressors (Rook, 1992), which Bolger, DeLongis, Kessler, and Schilling (1989) observed are "by far the most upsetting of all daily stressors" (p. 814). A combination of multiple, acute stressors may similarly erode coping efforts (Ebata & Moos, 1994).

We found, as have other investigators (see Abbey et al., 1995; Helgeson, 1993), that negative components of social ties are reported much less frequently than are positive features of relationships. This finding underscores the power of negative interactions. As Helgeson (1993) observed:

The relative infrequency with which most negative social interactions occur, and their unexpectedness after the onset of chronic illness, may make the experience more vivid and more consequential. (p. 838)

CONTROLLABILITY AS A MODERATOR

Some theorists have suggested that the adaptive significance of approach versus avoidance coping strategies may depend on the controllability of the stressors that are confronted (Cutrona & Russell, 1990; Folkman, 1984). For example, Moos and Schaefer (1993) argued:

Approach coping processes should be most effective in situations that are appraised as changeable and controllable.... An individual's coping style needs to fit the situation. (p. 251)

The controllability of life stressors may moderate the role of coping both by shaping the choice of coping strategies and by influencing coping outcomes. For example, when stressors are viewed as more controllable, individuals may use more approach and less avoidance coping (Folkman, Lazarus, Dunkle-Schetter, DeLongis, & Gruen, 1986; Forsythe & Compas, 1987; Scheier, Weintraub, & Carver, 1986). Similarly, an internal locus of control is associated with more direct coping efforts and less attempts at suppression (Parkes, 1984).

Moreover, some cross-sectional findings suggest that psychological outcomes are influenced by the fit between appraisals of controllability and the choice of coping strategies. For example, in nonpsychiatric samples, Vitaliano and his associates (Vitaliano, DeWolfe, Maiuro, Russo, & Katon, 1990) found that more reliance on problem-focused coping and less on emotion-focused coping predicted less depression only when stressors were appraised as controllable. Similarly, Forsythe and Compas (1987) reported that a higher proportion of active, problem-focused coping strategies was associated with less psychological distress only when events were viewed as controllable.

Coping with the College Transition

Thus, we conducted a study to refine our resources model of coping by examining the moderating role of appraisals of controllability on the coping process (Valentiner, Holahan, & Moos, 1994). We examined this more refined resources model in a 2-year prospective framework with 175 college students. During the transition from high school to college, the adaptive demands associated with becoming self-reliant require young adults to learn and execute active, problem-focused coping strategies (Compas, Malcarne, & Fondacaro, 1988; Zirkel, 1992). Moreover, this developmental transition presents significant adaptive challenges for many students (Compas, Wagner, Slavin, & Vannatta, 1986; Zirkel & Cantor, 1990).

Two groups were formed on the basis of students' appraisals of event controllability. A *controllable event* group was comprised of students who reported that they had considerable control over the most important problem they had faced ($n = 74$). An *uncontrollable event* group was comprised of students who reported that they had little control over the major problem they had faced ($n = 100$). Family support was indexed broadly to encompass maternal support, paternal support, and low marital conflict between parents.

The results of a multigroup LISREL analysis are presented graphically in Figure 8.2, which shows standardized estimates of parameters in the structural model. To simplify the presentation, the measurement model is not depicted. Parameter estimates for all hypothesized paths in the structural model are significant at the .01 level. As predicted, with controllable stressors, initial family support related to changes in psychological adjustment indirectly through coping strategies; with uncontrollable stressors, family support related directly to changes in adjustment. These results are consistent with research on the importance of the family environment to the adjustment of older adolescents (Phares & Compas, 1992; Rice, Cole, & Lapsley, 1990).

Especially important, these findings demonstrate that the role of coping in the stress process varies as a function of appraisals of event controllability. Appraisals of event controllability change both the degree to which social support influences coping and the association between coping and adjustment. When individuals confronted a

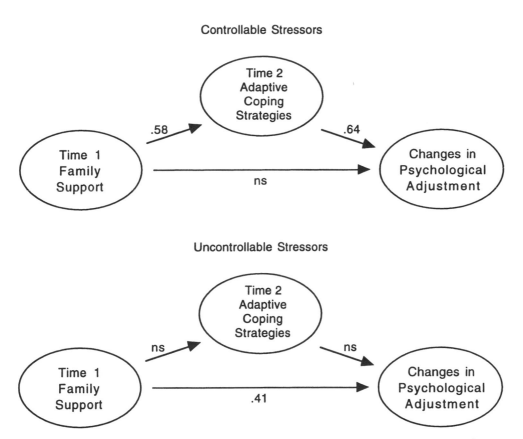

FIGURE 8.2 Results of the LISREL test of the structural equation model for a multisample analysis reflecting students who faced controllable versus uncontrollable life stressors (adapted from Valentiner et al., 1994). (*$p < .01$; *ns* indicates a nonsignificant parameter.)

controllable event, family social context supported adaptive coping. Moreover, the choice of coping strategy predicted changes in psychological adjustment.

When events were uncontrollable, however, the family context was not associated with adaptive coping, and coping was not linked with adjustment. Instead, family support was related directly to psychological adjustment.

This pattern of findings integrates research on controllability and coping choices (Folkman et al., 1986; Scheier et al., 1986) with research showing that psychological outcomes reflect the fit between stressor controllability and coping choices (Forsythe & Compas, 1987; Vitaliano et al., 1990). More generally, by pointing to the role of controllability in shaping coping effectiveness, these findings suggest that individuals who flexibly tailor their coping to situational constraints should show better adaptation than persons who rely consistently on a narrow coping repertoire (see Miller, 1992).

DIRECTIONS FOR FUTURE RESEARCH

More remains to be learned to achieve a full understanding of the role of personal and social resources in the stress and coping process. Especially important, the model needs to more fully reflect the dynamic and transactional nature of the coping process (see Lazarus & Folkman, 1984). This involves developing a more comprehensive picture of the links between personal and social resources, as well as among contextual variables. It also involves clarifying the underlying mechanisms through which resources shape coping responses.

INDIVIDUAL DIFFERENCES IN SOCIAL RESOURCES

Research is needed to examine individual differences in social resources. Although social support generally has been conceptualized as an environmental provision, data demonstrating considerable stability in social support and links to developmental precursors suggest that social support also may operate as an individual difference variable (Sarason, Sarason, & Shearin, 1986). For example, Cohen (1992) noted that individual differences play a role in the receipt of support; self-confident individuals with better social skills are more able to establish and utilize support networks.

Moreover, Lakey and Cassady (1990) argued that perceived social support functions partly as a cognitive personality variable that influences how supportive interactions are interpreted and remembered. Central to the salutary role of social relationships are people's *expectations* abut the likely receipt of support (Pierce et al., 1991). For example, Coyne et al., (1990) suggested that social support questionnaires may elicit general appraisals of the quality of aid and commitment across the history of a relationship rather than recent, specific, supportive interchanges.

In a similar vein, Sarason, Sarason, and Pierce (1990, 1994) noted that the meaning an individual attributes to the supportive efforts of network members shapes how these relationships influence an individuals' coping responses and adaptation. For example, Sarason et al. (1990) noted that "the most active ingredient of social support may be individuals' belief that they have people who value and care about them and who are willing to try to help them if they need assistance" (p. 137–138).

INTERDEPENDENCIES AMONG CONTEXTUAL FACTORS

Research also is needed to examine interdependencies among the predictive variables in the model. A full understanding of the coping process needs to reflect feedback influences among stressors, personal and social resources, and coping factors. Such feedback loops occur at every stage in the model and may be especially relevant to processes of change in the predictive variables (Holahan & Moos, 1994; Schaefer & Moos, 1992). For example, a dynamic interplay between coping resources and coping responses is central to crisis growth (Holahan & Moos, 1990).

Resilience develops from confronting stressful experiences and coping with them effectively; novel crisis situations promote new coping skills, which can lead to new personal and social resources (Schaefer & Moos, 1992). For example, self-reliance often increases when people acquire new coping skills, become more independent, and successfully manage new roles or seemingly overwhelming tasks and changes (Wallerstein, 1986). Similarly, life crises often necessitate help seeking that can foster deeper social bonds and enduring confidant relationships (Dhooper, 1983).

More research also is needed for a fuller understanding of how different types of life stressors and social resources influence each other. Life stressors can alter social support (Quittner, Glueckauf, & Jackson, 1990), and deficits in social support can increase the probability of experiencing life stressors (Russell & Cutrona, 1991). For example, Moos, Fenn, and Billings (1988) found that ongoing stressors and a lack of social resources predict new stressful events; in turn, such events contribute to a rise in chronic stressors and an erosion of social resources.

In terms of mutual influences between stressors and resources, stressors and a lack of support may often be closely connected in domains where there is a single source of both stressors and support. For example, in a sample of adults, Brennan and Moos (1990) found that ongoing difficulties involving finances, spouse, and children were associated with fewer resources in these domains. In contrast, in life domains where there are multiple sources of problems and assistance, such as friends, stressors and social resources were more independent.

A related issue that needs to be further explored involves interdependencies between the providers and recipients of support, such as between family members (Coyne & Smith, 1991). For example, Coyne et al. (1990) observed that deciding whether to give both emotional and practical help to a spouse versus only emotional support can be difficult. Offering practical assistance may feel rewarding to the provider, but in some circumstances, it can leave the recipient with a sense of helplessness.

In studying children and families, we discovered that factors that predict the health of one family member operate indirectly to affect the health of that family member's spouse and children (Cronkite & Moos, 1984; Holahan & Moos, 1987b). Not only are one spouse's symptoms stressful for the other, but each partner's personal resources and coping strategies affect the other partner's reaction to and selection of coping responses. The link between a partner's stressors and an individual's own depression may be mediated by a reduction in family support (Mitchell, Cronkite, & Moos, 1983).

EXPLANATORY MECHANISMS

In addition, research also is needed to identify the psychological mechanisms through which social resources foster adaptive coping. We have speculated (Holahan & Moos, 1991) that resources operate through relatively enduring patterns of self-referent thought. Both positive and negative aspects of social relationships likely relate to coping through the secondary appraisal process, in which the individual assesses what can be done to manage a stressor situation (see Lazarus & Folkman, 1984).

An especially promising construct in this regard is perceived self-efficacy (Sarason et al, 1990), that is, people's beliefs in their capability to execute the behaviors necessary to exercise control over adaptive demands (Bandura, 1982). Psychosocial assets may bolster perceptions of coping self-efficacy, which in turn aid in planning and executing more active coping efforts (Holahan & Moos, 1994). For example, self-efficacy for coping has been shown to mediate the effect of perceived social support on psychological adjustment among women in stressful circumstances (Cutrona & Troutman, 1986; Major et al., 1990). Conversely, psychosocial liabilities may erode coping self-efficacy by undercutting self-confidence, as well as by raising doubts about the availability of support (Krause, 1995).

Further, appraisals of event controllability likely influence the mechanisms through which perceived social support may function as a protective factor (Valentiner et al., 1994). With controllable challenges, perceptions of support may affect psychological adjustment indirectly by fostering self-efficacy. In contrast, with uncontrollable demands, perceived support may affect psychological adjustment directly by enhancing feelings of attachment and social integration, as well as by bolstering an individual's sense of self-esteem and self-worth (Krause & Borawski-Clark, 1994).

In considering the mechanisms through which social resources shape coping responses, it may be especially important to examine the source and type of social relationship (Cohen, 1992). Rook (1990) argued that more fine-grained analyses of both social support and social strain need to replace more global and undifferentiated conceptualizations. For example, measures of distinct, supportive behaviors form specific providers predict perceptions of being helped more accurately than do general indices of social support (Cutrona & Russell, 1990; Dakof and Taylor, 1990; Dean, Kolody, & Wood, 1990). These differences in perceived support may reflect correspondingly different underlying psychological processes.

CONCLUSIONS

Based on the pattern of findings reviewed here, we may summarize what we know presently about resources and coping. In general, the model integrates research on social support with research on the coping process. Most important, the findings demonstrate that coping plays a central mediating role in the link between adaptive resources and adjustment. Personal and social resources relate to psychological adjustment in part through fostering adaptive coping efforts, with the mediating role of coping responses especially apparent under high adaptive demands and in potentially controllable situations.

In addition, the model integrates knowledge about both positive and negative aspects of social relationships. Consistent with current reconceptualizations of social support, we found that negative aspects of relationships are as strongly related to less adaptive coping efforts and poor adjustment as positive aspects of relationships are related to more adaptive coping efforts and better adjustment.

Especially important, coping responses provide a common mechanism whereby both positive and negative components of relationships are linked to functioning. Whereas ongoing social support enhances coping efforts, ongoing social stressors erode coping efforts.

Furthermore, the model integrates current knowledge about the central role of appraisals of stressor controllability in the stress and coping process. Appraisals of event controllability moderate both the degree to which social support influences coping and the effectiveness of coping responses. With controllable stressors, social support relates to changes in adjustment indirectly through coping strategies; in contrast, with uncontrollable stressors, social support relates directly to changes in psychological adjustment.

More broadly, our findings are consistent with a stress-buffering conceptualization of social support. The resources model illustrates *how* social support functions as a health-protective factor under adversity. As Thoits (1992) noted, both conceptually and operationally, we view perceived support in the context of problems—as an expectation of help when needed. Sarason et al. (1990) similarly observed: "Knowing that one is loved and that others will do all they can when a problem arises may be the essence of social support" (p. 138).

At an applied level, the conceptualization of social support we have outlined also has implications for social and clinical interventions at both the individual and contextual levels. Each path in the model shown in Figure 8.1 identifies a process that is potentially alterable. An appreciation of the coping process can broaden our understanding of the determinants of psychiatric disorders and of the process of recovery from psychopathology and addiction (Moos, Finney, & Cronkite, 1990; Swindel, Cronkite, & Moos, 1989).

Recognizing that stressful or relapse-inducing life situations inevitably occur, clinicians can identify coping skills and associated coping resources that clients can utilize to help them deal with these situations more effectively (see Moos & Schaefer, 1993). Such information can be used in clinical case descriptions to help clinicians understand how their clients manage specific stressful circumstances, identify coping factors associated with symptom remission and relapse, and plan intervention programs that target clients' precise coping deficits.

Because a family member's stressors and maladaptive functioning present a health risk for his or her spouse and children, the framework also is relevant to treatment and preventive efforts within a family systems perspective (Holahan & Moos, 1994). Moreover, consistent with the resources model, prevention and treatment programs that strengthen social resources can promote effective coping as well.

We hope our findings can help to stimulate further inquiry in what promises to be an exciting new era of research on the nature and dynamics of social relationships. Especially important, a focus on coping and coping resources encourages a competence-enhancing view of people's adaptive strengths. Most central, the resources model illustrates the individual's potential for resilience and personal growth in the face of challenge. Yet, the model also recognizes that, in major part, the individual's capacity to thrive in the face of adversity is less a solitary effort than an expression of the shared strengths that constitute the human community.

ACKNOWLEDGMENTS

Parts of this chapter were adapted from Holahan and Moos (1994) and Holahan, Moos, and Schaefer (in press). The research summarized was supported in part by National Heart, Lung, and Blood Institute Grant No. 1-RO3-HL48063; NIAAA Grant No. AA06699; and by Department of Veterans Affairs Health Services Research and Development Service funds.

REFERENCES

Abbey, A., Andrews, F. M., & Halman, J. (1995). Provision and receipt of social support and disregard: What is their impact on the marital life quality of infertile and fertile couples? *Journal of Personality and Social Psychology, 68,* 455–469.

Aspinwall, L. G., & Taylor, S. E. (1992). Modeling cognitive adaptation: A longitudinal investigation of the impact of individual differences and coping on college adjustment and performance. *Journal of Personality and Social Psychology, 63,* 989–1003.

Bandura, A. (1982). Self-efficacy mechanism in human agency. *American Psychologist, 37,* 122–147.

Bennett, S. J. (1992). Perceived threats of individuals recovering from myocardial infarction. *Heart and Lung, 21,* 322–326.

Bolger, N., DeLongis, A., Kessler, R.C., & Schilling, E.A. (1989). Effects of daily stress on negative mood. *Journal of Personality and Social Psychology, 57,* 808–818.

Brennan, P. L., & Moos, R. H. (1990). Life stressors, social resources, and late-life problem drinking. *Psychology and Aging, 5,* 491–501.

Carpenter, B. N., & Scott, S. M. (1992). Interpersonal aspects of coping. In B. N. Carpenter (Ed.), *Personal Coping: Theory, research, and application* (pp. 93–109). New York: Praeger.

Carver, C. S., Pozo, C., Haris, S. D., Noriega, V., Scheier, M. F., Robinson, D. S., Ketcham, A. S., Moffat, F. L. Jr., & Clark, K. C. (1993). How coping mediates the effect of optimism on distress: A study of women with early stage breast cancer. *Journal of Personality and Social Psychology, 65,* 375–390.

Cohen, S. (1992). Stress, social support, and disorder. In H. O. F. Veiel & U. Baumann (Eds.), *The meaning and measurement of social support* (pp. 109–124). New York: Hemisphere.

Cohen, S., & Edwards, J. R. (1989). Personality characteristics as moderators of the relationship between stress and disorder. In R. W. J. Neufeld (Ed.), *Advances in the investigation of psychological stress* (pp. 235–283). New York: Wiley.

Cohen, S., & McKay, G. (1984). Social support, stress, and the buffering hypothesis: A theoretical analysis. In A. Baum, J. E. Singer, & S. E. Taylor (Eds.), *Handbook of psychology and health* (Vol. 4, pp. 253–267). Hillsdale, NJ: Erlbaum.

Cohen, S., & Williamson, G. M. (1991). Stress and infectious disease in humans. *Psychological Bulletin, 109,* 5–24.

Cohen S. & Wills, T. A. (1985). Stress, social support, and the buffering hypothesis. *Psychological Bulletin, 98,* 310–357.

Compas, B. E., Malcarne, V., & Fondacaro, K. (1988). Coping with stressful events in older children and young adolescents. *Journal of Consulting and Clinical Psychology,56,* 405–411.

Compas, B. E., Wagner, B. M., Slavin, L. A., & Vannatta, K. (1986). A prospective study of life events, social support, and psychological symptomology during the transition from high school to college. *American Journal of Community Psychology, 14,* 241-257.

Coyne, J. C., & DeLongis, A. (1986). Going beyond social support: The role of social relationships in adaptation. *Journal of Consulting and Clinical Psychology,54,* 454-460.

Coyne, J. C. & Downey, G. (1991). Social factors and psychopathology: Stress, social support, and coping processes. *Annual Review of Psychology, 42,* 401-425.

Coyne, J. C., Ellard, J. H., & Smith, D. A. F. (1990). Social support, interdependence, and the dilemmas of helping. In B. R. Sarason, I. G. Sarason, & G. R. Pierce (Eds.), *Social Support: An interactional view* (pp. 129-149). New York: Wiley.

Coyne, J. C., & Smith, D. A. F. (1991). Couples coping with a myocardial infarction: A contextual perspective on wives' distress. *Journal of Personality and Social Psychology,61,* 404-412.

Cronkite, R. C., & Moos, R. H. (1984). The role of predisposing and moderating factors in the stress-illness relationship. *Journal of Health and Social Behavior, 25,* 372-393.

Cutrona, C. E., & Russell, D. W. (1990). Type of social support and specific stress: Toward a theory of optimal matching. In B. R. Sarason, I. G. Sarason, & G. R. Pierce (Eds.), *Social support: An interactional view* (pp. 319-366). New York: Wiley.

Cutrona, C. E., & Troutman, B. R. (1986). Social support, infant temperament, and parenting self-efficacy: A mediational model of postpartum depression. *Child Development, 57,* 1507-1518.

Dakof, G., & Taylor, S. E. (1990). Victims' perceptions of social support: What is helpful from whom? *Journal of Personality and Social Psychology, 58,* 80-89.

Dean, A., Kolody, B., & Wood, P. (1990). Effects of social support from various sources on depression in elderly persons. *Journal of Health and Social Behavior, 31,* 148-161.

Dhooper, S. S. (1983). Family coping with the crisis of heart attack. *Social Work in Health Care, 9,* 15-31.

Ebata, A. T., & Moos, R. H. (1991). Coping and adjustment in distressed and healthy adolescents. *Journal of Applied Developmental Psychology, 12,* 33-54.

Ebata, A. T., & Moos, R. H. (1994). Personal, situational, and contextual determinations of coping in adolescents. *Journal of Research on Adolescence, 4,* 99-1225.

Ewart, C. K. (1990). A social problem-solving approach to behavior change in coronary heart disease. In S. Schumaker, E. Schron, & J. Ockene (Eds), *Handbook of health behavior change* (pp. 153-190). New York: Springer.

Folkman, S. (1984). Personal control and stress and coping processes: A theoretical analysis. *Journal of Personality and Social Psychology, 46,* 839-852.

Folkman, S., Lazarus, R. S., Dunkel-Schetter, C., DeLongis, A., & Gruen, R. J. (1986). Dynamics of a stressful encounter: Cognitive appraisal, coping, and encounter outcomes. *Journal of Personality and Social Psychology, 50,* 992-1003.

Fondacaro, M. R., & Moos, R. H. (1987). Social support and coping: A longitudinal analysis. *American Journal of Community Psychology, 15,* 653-673.

Fondacaro, M. R., & Moos, R. H. (1989). Life stressors and coping: A longitudinal analysis among depressed and nondepressed adults. *Journal of Community Psychology, 17,* 330-340.

Forsythe, C. J., & Compas, B. E. (1987). Interaction of cognitive appraisals of stressful events and coping: Testing the goodness of fit hypothesis. *Cognitive Therapy and Research, 11,* 473-485.

Havik, O. E., & Maelands, J. G. (1990). Patterns of emotional reactions after a myocardial infarction. *Journal of Psychosomatic Research, 34,* 271-285.

Helgeson, V. S. (1993). Two important distinctions in social support: Kind of support and perceived versus received. *Journal of Applied Social Psychology, 23,* 825-845.

Heller, K., Swindle, R. W., & Dusenbury, L. (1986). Component social support processes: Comments and integration. *Journal of Consulting and Clinical Psychology, 54,* 466-470.

Holahan, C. J., & Moos, R. H. (1981). Social support and psychological distress: A longitudinal analysis. *Journal of Abnormal Psychology, 90,* 365-370.

Holahan, C. J., & Moos, R. H. (1986). Personality, coping, and family resources in stress resistance: A longitudinal analysis. *Journal of Personality and Social Psychology, 52,* 389-395.

Holahan, C. J., & Moos, R. H. (1987a). Personal and contextual determinants of coping strategies. *Journal of Personality and Social Psychology, 52,* 946-955.

Holahan, C. J., & Moos, R. H. (1987b). Risk, resistance, and psychological distress: A longitudinal analysis with adults and children. *Journal of Abnormal Psychology, 96,* 3-13.

Holahan, C. J. & Moos, R. H. (1990). Life stressors, resistance factors, and psychological health: An extension of the stress resistance paradigm. *Journal of Personality and Social Psychology, 58*, 909-917.

Holahan, C. J., & Moos, R. H. (1991). Life stressors, personal and social resources, and depression: A four-year structural model. *Journal of Abnormal Psychology, 100*, 31-38.

Holahan, C. J., & Moos, R. H. (1994). Life stressors and mental health: Advances in conceptualizing stress resistance. In W. R. Avison & I. H. Gotlib (Eds.), *Stress and mental health:Contemporary issues and prospects for the future* (pp. 213-238). New York: Plenum.

Holahan, C. J., Moos, R. H., Holahan C. K., & Brennan, P. L. (1997). Social context, coping strategies, and depressive symptoms: An expanded model with cardiac patients. *Journal of Personality and Social Psychology, 72*, 918-928.

House, J. S., Landis, K. R., & Umberson, D. (1988). Social relationships and health. *Science, 241*, 540-545.

Jöreskog, K. G., & Sörbom, D. (1989). *LISREL 7: A guide to the program and applications* (2nd ed.). Chicago, Il.: SPSS Inc.

Kaplan, R. M. (1988). Health-related quality of life in cardiovascular disease. *Journal of Consulting and Clinical Psychology, 56*, 382-392.

Kessler, R. C., Price, R. H., & Wortman, C. B. (1985). Social factors in psychopathology: Stress, social support, and coping processes. *Annual Review of Psychology, 36*, 531-572.

King, K. B., Reis, H. T., Porter, L. A., & Norsen, L. H. (1993). Social support and the long-term recovery from coronary artery surgery: Effects on patients and spouses. *Health Psychology, 12*, 56-63.

Krause, N. (1995). Negative interaction and satisfaction with social support among older adults. *Journal of Gerontology: Psychological Sciences, 508*, 59-73.

Krause, N., & Borawski-Clark, E. (1994). Clarifying the functions of social support in later life. *Research on Aging, 16*, 251-279.

Lakey, B., & Cassady, P. B. (1990). Cognitive processes in perceived social support. *Journal of Personality and Social Psychology, 59*, 337-343.

Lazarus, R. S. & Folkman, S. (1984). *Stress, appraisal, and coping.* New York: Springer.

Lefcourt, H. M. (1992). Perceived control, personal effectiveness, and emotional states. In B. N. Carpenter (Ed.), *Personal coping: Theory, research, and application* (pp. 111-131). New York: Praeger.

Lepore, S. J., Evans, G. W., & Schneider, M. L. (1991). Dynamic role of social support in the link between chronic stress and psychological distress. *Journal of Personality and Social Psychology, 61*, 899-909.

Major, B., Cozzarelli, C., Sciacchitano, A. M., Cooper, M. L., Testa, M., & Mueller, P. M. (1990). Perceived social support, self-efficacy, and adjustment to abortion. *Journal of Personality and Social Psychology, 59*, 452-463.

Mann, S. L., & Zautra, A. J. (1989). Spouse criticism and support: Their association with coping and psychological adjustment among women with rheumatoid arthritis. *Journal of Personality and Social Psychology, 56*, 608-617.

Miller, S. M. (1992). Individual differences in the coping process: What we know and when we know it. In B. N. Carpenter (Ed.), *Personal coping: Theory, research, and application* (pp. 77-91). New York: Praeger.

Mitchell, R. E., Cronkite, R. C., & Moos, R. H. (1983). Stress, coping, and depression among married couples. *Journal of Abnormal Psychology, 92*, 433-448.

Moos, R. H., Brennan, P. L., Fondacaro, M., & Moos, B. S. (1990). Approach and avoidance coping responses among older problem and nonproblem drinkers. *Psychology and Aging, 5*, 31-40.

Moos, R. H., Fenn, C., & Billings, A. (1988). Life stressors and social resources: An integrated assessment approach. *Social Science and Medicine, 27*, 999-1002.

Moos, R. H., Finney, J. W., & Cronkite, R. C. (1990). *Alcoholism treatment: Process and outcome.* New York: Oxford University Press.

Moos, R. H., & Schaefer, J. A. (1993). Coping resources and processes: Current concepts and measures. In L. Goldberger & S. Breznitz (Eds.), *Handbook of stress: Theoretical and clinical aspects* (2nd ed., pp. 234-257). New York: Free Press.

Nolen-Hoeksema, S., Parker, L. E., & Larson, J. (1994). Ruminative coping with depressed mood following loss. *Journal of Personality and Social Psychology, 67*, 92-104.

Okun, M. A., Sandler, I. N., & Baumann, D. J. (1988). Buffer and booster effects as event-support transactions. *American Journal of Community Psychology, 16*, 435-449.

Pagel, M. D., Erdly, W. W., & Becker, J. (1987). Social networks: We get by with (and in spite of) a little help from our friends. *Journal of Personality and Social Psychology, 53*, 793-804.

Parkes, K. R. (1984). Locus of control, cognitive appraisal, and coping in stressful episodes. *Journal of Personality and Social Psychology, 46,* 655–668.

Parkes, K. R. (1986). Coping in stressful episodes: The role of individual differences, environmental factors, and situational characteristics. *Journal of Personality and Social Psychology, 51,* 1277–1292.

Phares, V., & Compas, B. E. (1992). The role of fathers in child and adolescent psychopathology: Make room for daddy. *Psychological Bulletin, 11,* 387–412.

Pierce, G. R., Sarason, I. G., & Sarason, B. R. (1991). General relationship-based perceptions of social support: Are two constructs better than one? *Journal of Personality and Social Psychology, 61,* 1028–1039.

Quittner, A. L., Glueckauf, R. L., & Jackson, D. N. (1990). Chronic parenting stress: Moderating versus mediating effects of social support. *Journal of Personality and Social Psychology, 59,* 1266–1279.

Rice, K. G., Cole, D. A., & Lapsley, D. K. (1990). Separation–individuation, family cohesion, and adjustment to college: Measurement validation and a test of a theoretical model. *Journal of Counseling Psychology, 37,* 195–202.

Rohde, P., Lewinsohn, P. M., Tilson, M., & Seeley, J. R. (1990). Dimensionality of coping and its relation to depression. *Journal of Personality and Social Psychology, 58,* 499–511.

Rook, K. S. (1990). Parallels in the study of social support and social strain. *Journal of Social and Clinical Psychology, 9,* 118–132.

Rook, K. S. (1992). Detrimental aspects of social relationships: Taking stock of an emerging literature. In H. O. F. Veiel & U. Baumann (Eds.), *The meaning and measurement of social support* (pp. 157–169). New York: Hemisphere.

Roth, S., & Cohen, L. J. (1986). Approach, avoidance, and coping with stress. *American Psychologist, 41,* 813–819.

Russell, D. W., & Cutrona, C. E. (1991). Social support, stress, and depressive symptoms among the elderly: Test of a process model. *Psychology and Aging, 6,* 190–201.

Sarason, I. G., Sarason, B. R., & Pierce, G. R. (1990). Social support: The search for theory. *Journal of Social and Clinical Psychology, 9,* 133–147.

Sarason, I. G., Sarason, B. R., & Pierce, G. R. (1994). Social support: Global and relationship-based levels of analysis. *Journal of Social and Personal Relationships, 11,* 295–312.

Sarason, I. G., Sarason, B. R., & Shearin, E. N. (1986). Social support as an individual difference variable: Its stability, origins, and relational aspects. *Journal of Personality and Social Psychology, 50,* 845–855.

Schaefer, J. A., & Moos, R. H. (1992). Life crises and personal growth. In B. N. Carpenter (Ed.), *Personal coping: Theory, research, and application* (pp. 149–170). New York: Praeger.

Scheier, M. F., Weintrab, J. K., & Carver, C. S. (1986). Coping with stress: Divergent strategies of optimists and pessimists. *Journal of Personality and Social Psychology, 51,* 1257–1262.

Schleifer, S., Macari-Hinson, M., Coyle, D., Slater, W., Kahn, M., Gorlin, R., & Zucker, H. (1989). The nature and course of depression following myocardial infarction. *Archives of Internal Medicine, 149,* 1785–1789.

Sherbourne, C. D., Hays, R. D., & Wells, K. B. (1995). Personal and psychosocial risk factors for physical and mental health outcomes and course of depression among depressed patients. *Journal of Consulting and Clinical Psychology, 63,* 345–355.

Stanton, A. L., & Snider, P. R. (1993). Coping with breast cancer diagnosis: A prospective study. *Health Psychology, 12,* 16–23.

Swindle, R. W., Cronkite, R. C., & Moos, R. H. (1989). Life stressors, social resources, coping, and the four-year course of unipolar depression. *Journal of Abnormal Psychology, 98,* 468–477.

Thoits, P. A. (1986). Social support and coping assistance. *Journal of Consulting and Clinical Psychology, 54,* 416–423.

Thoits, P. A. (1992). Social support functions and network structures: A supplemental view. In H. O. F. Veiel & U. Baumann (Eds.), *The meaning and measurement of social support* (pp. 57–62). New York: Hemisphere.

Thoits, P. A. (1995). Stress, coping, and social support processes: Where are we? What next? *Journal of Health and Social Behavior, 36,* 53–79.

Valentiner, D. P., Holahan, C. J., & Moos, R. H. (1994). Social support, appraisals of event controllability, and coping: An integrative model. *Journal of Personality and Social Psychology, 66,* 1094–1102.

Vinokur, A. D., & van Ryn, M. (1993). Social support and undermining in close relationships: Their independent effects on the mental health of unemployed persons. *Journal of Personality and Social Psychology, 65*, 350–359.

Vitaliano, P. P., DeWolfe, D. J., Maiuro, R. D., Russo, J., & Katon, W. (1990). Appraised changeability of a stressor as a modifier of the relationship between coping and depression: A test of the hypothesis of fit. *Journal of Personality and Social Psychology, 59*, 582–592.

Wallerstein, J. S. (1986). Women after divorce: Preliminary report from a ten-year follow-up. *American Journal of Orthopsychiatry, 56*, 65–77.

Wiedenfeld, S. A., O'Leary, A., Bandura, A., Brown, S., Levine, S., & Raska, K (1990). Impact of perceived self-efficacy in coping with stressors on components of the immune system. *Journal of Personality and Social Psychology, 59*, 1082–1094.

Wills, T. A. (1985). Supportive functions of interpersonal relationships. In S. Cohen & S. L. Syme (Eds.), *Social support and health* (pp. 61–82). New York: Academic Press.

Zirkel, S. (1992). Developing independence in a life transition: Investing the self in the concerns of the day. *Journal of Personality and Social Psychology, 62*, 506–521.

Zirkel, S., & Cantor, N. (1990). Personal construal of life tasks: Those who struggle for independence. *Journal of Personality and Social Psychology, 58*, 172–185.

Chapter 9

SOCIAL SUPPORT AND PERSONALITY IN DEPRESSION
IMPLICATIONS FROM QUANTITATIVE GENETICS

John E. Roberts and Ian H. Gotlib

Depression is a potentially debilitating disorder that affects a large segment of the population. Recent epidemiological studies indicate that depression is one of the most prevalent psychiatric disorders, affecting up to 2–3% of men and 5–9% of women each year (Kessler et al., 1994b). Over the course of a lifetime as many as 7–12% of men and 20–25% of women in the general population suffer from at least one clinically significant episode of depression (Kessler et al., 1994b). Furthermore, depression is frequently a recurrent disorder that troubles people intermittently throughout their lives. More specifically, it has been estimated that approximately 50% of those who recover from their first episode of depression will suffer from future episodes (Belsher & Costello, 1988), and that depression takes on a chronic course in 25% or more of persons who reach case level (Depue & Monroe, 1986). Beyond the emotional pain and troubling symptomatology that accompanies depression, this disorder is associated with a number of additional negative consequences, including cognitive impairments and biases (Gotlib, Roberts, & Gilboa, 1996), marital distress (Gotlib & Beach, 1995), social rejection (Joiner, Alfano, & Metalsky, 1993), and negative changes in personality functioning (Hirschfield et al., 1983b). Each of these effects can take a significant toll on individuals suffering from depression, as well as on those who have close relationships with them. Furthermore it is possible that these factors also play roles in the etiology and maintenance of depression. Although there is reason to believe that similar psychosocial processes are important in bipolar disorder, they may operate in a

John E. Roberts • Department of Psychology, State University of New York at Buffalo, Buffalo, New York 14260.   Ian H. Gotlib • Department of Psychology, Stanford University, Stanford, California 94305.

Sourcebook of Social Support and Personality, edited by Gregory R. Pierce, Brian Lakey, Irwin G. Sarason, and Barbara R. Sarason. Plenum Press, New York, 1997.

substantially different manner in this disorder (Johnson & Roberts, 1995). Consequently, in the current chapter, we focus on unipolar depression.

Clinicians and investigators have long believed that individuals with particular personality characteristics are at elevated risk for developing unipolar depression (e.g., Arieti & Bemporad, 1978; Beck, 1967; Hirschfeld & Klerman, 1979; Kraepelin, 1921). Similarly, the nature and quality of one's social relationships have been thought to play an important role in depression (e.g., Cohen & Wills, 1985; Gotlib & Whiffen, 1991). Nonetheless, it is still unclear whether, and how, personality and social support play *causal* roles in the etiology and maintenance of depression. As discussed by Hirschfeld and Shea (1992), several overarching models potentially represent the well-documented association between personality and depression. Predispositional models posit that particular personality features increase vulnerability for developing depression. These models assume that personality can play a causal role in the etiology of depression, perhaps in combination with environmental factors such as life stress. On the other hand, pathoplasty models posit that personality modifies the course or expression of depressive disorders, perhaps by prolonging episodes or by shaping particular symptom constellations. These models also suggest that personality can influence the social environment in ways that contribute to the maintenance of depression. In contrast, the complication or "scar" hypothesis presumes that the experience of depressive disorders modifies one's personality. According to this position, depression causes the negative personality features documented in depressed patients, rather than vice versa. Finally, the spectrum, or continuity, hypothesis suggests that certain personality features represent attenuated forms of major depression; that is, subclinical depression might be expressed in personality dimensions such as neuroticism and low self-esteem.

To a large extent, the relation between social support and depression can be represented by these types of models as well. Inadequate social support might contribute to vulnerability to depression, prolong the duration of depressive episodes, be a consequence of depression, or be a subclinical manifestation of the social withdrawal associated with depression. For example, consistent with predispositional models, a number of investigators have posited that low levels of social support contribute to the onset and recurrence of depression, perhaps by increasing the depressogenic impact of stressful life events. In pathoplasty models, social support is thought to play an important role in the recovery from depression, such that higher levels of support are associated with briefer episodes. In contrast to these positions, which each suggest that the arrow of causality points from low social support to depression, the complication hypothesis suggests that deficits in social support result from depression.

Despite progress in clarifying and evaluating theoretical models representing how social support and personality are each associated with depression, there have been few attempts to integrate these two domains of psychosocial functioning in depression. Investigators tend to focus exclusively either on the role of social support or on the role of personality in depression, without examining how social support, personality, and depression might be interrelated. Furthermore, there has been a failure to bridge these psychosocial levels of analysis with the expanding knowledge base concerning biological, and particularly genetic, contributions to depression. We believe that such bridges are critically important at the current stage of scientific progress.

In particular, recent developments in the field of quantitative genetics suggests that a major reevaluation of our models of the relations among social support, personality, and depression is warranted. Although it has been recognized for some time that depression runs in families, it has become increasingly clear that this relation is in large part due to genetic liability, rather than to shared family experiences (e.g., Kendler, 1993; but see also Gatz, Pedersen, Plomin, Nesselroade, & McClearn, 1992; McGuffin, Katz, & Rutherford, 1991). Furthermore, behavioral–genetic investigations are beginning to demonstrate that individual differences in many psychosocial factors implicated in depression, such as stressful life events, social support, and personality, are at least partly determined by genetic factors (e.g., Kendler, Neale, Kessler, Heath, & Eaves, 1993b,c). These findings obviously demand that researchers consider possible interrelations among support, personality, and depression that might be genetically mediated.

In this chapter we review plausible models of how social support and personality might each relate to depression. We also examine the role that genetic factors might play in affecting these associations. Finally, we discuss ways in which investigators might begin to integrate the constructs of social support, personality, and depression from the perspective of behavioral genetics.

SOCIAL SUPPORT

That the quality of one's social relationships affects emotional well-being is intuitively obvious. We have all experienced the emotional ups and downs associated with the vicissitudes of our intimate relationships. Indeed, Baumeister and Leary (1995) recently argued that the desire for close interpersonal relations is a fundamental human motivation that leads to a variety of negative psychological and biological sequelae when thwarted. Over the past three decades, researchers have accumulated a vast wealth of evidence that social support is related to a number of psychological and health outcomes, including cardiovascular reactivity (Kamarck, Manuck, & Jennings, 1990), birth outcomes (Collins, Dunkel-Schetter, Lobel, & Scrimshaw, 1993), immune functioning (Baron, Cutrona, Hicklin, Russell, & Lubaroff, 1990), and AIDS-related symptoms (Hays, Turner, & Coates, 1992). Deficits in social support have also been widely implicated in depression. Before summarizing the major findings from this body of research, it is important to discuss some of the varying definitions of social support that are found in this literature.

DEFINITIONAL AND MEASUREMENT ISSUES

In general, social support is treated as a broad concept that refers to many different aspects of one's interpersonal world. Consequently, investigators have operationally defined social support in a number of ways. Relatively objective measures of social support involve structural components, such as the number of members in one's social network, the frequency of club or church attendance, and marital status. Subjective measures include satisfaction with various domains of social support, such as self-esteem support, material support, and emotional support (Cohen & McKay, 1984). These types of measures are generally referred to as *perceived support* and seem to be the aspect of social support that is most robustly associated with psychological distress, such as depression (Cohen & Wills, 1985; Fiore, Coppel, Becker, & Cox, 1986; Sarason, Shearin, Pierce, & Sarason, 1987). Falling between relatively objective and subjective approaches are measures that request subjects to estimate the frequency with which their network members engage in various supportive behaviors. These types of measures are typically referred to as *enacted support*. Although enacted support would seem to be an intuitively obvious and important component of the social support construct, it is likely highly confounded with the *need* for support (Cohen & Wills, 1985; Coyne, Ellard, & Smith, 1990). Finally, there has been increasing interest in the concept of individual differences in support utilization. For example, given the same social support networks, some individuals might be more skilled than others at soliciting support. As we shall see later, the concept of support utilization brings with it the notion that social support is in important ways inextricably linked to personality differences that in part may be genetically determined.

Each of these approaches to conceptualizing and measuring social support emphasizes what appear to be stable aspects of one's social world; that is, social support is assumed to remain relatively constant over time. In contrast, Brown, Andrews, Harris, Adler, and Bridge (1986) highlighted the importance of discrepancies between one's expectations concerning support and the actual supportive behaviors that are received following major stressful life events. Brown et al. found that inadequate "crisis support" was associated with the onset of major depression. Indeed, depression was particularly likely when subjects were "let down" by their confidants. These women initially reported relatively high levels of support, reflected by their having trusted confidants. However, as time progressed, it became apparent that subjects' positive expectations of their confidants were not always met, and that these types of "let downs" played a critical role in the onset of depression. Other investigators have found that while under stress, individuals paradoxically report both higher levels of received support *and* higher levels of distress (Coyne et al., 1990). Apparently, distressed, needy, individuals are more likely to elicit support than are persons who are doing well and are in less need. Together, these findings suggest that dimensions of social support measured outside of dynamic environmental transactions, and treated essentially as static constants, are likely to be less informative in terms of understanding depression. Later, we discuss important methodological advantages of studying the effects of changes in social support over time within the same individuals.

In terms of the measurement of social support, depression poses several critical difficulties. First, depression is thought to be associated with a cognitive style involving negative biases in attention, perception, and memory (Beck, Rush, Shaw, & Emery, 1979; Gotlib et al., 1996). Accordingly, depressives' judgments about their social worlds cannot be uncritically accepted as veridical. Clearly objective indicators of network support, such as marital status, are much less likely to be influenced by such processes. However, self-report ratings of dissatisfaction with social support, perceptions about the availability of support, and even reports of the amount of received support all could be due, at least in part, to cognitive biases associated with depression rather than to actual differences in the quality of social supports.

In a similar manner, certain personality and cognitive styles might bias reports of social support. For example, individuals with borderline personality features might report extreme dissatisfaction with their support networks due to network members being unable to meet their excessive and unreasonable demands. In contrast, the actual behaviors of their network members might, in fact, be more supportive than is typically the case. Likewise, Lakey and Cassady (1990) found evidence that perceived social support operates like a cognitive personality construct. These investigators found perceived support to be more highly correlated with cognitive variables than was enacted support. Moreover, its association with symptoms of depression was rendered nonsignificant when cognitive variables were statistically controlled. In addition, perceived social support was associated with biases in the interpretation of novel supportive behaviors and with memory of supportive behaviors (Lakey & Cassady, 1990). Together, these concerns and findings suggest that, in addition to features of the actual social world, measures of perceived support are at least partly a reflection of characteristics and processes within the person. As noted by Monroe and Steiner (1986), "Social support is not simply a cause (of disorder) or buffer (of stress) but also a consequence and correlate of, and sometimes surrogate for, measures of these related constructs" (p. 29). Such issues obviously have important implications concerning the interpretation and meaning of findings linking perceived support and depression.

ASSOCIATIONS WITH DEPRESSION

Three major designs have been utilized in studying the naturalistic association of social support and depression. Cross-sectional designs either examine differences in various aspects of social support between currently depressed (typically clinically depressed) and nondepressed individuals, or examine the correlation between levels of depressive symptoms and social support. Remission designs test whether or not previously depressed individuals differ from never-depressed persons in social support, and prospective designs examine whether or not support predicts the onset or duration of depressive symptoms and disorders.

Not surprisingly, a vast number of cross-sectional studies have documented that various indices of social support are associated with depression (e.g., Billings, Cronkite, & Moos, 1983; Blazer, 1983; Mitchell & Moos, 1984). Higher levels of depression are associated with reports of fewer social contacts with friends and relatives (Roberts, Roberts, & Stevenson, 1982), less satisfaction with the quality of one's support (Blazer & Hughes, 1991; Pagel & Becker, 1987), particularly with support from one's relatives (Grant, Patterson, & Yager, 1988), and less frequent positive social contact with adults other than one's spouse (Beach, Arias, & O'Leary, 1986). Furthermore, clinically depressed patients report lower levels of perceived support than do normal controls, although psychiatric patients suffering from other conditions also tend to report deficits in many aspects of perceived support (Belsher & Costello, 1991). Similar results have been obtained in adolescent samples in which both peer and family support have significance (Barrera & Garrison-Jones, 1992). Depression also is associated with decreased marital satisfaction (Beach et al., 1986; Burns, Sayers, & Moras, 1994) and with increased rates of divorce (Beach, Sandeen, & O'Leary, 1990). Interestingly, it is possible that there are gender differences in the association between different forms of social support and depressive symptoms, with men's symptomatology being most directly linked to spousal support, but with women's symptomatology being associated with more diverse sources of support (Greenberger & O'Neil, 1993). Furthermore, it is apparent that negative aspects of one's social relationships (dissatisfaction) make a greater contribution to depressive symptoms than do the relative absence of positive aspects (satisfaction; Fiore, Becker, & Coppel, 1983; Rook, 1984).

Although the authors of these cross-sectional studies generally assume that inadequate support leads to depression, in fact, it is unclear what underlying causal processes are responsible for these associations. For example, as discussed earlier, it is plausible that the association between low levels of support and depression arise because depression negatively biases perceptions of support. In addition, there is evidence that depression contributes to *real* deteriorations in social support (Coyne, 1976; Joiner et al., 1993). In this case, depression might lead to breakdowns in social networks involving previously supportive individuals withdrawing from and rejecting depressed persons. Cross-sectional studies obviously are unable to rule out such alternative hypotheses. Remission and prospective designs are required to better address and clarify underlying causal processes.

To examine whether the cross-sectional findings discussed earlier simply represent the impact of "state depression" on social support, investigators have examined social support in previously depressed individuals. Differences between these remitted depressives and never-depressed individuals would suggest that deficits in social support reflect stable characteristics of depression that persist regardless of whether the individual is episodic or not (Barnett & Gotlib, 1988). Consistent with the stability hypothesis, Billings and Moos (1985) found that remitted depressives reported fewer friends, fewer close relationships, and less supportive family interactions than did never-depressed individuals. In contrast, no differences were found between these two groups in the quality of close relationships, work support, or size of social network. A number of other studies have found that clinically depressed individuals continue to report marital distress and conflict following recovery from their depressive episode (Hinchcliffe, Hooper, & Roberts, 1978; Merikangas, 1984; Paykel & Weissman, 1973). For example, Hinchcliffe et al. (1978) documented deviant communication patterns involving emotional discharge in previously depressed patients, and Paykel and Weissman (1973) found that previously depressed women exhibited inhibited communication and marital friction. However, it should be noted that there may be gender differences in the impact of depression on marital functioning, such that relationships tend to be more disturbed when wives, rather than husbands, have a history of depression (Gotlib, 1986).

Unfortunately, no research has yet investigated the impact of remitted depressives on others. As mentioned earlier, Coyne's (1976) interpersonal model of depression posits that depressives tend to drive other people away through their excessive demands (see Gotlib & Robinson, 1982). It is possible that some previously depressed persons continue to exhibit a negative interpersonal style, and that this style places them at risk for further deteriorations in their close relationships and perhaps clinical relapse or recurrence. Consistent with this possibility, prospective investigations of recovered depressives have found that negative emotionality and criticism from family members is associated with relapse of clinical episodes (Hooley, Orley, & Teasdale, 1986; Hooley & Teasdale, 1989).

Given potential confounds among measures of social support, personality, and depression, longitudinal prospective investigations are generally thought to better address causal issues than are cross-sectional studies. A number of longitudinal investigations have examined whether various dimensions of support are either associated with the onset of depressive symptoms or depressive episodes in initially non-depressed individuals (vulnerability models), or predict the course of disorder on initially depressed persons (pathoplasty models). In their review of this literature, Cohen and Wills (1985) focused largely on the issue of onset and concluded that perceived support buffers the impact of life stressors in the development of various forms of psychological distress, such as depression; that is, inadequate perceived support contributes to the onset of depression when persons experience stressful life events but has relatively little impact on symptomatology when persons are not faced with such environmental adversities (e.g., Brown et al., 1986; Phifer & Murrell, 1986; Turner, Kessler, & House, 1991). In contrast, structural aspects of support are thought generally to act as a main effect and not interact with stress; that is, factors such as a paucity of social network members or social interactions tend to lead to depression independent of life stress (e.g., Lin, Simeone, Ensel, & Kuo, 1979). Importantly, prospective findings involving both buffering and main effects indicate that inadequate social support contributes to *changes* in depressive symptoms over time (Cohen & Wills, 1985). Therefore, social support (both perceived and structural support) might play a causal role in the development of depression, rather than merely being a consequence or correlate of depression (see Barnett & Gotlib, 1988). In fact, Monroe, Bromet, Connell, and Steiner (1986) found that support was a stronger predictor of future depressive symptomatology in individuals who were relatively asymptomatic at the outset of the study than in those who were already mildly depressed.

In addition to prospective studies examining the *onset* of depression, a number of investigations also have found that social support prospectively predicts the *duration* of depressive episodes, suggesting that difficult interpersonal relationships might play a role in the maintenance of this disorder (George, Blazer, Hughes, & Fowler, 1989; Goering, Lancee, & Freeman, 1992; Keitner et al., 1995; Krantz & Moos, 1988). For example, Goering et al. (1992) found that depressed women's negative ratings of their current marital relationship, as well as their husbands' negative ratings of the premorbid marital relationship, were associated with a decreased likelihood of recovery 6 months later. In contrast, severity of symptomatology, age of onset, and family history of affective illness failed to predict recovery. In a study utilizing structural equation modeling, Burns et al. (1994) found that satisfaction with intimate relationships had only a small causal effect on the degree of recovery from depression, but that marital status strongly predicted improvement, even after controlling for satisfaction. Married patients showed greater improvement than single patients.

Issues of Causal Direction and Individual Differences

As reviewed earlier, it is clear that higher levels of social support are associated with a decreased risk for developing depression. Currently depressed (both symptomatically depressed and clinically depressed) individuals, previously depressed persons, and persons who develop future depressive symptomatology and disorders report lower levels of social support than do individuals who are not prone to depression. In addition, social support has been linked to recovery from episodes of depression. Despite these robust associations between social support and depression, the underlying mechanisms by which social support influences depression are not well documented. Although several theorists suggest that social support, particularly perceived support, leads to enhanced coping and appraisal processes (Cohen & Wills, 1985; Thoits, 1986), others have cautioned that relations between support and depression might be spurious. For example, Heller (1979; Heller & Swindle, 1983) suggested that the effects of social support might not be due to support *per se*, but to social competence; that is, persons with inadequate levels of social support might be socially incompetent. Similarly, Henderson, Byrne, and Duncan-Jones (1981) found evidence that neuroticism mediated the relation between support and depression. Individuals who reported lower levels of social support tended to score higher on neuroticism, and these higher levels of neuroticism were directly related to depressive symptomatology. Together, these investigators suggest that positive social support is not a random variable that some people are fortunate enough to have bestowed upon them. Instead, people are likely to differ in their ability to create and maintain adequate social support networks. As suggested by Lakey and Cassady (1990), people also differ in their cognitions about social relationships, and these cognitions are likely to influence their perceptions of social support. In summary, personality and cognitive styles are plausible third variables that likely influence levels of both social support and depression.

Consistent with the previously discussed complication hypothesis, it also is likely that depression leads to deteriorations in one's social relationships. As mentioned earlier, Coyne's (1976) interpersonal model of depression posits that depressed individuals have characteristics that are aversive to others and contribute to social isolation. In particular, depressed individuals are thought to excessively seek reassurance that others value and care about them, which induces dysphoric mood in persons who interact with them. Consequently, people tend to reject and avoid depressed persons, which over time leads to deficits in their social support networks. Rather than inadequate social support simply causing depression, depression also would lead to diminished support. Other investigators posit that depressives tend to seek negative feedback and rejection from others in order to maintain a stable, negative self-image (Swann, Wenzlaff, Krull, & Pelham, 1992). This research suggests that depressives actively elicit negative reactions and unsupportive behavior from others. Some evidence suggests that the combination of this negative-feedback seeking style *and* excessive reassurance seeking is most likely to lead to social rejection and isolation in depression (Joiner et al., 1993). This particular combination of behaviors is thought to be particularly aversive to others. Overall, this body of work suggests that not only do currently depressed persons negatively bias their perceptions of support, but that they also seek relationships with individuals who are unsupportive, and that they negatively affect the quality of their relationships with persons who might otherwise be supportive. These behaviors likely result from personality characteristics and needs, such as negative self-concept and dependence.

In addition, it is possible that social support differentially affects individuals who vary across certain personality dimensions (Roos & Cohen, 1987). In other words, personality could moderate the degree to which social support benefits particular individuals, and could determine which specific aspects of social support are most important to individuals. For example, a number of theorists have suggested that whereas some individuals who are vulnerable to depression base their self-worth and identity excessively on the maintenance of social relationships (sociotropy or dependence), others seem to be overinvested in achievement concerns (e.g., Arieti & Bemporad, 1978; Beck, 1983; Blatt & Zuroff, 1992). We expect that poor social support would take a greater toll on sociotropic individuals than on more autonomous persons. Furthermore, Panzarella and Alloy (1995) recently proposed that one important aspect of social support is the degree to which it counters negative attributional styles; that is, close, supportive, persons might influence the types of attributions that are made for stressful life events. Individuals who exhibit a characteristic negative attributional style are most likely to benefit from this function of social support. It is to the impact of personality and cognitive styles on depression and social support that we now turn.

PERSONALITY

Individual differences concerning social skills and competence, interpersonal style, and social needs are likely to be important determinants of the quality one's social support network and the amount and quality of support one has available. In fact, it may be that personality has its major influence on depression through such interpersonal channels. On the other hand, personality might have a more direct impact on depression that is relatively independent of its association with social relations. In this regard, it is widely believed that certain depression-prone personalities exist. Indeed, if there is a genetic liability to depression, it is quite reasonable to suppose that it might manifest itself in terms of premorbid personality functioning. One important issue involves the degree to which personality contributes to (i.e., causes) depression, as opposed to simply represents an underlying genetic vulnerability; that is, do personality features associated with depression better fit within vulnerability or spectrum models? Yet another way of stating this question is to ask: Do personality phenotypes contribute to depression beyond the effects of their genotypes (Carey & DiLalla, 1994)?

TRIPARTITE MODEL

According to Clark and Watson's (1991; Clark, Watson, & Mineka, 1994) tripartite model of anxiety and depression, negative affect (NA) is an element common to both disorders, whereas loss of positive affect (PA) is specific to depression. Importantly, these dimensions of affect are thought to arise from stable personality structures. NA has been theoretically associated with the behavioral inhibition system (BIS), a superordinate biobehavioral system that inhibits behavior in response to conditioned stimuli for punishment and frustrative nonreward, novel stimuli, and innate fear stimuli (Gray, 1987). The BIS and NA have been empirically related to personality constructs such as neuroticism (Costa & McCrae, 1980; Meyer & Shack, 1989; Watson & Clark, 1984), and are connected to the workings of the amygdala and the septohippocampal system (Gray, 1987). Relatively neurotic individuals are thought to have more active BISs and tend to experience higher levels of NA. In contrast, PA is thought to reflect the activation of the Behavioral Activation System (BAS), a superordinate biobehavioral system responsible for actively engaging the individual with the environment and with the expectation of reinforcement (Depue, Krauss, & Spoont, 1987; Fowles, 1994; Gray, 1987). As such, the BAS is critically important in reward-seeking behavior. The BAS and PA have been empirically associated with personality constructs such as extraversion (Meyer & Shack, 1989), and are related to dopaminergic systems in the brain (Depue & Iacono, 1988). Extraverted individuals are thought to have more active or vigorous BASs and tend to experience higher levels of PA.

Consistent with the tripartite model, neuroticism has been implicated in depression across numerous investigations (see Clark et al., 1994 for a review). Not only do currently depressed individuals report higher levels of neuroticism than do never-depressed persons (Kendell & DiScipio, 1968; Roberts & Gotlib, in press), but more interestingly, previously depressed individuals also report higher levels of neuroticism than do their never-depressed counterparts (Roberts, Gilboa, & Gotlib, 1997; Roberts & Gotlib, in press). Likewise, elevated levels of neuroticism have been found prospectively to predict both increases in depressive symptoms over time (Nolan, Roberts, & Gotlib, in press) and first episodes of clinical depression (Hirschfeld et al., 1989). Heightened neuroticism measured at remission (Duggan, Lee, & Murray, 1990), or after an initial clinical response (Weissman, Prusoff, & Klerman, 1978), also predicts poor long-term course of depression, particularly among nonendogenous depressives (Andrews, Neilson, Hunt, Stewart, & Kiloh, 1990). Neuroticism measured during an episode is associated with a decreased likelihood of recovery (Hirschfeld, Klerman, Andreasen, Clayton, & Keller, 1986). Elevated levels of neuroticism, therefore, appear to be a trait-characteristic of depression that is associated with increased vulnerability to the disorder. The nature of this association, though, remains a mystery.

Unfortunately, it is unclear what neuroticism scales actually measure. Factor-analytic studies of personality traits almost universally find a major dimension (factor) of personality represented by items involving moodiness, stress reactivity, irritability, worry, sleep difficulties, and loneliness that typically is labeled neuroticism or emotional stability–instability (Eysenck & Eysenck, 1985; McCrae & Costa, 1987; Norman, 1963). However, many of these items are so similar to the symptoms of depression and anxiety that it is unclear if persons who report high levels of neuroticism are simply indicating that they have been troubled by current or previous experiences of depression and anxiety. If so, it would be difficult to argue that neuroticism plays a causal role in depression. Instead, the association between depression and neuroticism would be better described by the spectrum or continuity hypothesis than by the vulnerability hypothesis; that is, neuroticism might simply reflect an attenuated form of depression, or a variant of depressive temperament, rather than an etiological agent (see Watson, Clark, & Harkness, 1994).

Although the association between neuroticism and depression borders dangerously close to tautology, there is reason to believe that neuroticism and depression are somewhat independent constructs. In particular, elevated levels of neuroticism predict the duration of depressive episodes and symptoms after statistically controlling for initial depressive symptomatology (Duggan et al., 1990; Hirschfeld et al., 1986; Nolan et al., 1996). In addition, elevated levels of neuroticism in previously depressed individuals remain statistically significant after controlling for current symptomatology (Roberts & Gotlib, in press). Furthermore, there is reason to believe that neuroticism contributes to depression indirectly by negatively biasing cognitive processes (Martin, 1985) and increasing ruminative focus (Nolen-Hoeksema, Parker, & Larson, 1994; Nolan et al., in press; Roberts et al., 1997). If neuroticism were merely an attenuated form of depression, we would expect it to have direct associations with depression, rather than indirect effects mediated through other psychological and behavioral processes. Also consistent with the possibility that neuroticism and depression are independent constructs, Kendler, Kessler, Neale, Heath, and Eaves (1993a) found that neuroticism contributed to vulnerability to depression independent of genetic liability to the disorder. We shall see shortly how other types of behavioral genetic analysis can help answer the question concerning the independence of neuroticism and depression.

The tripartite model (Clark et al., 1994) also suggests that deficits in the BAS might be particularly important in depression. Such deficits would result in impairments in reinforcement and goal-seeking behavior, and could contribute to anhedonia. Consistent with this possibility, behavioral theorists long have posited that deficits in reinforcement and reinforcement-seeking behavior are critical factors in the etiology and maintenance of depression. Interestingly, individual differences in the strength and activity of the BAS are thought to be represented in variations in Eysenck's personality dimension of introversion–extraversion (Eysenck & Eysenck, 1985). Introverts have a weaker BAS than do extraverts (Clark et al., 1994; Fowles, 1994). In this regard, a number of studies have reported that currently depressed individuals tend to report that they are more introverted than do nondepressed persons (Hirschfeld & Klerman, 1979; Kendell & DiScipio, 1968). Some studies also have obtained evidence that self-reported introversion persists following recovery from episodes of depression (Hirschfeld & Klerman, 1979; Hirschfeld, Klerman, Clayton, & Keller, 1983a). It is important to note here, however, that there have been a number of failures to replicate the latter findings (e.g., Roberts & Gotlib, in press), leading some theorists to question the reliability of these results (Clark et al., 1994).

Overall, although the evidence suggests that neuroticism is associated with vulnerability to depression, it is unclear whether neuroticism is causally related to depression or merely reflects an attenuated version of depression. The research is somewhat less clear with respect to introversion. Anhedonia and loss of social interest and engagement clearly are important characteristics of clinically depressed individuals. However, the findings are mixed concerning whether these characteristics can be found outside of symptomatic periods, let alone whether they play a causal role in depression. To the extent that introversion contributes to depression, findings linking social support and depression might be better accounted for in terms of this personality dimension and its concomitant deficits in reinforcement seeking and social engagement. On the other hand, it is possible that the association between introversion and depression results from introverts failing to obtain adequate social support.

NEGATIVE ATTRIBUTIONAL STYLE

Although the tripartite model focuses on two broad dimensions of personality derived through factor analysis, a number of more specific, narrow aspects of personality have been linked to depression. In particular, cognitive theorists have posited that stable individual differences in various cognitive processes, including attention, interpretation, and memory are associated with vulnerability to depression. The reformulated learned helplessness (Abramson, Seligman, & Teasdale, 1978) and hopelessness theories of depression (Abramson, Metalsky, & Alloy, 1989) have been among the most influential of these cognitive approaches. These theories posit that certain negative attributional styles make it more likely that an individual will develop depression following a stressful life event. In particular, individuals who attribute negative events to stable and global causes are more likely to develop hopelessness, which, in turn, is thought to be a proximal, sufficient cause of depression. Attributing negative events to internal causes is thought to contribute to the loss of self-esteem. Although this model suggests that particular, "on-line" attributions for actual life events lead to depression, it also assumes that there are stable individual differences in the types of attributions people tend to make for positive and negative life events in general; that is, persons with a negative attributional style will tend to make negative (global, stable) attributions to the majority of negative life events that they encounter in life. As discussed earlier, certain aspects of social support might operate to counter such a negative attributional style by providing the individual with more adaptive attributions (Panzarella & Alloy, 1995).

A number of studies have found support for some of the central hypotheses in this model. Cross-sectional investigations have tended to demonstrate that higher levels of depressive symptoms are associated with more negative attributional styles (Sweeney, Anderson, & Bailey, 1986). Prospective studies with nonclinical samples also have been generally supportive. For example, Metalsky, Halberstadt, and Abramson (1987) found that negative attributional style interacted with failure on a college exam to predict depressive mood reactions. Interestingly, these data supported the hypothesis that the particular attributions made for failure mediated these relations. More recently, these findings have been replicated, and support was obtained for the hypothesis that interaction of attributional style and failure was mediated by the onset of hopelessness (Metalsky, Joiner, Hardin, & Abramson, 1993; see also Metalsky & Joiner, 1992). Nonetheless, it is also apparent that negative attributional styles are at least partly state dependent and tend to return to normal levels upon remission from clinical depression (Dohr, Rush, & Bernstein, 1989; Hamilton & Abramson, 1983; Lewinsohn, Steinmetz, Larson, & Franklin, 1981).

DYSFUNCTIONAL SELF-ESTEEM REGULATION

Self-esteem also has been widely implicated as a risk factor for depression (see Roberts & Monroe, 1994). For example, low self-esteem was found to potentiate the effects of the interaction between negative attributional style and life stress in predicting the development of depressive symptoms in a nonclinical sample (Metalsky et al., 1993), and to predict the onset of cases of clinical depression in interaction with severe life stressors in a community study (Brown, Bifulco, & Andrews, 1990). Although it is clear that currently depressed individuals report diminished self-esteem, it is much less certain whether low self-esteem predicts the onset of depression or persists subsequent to recovery from depression (Bernet, Ingram, & Johnson, 1993). For example, one study found that individuals with high self-esteem tended to become *more* symptomatically depressed following stressful events than did persons with relatively low self-esteem (Whisman & Kwon, 1993), and a number of other investigations have failed to demonstrate any interactive effects of low self-esteem and life stress in predicting depression (Lakey, 1988; Lewinsohn, Hoberman, & Rosenbaum, 1988; Roberts & Monroe, 1992). Although several additional studies suggested that self-esteem is an important personal resource that buffers against the impact of stress (Hobfoll & Leiberman, 1987; Hobfoll & London, 1986), conclusions are difficult to draw, because self-esteem was measured concurrently with follow-up depressive symptomatology in these investigations.

On the other hand, there is growing and consistent evidence that it is not chronically low self-esteem that is associated with vulnerability to depression, but rather difficulties in regulating and maintaining stable levels of self-esteem. Persons with temporally unstable self-esteem (Roberts & Gotlib, in press; Roberts & Kassel, in press; Roberts & Monroe, 1992) or self-esteem that is highly reactive to minor daily events (Butler, Hokanson, & Flynn, 1994), are at risk for developing depressive symptoms following the occurrence of stressful life events. Furthermore, previously depressed individuals experience self-esteem that is more reactive to daily events than that of never-depressed persons (Butler et al., 1994). Together, these findings suggest that a tenuous sense of self-worth that is unstable over time, and that easily rises and falls in response to life's vicissitudes, is associated with depression proneness. Interestingly, the effects of instability in self-esteem remain significant after statistically controlling for affective instability (Roberts & Kassel, in press; Roberts & Monroe, 1992), and affective instability does not appear to predict changes in depressive symptoms, either alone or in interaction with stressful life events (Roberts & Gotlib, in press). Persons who are prone to developing depressive symptoms, therefore, might be better characterized as having labile self-esteem than as having chronically low self-esteem (Roberts & Monroe, 1994).

A related body of research suggests that individuals who overinvest their sense of self-esteem in either social or achievement domains are at increased risk for developing depression following life stress, particularly stressors that match these domains (see Nietzel & Harris, 1990). These findings suggest that it is possible that labile self-esteem reflects variations in environmental factors, such as fluctuations in the quality of one's interpersonal relationships or daily stressors related to achievement. As such, instability in self-esteem might be a marker of unstable environments. For example, individuals who overinvest their self-esteem in social relationships will experience unstable self-esteem to the extent that the quality of their interpersonal ties fluctuates over time. In order to examine this possibility, investigations need to assess the nature of daily stressors in addition to daily self-esteem (cf. Butler et al., 1994).

INTERPERSONAL ANTECEDENTS

Interestingly, some evidence suggests that certain personality characteristics associated with risk for depression, such as vulnerable self-esteem, result in part from interpersonal processes related to social support. For example, in a recent prospective study, we found that adult attachment insecurity contributed to dysfunctional contingencies of self-worth, which led to the development of depressive symptoms through the mediating role of depleted levels of self-esteem (Roberts, Gotlib, & Kassel, 1996);

that is, individuals with insecure adult attachment styles tended to develop depressive symptoms over time, but this relation was indirect and mediated by vulnerable self-esteem. In another study (Roberts & Gotlib, 1995), we found that individuals with preoccupied and fearful attachment styles were more symptomatically depressed than were secure and dismissing individuals, and that self-esteem accounted for these differences. Interestingly, preoccupied individuals were most likely to engage in excessive reassurance seeking and, therefore, were most likely to alienate their close relationships and lose social support (cf. Coyne, 1976). Consistent with these feelings, Collins (1996) recently reported that, in response to imagined interpersonal stressors, preoccupied individuals were more likely than were secure and avoidant persons to experience negative emotional reactions and behavioral intentions that would likely result in conflict. Other investigators have found that insecure adult attachment styles contribute to depression through the mediating role of negative cognitive styles (Whisman & McGarvey, 1995), and that perceptions of early childhood relationships with one's parents are crucial (Whisman & Kwon, 1992). Similar to other putative cognitive vulnerability factors, such as negative attributional style (Metalsky et al., 1987, 1993), some studies have found that attachment insecurity increases the depressogenic impact of life stressors (Hammen et al., 1995; Mikulincer, Florian, & Weller, 1993).

How might insecure attachment contribute to risk for depression? We suggest that attachment security first established in infancy and early childhood gives the individual a sense of unconditional acceptance and worth (cf. Rogers, 1961). Sensitive and responsive caregiving gives rise to working models of the self as being worthy and valued, and working models of others as being available. In contrast, insensitive and unresponsive caregiving leads to attachment insecurity and working models of the self as unworthy of support, or as only worthy if particular conditions are met. Self-esteem becomes contingent on the individual behaving in particular ways and is at risk of becoming depleted when these contingencies are not met. Consistent with this view, Sarason, Pierce, and Sarason (1990) hypothesized that perceived support (which appears to be most important in depression) is rooted in feelings of unconditional acceptance by important others and likely develops through security in attachment relationships. The degree to which feelings of unconditional acceptance and security are due to environmental transactions with caregivers versus innate characteristics is still debatable.

QUANTITATIVE GENETIC APPROACHES

As we have seen, it is clear that certain aspects of social support and personality are associated with vulnerability to depression. What is not clear, however, is the extent to which measures of social support actually assess the social environment versus stable personality characteristics, such as introversion, neuroticism, and depressive symptomatology (Monroe & Steiner, 1986). Likewise, it is unknown whether personality features associated with vulnerability to depression reflect true causal agents. To date, as we have reviewed, researchers have made some progress in disentangling these possibilities by employing prospective and remitted depressive designs. We view quantitative genetic investigations as providing an important and powerful complement to these strategies that can help address issues of causality. Quantitative genetic studies have provided some of the most intriguing and thought-provoking findings in the recent past concerning the relations among social support, personality, and depression.

Most generally, quantitative genetic investigations are concerned with determining the degree to which individual differences in various psychological and behavioral characteristics can be accounted for by genetic and environmental sources. Behavioral–genetic investigations are quasi experiments that examine the degree of resemblance between individuals who vary in terms of genetic and environmental relatedness (Plomin, DeFries, & McClearn, 1990). Quantitative genetic studies partition the variance in outcome measures to three sources: (1) genetic; (2) environmental effects that are shared among siblings (e.g., early loss of a parent, socioeconomic status); and (3) environmental effects that are nonshared and unique to a particular sibling (e.g., a negative relationship with an elementary school teacher; Loehlin, 1989). Shared environmental factors should make siblings similar to each other, whereas nonshared factors would contribute to differences between siblings. These types of studies also can help to determine the degree to which social support, personality features, and depression are determined by underlying common causes (genetic, shared environment, or nonshared environment). Shared determinants suggest that phenotypic correlations are to some extent spurious and due partly to these underlying third variables. Although it is generally not necessary to include actual measures of the environment, it is possible to model the contributions made by specified environmental agents (Kendler, 1993), and their inclusion substantially increases statistical power (e.g., Kendler, Neale, Kessler, Heath, & Eaves, 1992).

In this growing field, consensus is emerging that genetic factors account for at least moderate amounts of variance in many psychological individual difference variables (see Plomin et al., 1990, for a review). In addition, moderate environmental contributions are typically observed, suggesting that genetics alone cannot explain the development of most psychological characteristics. However, this research strongly suggests that the environmental factors that make a difference are to a large extent those that are nonshared among siblings. In contrast, shared family experiences generally are unable to explain individual differences in many psychological variables (Plomin & Daniels, 1987; Reiss, Plomin, & Hetherington, 1991; but see also Rose, 1988; Rose, Koskenvuo, Kaprio, Sarna, & Langinvainio, 1988). These findings suggest that the environment is primarily responsible for making siblings different from, rather than similar to, each other. This research also suggests that the critical environmental factors lie within, not between, families, and that more attention needs to be directed toward environmental differences within families (Reiss et al., 1991).

GENETICS OF DEPRESSION

Although bipolar disorder is generally thought to be influenced by genetic factors to a greater extent than is unipolar depression, there is growing evidence that unipolar depressive disorders, as well as subclinical levels of depressive symptoms, are in part genetically determined. For example, McGuffin et al. (1991) recently found that identical twins (who share 100% of their genes) were approximately twice as likely to be concordant for major depression as fraternal twins (who share 50% of their genes on average). With respect to subclinical depressive symptoms in older adults, Gatz et al. (1992) found that genetic factors accounted for 16% of the variance in total depression scores, whereas the shared environment accounted for 27%, and the nonshared environment accounted for 55% of the variance. Other investigators have found still larger genetic contributions to subclinical depressive symptoms (Jardine, Martin, & Henderson, 1984; Kendler, Heath, Martin, & Eaves, 1986; MacKinnon, Henderson, & Andrews, 1990; Tambs, 1991; Wierzbicki, 1987). In fact, Kendler et al. (1994) estimated that approximately 50% of the variance in subclinical depressive symptoms was genetically transmitted, whereas there was no evidence that risk for depression was environmentally transmitted by parents or resulted from shared environmental factors among siblings. Together, these findings indicate that even subclinical variations in depressive symptoms are partly determined by genetic factors.

It is obvious that researchers who are interested in psychosocial aspects of depression can no longer ignore or dismiss these findings, and furthermore, that they need to begin to develop and test models that integrate genetic and environmental vulnerabilities to this disorder. Likewise, quantitative genetic researchers need to move beyond simple demonstrations of genetic effects and begin to explore pathways by which genetic predispositions become translated into risk for depression. How do genes cause depression? Are their effects mediated entirely by the development of dysfunctional biological structures and processes that directly contribute to depression? Or might genetic effects in part be indirect and mediated by psychological and environmental processes? That is, could genes contribute to the development of distal outcomes (phenotypes), such as inadequate social support, neuroticism, and vulnerable self-esteem, that directly contribute to depression, independent of genetics? How might genetic and environmental predispositions conspire to bring about depression?

GENETICS OF PSYCHOSOCIAL RISK FACTORS

Researchers are only beginning to address questions concerning genetic contributions to putative psychosocial risk factors, such as social support and personality. For example, investigators have examined genetic and environmental contributions to individual differences in the experience of life stress. This research is based on the assumption that stressful life events are not randomly distributed in the population, but instead, that some individuals are more likely than others to experience these negative events. Consistent with this assumption, a number of studies have found that certain personality characteristics, such as high levels of neuroticism, are associated with a propensity to experience stressful life events (e.g., Magus, Diener, Fujita, & Pavot, 1993; Poulton & Andrews, 1992). In terms of genetic contributions, Kendler et al. (1993c) found that levels of life events were more highly correlated in identical twins than in fraternal twins. In this study, 26% of the variance in life events was accounted for by genetic factors, 18% by shared family environment, and 57% by the nonshared environment. Although this study incorporated sophisticated genetic modeling analyses and an unusually large sample of female twins, its self-report assessment of stressful life events was a major weakness (see Monroe & Roberts, 1990, for a critique of self-report measures of life stressors). Importantly, however, similar findings were reported by McGuffin, Katz, and Bebbington (1988), using a more objective, interview-based assessment of stressful life events. Although these investigators did not partition the variance in life stressors into genetic and shared environment components, they found that severe life events had a familial component. Furthermore, in addition to increasing the likelihood of exposure to stressful life events, it is apparent that genetic factors can contribute to vulnerability to depression by increasing one's sensitivity to stressful life events (Kendler et al., 1995a).

Other investigations have examined genetic contributions to parenting and support within the early childhood family environment. A number of studies have implicated perceptions of parental caregiving in depression. In particular, depressed adults report that their parents exhibited low levels of affection and high levels of control relative to nondepressed individuals (Parker, 1992). To some extent, these retrospective reports are not merely mood-state concomitants of depression, and they persist outside of episodic periods (Brewin, Andrews, & Gotlib, 1993; Gotlib, Mount, Cordy, & Whiffen, 1988). However, several behavioral–genetic investigations have determined that perceptions of affection (but not control) are genetically determined (Hur & Bouchard, 1995; Plomin, McClearn, Pederson, Nesselroade, & Bergeman, 1988; Rowe, 1983). Similar findings have been reported with objective measures of parental behaviors (Dunn & Plomin, 1986). The interesting, but as yet unaddressed, question is whether the relation between low perceived affection and depression is genetically mediated; that is, could genetic factors be a third variable that is responsible for the correlation between environmental measures and outcomes such as depression (Plomin, Loehlin, & Defries, 1985)?

It also is clear that certain aspects of social support in adulthood are genetically determined. For example, Bergeman, Plomin, Pederson, McClearn, and Nesselroade (1990) found that genetic factors were responsible for 30% of the variance in perceived support, whereas genetics made little contribution to individual differences in the overall quantity of enacted social support. These findings suggest that those aspects of social support that appear to be most directly related to depression (perceived support) are partly determined by genetics. More recently, Kessler, Kendler, Heath, Neale, and Eaves (1992) found similar genetic contributions to perceived support (in particular, perceived relative support, perceived friend support, and the presence of a confidant) in a large sample of female twins. In contrast to Bergeman et al.'s (1990) results, these investigators also found evidence that some forms of enacted support (in particular, frequency of church attendance and frequency of club attendance) also had genetic determinants. Together these findings suggest that measures that presumably assess the environment can be influenced by genetics (Plomin, DeFries, & Loehlin, 1977). The important point is that correlations between environmental agents and other characteristics of the person, such as depression, might not be due to the impact of the environment, but, rather, to genes that predispose to both the environmental factor and depression.

In a similar manner, correlations between personality features and depression also could be genetically mediated. A number of investigators have found that genetic factors make significant contributions to Minnesota Multiphasic Personality Inventory profiles (e.g., Loehlin, Willerman, & Horn, 1987; Pogue-Geile & Rose, 1985; Rose, 1988;

Rose et al., 1988). Of greater relevance, several researchers have used quantitative genetic designs to examine neuroticism and introversion/extraversion. For example, in a twin study, MacKinnon et al. (1990) found that, in females, genetics contributed to 67% of the variability in neuroticism scores, whereas the nonshared environment contributed to 33% of the variance. The shared environment failed to make a significant contribution. In contrast, in males, the nonshared environment contributed to 58% of the variance in neuroticism, whereas the shared environment contributed to 42%, genetic factors failed to make a significant contribution in males.

Although we are not aware of any behavioral genetic studies of aspects of vulnerable self-esteem, such as labile self-esteem, two twin studies have focused on affective lability. In the first study, Wierzbicki (1987) had twins complete measures of depressive mood and symptomatology on a daily basis for 2 weeks. Lability was defined as within-subject standard deviation scores in daily ratings. The mean intraclass correlation on affective lability for identical twins was .68 and .14 for fraternal twins, indicating strong genetic contributions, including nonadditive effects. In contrast, MacKinnon et al. (1990) measured depressive symptoms on five occasions separated by 4-month intervals but failed to demonstrate significant genetic contributions to affective lability. Unfortunately, we are not aware of any behavioral genetic studies of attributional style, sociotropy/autonomy, or attachment security. Obviously, future behavioral–genetic investigations of vulnerability to depression should target these variables.

GENETIC MEDIATION AMONG SOCIAL SUPPORT, PERSONALITY, AND DEPRESSION?

To what extent are relations that are observed among depression, social support, and personality at the phenotypic level due to shared, underlying genetic and environmental determinants? In this regard, we know that depression, support, and personality are correlated, and we also know that a moderate degree of variance in each is determined by genetic effects. To what degree do these genetic effects account for variance that is shared among these constructs? Of equal interest, are these relations mediated by environmental determinants that are common to support, personality, and depression? To the extent that phenotypic correlations among these measures are due to common, underlying genetic or environmental determinants, they are spurious and inconsistent with causal models. Instead, phenotypic associations would be due to third variables, residing either within one's chromosomes or within the environment.

With respect to social support, Bergeman, Plomin, Pederson, and McClearn (1991) replicated numerous previous findings that demonstrated a phenotypic association between cross-sectional measures of perceived social support and depressive symptoms. However, Bergeman et al. were also able to show with their adoption/twin data that, to some extent, this association was genetically mediated; that is, the same genetic factors that contributed to perceived support also led to depressive symptoms. Unfortunately, the authors did not indicate whether perceived support contributed to depression beyond these genetic effects. It is possible that phenotypic variance in perceived support played a causal role in depression, independent of this shared genotypic variance. In addition to this investigation, Kessler et al. (1992) found that the main effects of some aspects of social support on concurrent subclinical symptoms of depression were partly attributable to genes. Of even more interest, Kessler et al. also found that the buffering effects of social support were partly genetically mediated. Although it was apparent that the entire buffering effect was not spurious, Kessler et al. were unable to estimate how large the phenotypic effects were. In contrast, an analysis of longitudinal data from this same sample of twins found that the stress-buffering effects of perceived support on future episodes of clinical depression were *not* due to genetics. Buffering effects also could not be explained by other psychological factors such as coping or enacted support (Kessler et al., 1994a).

In an early study of genetic relations between personality and psychological distress, Jardine et al. (1984) found that genes played a large role in the shared variance among neuroticism, depression and anxiety; that is, for the most part, genes were responsible for phenotypic correlations among neuroticism, depression, and anxiety. These data were inconsistent with the hypothesis that neuroticism acts as a causal factor; instead, they suggest that its association with depression is spurious. As such, Jardine et al.'s findings were more consistent with spectrum models than with vulnerability or pathoplasty models. More recently, Kendler, Neale, Kessler, Heath, and Eaves (1993b) examined the role of personality in the onset of major depression using quantitative genetic analyses of longitudinal female twin data. Although extraversion was unrelated to lifetime history of major depression or to future onsets of the disorder, neuroticism was robustly associated with each of these outcomes. However, consistent with Jardine et al.'s findings, these associations were not due to a causal effect of neuroticism on depression. Instead, the phenotypic correlation between neuroticism and liability to major depression was due to shared genetic risk factors (70%), shared unique environmental risk factors (20%), and the causal effect of major depression on neuroticism (10%).

CONCLUSIONS AND FUTURE DIRECTIONS

As we have discussed, there is fairly strong evidence that vulnerability to depression is associated with deficits in various aspects of social support, particularly inadequate perceived support, and certain aspects of personality, such as neuroticism, negative attributional style, vulnerable self-esteem, and attachment insecurity. Cross-sectional studies typically demonstrate moderate-sized correlations between these putative risk factors and levels of depressive symptoms in nonclinical samples, and statistically significant elevations of these risk factors in clinically depressed individuals relative to nondepressed persons. In addition, remitted depressive and prospective designs have shown that several of these characteristics appear to act as stable, trait-like vulnerabilities to depression. However, given the inherent difficulties in conducting experimental studies with these types of constructs, this research is exclusively correlational in nature, rendering causality ambiguous. Correlational associations, even with prospective data that statistically control initial levels of depression, could result from third variables. Conceptual overlap among measures of social support, personality, and depression, and the fact that relations among these constructs are likely bidirectional, makes matters no easier. We believe that multivariate quantitative genetic analyses can help in sorting out these relations and in establishing causality. Although we have no final answers concerning the causal relations among social support, personality, and depression, we hope that we have given the reader a greater appreciation of the complexity of the issues at hand.

In our opinion, one of the most important and interesting questions concerns the extent to which psychosocial phenotypes, such as social support and personality, play causal roles in depression that are independent of their underlying genotypes (Carey & DiLalla, 1994). Are phenotypic correlations due to true causal connections or to third variables, such as common underlying genetic and environmental determinants? Multivariate genetic analyses can help answer these questions, particularly when prospective data are employed. Evidence for a causal relation between two phenotypic characteristics, such as neuroticism and depression, would be established by finding that the best fitting structural model included a significant direct path from one phenotype to another (e.g., neuroticism to depression), in addition to any paths involving shared genetic and environmental determinants (i.e., sources of variance of all possible third variables). Such a state of affairs would imply that, in addition to any third variables that might induce a correlation between the two phenotypes, a true causal relation exists. Prospective data with multiple assessments of each construct would be required to further determine the direction of causality (see Kendler et al., 1993b, for a recent application). One of the major strengths of behavioral genetic analyses of these kinds is that potential third variables can be left unmeasured. Any potential third variable would be captured in genetic, shared environmental, or nonshared environmental variance that is estimated by comparing relatives who vary in genetic and environmental similarity.

Several theorists have noted that many of the models discussed at the beginning of this chapter linking social support and personality to depression overlap and generally make similar empirical predictions (e.g., Clark et al., 1994). For example, at the phenotypic level, it is difficult to imagine that different predictions would be made by spectrum/continuity models and predispositional models. In contrast, quantitative genetic approaches would make specific differential predictions for these models. Whereas spectrum/continuity models would predict that personality (or social support) would be based on the same genetic or environmental determinants, without a direct phenotypic path, predisposition models would predict a direct path between the putative risk factor and depression that is independent of any shared underlying determinants. Predisposition models imply phenotypic causality, whereas spectrum/continuity models do not.

Although there are still few quantitative genetic studies that have examined the interrelations among social support, personality, and depression, we believe that such research holds considerable promise. Future studies would benefit from employing longitudinal designs that examine the onset of depressive symptoms or, better yet, clinical disorders. Such designs not only help establish the direction of causality, but also test–retest data can be used to further partition unique environmental variance into actual, unique environment variance, and variance due to error in measurement. In typical cross-sectional studies, the nonshared environment is treated as a residual category that includes all variance that cannot be attributed to genetics or the shared environment. As such, this category would include measurement error, which would lead to inflated estimates of the role of the nonshared environment. In addition, it will be important for future studies to investigate additional putative risk factors such as attributional style, vulnerable self-esteem, and attachment security.

There is also a need for investigators to specify and measure particular environmental factors. A number of studies suggest that the critical environmental factors lie within, not between, families. Unfortunately, most previous psychosocial research has focused on environmental differences between families. Consequently, there is now a critical need for the development of more refined measures of within-family environment factors and processes. Future research might then focus on examining within-family differences between siblings (or, better yet, twins) who are discordant on a given phenotype, such as depression. What family processes were associated with one sibling developing a particular phenotype (be it depression, inadequate social support, or some aspect of personality) and the other sibling developing a different phenotype?

Beyond quantitative genetic approaches, future studies could benefit by focusing more explicitly on within-subject analyses. For example, research could investigate the relation between *changes* in social support, life stress, and depression within individuals over time. The vast majority of extant studies have examined differences in social support *between* individuals, and are thus prone to the possibility that reports of support reflect stable differences between people. If social support *per se* plays a causal role in depression, then variations in support within an individual over time should predict changes in symptomatology. In a similar manner, experimental studies are critically important. Although we are not aware of any experimental manipulations of social support in the depression literature, Kamarck et al. (1990) conducted a creative study investigating the impact of support on cardiovascular reactivity. Social support was experimentally manipulated by having individuals participate in a stressful cognitive task in either the presence or the absence of a friend. Unfortunately, these within-person analyses and experimental manipulations are less applicable to personality, which is assumed to remain relatively stable over time.

In terms of integrating social support, personality, and depression, some theorists have argued that the health-promoting effect of social support largely involves the perception that one is accepted and loved (Sarason et al., 1990). Importantly, it appears that these perceptions of being lovable and accepted by others are critical in buffering against depression. Where do these perceptions come from? Given quantitative genetic findings, it is apparent that, in addition to actual positive, interpersonal transactions, genetic factors contribute to these feelings of social acceptance. We believe that it is unlikely that genes act in isolation; rather, they create a disposition to internalize positive social encounters. Beginning in infancy and early childhood, these interpersonal transactions become cognitively represented as internal working models, which in turn are important in regulating and maintaining feelings of self-worth and hope in the future. We also expect that genetics contributes to temperamental styles that first emerge in infancy and help shape the social environment throughout the life span. Temperament might influence the development of social supports and the likelihood of experiencing environmental adversities, such a stressful life events and difficulties. Perhaps genes contribute to depression through a developmental pathway in which difficult temperamental styles in infancy lead to affective dysregulation, insecure attachment, vulnerable self-esteem, inadequate social support, and increased exposure to life stressors, which in turn contribute to liability to depression (see Rothbart & Ahadi, 1994). It remains for future studies employing quantitative genetic approaches to further clarify these relations among social support, personality, and depression.

REFERENCES

Abramson, L. Y., Metalsky, G. I., & Alloy, L. B. (1989). Hopelessness depression: A theory-based subtype of depression. *Psychological Review, 96*, 358-372.

Abramson, L. Y., Seligman, M. E. P., & Teasdale, J. D. (1978). Learned helplessness in humans: Critique and reformulation. *Journal of Abnormal Psychology, 87*, 49-74.

Andrews, G., Neilson, M., Hunt, C., Stewart G., & Kiloh, L. G. (1990). Diagnosis, personality and the long-term outcome of depression. *British Journal of Psychiatry, 157*, 13-18.

Arieti, S. A., & Bemporad, J. (1978). *Severe and mild depression: The psychotherapeutic approach.* New York: Basic Books.

Barnett, P. A., & Gotlib, I. H. (1988). Psychosocial functioning and depression: Distinguishing among antecedents, concomitants, and consequences. *Psychological Bulletin, 104*, 97-126.

Baron, R. S., Cutrona, C. E., Hicklin, D., Russell, D. W., Lubaroff, D. M. (1990). Social support and immune function among spouses of cancer patients. *Journal of Personality and Social Psychology, 59*, 344-352.

Barrera, M., & Garrison-Jones, C. (1992). Family and peer social support as specific correlates of adolescent depressive symptoms. *Journal of Abnormal Child Psychology, 20*, 1-16.

Baumeister, R. F., & Leary, M. R. (1995). The need to belong: Desire for interpersonal attachments as a fundamental human motivation. *Psychological Bulletin, 117*, 497-529.

Beach, S. R. H., Arias, I., & O'Leary, K. D. (1986). The relationship of marital satisfaction and social support to depressive symptomatology. *Journal of Psychopathology and Behavioral Assessment, 8*, 305-316.

Beach, S. R. H., Sandeen, E. E., & O'Leary, K. D. (1990). *Depression in marriage.* New York: Guilford.

Beck, A. T. (1967). *Depression: Clinical, experimental and theoretical aspects.* New York: Harper & Row.

Beck, A. T. (1983). Cognitive therapy of depression: New perspectives. In P. J. Clayton & J. E. Barrett (Eds.), *Treatment of depression: Old controversies and new approaches* (pp. 265-290). New York: Raven Press.

Beck, A. T., Rush, A. J., Shaw, B. F., & Emery, G. (1979). *Cognitive therapy for depression.* New York: Guilford.

Belsher, G., & Costello, C. G. (1988). Relapse after recovery from unipolar depression: A critical review. *Psychological Bulletin, 104*, 84-96.

Belsher, G., & Costello, C. G. (1991). Do confidants of depressed women provide less social support than confidants of nondepressed women? *Journal of Abnormal Psychology, 4*, 516-525.

Bergeman, C. S., Plomin, R., Pederson, N. L., & McClearn, G. E. (1991). Genetic mediation of the relationship between social support and psychological well-being. *Psychology and Aging, 6*, 640-646.

Bergeman, C. S., Plomin, R., Pederson, N. L., McClearn, G. E., & Nesselroade, J. R. (1990). Genetic and environmental influences on social support: The Swedish Adoption/Twin Study of Aging (SALSA). *Journal of Gerontology, 45*, 101-106.

Bernet, C. Z., Ingram, R. E., & Johnson, B. R. (1993). Self-esteem. In C. G. Costello (Ed.), *Symptoms of depression* (pp. 141-159). New York: Wiley.

Billings, A. G., Cronkite, R. C., & Moos, R. H. (1983). Social-environmental factors in unipolar depression: Comparisons of depressed patients and nondepressed controls. *Journal of Abnormal Psychology, 92*, 119-133.

Billings, A. G., & Moos, R. H. (1985). Psychosocial processes of remission in unipolar depression: Comparing depressed patients with matched community controls. *Journal of Consulting and Clinical Psychology, 53*, 314-325.

Blatt, S. J., & Zuroff, D. C. (1992). Interpersonal relatedness and self-definition: Two prototypes for depression. *Clinical Psychology Review, 12*, 527-562.

Blazer, D. G. (1983). Impact of late life depression on the social network. *American Journal of Psychiatry, 140*, 162-166.

Blazer, D. G., & Hughes, D. C. (1991). Subjective social support and depressive symptoms: Separate phenomena or epiphenomena. *Journal of Psychiatric Research, 25*, 191-203.

Boyce, P., & Parker, G. (1985). Neuroticism as a predictor of outcome in depression. *Journal of Nervous and Mental Disease, 173*, 685-688.

Boyce, P., Parker, G., Barnett, B., Cooney, M., & Smith, F. (1991). Personality as a vulnerability factor to depression. *British Journal of Psychiatry, 159*, 106-114.

Brewin, C. R., Andrews, B., & Gotlib, I. H. (1993). Psychopathology and early experience: A reappraisal of retrospective reports. *Psychological Bulletin, 113*, 82–98.

Brown, G. W., Andrews, B., Harris, T., Adler, Z., & Bridge, L. (1986). Social support, self-esteem, and depression. *Psychological Medicine, 16*, 813–831.

Brown, G. W., Bifulco, A., & Andrews, B. (1990). Self-esteem and depression: III. Aetiological issues. *Social Psychiatry and Psychiatric Epidemiology, 25*, 235–243.

Burns, D. D., Sayers, S. L., & Moras, K. (1994). Intimate relationships and depression: Is there a causal connection? *Journal of Consulting and Clinical Psychology, 5*, 1033–1043.

Butler, A. C., Hokanson, J. E., & Flynn, H. A. (1994). A comparison of self-esteem lability and low trait self-esteem as vulnerability factors for depression. *Journal of Personality and Social Psychology, 66*, 166–177.

Carey, G., & DiLalla, D. L. (1994). Personality and psychopathology: Genetic perspectives. *Journal of Abnormal Psychology, 103*, 32–43.

Clark, L. A., & Watson, D. (1991). Tripartite model of anxiety and depression: Psychometric evidence and taxonomic implications. *Journal of Abnormal Psychology, 100*, 316–336.

Clark, L. A., Watson, D., & Mineka, S. (1994). Temperament, personality, and the mood and anxiety disorders. *Journal of Abnormal Psychology, 103*, 103–116.

Cohen, S., & McKay, G. (1984). Social support, stress and the buffering hypothesis: A theoretical analysis. In A. Baum, J. E. Singer, & S. E. Taylor (Eds.), *Handbook of psychology and health* (Vol. 4, pp. 253–267). Hillsdale, NJ: Erlbaum.

Cohen, S., & Wills, T. A. (1985). Stress, social support, and the buffering hypothesis. *Psychological Bulletin, 98*, 310–357.

Collins, N. L. (1996). Working models of attachment: Implications for explanation, emotion, and behavior. *Journal of Personality and Social Psychology, 71*, 810–832.

Collins, N. L., Dunkel-Schetter, C., Lobel, M., & Scrimshaw, C. M. (1993). Social support in pregnancy: Psychosocial correlates of birth outcomes and postpartum depression. *Journal of Personality and Social Psychology, 65*, 1243–1258.

Costa, P. T., & McCrae, R. R. (1980). Influence of extraversion and neuroticism on subjective well-being: Happy and unhappy people. *Journal of Personality and Social Psychology, 38*, 668–678.

Coyne, J. C. (1976). Toward an interactional description of depression. *Psychiatry, 39*, 28–40.

Coyne, J. C., Ellard, J. H., Smith, D. A. F. (1990). Social support, interdependence, and dilemmas of helping. In B. R. Sarason, I. G. Sarason, & G. R. Pierce (Eds.), *Social support: An interactional view* (pp. 129–149). New York: Wiley.

Depuc, R. A., & Iacono, W. G. (1988). Neurobehavioral aspects of affective disorders. *Annual Review of Psychology, 40*, 457–492.

Depue, R. A., Krauss, S., & Spoont, M. R. (1987). A two-dimensional threshold model of seasonal bipolar affective disorder. In D. Magnusson & A. Ohman (Eds.), *Psychopathology: An interactional perspective* (pp. 95–123). San Diego: Academic Press.

Depue, R. A., & Monroe, S. M. (1986). Conceptualization and measurement of human disorder in life stress research: The problem of chronic disturbance. *Psychological Bulletin, 99*, 36–51.

Dohr, K. B., Rush, A. J., & Bernstein, I. H. (1989). Cognitive bias and depression. *Journal of Abnormal Psychology, 98*, 263–267.

Duggan, C. F., Lee, A. S., & Murray, R. M. (1990). Does personality predict long-term outcome in depression? *British Journal of Psychiatry, 157*, 19–24.

Dunn, J., & Plomin, R. (1986). Determinants of maternal behavior towards 3-year-old siblings. *British Journal of Developmental Psychology, 4*, 127–137.

Eysenck, H. J., & Eysenck, M. W. (1985). *Personality and individual differences: A natural science approach*. New York: Plenum Press.

Fiore, J., Becker, J., & Copperl, D. B. (1983). Social network interactions: A buffer or a stress. *American Journal of Community Psychology, 11*, 423–439.

Fiore, J., Coppel, D. B., Becker, J., & Cox, G. B. (1986). Social support as a multifaceted concept: Examination of important dimensions for adjustment. *American Journal of Community Psychology, 14*, 93–111.

Fowles, D. C. (1994). A motivational theory of psychopathology. In W. D. Spaulding (Ed.), *Integrative views of motivation, cognition, and emotion: Volume 41 of the Nebraska Symposium on Motivation* (pp. 181–238). Lincoln: University of Nebraska Press.

Gatz, M., Pedersen, N. L., Plomin, R., Nesselroade, J. R., & McClearn, G. E. (1992). Importance of shared genes and shared environments for symptoms of depression in older adults. *Journal of Abnormal Psychology*, *101*, 701–708.

George, L. K., Blazer, D. G., Hughes, D. C., & Fowler, N. (1989). Social support and the outcome of major depression. *British Journal of Psychiatry*, *154*, 478–485.

Goering, P. N., Lancee, W. J., & Freeman, S. J. J. (1992). Marital support and recovery from depression. *British Journal of Psychiatry*, *160*, 76–82.

Gotlib, I. H. (1986, August). *Depression and marital interaction: A longitudinal perspective*. Paper presented at the annual convention of the American Psychological Association, Washington, DC.

Gotlib, I. H., & Beach, S. R. H. (1995). A marital/family discord model of depression: Implications for therapeutic intervention. In N. S. Jacobson & A. S. Gurman (Eds.), *Clinical handbook of couple therapy* (pp. 411–436). New York: Guilford.

Gotlib, I. H., Mount, J. H., Cordy, N. I., & Whiffen, V. E. (1988). Depressed mood and perceptions of early parenting: A longitudinal investigation. *British Journal of Psychiatry*, *152*, 24–27.

Gotlib, I. H., Roberts, J. E., Gilboa, E. (1996). Cognitive interference in depression. In I. G. Sarason, B. R. Sarason, & G. R. Pierce (Eds.), *Cognitive interference: Theories, methods, and findings* (pp. 347–377). Hillsdale, NJ: Erlbaum.

Gotlib, I. H., & Robinson, L. A. (1982). Responses to depressed individuals: Discrepancies between self-report and observer-rated behavior. *Journal of Abnormal Psychology*, *91*, 231–240.

Gotlib, I. H., & Whiffen, V. E. (1991). The interpersonal context of depression: Implications for theory and research. In W. H. Jones & D. Perlman (Eds.), *Advances in personal relationships* (Vol. 3, pp. 177–206). London: Jessica Kingsley Publishers.

Grant, I., Patterson, T. L., & Yager, J. (1988). Social supports in relation to physical health and symptoms of depression in the elderly. *American Journal of Pathology*, *145*, 1254–1258.

Gray, J. A. (1987). *The psychology of fear and stress*. New York: Cambridge University Press.

Greenberger, E., & O'Neil, R. (1993). Spouse, parent, worker: Role commitments and role-related experiences in the construction of adults' well-being. *Developmental Psychology*, *29*, 181–197.

Hamilton, E. W., & Abramson, L. Y. (1983). Cognitive patterns and major depressive disorder: A longitudinal study in a hospital setting. *Journal of Abnormal Psychology*, *92*, 173–184.

Hammen, C. L., Burge, D., Daley, S. E., Davila, J., Paley, B., & Rudolf, K. D. (1995). Interpersonal attachment cognitions and prediction of symptomatic responses to interpersonal stress. *Journal of Abnormal Psychology*, *104*, 436–443.

Hays, R. B., Turner, H., & Coates, T. J. (1992). Social support, AIDS-related symptoms, and depression among gay men. *Journal of Consulting and Clinical Psychology*, *60*, 463–469.

Heller, K. (1979). The effects of social support: Prevention and treatment implications. In A. P. Goldstein & F. H. Kanfer (Eds.), *Maximizing treatment gains: Transfer enhancement in psychotherapy* (pp. 353–382). San Diego: Academic Press.

Heller, K., & Swindle, R. V. (1983). Social networks, perceived social support, and coping with stress. In R. D. Felner, L. A. Jason, J. Moritsugu, & S. S. Farber (Eds.), *Preventive psychology: Research and practice in community intervention* (pp. 87–103). New York: Pergamon Press.

Henderson, S., Byrne, D. G., & Duncan-Jones, P. (1981). *Neurosis and the social environment*. San Diego: Academic Press.

Hinchcliffe, M., Hooper, D., & Roberts, F. J. (1978). *The melancholy marriage*. New York: Wiley.

Hirschfeld, R. M. A., & Klerman, G. L. (1979). Personality attributes and affective disorders. *American Journal of Psychiatry*, *136*, 67–70.

Hirschfeld, R. M. A., Klerman, G. L., Andreasen, N. C., Clayton, P. J., & Keller, M. B. (1986). Psycho-social predictors of chronicity in depressed patients. *British Journal of Psychiatry*, *148*, 648–654.

Hirschfeld, R. M. A., Klerman, G. L., Clayton, P. J., & Keller, M. B. (1983a). Personality and depression: Empirical findings. *Archives of General Psychiatry*, *40*, 993–998.

Hirschfeld, R. M. A., Klerman, G. L., Clayton, P. J., Keller, M. B., McDonald-Scott, P., & Larkin, B. H. (1983b). Assessing personality: Effects of the depressive state on trait measurement. *American Journal of Psychiatry*, *140*, 695–699.

Hirschfeld, R. M. A., Klerman, G. L., Lavori, P., Keller, M. B., Griffith, P., & Coryell, W. (1989). Premorbid personality assessments of first onset of major depression. *Archives of General Psychiatry*, *46*, 345–350.

Hirschfeld, R. M. A., & Shea, M. T. (1992). Personality. In E. S. Paykel (Ed.), *Handbook of affective disorders* (pp. 185-194). New York: Guilford

Hobfoll, S. E., & Leiberman, J. R. (1987). Personality and social resources in immediate and continued stress resistance among women. *Journal of Personality and Social Psychology, 52*, 18-26.

Hobfoll, S. E., & London, P. (1986). The relationship of self-concept and social support to emotional distress among women during war. *Journal of Social and Clinical Psychology, 4*, 189-203.

Hooley, J. M., Orley, J., & Teasdale, J. D. (1986). Levels of expressed emotion and relapse in depressed patients. *British Journal of Psychiatry, 148*, 642-647.

Hooley, J. M., & Teasdale, J. D. (1989). Predictors of relapse in unipolar depressives: Expressed emotion, marital distress and perceived criticism. *Journal of Abnormal Psychology, 98*, 229-235.

Hur, Y., & Bouchard, T. J. (1995). Genetic influences on perceptions of childhood family environment: A reared apart twin study. *Child Development, 66*, 330-345.

Jardine, R., Martin, N. G., & Henderson, A. S. (1984). Genetic covariation between neuroticism and symptoms of anxiety and depression. *Genetic Epidemiology, 1*, 89-107.

Johnson, S. L., & Roberts, J. E. (1995). Life events and bipolar disorder: Implications from biological theories. *Psychological Bulletin, 117*, 434-449.

Joiner, T. E., Alfano, M. S., & Metalsky, G. I. (1993). Caught in the crossfire: Depression, self-consistency, self-enhancement, and the response of others. *Journal of Social and Clinical Psychology, 12*, 114-135.

Kamarck, T. W., Manuck, S. B., & Jennings, J. R. (1990). Social support reduces cardiovascular reactivity to psychological challenge: A laboratory model. *Psychosomatic Medicine, 52*, 42-58.

Keitner, G. I., Ryan, C. E., Miller, I. W., Kohn, R., Bishop, D. S., & Epstein, N. B. (1995). Role of the family in recovery and major depression. *American Journal of Psychiatry, 152*, 1002-1008.

Kendell, R. E., & DiScipio, W. J. (1968). Eysenck Personality Inventory scores of patients with depressive illnesses. *British Journal of Psychiatry, 114*, 767-770.

Kendler, K. S. (1993). Twin studies of psychiatric illness. *Archives of General Psychiatry, 50*, 905-915.

Kendler, K. S., Heath, A., Martin, N. G., & Eaves, L. J. (1986). Symptoms of anxiety and depression in a volunteer twin population. *Archives of General Psychiatry, 43*, 213-221.

Kendler, K. S., Kessler, R. C., Neale, M. C., Heath, A. C., & Eaves, L. J. (1993a). The prediction of major depression in women: Toward an integrated etiologic model. *American Journal of Psychiatry, 150*, 1139-1148.

Kendler, K. S., Kessler, R. C., Walters, E. E., MacLean, C., Neale, M. C., Heath, A. C., & Eaves, L. J. (1995a). Stressful life events, genetic liability, and onset of an episode of major depression in women. *American Journal of Psychiatry, 152*, 833-842.

Kendler, K. S., Neale, M. C., Kessler, R. C., Heath, A. C., & Eaves, L. J. (1992). Childhood parental loss and adult psychopathology in women. *Archives of General Psychiatry, 49*, 109-116.

Kendler, K. S., Neale, M. C., Kessler, R. C., Heath, A. C., & Eaves, L. J. (1993b). A longitudinal twin study of personality and major depression in women. *Archives of General Psychiatry, 50*, 853-862.

Kendler, K. S., Neale, M., Kessler, R., Heath, A., & Eaves, L. (1993c). A twin study of recent life events and difficulties. *Archives of General Psychiatry, 50*, 789-796.

Kendler, K. S., Walters, E. E., Neale, M. C., Kessler, R. C., Heath, A. C., & Eaves, L. J. (1995b). The structure of the genetic and environmental risk factors for six major psychiatric disorders in women. *Archives of General Psychiatry, 52*, 374-383.

Kessler, R. C., Kendler, K. S., Heath, A., Neale, M. C. & Eaves, L. J. (1992). Social support, depressed mood, and adjustment to stress: A genetic epidemiological investigation. *Journal of Personality and Social Psychology, 62*, 257-272.

Kessler, R. C., Kendler, K. S., Heath, A., Neale, M. C., & Eaves, L. J. (1994a). Perceived support and adjustment to stress in a general population sample of female twins. *Psychological Medicine, 24*, 317-334.

Kessler, R. C., McGonagle, K. A., Zhao, S., Nelson, C. B., Hughes, M., Eshleman, S., Wittchen, H. U., & Kendler, K. S. (1994b). Lifetime and 12-month prevalence of DSM-III-R psychiatric disorders in the United States: Results from the National Comorbidity Survey. *Archives of General Psychiatry, 51*, 8-19.

Kraepelin, E. (1921). *Manic-depressive illness and paranoia*. Edinburgh, Scotland: E & S Livingstone.

Krantz, S. E., & Moos, R. H. (1988). Risk factors at intake predict nonremission among depressed patients. *Journal of Consulting and Clinical Psychology, 56*, 863-869.

Lakey, B. (1988). Self-esteem, control beliefs, and cognitive problem-solving skills as risk factors in the development of subsequent dysphoria. *Cognitive Therapy and Research, 12*, 409-420.

Lakey, B., & Cassady, P. B. (1990). Cognitive processes in perceived social support. *Journal of Personality and Social Psychology, 59,* 337–343.

Lewinsohn, P. M., Hoberman, H. M., & Rosenbaum, M. (1988). A prospective study of risk factors for unipolar depression. *Journal of Abnormal Psychology, 97,* 251–264.

Lewinsohn, P. M., Steinmetz, J. L., Larson, D. W., & Franklin, J. (1981). Depression-related cognitions: Antecedent or consequence? *Journal of Abnormal Psychology, 90,* 213–219.

Lin, N., Simeone, R. S., Ensel, W. M., & Kuo, W. (1979). Social support, stressful life events, and illness: A model and an empirical test. *Journal of Health and Social Behavior, 20,* 108–119.

Loehlin, J. C. (1989). Partitioning environmental and genetic contributions to behavioral development. *American Psychologist, 44,* 1285–1292.

Loehlin, J. C., Willerman, L., & Horn, J. M. (1987). Personality resemblance in adoptive families: A 10-year follow-up. *Journal of Personality and Social Psychology, 53,* 961–969.

MacKinnon, A. J., Henderson, A. S., & Andrews, G. (1990). Genetic and environmental determinants of the lability of trait neuroticism and the symptoms of anxiety and depression. *Psychological Medicine, 20,* 581–590.

Magnus, K., Diener, E., Fujita, F., & Pavot, W. (1993). Extroversion and neuroticism as predictors of objective life events: A longitudinal analysis. *Journal of Personality and Social Psychology, 65,* 1046–1053.

Martin, M. (1985). Neuroticism as predisposition toward depression: A cognitive mechanism. *Personality and Individual Differences, 6,* 353–365.

McCrae, R. R., & Costa, P. T. (1987). Validation of a five-factor model of personality across instruments and observers. *Journal of Personality and Social Psychology, 52,* 81–90.

McGuffin, P., Katz, R., & Bebbington, P. (1988). The Camberwell collaborative depression study, III: Depression and adversity in relatives of depressed probands. *British Journal of Psychiatry, 152,* 775–782.

McGuffin, P., Katz, R., & Rutherford, J. (1991). Nature, nurture and depression: A twin study. *Psychological Medicine, 21,* 329–335.

Merikangas, K. R. (1984). Divorce and assortative mating among depressed patients. *American Journal of Psychiatry, 141,* 74–76.

Metalsky, G. I., Halberstadt, L. J., & Abramson, L. Y. (1987). Vulnerability to depressive mood reactions: Toward a more powerful test of the diathesis–stress and causal mediation components of the reformulated theory of depression. *Journal of Personality and Social Psychology, 52,* 386–393.

Metalsky, G. I., & Joiner, T. E. (1992). Vulnerability to depressive symptomatology: A prospective test of the diathesis–stress and causal mediation components of the hopelessness theory of depression. *Journal of Personality and Social Psychology, 63,* 667–675.

Metalsky, G. I., Joiner, T. E., Hardin, T. S., & Abramson, L. Y. (1993). Depressive reactions to failure in a naturalistic setting: A test of the hopelessness and self-esteem theories of depression. *Journal of Abnormal Psychology, 102,* 101–109.

Meyer, G. J., & Shack, J. R. (1989). Structural convergence of mood and personality: Evidence for old and new directions. *Journal of Personality and Social Psychology, 57,* 691–706.

Mikulincer, M., Florian, V., & Weller, A. (1993). Attachment styles, coping strategies, and posttraumatic psychological distress: The impact of the Gulf War in Israel. *Journal of Personality and Social Psychology, 64,* 817–826.

Mitchell, R. E., & Moos, R. H. (1984). Deficiencies in social support among depressed patients: Antecedents or consequences of stress? *Journal of Health and Social Behavior, 25,* 438–452.

Monroe, S. M., Bromet, E. J., Connell, M. M., & Steiner, S. C. (1986). Social support, life events, and depressive symptoms: A one-year prospective study. *Journal of Consulting and Clinical Psychology, 54,* 424–431.

Monroe, S. M., & Roberts, J. E. (1990). Conceptualizing and measuring life stress: Problems, principles, procedures, progress. *Stress Medicine, 6,* 209–216.

Monroe, S. M., & Steiner, S. C. (1986). Social support and psychopathology: Interrelations with preexisting disorder, stress, and personality. *Journal of Abnormal Psychology, 95,* 29–39.

Nietzel, M. T., & Harris, M. J. (1990). Relationship of dependency and achievement/autonomy to depression. *Clinical Psychology Review, 10,* 279–297.

Nolan, S., Roberts, J. E., & Gotlib, I. H. (in press). Neuroticism and ruminative response style as predictors of change in depressive symptomatology. *Cognitive Therapy and Research.*

Nolen-Hoeksema, S., Parker, L. E., & Larson, J. (1994). Ruminative coping with depressed mood following loss. *Journal of Personality and Social Psychology, 67*, 92–104.

Norman, W. T. (1963). Toward an adequate taxonomy of personality attributes: Replicated factor structure. *Journal of Abnormal and Social Psychology, 66*, 574–583.

Pagel, M. D., & Becker, J. (1987). Depressive thinking and depression: Relations with personality and social resources. *Journal of Personality and Social Psychology, 52*, 1043–1052.

Panzarella, C., & Alloy, L. B. (1995, November). *Social support, hopelessness, and depression: An expanded hopelessness model.* Paper presented at a meeting of the Association for Advancement of Behavior Therapy, Washington, D.C.

Parker, G. (1992). Early environment. In E. S. Paykel (Ed.), *Handbook of affective disorders* (2nd ed., pp. 171–183). New York: Guilford.

Paykel, E. S., & Weissman, M. M. (1973). Social adjustment and depression: A longitudinal study. *Archives of General Psychiatry, 28*, 659–663.

Phifer, J. F., & Murrell, S. A. (1986). Etiologic factors in the onset of depressive symptoms in older adults. *Journal of Abnormal Psychology, 95*, 282–291.

Plomin, R., & Daniels, D. (1987). Why are children in the same family so different from one another? *Behavioral and Brain Sciences, 10*, 1–60.

Plomin, R., DeFries, J. C., & Loehlin, J. C. (1977). Genotype–environment interaction and correlation in the analysis of human behavior. *Psychological Bulletin, 84*, 309–322.

Plomin, R., DeFries, J. C., & McClearn, G. E. (1990). *Behavioral genetics: A primer.* New York: W. H. Freeman.

Plomin, R., Loehlin, J. C., & DeFries, J. C. (1985). Genetic and environmental components of "environmental" influences. *Developmental Psychology, 21*, 391–402.

Plomin, R., McClearn, G. E., Pederson, N. L., Nesselroade, J. R., & Bergeman, C. S. (1988). Genetic influence on childhood family environment perceived retrospectively from the last half of the life span. *Developmental Psychology, 24*, 738–745.

Pogue-Geile, M. F., & Rose, R. J. (1985). Developmental genetic studies of adult personality. *Developmental Psychology, 21*, 547–557.

Poulton, R. G., & Andrews, G. (1992). Personality as a cause of adverse life events. *Acta Psychiatrica Scandinavia, 85*, 35–38.

Reiss, D., Plomin, R., & Hetherington, E. M. (1991). Genetics and psychiatry: An unheralded window on the environment. *American Journal of Psychiatry, 148*, 283–291.

Roberts, C. R., Roberts, R. E., & Stevenson, J. M. (1982). Women, work, social support and psychiatric morbidity. *Social Psychiatry, 17*, 167–173.

Roberts, J. E., Gilboa, E., & Gotlib, I. H. (1997). *Ruminative response style and vulnerability to depressive episodes: Factor components, mediating processes, and episode duration.* Manuscript submitted for publication.

Roberts, J. E., & Gotlib, I. H. (in press). Vulnerability to episodes of depression: Gender, early childhood loss, and personality. *British Journal of Clinical Psychology.*

Roberts, J. E., & Gotlib, I. H. (in press). Temporal variability in global self-esteem and specific self-evaluation as prospective predictors of emotional distress: Specificity in predictors and outcome. *Journal of Abnormal Psychology.*

Roberts, J. E., & Gotlib, I. H. (1995, November). *Attachment insecurity and symptoms of depression: Breakdowns in self-esteem regulation?* Paper presented at the Association for the Advancement of Behavior Therapy, Washington, D.C.

Roberts, J. E., Gotlib, I. H., & Kassel, J. D. (1996). Adult attachment security and symptoms of depression: The mediating roles of dysfunctional attitudes and low self-esteem. *Journal of Personality and Social Psychology, 70*, 310–320.

Roberts, J. E., & Kassel, J. D. (in press). Labile self-esteem, stressful life events, and depressive symptoms: Prospective data testing a model of vulnerability. *Cognitive Therapy and Research.*

Roberts, J. E., & Monroe, S. M. (1992). Vulnerable self-esteem and depressive symptoms: Prospective findings comparing three alternative conceptualizations. *Journal of Personality and Social Psychology, 62*, 804–812.

Roberts, J. E., & Monroe, S. M. (1994). A multidimensional model of self-esteem in depression. *Clinical Psychology Review, 14*, 161–181.

Rogers, C. R. (1961). *On becoming a person*. Boston: Houghton Mifflin.

Rook, K. (1984). The negative side of social interactions: Impact on psychological well-being. *Journal of Personality and Social Psychology, 46*, 1097–1108.

Roos, P. E., & Cohen, L. H. (1987). Sex roles and social support as moderators of life stress adjustment. *Journal of Personality and Social Psychology, 52*, 576–585.

Rose, R. J. (1988). Genetic and environmental variance in content dimensions of the MMPI. *Journal of Personality and Social Psychology, 55*, 302–311.

Rose, R. J., Koskenvuo, Kaprio, J., Sarna, S., & Langinvainio, H. (1988). Shared genes, shared experiences, and similarity of personality: Data from 14,288 adult Finnish co-twins. *Journal of Personality and Social Psychology, 54*, 161–171.

Rothbart, M. K., & Ahadi, S. A. (1994). Temperament and the development of personality. *Journal of Abnormal Psychology, 103*, 55–66.

Rowe, D. C. (1983). A biometrical analysis of perceptions of family environment: A study of twin and singleton sibling kinships. *Child Development, 54*, 416–423.

Sarason, B. R., Pierce, G. R., & Sarason, I. G. (1990). Social support: The sense of acceptance and the role of relationships. In B. R. Sarason, I. G. Sarason, & G. R. Pierce (Eds.), *Social support: An interactional view* (pp. 97–128). New York: Wiley.

Sarason, B. R., Shearin, E. N., Pierce, G. R., & Sarason, I. G. (1987). Interrelations of social support measures: Theoretical and practical implications. *Journal of Personality and Social Psychology, 52*, 813–832.

Swann, W. B., Wenzlaff, R. M., Krull, D. S., & Pelham, B. W. (1992). Allure of negative feedback: Self-verification strivings among depressed persons. *Journal of Abnormal Psychology, 101*, 292–306.

Sweeney, P., Anderson, K., & Bailey, S. (1986). Attributional style in depression: A meta-analytic review. *Journal of Personality and Social Psychology, 50*, 974–991.

Tambs, K. (1991). Transmission of symptoms of anxiety and depression in nuclear families. *Journal of Affective Disorders, 21*, 117–126.

Thoits, P. A. (1986). Social support as coping assistance. *Journal of Consulting and Clinical Psychology, 54*, 416–423.

Turner, J. B., Kessler, R. C., & House, J. S. (1991). Factors facilitating adjustment to unemployment: Implication for intervention. *American Journal of Community Psychology, 19*, 521–542.

Watson, D., & Clark, L. A. (1984). Negative affectivity: The disposition to experience aversive emotional states. *Psychological Bulletin, 96*, 465–490.

Watson, D., Clark, L. A., & Harkness, A. R. (1994). Structures of personality and their relevance to psychopathology. *Journal of Abnormal Psychology, 103*, 18–31.

Weissman, M. M., Prusoff, B. A., & Klerman, G. L. (1978). Personality and the prediction of long-term outcome of depression. *American Journal of Psychiatry, 135*, 797–800.

Whisman, M. A., & Kwon, P. (1992). Parental representations, cognitive distortions, and mild depression. *Cognitive Therapy and Research, 16*, 557–568.

Whisman, M. A., & Kwon, P. (1993). Life stress and dysphoria: The role of self-esteem and hopelessness. *Journal of Personality and Social Psychology, 65*, 1054–1060.

Whisman, M. A., & McGarvey, A. L. (1995). Attachment, depressotypic cognitions, and dysphoria. *Cognitive Therapy and Research, 19*, 633–650.

Wierzbicki, M. (1987). Similarity of monozygotic and dizygotic child twins in level and lability of subclinically depressed mood. *American Journal of Orthopsychiatry, 57*, 33–40.

Chapter 10

SOCIAL SUPPORT, PERSONALITY, AND LIFE STRESS ADJUSTMENT

Lawrence H. Cohen, Tanya R. Hettler,
and Crystal L. Park

Research on the relationship between life stress and psychological and medical outcomes began approximately 30 years ago. Despite researchers' initial optimism, however, it soon became apparent that life stress accounted for only a small portion of variance, with correlations in the .30–.40 range. This led to an interest in variables that might moderate the stress–outcome relationship, that is, variables that might define the conditions affecting the predictive role of life events. Initially, the moderator variable of social support dominated research of this type; the empirical literature on the stress-buffering effects of social support is very large (Adler & Matthews, 1994; Cohen & Wills, 1985). In general, this literature provided some support for the stress-buffering role of perceived social support; received support and social network indices were found to be less consistent stress moderators (Cohen & Wills, 1985).

Social support was initially conceptualized as an "environmental" variable; therefore, the early research focused on environmental factors that influenced the stress–outcome relationship. Of course, researchers now recognize that social support, especially perceived support, is not simply an environmental variable, but rather is in part a consequence of, and confounded with, personality (Bolger & Eckenrode, 1991; Sarason, Pierce, & Sarason, 1994).

About 15 years ago, stress researchers began to examine the stress-moderating roles of various personality characteristics, such as locus of control, hardiness, and Type A behavior. This empirical literature is sizable, and there is modest support for the stress-buffering role of an "instrumental" personality style, broadly defined (Cohen &

Lawrence H. Cohen and Tanya R. Hettler • Department of Psychology, University of Delaware, Newark, Delaware 19716.   Crystal L. Park • Department of Psychology, Miami University, Oxford, Ohio 45056.

Sourcebook of Social Support and Personality, edited by Gregory R. Pierce, Brian Lakey, Irwin G. Sarason, and Barbara R. Sarason. Plenum Press, New York, 1997.

Edwards, 1989). Previous research with adults and adolescents has shown that instrumentality has concurrent and predictive relations with a relatively wide range of self-report and behavioral measures (e.g., Spence, 1984), including low levels of psychological distress and high self-esteem (e.g., Spence & Helmreich, 1978), and internal locus of control (e.g., Zeldow, Clark, & Daugherty, 1985).

Researchers tended to address these two questions regarding the stress-moderating role of social support and personality independently, without attempting to examine their joint influence on life stress adjustment. However, virtually all theories of human behavior emphasize the *interaction* between the environment and the person. Individuals' reactions to negative life events are similarly thought to result from the *combined* influences of environmental (e.g., social support) and personal (e.g., personality) variables (Lazarus & Folkman, 1984). With this in mind, approximately 10 years ago, researchers began to consider the *interactive* roles of social support and personality in life stress adjustment, that is, how social support and personality operate in unison to influence individuals' reactions to negative life experiences.

In this chapter, we address the *interactive* roles of social support and personality in life stress adjustment. Specifically, we discuss the issue of social support serving as a life stress buffer for individuals with certain personality characteristics. We should state at the outset that, surprisingly, the relevant empirical literature is sparse; there are relatively few studies that have tested the interactive roles of social support and personality in life stress adjustment. For this reason, we emphasize conceptual and methodological issues over a description of specific findings.

In the first section of the chapter, we clarify our use of the terms *social support*, *personality*, *life stress*, and *life stress adjustment*. In the second section, we review studies that have examined the interactive roles of social support and personality as life stress buffers. The third section provides a conceptual and methodological critique of these studies. We conclude with suggestions for future research.

DEFINITIONS OF TERMS

SOCIAL SUPPORT

There are several ways to conceptualize the construct of social support. Some researchers have emphasized the *structure* of individuals' social networks, with measurement of such variables as network size and network density (interrelatedness). Other researchers have studied the actual provision of supportive behaviors (i.e., *received* social support). Finally, many researchers have measured individuals' beliefs or perceptions of the availability of social support (i.e., *perceived* social support; Sarason, Sarason, & Pierce, 1990).

For both received support and perceived support, there is some consensus concerning the various potential *functions* of social support: (1) emotional support, in which others communicate to an individual that he or she is (will be) cared for in times of stress; (2) social integration or network support, in which an individual feels part of a group that has common interests and concerns; (3) esteem support, in which others reinforce an individual's sense of competence and self-esteem more generally;

(4) tangible aid, in which others provide instrumental assistance, such as money or physical help; and (5) informational support, in which an individual receives specific suggestions or guidance concerning solutions to a problem (Cutrona & Russell, 1990; Weiss, 1974).

For this chapter, we attempted an exhaustive review of the empirical literature on the interactive, stress-buffering roles of personality and social support. In these studies, social support was conceptualized as either perceived or received support. Research on the relationship between structural measures of support and psychological and health outcomes has yielded relatively weak findings (Sarason et al., 1990). A few studies examined the differential roles of the specific functions of support (e.g., emotional support vs. tangible aid), but most treated perceived or received support as a unitary construct. In all of the studies, social support was measured with a self-report questionnaire.

PERSONALITY

We use the term *personality* to refer to individual difference variables that are usually thought of as traits or dispositions, such as locus of control, sex-role orientation, and self-confidence. There is the assumption that these variables are relatively stable over time, and across situations. In all of the studies reviewed in this chapter, personality was measured with a self-report questionnaire. For the most part, we do not include studies that examined the stress-buffering roles of social support or personality in conjunction with *coping*, which is conceptualized as distinct from, although related to, both social support and personality (Lazarus & Folkman, 1984).

LIFE STRESS

Life stress can be defined as a discrete event (e.g., termination of a relationship) or chronic situation (e.g., unstable marriage) that is regarded as a threat, loss, or challenge, and that taxes an individual's ability to cope (Lazarus & Folkman, 1984). Most of the literature on life stress conceptualizes it in one of two ways: (1) As an accumulation of negative life events over time; in this model, individuals who experienced many negative events in the recent past would be classified as the "high-stress" group; high-stress individuals will vary in the specific nature of their negative events, but all will have experienced a relatively high number of them; (2) As the occurrence of a specific event; in this model, all participants will have experienced the same stressful event, for example, basic military training, or death of a spouse.

LIFE STRESS ADJUSTMENT

In the chapter, we are interested in how social support and personality, together, affect individuals' psychological adjustment to stressful life events. Life stress adjustment is typically conceptualized as clinical or subclinical outcomes, such as depression, anxiety, and general psychological distress. We limited our search to studies that measured psychological adjustment, although, to our knowledge, there is but one relevant study that measured physical health outcomes (Kobasa & Purcetti, 1983). In all of these studies, adjustment was assessed with self-report measures.

SOCIAL SUPPORT, PERSONALITY, AND STRESS MODERATION

Several models have been proposed to describe the roles that social support and personality play in life stress adjustment. Some models emphasize the causal path from stressors to social support (e.g., support mobilization model), whereas other models emphasize the causal path from social support to stressors (Barrera, 1988; Hobfoll & Vaux, 1993). The most influential, and widely researched, of these is the stress-buffering model. This model postulates that the relationship between stress and distress will vary as a function of values of a moderator variable (e.g., social support, personality). The stress-buffering model began to attract attention approximately 15 years ago, partly in response to a growing awareness that the relationship between accumulated life stress and mental health outcomes was relatively weak. Researchers hoped that inclusion of moderator variables would strengthen predictive models (Cohen & Edwards, 1989).

Before we consider specific studies that tested stress-buffering hypotheses, it is necessary to provide some background on the conceptual and methodological issues that are relevant to stress moderation in general. A stress moderator can be a qualitative (e.g., gender, race) or quantitative (e.g., social support, personality) variable that influences the direction and/or strength of the relationship between a predictor (e.g., stress) and a criterion (e.g., adjustment). Predictors (e.g., stress) and moderators (e.g., personality, social support) are conceptualized at the same level in regard to their role as causal variables antecedent to the criterion; in other words, moderators are always independent variables. Moderator variables are measured to help explain the conditions that affect the relationship between a predictor and a criterion; the focus of interest is on the predictor and its relationship to the criterion.

A variable is thought to function as a stress moderator by influencing primary or secondary appraisals of events (or both), and by influencing the reliance on specific coping strategies (Cohen & Edwards, 1989). For example, perceived social support might serve as a stress buffer because it (1) dampens evaluations of the potential threat inherent in an event; (2) enhances an individual's evaluations of his or her ability to cope with an event; and/or (3) influences an individual's reliance on adaptive coping strategies, such as problem solving and positive reinterpretation.

It is assumed that stress moderation occurs when there is a *match* between the needs elicited by stressful events and the resources inherent in the support and personality moderator variables (Cohen & Edwards, 1989). For example, a personality variable that promotes feelings of personal control should serve as a stress buffer for a negative event that threatens feelings of control.

Cohen and Edwards (1989) presented an excellent overview of methodological issues relevant to the study of stress moderation. From a methodological perspective, the "ideal" study would have adequate power and rely on a prospective design in which Time 1 life events, social support, and personality would predict Time 1–Time 2 change in the outcome measure. A regression model would be employed, and the important effect, for our purposes, would be that for life stress × social support × personality. The regression lines from this triple interaction would then be graphed and interpreted in accordance with principles outlined by Cohen and Cohen (1983) and Aiken and West

(1991). Aiken and West suggest *centering* the predictors (stress, personality, and social support); using deviation scores reduces the multicolinearity among them and helps in interpreting main effects. For statistical reasons, it is hoped that life stress, social support, and personality have low intercorrelations, and that both social support and personality have low correlations with the criterion variable (Baron & Kenney, 1986). However, because of limited power, it is often difficult to detect a significant triple-interaction effect in a regression analysis; this is especially true when a significant predictor–criterion relationship occurs only within a small subsample (Smith, Smoll, & Ptacek, 1990).

To our knowledge, virtually every study that has tested the interactive roles of social support and personality has focused on aspects of personality that can best be conceptualized as instrumentality. The major hypothesis has been that social support will serve as a life stress buffer for individuals who score high on instrumentality, but not for those who score low on instrumentality. The theory underlying this hypothesis has not been clearly articulated and varies in emphasis from study to study. For example, social support might be more helpful for instrumental individuals, because they solicit or attract more helpful types of support, or because of their behavior subsequent to the receipt of support. In the sections that follow, we review these empirical studies, beginning with those that examined locus of control.

LOCUS OF CONTROL AND SOCIAL SUPPORT AS STRESS MODERATORS

Sandler and Lakey (1982) sampled college students in a cross-sectional design. Students were chosen if they scored as very internal or very external on a locus of control scale (Mirels's [1970] 9-item version of Rotter's scale). *Received* social support was measured with the Inventory of Socially Supportive Behaviors (ISSB; Barrera, Sandler, & Ramsey, 1981), which yields only a total score. Life stress was assessed with an index of accumulated life events, specifically the 111-item College Student Life Event Schedule (CSLES; Sandler & Lakey, 1982). Depression and trait anxiety were the outcomes assessed. Because locus of control and received support were highly correlated, separate regression analyses were conducted for internal and external subjects, respectively. For the prediction of both depression and trait anxiety, there was a significant stress-buffering effect of received support for internal subjects, but not for external subjects. It is interesting to note that although external subjects had higher received support than internal subjects, received support served as a stress buffer only for the latter subjects; therefore, "more" support did not mean "better" support.

Lefcourt, Martin, and Saleh (1984) conducted a series of studies to test the interactive roles of locus of control and social support in life stress adjustment. In all three cross-sectional studies of college students, (1) life stress was assessed with the CSLES (Sandler & Lakey, 1982); (2) *received* support was measured with the ISSB; (3) the locus of control measure allowed for separate scores on achievement and affiliation dimensions, respectively; and (4) the outcome measure was the Profile of Mood States (McNair, Lorr, & Droppleman, 1971). Separate regression analyses were conducted for subjects who were high versus low on the respective scale of internality.

In Study 1, Lefcourt et al. (1984) found a stress-buffering effect of received support for subjects who were high on affiliation internality, but not for subjects who were low on this scale. When subjects were classified as high or low on achievement internality, the stress × social support effect was nonsignificant in both groups.

In Study 1, subjects also completed the Personality Research Form (PRF; Jackson, 1967). Two scales were examined: Needs for Affiliation, and Needs for Autonomy. When separate regression analyses were conducted, the findings revealed a stress-buffering role of received support for subjects who scored low, but not for those who scored high, on affiliation needs, and for subjects who scored high, but not for those who scored low, on autonomy needs.

Study 2 replicated the pattern involving affiliation internality. In addition, the stress-buffering effect of received support was also found for subjects who were high on achievement internality. Study 3 replicated this latter effect but not the former effect.

This series of studies suggests that received social support serves as a life stress buffer when coupled with an *instrumental* personality style: Internality and a high need for autonomy, and a low need for affiliation, seem to reflect an instrumental style (Lefcourt et al., 1984).

Cummins (1988) sampled older college students in a cross-sectional study. An index of accumulated hassles (Kanner, Coyne, Schaefer, & Lazarus, 1981) was used to assess life stress. Locus of control served as the personality variable, and it was measured by Levenson's (1974) 8-item scale. The ISSB was used to measure *received* social support. In addition, the Social Provisions Scale (Russell & Cutrona, 1985) was used to measure *perceived* social support. The Psychiatric Symptom Index (Derogatis, Lipman, Rickels, Uhlenhuth, & Covi, 1974) assessed life stress adjustment. Separate regression analyses were conducted for subjects who were high versus low on internality.

Cummins (1988) found a stress-buffering effect of received support for the high internal, but not low internal, subjects. On the other hand, he found that for high internal subjects, one of the perceived support scales (Reassurance of Worth) functioned as a stress *exacerbator*.

Cauce, Hannan, and Sargeant (1992) conducted a cross-sectional study of early adolescents. Life stress was measured with an index of accumulated life events for adolescents, the Junior High Life Experiences Survey (Swearingen & Cohen, 1985). Their locus of control scale (Intellectual Achievement Responsibility Scale; Crandall, Katkowsky, & Crandall, 1965) was specific to academic situations, and separate scores were computed for success and failure situations, respectively. The Social Support Rating Scale (SSRS; Cauce, Felner, & Primavera, 1982) was administered as a measure of *perceived* social support. This measure has separate subscales for the perceived helpfulness of peers, family, and school personnel (e.g., teachers, coaches). The dependent variables included a measure of state anxiety and Harter's (1982) Perceived Competence scale for children, which has subscales for perceived school competence, peer competence, physical competence, and overall competence.

Regression analyses revealed a significant stress × school support × locus of control (for success) effect in the prediction of perceived school competence. As predicted, school support served as a stress buffer for internal, but not for external, adolescents. Because their measure of perceived support had subscales for specific support sources, and one of their outcome measures had subscales for specific domains of functioning, Cauce et al. (1992) were able to document the specific nature of the social support × personality interaction.

Kobasa and Purcetti (1983) conducted a cross-sectional study of adult male business executives. They used a subscale (Cohesion) of the Family Environment Scale (FES; Moos & Moos, 1981) to assess perceived social support. Stress was assessed with an index of accumulated life events (a modification of Holmes & Rahe's [1967] Schedule of Recent Events). The personality variable was hardiness, which includes the construct of locus of control, and the dependent variable was an index of emotional and physical health problems. Using an analysis of variance model, they obtained an unexpected finding: The highest illness scores were obtained by subjects who had high stress scores, low hardiness scores, but *high* scores on family support. However, it should be noted that because the FES was not designed as a measure of perceived support *per se*, their study represented a weak test of the hypothesized relationship between hardiness and social support. In addition, their measure of hardiness combined the constructs of commitment and challenge, in addition to locus of control.

MASCULINITY AND SOCIAL SUPPORT AS STRESS MODERATORS

Two studies tested the interactive effects of social support and "masculinity" on life stress adjustment. Roos and Cohen (1987) conducted a longitudinal study of college students. Life stress was assessed with the CSLES (Sandler & Lakey, 1982), and depression and anxiety served as outcome variables. The Interpersonal Support Evaluation List (ISEL; Cohen & Hoberman, 1983) was used to assess *perceived* social support. The ISEL has subscales for tangible aid, belonging support, appraisal support, and self-esteem support. The Masculinity scale of the Personal Attributes Questionnaire (Spence & Helmreich, 1978) was administered as an index of instrumentality.

The major regression finding was a Time 2 stress × ISEL × masculinity effect, with initial (Time 1) distress controlled. This triple interaction was significant in the prediction of Time 1–Time 2 change in anxiety, and nearly significant in the prediction of Time 1–Time 2 change in depression. In both cases, perceived support served as a life stress buffer when combined with a high, but not with a low, level of masculinity. Separate analyses of the specific ISEL subscales revealed that this effect for anxiety was significant for the Tangible Aid subscale only. Roos and Cohen suggest that, of all the ISEL subscales, the Tangible Aid subscale is probably the most highly related to *received* support. Therefore, their finding concerning this ISEL subscale should be viewed as consistent with the findings of Sandler and Lakey (1982) and Lefcourt et al. (1984), who demonstrated the stress-buffering effect of received support for internal (instrumental), but not external, college students.

A strength of the Roos and Cohen (1987) study is its analysis of the separate ISEL subscales, demonstrating the specificity of the instrumentality × perceived support effect. Although their design is superior to a cross-sectional one, it is not prospective, because *Time 1* predictors (stress, perceived support, and masculinity) were not tested in the prediction of Time 1–Time 2 change in the criteria.

In a cross-sectional study of college students, Nezu, Nezu, and Peterson (1986) also tested the interactive roles of masculinity and social support. They assessed life stress with an index of accumulated life events (the Life Experiences Survey; Sarason, Johnson, & Siegel, 1978), and their outcome variable was depression. They used the Bem Sex-Role Inventory (BSRI; Bem, 1981) to assess "masculinity," which conceptually is synonymous with instrumentality (Spence & Helmreich, 1978). To measure *perceived* social support, they combined three subscales (Cohesion, Expressiveness, and Conflict) of the FES (Moos & Moos, 1981). Their regression analyses revealed an unexpected finding: Social support served as a life stress buffer when combined with *low* masculinity, but not with high masculinity.

Nezu et al.'s (1986) findings are inconsistent with those of Roos and Cohen (1987), and are difficult to explain. However, Nezu et al.'s study had a number of methodological problems. As mentioned previously, the FES was not designed as a measure of perceived support, and it assesses the quality of relationships with family members only. In addition, the version of the BSRI used in their study has been criticized on both conceptual and methodological grounds (Spence & Helmreich, 1981).

ASSERTIVENESS AND SOCIAL SUPPORT AS STRESS MODERATORS

Elliott and Gramling (1990) conducted two cross-sectional studies of college students to examine the interactive roles of assertiveness and perceived support as life stress moderators. In both studies, (1) an index of accumulated hassles (Kanner et al., 1981) was the measure of life stress, (2) assertiveness was the personality variable, (3) the Social Provisions Scale (SPS; Russell & Cutrona, 1985) was the measure of *perceived* social support, and (4) depression was an outcome variable. An overall measure of distress was also included as an outcome variable in Study 2. Separate regression analyses were conducted for the various SPS subscales (i.e., Attachment, Social Integration, Reassurance of Worth, Reliable Alliance, Guidance, and Opportunities for Nurturance/Care of Others).

In both studies, Elliott and Gramling (1990) found a significant stress × assertiveness × *social integration* effect in the prediction of depression. Study 2 also found this same effect on depression for the SPS subscale *Reassurance of Worth*, and on distress for the SPS subscale *Opportunity for Nurturance*. Each of these effects had the same pattern: Perceived social support served as a stress buffer only when combined with an assertive personality. A strength of this study is its examination of the separate support (SPS) functions.

SOCIOTROPY AND SOCIAL SUPPORT AS LIFE STRESS MODERATORS

Finally, Reynolds and Gilbert (1991) examined the interactive effect of social support and sociotropy (need for others). Subjects were unemployed men, presumed to be in a highly stressful situation. The outcome variable was depression. *Perceived* social support was measured by an "in-house" 5-item scale. These items assessed whether the respondent had someone to turn to for various forms of support (e.g., cheering up, providing advice). A total score was computed, reflecting the number of items endorsed. It was hypothesized that social support would be related to lower depression when combined with high sociotropy scores. It should be noted that Reynolds and Gilbert's hypothesis is opposite to that of the other studies previously discussed. Sociotropy and instrumentality are probably negatively correlated, and their hypothesis, therefore, predicts that social support will serve as a stress buffer when combined with low instrumentality. In any case, the sociotropy × social support effect was nonsignificant in their cross-sectional regression analysis.

CONCEPTUAL AND METHODOLOGICAL CRITIQUE

OVERVIEW OF FINDINGS

Three studies (Cummins, 1988; Lefcourt et al., 1984; Sandler & Lakey, 1982) tested the interactive roles of locus of control and received support (ISSB), and obtained significant findings in the expected direction. Cauce et al. (1992) obtained similar findings for the interaction between locus of control and perceived support. Roos and Cohen (1987) and Elliott and Gramling (1990) found the expected interaction between perceived support and instrumentality and assertiveness, respectively.

On the other hand, Kobasa and Purcetti (1983), Nezu et al. (1986), and Cummins (1988) obtained nonsignificant or unexpected effects for the interactive roles of perceived support and hardiness, masculinity, and locus of control, respectively. Reynolds and Gilbert (1991) tested the interactive roles of perceived support and sociotropy, and obtained nonsignificant results. However, all of the studies that obtained null or unexpected results, with the exception of Cummins (1988), used an inappropriate or weak measure of perceived social support. Specifically, Kobasa and Purcetti and Nezu et al. used subscales of the FES, and Reynolds and Gilbert used their own 5-item scale.

Of the studies that measured social support with an appropriate scale, all obtained findings that suggest that received or perceived support serves as a stress buffer when combined with an instrumental personality, the only exception being some of Cummins's (1988) analyses. However, it is important to note that none of these studies relied on a *prospective* methodology. All were cross-sectional, with the exception of Roos and Cohen (1987), who tested the effects of Time 2 stress × perceived support × instrumentality on Time 1–Time 2 change in distress. This is a very serious methodological limitation, rendering findings difficult to interpret. For example, research has shown that perceived support is highly related to initial dysphoria, and therefore the cross-sectional finding of a stress-buffering effect of perceived support might merely reflect the stress-buffering effect of low initial levels of distress (Lakey & Ross, 1994).

MEASUREMENT OF VARIABLES

With the exception of Reynolds and Gilbert (1991), all of the studies measured life stress with an index of accumulated life events or hassles. None attempted to categorize events into life domains (e.g., relationship, achievement, etc.). With the exception of studies by Cauce et al. (1992) and Lefcourt et al. (1984), both of which used dimensional measures of locus of control, all of the studies measured personality with a *global* or broadband scale. In every study, life stress adjustment (e.g., depression, anxiety) was assessed via self-report.

All of the studies measured social support with a self-report instrument. Sandler and Lakey (1982), Lefcourt et al. (1984), Kobasa and Purcetti (1983), Nezu et al. (1986), and Reynolds and Gilbert (1991) used global measures of received or perceived social support. The other studies had measures of perceived support that yielded separate scores for specific support functions or sources. But the findings are not very informative because of a lack of consistency. Specifically, Roos and Cohen (1987) reported a significant stress × perceived *tangible aid* × instrumentality effect. Cauce et al. (1992) obtained a significant stress × perceived *school support* × locus of control (for success) effect. Finally, Elliott and Gramling (1990) reported triple interactions involving stress, assertiveness, and perceptions of *social integration*, as well as *worth reassurance* and *opportunity for nurturance*.

Not one study measured subjects' appraisals of events or the reliance on specific coping strategies. Therefore, those studies that obtained significant stress × social support × personality effects cannot account for the *mechanisms* responsible for stress moderation. There is a sizable literature documenting the influence of personality and social support on stress appraisals and coping (Holahan & Moos, 1991; Major, Cozzarelli, Sciacchitano, Cooper, & Testa, 1990; Florian, Mikulincer, & Taubman, 1995; Parkes, 1986), but these studies do not address interactive effects.

Because these studies failed to assess possible mediating variables, the theory underlying the interactive stress-moderating roles of instrumentality and social support remains vague and essentially untested. There are a number of reasons why social support might serve as a stress buffer for instrumental individuals. It is possible that instrumental individuals have "better" or more "helpful" relationships with others; their friends might be more resourceful individuals than the friends of noninstrumental individuals, or their friends might be more invested in helping, because they anticipate eventual reciprocation (Elliott & Gramling, 1990). Compared to noninstrumental individuals, instrumental individuals might be more effective in requesting appropriate help and declining inappropriate help (Elliott & Gramling, 1990; Sandler & Lakey, 1982). Perhaps both attributional and coping differences mediate this effect: Instrumental individuals might be more likely to evaluate a negative event as controllable, and therefore might be more effective in translating social support into concrete action or problem solving (Cauce et al., 1992).

IMPLICATIONS FOR FUTURE RESEARCH

Understanding how personality and social support work together to influence individuals' reactions to negative life events is an important goal. We are surprised at the paucity of relevant research and disappointed in its quality. Although research to date suggests that social support serves as a stress buffer when combined with an instrumental personality, the mechanisms responsible for this effect remain unknown. Future research should examine differences in the social world of instrumental versus noninstrumental individuals, and should test the possible mediating roles of attributions and coping behavior.

It is possible that social support will be more helpful for noninstrumental individuals than instrumental individuals, depending on the nature of the stressor and the type of support received. For tragedies that are uncontrollable and require acceptance rather than problem solving (e.g., death of a child), noninstrumental individuals might "solicit" or receive emotional support, whereas instrumental individuals might solicit or receive more problem-oriented assistance. In this instance, social support should serve as a stress buffer for the former but not the latter individuals. Indeed, the matching model of stress moderation would predict this finding (Cohen & Edwards, 1989).

To date, the relevant empirical literature has focused on instrumentality, broadly defined, but there are other personality constructs that might interact with the stress-buffering role of specific types of social support, including self-complexity, introversion/extraversion, and sensation seeking. For example, complex individuals view themselves as having multiple identities that are relatively compartmentalized. Simple individuals view themselves as having a few overlapping identities. Previous research has shown that complex individuals fare better than simple individuals when confronted with life stress (e.g., Linville, 1987; Smith & Cohen, 1993). Although this effect has been explained in terms of self-complexity as an affect moderator, it is possible that social support is involved, perhaps in both type and *variety* of sources.

Future research will also need to be more *specific* and sensitive to context. As is discussed in other chapters in this book, measurement of social support, be it perceived or received, is moving toward assessment of specific relationship functions provided by specific sources. Similarly, a simple count of experienced life events should be replaced with categorization by domain or thematic implications, for example, relationship-negative events or achievement-negative events (Cutrona & Russell, 1990). There are some data that suggest that specific social support functions are differentially helpful for specific types of life events, such as controllable versus uncontrollable events, and threats versus losses (Bjorck & Cohen, 1993; Cutrona & Russell, 1990). However, this categorization is relatively crude, and it is imposed by investigators rather than created by the subjects themselves (Swindle, Heller, & Lakey, 1988). The analogue methodology used by Bjorck and Cohen (1993) might prove useful in studying stress × personality × social support interactions. They developed written vignettes for threat, loss, and challenge stressors, and asked subjects to report projected coping responses.

Virtually all of the studies that we reviewed tested the interactive effects of instrumentality, a personality variable that is conceptualized as broadband, with implications for most situations. If one assumes that most negative life events, regardless of domain, are potentially deleterious because they threaten feelings of esteem and personal control (Cohen & Edwards, 1989), then it makes sense that a broadband trait such as instrumentality will serve as a life stress buffer in most situations. However, as suggested by the findings of Cauce et al. (1992), more accurate prediction will require measurement of *situation-based* personality variables (as well as source-based social support variables; Swindle et al., 1988). Specifically, Cauce et al. measured locus of control for *academic* success and failure situations, respectively, and measured perceived social support from specific sources, including *school* personnel. In the prediction of perceived school competence, they found a significant effect for the stress × academic locus of control (for success) × school support interaction.

The empirical studies to date have addressed whether social support serves as a stress buffer when combined with a certain type of personality. As suggested by the preceding discussion, and by the model of "stress-resource matching" (Cohen & Edwards, 1989; Cutrona & Russell, 1990), a more appropriate question for research is: What situationally construed individual difference variables will facilitate the stress-buffering benefits of a specific relationship function, provided by a specific support source, in the context of a specific type of negative life event?

REFERENCES

Adler, N., & Matthews, K. (1994). Health psychology: Why do some people get sick and some stay well? *Annual Review of Psychology, 45*, 229-259.

Aiken, L., & West, S. (1991). *Multiple regression: Testing and interpreting interactions.* Newbury Park, CA: Sage.

Baron, R., & Kenny, D. (1986). The moderator-mediator variable distinction in social psychological research: Conceptual, strategic, and statistical considerations. *Journal of Personality and Social Psychology, 51*, 1173-1182.

Barrera, M. (1988). Models of social support and life stress: Beyond the buffering hypothesis. In L. Cohen (Ed.), *Life events and psychological functioning: Theoretical and methodological issues* (pp. 211-236). Newbury Park, CA: Sage.

Barrera, M., Sandler, I., & Ramsey, T. (1981). Preliminary development of a scale of social support: Studies on college students. *American Journal of Community Psychology, 9*, 435-447.

Bem, S. (1981). *Bem Sex Roles Inventory: A professional manual.* Palo Alto, CA: Consulting Psychologists Press.

Bjorck, J., & Cohen, L. H. (1993). Coping with threats, losses, and challenges. *Journal of Social and Clinical Psychology, 12*, 56-72.

Bolger, N., & Eckenrode, J. (1991). Social relationships, personality, and anxiety during a major stressful event. *Journal of Personality and Social Psychology, 61*, 440-449.

Cauce, A., Felner, R., & Primavera, J. (1982). Social support in high-risk adolescents. *American Journal of Community Psychology, 10*, 417-428.

Cauce, A., Hannan, K., & Sargeant, M. (1992). Life stress, social support, and locus of control during early adolescence: Interactive effects. *American Journal of Community Psychology, 20*, 787-797.

Cohen, J., & Cohen, P. (1983). *Applied multiple regression/correlation analysis for the behavioral sciences* (2nd ed.). Hillsdale, NJ: Erlbaum.

Cohen, S., & Edwards, J. (1989). Personality characteristics as moderators of the relationship between stress and disorder. In R. Neufeld (Ed.), *Advances in the investigation of psychological stress* (pp. 235-283). New York: Wiley.

Cohen, S., & Hoberman, H. (1983). Positive events and social supports as buffers of life change stress. *Journal of Applied Social Psychology, 13*, 99-125.

Cohen, S., & Wills, T. (1985). Stress, social support, and the buffering hypothesis. *Psychological Bulletin, 98*, 310-357.

Crandall, V., Katkowsky, W., & Crandall, V. (1965). Children's beliefs in their own control of reinforcements in intellectual-academic achievement situations. *Child Development, 36*, 91-109.

Cummins, R. (1988). Perceptions of social support, receipt of supportive behaviors, and locus of control as moderators of the effects of chronic stress. *American Journal of Community Psychology, 16*, 685-700.

Cutrona, C., & Russell, D. (1990). Type of social support and specific stress: Toward a theory of optimal matching. In B. Sarason, I. Sarason, & G. Pierce (Eds.), *Social support: An interactional view* (pp. 319-366). New York: Wiley.

Derogatis, L., Lipman, R., Rickels, K., Uhlenhuth, E., & Covi, L. (1974). The Hopkins Symptoms Checklist (HSCL): A self-report inventory. *Behavioral Science, 19*, 1-15.

Elliott, T., & Gramling, S. (1990). Personal assertiveness and the effects of social support among college students. *Journal of Counseling Psychology, 37*, 427-436.

Florian, V., Mikulincer, M., & Taubman, O. (1995). Does hardiness contribute to mental health during a stressful real-life situation? The roles of appraisal and coping. *Journal of Personality and Social Psychology, 68*, 687–695.

Harter, S. (1982). The Perceived Competence Scale for Children. *Child Development, 53*, 87–97.

Hobfoll, S., & Vaux, A. (1993). Social support: Social resources and social context. In L. Goldberger & S. Breznitz (Eds.), *Handbook of stress: Theoretical and clinical aspects* (pp. 685–705). New York: Free Press.

Holahan, C. J., & Moos, R. (1991). Life stressors, personal and social resources, and depression: A 4-year structural model. *Journal of Abnormal Psychology, 100*, 31–38.

Holmes, T., & Rahe, R. (1967). The Social Readjustment Rating Scale. *Journal of Psychosomatic Research, 11*, 213–218.

Jackson, D. (1967). *Personality Research Form*. Goshen, New York: Research Psychologists Press.

Kanner, A., Coyne, J., Schaefer, C., & Lazarus, R. (1981). Comparison of two modes of stress measurement: Daily hassles and uplifts versus major life events. *Journal of Behavioral Medicine, 4*, 1–39.

Kobasa, S., & Purcetti, M. (1983). Personality and social resources in stress resistance. *Journal of Personality and Social Psychology, 45*, 839–850.

Lakey, B., & Ross, L. (1994). Dependency and self-criticism as moderators of interpersonal stress: The role of initial dysphoria. *Cognitive Therapy and Research, 18*, 581–599.

Lazarus, R., & Folkman, S. (1984). *Stress, appraisal, and coping*. New York: Springer.

Lefcourt, H., Martin, R., & Saleh, W. (1984). Locus of control and social support: Interactive moderators of stress. *Journal of Personality and Social Psychology, 47*, 378–389.

Levenson, H. (1974). Activism and powerful others: Distinctions within the concept of internal–external control. *Journal of Personality Assessment, 38*, 377–383.

Linville, P. (1987). Self-complexity as a cognitive buffer against stress-related illness and depression. *Journal of Personality and Social Psychology, 52*, 663–676.

Major, B., Cozzarelli, C., Sciacchitano, A., Cooper, M., & Testa, M. (1990). Perceived social support, self-efficacy, and adjustment to abortion. *Journal of Personality and Social Psychology, 59*, 452–463.

McNair, D., Lorr, M., & Droppleman, L. (1971). *The Profile of Mood States*. San Diego, CA: Educational and Industrial Testing Service.

Mirels, H. (1970). Dimensions of internal versus external control. *Journal of Consulting and Clinical Psychology, 34*, 226–228.

Moos, R., & Moos, B. (1981). *Family Environment Scale manual*. Palo Alto, CA: Consulting Psychologists Press.

Nezu, A., Nezu, C., & Peterson, M. (1986). Negative life stress, social support, and depressive symptoms: Sex roles as a moderator variable. *Journal of Social Behavior and Personality, 1*, 599–609.

Parkes, K. R. (1986). Coping in stressful episodes: The role of individual differences, environmental factors, and situational characteristics. *Journal of Personality and Social Psychology, 51*, 1277–1292.

Reynolds, S., & Gilbert, P. (1991). Psychological impact of unemployment: Interactive effects of vulnerability and protective factors on depression. *Journal of Counseling Psychology, 38*, 76–84.

Roos, P., & Cohen, L. H. (1987). Sex roles and social support as moderators of life stress adjustment. *Journal of Personality and Social Psychology, 52*, 576–585.

Russell, D., & Cutrona, C. (1985). *The Social Provisions Scale*. Unpublished manuscript, Iowa State University.

Sandler, I., & Lakey, B. (1982). Locus of control as a stress moderator: The role of control perceptions and social support. *American Journal of Community Psychology, 10*, 65–80.

Sarason, I., Johnson, J., & Siegel, J. (1978). Assessing the impact of life changes: Development of the Life Experiences Survey. *Journal of Consulting and Clinical Psychology, 56*, 932–946.

Sarason, I., Pierce, G., & Sarason, B. (1994). General and specific perceptions of social support. In W. Avison & I. Gotlib (Eds.), *Stress and mental health: Contemporary issues and prospects for the future* (pp. 151–177). New York: Plenum.

Sarason, I., Sarason, B., & Pierce, G. (1990). Social support: The search for theory. *Journal of Social and Clinical Psychology, 9*, 133–147.

Smith, H., & Cohen, L. H. (1993). Self-complexity and reactions to a relationship breakup. *Journal of Social and Clinical Psychology, 12*, 367–384.

Smith, R., Smoll, R., & Ptacek, J. (1990). Conjunctive moderator variables in vulnerability and resiliency research: Life stress, social support and coping skills, and adolescent sport injuries. *Journal of Personality and Social Psychology, 58*, 360–370.

Spence, J. (1984). Masculinity, femininity, and gender-related traits: A conceptual analysis and critique of current research. In B. Maher & W. Maher (Eds.), *Progress in experimental personality research* (Vol. 13, pp. ••). New York: Academic Press.

Spence, J., & Helmreich, R. (1978). *Masculinity and femininity: Their psychological dimensions, correlates and antecedents*. Austin: University of Texas Press.

Spence, J., & Helmreich, R. (1981). Androgyny versus gender schema: A comment on Bem's gender schema theory. *Psychological Review, 88,* 365-368.

Swearingen, E., & Cohen, L. H. (1985). Measurement of adolescents' life events: The Junior High Life Experiences Survey. *American Journal of Community Psychology, 13,* 69-85.

Swindle, R., Heller, K., & Lakey, B. (1988). A conceptual reorientation to the study of personality and stressful life events. In L. Cohen (Ed.), *Life events and psychological functioning: Theoretical and methodological issues* (pp. 237-268). Newbury Park, CA: Sage Publications.

Weiss, R. (1974). The provision of social relationships. In Z. Rubin (Ed.), *Do unto others* (pp. 17-26). Englewood Cliffs, NJ: Prentice-Hall.

Zeldow, P., Clark, D., & Daugherty, S. (1985). Masculinity, femininity, Type A behavior, and psychological adjustment in medical students. *Journal of Personality and Social Psychology, 48,* 481-492.

Chapter 11

SOCIAL SUPPORT IN MARRIAGE
AN ANALYSIS OF INTRAINDIVIDUAL AND INTERPERSONAL COMPONENTS

Lauri A. Pasch, Thomas N. Bradbury, and Kieran T. Sullivan

INTRODUCTION AND BACKGROUND

Consider the following interactions in which a spouse talks with his or her partner about feeling irritable due to pressures at work.

Interaction 1: Jack and Karen

JACK: I think I just waste too much time and energy worrying about things I can't change. What I need to do is walk away without feeling so irritable that my whole day is ruined.

KAREN: Yeah, that's your problem.

JACK: Help me, try to help me with this ...

KAREN: I have tried to help you ... I've watched you for six years. You are just an irritable person. I don't know what to do about it.

JACK: I'm not saying I'm an angel and I do everything right.

KAREN: It kind of comes off that way when you talk.

Interaction 2: Jim and Kirsten

KIRSTEN: I just get really irritable. I know I'm a pain to live with.

JIM: Any common denominators when you feel most irritable?

LAURI A. PASCH • Department of Pediatrics, University of California at San Francisco, San Francisco, California 94143-0844.   THOMAS N. BRADBURY AND KIERAN T. SULLIVAN • Department of Psychology, University of California at Los Angeles, Los Angeles, California 90024.

Sourcebook of Social Support and Personality, edited by Gregory R. Pierce, Brian Lakey, Irwin G. Sarason, and Barbara R. Sarason. Plenum Press, New York, 1997.

> KIRSTEN: I just feel my life has been disrupted. Things that I normally did, I don't have time to do anymore.
>
> JIM: What do you think would make you happier? You sometimes talk about not having goals, not knowing what you really want to do.
>
> KIRSTEN: Yeah, that's true—I always had goals before, huh? I wonder what kind of goal I want to set.

We are interested in how spouses help each other contend with personal difficulties, and how they provide everyday support to one another. This might involve dealing with pressures at work, as in the foregoing examples, or wanting to lose weight, change careers, increase one's self-esteem, or any number of issues or problems individuals face. We believe that the quality of supportive exchanges between spouses has important implications for how well the spouse is able to cope with the problem at hand, and for the relationship itself. For example, consider the two interactions presented, which we observed in one of our studies on newlywed marriage. Notice that the interactions appear to differ not only in the likelihood that the problem (i.e., irritability from pressures at work) will be solved through the discussion, but also in the impact the discussion will have on each spouse's satisfaction with the relationship. Whereas Kirsten is likely to come away from her discussion with Jim feeling understood, leading her to feel more confident in the satisfying and supportive nature of her marriage, Jack is likely to come away feeling hurt and misunderstood, and he may question whether Karen is really the right person for him. In short, understanding the nature of supportive interactions in marriage may help us to understand variation in individual and interpersonal functioning.

Studying social support in marriage is of clear practical and theoretical importance. Spouses appear to play a critical role in the provision of support among married persons (Beach, Martin, Blum, & Roman, 1993; Dakof & Taylor, 1990; Reiss, 1990), and in many circumstances, support provided by a spouse or intimate partner appears to be particularly important (Brown & Harris, 1978). Theoretically, support between spouses has been described as a primary element of close relationships (e.g., Kelley et al., 1983; Stafford & Canary, 1991), and it plays a central role in models developed to understand and alleviate the clinical presentation of marital distress. For example, Weiss (1980, p. 201) included support—defined as "skills which provide companionship, comforting, and understanding"—as one of four essential "relationship accomplishments," and he maintained that the quality of a marriage is determined in part by the level of support and validation that spouses provide to each other. Similarly, Jacobson and Margolin (1979) argued that spousal exchange of helping behaviors facilitates closeness and caring, and that to the extent that individuals do not feel their partner is providing such help, intimacy decreases and marital strain becomes more likely.

Despite these theoretical developments, how social support operates in marriage has received relatively little research attention and remains vaguely understood. We argue that this is due in part to a lack of integration between social support and marital research. The reasons for this lack of integration are informative, and we consider them in this chapter in some detail. The importance of studying how support operates in marital relationships has been recognized recently among social support and relationship researchers (e.g., see Cutrona, Suhr, & MacFarlane, 1990; Fincham & Bradbury, 1990), and important advances in our knowledge in this area have begun to emerge (e.g., Cutrona & Suhr, 1994).

One important topic that may benefit from a unification of social support research and marital research is how intraindividual variables, most notably personality, influence the social support process. Although there is evidence that personality factors influence the support process in general (Sarason, Sarason, & Shearin, 1986), these influences have rarely been examined in the context of close relationships (cf. Cutrona & Suhr, 1994; Sarason, Pierce, & Sarason, 1994a). The purpose of this chapter is to consider how personality factors may influence how social support operates in marriage.

This chapter is organized in six sections. First, we illustrate how the development of these two research traditions has led to little interchange and why the time is now ripe for clarification of basic distinctions and for integration. Second, we summarize theory and research on intraindividual influences on the social support process, particularly in the context of marital or other intimate relationships. Third, we present the laboratory paradigm we developed to study the support process in married couples. Fourth, we describe a model of social support processes in marital relationships that incorporates the role of intraindividual influences. Fifth, we examine a set of empirical questions emerging from our model that address the interplay between global relationship quality, interactional behavior, and intraindividual characteristics in predicting how partners feel following support-based marital interactions. The chapter concludes with a summary and critique of key points.

A Lack of Interchange between Social Support and Marital Research

A lack of interchange between social support and marital research has been noted previously (Coyne & DeLongis, 1986; Fincham & Bradbury, 1990; Gottlieb, 1985). A decade ago, Coyne and DeLongis (1986) stated, "[T]he relevance of a large amount of literature concerning marital satisfaction and distress and marital therapy to an understanding of the role of social relationships in health [has] been all but ignored in discussions of social support" (p. 455). A comparable lack of attention to the importance of the supportive functions of marital relationships and to research on social support has been characteristic of marital research. Although the statement Coyne and DeLongis made is less true today than it was in the 1980s, these two research areas have yet to take full advantage of the advances each has made and create integrative research models. We next identify three key factors responsible for the lack of interchange between social support and marital research. Each factor has contributed to the lack of basic knowledge on how social support processes operate in marriage.

Outcomes of Interest

The first factor concerns the outcome of interest in the two research areas. From its inception, social support research has focused on individual outcomes. Early findings revealed that the quality of one's social contacts could have an effect on a broad range of outcomes, including mental health, physical health, and well-being (e.g., Cassel, 1976; Holahan & Moos, 1981; House, 1981). Although some researchers considered marriage to be an important source of social support (e.g., Brown & Harris, 1978), the focus of research was on improving outcomes for the individual. Thus, the relationship context in which social support influences occurred was not emphasized.

In contrast, most marital research has been directed at understanding and ameliorating marital distress, so that the quality and stability of the relationship itself is the outcome of interest. How relational processes influence individual outcomes has rarely been emphasized.

Level of Analysis

A second issue contributing to the lack of interchange concerns the basic conceptualization of how to best study events of interest within relationships. Within the social support literature, several studies demonstrated that *perceptions* of support available from one's social contacts were better predictors of adjustment than reported *receipt* of support (Wethington & Kessler, 1986). Researchers' interest in increasing their ability to predict individual adjustment led social support research toward measures of perceptions of available support from one's social network as a whole. It became widely accepted that social support is best regarded as a "personal experience, rather than a set of objective circumstances or even a set of interactional processes" (Turner, Frankel, & Levin, 1983, p. 74). Research findings indicating that perceived social support was related to personality characteristics (i.e., self-esteem, neuroticism) led some researchers in the field to consider perceived social support as a personality characteristic in itself (e.g., Lakey & Cassady, 1990; Sarason, Sarason, & Shearin, 1986). This so-called "cognitization" of the concept of social support (see Coyne & DeLongis, 1986) led the field away from direct analysis of how support was behaviorally enacted in specific relationships.

Whereas social support researchers emphasized the importance of perceptions of available social support, a number of early studies in the marital area revealed that spouses were poor reporters of events in their own relationship, and the more interactional the event, the less reliable they were (e.g., Sillars & Scott, 1983; Wills, Weiss, & Patterson, 1974). These findings, together with a growing concern over the lack of progress resulting from the sole use of self-report measures (e.g., see Raush, Barry, Hertel, & Swain, 1974), led marital researchers to question the validity of perceptions reported by spouses and to rely instead on observed behaviors of spouses as they interacted with one another. This focus on spousal exchange of specific behaviors led to a surge of behavioral research on marriage, based largely on a social learning model. Broadly, this model posited that rewarding or positive behaviors enhance global evaluations of the marriage, whereas punishing or negative behaviors detract (e.g., Jacobson & Margolin, 1979). Research based on this model has shown that distressed and nondistressed marriages can be distinguished by the behaviors spouses exhibit during marital problem-solving discussions (see Bradbury & Fincham, 1987; Weiss & Heyman, 1990). Thus, whereas models in the social support domain emphasized general perceived social support, models in marital research emphasized observable, interactional behavior and deemphasized individual spousal perceptions.

Domain of Emphasis

A further distinction between these two areas is the emphasis on prosocial aspects of relationships in research on social support versus the emphasis on conflictual aspects of relationships in research on marriage. Within the social support literature, social support was conceptualized originally as purely positive in nature, and it was believed that the more support people had available to them, the better off they were (see Coyne & DeLongis, 1986). The emphasis on the positive was reversed in research on marriage, which tended to focus on conflictual interactions between spouses. This emphasis on conflict probably emerged because of the salience of conflict in distressed marriages, particularly in clinical populations, and because negative behaviors were found to discriminate more strongly than positive behaviors between distressed and nondistressed marriages (see Weiss & Heyman, 1990). As a result, in virtually all laboratory interaction research, spouses were asked to discuss an area of conflict in their marriage. The surprisingly small amount of observational research on social support in marriage probably owes to the presumed significance of conflict in marriage as the prime determinant of marital outcomes and the mistaken view that social support necessarily involves positive behavior.

A TREND TOWARD INTEGRATION

Recent advances in marital and social support research have primed these areas for integration in the study of social support in marital relationships. With regard to differences in the outcome of interest, the need to consider support processes in the context of specific relationships has been recognized, and the notion that the quality of supportive exchanges may have implications for the relationship itself has been noted (see Barbee, 1990; Cutrona et al., 1990; Leatham & Duck, 1991; Steinberg & Gottlieb, 1994).

The issue of whether to study global perceptions or actual behaviors has also evolved in recent years in both domains, so that it is now clear that perceptions and behavior play important roles in understanding relationship processes. In the 1980s, marital researchers began to recognize that a behavior displayed by a spouse in marital interaction could vary in its effect on the partner, and possibly on the marriage, as a function of how the partner understood or interpreted the behavior; the realm of marital interaction research then expanded beyond a sole focus on behavior to include cognitive variables as well (Bradbury & Fincham, 1989; Weiss, 1984). For example, Bradbury and Fincham (1991) theorized that the attributions spouses make for partner behavior would be related to that spouse's subsequent behavior, and they hypothe-sized that, over time, the accumulation of experiences during and after interactions might gradually influence spouses' judgments of marital quality (cf. Bradbury & Fincham, 1992; Bradbury, Beach, Fincham, & Nelson, 1996). With these developments, spousal perceptions have regained a role in efforts to understand marital processes and outcomes. In keeping with the earlier findings, spousal perceptions are not considered accurate indicators of events in the relationship, but instead are considered part of a process whereby behaviors and cognition continuously affect one another, ultimately yielding change in marital satisfaction.

As spousal perceptions have received renewed importance in marital models, so too has actual behavior received renewed importance in social support research. Several researchers have heralded the need to include global perceptions, perceptions specific to important relationships, and the actual behaviors that might contribute to perceived support (e.g., Sarason, Sarason, & Pierce, 1994b). Thus, marital and social support researchers now advocate inclusion of cognitive and behavioral variables in understanding important relationship events. For example, Fincham and Bradbury (1990) have stated that "investigation of social support solely in terms of social interaction or perceived support seems ill-advised; it is only by including both that it is possible to determine their interrelations and relative contributions to well-being" (p. 33). To date, the interrelations between these elements of the support process have yet to be fully explored.

Last, regarding the domain of emphasis, social support researchers have now clearly acknowledged that the original conceptualization of social support as purely positive in nature was limited, and that the presence of negative aspects of support may be even more important than the presence of positive aspects (Pagel, Erdly, & Becker, 1987; Rook, 1984). Similarly, the importance of skills in the support domain has recently been suggested in marital research (e.g., Cutrona & Suhr, 1994). We have suggested that the strong focus on marital conflict in the marital interaction literature has limited the domain in which the social learning model was applied, neglecting an equally or perhaps more important domain of marital interaction (see Pasch and Bradbury, in press). As marital researchers, we adopt the view, following Weiss (1980), that marriage presents spouses with virtually limitless opportunities to provide support for and seek support from the partner, that some spouses and couples will take advantage of these opportunities more than others, and that some spouses and couples will be more effective at providing and soliciting support than others. Just as there is variation in how couples communicate regarding a marital problem, there is sure to be variation in the way they communicate in a support context. We have demonstrated that spouses' skills in providing help to each other with personal (nonmarital) problems predict changes in marital outcomes over a 2-year period, such that spouses with poor skills are more likely to experience deterioration in their marital quality and that skills in the support domain provide incremental information not available from examination of the conflict domain alone (see Pasch & Bradbury, in press).

Summary

We have attempted to illustrate how initial differences in the approach of social support and marital research have dissipated due to recent advances, making it easier to develop integrative research models. We believe that integration of these two areas is likely to speed progress in both. As mentioned earlier, the role of intraindividual variables, most notably personality, is an ideal domain in which to unite social support and marital research. Research from both arenas can be brought to bear on the question: To what extent and by what mechanisms do personality variables influence the social support process in marital relationships? Important developments relevant to this question, from both arenas, are highlighted below.

PERSONALITY AND THE SOCIAL SUPPORT PROCESS

Summary of Research

Within the social support literature, numerous studies suggest that personality factors influence the support process (e.g., Sarason & Sarason, 1982; Sarason et al., 1986). Research on the effect of personality can be divided into two categories:

personality characteristics affecting actual behaviors of either the spouse offering or soliciting help, and personality characteristics affecting the perception that support is available. Evidence pertaining to each category is summarized below.

First, there is evidence that intraindividual characteristics influence help-giving and help-seeking behavior. For example, individuals who are high in depression or low in self-esteem have been rated by observers as less effective support providers and seekers (e.g., Rook, Pietromonaco, & Lewis, 1994). A related question is whether intraindividual characteristics of one spouse influence the behavior of the other. For example, Sacco, Milana, and Dunn (1985) studied how individuals respond to a depressed individual's request for help, and found that requests for help from depressed persons elicited significantly more anger and social rejection but equal amounts of concern and willingness to help as requests for help from non-depressed individuals. Thus with regard to the influence of intraindividual characteristics on support behavior, research has addressed within-individual (i.e., an individual's characteristics affecting his or her own behavior) and cross-individual effects (an individual's characteristics affecting the other person's behavior).

Second, research has demonstrated that the personality of the support recipient is predictive of their perceived level of social support available from their social network (Procidano & Heller, 1983; Sarason, Sarason, Hacker, & Basham, 1985; Sarason et al., 1986). For example, people who show a tendency to evaluate themselves and their experiences in a negative light rate the support provided to them less favorably (Vinokur, Schul, & Caplan, 1987). Other personality characteristics that have been found to predict perceptions of social support include extraversion, self-esteem, depression, and neuroticism (see, e.g., Sarason, Levine, Basham, & Sarason, 1983). As discussed earlier, these findings led some researchers to consider perceived social support to be a personality characteristic itself.

Although much of the research discussed here is persuasive and informative, we see two critical problems with applying this research to support exchanged between marital partners. The first problem concerns the specific characteristics of close relationships, which compromise the generalizability of results from samples of nonintimate pairs. The second problem concerns the methodology employed. Most notable is the reliance on self-report measures, thus restricting the ability of research to speak to the interplay between personality, actual behavior, and perceptions. Each of these issues is next discussed in detail.

PERSONALITY INFLUENCES IN THE CONTEXT OF RELATIONSHIP HISTORY

Most important social interactions (i.e., those that are important in the long run for individual and relationship adjustment) occur in the context of ongoing, close relationships, such as marital or parent–child relationships. However, most of the research on social support has been conducted on college students, using only global perceptions of support without reference to particular relationships, or assessing interactions with strangers or friends. The complex relationship history that is characteristic of close relationships may mean that personality influences on behavior and the interpretation of behavior are less pronounced. This is not to say that personality was never an important influence on these relationships, as it may have originally played important roles in partner choice and in relationship formation. However, after the relationship is formed, it is an open question whether these personality influences persist, or whether behavior and perceptions are to a greater degree influenced by the relationship history (i.e., using social learning terms, the learning history) between provider and recipient. Because previous research has largely studied individuals interacting with others with whom they have at most a limited relationship history, we question the degree to which social psychological research on support behavior is relevant to support between spouses. If associations between personality and behavior do exist, we question whether they will remain once global relationship quality is taken into account.

METHODOLOGICAL ISSUES IN THE STUDY OF PERSONALITY AND SOCIAL SUPPORT

As discussed earlier, there have been two general lines of research on personality influences on social support—one in which the behavioral manifestations of various personality characteristics have been identified (i.e., depressed individuals are less positive support providers), and the other in which the personality characteristics of individuals high and low in perceived social support have been described (i.e., individuals with poor self-esteem perceive less available support). A lingering unanswered question in this research is the mechanism by which personality characteristics affect perceived support. Two pathways have been suggested (see Cutrona, 1989). First, certain personality characteristics may lead to a perceptual bias toward evaluating social relations negatively, and thus to appraise offerings of support, or support solicitation attempts, negatively. Second, certain personality characteristics may lead individuals to behave more negatively (i.e., rejecting helpful suggestions, ignoring legitimate requests for help). The resulting interaction may then be accurately perceived as unsupportive by the support solicitor or as frustrating by the support provider. It is also possible that both processes operate. Because actual support interactions and perceptions of those interactions have been studied together only rarely, the extent to which either of these pathways operates, and to what degree and in what combination, is unclear.

RESEARCH ON PERSONALITY INFLUENCES IN MARRIAGE

We have described two critical problems with applying existing research to support exchanged between marital partners. Specifically, the interplay between intraindividual variables, interactional behaviors, and perceptions of those behaviors, has not received systematic attention, nor has research addressed the complexity added in studying these variables in the context of close relationships (cf. Cutrona & Suhr, 1994; Hobfoll, Nadler, & Leiberman, 1986; Pierce, Sarason, & Sarason, 1992; Sarason et al., 1994a). Methods used in recent marital research on personality may be instructive in approaching these problems and in suggesting useful theoretical models.

Marital researchers have long been interested in the role of personality in determining marital outcomes (see Karney & Bradbury, 1995). For example, in a landmark study, Kelley and Conley (1987) demonstrated that individuals relatively high in neuroticism were more likely than individuals relatively low in neuroticism to be either in distressed relationships or have divorced 50 years later. The authors speculated that personality factors may exert their effect on relationship quality by affecting behaviors exhibited in marital interactions. The strong preference for observational data in the marital literature has left this hypothesis largely unaddressed. However, several studies have appeared recently that demonstrate relationships between personality characteristics and marital behavior. For example, Bradbury, Campbell, and Fincham (1995) asked married couples to have a laboratory discussion about an area of conflict in their marriage. These interactions were coded for the presence of various positive and negative behaviors. Spouses also completed self-report measures of personality. The results demonstrated that certain personality characteristics (in this case, masculinity and femininity) covaried with behavior in marital problem-solving interactions. Importantly, they demonstrate that while current relationship satisfaction was related to the behaviors exhibited, personality factors still accounted for unique variance after the contribution of relationship satisfaction was controlled. These results highlight the value of examining personality variables and interactional variables to understand marital processes. They also demonstrate that personality characteristics covary with marital behavior even in intimate relationships, when relationship quality is taken into account. This research examined personality influences on marital problem-solving skills, not social support provision and receipt. However, as we demonstrate in the next section, a similar methodology can be used to study how personality relates to support behaviors exchanged by marital partners.

The methodology described thus far will help us understand how personality can predict actual behaviors in intimate relationships. However, as we and others (i.e., Cutrona et al., 1990; Dunkel-Schetter, Blasband, Feinstein, & Herbert, 1992; Fincham & Bradbury, 1990; Vinokur et al., 1987) have argued, there is a need for models of personality and social support that incorporate both actual behaviors and perceptions of those behaviors. Both are essential components of the support process, and both may have influence on individual and marital outcomes. In previous research, we have studied spousal interpretations of behaviors by asking spouses to give their appraisal of a marital interaction immediately following it (see Bradbury, 1990) in order to study individual spousal perceptions. For example, spouses are asked to describe how they feel following a problem-solving discussion they just had with their spouse. A similar methodology can be used following laboratory support interactions. We have developed a research paradigm for studying social support in marriage that incorporates behavioral (behaviors exhibited during laboratory interactions) and cognitive variables (spousal appraisals following the interaction). This paradigm and its development are described in detail below.

MEASURING SOCIAL SUPPORT BEHAVIOR IN MARRIAGE: THE SOCIAL SUPPORT INTERACTION CODING SYSTEM

Our laboratory paradigm is similar to that used in standard behavioral research on marriage, in which couples are brought into the laboratory and asked to identify an important area of disagreement in their marriage and to discuss that topic for a specified period of time. The rationale underlying this task is that behaviors exhibited during these interactions are samples of the type of interaction that might occur under typical conditions in the marriage.

The procedure we have developed follows a similar structure with the exception that, rather than discuss a problem in their relationship, spouses are asked to each identify a personal issue, something about themselves they would like to change. They are specifically instructed to talk about personal problems that are not marital problems. Topics generated by subjects are typically issues such as exercising more, getting a better job, or changing a bad habit. Partners are asked to discuss this topic with their spouse for 10 minutes. The other spouse is told to respond in whatever way he or she wishes. These roles are then reversed so that, in two 10-minute interactions, spouses take turns as the support solicitor (what we call the *Helpee*) and the support provider (what we call the *Helper*).

We also ask spouses about their perceptions of these interactions after they are completed; for example, Helpees are asked how supported they feel, and Helpers are asked how valued and appreciated they feel. What is different about these perceptions of support compared to the standard measures of perceived social support used in the literature is that they are specific to this relationship and to the interaction that just occurred. Thus, they are less subject to inaccuracies or distortions in memories for past events (see Pierce et al., 1992).

We developed a microanalytic coding system for these interactions called the Social Support Interaction Coding System (SSICS; Bradbury & Pasch, 1992). The coding system is based on a normative standard conceptualization of social support, the idea that based on living in a particular culture, we develop norms concerning what types of behaviors are supportive and not, and that these can be generally agreed upon by members of that culture (see Dunkel-Schetter et al., 1992). We created a set of normative standards through group discussions and through a thorough review of social support research in which individuals had been queried regarding what behaviors they considered supportive and not in a variety of settings (e.g., Dunkel-Schetter et al., 1992; Lehman & Hemphill, 1990). This led to the development of definitions of positive and negative social support behaviors. An overview of the coding system, with examples of statements that might represent each code, is shown in Table 11.1. For Helpers, each speech turn is given one of six codes: Positive Instrumental, Positive Emotional, Positive Other, Negative, Neutral, or Off-Task. For Helpees, each speech turn is given one of four codes: Positive, Negative, Neutral, or Off-Task. Rates of each category of behavior can then be generated for husbands and wives in both the Helpee and the Helper roles.

A MODEL OF SOCIAL SUPPORT PROCESSES IN MARRIAGE

Our current understanding of the role of intraindividual variables in the support process in married couples is hampered by incomplete development of conceptual frameworks to guide research in this area. This shortcoming has been recognized for some time (e.g., Vinokur et al., 1987) and as a result, personality influences on social support processes in marriage and other intimate relationships remain poorly understood. We now outline a general model that might facilitate progress in understanding

TABLE 11.1. Description of Codes from the Social Support Interaction Coding System

Actor	Code label	Description and sample of code
Helper	Positive emotional	Reassures, consoles, or provides genuine encouragement to spouse; conveys that Helpee is loved, cared for, or esteemed; acknowledges Helpee's beliefs, interpretations, and feelings; encourages expression or clarification of feelings. *"So that should make you feel good, that you've taken steps to improve things!"*
Helper	Positive instrumental	Makes specific suggestions, gives helpful advice or access to information regarding the problem, asks specific questions aimed at narrowing or defining the problem, offers to assist in the development or enactment of a plan of action regarding the problem—all reflect consideration of Helpee's needs and opinions. *"When you feel nervous like that, do you think it might help to rehearse in your mind what you're going to say?"*
Helper	Positive other	All positive behaviors that do not fall specifically into the first two categories, including general analysis of the problem, summarizes, encourages continued discussion. *"Go on, talk more about how you would do that."*
Helper	Negative	Criticizes or blames the spouse; expresses negative affect at the spouse; insists that the Helpee employ his/her approach to the problem or recommendations; minimizes or maximizes the scope of the problem; expresses inappropriate pessimism or optimism; is inattentive or disengaged in the helping process; offers unhelpful or inconsiderate advice; discourages expression of feelings. *"You really just need to figure this out and stop complaining about it."*
Helper	Off-Task	All behaviors that involve matters not relevant to the problem under consideration.
Helper	Neutral	All other behaviors that relate to the problem under consideration or closely related issues.
Helpee	Positive	Offers specific, clear analysis of the problem, expresses feelings related to the problem, asks for help or states needs in a useful way, responds positively to Helper questions or suggestions. *"I know you love me either way, but I think my weight problem has been keeping me from feeling good about myself."*
Helpee	Negative	Makes demands for help, criticizes, blames or accuses Helper, expresses negative affect at the spouse, whines or complains. *"You're not even trying to help me. You're just turning it around to what you want to do. You never even asked me what I want."*
Helpee	Off-Task	All behaviors that involved matters not relevant to the problem under consideration.
Helpee	Neutral	All other behaviors that relate to the problem under consideration or closely related issues.

Note. The positive emotional, positive instrumental, and positive other codes can be summed to form a total positive code.

social support in marriage, and particularly, in understanding intraindividual influences on the support process. The basic model is shown in Figure 11.1.

The model posits that the quality of supportive exchanges between spouses may lead to deterioration, maintenance, or strengthening of the marital relationship (Path *g*). The basic tenet of the social learning model of marriage is the cornerstone of this model: The behaviors that spouses exchange when interacting with one another play a

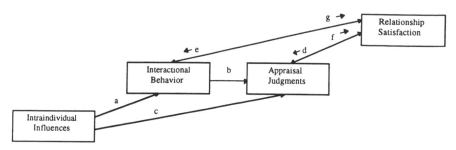

FIGURE 11.1. Model for the investigation of social support processes in marriage. According to this model, relationship satisfaction is affected by the rewarding and punishing nature of behaviors spouses exchange when helping each other to contend with personal difficulties. Behaviors also are hypothesized to affect relationship satisfaction through an effect on postinteraction appraisal judgments. Relationship satisfaction also has a reciprocal effect on future interactional behavior and appraisals. Intraindividual variables (i.e., personality, SES) have direct effects on appraisal judgments and indirect effects through an effect on behaviors spouses exchange. For clarity, depiction of the model has been simplified in several ways: Variables are not distinguished between husbands and wives; interactional behavior refers to both the support solicitor and the support provider. See text for further details.

key role in determining the degree of relationship satisfaction that spouses experience over time. Rewarding behaviors (e.g., in this case, offering reassurance, making helpful suggestions) are assumed to increase global evaluations of the marriage, and punishing behaviors (e.g., in this case, demanding help, offering inconsiderate advice) are assumed to decrease global evaluations. The model also highlights the importance of spouses' appraisal judgments following marital interactions. Specifically, it holds that following interactions with one's partner, spouses engage in internal evaluations of their spouse and of the relationship itself, which in the long run affect relationship satisfaction. Thus, interactional behaviors are also thought to influence relationship satisfaction over time by affecting spousal appraisal judgments (See Paths *b* and *f*).

To illustrate, consider again the scenarios presented earlier. Karen's statements to Jack contained several punishing elements (e.g., criticism, dismissal of his concerns). These elements are hypothesized to lead Jack to make negative appraisals of the completed interaction. For example, he may feel unsupported, and he may decide that his wife is not the helpful person he had earlier thought. If interactions and judgments such as these accumulate over time, they are hypothesized to affect negatively his assessment of the relationship itself. Similarly, Jack's statements to Karen contain several punishing elements (i.e., demands for help, sarcasm). These elements may lead Karen to make negative appraisals, such as thinking to herself that Jack is a demanding, difficult person. Over time, this type of interaction and resulting appraisals may lead to reductions in Karen's overall relationship satisfaction.

An additional feature of the model is that relationship satisfaction is not only hypothesized to be affected over time by the support process, but also to exert an effect on it. For example, if Kirsten goes into the interaction believing her relationship with her husband is satisfying, she may behave more openly and elicit support in more positive way (via Path *e*), and he may actually respond to her more positively. Also,

Kirsten's belief that she is in a satisfying relationship may affect the way she appraises her husband's behavior, regardless of what actually transpired; that is, prior beliefs about the quality of the relationship may create either positive or negative perceptual biases (Path *d*; see Beach, Fincham, Katz, and Bradbury, 1996). This formulation is consistent with the findings of Pierce et al. (1992), who showed that young adults' global evaluations of relationship quality with their parents predicted their reports of the quality of support received from their parents in a parent–child laboratory interaction. As Pierce et al. experimentally controlled behavior, it was not possible to examine the impact of the students' global evaluations of the relationship on actual behaviors.

The reciprocal effect of global relationship satisfaction is important, because it implies that each and every interaction between spouses is colored by the history of the relationship, as cumulated in spouses' global relationship satisfaction. In intimate relationships, this cumulated global relationship history may overpower more individually oriented variables that have been found to affect support behaviors and perceptions in previous research.

Intraindividual influences are incorporated into our model by two major pathways. First, intraindividual characteristics may influence appraisal judgments, independent of what actually occurs in the interaction (Path *c*, controlling for Path *b*). For example, Kirsten's generally high self-esteem may lead her to see Jim's suggestions as helpful, regardless of their actual nature. Or Jack's low self-esteem may lead him to see Karen's responses as critical, regardless of their actual nature. This pathway reflects the individual perceptual bias effect.

Second, intraindividual characteristics of either spouse may influence what actually transpires in the interaction (Path *a*), and what actually transpires may then affect appraisal judgments (Path *b*). This hypothesis suggests a mediational model. For example, suppose Jack is relatively high in neuroticism, the tendency "to report distress, discomfort, and dissatisfaction over time and regardless of the situation, even in the absence of any overt or objective source of stress" (Watson & Clark, 1984, p. 483). This tendency may lead him to behave more negatively (note the demands he makes for Karen to help him) and her to respond more negatively (note that Karen seems to be exasperated with offering help, perhaps because in the past her attempts have been rejected). Following the interaction, both spouses may feel negative about the interaction, with Jack feeling unsupported, and Karen feeling unappreciated. A second example might involve the intraindividual characteristics of the Helper. Suppose Karen is low in self-esteem. Perhaps because she is unable to focus on the partner's problems, she is relatively poor at providing support. An unproductive interaction may ensue that then causes both spouses to make negative appraisals of the interaction. Note that neither of these two last examples would be reflective of a perceptual bias, but instead, that the negative interaction is accurately judged to be more negative (via Path *b*).

In creating this model, our intention is not to describe a new formulation of the operation of social support processes, but instead to bring together previously hypothesized relationships among key variables into a comprehensive, testable framework. The framework draws heavily from social support and marital research traditions.

Importantly, both *objective* and *subjective* components of the process and their interrelations are included. By *objective*, we refer to the behaviors exhibited during interactions that have been coded by trained observers. By *subjective*, we refer to perceptions of what transpired.

THE CURRENT STUDY

Here we investigate the role of neuroticism in determining objective and subjective components of the support process in married couples. We chose neuroticism because it is the personality characteristic most often identified as a source of marital instability (see Karney & Bradbury, 1995) and because it has been shown to be related to perceiving less support available from one's social network (Sarason et al., 1983). Although previous research supports the particular importance of neuroticism in affecting the social support process, the results reported here should not be considered a complete test of our model or the research questions derived from it, but instead as an illustration of how our approach can be implemented to clarify key issues.

Specific Predictions

Five main outcomes are possible regarding the influence of global relationship quality, support behavior, and neuroticism on appraisal judgments. First, in the *relationship quality override model*, spouses' judgments of relationship quality will predict both interactional behaviors (Path *e*) and postinteraction appraisal judgments (Path *d*), whereas personality characteristics such as neuroticism will be less important. For example, how Kirsten behaves during a particular interaction with Jim, and how she interprets that interaction, may be determined by her general belief that her marriage is gratifying and close, and not so much by more distal variables such as the personality characteristics of either spouse. Second, in the *perceptual bias model*, neuroticism will predict postinteraction appraisal judgments (Path *c*) after controlling for relationship satisfaction (Path *d*), but behaviors exhibited in the interaction will not. Third, in the *interactional model*, behaviors exhibited in the interaction will predict postinteraction appraisal (Path *b*) after controlling for global relationship quality (Path *d*), but neuroticism will not. In the *integrated model*, both neuroticism and behaviors will account independently for variance in postinteraction appraisals, after controlling for global relationship quality. Finally, in the *mediational model*, behaviors exhibited in the interaction will predict appraisal judgments (Path *b*), and a previously significant association between neuroticism and appraisal judgments (Path *c*) will become nonsignificant after controlling for the association between neuroticism and interactional behaviors, and between behaviors and appraisal judgments (see Baron & Kenny, 1986). This *mediational model* would suggest that neuroticism has its effect on postinteraction appraisal judgments through its effect on the actual behaviors displayed.

These five possibilities are likely to oversimplify the actual pattern of results, because several models may be supported in part, or different models may be supported for husbands and wives, or for Helpee and Helper. Nevertheless, evaluation of the relative degree of support for each model will lead us to a clearer view of how social support processes might operate in marriage. This approach advances research to date in several ways: by studying support processes in actual intimate relationships; by including both behavioral and perceptual variables in the same analysis; and by allowing competing predictions to be made about how global relationship beliefs, intraindividual characteristics, and interactional behavior might affect spousal appraisal judgments. Previous theory and research provides limited support for each of the proposed models, but persuasive support for none, perhaps owing to variation in methodology and types of samples studied.

METHOD

The results reported here are part of a large longitudinal study of newlywed couples designed to understand the interplay between intraindividual variables (i.e., personality, family history), stressful life events (i.e., birth of a first child), and the couple's adaptive skills (i.e., marital interaction behaviors) in shaping relationship outcomes. More complete descriptions of the methods for this study are available in Pasch and Bradbury (in press).

In brief, 60 newlywed couples were recruited using newspaper advertisements to participate in a research project on marriage (see Karney et al., 1995, for details on this sampling method). All couples were married less than 6 months at the time of enrollment in the study. Husbands averaged 25.4 years of age ($SD = 3.4$), 15.6 years of formal education ($SD = 2.2$), and had a modal gross annual income between $11,000 and $20,000; wives averaged 24.0 years of age ($SD = 2.9$), 15.6 years of formal education ($SD = 1.6$), and also had a modal gross annual income between $11,000 and $20,000. Seventy-five percent of the sample were Caucasian, 10% were Hispanic, 7% were Asian, 5% were African-American, and 3% indicated "Other" for their race.

Each couple took part in a laboratory session in which the spouses provided demographic and questionnaire data, and participated in the social support task described earlier. The behaviors spouses exhibited were coded reliably using the SSICS described earlier (for Helpers, kappa = .69, percent agreement = 79%; for Helpees, kappa = .76, percent agreement = 87%). To control for variation across spouses in their number of speaking turns, the number of times each of the SSICS codes was emitted by each spouse in the interaction was divided by his or her number of speaking turns.

Immediately following each discussion, spouses rated a set of support-related adjectives to describe how they were feeling in consideration of the discussion they had just completed. Helpees rated four adjectives (supported, helped, valued, and respected) on a scale from 1 (*Not at all*) to 9 (*Very Much*). Helpees rated three adjectives (valued, appreciated, and respected) on the same scale. Composite indices were created, with higher scores indicating more positive appraisals. Coefficient alphas for Helpees were .93 for wives and .95 for husbands; for Helpers, .87 for wives and .96 for husbands.

Among the questionnaires spouses completed was the 15-item Marital Adjustment Test (MAT; Locke & Wallace, 1959), a widely used self-report measure commonly accepted as an adequate index of marital satisfaction. Husbands averaged 120.4 on the MAT ($SD = 17.4$) and wives averaged 119.7 ($SD = 17.3$). Spouses also completed the

Neuroticism scale of the Eysenck Personality Questionnaire (EPQ-N; Eysenck & Eysenck, 1978). Husbands averaged 8.4 on the EPQ-N ($SD = 5.0$), and wives averaged 11.2 ($SD = 5.1$).

RESULTS

Global Relationship Quality and Postinteraction Appraisal Judgments

First, the association between global relationship quality and appraisal judgments was investigated (Path d). For wives, MAT scores were significant predictors of how supported they felt following discussion of their own problem ($r = .40, p < .001$), and how appreciated they felt following discussion of her husband's problem ($r = .25, p < .05$). For husbands, MAT scores were not significant predictors of how supported they felt following discussion of their own problem ($r = .17$, ns) but they were significant predictors of how appreciated they felt following discussion of their wife's problem ($r = .32, p < .01$). Thus spouses' degree of satisfaction with their relationships tended to be associated with how they felt following interactions with their spouse.

Interactional Behaviors and Appraisal Judgments

The next two sets of analyses involve interactional behavior. Table 11.2 shows means and standard deviations for proportions of Helper and Helpee behaviors, for husbands and for wives. *T*-tests revealed no significant differences between husbands and wives in the proportions of each type of behavior, with the exception that husbands were significantly more neutral than wives as Helpees. An in-depth analysis of gender effects is available in Pasch, Bradbury, and Davila (in press). For simplicity, in the analyses below, four behavioral categories from the SSICS are examined—positive and negative Helpee behaviors, and positive and negative Helper behaviors. The positive

TABLE 11.2. Means and Standard Deviations for Proportions of Helper and Helpee Behaviors

| | Proportion of behavior | | | | |
| | Husbands | | Wives | | t (Husbands |
	M	SD	M	SD	vs. Wives)
Helper behaviors					
Positive	.34	.17	.32	.19	$-.62$, ns
Negative	.15	.18	.13	.18	$-.63$, ns
Off-task	.09	.13	.12	.19	1.73, ns
Neutral	.43	.15	.42	.19	$-.08$, ns
Helpee behaviors					
Positive	.43	.21	.48	.22	1.61, ns
Negative	.08	.13	.13	.18	1.80, ns
Off-task	.12	.19	.09	.13	-1.55, ns
Neutral	.37	.18	.31	.15	$-2.05, p < .05$

Note. $N = 58$ husbands, and $N = 58$ wives.

Helper category is a composite of Positive Instrumental, Positive Emotional, and Positive Other codes from the SSICS.

We examined the association between interactional behaviors and postinteraction appraisal judgments (Path *b*). The zero-order correlations between each behavior and postinteraction appraisals are shown in the left columns of Table 11.3, the correlations in the right columns show the same association with MAT scores partialed out, as they were shown earlier to be significant predictors of appraisal judgments (Path *d*). Before and after controlling for global relationship quality, the actual behaviors exhibited tended not to be significant predictors of postinteraction judgments when husbands were talking about their problems. However, during wives' problem discussions, wives tended to feel more supported after the discussion when their husbands were more positive and less negative as support providers, after accounting for the effect of wives' global relationship quality. Wives also tended to feel more supported after the discussion when they themselves were less negative as support solicitors, again controlling for the effect of their global relationship quality. Husbands tended to feel more valued if they were less negative as support providers, again, after controlling for their global relationship quality. Thus, what actually occurs in a support-based interaction tends to have some influence on both Helper and Helpee appraisal judgments, even after their global judgments about the quality of relationship are taken into account, although only when wives were presenting their problems.

Interactional Behaviors and Relationship Quality

The correlations between interactional behaviors and relationship satisfaction (Path *e*) are shown in Table 11.4. There was strong support for Path *e* for wives, such

TABLE 11.3. Correlations and Partial Correlations (Controlling for Marital Satisfaction) between Interactional Behavior and Postinteraction Appraisals for Husbands and Wives

	Wives' appraisal		Husbands' appraisal	
	r	Partial *r*	*r*	Partial *r*
Discussion of wives' topic				
Positive helpee	.34**	.18	.10	−.04
Negative helpee	−.56***	−.38**	−.33*	−.18
Positive helper	.41**	.31*	.14	.10
Negative helper	−.47***	−.31*	−.40**	−.32*
Discussion of husbands' topic				
Positive helpee	.21	.16	.16	.13
Negative helpee	−.10	−.06	−.27*	−.25
Positive helper	.12	.02	.16	.13
Negative helper	.06	.13	−.26*	−.24

Note. *N* = 58 husbands, and *N* = 58 wives.
*p < .05
**p < .01
***p < .001

TABLE 11.4. Correlations between Marital Satisfaction
and Interactional Behavior for Husbands and Wives

	Marital satisfaction		Marital satisfaction
Wives' behavior		Husbands' behavior	
Positive helper	.34**	Positive helper	.17
Negative helper	−.23*	Negative helper	−.35*
Positive helpee	.38***	Positive helpee	.17
Negative helpee	−.57***	Negative helpee	−.17

Note. N = 58 husbands, and N = 58 wives.
*$p < .05$
**$p < .01$
***$p < .001$.

that wives' MAT scores were strong predictors of their behavior, whereby wives who were more satisfied were more positive and less negative, both in the Helpee and the Helper role. There was weak support for Path *e* for husbands. Husbands' MAT scores were only significant predictors of their level of negative behavior as Helpers, such that husbands who were more satisfied were less negative support providers.

Neuroticism and Interactional Behavior

Next we investigated the association between each spouse's EPQ-N score and their behavior during the interaction in both roles (Path *a*). Results are shown in Table 11.5. Husbands' EPQ-N scores were not significant predictors of their behavior as Helpee or Helper, or their wives' behavior as Helpee or Helper. However, wives' EPQ-N scores were significant predictors of their own behavior as Helpers, such that wives with higher EPQ-N scores were less positive and more negative support providers, and more negative as support solicitors. Similarly, wives with higher EPQ-N scores received less positive and more negative support from their husbands.

Because our model also predicts that relationship quality would be reflected in interactional behavior (Path *e*), we investigated whether the association between neuroticism and interactional behaviors would remain once relationship quality was taken into account. The associations between neuroticism and interactional behavior, partialing out the effect of global relationship quality, appear in the right columns of Table 11.5. Two associations remained significant: Wives with higher EPQ-N scores were less positive when providing support to their husbands, and their husbands were less positive when providing support to them.

Neuroticism and Appraisal Judgments

We next investigated the association between neuroticism and postinteraction appraisal judgments (Path *c*). The correlations between EPQ-N scores and postinteraction appraisals before and after partialing out the effect of global relationship quality are shown in Table 11.6. There was almost no support for Path *c*. Neither wives' nor husbands' level of neuroticism was associated with their appraisal of the interaction. The only significant association was for husbands' EPQ-N and wives' postinteraction

TABLE 11.5. Correlations and Partial Correlations
(Controlling for Marital Satisfaction)
between Neuroticism and Interactional Behavior
for Husbands and Wives

	Wives' neuroticism		Husbands' neuroticism	
	r	Partial r	r	Partial r
Wives' behavior				
Positive helper	−.38**	−.35**	.07	.14
Negative helper	.26*	.23	.01	.04
Positive helpee	−.12	−.06	.03	.12
Negative helpee	.28*	.22	.19	.11
Husbands' behavior				
Positive helper	−.37**	−.35**	−.14	−.11
Negative helper	.25*	.19	.15	.09
Positive helpee	−.21	−.18	.12	.16
Negative helpee	.10	.06	.04	.01

Note. $N = 58$ husbands, and $N = 58$ wives.
*$p < .05$
**$p < .01$
***$p < .001$.

TABLE 11.6. Correlations and Partial Correlations
(Controlling for Marital Satisfaction)
between Neuroticism and Postinteraction Appraisals
for Husbands and Wives

	Wives' neuroticism		Husbands' neuroticism	
	r	Partial r	r	Partial r
Wives' appraisal				
Helpee	−.18	−.12	−.03	.05
Helper	−.01	.05	.26*	.33**
Husbands' appraisal				
Helpee	−.26*	−.23	−.07	−.04
Helper	−.25	−.19	.02	.07

Note. $N = 58$ husbands, and $N = 58$ wives.
*$p < .05$
**$p < .01$
***$p < .001$.

appraisals, and this was contrary to expectation. To the extent that husbands scored higher on neuroticism, their wives felt more valued in the Helper role.

Evaluation of the *Mediational Model*

According to the *mediational model*, neuroticism would have its effect on appraisal judgments through its effect on actual behaviors displayed. Only one association was found between neuroticism and appraisal judgments—wives felt more valued as Helpers to the extent that their husbands scored higher on neuroticism. In order to test for the mediating effect of behaviors, significant associations must be shown between neuroticism and at least one interactional behavior, and that same interactional behavior must be associated with wives' appraisal judgments as a Helper. Examination of these findings reveal no such behavior. Thus, all that could be concluded about the significant association between husbands' neuroticism and wives' postinteraction positive feelings as Helpers is that the relationship was not mediated by any of the behaviors studied.

Because this was such an unexpected finding, we wanted to investigate it further, and thus went back to our original interactional behavioral coding to see if some behavior we did not investigate here would be associated with both husbands' EPQ-N scores and wives' feeling more valued when helping their husbands. Such a behavior was identified—it was the tendency for wives to exhibit positive emotional support to their husbands, a behavior that we collapsed into the positive category along with positive instrumental and other positive support behaviors for the sake of simplicity. When husbands had higher EPQ-N scores, their wives displayed more positive emotional behavior, after controlling for MAT scores ($r = .32$, $p < .01$, partial $r = .44$, $p < .001$). Additionally, wives' display of positive emotional support was positively associated with their feeling valued after the interaction, after controlling for MAT scores ($r = .32$, $p < .01$, partial $r = .44$, $p < .001$). The final test of the mediational model is to demonstrate that the association between husbands' neuroticism and wives' appraisal judgments becomes nonsignificant once the associations between neuroticism and interactional behaviors, and between behaviors and appraisal judgments, are controlled. A hierarchical multiple regression was conducted in which wives' MAT was entered first, followed by wives' positive emotional behavior, followed by husbands' EPQ-N. This resulted in a nonsignificant effect of husbands' EPQ-N (partial $r = .25$, $p > .05$). Thus, when husbands were high in neuroticism, wives tended to provide them more emotional support, which, in turn, was related to wives feeling more valued after the interaction.

Further Analyses

Support for the association between relationship quality and interactional behavior (Path *e*), and between interactional behavior and appraisals (during the wives' discussions) (Path *b*), led us to ask a follow-up question that did not involve neuroticism at all: Does relationship satisfaction "influence" postinteraction appraisals by "influencing" the behaviors that spouses display, or do interactional behaviors and relationship satisfaction have independent effects on appraisals? To test this additional mediational model, we identified the interactional behaviors that were associated with both relationship satisfaction and appraisals made after the wives' discussion. For wives, these behaviors were their own positive and negative Helpee behaviors; for husbands, these behaviors were their own negative Helper behavior. We then tested whether the associations between relationship satisfaction and postinteraction appraisals would remain once the effects of the specific behaviors that were predictors of appraisal were partialed out. For the association between husbands' MAT and husbands' Helper appraisal, when husbands' negative Helper behavior was controlled, the association became nonsignificant, suggesting that husbands who were less satisfied with their marriage felt less appreciated and valued after discussing their wives' problem as a result of having been more negative during the discussion, partial $r = .23$, ns. Conversely, for wives, their relationship satisfaction and Helpee behaviors appeared to make independent contributions to how they felt after discussing their problem with their husband; that is, the association between wives' MAT and wives' Helpee appraisal remained significant after controlling for wives' positive Helpee behavior, partial $r = .43$, $p < .001$, and after controlling for wives' negative Helpee behavior, partial $r = .28$, $p < .05$.

SUMMARY AND CRITIQUE

RATIONALE AND SUMMARY OF RESULTS

We have argued that research to date has provided a limited understanding of how social support processes operate in marriage and other close relationships. Progress in this area has been limited by several key factors, the most notable of which are a tendency to study either behaviors exchanged or perceptions and not to examine them in relation to one another; a tendency to study individuals outside of the relationship context in which support occurs; and a relative focus on conflict resolution skills in the marital interaction literature and a lack of attention to support skills.

The approach we have taken tackles each of these problems and represents an integration of strengths from both social support and marital research traditions. We have developed a model for the investigation of social support processes in marital relationships that incorporates cognitive (i.e., perceptions) and behavioral elements (i.e., that which is available to be perceived) of the support process. What is most useful about such an approach is that it makes no assumptions about the relative importance of perceptions or actual behaviors, but instead provides a framework outlining their possible interrelations that can be empirically tested. It also then allows for specific models to be tested regarding the relative importance of intraindividual and global relationship influences on both cognitive and behavioral elements of the support process.

In the present study, we offered an example of how the model can be used to develop specific, competing predictions, using neuroticism as the intraindividual variable of interest. We are now in the position to evaluate the five possible outcomes regarding the interrelations among global relationship quality, neuroticism, support behavior, and appraisal judgments. The results revealed partial support for what we called the *relationship quality override model*, which predicted that global relationship quality would be an important predictor of both behavior and of appraisal judgments, and that personality would have less "influence," particularly after relationship quality was controlled. The idea that relationship quality would be reflected in the behaviors spouses exchange is consistent with the social learning model and actually supports the notion that the social learning model, previously investigated primarily with regard to marital problem-solving behaviors, applies equally well to behaviors in the support domain (see Pasch & Bradbury, in press, for further tests of the social learning model as it applies to the social support domain). The other portion of the relationship quality override model, that relationship quality would be an important predictor of postinteraction appraisals, was also supported.

No support was found for the *perceptual bias model*, in that one's own neuroticism did not predict one's own postinteraction appraisals; thus, neuroticism did not create a perceptual bias to viewing interactions in a particular way. Very limited support was found for the *mediational model*, only that when husbands were high in neuroticism, wives tended to provide them more emotional support, which, in turn, was related to wives feeling more valued after the interaction. Importantly, while two behaviors (husbands' and wives' Helper behavior) were associated with wives' EPQ-N scores, independent of relationship quality, wives' EPQ-N scores were not associated with either spouses' postappraisal judgments, so no mediational models could be tested with wives' neuroticism. No support was found for the *integrative model*, either, which proposed that interactional behaviors and personality would have independent "effects" on appraisal judgments. There were no associations between neuroticism and postinteraction judgments that were independent of behavior.

Some support was also found for the *interactional model*. During wives' problem discussions, but not during husbands' problem discussions, husbands' and wives' behavior was significantly associated with how they felt afterward, after controlling for relationship satisfaction. Thus, what actually occurred when wives presented their problems did add to our ability to predict how both partners felt afterward. It was further shown that, in some cases, relationship quality and behavior had independent associations with appraisals, and in other cases, the effect of relationship quality on appraisals appeared to be mediated by specific behaviors.

LIMITATIONS AND QUALIFICATIONS

The present study was not intended to fully explore intraindividual factors in the social support process but instead to illustrate how investigations can be conducted to test specific effects. Although past research suggested that neuroticism would be a particularly important first step, a full test of the model would involve a wide range of personality variables. Furthermore, we do not mean to imply that personality is the only important individual difference variable; other variables might include family of origin (e.g., Kobak & Hazan, 1991) or cultural and socioeconomic variables.

Although the use of a laboratory interaction task affords us the strength of being able to study actual support behaviors, its artificial nature may detract from the generalizability of our findings. For example, whereas support interactions probably normally occur in response to particular incidents (i.e., a difficult day at work), our research participants engage in these interactions following the direction of the researcher. Although research has tended to show that couples find laboratory inter-actions similar to interactions they normally have at home (Bradbury, 1994), neverthe-less, the affective experience that may instigate a discussion under normal circum-stances (i.e., distress, anger) may not be as strong, and the effect of this is unknown. The same criticism has been made of laboratory interactions in which couples are asked to resolve a marital problem, and it is probably a more serious criticism in that case, as the affective experience is presumably directed at the spouse, as opposed to at the external problem (i.e., a boss).

A more significant criticism regarding the artificial nature of our support task involves demand characteristics associated with the task that might lead individuals to alter their behavior based on the expectation that the researcher wants them to be supportive. To combat this possibility, spouses were not explicitly told to ask for help or to provide help. Nevertheless, demand characteristics may restrict the range of responses as compared to the natural environment. Some couples may rarely have conversations like the ones we ask them to have, or one partner may exit from the discussion by leaving the room. Importantly, intraindividual and relationship variables may influence the extent to which support-based discussions occur. For example, distressed couples may be experiencing so much conflict that they seldom feel comfortable enough to bring up personal problems with each other. Similarly, person-ality characteristics might influence the extent to which a spouse ever initiates a discussion of personal problems.

The model we have presented could be further expanded to include forces external to the couple in determining their ability to provide support to one another. It seems reasonable to propose that stressors can decrease spouses' abilities to offer support to each other (see Christensen & Pasch, 1993). Experimental data have shown that stress tends to lead individuals to focus on their own problems or concerns, and to have more difficulty with problem solving (e.g., Wood, Saltzberg, & Goldsamt, 1990).

Additionally, external stressors might increase the magnitude of the problem for which help is needed. Couples facing more difficult issues may have more difficulty with the task, and it may be harder to effectively define the problem and to offer support. For example, while a wife may find it relatively easy to support her husband's desire to get more exercise, she may experience significant difficulty supporting his desire to quit his job. This difficulty may be particularly pronounced in close relation-ships. It seems reasonable to hypothesize that the level of interdependence between spouses make the stakes higher—it may be much easier to support a friend's desire to quit her job than to support one's spouse with the same desire. The likelihood that a spouse will be affected personally is much greater than the likelihood that a friend will be affected personally. This is consistent with findings of Barker and Lemle (1987), who found that spouses were more negative in the helping role than were strangers, as spouses seemed to have difficulty separating their own needs from their spouse's needs. Accordingly, incorporating external stressors into our understanding of how support operates in marriage is an important avenue for future research.

IMPLICATIONS FOR THEORY AND RESEARCH

The results of these analyses suggest that theory and empirical findings concern-ing social support processes in nonintimate pairs may not be easily generalized to the operation of these processes in marital or other intimate, close relationships (i.e., parent–child, sibling), as the history of the relationship between provider and recipient has been largely overlooked (cf. Pierce et al., 1992; Sarason et al., 1994b). This issue is of particular importance in consideration of intraindividual influences. Intraindividual influences on the support process may not be as apparent in support interactions in close relationships, as they may in some cases be overshadowed by the history of the relationship between provider and recipient. As Sarason et al. (1994a) have said of their own similar findings with regard to the effects of personality on interactions between parent–child dyads, "characteristics of personality may have been subsumed into their views of their joint relationship to the extent that these no longer play direct or easily discernible roles in their dyadic behavior" (p. 29). Our results do not suggest that neuroticism no longer plays a discernible role, as wives' neuroticism was associated with both spouses' behavior during discussion of wives' problems, even after relationship quality was controlled. However, our results do suggest that theory and research on social support in marriage that excludes relationship satisfaction will result in an incomplete, and in some cases, misleading picture.

It is also critically important to consider these findings into the context of relationship development and functioning over time. Variables or processes that are salient and influential at certain points in relationship development may be less important at other points. For example, personality may be of critical importance in determining partner choice, early interactional processes, and whether a relationship develops at all between two people. As the relationship develops, personality influences may appear less obvious, because the history of that particular relationship may determine behavioral interactions and resulting appraisals more than broader personality characteristics. As relationships develop beyond the early stages, negative personality traits may have a clearer impact on behavior, as initially reinforcing interaction patterns may deteriorate. For example, consider the finding in the present study that, regardless of the quality of the marriage, wives who had husbands who were relatively high in neuroticism felt *more* appreciated and valued after discussing his problem. Given the finding that neuroticism has negative implications for marital outcomes (Kelley & Conley, 1987), this seems to be an odd finding. In retrospect, it seems plausible that husbands who were relatively high in neuroticism were more in need of support, and were perhaps more disclosing than husbands relatively low in neuroticism, thus giving their wives a sense of being needed. This is supported by the finding that husbands' neuroticism was related to wives' offering more emotional support; perhaps the opportunity to offer emotional support was valued by wives. However, it also seems plausible that this set of relationships could be unique to newlywed couples, and that over time in the marriage, the husband's neuroticism would begin to have the predicted negative effect. Perhaps eventually wives would tire of offering emotional support, particularly if their husbands did not seem to benefit from it, resulting in more negative Helper behavior, more negative Helpee behavior, thus over time decreasing the sense of appreciation wives felt and their assessment of the marriage in general. We do not mean to suggest that this specific process occurs, but instead, to highlight the importance of considering social support processes in close relationships over time. Personality characteristics may affect the support process differently at various points over the course of the relationship.

The present study did not address the elements of the support process in relation to *changes* in the quality of the relationship over time (Paths *g* and *f*), but instead focused on the determinants of these elements themselves. As described earlier, in another source, we show that the quality of marital support interactions predict changes in the quality of the marriage 2 years later, controlling for initial marital quality (Pasch & Bradbury, in press). What we do not know is the process by which behaviors and appraisals of those behaviors determine these outcomes. Our model is based on a reciprocal process whereby spouses make judgments about their partners and the relationship based on previous interactions; those judgments then affect actual behaviors, which in turn affect appraisals and so on, either leading to improving, declining, or maintaining relationship satisfaction (Bradbury & Fincham, 1991). Testing this portion of the model will no doubt prove difficult, due to the reciprocal nature of effects, and must involve multiple assessments, including repeated analyses of behavior.

ACKNOWLEDGMENTS

Preparation of this chapter was supported by training Grant No. MH19391 received by Lauri A. Pasch, by Grant No. 4-564040-19900-07 from the Committee on Research of the UCLA Academic Senate, and by Grant No. R29 MH48674, awarded to Thomas N. Bradbury, and by Grant No. F31 MH10779, awarded to Kieran T. Sullivan.

REFERENCES

Barbee, A. P. (1990). Interactive coping: The cheering-up process in close relationships. In S. Duck (Ed.), *Personal relationships and social support* (pp. 46–65). London: Sage.

Barker, C., & Lemle, R. (1987). Informal helping in partner and stranger dyads. *Journal of Marriage and Family, 49,* 541–547.

Baron, R. M., & Kenny, D. A. (1986). The moderator–mediator variable distinction in social psychological research: Conceptual, strategic, and statistical considerations. *Journal of Personality and Social Psychology, 51,* 1173–1182.

Beach, S. R. H., Fincham, F. D., Katz, J., & Bradbury, T. N. (1996). Social support in marriage: A cognitive perspective. In G. R. Pierce, B. R. Sarason, & I. G. Sarason (Eds.), *Handbook of social support and the family* (pp. 43–65). New York: Plenum.

Beach, S. R. H., Martin, J. K., Blum, T. C., & Roman, P. M. (1993). Effects of marital and co-worker relationships on negative affect: Testing the central role of marriage. *American Journal of Family Therapy, 21,* 312–322.

Bradbury, T. N. (1989). *Cognition, emotion, and interaction in distressed and nondistressed couples.* Unpublished dissertation, University of Illinois at Urbana–Champaign.

Bradbury, T. N. (1994). Unintended effects of marital research on marital relationships. *Journal of Family Psychology, 8*(2), 187–201.

Bradbury, T. N., Beach, S. R. H., Fincham, F. D., & Nelson, G. M. (1996). Attributions and behavior in functional and dysfunctional marriages. *Journal of Consulting and Clinical Psychology, 64,* 569–576.

Bradbury, T. N., Campbell, S. M., & Fincham, F. D. (1995). Longitudinal and behavioral analysis of masculinity and femininity in marriage. *Journal of Personality and Social Psychology, 68,* 328–341.

Bradbury, T. N., & Fincham, F. D. (1987). Assessment of affect in marriage. In K. D. O'Leary (Ed.), *Assessment of marital discord* (pp. 59–108). Hillsdale, NJ: Erlbaum.

Bradbury, T. N., & Fincham, F. D. (1989). Behavior and satisfaction in marriage: Prospective mediating processes. *Review of Personality and Social Psychology, 10,* 119–143.

Bradbury, T. N., & Fincham, F. D. (1991). A contextual model for advancing the study of marital interaction. In G. J. O. Fletcher & F. D. Fincham (Eds.), *Cognition in close relationships* (pp. 127–147). Hillsdale, NJ: Erlbaum.

Bradbury, T. N., & Fincham, F. D. (1992). Attributions and behavior in marital interaction. *Journal of Personality and Social Psychology*, *63*, 613–628.

Bradbury, T. N., & Pasch, L. A. (1992). The Social Support Interaction Coding System. Unpublished coding manual. University of California, Los Angeles.

Brown, G. W., & Harris, T. O. (1978). *Social origins of depression: A study of psychiatric disorder in women*. New York: Free Press.

Cassel, J. (1976). The contribution of social environment to host resistance. *American Journal of Epidemiology*, *102*(2), 107–123.

Christensen, A., & Pasch, L. (1993). The sequence of marital conflict: An analysis of seven phases of marital conflict in distressed and nondistressed couples. *Clinical Psychology Review*, *13*, 3–14.

Coyne, J. C., & DeLongis, A. (1986). Going beyond social support: The role of social relationships in adaptation. *Journal of Consulting and Clinical Psychology*, *54*(4), 454–460.

Cutrona, C. E. (1989). Ratings of social support by adolescents and adult informants: Degree of correspondence and prediction of depressive symptoms. *Journal of Personality and Social Psychology*, *57*, 723–730.

Cutrona, C. E., & Suhr, J. A. (1994). Social support communication in the context of marriage: An analysis of couples' supportive interactions. In B. Burleson, T. Albrecht, & I. Sarason (Eds.), *The communication of social support: Messages, interactions, and community* (pp. 113–135). Thousand Oaks, CA: Sage.

Cutrona, C. E., Suhr, J. A., & MacFarlane, R. (1990). Interpersonal transactions and the psychological sense of support. In S. Duck & R. Silver (Eds.), *Personal relationships and social support* (pp. 30–45). London: Sage.

Dakof, G. A., & Taylor, S. E. (1990). Victim's perceptions of social support: What is helpful from whom? *Journal of Personality and Social Psychology*, *58*, 80–89.

Dunkel-Schetter, C., Blasband, D. E., Feinstein, L. G., & Herbert, T. B. (1992). Elements of supportive interactions: When are attempts to help effective? In S. Spacapan & S. Oskamp (Eds.), *Helping and being helped in the real world* (pp. 83–114). Newbury Park, CA: Sage Publications.

Eysenck, H. J., & Eysenck, S. B. (1978). *Manual for the Eysenck Personality Questionnaire*. Kent, England: Hodder and Stoughton.

Fincham, F. D., & Bradbury, T. N. (1990). Social support in marriage: The role of social cognition. *Journal of Social and Clinical Psychology*, *9*(1), 31–42.

Gottlieb, B. H. (1985). Social support and the study of personal relationships. *Journal of Social and Personal Relationships*, *2*, 351–375.

Hobfoll, S. E., Nadler, A., & Leiberman, B. G. (1986). Satisfaction with social support during a crisis: Intimacy and self-esteem as critical determinants. *Journal of Personality and Social Psychology*, *51*, 296–304.

Holahan, C. J., & Moos, R. H. (1981). Social support and psychological distress: A longitudinal analysis. *Journal of Abnormal Psychology*, *90*, 365–370.

House, J. S. (1981). *Work stress and social support*. Reading, MA: Addison-Wesley.

Jacobson, N. S., & Margolin, G. (1979). *Marital therapy: Strategies based on social learning and behavior exchange principles*. New York: Brunner/Mazel.

Karney, B. R., & Bradbury, T. N. (1995). The longitudinal course of marital quality and stability: A review of theory, method, and research. *Psychological Bulletin*, *118*, 3–34.

Karney, B. R., Davila, J., Cohan, C. L., Sullivan, K. T., Johnson, M. D., & Bradbury, T. N. (1995). An empirical investigation of sampling strategies in marital research. *Journal of Marriage and the Family*, *57*(4), 909–920.

Kelley, H. H., Berscheid, E., Christensen, A., Harvey, J. H., Huston, T. L., Levinger, G., McClintock, E., Peplau, L. A., & Peterson, D. R. (1983). *Close relationships*. New York: Freeman.

Kelley, E. L., & Conley, J. J. (1987). Personality and compatibility: A prospective analysis of marital stability and marital satisfaction. *Journal of Personality and Social Psychology*, *52*, 27–40.

Kobak, R. R., & Hazan, C. (1991). Attachment in marriage: Effects of security and accuracy of working models. *Journal of Personality and Social Psychology*, *60*, 861–869.

Lakey, B., & Cassady, P. B. (1990). Cognitive processes in perceived social support. *Journal of Personality and Social Psychology*, *59*, 337–343.

Leatham, G., & Duck, S. (1991). Conversations with friends and the dynamics of social support. In S. Duck & R. C. Silver (Eds.), *Personal relationships and social support* (pp. 1-29). London: Sage.

Lehman, D. R., & Hemphill, K. J. (1990). Recipients' perceptions of support attempts and attributions for support attempts that fail. *Journal of Social and Personal Relationships, 7*, 563-574.

Locke, H., & Wallace, K. (1959). Short marital adjustment and prediction tests: Their reliability and validity. *Marriage and Family Living, 21*, 251-255.

Pagel, M. D., Erdly, W. W., & Becker, J. (1987). Social networks: We get by with (and in spite of) a little help from our friends. *Journal of Personality and Social Psychology, 53*, 793-804.

Pasch, L. A., & Bradbury, T. N. (in press). Social support, conflict, and the development of marital dysfunction. *Journal of Consulting and Clinical Psychology*.

Pasch, L. A., Bradbury, T. N., & Davila, J. (in press). Gender, negative affectivity, and observed social support behavior in marital interaction. *Personal Relationships*.

Pierce, G. R., Sarason, B. R., & Sarason, I. G. (1992). General and specific support expectations and stress as predictors of perceived supportiveness: An experimental study. *Journal of Personality and Social Psychology, 63*, 297-307.

Procidano, M., & Heller, K. (1983). Measures of perceived social support from friends and family: Three validation studies. *American Journal of Community Psychology, 11*, 1-24.

Raush, H. L., Barry, W. A., Hertel, R. K., & Swain, M. A. (1974). *Communication, conflict, and marriage*. San Francisco: Jossey-Bass.

Reiss, H. T. (1990). The role of intimacy in interpersonal relations. *Journal of Social and Clinical Psychology, 9*, 15-30.

Rook, K. S. (1984). The negative side of social interaction: Impact in psychological well-being. *Journal of Personality and Social Psychology, 46*, 109-118.

Rook, K. S., Pietromonaco, P. R., & Lewis, M. A. (1994). When are dysphoric individuals distressing to others and vice versa? Effects of friendship, similarity, and interaction task. *Journal of Personality and Social Psychology, 67*(3), 548-559.

Sacco, W. P., Milana, S., & Dunn, V. K. (1985). Effect of depression level and length of acquaintance on reactions of others to a request for help. *Journal of Personality and Social Psychology, 49*(6), 1728-1737.

Sarason, I. G., Levine, H. M., Basham, R. B., & Sarason, B. R. (1983). Assessing social support: The social support questionnaire. *Journal of Personality and Social Psychology, 44*, 127-139.

Sarason, B. R., Pierce, G. R., & Sarason, I. G. (1994a). Personality, relationship, and task-related factors in parent-child interactions: Two observational studies. Manuscript submitted for publication.

Sarason, I. G., & Sarason, B. R. (1982). Concomitants of social support: Attitudes, personality characteristics, and life experiences. *Journal of Personality, 50*, 331-344.

Sarason, B. R., Sarason, I. G., Hacker, T., & Basham, R. (1985). Concomitants of social support: Social skills, physical attractiveness, and gender. *Journal of Personality and Social Psychology, 49*, 469-480.

Sarason, I. G., Sarason, B. R., & Pierce, G. R. (1994b). Relationship-specific social support: Toward a model for the analysis of supportive interactions. In B. Burleson, T. Albrecht, & I. Sarason (Eds.), *The communication of social support: Messages, interactions, and community* (pp. 91-112). Thousand Oaks, CA: Sage.

Sarason, I. G., Sarason, B., & Shearin, E. (1986). Social support as an individual difference variable: Its stability, origins, and relational aspects. *Journal of Personality and Social Psychology, 50*, 1222-1225.

Sillars, A., & Scott, M. (1983). Interpersonal perception between intimates: An integrative review. *Human Communications Research, 10*, 153-176.

Stafford, L., & Canary, D. J. (1991). Maintenance strategies and romantic relationship type, gender and relational characteristics. *Journal of Social and Personal Relationships, 8*, 217-242.

Steinberg, M., & Gottlieb, B. H. (1994). The appraisal of spousal support by women facing conflicts between work and family. In B. R. Burleson, T. L. Albrecht, & I. G. Sarason (Eds.), *Communication of social support: Messages, interactions, relationships, and community* (pp. 152-172). Thousand Oaks, CA: Sage.

Turner, R. J., Frankel, B. G., & Levin, D. M. (1983). Social support: Conceptualization, measurement, and implications for mental health. In J. Greeley (Ed.), *Research in community and mental health* (Vol. 3, pp. 67-111). Greenwich, CT: JAI Press.

Vinokur, A., Schul, Y., & Caplan, R. D. (1987). Determinants of perceived social support: Interpersonal transactions, personal outlook, and transient affect states. *Journal of Personality and Social Psychology, 53,* 1137-1145.

Watson, D., & Clark, L. A. (1984). Negative affectivity: The disposition to experience aversive emotional states. *Psychological Bulletin, 96,* 465-490.

Weiss, R. L. (1980). Strategic behavioral marital therapy: Toward a model for assessment and intervention. In J. P. Vincent (Ed.), *Advances in family intervention, assessment, and theory* (Vol. 1, pp. 229-271). Greenwich, CT: JAI Press.

Weiss, R. L. (1984). Cognitive and behavioral measures of marital interaction. In K. Hahlweg & N. S. Jacobson (Eds.), *Marital interaction: Analysis and modification* (pp. 232-252). New York: Guilford.

Weiss, R. L., & Heyman, R. E. (1990). Observation of marital interaction. In F. D. Fincham & T. N. Bradbury (Eds.), *The psychology of marriage* (pp. 87-119). New York: Guilford.

Wethington, E., & Kessler, R. C. (1986). Perceived support, received support, and adjustment to life events. *Journal of Health and Social Behavior, 27,* 78-89.

Wills, T., Weiss, R., & Patterson, G. (1974). A behavioral analysis of the determinants of marital satisfaction. *Journal of Consulting and Clinical Psychology, 42,* 802-811.

Wood, J. V., Saltzberg, J. A., & Goldsamt, L. A. (1990). Does affect induce self-focused attention? *Journal of Personality and Social Psychology, 58,* 899-908.

CHAPTER 12

PERSONALITY AND THE MARITAL CONTEXT

THE CASE FOR INTERACTIVE CONCEPTUALIZATIONS OF NEEDS FOR SPOUSAL SUPPORT

JENNIFER KATZ, STEVEN R. H. BEACH, DAVID A. SMITH, AND LISA B. MYERS

Clearly, the marital relationship is an important source of social support. Three out of four married people name their spouse as their best friend, and four out of five married people say they would marry the same person again (Greely, 1991). Marital partners often are named as the persons most likely turned to for support in times of need (Berg-Cross, 1974; Dakof & Taylor, 1990), and marital partners are more effective than others at providing many aspects of this support (Cutrona, 1986). In addition, spouses are most likely to be named as confidants and as primary sources of social support and companionship (Beach, Martin, Blum, & Roman, 1993).

The importance of marriage to the realm of social support is clear. Equally apparent, however, is the fact that there are individual differences in the levels of

JENNIFER KATZ AND STEVEN R. H. BEACH • Department of Psychology, University of Georgia, Athens, Georgia 30602.   DAVID A. SMITH AND LISA B. MYERS • Department of Psychology, Ohio State University, Columbus, Ohio 43210.

Sourcebook of Social Support and Personality, edited by Gregory R. Pierce, Brian Lakey, Irwin G. Sarason, and Barbara R. Sarason. Plenum Press, New York, 1997.

support expected and needed from marriage, levels of marital support experienced, and the effectiveness of marital support. These differences may be associated with differences in personality styles. Such personality styles are evidenced in marital support processes in at least three primary ways. First, people with different personality styles may elicit different kinds of support from their partners. This may be due, in part, to behavioral tendencies associated with personality styles such as willingness to self-disclose or propensity to display emotion in response to stressful life circumstances (e.g., Simpson, Rholes, & Nelligan, 1991). Second, people with different personality styles may interpret partner behaviors differently (e.g., Beach, Fincham, Katz, & Bradbury, 1996), resulting in different levels of perceived support across individuals, even when their partners' behaviors are identical. Finally, personality may influence the types of social support offered to or sought from partners (e.g., Swann & Predmore, 1985), leading to differing patterns of exchange for persons with different personality styles. Thus, personality may influence support in marriage through a variety of different mechanisms.

The thesis of the current chapter is that a comprehensive understanding of social support in marriage requires the adoption of an interactionist perspective (Bem & Allen, 1974) that encompasses the interplay of marital support, personality, and individual outcomes. We structure our analysis of this thesis around the marital environment (i.e., supportive, nonsupportive, and discordant behaviors) and personality factors postulated to increase the likelihood of a specific outcome among married people. Restricting attention to the interactive effects of personality and social support in marriage increases the homogeneity of the situational side of the interaction and helps focus the search for relevant personality variables. To further refine our discussion, we concentrate on depression as an outcome that is well-suited in illustrating the potentially independent and interactive effects of support and personality.

We begin by reviewing studies from the marriage and social support literature that emphasize situational vulnerabilities to depression. We then review several individual differences that may influence or moderate the effects of social support processes in marriage. In each case, we attempt to draw out the implications for level of support received or experienced in light of an interactionist framework. Next, we examine various problems with current characterizations of personality diatheses for depression, as recently outlined by Coyne and Whiffen (1995). The problems highlighted represent serious challenges to many, if not all, the current formulations of the interactionist perspective in the marital/depression area. Finally, we discuss a reformulation of "personality" that may provide a more satisfactory account of the ways in which personality processes influence the association between social support and depression. Three emerging approaches are briefly analyzed from the standpoint of this reformulation: self-esteem maintenance, self-verification, and cognitive accessibility of relationship schemas. Although very different from each other, theory and research within each of these domains take into consideration both social–environmental influences and individual differences in thoughts, feelings, and behaviors in a way that merits broader attention in the marital literature. As such, they represent an approach to "personality" that may be less subject to the theoretical and methodological criticisms appropriately directed toward current formulations.

THE MARITAL CONTEXT FOR THE INTERPLAY
OF SOCIAL SUPPORT, DEPRESSION, AND PERSONALITY

Marital status and quality are both strongly related to general subjective well-being. For example, whereas only 24% of never-married adults are willing to characterize themselves as very happy, 39% of married people are willing to characterize themselves that way (Lee, Seccombe, & Shehan, 1991). In keeping with the social support interpretation of these data, it appears that the advantage of being married relative to being single is attributable to being happily married, with no advantage being conferred to the unhappily married (Ross, 1995). Indeed, a large body of empirical evidence encompassing a wide array of research designs and assessment strategies has documented a robust association between marital distress and depression in the general population (cf. Beach, Smith, & Fincham, 1995). Although a complete review of this literature is beyond the scope of this chapter, the following recent study may be viewed as representative of this literature.

In a random probability sample of 2,031 adults aged 18 to 90, Ross (1995) assessed depression among people who were married, in romantic relationships but unmarried, or not in romantic relationships. This allowed a direct comparison of people with and without an intimate partner, as well as comparisons on the basis of relationship quality. The study showed that people without partners reported a somewhat higher level of depression than the sample as a whole. People not in romantic relationships, however, were better off than people in unhappy relationships, regardless of marital status. Conversely, people in moderately or very happy romantic relationships reported less depressive symptoms than those with no partner. These effects could not be accounted for by differences associated simply with living with other adults or with children. Furthermore, the effect of not having an intimate partner, in conjunction with the decreased availability of emotional support, fully accounted for the apparent effect of being single on elevated depressive symptomatology (Ross, 1995). The two key points underscored by this investigation are that romantic partners may be uniquely important with regard to depressive symptomatology, and that much of this importance has to do with the provision of support.

SOCIAL SUPPORT IN THE MARITAL CONTEXT

People in distressed marriages rarely report that their spouses are dependable sources of support (Weiss, 1978). This suggests that discordant couples may be especially unlikely to provide their partners with support that could ameliorate depressive symptomatology (Beach, Arias, & O'Leary, 1986). Such broad associations invite speculation about mechanisms through which this occurs. How does marital discord reduce support in marriage?

Marital discord may directly lead to attenuated levels of available partner support in several ways. For instance, discordant partners might be less willing to provide support to their partners because of feelings of hostility or attributions of blame (Bradbury & Fincham, 1992). When opportunities for support arise, a discordant partner may be more likely to engage in punitive or disruptive behavior rather than support. Alternatively, spouses may be less likely to elicit support from their partners when feeling maritally dissatisfied, electing instead to withdraw from the relationship and turn to other sources of support (Burger & Milardo, 1995).

Marital problems also indirectly lead to attenuated partner support by increasing the likelihood that potentially supportive partner behaviors (e.g., problem-focused advice giving) will be interpreted negatively (e.g., as invalidation). For instance, a husband's silence while he considers how best to respond to his wife's need for support might be interpreted differently depending on her level of marital satisfaction. If satisfied, his wife might interpret the husband's silence as a sign of careful considera- tion. If discordant, his wife might interpret his silence as a hostile, withdrawing act. In brief, marital distress may directly weaken levels of available spousal support and reduce the impact of support that is offered by increasing negative interpretations. The context of discord may have a salient effect on support processes, rivaling the effects of individual differences in determining support effectiveness.

DEPRESSION IN THE MARITAL CONTEXT

Over the past 20 years, Brown and colleagues have systematically advanced the study of social support and intimate relationships in forming a social causation model of depression (cf. Brown & Harris, 1989). For instance, using interviewer ratings of relationship quality, Brown and Harris (1978) found that lack of a confiding relationship with a boyfriend or spouse was a significant vulnerability factor in the development of depression among women. A number of the stressors found to precipitate the onset of women's major depressive episodes were marital events.

In a prototypical investigation, Brown, Andrews, Hams, Adler, and Bridge (1986) evaluated the prospective effect of marital support on depression in a study of 400 women. They found that negative marital interaction (e.g., arguing, strain, coldness, violence) at the time of the initial interview predicted much greater vulnerability to depression. Women confronted with a severe difficulty or negative life event were more than three times as likely to become depressed if their marriage previously had been characterized by negative marital interaction. Interestingly, retrospective inter- views suggested that much of this effect was attributable to lack of support from the partner in times of crisis, particularly if support had been expected but was not forthcoming.

These data suggest that one causal mechanism linking marital discord and depres- sion could be the lack of needed support associated with being in a discordant marital relationship during difficult times. Alternatively, or in addition, negative marital inter- actions might themselves sometimes constitute severe negative events. Negative mari- tal interactions that functionally disrupt normal social support processes between spouses are, therefore, likely to be particularly depressogenic (Coyne, Kahn, & Gotlib, 1987).

More recent research by Brown and colleagues has demonstrated the potential importance of marital events during recovery from episodes of depression. In particu- lar, they found that a "fresh start" episode or dramatic improvement in a marital problem (e.g., reconciliation following a separation) may prompt recovery from a depressive episode that has become chronic (Brown, Adler, & Bifulco, 1988; Brown, Lemyre, & Bifulco, 1992). This again suggests that marital changes may sometimes precede and produce improvement in depression. If a woman's partner who was previously viewed as unsupportive, unapproachable, and undependable comes to be viewed as warm and supportive, in some cases, this change may be sufficient to precipitate the woman's recovery from a chronic depressive episode.

MODERATING EFFECTS OF PERSONALITY

In addition to data showing that the availability of a confiding, nonjudgmental relationship decreases the probability of becoming depressed in response to a negative life event (Brown & Harris, 1978, 1986), more recent research by Brown and colleagues has singled out a particularly important individual difference variable: negative self-evaluation. They found that less negative self-evaluations decrease the probability of depression in response to a negative life event (Brown, Bifulco, & Andrews, 1990b). Accordingly, consistent with the interactionist perspective, we can conclude that both social support and individual differences may interact with severe events in predicting the likelihood of a depressive episode.

In particular, there is a subset of people at risk to experience especially negative affective outcomes in response to various threatening events (Brown, Bifulco, & Andrews, 1990b). The mechanism for this elevated risk may be increased vulnerability to situations involving direct attack on one's self-evaluation (Gilbert, 1992). Social support may change risk of a successful attack in one way, whereas personality does so in another. Furthermore, it seems clear as well that personality and social support could influence or interact with each other.

In a test of the central role of successful attacks on self-evaluation in producing depression, Brown, Harris, and Hepworth (1995) contrasted the effects of various types of events deemed severely stressful. They found that the experience of humiliation and entrapment was associated with a far greater risk of depression than were experiences of loss or danger that did not produce humiliation or entrapment. In keeping with Christian, O'Leary, and Avery (1993), discoveries of infidelity were treated as instances of humiliation. In fact, over half of the "humiliation events" that posed a direct threat to the individual's self-esteem involved spouses or lovers. Because "humiliation" experiences are such potent precipitants of depression, it would seem prudent to search for general individual differences such as negative self-evaluation that predispose to humiliation. For instance, it might be particularly valuable to identify personal characteristics that create increased risk for the simultaneous loss of social status (i.e., stressor) and the experience of social exclusion (i.e., lack of support; Gilbert, 1992).

Of particular relevance to our discussion of personality, social support, and vulnerability to depression is a recent study by Andrews and Brown (1995) that demonstrates the reverse process. In a sample of 102 women assessed over 7 years, half of the 36 women initially found to have high levels of negative self-evaluation had more positive self-evaluations as follow-up. One important predictor of these positive changes was improvement in the quality of close relationships and associated marital support. Accordingly, it appears that when close relationships and the quality of partner support behaviors improve, they may have the potential to affect individual difference factors that create vulnerability to depression (cf. Coyne & Whiffen, 1995).

GENDER AND SOCIAL SUPPORT IN THE MARITAL CONTEXT

Gender has been found to be related to social support processes in important ways, and so no discussion of the interactions among these factors would be complete without brief mention of some gender-related issues. Two broad themes can be discerned in this literature: the provision of support, and the elicitation and receipt of support. Each of which will be discussed in turn.

GENDER AND SUPPORT PROVISION

Derlega, Metts, Petronio, and Margulis (1993) argue that gender differences in relationship behaviors can be attributed to men and women experiencing "different subcultures." These subcultures result from socialization processes in which males and females are reinforced for holding certain values about social support, and for behaving accordingly. There is now a large body of research on how men and women differentially define problem sharing and intimacy in their relationships (e.g., Caldwell & Peplau, 1982; Reis, Senchak, & Solomon, 1985). These differences in definitions of relationship intimacy by gender logically influence gender-specific definitions of support in marriage as well as actual enactments of support. For instance, women tend to ask questions to indicate interest, whereas men may ask questions to find out specific facts (Fincham, Fernandes, & Humphreys, 1993). Accordingly, although many wives discuss problem situations in an attempt to be close and supportive, many husbands dislike discussions that involve dwelling on negative and/or minor details. Consequently, inquiries, problem sharing, and problem discussions by women might be perceived as inane and pointless by men, whereas the absence of these behaviors by husbands might cause wives to infer a lack of interest, support, and caring. In brief, intended versus perceived meanings of the same actions may differ depending on the gender of the communicator and the gender of the recipient. Differential perceptions about "what is supportive," then, easily could influence both the provision of support and the perception of support that is offered. This may lead both husbands and wives to feel undersupported or to offer support that will not be experienced as helpful by their partners in some cases.

GENDER AND THE ELICITATION, RECEIPT, AND USE OF SUPPORT

To the extent that men and women have internalized the gender roles prescribed by society, they are more likely to experience support in marriage according to societal norms. Although sex is biologically driven, gender roles are not, and it is reasonable to assume that gender-role behaviors are influenced, at least in part, by social learning histories.

One important individual difference between men and women in relationships involves level of self-disclosure. Self-disclosing a problem situation and expressing one's needs is one fundamental method of eliciting social support. Self-disclosure itself often elicits affirmation and acceptance, important types of socioemotional support within marriage (Christensen, Jacobson, & Babcock, 1995). In general, women tend to self-disclose at more intimate levels and to value self-disclosure more than men (Aries & Johnson, 1983; Caldwell & Peplau, 1982; Derlega, Winstead, Wong, & Hunter, 1985; Reis et al., 1985). In contrast, men's self-disclosures tend to center on shared activities or interests, including work, sports, and shared expertise (Caldwell & Peplau, 1982; Rubin, 1983). Women also tend to gauge their marital adjustment by their self-disclosure about personal facts, feelings, communication, and affection, whereas men gauge their marital adjustment by sexual satisfaction and shared pleasurable activities (Peplau & Gordon, 1985). Although disclosure is valued by both men and women in their marriages, intimate disclosure is related more strongly to women's marital adjustment than men's (Hendrick, 1981; Hendrick, Hendrick, & Adler, 1988; Jones, 1991). Alternatively, some forms of social support, particularly those associated with intimate self-disclosure, may be more powerful for women than for men.

Other types of supportive behaviors also may be related differentially to men's and women's marital adjustment. Relative to men, women have been found to prefer verbal and nonverbal demonstrations of affection, more direct communication and disclosure of thoughts and feelings, and equality of decision making and control of resources (Hawkins, Weisberg, & Ray, 1980; Madden & Janoff-Bulman, 1981; Noller, 1987; Wills, Weiss, & Patterson, 1974). Furthermore, with regard to conflict within the marriage, findings suggest that women prefer their partner to be actively involved in problem discussions, whereas men prefer not to dwell on discussion of negative events (Fincham et al., 1993). This may be particularly true when discussing events that are perceived as uncontrollable (e.g., a chronic illness). These preferences also may combine to create gender differences in broader patterns of interacting.

The demand–withdraw dynamic, an escalating pattern of attempts to change partner behaviors and subsequent partner withdrawal, may reflect differences in preferences associated with gender. Findings to date indicate that women more often take the role of the "demander," and men more often take the role of the "withdrawer." This dynamic is robustly related to marital discord and relationship dissolution (Christensen & Heavey, 1990). In contrast, when men and women are satisfied with their problem discussions, both genders report higher levels of satisfaction with their relationships (Heavey, Layne, & Christensen, 1993).

In brief, gender provides several examples of the way in which individual difference variables may influence both the provision and perception of social support offered by the partner. In turn, these differences may lead to subtly different effects of social support (or its absence) on the formation and maintenance of depressive symptomatology. We turn now to variables more traditionally dealt with as individual differences.

INDIVIDUAL DIFFERENCES, SOCIAL SUPPORT, AND DEPRESSION

Personality characteristics have long been hypothesized to be related to depression (cf., Frank, Kupfer, Jacob, & Jarrett, 1987; Gotlib & Hooley, 1988). Depressed people often display characteristic personalities or even diagnosable personality disorders (Zimmerman, Pfohl, Coryell, Corenthal, & Stangl, 1991). What is less clear is the extent to which various personality characteristics (1) directly predispose people to depression through an increase in negative life events or decrease social support, (2) are simply a product or reflection of depression, or (3) interact with life events or social support to produce increased risk for depression. Without resolving or diminishing the potential importance of the first two of these mechanisms, it is the last mechanism on which we are focused. In particular, we explore the possibility that individual differences may introduce variability in response to negative life events and available support.

For what follows, it bears emphasizing that individual differences, gender included, are not causes; at most, they are correlates of other causes. Attention to individual differences, however, helps broaden empirical inquiry to encompass a more diverse array of causes. Thus, by studying the personality characteristics of their subjects, researchers may account for more of the variance in such notoriously heterogeneous conditions as marital discord and depression (cf. Bradbury & Karney, 1993). This important point will be one focus of the "reformulation" of personality to be discussed later.

The fundamental premise of the individual differences perspective is that marital problems are not equally depressogenic for all people. Rather, marital problems are more or less depressogenic when they are experienced by spouses who are, for whatever reasons, more or less vulnerable to these kinds of events. According to this view, some people possess a specific vulnerability to interpersonal stress or failure, or perhaps special sensitivity to the presence or absence of social support. Others may, instead, be vulnerable to events of a different nature (i.e., achievement- or work-related stress or failure). Because we believe "personality" is affected by ongoing social realities rather than being strictly internal to the individual, we will emphasize this view in our discussion of social processes related to individual differences, negative events, social support, and depression.

We will discuss neuroticism and affective style, vulnerability to interpersonal events, attachment style, and negative self-evaluations as representative characteristics that may moderate the association between marital support and depression. These moderating factors may influence reactions to negative events, support use, and/or the efficacy of social support. In part, these personality characteristics are all conceptually related. The ways in which people cope with life stress may differ as a function of their self-definitions, needs for support, and support-eliciting behaviors. These variables have been chosen for illustrative purposes, and it should be noted that by no means have we exhausted the set of personality characteristics associated with increased vulnerability to depression.

NEUROTICISM AND AFFECTIVE STYLE

Since the earliest systematic investigations into the determinants of marital adjustment (e.g., Adams, 1946), individual differences in neuroticism (e.g., emotional instability, irritability) have been linked with poor marital adjustment (Bentler & Newcomb,

1978; Kelly & Conley, 1987; Terman & Oden, 1947). Theoretically, neuroticism should be related to subsequent depressive symptomatology through its connection with more enduring negative affective styles (Clark & Watson, 1991). Therefore, one might expect dysphoria, particularly when it endures over a long period of time, to be associated with both declines in support received in the marriage and greater emotional reaction if negative changes in the marital relationship occur.

Recently, the utility of dysphoria in predicting subsequent marital adjustment and the development of depressive symptoms has been examined directly. Elevated symptoms of depression were found to (1) be a significant risk factor for the development of a first episode of major depression (Horwath, Johnson, Klerman, & Weissman, 1992), (2) lead both to heightened reactivity to stressors in general (Hammen, Marks, Mayol, & de Mayo, 1985), and (3) heightened reactivity to marital discord in particular (Beach & O'Leary, 1993a). This heightened reactivity may largely account for the finding that people who are dysphoric early in their relationships subsequently show greater declines in marital adjustment than those who are not (Beach & O'Leary, 1993b).

Three separate effects of affective style (i.e., chronic dysphoria and/or neuroticism) on the association between marital discord and depression can be envisioned. First, affective style might influence the occurrence of numerous relationship-enhancing or relationship-diminishing behaviors. This influence may in turn lead affective style to be associated with various relationship processes, and with relationship adjustment. More specifically, individuals with negative affective styles may engage in fewer constructive (e.g., support provision) and more frequent destructive (e.g., excessive demands for reassurance and support) behaviors associated with poor marital quality. Second, affective style might have a direct effect on the probability of displaying dysphoria and symptoms of depression. And finally, affective style might moderate the impact of marital discord on depressive symptoms, rendering those high in negative affect more vulnerable to negative marital interaction and negative changes in the marital relationship (Beach & Fincham, 1994). As discussed previously, marital problems are often associated with less marital support, a resource that might be particularly needed by chronically distressed individuals experiencing marital difficulties. In brief, a neurotic or negative affective style may predispose spouses to be in need of support due to vulnerability to both negative affective and marital outcomes. Individuals with such a style, however, may be unlikely to elicit supportive partner behaviors, and perhaps less likely to experience support offered to them as positive.

VULNERABILITY TO INTERPERSONAL EVENTS

Investigations of individual differences and depressogenic vulnerability to specific kinds of events can be found within three research traditions: (1) Beck, Epstein, Harrison, and Emery's (1983) distinction between sociotropy (i.e., having dysfunctional beliefs centered on the need for approval or love), and autonomy (i.e., having dysfunctional beliefs centered on perfectionism; Robins, 1990); (2) Blatt's work (1974) on anaclitic (dependence-based) and introjective (autonomy-based) types of depressive experiences; and (3) Hammen's work (e.g., Hammen et al., 1985) on dependent versus self-critical cognitive schemas. Common to these perspectives is the view that an important liability, possessed only by some people, accounts for the association between interpersonal stress or achievement-related failure and depression. For instance, sociotropic depressed patients report more recent negative interpersonal events than autonomy events, and more negative interpersonal events than non-sociotropic depressed patients (Robins, 1990). Dependence (e.g., "I am very sensitive to others for signs of rejection") emerges as an important theme in surveys of the phenomenology of depressive experiences (Blatt & Zurroff, 1992). Furthermore, people identified as schematic for dependence were later more strongly affected by interpersonal events than by other types of events (Hammen et al., 1985). Additional research of this type has been discussed in several excellent reviews (Blatt & Zurroff, 1992; Coyne & Whiffen, 1995; Gotlib & Hammen, 1992).

Due to dysfunctional beliefs about their self-definitions, interpersonally vulnerable people may be more likely than others to experience available support as deficient and to perceive marital interactions as negative. As such, they may be particularly vulnerable to both marital discord and depression, given that negative marital relations are associated with deficient spousal support and stressful marital interactions and events.

We do not mean to imply, however, that beliefs about deficient support are necessarily distortions of reality. It may also be the case that these beliefs are accurate, since behaviors characteristic of interpersonally vulnerable people (e.g., clinging, reassurance-seeking) may function to isolate the relationship partner and preclude partner support provision.

ATTACHMENT STYLE

Adult attachment styles have also recently attracted the attention of researchers seeking to predict variability in relationship and personal adjustment with more precision. This line of inquiry is distinguished not only for its attention to the individual differences people bring to their interpersonal relationships, but also for its attention to mechanisms through which individual differences influence relationship functioning.

Ever since Hazan and Shaver's seminal study (1987), it has become increasingly clear that adult relationships can be described in terms similar to those used to describe infant–mother attachment relationships (Shaver, Hazan, & Bradshaw, 1988), and that attachment style may not be readily reducible to common personality constructs (Shaver & Brennan, 1992). Within intimate relationships, people with particular attachment styles think, feel, and behave in different ways during times of stress (Simpson et al., 1991). These behaviors are likely to impact the social support elicited by the partner, as well as appraisals of available support.

In general, securely attached people endorse positive relationship characteristics (e.g., "I find it relatively easy to get close to others and am comfortable depending on them and having them depend on me"), people with dismissive- or fearful–avoidant attachment express greater mistrust (e.g., "I am nervous when anyone gets too close, and often, love partners want me to be more intimate than I feel comfortable being"), and anxiously attached–preoccupied adults are typically more dependent and needy (e.g., "I want to merge completely with another person, and this desire sometimes scares people away"; Bartholomew & Horowitz, 1991; Hazan & Shaver, 1987; Hendrick & Hendrick, 1989; Levy & Davis, 1988). Of particular interest in the current context, childhood experiences of attachment to a parent have been shown to be associated with adult attachment style (Feeney & Noller, 1990). Thus, there is a basis in these studies for hypothesizing that people bring to their marriages broadly based working models of the self and relationships that may then influence the development of marital quality.

But how do attachment styles, identifiable in spouses before they are married, exert an influence on later marital functioning? Recent research indicates a tendency toward assortive pairing with regard to attachment style (Senchak & Leonard, 1992). Accordingly, it is often the case that spouses with secure attachment styles will be paired with spouses who also have secure attachment styles. Such couples report significantly more intimacy than couples containing one or two insecure spouses. Of particular interest from the standpoint of the development of depression is the question of whether those with fearful–avoidant attachment styles, who may enter marriage more dysphoric and with a less positive view of their partner (Feeney & Noller, 1991), are at greater or lesser risk of depression in response to marital discord than are the anxiously attached, who may enter marriage with an overidealized view of the partner. Evidence to date indicates that both styles are associated with depression, with a stronger association among the fearful–avoidant (Carnelley, Pietromonaco & Jaffe, 1994; Katz, Beach, & Wakefield, 1996). Given that this attachment style is characterized by negative internal models of the self and of others (Bartholomew & Horowitz, 1991), it is likely that these persons view themselves as in need of support from others but do not perceive others as reliable sources of social support.

Finally, attachment styles appear to influence the interactional behaviors of couples. For instance, in a study of social support in dating couples, Simpson et al. (1991) showed that when they were nervous, securely attached women sought more support from their partners, whereas avoidant women sought less. The securely attached men in this study offered more support to their nervous partners, whereas those who were more avoidant offered less. A connection between attachment styles and interactional behaviors was also reported by Senchak and Leonard (1992) and Kobak and Hazan (1991). Senchak and Leonard (1992) found that secure married couples reported less withdrawal and verbal aggression than couples containing an insecure spouse. Withdrawal behaviors might in turn predict later deterioration in marital adjustment (Gottman, 1993; Smith, Vivian, & O'Leary, 1990, 1991). Kobak and Hazan (1991) found husbands' security negatively correlated with wives' rejection during problem solving, whereas wives' security positively correlated with husbands' listening while confiding.

There is considerable descriptive overlap between the anxious–preoccupied attachment style and the previously discussed sociotropic, dependent, and anaclitic individual differences formulations. Likewise, there may be considerable overlap between the dismissive and fearful–avoidant attachment styles and the autonomous, self-critical, and introjective formulations. The application of these constructs to the study of the covariation between marital discord and depression might, therefore, be streamlined by emphasizing these similarities, and by seeking to identify those people for whom marital disruptions may be particularly depressing (cf. Cummings, 1995).

NEGATIVE SELF-EVALUATION

Negative self-evaluation appears to be another vulnerability factor for depression, making it more likely that a depressive episode will occur in response to severe negative events or adverse circumstances (e.g., Brown, Andrews, Bifulco, & Veiel, 1990a; Brown et al., 1986). With regard to intimate relationships, recent work suggests that a negative self-evaluation, in combination with marital discord, is predictive of depressive symptomatology (Culp & Beach, 1993). It also appears that negative self-evaluations are associated with negative interpersonal behaviors (e.g., deficient social support, conflict; Rusbult, Morrow, & Johnson, 1987). Accordingly, negative self-evaluations may precipitate episodes of depression and extreme vulnerability for depressive episodes, given the occurrence of negative marital events (Brown et al., 1990b). Available work in this area suggests that it is important to consider separately positive and negative attitudes about the self, as it is only negative self-attitudes (rather than positive attitudes or global evaluations) that are likely to predict greater vulnerability to depression (Brown et al., 1990b).

It also appears that negative self-evaluations are particularly prevalent among people reporting a poor relationship with their parents, suggesting some overlap with attachment style (Brown, Bifulco, Veiel, & Andrews, 1990c). Researchers in the area of adult attachment have studied internal models of the "self" and the "other" individually, finding only a moderate correspondence between negative internal self-models and low self-esteem (Collins & Reed, 1990; Feeney & Noller, 1990). Furthermore, studies suggest that women with attachment styles characterized by negative internal self-models may be more vulnerable to depression. One study found that both mildly depressed undergraduate women and clinically depressed married women were characterized by greater preoccupation and greater fearful avoidance than non-depressed women (Carnelley et al., 1994). Likewise, recent work by Katz et al. (1996) suggests that relationship satisfaction and dysphoria are more likely to covary among women characterized by negative internal self-models, even after controlling for global self-esteem level. It may be that the self-model dimension of attachment serves as a more powerful predictor of the covariation between discord and depression than traditional measures of global self-esteem.

Taken together, this brief survey of individual differences suggests considerable potential for research to specify with greater precision people who may be at greatest risk for depression in response to marital discord. Because individual differences are not "causes," it will be important to launch companion research efforts to specify the mechanisms through which these individual differences operate and the social conditions that may maintain them. Such endeavors would allow for the identification of the ways in which these risks are manifested. Personality and individual differences appear to have an as yet untapped potential to identify those who are (1) more likely to experience particular types of problems in their relationships, (2) most likely to utilize effectively the social resources available to them, and (3) most vulnerable to depressive reactions, should problems materialize.

To conclude our discussion of individual differences that may moderate the effects of support on individual outcomes, we discuss some problems with current characterizations of these personality diatheses. Specifically, we alert readers to three important shortcomings of current formulations of this interaction as recently outlined by Coyne and Whiffen (1995).

CRITIQUE OF CURRENT PERSONALITY APPROACHES

First among problems with current personality diatheses to depression are the strong interrelationships among the many proposed diatheses. At a minimum, the current level of overlap in various proposed diatheses creates a problem of discriminant validity. It is readily apparent that various individual difference variables often account for the same variance in depression. In some cases, there is obvious and benign conceptual overlap among proposed personality mediators. For instance, neuroticism, negative affectivity, negative self-evaluation, and self-criticism all contain negatively valenced affect or behavior as their defining characteristics (Clark & Watson, 1991). More disturbing, however, are those personality styles that are not conceptually similar but nevertheless reveal substantial redundancy under empirical scrutiny. For example, one study found that Beck et al.'s (1983) concept of sociotropy was related positively to the Big Five factors of neuroticism and negatively to openness to experience (Cappeliez, 1993). To the extent that reality can be captured by fewer constructs than are currently being investigated, progress in this area will be enhanced. Clearly, conceptual clarity is better served if we recognize overlapping aspects of various constructs and consolidate our conceptualization of them.

Second, Coyne and Whiffen (1995) argue that it is difficult to distinguish many proposed risk factors from the experience of depression itself. In particular, low self-esteem, self-critical tendencies, and neuroticism show very high overlap with depressive symptomatology. Additional concern about the need for distinct personality dimensions is raised by findings that subclinical depression may predict greater reactivity to both stressors in general (Hammen, 1991) and to marital discord in particular (Beach & O'Leary, 1993a). Furthermore, the assessment of personality upon recovery from depression does not disentangle personality and depression, because residual symptoms or related difficulties may affect subsequent personality functioning (Hirschfeld, Klerman, & Korchin, 1989).

Third, Coyne and Whiffen (1995) note that current conceptualizations of personality diatheses insufficiently account for the effects of the social context. For example, a recent study defined interpersonal sensitivity as composed of several factors, including need for approval, separation anxiety, and fragile inner-self (Boyce, Parker, Barnett, Cooney, & Smith, 1991). Boyce et al. found that for nondepressed women in a stable relationship, the risk of depression at 6-month follow-up was increased up to ten-times by high interpersonal sensitivity, and threetimes by neuroticism. Clearly, however, the social context can directly affect the expression of interpersonal sensitivity or neuroticism. This may occur, for instance, when a critical, nonsupportive spouse engenders increased self-criticism, or when a partner's repeated extramarital affairs produce increased preoccupation with the availability and dependability of the partner. As observed by Leff and Vaughn (1985), few chronically insecure people live with supportive and sympathetic partners. If other "personality" diatheses for depression are related to recent interpersonal experiences, we may find that we must recast them as interpersonal process variables rather than as static person variables. If we successfully recast personality in this way, we should enjoy considerably enhanced predictive power and better grounded therapeutic interventions.

REFORMULATION OF "PERSONALITY" AS A PROCESS

The widely accepted interactionist perspective posits that behavior is a joint function of the situation and the person (Bem & Allen, 1974). The transactional form of this approach (Endler & Magnussen, 1976) refers to the reciprocal interactions between people and situations. According to this model, people select situations and bring their own unique personality characteristics to them. These characteristics influence how the situation is then perceived and the reactions that are elicited from others. Reactions from others and other environmental factors, in turn, may impact subsequent perceptions, behaviors, and personality factors. Because outcomes such as depression can best be understood by examining both the main and interactive effects of personality and the social environment, variation in behavior is best accounted for by considering both the person and the environment simultaneously.

It may appear that the interactionist perspective hardly requires special emphasis given its widely accepted role in the social psychology literature. Our review of the social support and personality literatures relevant to marriage and depression, however, suggests that this perspective warrants stronger consideration in the design of studies investigating social support and marriage. To simplify their work, many researchers seem to concentrate on the effects of the situation and ignore differences in personal attributes. Conversely, other researchers focus on individual differences while ignoring situational factors.

The search for mechanisms that better explain how personality processes create vulnerability to depression has barely begun, yet such a search is clearly desirable. In this section, we outline three mechanisms that may account for important individual differences in vulnerability to depression. Each of these approaches emphasizes individual differences and how they are affected by the marital context to produce different thoughts, feelings, and behaviors.

SELF-EVALUATION MAINTENANCE PROCESSES

The self-evaluation maintenance (SEM) model assumes that people are motivated to maintain a positive self-view and behave in ways to preserve this view (Tesser, 1988). The model proposes that self-view is influenced via two social psychological processes: reflection and comparison. The reflection process is one in which person's enhance their self-views by basking in the glory of another's outstanding performance (Cialdini et al., 1976). The comparison process is one in which persons' self-views are threatened by the outstanding performance of a close other.

Reflection and comparison processes are influenced by three factors: performance, closeness, and relevance. *Performance* refers to how well one accomplishes a particular task relative to others. *Closeness* refers to the degree of association between the self and other. *Relevance* refers to the importance of the performance dimension to one's self-definition (Pilkington, Tesser, & Stephens, 1989). According to the SEM model, people are threatened by the good performance of others who outperform them on self-relevant tasks. When a task is not self-relevant, however, people can have their self-evaluations enhanced by the good performance of others who outperform them via reflection. Both comparison and reflection processes are intensified by psychological closeness.

The SEM model highlights the potential for people to experience more intense affective reactions when the comparisons involve a close other. Indeed, being outperformed by a partner in a self-relevant area may be especially distressing for some people. However, more common routes to depression may be due to indirect effects of SEM processes on marital relationship quality or changes in self-definition. The effect on relationship quality would be expected to occur as a defensive response to being outperformed by the partner. One way to alleviate negative affect in such a situation is to reduce levels of perceived closeness or intimacy with the partner. If so, an important resource used to buffer the effects of negative life events and maximize the benefits of relationship support may often be sacrificed to maintain self-evaluation. The more subtle effects of SEM processes on increasing vulnerability to depression are discussed next in the context of effects that may be particularly relevant to women.

Women's Potentially Increased Vulnerability to Humiliation/Depression

Beach and Tesser (1995) outlined ways that each partner's attempts to protect his or her self-evaluation could lead to lower global self-esteem and increased vulnerability to depression over time. Interestingly, their analysis provides a plausible mechanism for women's greater vulnerability to depression. Specifically, they note that the pattern of slightly older males marrying somewhat younger females may be sufficient to (1) create differential earnings potential, (2) engender deference with regard to decision making in important areas, and (3) support a performance differential in favor of husbands across many areas (Baumeister, 1991). Such performance differentials may sometimes cause negative affect directly. However, they also may lead wives to reassess the self-relevance of areas on which they are outperformed by their partner, leading them to view these areas as less central to their self-definition (Tesser, 1988). The exclusion of a large range of performance domains from one's self-definition, however, should render the self more vulnerable to subsequent challenges by limiting the complexity of future selves (e.g., Linville, 1985; Niedenthal, Setterlund, & Wherry, 1992). Accordingly, to the extent that relationships reduce cognitive complexity and the range of functional competence, even happy marriages might undermine women's capacity to remain free of depression when faced with negative life events. If so, these considerations underscore the potential importance of a gender-sensitive approach to investigating relationship effects in depression, as well as recommending marital interventions for the treatment of depression (cf. Kaslow & Carter, 1991).

PARTNER SELECTION AND SELF-VERIFICATION PROCESSES

Another process that may connect individual differences to the association between marital discord and depression is described by self-verification theory (Swann, 1983). Self-verification theory suggests that people are motivated to confirm both favorable and unfavorable self-conceptions. Thus, although people seek and value positive feedback about positive self-views, they also seek and value negative information about negative self-views. The confirmation of self-views, even when negative, may lead to greater perceptions of predictability and control of oneself and the environment, as the self-verification motive is driven by both intrapsychic ("I really do know myself") and interpersonal ("My spouse really does know me") factors (Swann, Hixon, & De La Ronde, 1992a).

Swann, Wenzlaff, Krull, and Pelham (1992b) showed that depressed people will, in fact, gravitate toward people who evaluate them unfavorably. They also showed that depressed people are more likely both to solicit unfavorable feedback and to be rejected. Similar findings were reported by Joiner, Alfano, and Metalsky (1993), who found that levels of depressive symptoms, reassurance seeking, and negative-feedback seeking were predictive of rejection by same-sex roommates (see also Joiner & Metalsky, 1995). Of note, Katz and Beach (in press) recently replicated the Joiner et al. (1993) findings among dating couples, predicting partner dissatisfaction from the three-way interaction of depression, reassurance, and negative-feedback seeking.

Using a married sample to test the connection between self-verification processes and both marital and personal adjustment, Swann et al. (1992a) showed that spouses with positive self-concepts were more committed to their marriages to the extent that their partners appraised them favorably. Likewise, perceptions of partner support that confirm preexisting self-evaluations are associated with greater marital adjustment (Katz, Beach, & Anderson, 1996). Another striking finding, however, was Swann et al.'s (1992a) conclusion that spouses with negative self-concepts were more committed to their marriages to the extent that their partners thought *unfavorably* of them.

In another study, it was found that women predisposed toward self-criticism tend to date men who placed little value on intimacy, thereby ensuring a less nurturant environment (Zurroff & de Lorimier, 1989). It appears that spouses with some types of depressed partners find it difficult to challenge the other's depressogenic guilt or negative self-perceptions, either because they lack the ability and inclination, or because this might decrease the partner's relationship commitment. Indeed, some research on attributions for depressed people's behavior suggests that partners of depressives may be less likely to provide support by virtue of their partner's depression. In assessing attributions for failure or success ascribed to hypothetical depressed people, Sacco and Dunn (1990) found that failures were judged to be controllable and due to internal and global characteristics of the depressed person. In contrast, successes were attributed to unstable, external, and uncontrollable factors. Subjects also indicated that they were more likely to experience resentment and anger at being support providers for depressed persons. Given that attributions appear to influence motivation to provide support, spouses of depressives may provide less than adequate support due, in part, to negative attributional processes (e.g., "He's the one who got himself into this mess—I'm not going to waste my time helping him out!"). In addition, interpersonal reactions to depressed people, in some cases, may lead to the development and maintenance of decreased partner marital satisfaction.

COGNITIVE ACCESSIBILITY

A final dimension of importance in explaining the connection between spousal support, personality, and vulnerability to depression is cognitive accessibility. Knowledge structures that have been recently primed, or that are chronically primed, will be most potent in structuring the interpretation of events (Bargh & Pietromonaco, 1982). To the extent that a situation is ambiguous, missing information will be supplied by the general knowledge structure that has been activated (Uleman & Bargh, 1989). Likewise, over time, information that was inferred may become indistinguishable from information that exists, leading to the fabrication of compelling evidence in support of one's initial biases (O'Sullivan & Durso, 1984). Accordingly, the more chronically activated a particular schema regarding partner supportiveness, the greater its potential impact on the perception of the partner and the development of the relationship with the partner.

One of the most robust findings in the cognitive and social-cognitive literatures is that knowledge structures in memory that are made available through situational manipulations (e.g., priming) or naturally occurring states (e.g., depression) can influence the encoding of new information, judgments made about the information, and responses to it (e.g., Srull & Wyer, 1979). Concepts easily accessed from memory can, therefore, have a pervasive impact on spousal information processing, judgments, and behavior. When information processing occurs, however, not all concepts are equally accessible or brought to mind with equal ease. In fact, the importance of individual differences in concept accessibility is well documented (Markus & Smith, 1981). Thus, even if a concept is chronically accessible to all spouses, individual differences in accessibility may still exist.

Not all people should be expected to have equal access to their assumptions about partner availability and supportiveness, and ratings of the partner for people with readily accessible knowledge structures about spouse supportiveness should be more stable and more robust across changing circumstances than the ratings of people with less readily accessible knowledge structures regarding partner supportiveness. For those with more accessible knowledge structures, prior beliefs should exert an ongoing conservative effect with regard to beliefs about the spouse. Therefore, highly accessible beliefs may differentiate persons who expect more negative, as opposed to more positive, behavior when preparing to interact with their partner (e.g., Fincham, Beach, & Kemp-Fincham, in press), and may influence as well the extent to which individuals engage in self-fulfilling prophecies; that is, cognitive accessibility should influence the likelihood of a knowledge structure contributing to vulnerability to negative marital interactions, perceived loss of support from the spouse, and perhaps negative conclusions about the self in response to negative partner behavior. Although the role of cognitive accessibility remains understudied in the marital area, it is an emerging realm with considerable potential to enhance reformulation of current personality constructs and even reformulation of the construct of marital satisfaction (Fincham et al., in press).

Accordingly, to the extent that certain cognitive contents can be shown to be more readily accessible for some individuals, we should anticipate a wide range of effects on the influences of stressors and social support to depressive outcomes.

SUMMARY

People differ with regard to their specific support needs and the types of support that effectively preserve their emotional well-being. Within the marital context, these differences may have important implications for the prevention of depression in response to negative life events. Concerns about current personality conceptualizations become more tractable when traditional conceptions of personality give way to processes encompassing both individual differences and the social context. Examples of such mechanisms discussed include self-evaluation maintenance processes (Tesser, 1988), self-verification processes (Swann, 1983), and cognitive accessibility (Fincham, Garnier, Gano-Phillips, & Osborne, 1995). In particular, these perspectives allow personality styles to be conceptualized in terms of more basic, transactional processes. Within each viewpoint, personality is reconceptualized at a different level of analysis that is largely nonoverlapping with symptoms of depression. These perspectives naturally reduce the proliferation of personality-style diatheses to a few basic process dimensions of importance. Process-oriented perspectives that consider both individual and situational factors may then be better equipped to highlight the important effects of personality styles in changing the impact of marital support on depressive outcomes. In particular, we propose that current diathesis–stress support models of depression be reformulated to better reflect the core processes and transactions that are partially captured in current, static formulations. Toward this end, theorists may do well to consider self-protective processes, self-verification processes, and basic cognitive processes as they move toward the next generation of theories encompassing personality, social support, and depression.

REFERENCES

Adams, C. R. (1946). The prediction of adjustment in marriage. *Educational and Psychological Measurement, 6*, 185–193.

Andrews, B., & Brown, G. W. (1995). Stability and change in low self-esteem: The role of psychosocial factors. *Psychological Medicine, 25*, 23–31.

Aries, E. J., & Johnson, F. L. (1983). Close friendship in adulthood: Conversational content between same-sex friends. *Sex Roles, 9*, 1183–1196.

Bargh, J. A., & Pietromonaco, P. (1982). Automatic information processing and social perceptions: The influence of trait information presented outside of conscious awareness on impression formation. *Journal of Personality and Social Psychology, 43*, 437–449.

Bartholomew, K., & Horowitz, L. M. (1991). Attachment styles among young adults: A test of a four category model. *Journal of Personality and Social Psychology, 61*, 226–244.

Baumeister, R. F. (1991). *Escaping the self.* New York: Basic Books.

Beach, S. R. H., Arias, I., & O'Leary, K. D. (1986). The relationship of marital satisfaction and social support to depressive symptomatology. *Journal of Psychopathology and Behavioral Assessment, 8*, 305–316.

Beach, S. R. H., & Fincham, F. D. (1994). Towards an integrated model of negative affectivity in marriage. In S. M. Johnson & L. S. Greenberg (Eds.), *Emotion in marriage and marital therapy.* New York: Brunner/ Mazel.

Beach, S. R. H., Fincham, F. D., Katz, J., & Bradbury, T. (1996). Social support in marriage: A cognitive perspective. In G. R. Pierce, B. R. Sarason, & I. G. Sarason (Eds.), *Handbook of social support and the family* (pp. 43–65). New York: Plenum.

Beach, S. R. H., Martin, J., Blum, T., & Roman, P. (1993). Effects of marital and co-worker relationships on negative affect: Testing the central role of marriage. *American Journal of Family Therapy, 21*, 213–322.

Beach, S. R. H., & O'Leary, K. D. (1993a). Marital discord and dysphoria: For whom does the marital relationship predict depressive symptomatology? *Journal of Personal and Social Relations, 10*, 405–420.

Beach, S. R. H., & O'Leary, K. D. (1993b). Dysphoria and marital discord: Are dysphoric individuals at risk for marital maladjustment? *Journal of Marital and Family Therapy, 19*, 355–368.

Beach, S. R. H., Smith, D. A., & Fincham, F. D. (1995). Marital interventions for depression: Empirical foundation and future prospects. *Applied and Preventive Psychology, 3*, 233–250.

Beach, S. R. H., & Tesser, A. (1995). Self-esteem and the extended self-evaluation maintenance model: The self in social context. In M. H. Kernis (Ed.), *Efficacy, agency, and self-esteem* (pp. 145-170). New York: Plenum.

Beck, A. T., Epstein, N., Harrison, R. P., & Emery, G. (1983). Development of the Sociotropy/Autonomy Scale: A measure of personality factors in psychopathology. Unpublished manuscript, University of Pennsylvania, PA.

Bem, D. J., & Allen, A. (1974). On predicting some of the people some of the time: The search for cross-situational consistencies in behavior. *Psychological Review, 81*, 505-520.

Bentler, P. M., & Newcomb, M. D. (1978). Longitudinal study of marital success and failure. *Journal of Consulting and Clinical Psychology, 46*, 1053-1070.

Berg-Cross, L. (1974). *Basic concepts in family therapy*. New York: Horwath.

Blatt, S. J. (1974). Level of object representation in anaclitic and introjective depression. *Psychoanalytic Study of the Child, 29*, 107-157.

Blatt, S. J., & Zurroff, D. C. (1992). Interpersonal relatedness and self-definition: Two prototypes for depression. *Clinical Psychology Review, 12*, 527-562.

Boyce, P., Parker, G., Barnett, B., Cooney, M., & Smith, F. (1991). Personality as a vulnerability factor to depression. *British Journal of Psychiatry, 159*, 106-114.

Bradbury, T. N., & Fincham, F. D. (1992). Attributions and behavior in marital interaction. *Journal of Personality and Social Psychology, 51*, 1173-1182.

Bradbury, T. N., & Karney, B. R. (1993). Longitudinal study of marital interaction and dysfunction: Review and analysis. *Clinical Psychology Review, 13*, 15-27.

Brown, G. W., Adler, Z., & Bifulco, A. (1988). Life events, difficulties and recovery from chronic depression. *British Journal of Psychiatry, 152*, 487-498.

Brown, G. W., Andrews, B., Bifulco, A., & Veiel, H. (1990a). Self-esteem and depression: I. Measurement issues and prediction of onset. *Social Psychiatry and Psychiatric Epidemiology, 25*, 200-209.

Brown, G. W., Andrews, B., Hams, T., Adler, Z., & Bridge, L. (1986). Social support, self-esteem, and depression. *Psychological Medicine, 16*, 813-831.

Brown, G. W., Bifulco, A., & Andrews, B. (1990b). Self-esteem and depression: III. Aetiological issues. *Social Psychiatry and Psychiatric Epidemiology, 25*, 235-243.

Brown, G. W., Bifulco, A., Veiel, H., & Andrews, B. (1990c). Self-esteem and depression: II. Social correlates of self-esteem. *Social Psychiatry and Psychiatric Epidemiology, 25*, 225-234.

Brown, G. W., & Harris, T. O. (1978). *The social origins of depression*. London: Tavistock.

Brown, G. W., & Harris, T. (1986). Establishing causal links: The Bedford College studies of depression. In H. Katschnig (Ed.), *Life events and psychiatric disorders: Controversial issues* (pp. 107-187). Cambridge, UK: Cambridge University Press.

Brown, G. W., & Harris, T. O. (Eds.), (1989). *Life events and illness*. New York: Guilford.

Brown, G. W., Harris, T. O., & Hepworth, C. (1995). Loss, humiliation and entrapment among women developing depression: A patient and non-patient comparison. *Psychological Medicine, 25*, 7-21.

Brown, G. W., Lemyre, L., & Bifulco, A. (1992). Social factors and recovery from anxiety and depressive disorder: A test of specificity. *British Journal of Psychiatry, 161*, 44-54.

Burger, E., & Milardo, R. M. (1995). Marital independence and social networks. *Journal of Social and Personal Relationships, 12*, 403-415.

Buss, D. M. (1994). Personality evoked: The evolutionary psychology of stability and change. In T. F. Hetherington & J. L. Weinberger (Eds.), *Can personality change?* Washington, DC: American Psychological Association.

Caldwell, M. A., & Peplau, L. A. (1982). Sex differences in same-sex friendship. *Sex Roles, 8*, 721-732.

Cappeliez, P. (1993). The relationship between Beck's concepts of sociotropy and autonomy and the NEO-Personality Inventory. *British Journal of Clinical Psychology, 32*, 78-80.

Carnelley, K., Pietromonaco, P. R., & Jaffe, K. (1994). Depression, working models of others, and relationship functioning. *Journal of Personality and Social Psychology, 66*, 127-140.

Christensen, A., & Heavey, C. L. (1990). Gender and social structure in the demand/withdraw pattern of marital conflict. *Journal of Personality and Social Psychology, 59*, 73-81.

Christensen, A., Jacobson, N. S., & Babcock, J. (1995). Integrative behavioral couple therapy. In N. S. Jacobson & A. S. Gurman (Eds.), *Clinical handbook of couple therapy*. New York: Guilford.

Christian, J. L., O'Leary, K. D., & Avery, S. (1993). *The impact of negative events in marriage and depression*. Unpublished manuscript, the University at Stony Brook, Stony Brook, NY.

Cialdini, R. B., Borden, R. J., Thorne, A., Walker, M. R., Freeman, S., & Sloan, L. R. (1976). Basking in reflected glory: Three (football) field studies. *Journal of Personality and Social Psychology, 34*, 366-375.

Clark, L. A., & Watson, D. (1991). General affective dispositions in physical and psychological health. In C. R. Snyder & D. R. Forsyth (Eds.), *Handbook of social and clinical psychology* (pp. 221-245). New York: Pergamon.

Collins, N. L., & Read, S. J. (1990). Adult attachment, working models, and relationship quality in dating couples. *Journal of Personality and Social Psychology, 58,* 644-663.

Coyne, J. C., Kahn, J., & Gotlib, I. E. (1987). Depression. In T. Jacob (Ed.), *Family interaction and psychopathology* (pp. 509-533). New York: Plenum.

Coyne, J. C., & Whiffen, V. E. (1995). Issues in personality as diathesis for depression: The case of sociotropy/dependency and autonomy/self-criticism. *Psychological Bulletin, 118,* 358-378.

Culp, L. N., & Beach, S. R. H. (November, 1993). *Marital discord, dysphoria, and thoughts of divorce: Examining the moderating role of self-esteem.* Presented at Association for Advancement of Behavior Therapy, Atlanta, GA.

Cummings, E. M. (1995). Security, emotionality, and parental depression: A commentary. *Developmental Psychology, 31,* 425-427.

Cutrona, C. E. (1986). Objective determinants of perceived social support. *Journal of Personality and Social Psychology, 50,* 349-355.

Dakof, G. A., & Taylor, S. E. (1990). Victims' perceptions of social support: What is helpful from whom? *Journal of Personality and Social Psychology, 58,* 80-89.

Derlega, V. J., Metts, S., Petronio, S., & Margulis, S. T. (1993). *Self-disclosure.* Newbury Park, CA: Sage.

Derlega, V. J., Winstead, B. A., Wong, P. T. P., & Hunter, S. (1985). Gender effects in an initial encounter: A case where men exceed women in disclosure. *Journal of Social and Personal Relationships, 2,* 25-44.

Endler, N. S., & Magnussen, D. (1976). *Interactional psychology and personality.* Washington, DC: Hemisphere.

Feeney, J. A., & Noller, P. (1990). Attachment style as a predictor of adult romantic relationships. *Journal of Personality and Social Psychology, 58,* 281-291.

Feeney, J. A., & Noller, P. (1991). Attachment style and verbal descriptions of romantic partners. *Journal of Social and Personal Relationships, 8,* 187-215.

Fincham, F. D., Beach, S. R. H., & Kemp-Fincham, S. I. (in press). Marital quality: A new theoretical perspective. In R. J. Sternberg & M. Hojjat (Eds.), *Satisfaction in close relationships.* New York: Guilford.

Fincham, F. D., Fernandes, L. O. L., & Humphreys, K. (1993). *Communicating in relationships: A guide for couples and professionals.* Champaign, IL: Research Press.

Fincham, F. D., Garnier, P. C., Gano-Phillips, S., & Osborne, L. N. (1995). Preinteraction expectations, marital satisfaction, and accessibility: A new look at sentiment override. *Journal of Family Psychology, 9,* 3-14.

Frank, E., Kupfer, D. J., Jacob, M., & Jarrett, D. (1987). Personality features and response to acute treatment in recurrent depression. *Journal of Personality Disorders, 1,* 14-26.

Gilbert, P. (1992). *Depression: The evolution of powerlessness.* New York: Guilford.

Gotlib, I. H., & Hammen, C. L. (1992). *Psychological aspects of depression: Toward a cognitive-interpersonal integration.* New York: Wiley.

Gotlib, I. H., & Hooley, J. M. (1988). Depression and marital distress: Current status and future directions. In S. Duck (Ed.), *Handbook of personal relationships: Theory, research, and interventions* (pp. 543-570). Chicester, UK: Wiley.

Gottman, J. M. (1993). The roles of conflict engagement, escalation, or avoidance in marital interaction: A longitudinal view of five types of couples. *Journal of Consulting and Clinical Psychology, 61,* 6-15.

Greely, A. M. (1991). *Faithful attraction.* New York: Tor Books.

Hammen, C. (1991). Generation of stress in the course of unipolar depression. *Journal of Abnormal Psychology, 100,* 555-561.

Hammen, C., Marks, T., Mayol, A., & de Mayo, R. (1985). Depressive self-schemes, life stress, and vulnerability to depression. *Journal of Abnormal Psychology, 94,* 308-319.

Hawkins, J. L., Weisberg, C., & Ray, D. W. (1980). Spouse differences in communication style: Preference, perception, behavior. *Journal of Marriage and the Family, 42,* 585-593.

Hazan, C., & Shaver, P. (1987). Conceptualizing romantic love as an attachment process. *Journal of Personality and Social Psychology, 52,* 511-524.

Heavey, C. L., Layne, C., & Christensen, A. (1993). Gender and conflict structure in marital interaction: A replication and extension. *Journal of Consulting and Clinical Psychology, 61,* 16-27.

Hendrick, C., & Hendrick, S. S. (1989). Research on love: Does it measure up? *Journal of Personality and Social Psychology, 52*, 784–794.

Hendrick, S. S. (1981). Self-disclosure and marital satisfaction. *Journal of Personality and Social Psychology, 40*, 1150–1159.

Hendrick, S. S., Hendrick, C., & Adler, N. L. (1988). Romantic relationships: Love, satisfaction, and staying together. *Journal of Personality and Social Psychology, 54*, 980–988.

Hirschfeld, R. M. A., Klerman, G. L., & Korchin, S. (1989). Dependency, self-esteem, and clinical depression. *Journal of the American Academy of Psychoanalysis, 4*, 373–388.

Horwath, E., Johnson, J., Klerman, G. L., & Weissman, M. M. (1992). Depressive symptoms as relative and attributable risk factors for first-onset major depression. *Archives of General Psychiatry, 49*, 817–823.

Joiner, T. E., Alfano, M. S., & Metalsky, G. I. (1993). Caught in the crossfire: Depression, self-consistency, self-enhancement, and the response of others. *Journal of Social and Clinical Psychology, 12*, 113–134.

Joiner, T. E., & Metalsky, G. I. (1995). A prospective test of an integrative interpersonal theory of depression: A naturalistic study of college roommates. *Journal of Personality and Social Psychology, 69*, 778–788.

Jones, D. C. (1991). Friendship satisfaction and gender: An examination of sex differences in contributors to friendship satisfaction. *Journal of Social and Personal Relationships, 8*, 167–185.

Kaslow, N. J., & Carter, A. (1991). Gender-sensitive object relational family therapy with depressed women. *Journal of Family Psychology, 5*, 116–135.

Katz, J., Beach, S. R. H. (in press). Romance in the crossfire: When do women's depressive symptoms influence partner relationship satisfaction? *Journal of Social and Clinical Psychology.*

Katz, J., Beach, S. R. H., & Anderson, P. (1996). Self-enhancement versus self-verification: Does spousal support always help? *Cognitive Therapy and Research, 20*, 345–360.

Katz, J., & Beach, S. R. H., & Wakefield, R. (1996). *Dysphoria and relationship satisfaction: Moderating effects of internal models of self.* Unpublished manuscript, University of Georgia, Athens, GA.

Kelly, E. L., & Conley, J. J. (1987). Personality and compatibility: A prospective analysis of marital stability and marital satisfaction. *Journal of Personality and Social Psychology, 52*, 27–40.

Kobak, R. R., & Hazan, C. (1991). Attachment in marriage: Effects of security and accuracy of working models. *Journal of Personality and Social Psychology, 60*, 861–869.

Lee, G. R., Seccombe, K., & Shehan, C. L. (1991). Marital status and personal happiness: An analysis of trend data. *Journal of Marriage and the Family, 52*, 839–844.

Leff, J., & Vaughn, C. E. (1985). *Expressed emotion in families: Its significance for mental illness.* New York: Guilford.

Levy, M. B., & Davis, K. E. (1988). Lovestyles and attachment styles compared: Their relations to each other and to various relationship characteristics. *Journal of Social and Personal Relationships, 5*, 439–471.

Linville, P. (1985). Self-complexity and affective extremity: Don't put all your eggs into one cognitive basket. *Social Cognition, 3*, 94–124.

Madden, M. E., & Janoff-Bulman, R. (1981). Blame, control, and marital satisfaction: Wives' attributions for conflict in marriage. *Journal of Marriage and the Family, 43*, 663–674.

Markus, H., & Smith, J. (1981). The influence of self-schemata on the perception of others. In N. Cantor & J. F. Kihlstrom (Eds.), *Personality, cognition, and social interaction* (pp. 233–262). Hillsdale, NJ: Erlbaum.

Niedenthal, P. M., Setterlund, M. B., & Wherry, M. B. (1992). Possible self-complexity and affective reactions to goal-relevant evaluation. *Journal of Personality and Social Psychology, 63*, 17–29.

Noller, P. (1987). Nonverbal communication in marriage. In D. Perlman & S. Duck (Eds.), *Intimate relationships: Development, dynamics, and deterioration* (pp. 149–175). Beverly Hills, CA: Sage.

O'Sullivan, C. S., & Durso, F. T. (1984). Effects of schema-incongruent information on memory for stereotypical attributes. *Journal of Personality and Social Psychology, 47*, 55–70.

Peplau, L. A., & Gordon, S. L. (1985). Women and men in love: Gender differences in close heterosexual relationships. In V. E. O'Leary, R. K. Unger, & B. S. Wallston (Eds.), *Women, gender, and social psychology* (pp. 257–291). Hillsdale, NJ: Erlbaum.

Pilkington, C. J., Tesser, A., & Stephens, D. (1989, April). *Self-evaluation maintenance in romantic relationships: Considering your partner's welfare.* Paper presented at the annual meeting of the Midwestern Psychological Association, Chicago, IL.

Reis, H. T., Senchak, M., & Solomon, B. (1985). Sex differences in the intimacy of social interaction: Further examination of potential explanations. *Journal of Personality and Social Psychology, 48*, 1204–1217.

Robins, C. J. (1990). Congruence of personality and life events in depression. *Journal of Abnormal Psychology, 99*, 393–397.

Ross, C. E. (1995). Reconceptualizing marital status as a continuum of social attachment. *Journal of Marriage and the Family, 57,* 129–140.

Rubin, L. B. (1983). *Intimate strangers: Men and women together.* New York: Free Press.

Rusbult, C. E., Morrow, G. D., & Johnson, D. J. (1987). Self-esteem and problem-solving behaviors in close relationships. *British Journal of Social Psychology, 26,* 293–303.

Sacco, W. P., & Dunn, V. K. (1990). Effect of actor depression on observer attributions: Existence and impact of negative attributions toward the depressed. *Journal of Personality and Social Psychology, 59,* 517–524.

Senchak, M., & Leonard, K. E. (1992). Attachment styles and marital adjustment among newlywed couples. *Journal of Social and Personal Relationships, 9,* 51–64.

Shaver, P. R., & Brennan, K. A. (1992). Attachment styles and the "Big Five" personality traits: Their connections with each other and with romantic relationship outcomes. *Personality and Social Psychology Bulletin, 18,* 536–545.

Shaver, P. R., Hazan, C., & Bradshaw, D. (1988). Love as attachment: The integration of three behavioral systems. In R. Sternberg and M. Barnes (Eds.), *The anatomy of love* (pp. 68–99). New Haven, CT: Yale University Press.

Simpson, J. A., Rholes, W. S., & Nelligan, J. S. (1991). Support-seeking and support-giving within couples in an anxiety-provoking situation: The role of attachment styles. *Journal of Personality and Social Psychology, 62,* 434–446.

Smith, D. A., Vivian, D., & O'Leary, K. D. (1990). Longitudinal prediction of marital discord from premarital expression of affect. *Journal of Consulting and Clinical Psychology, 58,* 790–798.

Smith, D. A., Vivian, D., & O'Leary, K. D. (1991). The misnomer proposition: A critical reappraisal of the longitudinal status of "negativity" in marital communication. *Behavioral Assessment, 13,* 7–24.

Srull, T. K., & Wyer, R. S. Jr. (1979). The role of category accessibility in the interpretation of information about persons: Some determinants and implications. *Journal of Personality and Social Psychology, 37,* 1660–1672.

Swann, W. B. Jr. (1983). Self-verification: Bringing social reality into harmony with the self. In J. Suls & A. G. Greenwald (Eds.), *Social psychological perspectives on the self* (Vol. 2, pp. 33–66). Hillsdale, NJ: Erlbaum.

Swann, W. B. Jr., Hixon, J. G., & De La Ronde, C. (1992a). Embracing the bitter "truth": Negative self-concepts and marital commitment. *Psychological Science, 3,* 118–121.

Swann, W. B. Jr., & Predmore, S. C. (1985). Intimates as agents of social support: Sources of consolation or despair? *Journal of Personality and Social Psychology, 49,* 1609–1617.

Swann, W. B. Jr., Wenzlaff, R. M., Krull, D. S., & Pelham, B. W. (1992b). Allure of negative feedback: Self-verification strivings among depressed persons. *Journal of Abnormal Psychology, 101,* 293–233.

Terman, L. M., & Oden, M. H. (1947). *The gifted child grows up: Twenty-five year follow-up of a superior group.* Stanford, CA: Stanford University Press.

Tesser, A. (1988). Toward a self-evaluation maintenance model of social behavior. In L. Berkowitz (Ed.), *Advances in experimental social psychology,* Vol. 21 (pp. 181–227). New York: Academic Press.

Uleman, J. S., & Bargh, J. A. (1989). *Unintended thought.* New York: Guilford.

Weiss, R. L. (1978). The conceptualization of marriage from a behavioral perspective. In T. Paolino, Jr. & B. McCrady (Eds.), *Marriage and marital therapy: Psychoanalytic, behavioral, and systems theory perspectives* (pp. 165–239). New York: Brunner/Mazel.

Weissman, M. M. (1987). Advances in psychiatric epidemiology: Rates and risks for major depression. *American Journal of Public Health, 77,* 445–451.

Wills, T. A., Weiss, R. L., & Patterson, G. R. (1974). A behavioral analysis of determinants of marital satisfaction. *Journal of Consulting and Clinical Psychology, 46,* 802–811.

Zimmerman, M., Pfohl, B., Coryell, W. H., Corenthal, C., & Stangl, D. (1991). Major depression and personality disorder. *Journal of Affective Disorders, 22,* 199–241.

Zurroff, D. C., & Lorimier, S. (1989). Dependency and self-criticism as predictors of the personality characteristics of women's ideal boyfriends and their satisfaction with actual boyfriends. *Journal of Personality, 17,* 226–241.

CHAPTER 13

SOCIAL SUPPORT

CAUSE OR CONSEQUENCE OF POOR HEALTH OUTCOMES IN MEN WITH HIV INFECTION?

ROBERT M. KAPLAN, THOMAS L. PATTERSON, DAVID KERNER, IGOR GRANT, AND THE HIV NEUROBEHAVIORAL RESEARCH CENTER

A substantial literature argues that people who have smaller social networks experience increased risk of death and other negative health outcomes. Early sociological research, for instance, found a link between social support and suicide risk (Durkheim, 1951). Since that early observation, researchers have probed the link between social support and health in a variety of ways. The literature, on the relationship between social support and a variety of different causes of death has evolved over a course of 20

The San Diego HIV Neurobehavioral Research Center (HNRC) group is affiliated with the University of California, San Diego; the Naval Hospital, San Diego, and the San Diego VA Medical Center, and includes Igor Grant, M.D., Director; J. Hampton Atkinson, M.D., Codirector; Robert A Velin, Ph.D., Center Manager; Edward C. Oldfield III, M.D., James L. Chandler, M.D., Mark R. Wallace, M.D., and Joseph Malone, M.D., Coinvestigators Naval Hospital San Diego; J. Allen McCutchan, M.D., P.I. Medical Core; Stephen A. Spector, M.D., P.I. Virology Core; Leon Thal, M.D., P.I. Neurology Core; Robert K. Heaton, Ph.D., P.I. Neuropsychology Core; John Hesselink, M.D. and Terry Jernigan, Ph.D., Co-P.I.s Imaging Core; J. Hampton Atkinson, M.D., P.I. Psychiatry Core; Clayton A. Wiley, M.D., Ph.D., P.I. Neuropathology Core; Richard Olshen, Ph.D. and Ian Abramson, Ph.D., Co-P.I.s Biostatistics Core; Nelson Butters, Ph.D., P.I. Memory Project; Renée Dupont, M.D., P.I. SPECT Project; Dilip Jeste, M.D., P.I. Psychosis Project; Hans Sieburg, Ph.D., P.I. Dynamical Systems Project; and James D. Weinrich, Ph.D., P.I. Sexology Project.

ROBERT M. KAPLAN • Department of Family and Preventive Medicine, University of California, San Diego, La Jolla, California 92093-0622.   THOMAS L. PATTERSON AND IGOR GRANT • Department of Psychiatry, University of California, San Diego, La Jolla, California 92092-0622.   DAVID KERNER • SDSU/UCSD Joiny Doctoral Program in Clinical Psychology, University of California, San Diego, La Jolla, California 92092-0622.

Sourcebook of Social Support and Personality, edited by Gregory R. Pierce, Brian Lakey, Irwin G. Sarason, and Barbara R. Sarason. Plenum Press, New York, 1997.

years (Berkman, 1995). However, the literature on social support and health outcome leaves many questions unanswered. For example, most studies relating social support to mortality outcomes define social support in terms of network size. Current definitions of social support include qualitative (emotional), quantitative (adequacy), as well as measures of social network size.

One of the difficulties in separating explanations for the relationship between social support and health outcome is that most of the studies are cross-sectional. In this chapter, we present longitudinal data in which health-outcome data and social support are measured at multiple points in time. Longitudinal studies are needed, because social support may be determined by health variables, as opposed to being a determinant of health outcomes. This chapter focuses on outcomes for men with HIV disease. After a brief introduction to epidemiology, we will review the HIV epidemic. Then, we will briefly review the literature linking stress, social support, and immune status in HIV patients. The remainder of the chapter presents original data evaluating the causal direction of social support and immune status in HIV-infected patients. We are interested in separating two causal pathways. In particular, we consider whether poor social support causes reductions in immune status against the alternative explanation that declining health causes reductions in social networks. Most studies begin with the assumption that social support is a predictor of health outcome and fail to test the alternative directional hypothesis. We suggest that the causal pathway between social support and health outcome may be bidirectional.

EPIDEMIOLOGY OF SOCIAL SUPPORT AND HEALTH OUTCOMES

Epidemiology is the study of the determinants and distribution of disease. The hallmark of epidemiological methodology is the prospective/longitudinal cohort study. Major investigations, such as the Framingham Heart Study, attempted to establish prospective predictors of mortality in a random sample from the general population. For example, the Framingham Study began with 5,127 participants who had no visible signs of heart disease. Each participant was given a physical examination and a detailed interview that included lifestyle and demographic characteristics. Then, each participant was followed every other year (Kannel, 1987). Other major epidemiological investigations have used similar methodologies.

Most epidemiological studies were started some years ago, before formal measures of social support had been developed. Nevertheless, simple measures of social network, often extracted *post hoc* from a database, appeared to be predictive of health outcomes in a variety of studies. The Alameda County Population Monitoring Study demonstrated that a simple measure of social network was a significant predictor of longevity. The measures of social support included marital status, number of close family and friends, church membership, and group membership. Men with weak social networks were nearly 2.5 times as likely to die within a defined time period as men with extensive networks. Women benefited even more from established social networks (Berkman & Breslow, 1983).

Similar results were obtained in Tecumseh, Michigan, where 2,754 men and women were studied. In this investigation, men who were married, who attended church, and who participated in voluntary organizations and community activities were significantly less likely to die within a 10-year period than were men who were disconnected. However, the Tecumseh Study did not show similar relationships for women (House, Robbins, & Metzner, 1982). In contrast to the findings of Berkman and Breslow (1983) and House et al., in the Durham County, North Carolina study (Blazer, 1982), no consistent pattern of increased mortality rates were associated with a progressive decrease in social support. Rather, in this data set, there appeared to be a threshold effect in which only those individuals, either male or female, who were at the extreme end of the continuum in terms of the least amount of social support, had increased mortality rates. In a study of residents of Evans County, Georgia, those with the fewest ties were at increased risk for mortality. The findings reported were significant for older white males only and not for black individuals and white females (Schoenbach, Kaplan, Fredman, & Kleinbaum, 1986).

Several studies have suggested that the combination of high stress and low social support is a particularly strong predictor of negative outcome. For example, 142 women in the Framingham Heart Study had more cardiovascular disease if they worked in clerical roles and had nonsupportive spouses (Haynes & Feinleib, 1980). A study of Swedish workers revealed that risk for cardiovascular disease was excessive among workers who had low social support, perceived their jobs to be stressful, and felt they had little control over their work environment (Welin et al., 1985). In one study of survivors of myocardial infarction, survivors were classified according to social isolation and stress, and then followed prospectively. Those who experienced low stress and were socially connected had one-fourth the rate of mortality in comparison to those who were under high stress and were isolated (Ruberman, Weinblatt, Goldberg, & Chaudhary, 1984). Despite these strong results, some studies have also failed to show a relationship between social support, stress, and health outcomes (Cohen & Syme, 1985). Many studies focus on the impact of social support on only one disease state or outcome variable. Aneshensel, Rutter, and Lachenbruch (1991) argued that the impact of stress and social support on health may be underestimated if the range of outcomes is limited. An alternative is to go beyond mortality to consider disease stage and measures of disability and health-related quality of life.

It is difficult to make comparisons across studies that have different conceptualization of health outcome. Populations varied greatly from study to study, as did definitions of social support. The measures of social support were usually crude. Some studies merely recorded the presence of a spouse or participation in group activities. In addition, the degree of satisfaction associated with these relationships in specific types of support received were often not considered. Nevertheless, these studies generally show a relationship between social relationships and longevity (Berkman, 1995; Davidson & Shumaker, 1987). These findings have intrigued epidemiologists and have supported the notion that friends and family are health assets.

Although the relationship between social support and mortality may seem impressive, these relationships are primarily correlational. There are at least three rival explanations for the association between the presence of social relationships and health. First, there is the assumed explanation that the correlation between social support and disease is causal—high support protects against illness. The second explanation is that individuals who are sick drive away their social support system.

This suggests that early illness causes changes in social support. A third explanation is that a third variable, such as social class, personality, and so on, causes both poor social support and poor health outcomes.

It is important to emphasize that epidemiological studies use different measures than do psychological investigations. The psychological construct *support* is usually defined as the number of social contacts, and *health* is most often defined as survival or mortality. Most support for the argument that social support protects against illness comes from epidemiological studies. However, these observational studies do not establish the causal relationship between network size and mortality. Furthermore, the epidemiology studies have rarely considered satisfaction with social support. As a result, many of the inferences about the relationship between support satisfaction and mortality remain highly speculative. The epidemiological studies have stimulated interest in the relationship between social support and health, but provide only a very small piece of the puzzle. To follow up on the suggestive evidence from epidemiological studies, we need to focus on a wider array of health outcomes and learn more about the nature of social interactions among those with serious illness. This chapter focuses on social support among men infected with the human immunodeficiency virus (HIV). HIV disease will be reviewed briefly in the next section.

HIV DISEASE

The acquired immune deficiency syndrome (AIDS) has directly affected millions of people worldwide and indirectly affects virtually every one of us. HIV, a retrovirus of the T-cell leukemia/lymphoma line, reduces the immune system's ability to recognize and destroy infectious agents. For healthy individuals, the immune system is capable of overcoming many common infections. As HIV disease progresses, an overall loss of immune competence leaves HIV-infected individuals susceptible to a variety of opportunistic infections.

As of June 1995, 470,228 cases of HIV infection had been reported in the United States. Among these, approximately half (52%) were among men who have sex with other men. Another 25% were reported among those who inject nonprescription drugs. About 7% of the cases were men who have sex with other men and also inject drugs. Most of the other cases were among those who have received blood products because of hemophilia (1%) or transfusion (2%). A growing number of cases were associated with heterosexual contact (8%), especially among intravenous (IV) drug users (data from Centers for Disease Control HIV/AIDS Surveillance Report 1995, 1997, No. 1). In addition to the medical issues, HIV infection has serious social consequences. Infected individuals are told to change the most central aspects of their lifestyles, and fear of infection may disrupt many social relationships. The stigma associated with the illness may cause disruptions in employment, housing, and friendships. In the next section, the impact of the illness on the immune system will be briefly reviewed.

PSYCHONEUROIMMUNOLOGY AND HIV INFECTION

In the 1980s, medical and social science researchers from the field of psychoneuroimmunology recognized HIV disease as an appropriate model for testing the effects of psychosocial variables on physical illness (Glaser & Kiecolt-Glaser, 1987). Both the immune and neural systems appeared to be central to HIV progression, and the course of HIV illness varied substantially among infected individuals, suggesting that a variety of factors were related to disease progression. The psychoneuroimmunological hypothesis in HIV has been tested empirically, using a variety of markers of HIV disease progression. HIV infection is detected by observing antibodies to the virus in serum, and is characterized by depletion and infection of CD4+ T-cells, which leaves the immune system compromised and prone to contracting opportunistic infections (signaling disease progression).

The basic premise of the psychoneuroimmunological hypothesis is that the immune systems of individuals who experience major stress in their lives are compromised. The way this works in HIV is as follows. When someone contracts the HIV virus, the virus attaches and enters cells in the host's body, usually CD4+ helper/inducer T-cell lymphocytes. The CD4+ lymphocytes are white blood cells that activate the immune system in order to combat foreign invaders, known as foreign *antigens*, in the body. HIV multiplies in the body when these CD4+ cells replicate in response to contact with an antigen, such as a cold virus. Thus, the life cycle of HIV consists of a series of steps in which the virus uses the host's own cells to reproduce enormous numbers of new viruses. As more and more CD4+ cells become infected, the immune system becomes unable to respond to infectious agents. Individuals die, therefore, from other infections that the body is no longer able to fight off, not from the HIV virus itself. In addition to destroying the CD4+ lymphocytes, HIV infects a number of other cells, including macrophages, skin, lymph nodes, and endothelial cells of the brain. Thus, the picture of the infection is more complicated than can be presented here. A central premise underlying the observed association between life adversity and health status is that stress exerts a suppressive effect on immune functioning. Studies from several laboratories have shown that a variety of stressors affect the immune response in animals as well as humans (Borysenko & Borysenko, 1982; Palmblad, 1981). Because HIV disease is by nature an immunosuppressive disorder, it has been an especially fertile ground for the study of the impact of psychoneuroimmunological factors in health.

DOES THE HEALTH OF HIV-POSITIVE INDIVIDUALS WHO EXPERIENCE GREATER STRESS IN THEIR LIVES DECLINE MORE RAPIDLY COMPARED TO LESS STRESSED INDIVIDUALS?

Currently, the best prognostic indicators of increased HIV-disease symptomatology are absolute CD4+ cell number (Fahey et al., 1990; Pederson et al., 1990) and presence of circulating P_{24} antigen (among advanced HIV disease stages), although elevated β_2-microglobulin levels have also been noted to rise with disease progression (Volberding & McCutchan, 1989). Psychoneuroimmunological studies have used a number of outcomes including CD4+ lymphocyte count (Perry, Fishman, Jacobsberg, & Frances, 1992; Rabkin, Remien, Katoff, & Williams, 1993), percent CD4+ lymphocytes (Patterson et al., 1995), CD4+/CD8+ ratio (Antoni et al., 1990; Goodkin et al., 1992), natural killer (NK) cell cytotoxicity (Antoni et al., 1990; Goodkin et al., 1992), absolute NK cell count (Sahs et al., 1994), time from seroconversion to AIDS diagnosis (Goodkin et al., 1992), survival time (Greco & Stazi, 1987), symptoms of HIV illness

(Kessler et al., 1991; Rabkin et al., 1991), degree of physical impairment (Rabkin et al., 1993), as well as a host of other biological markers for HIV-disease progression. Of these outcome measures, the most frequently used is CD4+ cell count, the immune marker most closely linked to the clinical consequences of HIV infection (Moss et al., 1988). Enumeration of CD4+ cells and other lymphocyte subsets have served as laboratory outcome measures in recent studies of HIV, life adversity, psychosocial moderators, and physical and mental health outcome. Preliminary analysis of data from an intensive psychoimmunological study of men with AIDS indicated significant negative correlations between absolute number of CD4+ helper cells and less tension-anxiety, depression–dejection, fatigue–inertia, and anger–hostility on the Profile of Mood States (POMS; Solomon, Temoshok, O'Leary, & Zich, 1987). Furthermore, Solomon and colleagues found self-rated "ability to say 'no' to unwanted favors" to be positively related to absolute number of NK cells, which are important in fighting neoplastic disease, and this ability was the best predictor of "positive" immune parameters overall. However, the results from other studies have been mixed. Rabkin et al. (1991) found no relationship between immune status as measured by CD4+ and CD8+ cell subsets and depression, distress, and negative life events, consistent with Kessler et al.'s (1991) report of no relationship between stress and percentage decrease of CD4+ cells or development of thrush and/or fever.

Previously Rabkin, Williams, Neugebauer, Remien, and Goetz (1990) reported a relationship between high levels of hopelessness and low levels of social support and more depressive symptoms, but no relationship was found between hopelessness, HIV symptoms, and negative life events. In contrast, Blaney et al. (1991) reported that both negative life events and social support were significant predictors of psychological distress (main effects only, no interaction effects), but immune and physical health outcomes were not reported. Similarly, Dew, Ragni, and Nimorwicz (1990) found depressive symptoms in HIV seropositive men to be related to recent loss events and current unemployment, and history of personal or family psychiatric treatment, but detected no interaction effects between "vulnerability factors" and symptoms.

In summary, there is a lot of excitement about psychoneuroimmunology. Some evidence suggests that HIV patients who experience serious life stress have poorer prognoses than those who experience less stress. However, studies investigating these issues have produced inconsistent results. Currently, we are unable to say with confidence that life stress is a significant factor in the progression of HIV disease.

HIV AND SOCIAL SUPPORT

Social support is another psychosocial variable that has been examined as a moderator of HIV disease progression. Although social support is consistently related in an inverse direction to psychological distress among asymptomatic, HIV-positive gay males (Blaney et al., 1991; Patterson et al., 1993), associations with physical symptoms are less supported. It is believed that social support may act indirectly on physical health by easing the emotional or tangible burden of increased physical symptoms (Hays, Turner, & Coates, 1992); however, this stress-buffering hypothesis has not been tested prospectively among HIV-positive individuals. We previously studied 414 HIV-positive males using survival analysis (Patterson et al., 1996). Our analysis was based on the existing empirical evidence that psychosocial variables may predict the course of HIV-illness disease progression (described by advance in symptoms, decline in CD4+ cell count, and mortality). We found that depressive symptoms predicted shorter longevity after controlling for symptoms and CD4+ cell count. Large social network sizes predicted longevity among those with AIDS-defining symptoms at baseline, but not among other subjects. Therefore, psychosocial variables and affective states may be related to disease outcome only during later stages of HIV disease. Although the results provide support for psychoneuroimmunological effects in HIV, other confounding explanations may still apply. More longitudinal research is needed to assess the impact stressful life adversity, social support, and affective feeling states may have on HIV-disease progression above and beyond that which is determined by the natural course of HIV diseases and demographic or background characteristics that may influence health status, such as age and socioeconomic status.

Although social support is likely to play a similar role with the context of HIV-related disease as it does with other health problems, only a handful of studies have reported beneficial effects of social support, and longitudinal data are even more scarce. In a cross-sectional study, Wolf et al. (1991) found that less perceived available social support was associated with more use of avoidant coping and greater mood disturbance, including higher levels of self-reported depression and anxiety, and lower levels of vigor among HIV-infected men (half medically asymptomatic, half symptomatic with AIDS or AIDS-related conditions). Similarly, Namir, Wolcott, and Fawzy (1989) found social support to be related to physical and mental health within their sample of 50 men with AIDS. Specifically, instrumental or tangible support was the only variable to significantly predict physical health scores, and it was significantly associated with mood disturbance as well.

It is possible that the type of social support most associated with physical illness varies according to disease stage or level of disability. Thus, in Namir et al.'s (1989) sample of men with full AIDS diagnoses, tangible support was most associated with physical health, perhaps reflecting more progressed disease and increased disability. Furthermore, Zich and Temoshok (1987) found that less available social support was associated with more physical symptoms for men with AIDS, but not for men with AIDS-related conditions (ARC) or HIV-positive asymptomatics. However, less available social support was related to higher levels of hopelessness and depression for all HIV-infected men in their sample. Among asymptomatic HIV-infected men, Blaney et al. (1991) found main effects for negative life events and emotional support. Together, these findings suggest that the domains of social support most closely associated with physical symptomatology may depend on disease status or level of physical dysfunction. Although satisfaction with emotional support appears to be a good predictor of mood and possibly physical symptoms, specific characteristics of emotional support, such as availability of a close companion and reciprocity of social support, warrant further study.

SUMMARY

In summary, studies consistently show that smaller social support network size is associated with poor health outcomes. Fewer studies show that instrumental social support protects against failing health. However, most current studies have used cross-sectional designs. Most authors believe that social support either directly causes poor health outcomes or provides an inadequate buffer against life stresses. An alternative explanation is that low social support is a consequence rather than a cause of poor health status. The remainder of this chapter evaluates these alternative explanations, using a longitudinal cohort of men with HIV infection. The male participants in this study were evaluated at 6-month intervals over the course of 18 months. At each evaluation, measures of social support and immune status were gathered.

METHOD

SUBJECTS AND PROCEDURE

For the present analyses, the sample comprised 397 HIV-positive heterosexual and gay men who were participating in a longitudinal cohort study at the HIV Neuro-behavioral Research Center (HNRC), University of California, San Diego. The sample was recruited from military personnel seen at the Naval Medical Center, San Diego, as well as from the civilian community in the greater San Diego area. Inclusionary criteria of the HNRC required that participants be male residents of San Diego County with at least 10 years of formal education, and willing to undergo extensive evaluations semiannually for up to 5 years. Individuals were excluded if their medical history might confound interpretation of neurological or neuropsychological findings, such as a history of IV drug use, head injury with loss of consciousness exceeding 30 minutes, or a primary diagnosis of thought disorder. The present sample was selected from the HNRC main cohort, based on two additional criteria: (1) availability of psychological variables from four consecutive measures, 6 months apart; and (2) participation in the study for at least 1 year.

Demographic characteristics for the sample are shown in Table 13.1. The average participant was 32.7 years of age ($SD = 7.1$), had 14 years of formal education, and had known of his HIV-positive status for 2 years. Reflecting the epidemiological characteristics of the epidemic present when the study began, the sample was largely Caucasian (76%), and of lower middle-class socioeconomic (SES) background (a Hollingshead SES rating of 4). Participants with more severe HIV symptoms were older, had known of their HIV-positive status longer, but they were not different in background, education, ethnicity, and SES. As expected, differences in CD4+ cell count and serum β_2-micro-globulin levels differed significantly between baseline and 1-year follow-up (see Table 13.1).

Stage of HIV infection was determined at baseline using the 1993 Revised Classification System for HIV Infection (Centers for Disease Control, 1993). As shown in Table 13.1, the majority of participants (73%) were asymptomatic at baseline (symptom category A). Using the bidimensional definition for an actual AIDS diagnosis (CD4+ less than 200/mL and/or AIDS-indicator opportunistic infections), 40 participants (10%) had reached these criteria prior to or concurrent with their baseline assessment. Of the total sample, 16 (4%) had CD4+ cell counts less than 200/mL. The distribution of HIV severity in the sample might be described as somewhat bimodal: a large cluster of mostly asymptomatic cases with varying levels of immune function, and a smaller

TABLE 13.1. Demographic and Background
Characteristics of Sample (n = 397)
at Baseline and 1-Year Following

	Baseline	One year
Age	32.7 (7.1)	—
Years of education	14.0 (2.1)	—
Hollingshead SES (1–5)	3.7	—
Years HIV+	2.0 (1.4)	—
CD4+ count	473.5 (260.7)	365.4 (278.4)*
Beta-2 Microglobulin	2.98 (1.44)	3.36 (1.55)*
Ethnicity		
Caucasian	76%	—
African-American	15%	—
Latino	7%	—
Other	2%	—
CDC		
A	73%	45%
B	23%	38%
C	4%	17%

*$p < .05$

cluster of cases with an AIDS diagnosis and severely compromised immune function. All participants completed a 2-hour psychosocial battery, including measures of life stress, coping, social support, and depressive symptoms.

MEASURES

Depressive Symptoms

The clinician-rated Hamilton Rating Scale for Depression (HRSD) is a 21-item clinical instrument for assessing depressive symptoms based on 3- or 5-point Likert-type scale responses. The HRSD has well-documented validity (Endicott et al., 1981), and it has been used extensively in clinical trials of antidepressant drugs. Interrater reliability has been found to be in the range of 0.80 to 0.91 (Hamilton, 1969; 1974).

The Beck Depression Inventory (BDI) was also given to all participants. The BDI is a self-administered questionnaire consisting of 21 items, each having four graded statements pertaining to how the subject has been feeling during the past week (Beck, 1967). The statements within a question are ordered (0 to 3) to show increasing depressive symptomatology. Summary scores are calculated (range, 0 to 63). The items of the BDI are clinically derived and have undergone extensive reliability and validation studies (Beck, 1976). Internal consistency assessments of reliability have been high (> .90) in most evaluations.

Social Support

Social support was assessed using the Social Support Questionnaire, a 5-item self-report measure developed by Schaefer, Coyne, and Lazarus (1981). Participants identify individuals who provide support and rate them on a 5-point Likert-type scale for the degree of useful information, reliable help, emotional uplift, caring, and trust they receive from them. Mean ratings across relationship categories yielded summary scores for emotional and informational support. Social network size was calculated as the total number of all social support contacts listed. Test–retest reliability is .66 and internal consistency (alpha) is .95.

HIV-Disease Classifications

The 1993 Centers for Disease Control (CDC) classification system for HIV infection was used to classify subjects within the 3×3 matrix of CDC classifications ranging from A1 (asymptomatic, with CD4+ cell count greater than or equal to 500 mL) to C3 (AIDS-indicated symptoms, with CD4+ cell count less than 200/mL).

RESULTS

Several analyses were conducted to address the causal relationship between social support and outcomes in HIV disease. These analyses used four waves of HNRC data. These data were collected at baseline, 6 months, 12 months, and 18 months.

The initial analyses involved simple bivariate correlations between CD4+ cells and size of social network. At each evaluation, there was a significant (or marginally significant) correlation between network size and immune status (i.e., CD4+ cell number). At baseline, the relationship was $r = .15, p = .008$; at 6 months, it was $r = .10, p = .08$; at 1 year, it was $r = .25, p = .001$; and at 18 months, the association was $r = .34, p = .001$. These findings confirm that social support and immune status are correlated at each point in time.

In order to investigate the causal pathway, a cross-lagged correlational model was employed. The cross-lagged correlation model attempts to determine the direction of causation. The model evaluates causation by examining asymmetries in the correlations between two variables over time. The basic question is whether network size is a strong predictor of CD4+ cells, or the alternative explanation, that CD4+ cells are a strong predictor of network size. The model considers the temporal sequence (Does the measurement of the predictor precede the measurement of the outcome?), the synchronous correlations, and the stability of the measures over time.

The model is shown in Figure 13.1. According to the logic of the cross-lagged model (Kenny, 1975), lagged correlations can suggest direction of causation. The lagged correlations are shown as diagonals on the figure. Figure 13.1 shows that baseline social support network size is not predictive of network size 18 months later ($r = .08, p = $ ns). On the other hand, CD4+ cell counts at baseline do predict these values 18 months later. Of particular importance are the diagonals in the figure. Baseline social support network size is uncorrelated with CD4+ cell number 18 months later. Conversely, baseline CD4+ cell level is a strong, significant predictor of network size 18 months following the initial evaluation ($r = .26, p = .002$). The temporal relationship favors the explanation that illness causes decline in social support over the alternative that low support causes progression of illness.

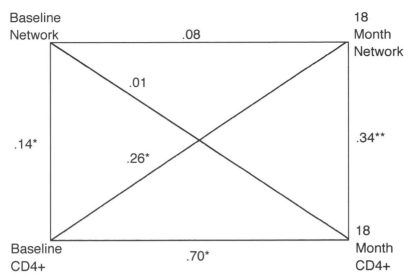

FIGURE 1. Cross-lagged panel model for network size and disease severity.

A variety of analyses were performed in order to evaluate this issue in greater detail. One approach involved breaking the subjects into smaller groups, based on their change in immune status over the 18-month evaluation. Since the study is still in progress, this allowed us to use only 78 subjects for whom data were complete. The four groups were those whose immune status was relatively high and stable (stable/ high group, $n = 14$), those whose immune status was relatively low but stable (stable/ low group, $n = 35$), those who began the study with relatively low immune status and declined slowly (slow-decline group, $n = 21$), and those who began the study with relatively high immune status and declined rapidly (rapid-decline group, $n = 8$). Figure 13.2 shows changes in CD4+ cells for these four groups. The lines for the two stable groups are relatively flat over the 18 months of follow-up. The rapid-decline groups shows a sharp fall over time, whereas the slow-decline group starts at a lower level and declines to levels reflecting more serious illness.

Figure 13.3 describes changes in social support network size for these four groups. The most important feature of Figure 13.3 is the line for the rapid-decline group. As demonstrated, those who have rapidly declining levels of immune status also show a significant decline in social support network size. As might be predicted, those with stable, higher levels of immune status maintain a relatively stable social support network size. Those with stable, low immune status begin with lower levels of social support, but show some nonsignificant increase over the course of time. The slow-decline group reflects the expected pattern through the first year of evaluation. However, this group does show an unexpected increase in network size (although not statistically significant) at the final follow-up. Overall, this analysis suggests that progression of illness, particularly for those with rapid changes in immune status, is followed by reductions in network size. Those with stable illness tend to have more stable social networks.

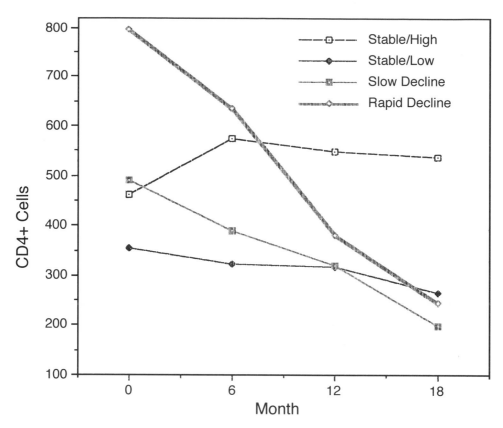

FIGURE 2. Changes in CD4+ cells for four CD4+ groups: Stable/High, Stable/Low, Rapid Decline, Slow Decline.

Detailed evaluations for measures of instrumental and emotional–social support did not reveal consistent patterns. Similarly, all evaluations for the HRSD were nonsignificant. Figure 13.4 shows the outcomes for the BDI. Interestingly, at all time periods, the rapidly declining group had the lowest BDI scores, and the slowly declining group had the highest BDI scores. These differences were not statistically significant at baseline or at 6 months. However, the differences between these two groups were statistically significant (as evaluated by analysis of variance) at the 12-month ($p < .02$) and the 18-month ($p < .05$) evaluations. The finding suggests that depression is related to the stability groupings. Furthermore, those with rapidly declining immune status started and ended the study with greater levels of depression than those whose illness progressed slowly. These data may suggest that depression is related to poorer prognosis. However, it is not possible to infer direction of causation from these results.

In order to investigate the relationship between advancing illness and social support further, we performed more detailed analyses on 52 subjects who had less than 200 CD4+ cells at the third visit. The threshold of 200 CD4+ cells was chosen, because this represents entry into the terminal stage of the illness. This stage, which may

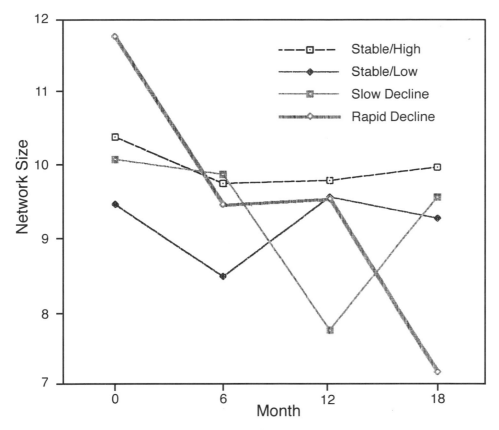

FIGURE 3. Changes in social network size for four CD4+ groups: Stable/High, Stable/Low, Rapid Decline, Slow Decline.

last for some years, is typically referred to as AIDS. These analyses focused on 31 subjects who made the transition from 200–500 CD4+ cells to the AIDS (less than 200 cells) category between the first and third visits. We refer to these subjects as the Transition group. For comparison, we considered 21 subjects who were in the AIDS category at both the initial and third visit (AIDS group).

Figure 13.5 shows the network size for the men at the initial and third visits. The figure demonstrates that, at the initial visit, the AIDS patients had smaller social networks than their peers, who, at the time, had not reached the diagnosis of AIDS ($t = 2.01$, $df = 51$, $p = .05$). At the third visit, when both groups were in the AIDS category, the network sizes were nearly identical ($t = -.11$, $df = 51$, $p = .91$). These findings provide more evidence that worsening illness causes network size to decline.

The findings for instrumental support are summarized in Figure 13.6. In contrast to network size, AIDS patients appear to receive more instrumental support than their peers in earlier stages of the illness. At the initial visit, instrumental support scores were significantly higher for AIDS patients ($t = -2.35$, $df = 51$, $p = .025$). However, at the follow-up, the instrumental support for those subjects making the transition from

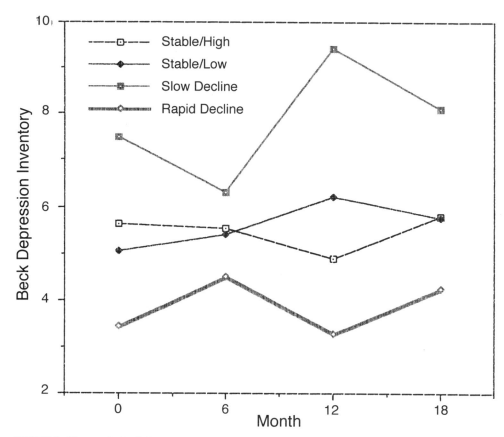

FIGURE 4. Changes in Beck Depression Inventory scores for four CD4+ groups: Stable/High, Stable/Low, Rapid Decline, Slow Decline.

HIV-positive to AIDS increased, whereas it remained steady for those who remained in the AIDS category. At the third visit, differences in instrumental support between these two groups were nonsignificant ($t = -.54$, $df = 51$, $p = .59$).

These differences could not be explained by differences in depression. Table 13.2 summarizes the depression outcomes. As the table shows, scores on both HRSD and BDI measures were comparable between these groups at each assessment. Furthermore, there were no differences in emotional support.

Summary of Results

In summary, we conducted a series of different analyses designed to investigate the relationship between social support and immune status. The cross-lagged correlation model attempted to evaluate the strength of two alternative causal pathways. The first pathway was that low social support caused reductions in immune status. Little evidence was provided to support this hypothesis. Alternatively, the model provided more evidence for the hypothesis that declining immune status causes reductions in

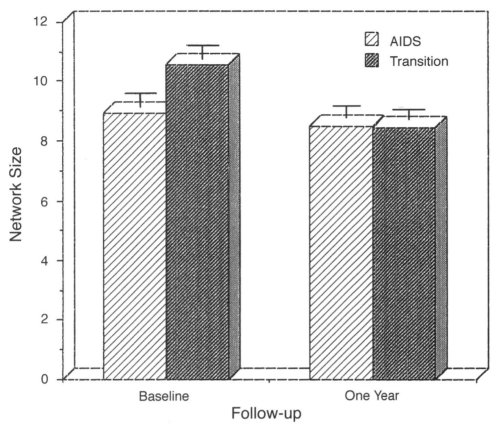

FIGURE 5. Network size for the men who had AIDS at the initial and third visit, and for those who made the transition to AIDS between the first and third visit.

social support network size. There are many problems with the crossed-lagged correlational model. One problem is that network size was not stable over the course of time. The low correlation between network size at baseline and at follow-up may indicate that network is measured with error. This problem could hinder the interpretation of the model.

A series of other analyses tended to support the hypothesis that declining health status causes reductions in social network size. For example, the group of patients with rapidly declining immune status also experienced systematic reductions in network size over the course of four evaluations that were spread over 18 months. Among patients who made the transition to AIDS status during the study, network size declined significantly. Although patients with rapid decline in immune status tended to be depressed throughout the study, the depression remained relatively stable. Thus, changes in depression could not explain changes in network size. Overall, these data appear to support the hypothesis that reductions in immune status and progression of HIV infection cause reductions in social support network size.

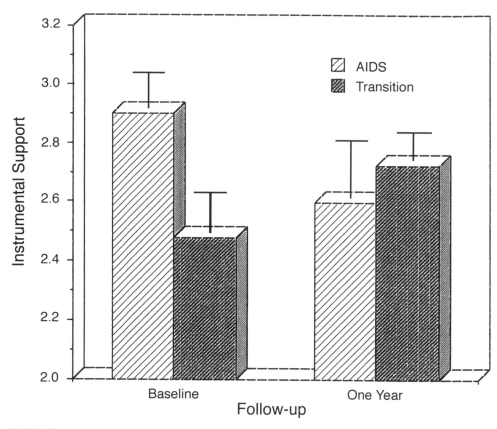

FIGURE 6. Instrumental support for the men who had AIDS at the initial and third visit, and for those who made the transition to AIDS between the first and third visit.

DISCUSSION

A substantial literature argues that people with small social networks are at risk for poor health outcomes (Berkman, 1995). In this chapter, we suggest an alternative explanation for the relationship between social support and health outcome. Specifically, we suggest that illness can cause modifications in the social environment. Studies of asthma, cancer, and other diseases are common stimuli for alterations in family

TABLE 13.2. Depression Changes for AIDS and Transition to AIDS Subjects

Measure	Baseline				One year			
	AIDS	Transition	t	p	AIDS	Transition	t	p
Beck	9.88 (8.66)	8.65 (9.55)	−.45	.66	10.25 (8.67)	9.83 (7.22)	−.18	.85
Hamilton	5.85 (5.92)	6.35 (6.60)	.28	.78	7.52 (6.48)	5.52 (4.14)	−1.36	.18

environment. For example, AIDS patients may be victimized by family members and friends. These potential supporters may feel uncomfortable interacting with someone who has an infectious disease. Disturbance in marital relationships often follow diagnosis and treatment of serious conditions such as heart disease. In discases such as HIV infection, the illness almost certainly will interfere with intimate relationships (Semple et al., 1993).

Our findings are limited to HIV-infected men, and we are uncertain how well they generalize to other chronic disease groups. Nevertheless, we do feel they have some important implications. HIV-infected individuals represent an interesting population for the study of social support and health. They share much in common with other disease groups (e.g., deterioration of health status, reduced quality of life, increased contact with the healthcare system). However, HIV disease differs in interesting ways from other chronic disease groups, such as heart disease and cancer. Unlike other diseases, HIV is primary seen in young people who have not typically begun to come to terms with their own mortality. In addition, HIV carries a stigma that other diseases do not, due to its association with homosexuality and drug use. HIV-infected individuals are also likely to be poor and are often members of minority groups. Thus, HIV may be associated with a unique set of stressors not seen in other chronic disease groups. For many HIV-infected individuals, certain important aspects of social support may be less available then in other chronic diseases. This is especially true for the homosexual men, such as those who participated in this study. Marriage, for instance, one of the primary sources of structural support, is typically not available for this group (although significant partnership may be). In addition, many HIV-positive individuals lose many friends to the epidemic, further reducing their ability to receive social support.

Epidemiological studies usually attempt to control for disease severity. However, measures of disease severity are often inadequate. When controls for health status are entered into multivariate equations, it is likely that the analyses will underadjust, because the measures of health status simply do not reliably capture the construct. Another issue is that early phases of illness may interfere with social relationships. As people progress through illness, they may not be interested in walking, dancing, or leisure activities, and these may be the early symptoms of an undiagnosed condition.

CRITERIA FOR CAUSAL DIRECTION

Epidemiologists consider five criteria for establishing causal relationships. These are temporality, strength, consistency, gradient, and plausibility. We will address each of these briefly.

TEMPORALITY

Temporality occurs when the cause precedes the outcome. The crossed-lagged correlations and the analyses of specific groups suggest that reduced CD4+ cells occurs prior to reductions in social support network. Thus, the temporality data appear to support the alternative hypothesis that illness causes low support.

STRENGTH

The strength of association between social support network size and immune status is relatively weak. However, the magnitude of the relationship is approximately equal to that of other epidemiological associations.

CONSISTENCY

Epidemiologists argue that causal relationships must be established consistently across studies. Our data are preliminary. We are unaware of other studies that have reported this same relationship. Thus, the consistency criterion is not met by our observations. We encourage other investigators to evaluate this hypothesis using longitudinal data.

GRADIENT

For some, but not all, biological outcomes, there is a gradient between the causal factor and the outcome. For example, there is a systematic relationship between the number of cigarettes smoked and mortality. The data we present here suggest there is a systematic relationship between network size and immune status. Furthermore, this relationship becomes stronger over the lagged observations. Over the course of time, network size declines substantially, corresponding to reductions in CD4+ cells. This observation tends to argue in favor of the hypothesis that increasing illness causes reductions in social support network size.

PLAUSIBILITY

Epidemiologist argue that there must be some reasonable hypothesis that explains the relationship between a causal factor and an outcome. Many authors have argued that social support buffers stress, thus resulting in reduced disease impact. The alternative explanation suggests that illness limits social activity. For example, health outcomes are largely behavioral (Kaplan, 1990). As illness progresses, capabilities for performing activities of daily living decline. For example, men with advanced HIV infection may not have enough energy to attend parties, gather with friends, or perform usual role activities. Furthermore, the illness and the associated stigma may result in avoidance by friends and peers. Thus, the alternative hypothesis seems logically plausible. Indeed, it requires fewer assumptions than the stress-buffering model.

RELATED STUDIES

It would appear that our results are in contrast to the majority of published studies. However, upon reexamination, many studies could be reinterpreted within this framework. For example, in a recent study, we administered the social support questionnaire to adults with advanced lung disease. These patients were then followed prospectively over the course of 6 years. Using a Cox Proportional Hazard Model, social support satisfaction significantly predicted survival up to 6 years. However, when the data were analyzed in more detail, it was noted that network size was related to disease severity at baseline. It is possible that increased severity of illness may interfere with an individual's ability to elicit, make use of, or be satisfied with the support that is obtained from others. In turn, this may deepen the sense of social isolation (Grodner et al., 1996).

A related study evaluated predictors of survival following cardiac surgery in the elderly. In this study, older adults who did not participate in community groups or feel comfort from religion were more likely to die within 6 months of surgery than those who were more socially active. The authors adjusted for biological variables and presurgical activity. However, these typically serve as an underadjustment in multivariate analysis. Nonparticipation in social activities may be a sensitive measure of severity of illness. Thus, we would expect that those who fail to participate in community groups may be more severely ill than those who are more active. Furthermore, those with declining health status may also feel less comfortable with religion (Oxman, Freeman, & Manheimer, 1995).

There have been relatively few studies of the progression of HIV illness in relation to social support. A report by Theorell and colleagues (1995) may, at first, appear inconsistent with our findings. These investigators studied a group of hemophiliacs in Sweden who were infected with the HIV virus. The subjects were divided into those with high or low availability of attachment. Subjects with high availability of attachment progressed more slowly than their peers with low availability of attachment. When considering these results, it is worth noting that availability of attachment is more similar to our instrumental social support variable than to network size. Indeed, our data show that instrumental support actually improves with severity of illness. In other words, availability of instrumental support may also be a consequence rather than a cause of HIV progression. Had we measured availability of attachment, we might have expected it to increase with advancing disease. It is also possible that social support functions differently among Swedish hemophiliacs than among American homosexual men.

SUMMARY

An extensive literature argues that high levels of social support provide protection against disease progression. An alternative explanation is that decreased social activity is a consequence rather than a cause of illness. Cohort data from HIV-infected men suggest that social network size declines as men become progressively more ill. Furthermore, our data indicate that illness progression precedes rather than antecedes declines in social network. Most published studies are based on cross-sectional observations that are unable to disentangle cause and effect. Our data suggest that social support should not always be conceptualized and investigated as a predictor of health outcome. Indeed, changes in social support may also be a consequence of illness. Furthermore, there may be reciprocal influences. The relationship between social support and outcome may be bidirectional.

We offer these observations to stimulate discussion. The study has many significant limitations. First, this study is based on a relatively small group of HIV-infected men. We are uncertain as to whether these observations have any relevance for women or will be generalizable to larger groups. Another concern is that these data are based exclusively on HIV-infected men. HIV disease may represent a unique illness that is not like other chronic diseases. There is a serious social stigma associated with this illness that may not generalize to other diseases. Furthermore, HIV may be unique, in that it will almost certainly disrupt intimate relationships. Another problem is that HIV-infected men tend to associate with others with the same condition. Some of the reduction in social support network size may reflect losses in friends and lovers due to death. Unfortunately, we cannot determine this from the data available to us in the HNRC project.

Finally, it is important to emphasize that our findings apply only to social network size. Some of our evidence suggests that instrumental social support actually improves with advancing infection. In other words, as disease progresses, HIV-infected men may have fewer people in their support network. However, those who remain in the network can be counted on more than those who are lost.

In conclusion, there is sufficient evidence to believe that there is an association between social support and health outcomes. However, determination of the causal direction is deserving of further study.

DIRECTIONS FOR FUTURE RESEARCH

The relationship between social support and health outcome has fascinated investigators for several decades. However, few studies have performed longitudinal evaluations. Longitudinal studies are necessary in order to separate the causal pathways between support and health outcome. Most investigators believe that low social support causes poor health outcomes by providing an inadequate buffer against life stress. Data from patients with HIV infection suggest that the progression of illness may cause reductions in social support network size. We believe that the direction of causation may be even more complex. For example, life stress may inhibit immune status, allowing the disease to progress. Once the disease progresses, social support may be reduced. In turn, this may lead to an even poorer buffer against life stresses. Additional research is necessary in order to investigate these questions. We encourage investigators to include measures of social support in ongoing studies. Measurement of social process in epidemiological studies is typically inadequate. Few studies have considered satisfaction with support, and even fewer have attempted to build models that examine causal pathways.

In conclusion, few data are available to address the relationship between social support and health outcome. We believe this is a rich field for future investigation, and we encourage continuing explorations of these problems.

ACKNOWLEDGMENTS

The principal support for the HNRC is provided by NIMH Center Grant No. 5 P50 MH45294 (HIV Neurobehavioral Research Center). Additional support is provided by Grant No. 5 R01 MH43298 (Neuropsychiatric Sequelae of HTLV-III Infections), Grant

No. 5 R29 MH45688 (Object-Oriented Simulation of HIV and CNS/HIV Infection, Grant No. 1 R01 MH46255 (Psychosocial Moderators of Disease Progression in AIDS), Grant No. 1 R01 NS27810 (Role of Immune Responsiveness in HIV Encephalopathy), and the Henry M. Jackson Foundation (Psychiatric Natural History Study: Factors Related to Human Immunodeficiency Virus Transmission and Morbidity). The views expressed in this article are those of the authors and do not reflect the official policy or position of the Department of the Navy, Department of Defense, or the United States Government.

REFERENCES

Aneshensel, C. S., Rutter, C. M., & Lachenbruch, P. A. (1991). Social structure, stress, and mental health: Competing conceptual and analytic models. International Conference on Social Stress Research (1990, London, England). *American Sociological Review*, *56*(2), 166-178.

Antoni, M. H., August, S., LaPerriere, A., Bagett, H. L., Klimas, N., Ironson, G., Schneiderman, N., & Fletcher, M. A. (1990). Psychological and neuroendocrine measures related to functional immune changes in anticipation of HIV-1 serostatus notification. *Psychosomatic Medicine*, *52*, 496-510.

Beck, A. T. (1967). *Depression: Clinical, experimental, and theoretical aspects*. New York: Harper & Row.

Beck, A. T. (1976). *Cognitive therapy and emotional disorder*. New York: International Universities Press.

Berkman, L. F. (1995). The role of social relations in health promotion. *Psychosomatic Medicine*, *57*(3), 245-254.

Berkman, L. F., & Breslow, L. (1983). *Health and ways of living: Findings from the Alameda County study*. New York: Oxford University Press.

Blaney, N. T., Goodkin, K., Morgan, R. O., Feaster, D., Millon, C., Szapocznik, J., & Eisdorfer, C. (1991). A stress-moderator model of distress in early HIV-1 infection: Concurrent analysis of life events, hardiness and social support. *Journal of Psychosomatic Research*, *35*, 297-305.

Blazer, D. (1982). Social support and mortality in an elderly community population. *American Journal of Epidemiology*, *115*, 684-694.

Borysenko, M., & Borysenko, J. (1982). Stress, behavior, and immunity: Animal models and mediating mechanisms. *General Hospital Psychiatry*, *4*, 56-67.

Centers for Disease Control and Prevention (1995). HIV/AIDS Surveillance Report. *Morbidity and Mortality Weekly*, 7.

Centers for Disease Control and Prevention (1993). Revised classification system for HIV Infection and expanded surveillance case definition for AIDS among adolescents and adults. *Morbidity and Mortality Weekly Reports*, *41* (RR-17), 1-20.

Cohen, S., & Syme, S. L. (1985). *Social support and health*. San Francisco: Academic Press.

Davidson, D. M., & Shumaker, S. A. (1987). Social support and cardiovascular disease. *Atherosclerosis*, *7*, 101-104.

Dew, M. A., Ragni, M. V., & Nimorwicz, P. (1990). Infection with human immunodeficiency virus and vulnerability to psychiatric distress. *Archives of General Psychiatry*, *47*, 737-744.

Durkheim, E. (1951). *Suicide*. New York: Free Press.

Endicott, J., Cohen, J., Nee, J., Fleiss, J., & Sarantakos, S. (1981). Hamilton Depression Rating Scale: Extracted from regular and change versions of the schedule for affective disorders and schizophrenia. *Archives of General Psychiatry*, *38*, 98-103.

Evans, D., Petitto, J., Leserman, J., Perkins, D., Stern, R., Folds, J., Ozer, H., & Golden, R. (1992). Stress, depression and natural killer cells: Potential clinical relevance. *Clinical Neuropharmacology*, *15* (Suppl. 1A), 656A-657A.

Fahey, J. L., Taylor, J. M. G., Detels, R., Hofmann, B., Melmed, R. M., Nishanian, P., & Giorgi, J. V. (1990). The prognostic value of cellular and serologic markers in infection with human immunodeficiency virus type 1. *New England Journal of Medicine*, *322*, 166-172.

Glaser, R., & Kiecolt-Glaser, J. (1987). Stress-associated depression in cellular immunity: Implications for acquired immune deficiency syndrome (AIDS). *Brain, Behavior, and Immunity*, *1*, 107-112.

Goodkin, K., Blaney, N. T., Feaster, D., Fletcher, M. A., Baum, M. K., Mantero-Atienza, E., Klimas, N. G., Millon,

C., Szapocznik, J., & Eisdorfer, C. (1992). Active coping style is associated with natural killer cell cytotoxicity in asymptomatic HIV-1 seropositive homosexual men. *Journal of Psychosomatic Research, 36,* 635–650.

Goodkin, K., Fuchs, I., Feaster, D., Leeka, J., & Dickson-Rishel, D. (1992). Life stressors and coping style are associated with immune measures in HIV-1 infection—a preliminary report. *International Journal of Psychiatry in Medicine, 22,* 155–172.

Greco, D., & Stazi, M. A. (1987). Length of survival of patients with AIDS. *British Medical Journal, 293,* 451–452.

Grodner, S., Prewitt, L. M., Jaworski, B. A., Myers, R., Kaplan, R. M., & Ries, A. L. (1996). The impact of social support in pulmonary rehabilitation of patients with chronic obstructive pulmonary disease. *Annals of Behavioral Medicine, 18,* 139–145.

Hamilton, M. (1969). Standardised assessment and recording of depressive symptoms. *Psychiatric Neurologial Neurochiropracty, 72,* 201–205.

Hamilton, M. (1974). General problems of psychiatric rating scales (especially for depression). *Modern Problems of Pharmopsychiatry, 7,* 125–138.

Haynes, S. G., & Feinleib, M. (1980). Women, work, and coronary heart disease: Prospective findings from the Framingham Heart Study. *American Journal of Public Health, 70,* 133–141.

Hays, R. B., Turner, H., & Coates, T. J. (1992). Social support, AIDS-related symptoms, and depression among gay men. *Journal of Consulting and Clinical Psychology, 60,* 463–469.

House, J. S., Robbins, C., & Metzner, H. L. (1982). The association of social relationships and activities with mortality: Prospective evidence from the Tecumseh Community Health Study. *American Journal of Epidemiology, 116,* 123–140.

Kannel, W. B. (1987). New perspectives on cardiovascular risk factors. *American Heart Journal, 114,* 213–219.

Kaplan, R. M. (1990). Behavior as the central outcome in health care. *American Psychologist, 45,* 1211–1220.

Kenny, D. A. (1975). Cross-lagged panel correlation: A test for spuriousness. *Psychological Bulletin, 82*(6), 887–903.

Kessler, J. R., Joseph, J., Ostrow, D., Phair, J., Chmiel, J., & Rush, C. (1989, June). *Psychosocial co-factors in illness onset among HIV-positive men.* International AIDS Conference, Montreal, Canada.

Kessler, R. C., Foster, C., Joseph, J., Ostrow, D., Wortman, C., Phair, J., & Chmiel, J. (1991). Stressful life events and symptom onset in HIV infection. *American Journal of Psychiatry, 148,* 733–738.

Moss, A. R., Bacchetti, P., Osmond, D., Krampf, W., Chaisson, R. E., Stites, D., Wilber, J., Allain, J. P., Carlson, J. (1988). Seropositivity for HIV and the development of AIDS or AIDS-related condition: Three-year follow up of the San Francisco General Hospital cohort. *British Medical Journal, 296,* 745–750.

Namir, S., Wolcott, E. L., & Fawzy, F. I. (1989). Social support and HIV spectrum disease: Clinical and research perspectives. *Psychiatric Medicine, 7,* 97–105.

Oxman, T. E., Freeman, D. H. Jr., & Manheimer, E. D. (1995). Lack of social participation or religious strength and comfort as risk factors for death after cardiac surgery in the elderly. *Psychosomatic Medicine, 57*(1), 5–15.

Palmblad, J. (1981). Stress and immunocompetence: Studies in man. In R. Ader (Ed.), *Psychoneuroimmunology* (pp. 229–257). New York: Academic Press.

Patterson, T. L., Semple, S. J., Temoshok, L. R., Atkinson, J. H., McCutchan, J. A., Straits-Tröster, K. A., Chandler, J. L., & Grant, I. (1993). Depressive symptoms among HIV+ men: Life stress, coping, and social support. *Journal of Applied Biobehavioral Research, 1*(1), 64–87.

Patterson, T. L., Semple, S. J., Temoshok, L. R., Atkinson, J. H., McCutchan, J. A., Straits-Tröster, K., Chandler, J. L., Grant, I., & the HIV Neurobehavioral Research Center Group (1995). Stress and depressive symptoms prospectively predict immune change among HIV-seropositive men. *Psychiatry: Interpersonal and Biological Processes, 58,* 299–312.

Patterson, T. L., Shaw, W. S., Semple, S. J., Cherner, M., Nannis, E., McCutchan, J. A., Atkinson, J. H., Grant, I., and the HIV Neurobehavioral Research Center (HNRC) Group (1996). Relationship of psychosocial factors to HIV disease progression. *Annals of Behavioral Medicine, 18,* 30–39.

Pederson, C., Dickmeiss, E., Gaub, J., Ryder, L. P., Lindhardt, B. O., & Lundgren, J. D. (1990). T-cell subset alterations and lymphocyte responsiveness to mitogens and antigen during severe primary infection with HIV: A case series of seven consecutive HIV seroconverters. *AIDS, 4,* 523–526.

Perry, S., Fishman, B., Jacobsberg, L., & Frances, A. (1992). Relationships over one year between lymphocyte subsets and psychosocial variables among adults with infection by human immunodeficiency virus. *Archives of General Psychiatry, 49*, 396–401.

Polk, B. F., Fox, R., Brookmeyer, R., Kanchanarksa, S., Kaslow, R., Visscher, B., Rinaldo, C., & Phair, J. (1987). Predictors of the acquired immunodeficiency syndrome developing in a cohort of seropositive homosexual men. *New England Journal of Medicine, 316*, 61–66.

Rabkin, J. G., Remien, R., Katoff, L., & Williams, J. B. (1993). Resilience in adversity among long-term survivors of AIDS. *Hospital and Community Psychiatry, 44*, 162–167.

Rabkin, J. G., Williams, J. B. W., Neugebauer, R., Remien, R. H., & Goetz, R. (1990). Maintenance of hope in HIV-spectrum homosexual men. *American Journal of Psychiatry, 147*, 1322-1326.

Rabkin, J. G., Williams, J. B. W., Remien, R. H., Goetz, R., Kertzner, R., & Gorman, J. M. (1991). Depression, distress, lymphocyte subsets, and human immunodeficiency virus symptoms on two occasions in HIV-positive homosexual men. *Archives of General Psychiatry, 48*, 111-119.

Rubermen, W., Weinblatt, E., Goldberg, J. D., & Chaudhary, B. S. (1984). Psychosocial influences on mortality after myocardial infarction. *New England Journal of Medicine, 311*, 552-559.

Sahs, J. A., Goetz, R., Reddy, M., Rabkin, J. G., Williams, J. B. W., Kertzner, R., & Gorman, J. M. (1994). Psychological distress and natural killer cells in gay men with and without HIV infection. *American Journal of Psychiatry, 151*, 1479-1484.

Schaefer, C., Coyne, J. C., & Lazarus, R. S. (1981). The health-related functions of social support. *Journal of Behavioral Medicine, 4*, 381-406.

Schoenbach, V. J., Kaplan, B. H., Fredman, L., & Kleinbaum, D. G. (1986). Social ties and mortality in Evans County, Georgia. *American Journal of Epidemiology, 123*(4), 577-591.

Semple, S. J., Patterson, T. L., Temoshok, L. R., McCutchan, J. A., Straits-Troster, K. A., Chandler, J. L., & Grant, I. (1993). Identification of psychobiological stressors among HIV-positive women. *Women and Health, 20*(4), 15-36.

Solomon, G. F., Temoshok, L., O'Leary, A., & Zich, J. (1987). An intensive psychoimmunologic study of long-surviving persons with AIDS: Pilot work, background studies, hypothesis, and methods. *Annals of the New York Academy of Sciences, 496*, 567-575.

Taylor, J. M. G., Schwartz, K., & Detels, R. (1986). The time from infection with human immunodeficiency virus (HIV) to the onset of AIDS. *Journal of Infectious Diseases, 154*, 694-697.

Theorell, T., Blomkvist, V., Jonsson, H., Schulman, S., Berntorp, E., Stigendal, L. (1995). Social support and the development of immune function in human immunodeficiency virus infection. *Psychosomatic Medicine, 57*(1), 32-36.

Volberding, P. A., McCutchan, J. A. (1989). The HIV epidemic: Medical and social challenges. *Biochimica et Biophysica Acta, 989*, 227.

Welin, L., Svardsudd, K., Ander-Peciva, S., Tibblin, G., Tibblin, B., & Larsson, G. (1985). Prospective study of social influences on mortality. *Lancet, 2*, 915-918.

Wolcott, D. L., Namir, S., Fawzy, F. I., Gottlieb, M. S., & Mitsuyasu, R. T. (1986). Illness concerns, attitudes toward homosexuality and social support in gay men with AIDS. *General Hospital Psychiatry, 8*, 395-403.

Wolf, T. M., Balson, P. M., Morse, E. V., Simon, P. M., Gaumer, R. H., Dralle, P. W., & Williams, M. H. (1991). Relationship of coping style to affective state and perceived social support in asymptomatic and symptomatic HIV-infected persons: Implications for clinical management. *Journal of Clinical Psychiatry, 52*, 171-173.

Zich, J., & Temoshok, L. (1987). Perceptions of social support in men with AIDS and ARC: Relationships with distress and hardiness. *Journal of Applied Social Psychology, 17*, 193-215.

Chapter 14

SOCIAL SUPPORT, SELF-ESTEEM, SOCIAL CONFORMITY, AND GREGARIOUSNESS

DEVELOPMENTAL PATTERNS ACROSS TWELVE YEARS

Michael D. Newcomb and Keunho Keefe

Social support has generally beneficial effects on physical health and emotional well-being (e.g., Cohen & Wills, 1985), although some problem or negative effects have been observed under certain circumstances (e.g., Rook, 1984). Many studies have revealed that people with supportive, close relationships with spouses, family, and friends have better health and lower mortality than those with fewer supportive ties. For example, Newcomb and Bentler (1988b) found that social support during adolescence reduced problems in several areas of functioning in young adulthood. In particular, social support in late adolescence ameliorated problems with drugs, psychosomatic complaints, emotional distress, intimate relations, health, and family 4 years later.

In this chapter, we review theory and research on the relationships between perceived social support and personality. We focus specifically on three personality traits: Self-esteem, gregariousness (extraversion), and social conformity. Based within a developmental framework, we examine empirically how these personal and social-environmental characteristics influence each other over a 12-year period from late adolescence to adulthood at 4-year intervals. Finally, these new results are interpreted

MICHAEL D. NEWCOMB • Division of Counseling Psychology, University of Southern California, Los Angeles, California 90089-0031.   KEUNHO KEEFE • Reiss-Davis Child Study Center, Los Angeles, California 90034.

Sourcebook of Social Support and Personality, edited by Gregory R. Pierce, Brian Lakey, Irwin G. Sarason, and Barbara R. Sarason. Plenum Press, New York, 1997.

in light of prior theory and research to characterize more precisely and accurately the interplay between personality and social support at different development stages of life.

THEORETICAL CONSIDERATION
OF PERSONALITY AND SOCIAL SUPPORT

Social support is defined here not as a static construct, but as a resource that evolves throughout life. Social support is shaped through reciprocal and transactional processes between characteristics of the individual and those of other people in his or her social environment (Newcomb, 1990a). More specifically, we limit our attention to perceived social support, rather than received or actual support (e.g., Newcomb & Chou, 1989), and to the quality of perceived support rather than assessments of quantity (e.g., Newcomb, 1990c). Finally, we also limit our empirical consideration to perceived quality of support from peers and parents, rather than other possible sources such as professionals or agencies (e.g., Newcomb & Chou, 1989). We define *social support* as "an interwoven network of interpersonal relationships that provide companionship, assistance, attachment, and emotional nourishment to the individual" (Newcomb & Bentler, 1986, p. 521). This definition is largely consistent with that of Sarason, Levine, Basham, and Sarason (1983), that social support is "the existence or availability of people on whom we can rely, people who let us know that they care about, value, and love us" (p. 127).

In prior research, social support has typically been studied as a provision that is given from the external social environment to the individual (e.g., Newcomb, 1990a). Individual characteristics that may contribute to creating and maintaining a social environment have been largely ignored until recently. Sarason, Sarason, and Pierce (1990b) compiled and presented a wealth of theory and research knowledge suggesting that, in fact, social support is closely interrelated with personal aspects of the individual. Personal characteristics help shape and form one's social environment and, particularly, the nature of one's social support system.

In social-cognitive theories, individual differences in patterns of behavior across situations reflect such underlying person variables as the individuals' encoding or construction of their experiences (e.g., Mischel, 1973, 1990). These relatively enduring person variables within the individual interact with situational characteristics to generate stable but discriminative patterns of behavior. Different persons evoke different responses from social and physical environments. The responses from others, in turn, further shape, reinforce, and extend the pattern of personal or individual development.

As one central personal characteristic, personality has been linked both theoretically and empirically to social support. Personality variables such as shyness, introversion, sociability, self-esteem, and assertiveness have been repeatedly correlated with perceived social support (Jones, 1985; Newcomb, 1990a; Procidano & Heller, 1983; Sarason et al., 1983; Vinokur, Schul, & Caplan, 1987). More precisely, personality can reflect numerous and diverse aspects of individual functioning. Certainly, there is no one quality or trait that denotes personality. In fact, substantial controversy exists regarding the specific components and dimensions that encompass personality (e.g., Katigbak, Church, & Akamine, 1996).

We consider personality as several types or aspects of individual psychological functioning that develop early in life, become more stable with increasing age, are cross-situationally consistent, and reflect the unique characteristics, attitudes, affect, and propensities of an individual. This is a broad construction of personality that subsumes various aspects of personal, nonbehavioral characteristics. To capture several aspects of this multitude of individual differences, we have selected three traits that represent diverse components of individual functioning. Self-esteem was chosen as a critical component of self-evaluative processes that reflect important features of self-concept (e.g., Marsh & Hocevar, 1985). Furthermore, low self-esteem denotes an adverse emotional state often considered as psychological or emotional distress (Scheier & Newcomb, 1993). Gregariousness, or extraversion, was selected to characterize individual propensities, proclivities, or comfort with social interactions and transactions. Finally, social conformity was included to reflect an attitudinal dimension of personality that captures adherence to conventional norms and values. Taken together, these three constructs, reflecting diverse aspects of personality, capture affective, social, and attitudinal components of individual functioning.

We expect personality and social support to have a reciprocal influence on each other throughout one's life through two different processes: evocative and active processes (Scarr & McCartney, 1983). In terms of evocative processes, people with differing personalities elicit different responses from their social and physical environments. For example, an individual who is friendly and outgoing is likely to receive positive interpersonal feedback from others. In contrast, a shy person is likely to evoke fewer and less positive responses from others. These responses from one's environments, in turn, further shape, reinforce, and extend the pattern of personality development. The transactions between individuals and their environments continue throughout their lives. The latter processes, active processes, refer to an individual's selection of environments that are compatible with his or her personality. A person is actively led to find a particular environment that matches his or her personality. This active selection process, in turn, might reinforce and maintain the personality (Scarr & McCartney, 1983). The active kinds of processes become more important with increasing age, as the individual has more freedom to choose or to create his or her own environment.

Based on these theories, we derived the following hypotheses: First, personality constructs and social support will have reciprocal influences on each other; second, the influence of personality constructs on social support will be stronger than that of social support on personality with increasing age.

Self-Esteem and Social Support

Self-esteem correlates positively with perceived adequacy and availability of social support (Brown, Andrews, Harris, Adler, & Bridge, 1986; Dunkel-Schetter, Folkman, & Lazarus, 1987; Hansson, Jones, & Carpenter, 1984; Newcomb, 1990a; Sarason, Sarason, & Shearin, 1986; Sarason et al., 1983, 1990a). For example, those higher in social support described themselves more positively than did those lower in social support

(Sarason, Pierce, Shearin, Sarason, Waltz, & Poppe, 1991). In the same vein, lack of perceived social support was related to such negative affect as feelings of personal inadequacy, anxiety, and social rejection (Sarason et al., 1991). Most of these studies have been cross-sectional.

Close relationships increase the individual's self-worth and assertiveness by rendering the support, understanding, and positive regard of others. Various theorists have emphasized the role of other people in developing a person's sense of self (Cooley, 1902; Mead, 1934; Rosenberg, 1979). For example, Bowlby (1988) postulated that early attachment experiences with a primary caregiver contribute to the formation of self-concept and personality. Symbolic interactionists such as Cooley (1902) and Mead (1934) postulate that the self is basically the internalization of what we perceive others think of us; that is, the individual defines the sense of self based on feedback from significant others in his or her social environment. Consistent with the view of symbolic interactionists, adolescents' perceptions of the attitudes of significant others were shown to highly relate to their self-esteem (Harter, 1986, 1987; Rosenberg, 1979).

Although we have emphasized that high self-esteem results from social support, positive self-regard may in turn help initiate and nourish a supportive network. Those who feel confident in the support and responsiveness of significant others are likely to increase social bonds and solidify existing attachment relationships. Various studies have found that positive affective experiences increase social ties (see Baumeister & Leary, 1995). By contrast, those with low self-esteem may feel inhibited from initiating or maintaining social contacts with others.

Correlational studies cannot establish causal relations between self-esteem and perceived social support (Newcomb, 1990c). As a rare exception, Newcomb (1990a) examined reciprocal relationships between self-esteem and social support in adolescents by using a longitudinal design. Earlier self-esteem improved the quality of peer support 1-year later for both adolescent boys and girls. In addition, self-esteem increased parent and family support for boys, whereas self-esteem increased peer support for girls. Conversely, perceived support from adults improved subsequent self-esteem for both boys and girls. Furthermore, perceived support from family and adults enhanced later self-esteem among boys. These findings suggest that there are dynamic reciprocal relations between social support and self-esteem at least during adolescence. Because Newcomb only dealt with changes during a 1-year period in adolescence, it is uncertain whether reciprocal relations between the two constructs can be generalized to other periods of life.

GREGARIOUSNESS AND SOCIAL SUPPORT

Social support has also been shown to correlate with outgoing, extraverted, or generally gregarious tendencies. Extraverts tend to have larger social networks with more people to whom they feel close than do introverts (Jones, Freeman, & Goswick, 1981; Sarason et al., 1983; Stokes, 1985). On the other hand, introverts are more likely to report fewer friends and lower satisfaction with their social participation, and are more likely to regard their friendships and social networks as less supportive and less satisfying (DePaulo, Dull, Greenberg, & Swaim, 1989; Jones, 1985).

Those who are extraverted and outgoing tend to seek out opportunities for social interaction and select themselves into environments where they can create and intensify close ties. Having success in forming and maintaining close relationships may, in turn, reinforce individuals' tendencies to be sociable and gregarious by increasing their self-competence in the social domain. Conversely, a shy person tends to avoid and withdraw from social interactions out of fear of social rejection or embarrassment (see Baumeister & Leary, 1995). As a consequence, shy individuals reduce their chances of creating and nourishing supportive ties. Thus, these individuals miss out on an opportunity to develop social skills and to gain relational experiences. This lack of social experiences, along with deficits in social skills will in turn reinforce and maintain shyness in the person. Consistent with this hypothesis, shyness in late childhood has been shown to predict delay in marriage and in fatherhood (Caspi, Elder, & Bem, 1988). Those who were shy as children had interactional difficulties, and had trouble making transitions to marriage and parenthood in later years. Although there are no longitudinal data on the relationship between extraversion and social support, such a dynamic developmental process seems likely.

Social Conformity and Social Support

Social conformity has been shown to be negatively related to problems with interpersonal relationships and to drug use among adolescents and young adults (Newcomb, 1988; Newcomb & Bentler, 1988a, 1988b, 1988c), as well as a central attitudinal or personality dimension of general deviance (McGee & Newcomb, 1992) and risky behavior relative to AIDS (Stein, Newcomb, & Bentler, 1994). Newcomb and Bentler (1988a, 1988b) also found that social conformity was positively correlated with perceived social support during adolescence and young adulthood.

Socially conforming attitudes and lack of deviant orientations can facilitate amiable relations with other people. Deviant individuals may be rejected as potential relationship partners. Conversely, it is also possible that the presence of supportive social networks may reduce deviant attitudes and values. According to Durkheim's (1897/1951) theory of social integration, social relationships contribute to maintaining social order by inhibiting deviant or maladaptive behavior. Thus, close relationships may serve as a source of social norms that regulate people's behaviors. These social norms may then be internalized in the form of personality traits or attitudinal predispositions. As a result, supportive relationships may help people maintain more stable functioning and reduce the probability of problematic, deviant, or maladaptive behaviors.

Consistent with social integration theory (Durkheim, 1897/1951), Newcomb and Bentler (1988b) showed with longitudinal design that social support during adolescence reduced problems with drug use in young adulthood. However, Newcomb and Bentler did not directly examine whether adolescent social support increased adult social conformity. There is little direct evidence on the relations between social support and social conformity over time.

DEVELOPMENTAL PATTERNS

Developmental aspects of how personality and social support might mutually influence each other can be understood in regard to two components. First are the demand characteristics of various developmental transitions. We focus on the periods from adolescence into young adulthood, and also from young adulthood into adulthood. Second are the stability effects that transcend developmental transitions that reflect state dependency or continuity of development. Finally, transactions and reciprocal influences between social support and personality may be more apparent or salient at certain developmental periods than other periods.

TRANSITION FROM ADOLESCENCE TO ADULTHOOD

Transition from adolescence to adulthood can be divided into two periods: from adolescence to young adulthood, and from young adulthood to adulthood. Between adolescence and young adulthood, a major developmental task is to achieve independence and autonomy from parents, teachers, and other authority figures. During this period, many individuals complete their formal education and embark on their first full-time jobs. Entering an occupation signals the beginning of new roles. Meeting the expectations of a career and adjusting to a new role are crucial for the individual at this time. It is also a time when an individual tries out many different roles, explores alternative career goals, and considers various relationships and lifestyles. During the transition from young adulthood to adulthood, an individual shifts away from tentative choices concerning many important issues in life to more or less permanent ones. The individual who enters adulthood has made decisions about a career, values and goals, family and relationships, and lifestyle. During this period, many individuals get married, become parents, and settle down in their careers.

The two developmental transitional periods involve a number of important role changes and shifts in life experiences (Mortimer, Finch, & Kumka, 1982; Pearlin, 1985). These are the periods in which the abandonment of old roles and the achievement of new ones take place at a fairly rapid pace (Pearlin, 1985). As an individual progresses through these developmental transitions, his or her social support can contract, expand, or be substituted. Because most of the past studies on social support are cross-sectional, the dynamic nature of social support through the life course has not been well understood.

DEVELOPMENTAL STABILITY

Recent research on close relationships and social cognition has suggested that people develop an internal representation of relationships based on their early interpersonal experiences (see Baldwin, 1992; Baumeister & Leary, 1995). The internalized relationships function as a stable and systematic belief system or expectations about the extent and quality of the person's relationships. These beliefs or expectations are likely to lead to biased interpretation of social interactions and to affect the formation and maintenance of social ties; that is, individuals are likely to interpret ambiguous social information according to their belief system, or seek out relational experiences that are congruent with their belief system or relational expectations.

Various studies have suggested that through such expectations or belief systems, one's perceived social support may remain relatively stable across situations and over time. Early attachment style has been shown to relate to peer relationships during preschool years and to romantic relationships in adulthood (Hazan & Shaver, 1987; see Rutter & Garmezy, 1983). Similarly, Sarason et al. (1986) found that perceived social support showed considerable stability during radical changes in social environment. Sarason et al. assessed college students' perceived availability of, and satisfaction with, their social support on four occasions over a 3-year period: during the first 2 weeks of the first quarter, at 2 months, at 5 months into the freshman year, and after 36 months. The stability of perceived social support during this period is noteworthy, because transition from high school to college often involves major changes in one's interpersonal networks, accompanied by changes in living situations.

Parent–child relationships are also highly stable throughout childhood and adolescence (Hunt & Eichorn, 1972). Network size and frequency of contacts with close relatives are shown to remain stable across the life span (see Schulz & Rau, 1985). Stueve and Gerson (1977), for example, showed that the number of kin in one's social network remains stable from ages 21 to 64. Stueve and Gerson also found that although there was a considerable change of best friends during early adult years, best friendships remained stable in later years among their male samples.

Personality stability increases with age well into adulthood. Stein, Newcomb, and Bentler (1986a) showed in their 8-year longitudinal study that personality stability was greater between late adolescence and young adulthood than it was between early and late adolescence. Between late adolescence and adulthood, personality traits appear to be firmly established (Conley, 1984a, 1984b; Moss & Susman, 1980; Nesselrode & Baltes, 1974; Stein et al., 1986a). For example, Conley (1984a) showed a substantial continuity in personality traits over a 40-year span of adulthood. Block (1971) also found that the average stability correlation of personality traits was .55 between senior high school and adulthood. In the same vein, Bachman, O'Malley, and Johnston (1978) showed more stability than change in personality among males during an 8-year period from 10th grade to young adulthood. The results of these longitudinal studies indicate that personality and other individual characteristics increase in stability over time and thereby become more recalcitrant to change with age. The stability of self-esteem, however, seems to depends on the stability of environmental demands, performance expectations, and social comparison groups. When there are changes in these factors, such as during transition to junior high school, changes in one's self-esteem follow (Harter, 1983).

Only a few longitudinal studies have followed individuals from late adolescence into adulthood (Moritmer et al., 1982). This time period often involves major transitions and role changes. It is thus important to examine how social support and personality traits influence each other during this developmental period.

CRITICAL STAGES

The record of research across the life span indicates that different stages of development may be more vulnerable to changes among personality and social interactions than other stages. At a global level, it seems that with advancing age, the likelihood of either personal or social-environmental changes diminishes. For instance, although the particular pattern and participants of social support for an individual may shift from one stage in life to another (Newcomb, 1990b), as well as underlying individual propensities (Newcomb, 1997), many of the socialpsychological developmental trajectories established early in life may simply become more entrenched and specific with advancing age. Thus, the period between late adolescence and adulthood may not be the "critical period" for the energetic reciprocal influences between personality and social support. However, major normative life changes may make these trajectories more malleable and open to reciprocal influence.

A PROSPECTIVE EMPIRICAL CONSIDERATION
OF PERSONALITY AND SOCIAL SUPPORT

As an empirical test of the prospective relations between social support and various aspects of personality, we focus on a 12-year period from late adolescence into adulthood. This life period includes numerous normative developmental changes that are stressful and entail profound shifts in environment, living arrangements, and role responsibilities (Newcomb, 1996).

The research evidence we have reviewed suggests that there may be reciprocal relationships between social support and some of the personality constructs. An individual's early social environment influences his or her personality. One's personality, in turn, may contribute to the further course of development of his or her social environment. In cross-sectional research, it is impossible to draw a conclusion on the dynamic and reciprocal relationship between these two domains of variables. A longitudinal study is an effective method for uncovering causal relations between personality and social support.

We examine the relationships between three personality traits and social support by using a long-term longitudinal design. Cross-lagged latent-variable structural models are used to determine the impact of personality on perceived social support and the impact of perceived social support on personality over time. A cross-lagged longitudinal analysis is a powerful method for determining causal relationships in real-world data (Newcomb, 1990c). The methodology controls for contemporaneous associations, incorporates the stability of the constructs over time, and controls for initial levels of all constructs (Newcomb, 1994a; Stein, Newcomb, & Bentler, 1986b). Several different measures are used to reflect latent personality traits of Self-Esteem, Gregariousness, and Social Conformity. Perceived support from parents and peers is used to reflect a latent factor of Social Support. Although social support can be obtained from many diverse individuals and institutions, parents and peers/friends are for most people the most prominent and critical agents of support, and are also highly related to other forms or sources of social support (e.g., Newcomb, 1990c; Newcomb & Chou, 1989).

The transitional period between late adolescence and adulthood is certainly demanding, since it is a time to establish personal and economic independence, and is often a time of taking on the challenges of a marriage and parenthood (e.g., Newcomb, in press a). It is thus important to examine how social support and personality traits influence each other during this time period; therefore, we focus on this age period. Four data-collection points from the UCLA Study of Adolescent Growth and Adult Development longitudinal data are used: Year 5, Year 9, Year 13, and Year 17 (Newcomb, 1997).

Participants

This study was begun in 1976 with a sample of 7th-, 8th-, and 9th-grade students gathered from 11 Los Angeles County schools. Sites were chosen to oversample lower socioeconomic scale (SES) and minority areas. The first years of the project examined and tested many psychosocial predictors of drug initiation (Newcomb, 1997; Newcomb & Bentler, 1988c; Newcomb, Maddahian, & Bentler, 1986). The study has continued into adulthood, with assessments occurring every 4 years after the Year 5 late-adolescent wave of data collection.

Sufficient data on social support and personality to conduct the present study were not included in the assessments until Year 5 of this project. Therefore, the present analyses focus on the last 12 years of the study that spans late adolescence to adulthood, including four assessments points gathered at 4-year intervals (Year 5, Year 9, Year 13, and Year 17).

In Year 17, we received completed questionnaires from 552 subjects. This reflects a 34% retention rate over this 16-year period. Although this figure is lower than some other, shorter prospective studies, it is only 5% less than 4 years ago, and most subject loss occurred in the first 5 years of the study, when the population was oversampled to accrue sufficient numbers of parent, best friend, and subject triads (Newcomb, 1997).

Fewer than five individuals refused to continue in the study by returning their unsigned consent form with the withdrawal box checked. The vast majority of lost subjects was attributable to our inability to obtain a current address for them. In other words, the loss of individuals in this follow-up was primarily the result of our inability to contact them and *not* their voluntary withdrawal from the study.

Descriptive information on the sample from the Year 17 data collection is provided in Table 14.1 for all subjects, and for men and women separately. Ages ranged between 28 and 32 years; 67% of the sample is White and the remaining 33% is roughly spread across Asians, Hispanics, and Blacks. The average education level was about 2 years of college and ranged from the ninth grade to doctoral degree. Most were employed in full-time jobs, and the modal income was over $50,000, although similar percentages were in the $10,000–30,000 range, and the $30,000–50,000 range. The most prevalent living arrangement was living with a spouse, and almost half of the sample were parents.

An extensive series of attrition analyses have been conducted to determine whether, and in what manner, systematic withdrawal from the study may have occurred (Newcomb, 1997). These were conducted in several ways but generally revealed that only a very small percentage of attrition could be accounted for by numerous personality and drug-use variables, and that the remaining sample is quite similar to general population surveys regarding prevalence of drug use.

Measures

Eleven identical scales were assessed repeatedly at each of the four data waves. Each scale is composed of four bipolar items, two on each scale reverse-coded to control for acquiescent response style. These 11 scales were selected to reflect four latent constructs and are described in regard to each of these. The social support scales

TABLE 14.1. Description of Sample in Year 17

Variable	Male (N = 106)	Female (N = 284)	Total (N = 390)
Age (years)			
M	29.92	29.88	29.89
Range	29–32	28–32	28–32
Ethnicity (%)			
Black	7	15	13
Hispanic	9	10	10
White	75	65	67
Asian	9	10	10
Education (years)			
Mean	14.86	14.26	14.48
Range	10–18	9–18	9–18
Number of children (%)			
None	54	46	49
One	23	24	24
Two	19	18	18
Three or more	4	12	9
Income for past year (%)			
Under $10,000	2	10	8
$10,000 to $30,000	21	27	25
$30,000 to $50,000	33	28	30
Over $50,000	44	35	37
Living situation (%)			
Alone	6	11	10
Parents	7	9	9
Spouse	71	54	58
Cohabitation	4	9	7
Dormitory	1	0	0
Roommates	11	8	9
Single parent	0	9	6
No regular place	0	1	1
Current life activity (%)			
Unemployed, laid off, fired	2	5	4
Military	4	0	1
College	4	2	3
Childrearing/part-time job	0	9	7
Part-time job	5	7	6
Full-time job	80	63	68
Childrearing/homemaker	0	13	9
None	5	1	2

are discussed more completely elsewhere (e.g., Newcomb & Bentler, 1986, 1988b), as are the personality scales (Stein et al., 1986a).

Social Support

The construct of Social Support was reflected in two scales assessing the perceived supportiveness of particular personal relationships (Newcomb & Bentler, 1986). These scales include good relationship with parents and good relationship with peers. These scales were selected to capture two critical aspects of the social environment: that of friends and peers, and that of the family as reflected in parents.

Self-Esteem

This construct was reflected in three measured variables or personality scales (Stein et al., 1986b): invulnerability, self-acceptance, and (low) depression.

Social Conformity

This latent factor has been a critical construct throughout this multiyear project (Newcomb, 1997) and reflects attitudes toward conventional norms. Three scales reflected this construct (Castro, Maddahian, Newcomb, & Bentler, 1987; Newcomb & Bentler, 1988a): law abidance, (low) liberalism, and religiosity.

Gregariousness

This construct captures the personality tendency toward outgoing and confident interpersonal relationships. Three scales were chosen to reflect this latent factor: ambition, extraversion, and leadership.

ANALYSIS SUMMARY

Three sets of analyses are used to analyze and describe these data. The first set examines the gender and time effects for each of the 11 scales. Next, confirmatory factor analyses (CFAs) are used to verify the hypothesized factor structure, examine the latent factor intercorrelations, and test from sex differences on factor loadings and intercorrelations using multiple-group models. Finally, structural or path models are constructed to elucidate the significant-across-time effects between social support and the three types of personality reflected in the data.

MEAN DIFFERENCES

Repeated-measures ANOVAs, with gender as a second independent variable, were conducted on each of the 11 social support and personality scales. The means and significance levels for these analyses are presented in Table 14.2.

There were seven significant gender differences from these analyses. Compared to the men, women reported significantly less invulnerability, less self-acceptance, more depression, more law abidance, more religiosity, less ambition, and fewer leadership qualities.

There were also seven significant time effects among the 11 variables. Over time, good relationship with peers decreased, good relationship with parents increased, law abidance increased, liberalism decreased, ambition decreased, extraversion decreased, and leadership increased.

Finally, there were two significant interaction between time and gender. Figure 14.1 graphically depicts these two significant interactions. Although law abidance increased for both men and women, it rose much more sharply for the men, whereas at

TABLE 14.2. Repeated-Measure ANOVAs by Gender for All Manifest Variables

	Means				Significance of F-test		
	Y5	Y9	Y13	Y17	Sex	Time	Sex × Time
Social support							
Good relationship with peers							
Male	16.53	16.60	16.19	16.11	—	*	—
Female	16.82	16.36	16.39	16.32			
Good relationship with parents							
Male	16.02	16.72	16.71	16.92	—	*	—
Female	16.05	16.86	16.90	16.75			
Self-esteem							
Invulnerability							
Male	14.68	14.35	14.77	14.76	*	—	—
Female	12.81	12.67	12.68	12.54			
Self-acceptance							
Male	16.03	16.46	16.39	16.22	*	—	—
Female	15.77	15.70	16.09	15.65			
Depression							
Male	7.39	7.10	7.03	7.18	*	—	—
Female	7.78	7.55	7.25	7.55			
Social conformity							
Law abidance							
Male	12.42	13.39	14.98	15.66	*	***	**
Female	13.58	14.38	15.09	15.77			
Liberalism							
Male	9.75	9.49	9.21	9.25	—	**	—
Female	10.01	9.37	9.63	9.52			
Religosity							
Male	14.45	14.27	14.21	14.66	***	—	—
Female	15.71	15.89	15.75	15.55			
Gregariousness							
Ambition							
Male	16.03	15.82	15.19	14.91	***	***	*
Female	14.33	14.27	13.54	12.43			
Extraversion							
Male	13.33	12.90	12.85	12.58	—	***	—
Female	13.15	12.93	12.51	12.86			
Leadership							
Male	14.90	14.95	14.99	15.21	**	*	—
Female	13.94	14.12	14.39	14.38			

*p < .05
**p < .01
***p < .001

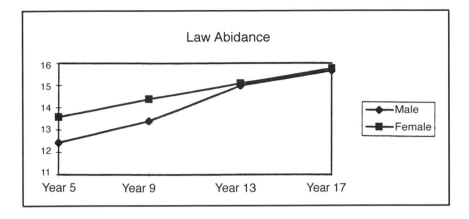

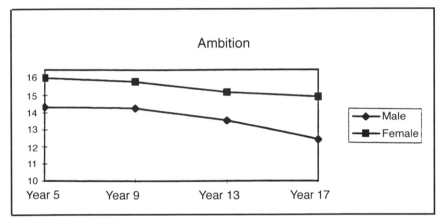

FIGURE 14.1. Plots of significant interactions. Dependent measures are Ambition and Law Abidance. Independent variables are Sex and Year assessed (repeated measure).

Year 13 and Year 17, gender differences were only minimal. Conversely, although ambition declined with age for both genders, it decreased more precipitously for the women and at Year 17, the greatest absolute gender difference was noted.

CONFIRMATORY FACTOR ANALYSES

For analyses of the CFA and path models, latent-variable structural equation modeling was used (structural equation modeling [SEM]: e.g., Bentler, 1980; Newcomb, 1990c, 1994a). Analyses were performed using the EQS structural equations program (Bentler, 1995). All models are run simultaneously, with every variable included at once.

Fit Criteria

Although a nonsignificant p-value associated with a chi-square test is a common criteria for not rejecting a SEM, the chi-square statistic is sensitive to the number of variables and the sample size. Other fit indices have been developed to control for these problems. In this study, models are accepted if the chi-square statistic is less than two times the degrees of freedom and the comparative fit index (CFI: Bentler, 1990) is greater than .90 (Newcomb, 1990c, 1994a). The nonnormed fit index (NNFI) is also presented, since it is correct for degrees of freedom, is commonly used, and is identical to the Tucker–Lewis index (Bentler, 1995).

First-Order Confirmatory Factor Analyses

Prior to constructing the across-time path models, CFAs were run to determine whether the measured variables chosen to capture the latent constructs did so in a statistically reliable manner. Correlations among the latent constructs were also presented. In the CFA model, all factor loadings were freed, factor variances were constrained at 1.00 (to identify the constructs), all factors were allowed to correlate freely, and the uniqueness or residual variables of repeated measures were allowed to correlate (i.e., the residual of extraversion Year 5 was allowed to correlate with the residual of extraversion at Year 9). Furthermore, identical factor loadings over time were constrained to equality in order to guarantee that each of the repeatedly assessed latent constructs were constituted in a similar manner over time (e.g., Aiken, Stein, & Bentler, 1994).

The initial CFA model fit the data quite well according to the criteria delineated here, $X^2/df = 1.44$, $p < .001$, CFI = .96, NNFI = .97. All hypothesized factor loadings were substantial and significant in the expected directions. These are graphically depicted in Figure 14.2 in standardized form.

Factor intercorrelations for this CFA model are given in Table 14.3. Social Support was significantly and positively correlated with each of the three personality constructs at each wave of data. The highest correlations within time were between Social Support and Self-Esteem (ranging from .88 to .94). To determine whether Social Support and Self-Esteem were in fact capturing the identical construct, an additional model was run. In this model, the correlations between Self-Esteem and Social Support within each time were forced to 1.00. A nested test revealed that this imposition significantly degraded the model ($p < .001$). This verifies that despite the high correlation between these constructs, they are not identical and must be considered separately.

The three personality constructs were all positively correlated except for Social Conformity and Gregariousness, which were negatively correlated and, at times, significantly so. Finally, stability correlations were quite high between repeatedly assessed constructs. The highest of these 4-year stability correlations was for Social Support (ranging from .79 to .93), followed by Social Conformity (ranging from .80 to .89) and Gregariousness (ranging from .78 to .89), with far lower stability correlations for Self-Esteem (ranging from .49 to .67).

These CFA analyses confirm that the measured-variable indicators hypothesized to reflect the latent constructs were reliable and significant. They also provide important information regarding the degree of association among these latent factors, providing a basis for understanding the path models to follow. Prior to this, however, the mean differences for gender suggest that we must consider whether different factor structures and factor intercorrelations exist for men and women.

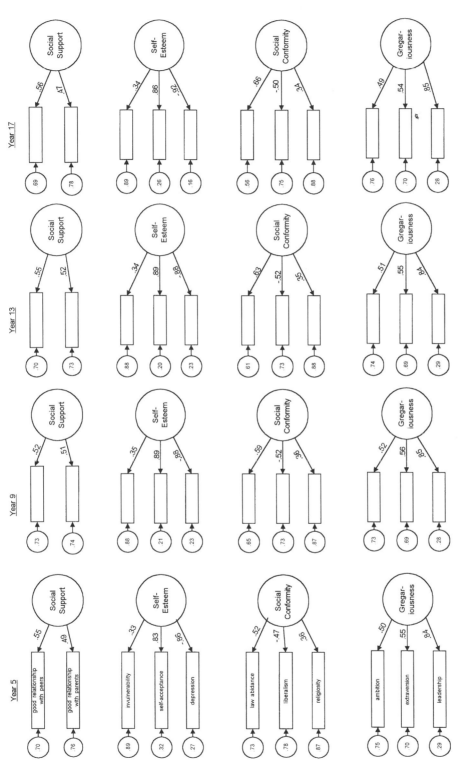

FIGURE 14.2. Latent factor structure. Measurement model from the confirmatory factor analysis (CFA). Rectangles are measured variables (repeatedly measured across the 4 years), large circles are latent constructs, and small circles are residual variances. All factor loadings are standardized and significant ($p < .001$). Correlations among all latent constructs from this CFA model are presented in Table 14.3.

TABLE 14.3. Factor Intercorrelations between Social Support and Personality Factors

Factor	1	2	3	4	5	6	7	8	9	10	11	12	13	14	15	16
Year 5																
1. Social support	—															
2. Self-esteem	.89***	—														
3. Social conformity	.63***	.44***	—													
4. Gregariousness	.42***	.44***	-.12	—												
Year 9																
5. Social support	.82***	.50***	.50***	.26***	—											
6. Self-esteem	.68***	.49***	.32***	.32***	.94***	—										
7. Social conformity	.33**	.20**	.80***	-.16*	.38***	.26***	—									
8. Gregariousness	.31***	.33***	-.10	.78***	.30***	.36***	-.22**	—								
Year 13																
9. Social support	.76***	.46***	.50***	.32***	.93***	.72***	.44***	.36***	—							
10. Self-esteem	.46***	.46***	.30***	.25***	.57***	.53***	.25***	.29***	.89***	—						
11. Social conformity	.21*	.24**	.69***	-.17*	.22*	.19**	.89***	-.12	.46***	.40***	—					
12. Gregariousness	.26**	.26***	-.08	.73***	.18*	.23***	-.22**	.84***	.42***	.39***	-.13	—				
Year 17																
13. Social support	.69***	.52***	.42***	.34***	.81***	.66***	.20	.41***	.79***	.60***	.20*	.30***	—			
14. Self-esteem	.49***	.39***	.36***	.24***	.54***	.48***	.24***	.30***	.69***	.67***	.37***	.34***	.88***	—		
15. Social conformity	.15	.11	.72***	-.17*	.16	.07	.80***	-.13	.27***	.23***	.89***	-.14	.21*	.34***	—	
16. Gregariousness	.26**	.29***	-.02	.70***	.17*	.23***	-.15*	.79***	.35***	.31***	-.04	.89***	.40***	.42***	-.05	—

*p < .05
**p < .01
***p < .001

Multiple-Group CFA Model

Since it is possible that either the factor structure or factor intercorrelations may be different for men and women, a series of multiple-group models were run (Newcomb, 1994a). The two groups were men and women, and the model tested was the final CFA model. Three models were run and difference X^2 tests used to evaluate factorial invariance and factor correlation differences.

The first multiple-group CFA model imposed no constraints between the groups. The second model imposed equality constraints on identical factor loadings for men and women. This model was slightly worse than the first model ($p < .05$). An examination of the Lagrangian Multiplier test (Chou & Bentler, 1990) revealed that two factor loadings were different for men compared to women. These were for good relationship with peers on Social Support (men = .59, women = .48) and law abidance on Social Conformity (men = .81, women = .62). These differences were not substantial and should not bias results based on a combined sample of men and women. Finally, we imposed equality constraints on both the factor loadings and all factor intercorrelations. This more constrained model did not differ significantly from either the factor-loadings-constrained model ($p > .50$) or the totally unconstrained model ($p > .50$).

Based on these findings, it is clear that very few, and minor, differences exist between the CFA models for men and women. Therefore, the samples of men and women were combined for the structural or path analyses to follow.

STRUCTURAL OR PATH MODELS

The latent factor structure confirmed in the CFA model was used as the foundation for the initial structural (STR), or path models. All within-time constructs (or their disturbance terms) were allowed to correlate freely; no within-time directional paths were allowed (only the correlations), since these are purely speculative, based only on theory, cannot establish any true causal order, and can bias or misspecify the model when they are imposed (Newcomb, 1990c, 1994a). In this first path model, only 4-year stability paths for repeated constructs were initially included.

As described elsewhere (Newcomb, 1994a), there are basically three approaches to testing paths among latent constructs. One technique is to test only hypothesized paths. The advantage of this approach is that it is theoretically driven. The disadvantage of this approach is that it capitalizes on hubris of the theory and researcher, since no other possible paths or lack of path (hypothesized no relation) are considered or directly tested (Newcomb, 1994b). A second technique is an additive (or forward-stepping) approach in which only the paths that have been hypothesized are included in the initial STR model. The next step in such an approach is to test all paths that were held at zero to determine if they are significant (Newcomb, 1994b). If any of these are significant, they are then added to the path model. The third approach is a subtractive (or step-down) method. In this approach, all paths (whether hypothesized or not) are included in the initial STR model. Then, all nonsignificant paths are removed.

The totally theory-driven method cannot be used here, since it allows no competing or unanticipated results and cannot be trusted, due to likely spurious conclusions (Newcomb, 1994b). Although the subtractive method has certain advantages (Newcomb, 1994a), the additive approach was chosen for the current analyses. This was due

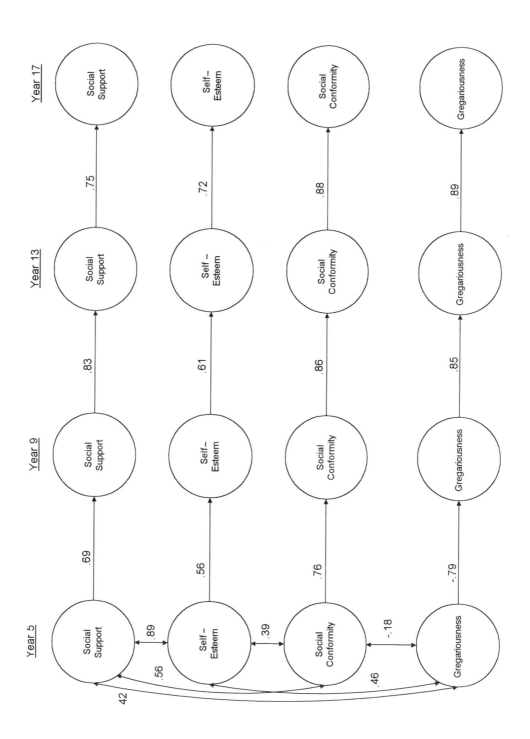

to the very high associations among most of the latent constructs, which often lead to estimation difficulties, colinearities, and uninterpretable suppression effects.

The initial STR model estimated only included stability paths across time (although within-time correlations were also estimated). These stability paths were the only strongly expected or hypothesized across-time effects. This model fit the data well, $X^2/df = 1.46$, $p < .001$, CFI = .96, NNFI = .96, and is graphically depicted in Figure 14.3. As evident, all 4-year stability effects were positive and significant, ranging from a low for Self-Esteem from Year 5 to Year 9 (.56) to a high for Gregariousness from Year 13 to Year 17 (.89). In general, the magnitude of the stability paths increased with advancing age.

The final STR model was generated by adding paths to the initial stability–only STR model. Modification indices were used to add standard paths between latent constructs over time, as well as specific or nonstandard effects to the model (Chou & Bentler, 1990; Newcomb, 1994a). All significant paths between latent constructs over time were also added.

The specific paths were limited to three types of across-time effects, not strictly between latent variables. These possible paths were restricted to those (1) from earlier measured variables (or their residuals) to later latent constructs; (2) from earlier latent constructs to later measured variables; and (3) from earlier measured variables (or their residuals) to later measured variables (Newcomb, 1994a). Since the focus of this investigation is on the effects between social support and personality, a further limitation was imposed on the inclusion of specific effects. Only those specific paths between social support and its variables, and the personality constructs and their variables were included. No social support-to-social support or personality-to-personality specific effects were added to the model.

Six latent variable-to-latent variable paths and 14 specific effects were added to the model. Then, all nonsignificant parameters were removed, as guided by the Wald Test (Chou & Bentler, 1990). This final STR model fit the data quite well; $X^2df = 1.32$, $p < .001$, CFI = .97, NNFI = .97. Figure 14.4 depicts the significant paths between the latent factors, and the 14 specific effects are listed in Table 14.4. The information provided in Figure 14.4 and Table 14.4 are taken from the same final STR model and must be considered in conjunction with each other; they are only presented separately for the sake of clarity. The findings presented in Figure 14.4 are strictly factor-to-factor results, whereas those findings reported in Table 14.4 are all specific or nonstandard effects.

In Figure 14.4, it can be seen that Year 5 Gregariousness reduced Year 9 Social Conformity, and Year 5 Social Conformity increased Year 13 Self-Esteem and Year 17 Social Support. The most interesting aspects of this figure are the significant positive paths from earlier Social Support to later Self-Esteem, in conjunction with the deletion of the Self-Esteem stability paths. This pattern was evident for all three time spans. A careful examination of the CFA intercorrelation matrix helps explain these unusual

---

FIGURE 14.3. Initial path or structural model. This model includes only stability paths over time; no cross-lagged effects were initially included. Correlations among the disturbance terms at each assessment were allowed but are not depicted for the sake of clarity (their magnitudes are similar to the correlations among independent constructs included in the figure). Path coefficients are standardized, and all parameter estimates are significant ($p < .001$).

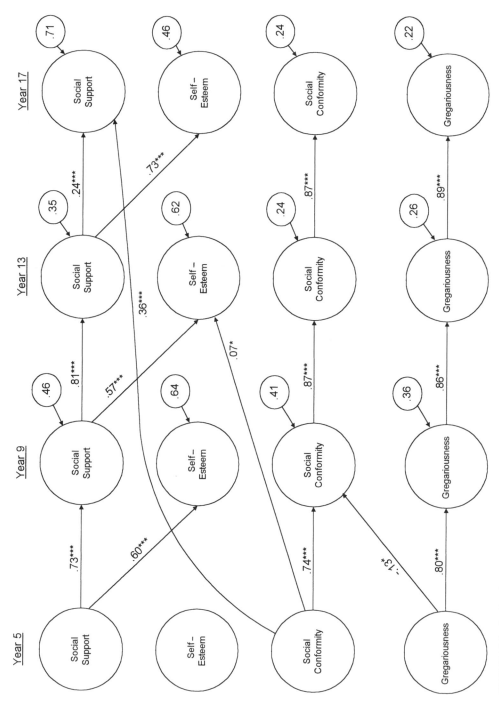

FIGURE 14.4. Final path or structural model. This figure includes only significant across-time effects between latent constructs; specific or nonstandard effects from this same final model are presented in Table 14.4. All path coefficients are standardized (*p < .05; ***p < .001).

TABLE 14.4. Specific Effects for the Final Structural or Path Model

Predictor	Outcome	Standardized parameter estimate
Religiosity 5 (R)	Social Support 9	.10**
Ambition 5 (R)	Good relationship with peers 9	.06*
Depression 5 (R)	Good relationship with peers 13	−.10*
Law abidance 5 (R)	Good relationship with peers 13	.11**
Religiosity 5 (R)	Good relationship with peers 13	.09**
Extraversion 5 (R)	Good relationship with peers 13	.11***
Law Abidance 9 (R)	Good relationship with peers 13	.08*
Ambition 9 (R)	Good relationship with parents 13	.10***
Social support 9	Self-acceptance 13	.06*
Good relationship with parents 5 (R)	Depression 13	−.04*
Good relationship with peers 5 (R)	Extraversion 13	.06*
Self-esteem 9	Good relationship with peers 17	.28***
Self-esteem 9	Good relationship with parents 17	.21***
Ambition 13 (R)	Good relationship with parents 17	.11**

*$p < .05$
**$p < .01$
***$p < .001$

and unexpected effects. What is noticed is that at each interval, later Self-Esteem was more highly correlated with earlier Social Support than with earlier Self-Esteem. In other words, the cross-lagged correlations between prior Social Support and later Self-Esteem were consistently stronger than were the stability effects for Self-Esteem. Therefore, when these cross-lagged paths were entered into the STR model, the stability paths for Self-Esteem became nonsignificant.

By combining the results from Figure 14.4 with the 14 significant specific or nonstandard effects from Table 14.4 and focusing on cross-lagged effects between social support and personality, the following six possible types of relationships can be examined: (1) five from earlier Social Support to later Self-Esteem variables; (2) none from earlier Social Support to later Social Conformity variables; (3) one from earlier Social Support to later Gregariousness measures; (4) three from earlier Self-Esteem to later Social Support variables; (5) five from earlier Social Conformity to later Social Support variables; and (6) four from earlier Gregariousness to later Social Support variables.

INTEGRATION OF FINDINGS AND THEORY

These results present some intriguing, informative, and theoretically meaningful associations and plausible causal relationships between social support and personality, both within-time and over time. Each of these are reviewed.

The three constructs were selected to reflect different domains of personality and individual differences, including affect and self-evaluation (Self-Esteem), attitudes toward conventionality (Social Conformity), and interpersonal adeptness (Gregariousness). These personality constructs were modestly to moderately correlated, verifying that each captures unique aspects of intrapersonal functioning.

The most surprising finding was the very few, significant cross-lagged paths between the latent construct of Social Support and the three personality constructs. Based on theory and prior research, we had expected more significant effects between these constructs over time. Social Support and the three personality factors were significantly correlated within each time but had few reciprocal effects across time. Nevertheless, there were several intriguing specific or nonstandard prospective effects between indicators of these constructs. Numerous explanations may account for these results.

These new findings are discussed in regard to several themes that include stability effects, associations among personality and social support constructs, reciprocal effects between these two domains, theoretical implications, developmental period, and time lags. Each of these topics are considered in turn.

STABILITY EFFECTS

All across-time stability effects were highly significant for both personality and social support latent variables, indicating a high degree of continuity in personality and perceived adequacy of social support over a 12-year period. Self-Esteem appeared to be less stable over time than the other two personality traits, Social Conformity and Gregariousness, which is consistent with past results (Stein et al., 1986a; Conley, 1984b). Social Conformity reflects one's attitudes toward society and traditional values, whereas Gregariousness is one's interactional style toward other people and the world. On the other hand, Self-Esteem partly reflects affect or self-feelings that perceived judgement of others invokes in the self. Because of this affective component, one's self-theory, or Self-Esteem, seems to be less stable across time compared to Social Conformity or Gregariousness. In other words, the affective components of Self-Esteem make it relatively more state-like than trait-like, particularly in comparison to the other two personality constructs (e.g., Hertzog & Nesselroade, 1987). However, the operative word here is *relatively*, since, clearly, even Self-Esteem has substantial stability over these 12 years, and therefore is certainly a personality trait within a more global perspective. Nevertheless, this does suggest that the personality construct of Self-Esteem has more room for change (due to its lower stability paths) compared to Social Conformity and Gregariousness, where the stability effects are so high that there is little variance left to be influenced by other factors.

ASSOCIATIONS BETWEEN PERSONALITY AND SOCIAL SUPPORT

There were significant and positive intercorrelations between Social Support and the three personality latent constructs at each period of measurement. These reflect cross-sectional associations and cannot establish any causal priority.

As previous research has demonstrated, Social Support was closely linked to Self-Esteem, Social Conformity, and Gregariousness. Especially, the relation of Social Support to Self-Esteem was considerably high, indicating a substantial degree of association between perceived inadequacy of social support and self-evaluations (Newcomb, 1990a). Although lower in magnitude in regard to correlations, Social Support was also associated with greater Social Conformity and more Gregariousness.

The strong association between Social Support and Self-Esteem may perhaps be due in part to the more affective component of Self-Esteem, which may parallel the affective aspects of Social Support that result from the satisfaction and quality of such interpersonal contact. It is possible that self-evaluations (i.e., self-esteem) are partly influenced by reactions of others to the person (as reflected in social support). Similarly, others may be more supportive when they perceive a person as confident and self-assured.

Since Gregariousness also implies the manner in which one interacts with others, it is somewhat surprising that it was only moderately correlated with Social Support. However, the perceived valence (positive or negative) of this Gregariousness was not captured in the construct, and certainly ambition and leadership can be expressed in invasive, intrusive, and obnoxious ways. Therefore, this ambiguity may have attenuated the association between these constructs, despite their apparent similarity in dealing with others. Nevertheless, it remains clear that those who perceive themselves as more gregarious also perceive a more supportive social network of parents and peers.

Finally, Social Support was also moderately related to greater Social Conformity. In other words, those who conform to traditional values also perceive greater support from important others. This is not surprising and may reflect either a selection process, socialization process, or both. A selection process might occur, whereby conforming individuals attract greater support from others, since they are more predictable, reliable, and in harmony with traditional social norms. A socialization process may occur, whereby individuals may become more social conforming in response to the supportiveness of others, in order to fit in and be even more accepted.

Reciprocal Effects

Each of these positions suggest that reciprocal effects should have been found between Social Support and the three personality constructs over time. Although several of these were found, the larger conclusions are that these constructs are highly intercorrelated within time and highly stable across time.

The major goal of this chapter is to consider the reciprocal and potential relations between three aspects of personality and social support during a 12-year period in which major life changes take place. Our findings reveal some support that bidirectional relations exist between these domains of psychosocial functioning between late adolescence and adulthood.

Self-Esteem and Social Support

Most interesting and rather surprising, the latent construct of Social Support consistently predicted later Self-Esteem at each of the developmental spans. However, when this occurred, the stability paths for Self-Esteem were reduced to nonsignificance. As discussed, earlier Social Support was a better predictor of later Self-Esteem than was earlier Self-Esteem. This clearly demonstrates the vital role of the social environment on shaping an individual's affective, self-appraisal form of personality we are calling self-esteem.

These findings are consistent with the "looking-glass" theory (Cooley, 1902; Mead, 1934). Social interactions with significant others in various settings provide important evaluative feedback for an individual. By internalizing these evaluative judgments of others, individuals define themselves in terms of responses they arouse in others. Affect or self-feelings that the judgment of others invoke in the self also become an important part of the self-concept (see Harter, 1983). Even during late adolescence and early adulthood, the degree to which one felt accepted and supported by one's parents and friends led to positive feelings about, and evaluations of, the self.

In fact, external stressors create instability and fluctuations in self-esteem (Harter, 1983). The life transitions from adolescence to young adulthood, and young adulthood to adulthood, are fraught with external changes and new life demands in terms of occupation and interpersonal roles (e.g., Newcomb, 1996). Therefore, these critical stages may be particularly sensitive to changes and influences on self-esteem due to the new external demands and changes. The perceived quality of social relationships with peers and parents clearly affects self-feelings and evaluations during these developmental stages.

Conversely, the construct of Self-Esteem did not significantly influence Social Support at any interval. However, several specific effects lent some support for a reverse pathway from Self-Esteem to some of the indicators of Social Support, which is consistent with the findings of Newcomb (1990a). For instance, earlier depression reduced the quality of later peer relationships. Similarly, earlier Self-Esteem increased later support from both peers and parents. The hypothesis that Self-Esteem and Social Support influence each other in a bidirectional manner was thus confirmed (not with the paths between the latent constructs but with the specific or nonstandard paths).

Gregariousness and Social Support

All possible pathways between the Gregariousness and Social Support latent variables across time were nonsignificant over all intervals. However, several significant effects emerged between indicators of these two constructs. There were more specific effects from the indicators of Gregariousness to the indicators of Social Support, rather than the reverse effect from the latter to the former. Extraversion is one of the personality traits that are highly stable over time and are fairly well established in early childhood (Emmerich, 1964). Extraversion was also shown to change little between early adolescence and young adulthood (Stein et al., 1986b). Thus, the relatively strong effects of Gregariousness on Social Support seem to be consistent with Scarr and McCartney's (1983) active genotype–environment effect hypothesis. According to this view, a gregarious individual actively seeks out a niche that is compatible with his or her disposition. For example, an outgoing person may find a job in which considerable social skills are required. Obtaining this job may further help the person to build up and maintain social networks with rewarding ties.

Social Conformity and Social Support

The paths between the Social Conformity and Social Support latent variables showed that the former in Year 5 significantly influenced the latter in Year 17. But the reverse pathway from Social Support to Social Conformity was not significant at any interval. The effect of social conformity in late adolescence was not immediately apparent but only appeared after more than a decade had passed. The socially conforming attitudes seem to have accumulating effects on the trajectory of an individual over time. Lack of social conformity is likely to lead adolescents to get involved in drug use and other problem behaviors such as school dropout, delinquent behaviors, and precocious sexual involvement (e.g., McGee & Newcomb, 1992; Newcomb & Bentler, 1988a). By the progressive accumulation of the consequences of deviant behaviors, these youths increasingly select themselves into life circumstances that further reinforce their deviant tendencies (Caspi, Elder, & Bem, 1988; Kaplan, 1980, 1986; Scarr & McCartney, 1983). Deviant orientations and behavior are likely to alienate an individual from traditional social institutions such as family. There was, however, no evidence that social support increases social conformity over time, which is inconsistent with Durkheim's (1897/1951) social integration theory.

The lack of significant paths from Social Support to Social Conformity may be due to the developmental periods on which we focused in the present study. Past research has emphasized the importance of quality of the early parent–child relationship, parenting style, and family environment for a child's readiness to be socialized (see Maccoby & Martin, 1983). Family disruptions and maternal drug use, for example, have been shown to contribute to early adolescents' deviant or nontraditional attitudes (Newcomb & Bentler, 1988c). It is plausible that by late adolescence, an individual's deviant or socially nonconforming attitudes are already well established and are unlikely to be influenced by social support.

THEORETICAL IMPLICATIONS

Modest support for bidirectional relations between Self-Esteem and Social Support, and between Gregariousness and Social Support (not with the paths between the latent constructs, but with the nonstandard paths) provides evidence for reciprocal transactions between the person and the environment (Mischel, 1973, 1990). For example, a gregarious and outgoing person is likely to be friendly and sociable toward other people. These behaviors, in turn, may evoke positive and accepting responses from her or his social environment. This positive feedback further maintains and reinforces the person's gregarious or extraverted tendencies.

More generally, however, a tentative theoretical model can be proposed based on the present evidence. Analyses clearly demonstrate a distinction among the personality constructs. Self-Esteem appears to be more unstable and includes a substantial degree of affect and self-evaluation. Gregariousness and Social Conformity are different to the extent that they are more enduring and stable across time, lack an affective or self-evaluative component, are more attitudinal and interpersonally oriented, and may be more family established earlier in life than Self-Esteem.

Based on these distinctions and the results of the present study, it appears that gregariousness and social conformity precede and help shape and establish social support (and not the reverse). Sequentially, social support influences self-esteem, which in turn contributes to construction of a social support network. In other words, traditional personality traits of social conformity and gregariousness lead to social support, which then contributes to self-esteem, which in a feedback loop, also helps mold one's social environment in terms of social support. This may be an interesting model that should be explored in future developmental research.

DEVELOPMENTAL PERIOD

As suggested earlier, there may be critical periods for the optimal and salient mutual influence of social psychological factors on each other over time. Based on theory and empirical evidence (e.g., Mischel, 1973; Newcomb, 1990a), and abundant anecdotal evidence going back to Freud and even earlier, we know that the social environment shapes individuals, and that individuals help select and modify their social milieu. In this particular instance of social support and personality, it appears that much of this cross-fertilization occurs prior to late adolescence, and that reciprocal effects subsequent to adolescence are few.

The energetic and volatile cross-influence between personality and social support apparently occur at earlier stages in life, either in childhood or young adolescence. The current approach of using SEMs should be an appropriate technique to elucidate such processes with appropriate samples and data (e.g., Connell, 1987). In other words, we remain convinced that social support and personality do influence and shape each other much more than revealed in the present analyses. However, we expect these effects to occur at younger ages or more sensitive or critical periods when these characteristics are more malleable and less entrenched. Therefore, our focus should shift to earlier developmental periods to establish more precisely whether reciprocal processes help develop both personality and social support.

The evidence for this conclusion is based on two prominent features of the current analyses. The first piece of evidence is the substantial correlations between social support and the personality traits even during late adolescence, demonstrating that they are highly related. This suggests that they may have been mutually influential at a younger age, or that a third or spurious influence generated them both (Newcomb, 1990c). Without additional data, it is impossible to confirm or disconfirm either of these possibilities. The second piece of evidence is the high stability effects of all constructs. As discussed earlier, this high degree of state dependence, or stability, reduces the potential influence any other variable may have on them. However, since stability tends to increase with age (e.g., Stein et al., 1986a), it is likely that these psychosocial constructs may have been more malleable and amenable to change at younger ages.

Finally, the concerns raised by Hertzog and Nesselroade (1987) are not really applicable here, since all of the constructs under study conform to trait rather than state definitions. Although some may be considered relatively more state-like than others (i.e., Self-Esteem), they are all traits in the traditional sense, which is confirmed by their high degrees of across-time stability.

TIME LAGS

When trying to establish causal inferences in nonexperimental, naturally occurring data, the time lag between the cause and effect becomes critical. Not all causal processes occur within similar temporal frames. Some processes occur almost simultaneously, whereas others may take years and decades to emerge. Unfortunately, most research designs fail to take these variations in the causal process into consideration (Gollob & Reichardt, 1987).

In the present study, we incorporated 4-year time lags. We anticipated that as our subjects matured, it would take longer for causal effects and processes to occur. Given the relatively moderate to high stability paths, this assumption seems well founded. As we know, stability decreases with increasing time. Given that we considered effects from a minimum of a 4-year to a 12-year time lag, the present design appears appropriate.

However, if the causal effects between social support and personality occur at much shorter and nearly instantaneous intervals (Gollob & Reichardt, 1987), we clearly have missed them. These processes are probably more relevant for state rather than trait characteristics (Hertzog & Nesselroade, 1987), which is not relevant to the present constructs. Furthermore, shorter time intervals seem appropriate when studying these same constructs at much younger ages and should be examined in future research.

CONCLUSIONS

Our findings clearly show that Self-Esteem, Gregariousness, and Social Conformity tap different aspects of personality, which are differentially related to Social Support. Although the effects were few and weak, there was some support for a bidirectional and reciprocal relation between both Self-Esteem and Gregariousness, and Social Support. The consistent effects of Social Support on Self-Esteem across the three time-intervals provide further understanding of how social support produces beneficial effects in people.

Although several mean differences were noted for gender and time, very few structural differences were found for men compared to women. In the paths models, there were two clear conclusions: (1) that Social Support was highly correlated with higher Self-Esteem, greater Gregariousness, and more Social Conformity; and (2) that all constructs were quite stable over the 12-year period under study from late adolescence to adulthood.

The study of the interactional and causal processes between social support and personality is a very fertile area of inquiry. In this chapter, we have found that these psychosocial constructs are highly related, have some modest reciprocal effects from late adolescence to adulthood, are quite stable, and are probably more fluidly related and mutually influential during childhood and early adolescence.

ACKNOWLEDGMENTS

This research was supported by Grant No. DA 01070 from the National Institute on Drug Abuse. The assistance of Wendy Sallin and Julio Angulo is warmly appreciated.

REFERENCES

Aiken, L. S., Stein, J. A., & Bentler, P. M. (1994). Structural equation analyses of clinical subpopulation differences and comparative treatment outcomes: Characterizing the daily lives of drug addicts. *Journal of Consulting and Clinical Psychology, 62*, 488–499.

Bachman, J. G., O'Malley, P. M., & Johnston, J. (1978). *Adolescence to adulthood: Change and stability in the lives of young men.* Ann Arbor, MI: Institute for Sociological Research.

Baldwin, M. K. (1992). Relational schemas and the processing of social information. *Psychological Bulletin, 112,* 461–484.

Baumeister, R. F., & Leary, M. R. (1995). The need to belong: Desire for interpersonal attachments as a fundamental human motivation. *Psychological Bulletin, 117,* 497–529.

Bentler, P. M. (1980). Multivariate analysis with latent variables: Causal modeling. *Annual Review of Psychology, 31,* 419–456.

Bentler, P. M. (1990). Comparative fit indexes in structural models. *Psychological Bulletin, 107,* 238–246.

Bentler, P. M. (1995). *EQS Structural Equations Program Manual.* Encino, CA: Multivariate Software, Inc.

Block, J. (1971). *Lives through time.* Berkeley, CA: Bancroft Books.

Bowlby, J. (1988). Developmental psychiatry comes of age. *American Journal of Psychiatry, 145,* 1–10.

Brown, G. W., Andrews, B., Harris, T., Adler, Z., & Bridge, L. (1986). Social support, self-esteem and depression. *Psychological Medicine, 16,* 813–831.

Caspi, A., Elder, G. H. Jr., & Bem, D. J. (1988). Moving away from the world: Life-course patterns of shy children. *Developmental Psychology, 24,* 824–831.

Castro, F. G., Maddahian, E., Newcomb, M. D., & Bentler, P. M. (1987). A multivariate model of the determinants of cigarette smoking among adolescents. *Journal of Health and Social Behavior, 28,* 273–289.

Chou, C.-P., & Bentler, P. M. (1990). Model modification in covariance structure modeling: A comparison among likelihood ratio, Lagrange Multiplier, and Wald tests. *Multivariate Behavioral Research, 25,* 115–136.

Cohen, S., & Wills, T. A. (1985). Stress, social support, and the buffering hypothesis. *Psychological Bulletin, 98,* 310–357.

Conley, J. J. (1984a). Longitudinal consistency of adult personality: Self-reported psychological characteristics across 45 years. *Journal of Personality and Social Psychology, 47,* 1325–1333.

Conley, J. J. (1984b). The hierarchy of consistency: A review and model of the longitudinal findings on adult and individual differences in intelligence, personality and self-opinion. *Personality and Individual Differences, 5,* 11–25.

Connell, J. P. (1987). Structural equation modeling and the study of child development: A question of goodness of fit. *Child Development, 58,* 167–175.

Cooley, C. H. (1902). *Human nature and the social order.* New York: Schocken.

Cooley, C. H. (1909). *Social organization.* New York: Scribner's.

DePaulo, B. M., Dull, W. R., Greenberg, J. M., & Swaim, G. W. (1989). Are shy people reluctant to ask for help? *Journal of Personality and Social Psychology, 56,* 834–844.

Dunkel-Schetter, C., Folkman, S., & Lazarus, R. S. (1987). Correlates of social support receipt. *Journal of Personality and Social Psychology, 53,* 71–80.

Durkheim, E. (1951). *Suicide: A study in sociology.* Translated by J. A. Spaulding & G. Simpson. New York: Free Press. (Original published in 1897)

Emmerich, W. (1964). Continuity and stability in early social development. *Child Development, 35,* 311–332.

Gollob, H. F., & Reichardt, C. S. (1987). Taking account of time lags in causal models. *Child Development, 58,* 80–92.

Hansson, R. O., Jones, W. H., & Carpenter, B. N. (1984). Relational competence and social support. In P. Shaver (Ed.), *Review of personality and social psychology* (pp. 265–284). Beverly Hills: Sage.

Harter, S. (1983). Developmental perspectives on the self-system. In E. M. Hetherington (Ed.), *Handbook of child psychology: Vol. 4. Socialization, personality, and social development* (pp. 275–386). New York: Wiley.

Harter, S. (1986). Processes underlying the construction, maintenance, and enhancement of the self-concept in children. In J. Suls & A. Greenwald (Eds.), *Psychological perspectives on the self* (Vol. 3, pp. 137–181). Hillsdale, NJ: Erlbaum.

Harter, S. (1987). The determinants and mediational role of global self-worth in children. In N. Eisenberg (Ed.), *Contemporary issues in developmental psychology* (pp. 219–242). New York: Wiley.

Hazan, C., & Shaver, P. (1987). Romantic love conceptualized as an attachment process. *Journal of Personality and Social Psychology, 52,* 511–524.

Hertzog, C., & Nesselroade, J. R. (1987). Beyond autoregressive models: Some implications of the trait–state distinction for structural modeling of developmental change. *Child Development*, *58*, 93–109.

Hoffman, M. A., Levy-Shiff, R., & Ushpiz, V. (1993). Moderating effects of adolescent social orientation on the relation between social support and self-esteem. *Journal of Youth and Adolescence*, *22*, 23–31.

Hunt, J. V., & Eichorn, D. H. (1972). Material and child behaviors: A review of data from the Berkeley growth study. *Seminars in Psychiatry*, *4*, 4.

Jones, W. H. (1985). The psychology of loneliness: Some personality issues in the study of social support. In I. R. Sarason & B. R. Sarason (Eds.), *Social support: Theory, research and applications* (pp. 225–242). Dordrecht, The Netherlands: Martinus Nijhoff.

Jones, W. H., Freeman, J. E., & Goswick, R. A. (1981). Loneliness and social skill deficits. *Journal of Personality and Social Psychology*, *42*, 682–689.

Kaplan, H. B. (1980). *Deviant behavior in defense of self*. New York: Academic Press.

Kaplan, H. B. (1986). *Social psychological self-reference behavior*. New York: Plenum.

Katigbak, M. S., Church, T., & Akamine, T. X. (1996). Cross-cultural generalizability of personality dimensions: Relating indigenous and imported dimensions in two cultures. *Journal of Personality and Social Psychology*, *70*, 99–114.

Maccoby, E. E., & Martin, J. A. (1983). Socialization in the context of the family: Parent–child interaction. In E. M. Hetherington (Ed.), *Handbook of child psychology: Vol. 4. Socialization, personality, and social development* (pp. 1–102). New York: Wiley.

Marsh, H., & Hocevar, D. (1985). The application of confirmatory factor analysis to the study of self concept: First and higher-order factor structures and their invariance across groups. *Psychological Bulletin*, *97*, 565–582.

McGee, L., & Newcomb, M. D. (1992). General deviance syndrome: Expanded hierarchical evaluations at four ages from early adolescence to adulthood. *Journal of Consulting and Clinical Psychology*, *60*, 766–776.

Mead, G. H. (1934). *Mind, self, and society*. Chicago: University of Chicago Press.

Mischel, W. (1973). Toward a cognitive social learning reconceptualization of personality. *Psychological Review*, *80*, 252–283.

Mischel, W. (1990). Personality dispositions revisited and revised: A view after three decades. In L. A. Pervin (Ed.), *Handbook of personality: Theory and research* (pp. 111–134). New York: Guilford.

Mortimer, J. T., Finch, M. D., & Kumka, D. (1982). Persistence and change in development: The multidimensional self-concept. In P. B. Bates & O. G. Brim Jr. (Eds.), *Life-span development and behavior* (pp. 264–313). New York: Academic Press.

Moss, H. A., & Susman, E. J. (1980). Longitudinal study of personality development. In O. G. Brim Jr. & J. Kagan (Eds.), *Constancy and change in human development* (pp. 530–595). Cambridge, MA: Harvard University Press.

Nesselroade, J. R., & Baltes, P. B. (1974). Adolescent personality development and historical change: 1970–1972. *Monographs of the Society for Research in Child Development*, *39*, 1–79.

Newcomb, M. D. (1988). *Drug use in the workplace: Risk factors for disruptive drug use among young adults*. Dover, MA: Auburn House.

Newcomb, M. D. (1990a). Social support and personal characteristics: A developmental and interactional perspective. *Journal of Social and Clinical Psychology*, *9*, 54–68.

Newcomb, M. D. (1990b). Social support by many other names: Toward a unified conceptualization. *Journal of Social and Personal Relationships*, *7*, 479–494.

Newcomb, M. D. (1990c). What structural modeling techniques can tell us about social support. In I. G. Sarason, B. R. Sarason, & G. R. Pierce (Eds.), *Social support: An interactive view* (pp. 26–63). New York: Wiley.

Newcomb, M. D. (1994a). Drug use and intimate relationships among women and men: Separating specific from general effects in prospective data using structural equations models. *Journal of Consulting and Clinical Psychology*, *62*, 463–476.

Newcomb, M. D. (1994b). Families, peers, and adolescent alcohol abuse: A paradigm to study multiple causes, mechanisms, and outcomes. In R. A. Zucker, G. M. Boyd, & J. Howard (Eds.), *Development of alcohol problems: Exploring the biopsychosocial matrix of risk* (pp. 157–168). Rockville, MD: National Institute on Alcohol Abuse and Alcoholism.

Newcomb, M. D. (1996). Pseudomaturity among adolescents: Construct validation, sex differences, and associations in adulthood. *Journal of Drug Issues*.

Newcomb, M. D. (1997). Psychosocial predictors and consequences of drug use: A developmental perspective within a prospective study. *Journal of Addictive Disease*.

Newcomb, M. D., & Bentler, P. M. (1986). Loneliness and social support: A confirmatory hierarchical analysis. *Personality and Social Psychology Bulletin, 12*, 520-535.

Newcomb, M. D., & Bentler, P. M. (1988a). *Consequences of adolescent drug use: Impact on the lives of young adults*. Beverly Hills, CA: Sage Publications.

Newcomb, M. D., & Bentler, P. M. (1988b). Impact of adolescent drug use and social support on problems of young adults: A longitudinal study. *Journal of Abnormal Psychology, 97*, 64-75.

Newcomb, M. D., & Bentler, P. M. (1988c). The impact of family context, deviant attitudes, and emotional distress on adolescent drug use: Longitudinal latent-variable analyses of mothers and their children. *Journal of Research in Personality, 22*, 154-176.

Newcomb, M. D., & Chou, C.-P. (1989). Social support among young adults: Latent-variable models of quantity and satisfaction within six life areas. *Multivariate Behavior Research, 24*, 233-256.

Newcomb, M. D., Maddahian, E., & Bentler, P. M. (1986). Risk factors for drug use among adolescents: Concurrent and longitudinal analyses. *American Journal of Public Health, 76*, 525-531.

Parker, J. G., & Asher, S. R. (1987). Peer relations and later personal adjustment: Are low-accepted children at risk? *Psychological Bulletin, 102*, 357-389.

Pearlin, L. I. (1985). Social structure and processes of social support. In S. Cohen & S. L. Syme (Eds.), *Social support and health* (pp. 43-60). Orlando, FL: Academic Press.

Procidano, M. F., & Heller, K. (1983). Measures of perceived social support from friends and from family: Three validation studies. *American Journal of Community Psychology, 11*, 1-24.

Rook, K. S. (1984). The negative side of social interaction: Impact on psychological well-being. *Journal of Personality and Social Psychology, 46*, 1097-1108.

Rosenberg, M. (1979). Which significant others? *American Behavioral Scientist, 16*, 829-860.

Rutter, M., & Garmezy, N. (1983). Developmental psychopathology. In E. M. Hetherington (Ed.), *Handbook of child psychology: Vol. 4. Socialization, personality, and social development* (pp. 775-911). New York: Wiley.

Sarason, B. R., Pierce, G. R., & Sarason, I. G. (1990a). Social support: The sense of acceptance and the role of relationships. In *Social support: An interactive view* (pp. 97-128). New York: Wiley.

Sarason, I. G., Levine, H. M., Basham, R. B., & Sarason, B. R. (1983). Assessing social support: The Social Support Questionnaire. *Journal of Personality and Social Psychology, 44*, 127-139.

Sarason, B. R., Pierce, G. R., Shearin, E. N., Sarason, I. G., Waltz, J. A., & Poppe, L. (1991). Perceived social support and working models of self and actual others. *Journal of Personality and Social Psychology, 60*, 273-283.

Sarason, I. G., Sarason, B. R., & Pierce, G. R. (Eds.). (1990b). *Social support: An interactive view*. New York: Wiley.

Sarason, I. G., Sarason, B. R., & Shearin, E. N. (1986). Social support as an individual difference variable. *Journal of Personality and Social Psychology, 50*, 845-855.

Scarr, S., & McCartney, K. (1983). How people make their own environments: A theory of genotype-environment effects. *Child Development, 54*, 424-435.

Scheier, L. M., & Newcomb, M. D. (1993). Multiple dimensions of affective and cognitive disturbance: Latent variable models in a community sample. *Psychological Assessment: A Journal of Consulting and Clinical Psychology, 5*, 230-234.

Schulz, R., & Rau, M. T. (1985). Social support through the life course. In S. Cohen & S. L. Syme (Eds.), *Social support and health* (pp. 129-149). Orlando, FL: Academic Press.

Stein, J. A., Newcomb, M. D., & Bentler, P. M. (1986a). Stability and change in personality: A longitudinal study from early adolescence to young adulthood. *Journal of Research in Personality, 20*, 276-291.

Stein, J. A., Newcomb, M. D., & Bentler, P. M. (1986b). The relationship of gender, social conformity, and substance use: A longitudinal study. *Bulletin of the Society of Psychologists in Addictive Behaviors, 5*, 125-138.

Stein, J. A., Newcomb, M. D., & Bentler, P. M. (1987). Personality and drug use: Reciprocal effects across four years. *Personality and Individual Differences, 8*, 419-430.

Stein, J. A., Newcomb, M. D., & Bentler, P. M. (1994). Psychosocial correlates of AIDS risk behaviors, abortion, and drug use among a community sample of young adult women. *Health Psychology, 13,* 308–318.

Stokes, J. P. (1985). The relation of social network and individual difference variables to loneliness. *Journal of Personality and Social Psychology, 8,* 981–990.

Stueve, C. A., & Gerson, K. (1977). Personal relations across the life cycle. In C. S. Fisher, R. M. Jackson, C. A. Stueve, K. Gerson, L. M. Jones, & M. Baldassare (Eds.), *Networks and places: Social relations in the urban setting* (pp. 79–98). New York: Free Press.

Sullivan, H. S. (1953). *The interpersonal theory of psychiatry.* New York: Norton.

Vinokur, A., Schul, Y., & Caplan, R. D. (1987). Determinants of perceived social support: Interpersonal transactions, personal outlook, and transient affective states. *Journal of Personality and Social Psychology, 53,* 1137–1145.

CHAPTER 15

SOCIAL SUPPORT AND FEELINGS OF PERSONAL CONTROL IN LATER LIFE

NEAL KRAUSE

The purpose of this chapter is to explore the interface between feelings of personal control and social support in later life. As a number of researchers have pointed out (e.g., Rodin, 1990; Turner & Roszell, 1994), the construct of control has been operationalized in many different ways. Among the specific variables subsumed under this broad rubric are mastery (Pearlin & Schooler, 1978), fatalism (Wheaton, 1983), and locus-of-control orientation (Rotter, 1966). Although there are differences in the way these variables have been defined and measured, they nevertheless share a common conceptual core. Embedded within each measure is the notion that individuals with a strong sense of control believe that changes in their social environment are responsive to and contingent upon their own choices, efforts, and actions. In contrast, people with a weak sense of control believe that the events in their lives are shaped by forces outside their influence, and that they have little ability to affect the things that happen to them.

There has been a long-standing debate in the social and behavioral sciences on whether feelings of control decline in later life (e.g., Schulz, Heckhausen, & Locher, 1991). Although many investigators argue that people maintain a fairly stable sense of control over the life course (e.g., Brandtstadter & Rothermund, 1994), recent evidence suggests that there may be a nonlinear relationship between these constructs, and that feelings of control decline in an accelerating fashion with age (Mirowsky, 1995). The debate on changes in control over the life course has attracted considerable attention, because there is an extensive body of research linking feelings of personal control with

NEAL KRAUSE • School of Public Health and Institute of Gerontology, University of Michigan, Ann Arbor, Michigan 48109.

Sourcebook of Social Support and Personality, edited by Gregory R. Pierce, Brian Lakey, Irwin G. Sarason, and Barbara R. Sarason. Plenum Press, New York, 1997.

a wide range of health-related outcomes, including healthcare utilization, physical illness, psychological well-being, and numerous other types of health behavior (for reviews of this research see Rodin, Timko, & Harris, 1985; Schulz et al., 1991).

Given the central role played by the construct of control in gerontological research, it is not surprising to find that a number of investigators have tried to identify factors that promote (or erode) feelings of personal control in elderly people. One intriguing line of research focuses on the potentially important influence of social support. However, at least two major theoretical orientations divide this literature. According to proponents of the first perspective, feelings of control are shaped by the behavior and influence of significant others (e.g., Antonovsky, 1991; Krause, 1990). In contrast, adherents of the second view suggest that feelings of control affect social support, and that individuals with a strong sense of personal control subsequently utilize their social networks more often and more effectively than people who feel they can exert little control over their environment (e.g., Eckenrode, 1983; Sandler & Lakey, 1982). Even though the proponents of both perspectives make many valid points, the goal of this chapter is to show that it is important to take life-course factors into consideration, and that the first perspective may be especially relevant for the study of control in later life.

The discussion that follows is divided into four main sections. Conventional thinking on how social support may influence feelings of personal control is reviewed first. Following this, recent theoretical elaborations and extensions are presented. Next, issues in the conceptualization and measurement of personal control, as well as social support, are examined, with an eye toward refining the emerging theoretical framework. Finally, the chapter concludes by briefly evaluating a third perspective, which suggests that there may be a reciprocal relationship between control and social support. An effort is made at this juncture to reconcile the competing perspectives by bringing the critical element of timing to the foreground.

PREVAILING VIEWS ON HOW SUPPORT MAY AFFECT CONTROL

The idea that significant others bolster feelings of personal control rests on a fairly well-developed theoretical perspective that has its roots in the symbolic interaction tradition in sociology. Stated simply, self-assessments of one's abilities and competencies are thought to be the product of feedback received from significant others. This view is expressed unequivocally in the work of Cooley (1931, p. 198), who argues, "We have no means of knowing our self except by observing how others respond to it, and we can be assuredly ourselves only when we have had long experience of a certain kind of response."

Although these fundamental insights are useful (and even provocative), they fail to provide a sense of when and under what circumstances assistance from significant others tends to increase feelings of personal control. A necessary first step in developing this perspective is to briefly consider the different ways of classifying how individuals relate to their network members. Although there are many ways to handle this task, Rook's (1987) distinction between crisis support and companionship is especially useful. Crisis support refers to assistance that is given to help a person confront and resolve a stressful life event. In contrast, companionship involves relationships that are not oriented to problem solving but are instead pursued purely for the joy of self-expression and the enhancement of mutual interests.

A basic premise in this chapter is that both companionship and crisis support bolster feelings of control in later life. As Rook (1987) points out, companionship provides the opportunity to discuss aspirations and goals for the future. In the process of exploring these issues with intimate others, older adults may get valuable insights into how best to realize their goals. For example, elders may get good advice on how to best manage their financial plans, even though they are not currently experiencing an economic problem. Acting on this advice and enjoying the success that follows may enhance their sense of control over their economic future.

Although a plausible argument may be presented for showing that companionship enhances control, the main thrust of this chapter is on crisis support, because the impact of social relationships is perhaps most evident in this context. The work of Caplan (1981) provides a useful point of departure for showing why the life-stress perspective provides an especially useful forum for assessing this relationship. Caplan begins with the observation that undesirable stressors tend to erode an individual's cognitive and problem-solving capabilities. Due in part to the compromising of these important cognitive functions, Caplan comes to the now-familiar conclusion that stressful events erode feelings of mastery or control (see also Krause, 1987a; Pearlin, Menaghan, Lieberman, & Mullan, 1981).

According to Caplan's (1981) perspective, one of the primary functions of supportive others is to bolster and restore feelings of control that have been depleted by stressful events. In particular, he argues that social network members help to define the problem situation, develop a plan of action, assist in implementing the plan, and provide feedback and guidance as the plan is being executed. As a result of receiving this assistance, the stressed individual comes to believe that the problem situation can be overcome or controlled.

The framework developed by Caplan (1981) is important, because it has clear implications for the way that models are developed to assess the relationship between social support and feelings of personal control. If stress affects both support and control, but measures of life events are excluded from the model, then the observed correlation between support and control will contain variance that is due to the common dependence of these constructs on stress. Stated another way, if measures of stress are not included in the model, then researchers run the risk of observing a spurious relationship between social support and feelings of personal control.

Despite the intuitive appeal of Caplan's (1981) theoretical framework, empirical studies on the relationships among stress, social support, and feelings of personal control have failed to produce consistent results. Whereas some investigators find evidence that social support operates, as least in part, by replenishing feelings of control that have been depleted by stressful experiences, other researchers are unable to replicate these findings (see Cohen & Edwards, 1989, for a review of this research).

THEORETICAL EXTENSIONS AND ELABORATIONS

As the literature has evolved, it is becoming increasingly clear that the perspective developed by Caplan (1981) is incomplete, because it creates an overly optimistic view of the social support process. In particular, this framework conveys a sense that significant others are always willing to offer assistance, that support provided by social network members is always appropriate for the problem at hand, and that the stressed individual actively seeks out and gratefully receives this help. Three closely related bodies of research are reviewed here in order to provide a more balanced view of potentially supportive exchanges in later life. In the process, an effort is made to show how the insights provided by this literature further enrich our understanding of the potential control-enhancing functions of supportive social ties. The first line of thinking recognizes that there may be limits to the beneficial effects of support, and that increased assistance from others does not always promote greater feelings of personal control among older adults. The second group of studies suggests that significant others are not always a source of support, and that at times, negative feedback from social network members may actually tend to diminish perceptions of control. The final view indicates that social support may bolster feelings of control, but only when certain types of stressful events emerge.

LIMITS TO THE BENEFITS OF SOCIAL SUPPORT

Most researchers who examine the interface between social support and feelings of personal control specify and test for linear effects. Implicit in this strategy is the notion that more assistance is always better, and that individuals who receive the most support will experience the greatest benefits. However, research by Krause (1987b) suggests that there may be problems with this specification, because the relationship between support and control may be captured more accurately by estimating a nonlinear model. In essence, this nonlinear model predicts that, initially, increments in support from others will serve to bolster feelings of control. However, beyond a certain threshold point, receiving additional assistance from social network members may actually tend to erode control perceptions in later life. As Wheaton (1985) observes, there can be too much of a good thing. Longitudinal data gathered by Krause (1987b) from a sample of older adults provide empirical support for this nonlinear specification (see also Krause, 1995a).

There are at least two explanations for the findings observed by Krause (1987b): The first has to do with the potentially beneficial effects of stressful events, whereas the second involves general norms that are thought to govern social exchanges in later life. Even though stress is often thought of as a wholly negative experience, several investigators have argued that successfully confronting and resolving difficult life experiences may provide an opportunity for personal growth and development (e.g., Moos & Schaefer, 1986). However, it is important to identify how these positive effects may emerge. As Krause and Borawski-Clark (1994) point out, social support is sometimes thought of as helping people to help themselves. This means that although others are willing to assist persons in need, they do not (or often cannot) do everything for them. Instead, significant others may provide encouragement, advice, and even tangible resources needed to confront a difficult situation, but they often leave the main burden of resolving the problem up to the stressed individual. Feelings of control are especially likely to flourish in this context, because in the process of helping themselves, elderly people may come to feel as though they can control the course of events in their lives. In contrast, having significant others take complete charge of the problem situation is likely to foster feelings of dependence and enmeshment that may ultimately erode feelings of personal control.

It may also be especially important to consider the norms governing supportive exchanges in later life, because research reviewed by Lee (1985) suggests that older adults adhere strongly to the norm of reciprocity, and they actively try to avoid becoming overly dependent on others. It seems that the violation of this norm, coupled with the feelings of dependence discussed earlier, may serve to diminish feelings of control among elderly people.

Negative Interaction and Personal Control

An increasing number of studies that focus on older subjects suggest that interaction with others is not always positive, and that social network members may also be a source of unpleasant or negative interaction (e.g., Rook, 1984; Krause, 1995b). It is especially important for the purposes of this discussion to note that stress may play a potentially important role in promoting these undesirable encounters. For example, as Krause (1991) points out, significant others may be critical of an older adult for allowing the problem situation to arise, or for not adopting efficacious coping strategies to reduce the noxious effects of events after they have taken place.

Coyne, Wortman, and Lehman (1988) provide an interesting explanation for why significant others may react in a negative manner. According to these investigators, stressful events often affect social network members as well as the focal person. This means, for example, that if a man experiences financial difficulties, it is likely that his wife will be influenced by this event as well. Since wives are especially likely to be a primary source of support for men in later life (Antonucci, 1985), the spillover effect of this stressor may influence the nature of the assistance provided by the wife. In this instance, the wife has a stake in the successful resolution of the event. If her husband fails to resolve the financial crisis, in spite of her support, she may become emotionally overinvolved in the situation and inadvertently provide feedback that makes her husband feel guilty, incompetent, or even coerced into taking additional actions he may prefer not to pursue.

Regardless of the underlying mechanisms driving this process, being rebuffed by social network members during stressful times may be especially likely to affect feelings of personal control, because, as Caplan's (1981) research suggests, this is precisely the time when control-enhancing assistance is needed most. This view is consistent with the notion that requesting assistance and not receiving it may have more deleterious effects than never asking for help in the first place (Eckenrode & Wethington, 1990).

By extending Baltes's work on the support-dependence script, it is possible to provide evidence of yet another way in which the negative behavior of significant others can reduce feelings of control in later life (Baltes & Wahl, 1992). This research involves how significant others responded to older adults who were either suffering from chronic health problems, or who needed assistance with basic activities of daily living. In a sense, this study focuses on the response of network members to a particular type of stressor—chronic illness. The opportunity to engage in self-care activities (e.g., getting dressed without the assistance of others) is an important way to cope with chronic illness, because it represents one way of maintaining a sense of autonomy, independence, and control in the face of a debilitating problem. The goal of the study by Baltes and Wahl was to see how significant others react when older adults attempt to engage in self-care behaviors. Unfortunately, the findings reveal that social network members often respond to dependent behavior in an encouraging fashion, while ignoring or even explicitly disapproving independent self-care behaviors. This means, for example, that significant others discourage older adults from attempting to get dressed by themselves, and encourage dependent behaviors such as being fed by someone else. Baltes and Wahl point out that complying with these demands and engaging in dependent behavior tends to reduce competence and feelings of autonomy in older adults. Although the construct of control was not measured explicitly in this study, research suggests that encouragement of dependence tends to reduce feelings of personal control in later life (e.g., Rodin & Langer, 1977).

Assessing the Effects of Particular Types of Stressors

Up to this point, an emphasis has been placed on identifying the ways in which prevailing conceptions of social support may limit our understanding of how feelings of personal control emerge and are maintained in later life. However, limitations in the conceptualization and measurement of stress create similar problems as well. Researchers who examine the relationship between support and feelings of control within a life-stress perspective frequently rely on global checklists of stressors that assess exposure to a diverse range of life events. Implicit in this measurement strategy is the notion that all stressors are capable of eroding feelings of control, and that the noxious effects of virtually every kind of life event are offset effectively by assistance from social network members. However, as the discussion of negative interaction in the previous section reveals, this is a dubious assumption. Instead, greater insights may be gained by disaggregating global checklists and assessing whether social support has beneficial effects in the face of some types of stressors but not others.

A persistent problem facing those who wish to disaggregate global stress indices is how to develop meaningful alternative measures. Outside the work of Kessler and his associates (e.g., Kessler, McLeod, & Wethington, 1985), there has been little guidance in the literature. Part of the problem arises from the fact that investigators do not have a compelling theoretical framework to serve as the basis for partitioning life events into substantively meaningful categories. Fortunately, recent extensions of identity theory provide a promising way to begin resolving this problem (Burke, 1991; Thoits, 1987).

Social roles, and the identities associated with these roles, form the core of identity theory (see McCall & Simmons, 1966, for a detailed discussion of this perspective). A *social role* is defined structurally as a position in a group (e.g., father, husband, university faculty member). An *identity* is a self-evaluation that emerges from occupying a given role. For example, fatherhood becomes part of a man's identity when he becomes a father and begins to think of himself in that way. Associated with each role are clusters of norms or behavioral expectations. These norms specify the appropriate behavior for a given role and serve as the basis for evaluating whether role performance is adequate. This basic regulatory function provides guidance, meaning, and purpose in life. According to Thoits (1991), stressors arising in certain roles may exert an especially noxious effect, because they have the potential to undermine the identity associated with that role.

A major premise in this extension of identity theory is that all stressors do not exert a similar effect. Individuals typically occupy a number of different roles. Consequently, there is a separate identity associated with each of these social positions. However, some roles are valued more highly than others. In fact, social psychologists have argued for some time that these individual identities are organized into a salience hierarchy reflecting various levels of commitment to and investment in the roles associated with these identities (e.g., Stryker, 1987). Thoits (1991) and Burke (1991) maintain that if some roles are valued more highly than others, then the impact of stressors arising in various roles depends upon where these roles are located in the salience hierarchy: Stressors emerging in roles that are valued highly will have a more deleterious effect than events that arise in roles that are less important to an individual.

The work of Erikson (1959) provides a basis for arguing that stressors arising in salient roles may exert an especially noxious impact in later life. His widely cited theory of aging specifies that the life course may be divided into eight stages, each posing unique developmental challenges. The final stage to emerge in later life is characterized by the crisis of integrity versus despair. This is a time of introspection and life review, when an individual comes to grips with the kind of person he or she has become over the years. Cast in the language of identity theory, the eighth stage may be described as a time for reconciling the ideal self and the real self by coming to grips with the inevitable gap between role prescriptions and actual role enactments. Older adults may be especially vulnerable to events arising in salient roles, because these life events may drive a wedge between the real and ideal selves, thereby compromising the process of identity crystallization that is supposed to take place during this time. Perhaps failure to meet the developmental challenge identified by Erikson increases the probability that an elderly person will slip into despair.

Despite the intuitive appeal of the theoretical framework provided by identity theory, subsequent empirical tests of this perspective have produced inconsistent results. Whereas research by Krause (1994) tends to support the basic tenets embedded in this perspective, Thoits (1995) has been unable to demonstrate that stressors arising in highly valued roles have a disproportionately greater effect. Although there are undoubtedly many reasons for these inconclusive findings, one potential explanation is especially relevant for the purposes of this chapter. In particular, Thoits focuses solely on the direct effects of stress on well-being, without exploring the potentially important role that social support and feelings of personal control may play in this process. By examining this issue in an identity theory framework, it may be possible to provide a more fully articulated view of how social support influences feelings of personal control in later life.

The discussion that follows elaborates and extends recent work by Krause and Borawski-Clark (1994). This study was designed to test the hypothesis that social support offsets the noxious effects of salient role stressors on feelings of personal control, but that comparable buffering effects will not emerge when events arise in roles that are valued less highly by elderly people. Three lines of research that developed in a largely independent manner form the theoretical underpinnings of this proposition: The first is reviewed by Eckenrode and Wethington (1990), the second may be found in the work of Hobfoll (1989), and the third comes from extensive research by Baltes and Baltes (1990).

Eckenrode and Wethington (1990) note that when stressors arise, individuals seek out assistance from others only after they have been unable to resolve the problem situation on their own. Although the reasons for this finding are not entirely clear, perhaps part of the explanation may be found by examining the norms surrounding the social support process. Social support is not an unlimited resource. Consequently, significant interpersonal costs may be incurred if repeated requests for assistance are made, because significant others may feel that they are being taken advantage of (see, e.g., La Gaipa, 1990). Because of the potential costs associated with mobilizing support from others, older adults must decide when to spend their social capital. Unfortunately, the factors that influence this decision have not been described fully in the literature.

Hobfoll's (1989) conservation of resources perspective provides a potentially useful explanation for determining when social support networks will be mobilized. According to this view, people are especially motivated to actively confront the effects of life events that threaten things they value highly. Further insights into the process of support mobilization may be found by extending the concept of selective optimization that was developed by Baltes and Baltes (1990). These investigators note that although there is considerable variation in the process of aging, people nevertheless encounter a disproportionately greater number of undesirable changes as they age. For example, Baltes (1991) reviews research that indicates the loss of certain cognitive functions with advanced age. Even so, Baltes and Baltes (1990) maintain that most elders cope successfully with these losses by focusing their efforts on the life domains of greatest importance, while simultaneously investing less effort and resources in domains that are valued less highly.

The common thread that unites the work of Hobfoll (1989) and Baltes and Baltes (1990) is that individuals will focus their efforts on those life domains that are most important to them. By merging these insights with the work reviewed by Eckenrode and Wethington (1990), it may be possible to more clearly specify when older adults will turn to others for assistance. Whereas older adults may be especially inclined to seek help when events arise in roles they value highly, they may be less willing to run the risk of encountering resentment and rejection by requesting assistance with life events that arise in domains that are not as important to them.

Krause and Borawski-Clark (1994) develop this perspective further by arguing that the potential benefits associated with receiving assistance from others may be maximized when older adults receive help with events that arise in highly valued roles. These investigators suggest that the concerted efforts exerted by elders to confront salient role stressors may be enhanced by an added sensitivity on the part of support providers. In particular, significant others may be more willing to afford great latitude to the stressed person when they are aware that these individuals are grappling with an event that is highly salient, and that threatens core elements in their identity. Instead of being quick to affix blame, social network members may be more willing to overlook and even downplay any part the stressed person may have played in bringing on his or her problem. Moreover, support providers may be less critical of failed coping efforts when the precipitating event arises in a highly salient role. It seems that the control-enhancing function of social support systems identified by Caplan (1981) should be especially likely to emerge under these circumstances.

Using data provided by a nationwide sample of older adults, Krause and Borawski-Clark (1994) found support for this theoretical rationale. In particular, this research revealed that social support tends to buffer the effects of salient role stressors on feelings of personal control, but assistance from others does not reduce the noxious effects of events arising in roles that are valued less highly.

Taken as a whole, the research reviewed in this section begins to lay the groundwork for developing a plausible rationale for linking social support with feelings of control in later life. Beginning with the simple proposition that assistance from others serves to restore and enhance control perceptions, this perspective aims to tease out the fine points of the social support process by specifying when help from others is beneficial, and when it may be less efficacious. Although this discussion may have provided some useful insights, it still remains underdeveloped. Up until this point, social support, as well as feelings of personal control, have been discussed in a general way, without specifically paying attention to measurement issues. A central premise of this chapter is that if further advances are to be made, then issues in the conceptualization and measurement must be addressed head-on. The intent of the next section is briefly to pursue this issue.

ISSUES IN THE MEASUREMENT OF CONTROL AND SUPPORT

Social support and feelings of personal control are not precise constructs that refer to distinct and clearly circumscribed entities. Instead, they are umbrella terms that subsume a rather broad range of related yet discernible conceptualizations. Although it is not possible to explore all of the ways in which these constructs have been used in the literature, the goal of this section is to highlight a few applications that may be especially relevant for studying the interface between support and control in later life.

ALTERNATIVE SPECIFICATIONS OF CONTROL

Researchers investigating the interface between stress, social support, and feelings of control typically rely on global measures that are thought to assess feelings of control over life as a whole. The Internal–External Locus of Control (I-E) Scale developed by Rotter (1966) is used frequently in these studies. There are at least two problems with this approach. First, it overlooks the possibility that older adults may feel as though they can exercise more control in some areas or domains of their life than in others. Second, the use of standard measures may not be sensitive to the ways in which people strive to maintain feelings of control in later life. In particular, recent efforts to introduce the notion of secondary control (i.e., accommodating oneself to the environment rather than attempting to change it) provide an opportunity to further delineate the social foundations of control perceptions in elderly populations. The theoretical rationale for focusing on domain-specific measures of control, as well as the utility of examining secondary control, is presented later.

There is growing evidence in the gerontological literature that feelings of personal control may not be consistent across all areas of life, and that elderly people may feel that they can exercise more control in some domains than in others (see Schulz et al., 1991, for a review of this research). For example, some older adults may feel that they have more control over their interpersonal relationships than their personal financial circumstances. This may be especially true for elderly people who are retired and living on fixed incomes. If this perspective is valid, then fundamental questions must be raised about what is captured by global control items.

Many global scales of control contain some variant of the following item: "When I make plans, I am almost certain I can make them work" (Rotter, 1966). Unfortunately, the cognitive processes that respondents engage in when answering this type of question have not been examined fully. If the research reviewed by Schulz et al. (1991) is accurate, then study participants may think about their ability to exercise control in various areas or domains of life, and then perform some sort of mental arithmetic to arrive at a global or overall evaluation. However, it is not known whether some domains are differentially weighted in this process.

The possibility that feelings of control may vary across different domains has important implications for studies on the interface between stress, social support, and feelings of personal control in later life. In particular, relying on more focused measures of control may provide greater insight into the relationship between stress and control, as well as the role played by significant others in bolstering feelings of control that have been depleted by stressful life events.

When an event arises in a given area in life, it seems reasonable to look for the impact of that stressor on feelings of control over the same domain. For example, financial difficulty may have the greatest effect on feelings of control over one's personal finances. In contrast, the use of a global control measure may produce less dramatic results, because these assessments are presumably based on a wide range of experiences arising in roles that may not be affected directly by a given stressor.

Empirical support for focusing on domain-specific measures of control is provided in a recent study by Krause (1994). This research contrasts the effects of salient role stressors on global control, as well as feelings of control that are associated with the same domains in which the salient events emerged. The findings suggest that the impact of salient role stressors on domain-specific measures of control is considerably greater than the corresponding effect on feelings of control over life as a whole.

Focusing on domain-specific measures of control may also assist us in thinking about how significant others may help to enhance feelings of control in later life. Even a moment's reflection suggests that when specific stressors emerge, older adults turn to significant others to help resolve the particular problem at hand. Put another way, it seems unlikely that elders are deliberately looking for others to change their worldview by bolstering their feelings of control over life as a whole. Similarly, it is doubtful that significant others offer assistance with the intent of influencing the global perceptions of the elder in need. Instead, as the theoretical insights provided by Caplan (1981) suggest, assistance from others is very problem focused and geared specifically toward resolving the particular stressor that has emerged. Given the goals and orientations of the support provider as well as the support recipient, it seems that researchers are likely to observe the greatest impact of support on control if they focus on feelings of control over the same domain in which the stressor emerged. The intent here is not to imply that support cannot influence global perceptions of control. As noted earlier, existing research suggests otherwise. Rather, the point is that if one is searching for the more immediate and perhaps the strongest effects of support, then it may be especially helpful to work with domain-specific measures of control. Empirical support for this view is provided by Krause and Borawski-Clark (1994). Their work indicates that support offsets the deleterious effects of salient role stressors on domain-specific measures of control. However, similar stress-buffering functions were not observed when a global measure of control served as the dependent variable.

Recent research by Schulz and his colleagues on the distinction between primary and secondary control provides yet another way to highlight the social underpinnings of control perceptions in later life (e.g., Schulz et al., 1991; Heckhausen & Schulz, 1993). Primary control refers to efforts that are aimed at changing or shaping the social environment to fit the goals or needs of the individual. In contrast, secondary control involves changing internal goals, expectancies, and causal attributions in order to accommodate oneself to the external world. Although secondary control can be achieved in a number of ways, one is especially relevant for the purposes of this chapter. In particular, older adults can derive a sense of secondary control by aligning themselves with powerful others. This specific application is closely akin to Antonovsky's (1979) notion of a sense of coherence. According to this view, control is relinquished to a significant other, who then acts in the best interest of the focal person. This means, for example, that an elderly widow may be able to preserve a sense of control over her financial situation by having her son manage her fiscal affairs. In this way, she is able to maintain a sense that "things are under control," even though she is not personally in charge of the situation herself (Antonovsky, 1979, p. 155).

There are three reasons why focusing on secondary control may provide useful insights into the social support process in later life. First, given the physical and cognitive declines that are encountered frequently in later life, Schulz et al. (1991) argue that people are increasingly likely to turn to secondary control strategies as they age. Second, as Heckhausen and Schulz (1993) point out, the goal of engaging in and pursuing secondary control is to enhance primary control efforts in other areas. More specifically, relinquishing control in some domains to benevolent significant others makes it possible to devote limited resources to the maintenance of primary control in other areas that are valued highly. Third, and perhaps most important, the whole notion of deriving control from the benevolent actions of significant others serves to firmly anchor the genesis of control beliefs in a social support context: If significant others are not available or willing to act on behalf of an older adult, then it would not be possible to exercise secondary control.

ALTERNATIVE SPECIFICATIONS OF SUPPORT

The discussion that has been provided up to this juncture has taken a rather narrow view of the support process. As the literature has evolved, researchers have developed a number of different ways to conceptualize and measure supportive exchanges with others. In order to more clearly understand how support may influence feelings of personal control among older adults, it may be helpful to examine three facets, or dimensions, of the support process that are frequently overlooked: The first involves the potential control-enhancing benefits associated with providing assistance to others; the second is concerned with the important role played by formal sources of support in later life; and the third has to do with the perceived availability of support.

The wide majority of studies on the supportive social ties of elderly people focus exclusively on the benefits of receiving assistance from others (see Krause, 1989, for a review of this research). In contrast, relatively few studies have examined the potential advantages of providing support to others. This somewhat narrow orientation overlooks the basic fact that people strive to maintain a sense of balance or equity in their relations with others (e.g., Dowd, 1975), and that older adults may benefit from giving as well as receiving assistance from others. The lack of research on support provided to others is surprising, because over 20 years ago, Weiss (1975) included this dimension in his well-known work on the six provisions of social relationships. Moreover, a small cluster of studies provide empirical evidence attesting to the importance of focusing on support that is given to others (e.g., Cutrona & Russell, 1987). It is especially important to point out that some of this empirical work explicitly links providing support to others with increased feelings of personal control in later life (e.g., Krause, 1987a; Krause, Herzog & Baker, 1992).

For some time, mental health professionals have reported that individuals who give assistance to others often benefit themselves from the help-giving role (e.g., Reisman, 1965). In fact, this so-called "helper principle" forms the basis of many self-help groups, such as Alcoholics Anonymous. According to this view, giving help to other people, and observing that this assistance can improve the situation of the needy other, may lead the help-provider to realize that it is possible for his or her own problems to be overcome in a similar manner. The realization that action may lead to the improvement of problem situations may in turn bolster feelings of personal control in the support provider. Empirical support for this view is provided by Krause (1987a) and Krause et al. (1992).

Research on the social support process overwhelmingly focuses on informal social exchanges among relatives, friends, and neighbors. This bias toward strong informal ties promotes an "ideology of intimacy" that implicitly deemphasizes and devalues the benefits associated with relationships that arise in formal settings (Adelman, Parks, & Albrecht, 1987). As Jung (1984) and others maintain, it is not sufficient to base measures of support solely on informal sources when it is evident that individuals can and do obtain assistance in formal settings as well.

Failure to consider formal support in conjunction with informal assistance has important data-analytic implications. Assume that a study is conducted to investigate the relationships among stress, social support, and feelings of personal control. In addition, suppose that only informal sources of support are taken into consideration, even though study participants are receiving assistance from formal sources as well. Under these circumstances, subsequent data analysis may lead to an inappropriate rejection of the stress-buffering hypothesis, because those individuals with little informal support may not report diminished feelings of personal control. Rather than rejecting the stress-buffering hypothesis, however, the reasons for the nonsignificant relationship may be attributed to the fact that control-enhancing assistance for coping with stress was obtained in formal settings.

There are compelling reasons why it may be especially important to consider formal sources of support when working with samples consisting of older adults. As mentioned earlier, research reviewed by Lee (1985) indicates that elderly people adhere strongly to the norm of reciprocity, and they do not want to receive support unless they can reciprocate. Consequently, Lee suggests that elders may actually prefer to receive assistance from formal sources, because they do not have to worry about repayment for this help. Lee argues that as a result, formal sources may increase their sense of autonomy and allow elders to avoid becoming overly dependent upon others. As noted earlier, feelings of control should be enhanced under these circumstances.

Although older adults may receive assistance in a number of different formal settings, briefly reviewing research on the role of religious institutions in later life provides one way to illustrate the general principles that are developed in this section. The study of religious organizations may be especially useful, because a substantial number of studies indicate that people become more religious as they age (e.g., Koenig, Smiley, & Gonzales, 1988). Although a number of benefits have been associated with increased religious involvement, research on the potentially important role played by religion in the stress process is particularly pertinent to the present discussion.

As many investigators have pointed out, one of the chief functions of religion is to help offset the noxious effects of stress (see Koenig, 1994, for a recent review of this research). A key issue is how these beneficial effects emerge. One line of thinking suggests that through counseling and formal religious instruction, clergy provide access to basic religious tenets that reveal time-honored ways of coping with stressful events. Perhaps more important, these beneficial, restorative properties are thought to operate at least in part by bolstering feelings of control. For example, Krause and Tran (1989) argue that religious beliefs provide reassurance that problematic aspects of life can be overcome, and that God intervenes to ensure that difficult situations will be resolved. Stated another way, individuals with strong religious convictions may be especially likely to believe that, with God's help, stressful events and their sequelae can be controlled and overcome. Empirical support for this view is provided by Krause and Tran (1989). One potential problem with this research is that informal social systems tend to emerge and flourish within religious institutions, and as a result, the beneficial effects of religion may really be due to the influence of informal social relationships. However, research by Krause (1992) helps to allay this concern. This work suggests that religiosity tends to enhance feelings of control, even after the effects of informal social support have been controlled statistically.

Up to this point, the discussion has focused solely on the actual exchange of resources between network members. However, a small but compelling body of research indicates that perceptions of support availability may play an even greater role in shaping subsequent behavior than actual or enacted support (e.g., Krause, Liang, & Keith, 1990). As defined by Wethington and Kessler (1986), perceptions of support availability (i.e., anticipated support) refer to the belief that assistance will be forthcoming in the future should the need arise. In order to see how anticipated support may enhance feelings of control, it is helpful to briefly return to the work of Caplan (1981). As discussed earlier, Caplan argues that undesirable stressors erode cognitive and problem-solving capabilities. This leads to inertia in the face of life events, precisely at the time when decisive action is required. Anticipated support may function as a powerful antidote in this situation. Knowing that others are available creates a backup or social safety net that promotes risk taking. Risk taking, in turn, encourages exploration, personal growth, and the implementation of self-initiated coping responses. It seems that feelings of control are likely to thrive in this context, because successfully resolving a problem without direct intervention from others should greatly enhance the belief that the environment is responsive to one's own actions. Moreover, the self-reliance afforded by anticipated support may help elders avoid feelings of dependence and enmeshment that can characterize social ties in later life (Lee, 1985).

As this research review indicates, receiving informal assistance from others represents just one aspect of a larger social process. Focusing solely on received, informal support serves to reduce the complexity that is inherent in studying social ties, but this simplification may come at a cost. Social life is a seamless whole that encompasses giving and receiving, and that takes place within formal as well as informal settings. The distinction between perceived and actual support serves to further highlight the scope and complexity of the social environment. As research reviewed in this section suggests, considering only one facet or dimension may lead to a myopic view of the interface between supportive social ties and feelings of personal control in later life.

RECIPROCAL LINKAGES BETWEEN SUPPORT AND CONTROL

An emphasis had been placed throughout this chapter on how social support enhances feelings of control among older adults. However, as discussed earlier, there is a competing view on the nature of the relationship between these constructs. More specifically, the work of Lakey and his colleagues (e.g., Sandler & Lakey, 1982) indicates that individuals with a strong sense of control may utilize their support networks more effectively than people who believe that their environment is less responsive to their demands. Simply put, this research specifies that control affects support. Given the high quality of this research, as well as the power of mere observation, it is hard to refute this position. One obvious resolution is to argue that there is a reciprocal relationship between support and control, and that both perspectives are correct. There appears to be some merit in this approach. However, it is important to reflect carefully on the precise nature of this reciprocal relationship.

When researchers think in terms of reciprocal effects, they typically rely on models like the one shown in Figure 15.1. Speaking in more technical terms, this conceptual scheme focuses solely on contemporaneous effects. This means that the impact of support on control, as well as the influence of control on support, occur either simultaneously or within a relatively short period of time. There are, however, other ways to think about the nature of this relationship. The model contained in Figure 15.2 represents another possibility that relies on lagged as well as contemporaneous effects. According to this specification, the effects of support on control arise within a relatively short time, whereas the impact of control on support takes relatively longer to become manifest. The goal of the discussion that follows is to suggest that the model depicted in Figure 15.2 may be more useful for exploring the reciprocal effects between support and control in elderly populations.

Many of the studies showing that feelings of control affect the amount of sup-

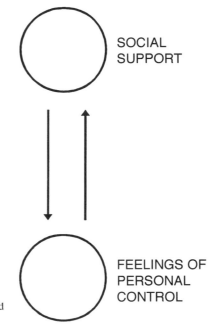

SOCIAL
SUPPORT

FEELINGS OF
PERSONAL
CONTROL

FIGURE 15.1 A contemporaneous model of control and support.

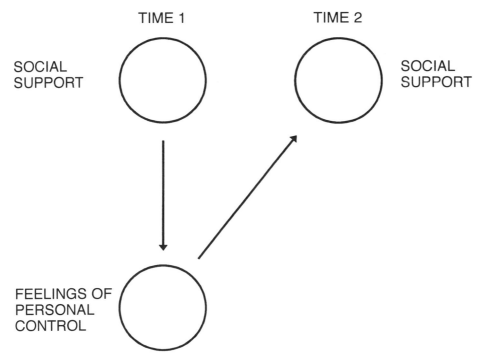

TIME 1

TIME 2

SOCIAL
SUPPORT

SOCIAL
SUPPORT

FEELINGS OF
PERSONAL
CONTROL

FIGURE 15.2 A lagged model of control and support.

port received from others rely on data gathered from college students (e.g., Sandler & Lakey, 1982). However, it is necessary to take the nature of the sample into consideration, because social networks may be more malleable at this stage in the life course, due to the fact that they contain a disproportionately large number of friends. This point is important, because friendship ties are formed on a voluntary basis, and as a result, they may be initiated and dissolved with relative ease. Under these circumstances, the impact of control on changes in support should be evident in a relatively short period of time. Consequently, the model contained in Figure 15.1 may be more appropriate for investigating the reciprocal link between support and control in samples consisting of younger people. However, there are two reasons why it may take longer for feelings of control to bring about changes in support in elderly populations: The first has to do with Carstensen's (1992) theory of socioemotional selectivity, and the second involves Antonucci's (1985) notion of the support bank.

One of the long-standing theories in social gerontology (i.e., disengagement theory) specifies that the size of social networks diminishes with age (Cumming & Henry, 1961). This is thought to occur in part because of role loss (e.g., retirement, widowhood). As originally specified, this perspective suggests that social network loss occurs across the board, and that diminished contact is evident among family as well as friends.

Recently, intriguing research by Carstensen (1992) has challenged the views of disengagement theorists. According to her socioemotional theory of selectivity, network attrition occurs largely on the periphery wherein contact with casual acquaintances declines, but relationships with core network members remain largely intact (see also Lang & Carstensen, 1994). It is especially important for the purposes of this chapter to examine the composition of the innermost circle of these social networks. Research by Lang and Carstensen indicates that when nuclear family members are available, they typically are placed in the innermost circle. If nuclear family members are not present, subjects tend to place other kin in their inner circle. The key point is that family members are often the most important social network members in later life. This is important for two reasons. First, rather than being formed on a voluntary basis, family ties rest on a sense of obligation. This suggests that the actions of elders are less likely to affect subsequent provisions of support, because the impetus for providing assistance is based more on a sense of duty and less on the current behaviors of the support recipient. Second relations with family members are likely to emerge over a relatively long period of time. As research discussed later suggests, the history of specific social relationships may have a bearing on the extent to which current perceptions of control may influence changes in the nature and amount of assistance that is provided.

The importance of focusing on the history of social relationships may be highlighted by examining Antonucci's conceptualization of the support bank (Antonucci, 1985). This view, which is derived from social exchange theory, is best described by focusing on the relationship between elderly people and their adult offspring. Early in life, parents make a substantial investment in their children without receiving compensation that is commensurate with their efforts. Even so, they are building up support credits that may be cashed in during later life. In particular, when the parents reach old age, the balance of supportive exchanges tips, and they begin to receive substantially more support than they provide. Nevertheless, this unbalanced exchange is not problematic, because both elders and their children recognize that the children are merely making repayments for assistance that was provided decades earlier. The concept of the support bank is useful, because it shows how support received from grown offspring in later life is less likely to be affected by the actions of older adults at the present time and is instead more likely to be influenced by the long history of the parent–child relationship.

Although this conceptual framework is plausible, care must be taken not to overstate the case. Elders do indeed influence the composition of their networks and the nature of the exchanges that take place within them. In fact, one of the main tenets in Carstensen's (1992) socioemotional selectivity theory maintains that older adults actively cultivate and shape their inner support systems in order to optimize the amount of assistance obtained from them. Even so, the intent of the discussion provided earlier is to highlight relative differences in the degree of influence that can be exerted across the life course and the time it takes for these differences to become manifest. Compared to college students, it seems that the disproportionately greater number of family members in the networks of older adults, coupled with the long history of relations with these individuals, serves to delimit the extent to which current perceptions of control can exert a rapid influence on the nature of exchanges that take place. The issue here is not whether control affects support *per se*. Instead, the crux of the problem is how best to capture this effect. Given the literature reviewed earlier, it would appear that the model in Figure 15.2 may be more appropriate for older populations, whereas the model in Figure 15.1 may provide better estimates for samples consisting of younger adults.

CONCLUSIONS

As Monroe and Steiner (1986) point out, social support, stress, and personality form part of an immensely complex process. When viewed at the broadest level, the intent of this chapter has been to selectively unravel some of the intricacies involved in the relationship among these constructs. Beginning with the premise that significant others play a substantial role in shaping perceptions of control, an effort was made to identify factors that either promote or inhibit the expression of this simple principle in social life. Salient role stressors, domain-specific measures of control, negative inter-action, and support obtained in formal settings figure prominently in this respect. Throughout, an effort was made to ground recent empirical work in a firm theoretical foundation by drawing upon identity theory as well as select conceptual formulations in the gerontological literature. The emphasis on gerontological theory serves to highlight important life-course issues that are frequently overlooked when the relation-ship between control and support is discussed.

Even though a lot of ground was covered, many important issues remained unexamined. Three are identified briefly below.

First, only one facet or dimension of personality was considered—feelings of personal control. Although a case was made for identifying the social roots of this construct, it is not clear whether the same argument applies to other personality traits as well. For example, a number of studies link introversion–extroversion with social relationships and support (e.g., Diener, Larsen, & Emmons, 1984). However, given recent evidence on the genetic basis of this personality trait, it seems that social support may not affect extroversion to the same extent that it may influence feelings of personal control (Stelmack, 1990).

Second, this chapter has, of necessity, focused on all elderly people taken as a whole. Consequently, this may have created the impression that a decline in control with age is inevitable. However, it is possible that there are substantial individual variations in the way that feelings of control change over the life course. Although their work is not cast explicitly within a stress context, research by Baltes and Baltes (1990) on the principles of selection, optimization, and compensation illustrates a number of ways that people maintain and enhance their sense of control as they age.

Third, the discussion provided earlier focuses solely on conceptual and measurement issues relating to feelings of control in later life. However, nothing has been said about the data-analytic issues and procedures needed to evaluate this perspective empirically. As a recent study by Krause (1995a) reveals, the statistical challenges facing those wishing to accurately estimate the effects of supportive social relationships can be formidable.

The emphasis on the primacy of the social context differs from the themes that emerge from other chapters in this volume. This reflects the training and objective of the author(s). By bringing social factors to the foreground, the intent is to illuminate the crosscutting currents that must be reconciled by those who wish to model two of the most fundamental building blocks of social existence. Although this is a daunting task, the sheer volume of material in the literature, coupled with the increased sophistication of recent empirical studies, suggests that substantial progress is being made, and that even greater advances await those who are diligent.

REFERENCES

Adelman, M., Parks, M., & Albrecht, T. (1987). Beyond close relationships: Support in weak ties. In T. Albrecht & M. Adelman (Eds.), *Communicating social support* (pp. 126–147). Beverly Hills, CA: Sage.

Antonovsky, A. (1979). *Health, stress, and coping.* San Francisco: Jossey-Bass.

Antonovsky, A. (1991). The structural sources of salutogenic strengths. In C. L. Cooper & R. Payne (Eds.), *Personality and stress: Individual differences in the stress process* (pp. 67–104). New York: Wiley.

Antonucci, T. C. (1985). Personal characteristics, social support, and social behavior. In R. H. Binstock & E. Shanas (Eds.), *Handbook of aging and the social sciences* (pp. 94–128). New York: Van Nostrand Reinhold.

Baltes, P. B. (1991). The many faces of human aging: Toward a psychological culture of older age. *Psychological Medicine, 21,* 837–854.

Baltes, P. B., & Baltes, M. M. (1990). Psychological perspectives on successful aging: The model of selective optimization and compensation. In P. B. Baltes & M. M. Baltes (Eds.), *Successful aging: Perspectives from the behavioral sciences* (pp. 1–34). New York: Cambridge University Press.

Baltes, M. M. & Wahl, H. W. (1992). The dependency–support script in institutions: Generalization to community settings. *Psychology and Aging, 7,* 409–418.

Brandtstadter, J., & Rothermund, K. (1994). Self-percepts of control in middle and later adulthood: Buffering losses by rescaling goals. *Psychology and Aging, 9,* 265–273.

Burke, P. J. (1991). Identity process and social stress. *American Sociological Review, 56,* 839–849.

Caplan, G. (1981). Mastery of stress: Psychosocial aspects. *American Journal of Psychiatry, 138,* 413–420.

Carstensen, L. I. (1992). Social and emotional patterns in adulthood: Support for socioemotional selectivity theory. *Psychology and Aging, 7*, 331-338.

Cohen, S., & Edwards, J. R. (1989). Personality characteristics as moderators of the relationship between stress and disorder. In R. W. J. Neufeld (Ed.), *Advances in the investigation of psychological stress* (pp. 235-283). New York: Wiley.

Cooley, C. H. (1931). *Life and the student: Roadside notes on human nature, society, and letters.* New York: Alfred Knopf.

Coyne, J. C. Wortman. C. B., & Lehman, D. R. (1988). The other side of support: Emotional overinvolvement and miscarried helping. In B. H. Gottlieb (Ed.), *Marshaling social support: Formats, processes, and effects* (pp. 305-330). Newbury Park, CA: Sage.

Cumming, E., & Henry, W. H. (1961). *Growing old: The process of disengagement.* New York: Basic Books.

Cutrona, C. E., & Russell, D. (1987). The provisions of social relationships and adaptation to stress. In W. H. Jones & D. Perlman (Eds.), *Advances in personal relationships* (Vol. 1, pp. 37-67). Greenwich, CT: JAI Press.

Diener, E. Larsen, R. J., & Emmons, R. A. (1984). Person X situation interactions: Choice of situations and congruence response models. *Journal of Personality and Social Psychology, 47*, 580-592.

Dowd, J. J. (1975). Aging as exchange: A preface to theory. *Journal of Gerontology, 30*, 584-594.

Eckenrode, J. (1983). The mobilization of social supports: Some individual constraints. *American Journal of Community Psychology, 11*, 509-528.

Eckenrode, J., & Wethington, E. (1990). The process and outcome of mobilizing social support. In S. Duck (Ed.), *Personal relationships and social support* (pp. 83-103). Newbury Park, CA: Sage.

Erikson, E. (1959). *Identity and the life cycle.* New York: International University Press.

Heckhausen, J., & Schulz, R. (1993). Optimisation by selection and compensation: Balancing primary and secondary control in life span development. *International Journal of Behavioral Development, 16*, 287-303.

Hobfoll, S. E. (1989). Conservation of resources: A new attempt at conceptualizing stress. *American Psychologist, 44*, 513-524.

Jung, J. (1984). Social support and its relation to health. *Basic and Applied Social Psychology, 5*, 143-169.

Kessler, R. C., McLeod, J. D., & Wethington, E. (1985). The costs of caring: A perspective on the relationship between sex and psychological distress. In I. G. Sarason & B. R. Sarason (Eds.), *Social support: Theory, research, and applications* (pp. 491-506). The Hague, The Netherlands: Martinus Nijhoff.

Koenig, H. G. (1994). *Aging and God: Spiritual pathways to mental health in midlife and later years.* New York: Hawthorn Press.

Koenig, H. G., Smiley, M., & Gonzales, J. A. (1988). *Religion, health, and aging.* New York: Greenwood.

Krause, N. (1987a). Chronic financial strain, social support, and depressive symptoms among older adults. *Psychology and Aging, 2*, 185-192.

Krause, N. (1987b). Understanding the stress process: Linking social support with locus of control beliefs. *Journal of Gerontology, 42*, 589-593.

Krause, N. (1989). Issues of measurement and analysis in studies of social support, aging, and health. In K. S. Markides & C. L. Cooper (Eds.), *Aging, stress, social support, and health* (pp. 43-66). New York: Wiley.

Krause, N. (1990). Stress, social support, and well-being: Focusing on salient social roles. In M. A. P. Stephens, J. H. Crowther, S. E. Hobfoll, & D. L. Tennenbaum (Eds.), *Stress and coping in later life families* (pp. 71-97). Washington, DC: Hemisphere.

Krause, N. (1991). Stress and isolation from close ties in later life. *Journal of Gerontology: Social Sciences, 46*, S183-S194.

Krause, N. (1992). Stress, religiosity, and psychological well-being among older blacks. *Journal of Aging and Health, 4*, 412-439.

Krause, N. (1994). Stressors in salient social roles and well-being in later life. *Journal of Gerontology: Psychological Sciences, 49*, P137-P148.

Krause, N. (1995a). Assessing stress-buffering effects: A cautionary note. *Psychology and Aging, 10*, 518-526.

Krause, N. (1995b). Negative interaction and satisfaction with social support among older adults. *Journal of Gerontology: Psychological Sciences, 50B*, P59-P73.

Krause, N., & Borawski-Clark, E. (1994). Clarifying the functions of social support in later life. *Research on Aging, 16*, 251-279.

Krause, N., Herzog, A. R., & Baker, E. (1992). Providing support to others and well-being in later life. *Journal of Gerontology: Psychological Sciences*, *47*, P300–P311.

Krause, N., Liang, J., & Keith, V. (1990). Personality, social support, and psychological distress in later life. *Psychology and Aging*, *5*, 315–326.

Krause, N., & Tran, T. V. (1989). Stress and religious involvement among older blacks. *Journal of Gerontology: Social Sciences*, *44*, S4–S13.

La Gaipa, J. J. (1990). The negative effects of informal support systems. In S. Duck (Ed.), *Personal relationships and social support* (pp. 122–139). Newbury Park, CA: Sage.

Lang, F. R., & Cartensen, L. I. (1994). Close emotional relationships in later life: Further support for proactive aging in the social domain. *Psychology and Aging*, *9*, 315–324.

Lee, G. R. (1985). Kinship and social support of the elderly: The case of the United States. *Ageing and Society*, *5*, 19–38.

McCall, G. J., & Simmons, J. L. (1966). *Identities and interaction*. New York: Free Press.

Mirowsky, J. (1995). Age and sense of control. *Social Psychology Quarterly*, *56*, 31–43.

Monroe, S. M., & Steiner, S. C. (1986). Social support and psychopathology: Interrelations with preexisting disorder, stress, and personality. *Journal of Abnormal Psychology*, *95*, 29–39.

Moos, R. H., & Schaefer, J. A. (1986). Life transitions and crises: A conceptual overview. In R. H. Moos (Ed.), *Coping with life crises: An integrated approach* (pp. 3–28). New York: Plenum Press.

Pearlin, L. I., & Schooler, C. (1978). The structure of coping. *Journal of Health and Social Behavior*, *19*, 2–21.

Pearlin, L. I., Menaghan, E., Lieberman, M., & Mullan, J. (1981). The stress process. *Journal of Health and Social Behavior*, *22*, 337–356.

Reisman, F. (1965). The helper therapy principle. *Social Work*, *10*, 27–32.

Rodin, J. (1990). Control by any other name: Definitions, concepts, and processes. In J. Rodin, C. Schooler, & K. W. Schaie (Eds.), *Self-directedness: Cause and effects through the life course* (pp. 1–17). Hillsdale, NJ: Erlbaum.

Rodin, J., & Langer, E. J. (1977). Long-term effects of control-relevant intervention with the institutionalized aged. *Journal of Personality and Social Psychology*, *35*, 897–903.

Rodin, J., Timko, C., & Harris, S. (1985). The construct of control. In M. P. Lawton & G. L. Maddox (Eds.), *Annual review of gerontology and geriatrics* (Vol. 5, pp. 3–55). New York: Springer.

Rook, K. S. (1984). The negative side of social interaction: Impact on psychological well-being. *Journal of Personality and Social Psychology*, *46*, 1097–1108.

Rook, K. S. (1987). Social support versus companionship: Effects on life stress, loneliness, and evaluations by others. *Journal of Personality and Social Psychology*, *52*, 1132–1147.

Rotter, J. B. (1966). Generalized expectancies for internal versus external control of reinforcement. *Psychological Monographs*, *80*, (Whole No. 609).

Sandler, I. N., & Lakey, B. (1982). Locus of control as a stress moderator: The role of control perceptions and social support. *American Journal of Community Psychology*, *10*, 61–80.

Sarason, I. G., Sarason, B. R., & Pierce, G. R. (1994). Relationship-specific social support: Toward a model for the analysis of supportive interactions. In B. R. Burleson, T. L. Albrecht, & I. G. Sarason (Eds.), *Communication of social support: Messages, interactions, relationships, and community* (pp. 91–112). Thousand Oaks, CA: Sage.

Schulz, R., Heckhausen, J., & Locher, J. L. (1991). Adult development, control, and adaptive functioning. *Journal of Social Issues*, *47*, 117–196.

Stelmack, R. M. (1990). Biological basis of extraversion. *Journal of Personality*, *58*, 293–311.

Stryker, S. (1987). Identity theory: Developments and extensions. In K. Yardley & T. Honess (Eds.), *Self and identity: Psychosocial perspectives* (pp. 89–104). Chichester, UK: Wiley.

Thoits, P. A. (1987). Gender and marital status differences in control and distress: Common stress versus unique stress explanations. *Journal of Health and Social Behavior*, *28*, 7–22.

Thoits, P. A. (1991). On merging identity theory and stress research. *Social Psychology Quarterly*, *54*, 101–112.

Thoits, P. A. (1995). Identity-relevant events and psychological symptoms: A cautionary tale. *Journal of Health and Social Behavior*, *36*, 72–82.

Turner, R. J., & Roszell, S. O. (1994). Psychosocial resources and the stress process. In W. R. Avison & I. H. Gotlib (Eds.), *Stress and mental health: Contemporary issues and prospects for the future* (pp. 179–210). New York: Plenum.

Weiss, R. S. (1975). The provisions of social relationships. In Z. Rubin (Ed.), *Doing unto others* (pp. 17–26). Englewood Cliffs, NJ: Prentice-Hall.

Wethington, E., & Kessler, R. C. (1986). Perceived support, received support, and adjustment to stressful life events. *Journal of Health and Social Behavior, 27,* 78–89.

Wheaton, B. (1983). Stress, personal coping resources, and psychiatric symptoms: An investigation of interactive models. *Journal of Health and Social Behavior, 24,* 208–229.

Wheaton, B. (1985). Personal resources and mental health: Can there be too much of a good thing? In J. R. Greenley (Ed.), *Research in community and mental health* (Vol. 5, pp. 139–184). Greenwich, CT: JAI Press.

PART III

SOCIAL SUPPORT, PERSONALITY, AND SUPPORTIVE INTERACTIONS

CHAPTER 16

ADULT ATTACHMENT PATTERNS AND SOCIAL SUPPORT PROCESSES

Kim Bartholomew, Rebecca J. Cobb, and Jennifer A. Poole

In this chapter, we explore the links between individual differences in adult attachment and social support processes. First, we review attachment theory and research, and the theoretical and empirical links between attachment and social support in adulthood. We then present a model of the processes through which attachment may impact upon various aspects of social support. Drawing on this model, we describe how we expect each of four distinct attachment patterns to be associated with social support processes, incorporating case studies to illustrate our hypotheses. Finally, we discuss the limitations of our model.

ATTACHMENT

Bowlby proposed that an innate behavioral system underlies the tendency of infants and children to form strong emotional ties with caregivers, their *attachment figures*. This system prompts infants to seek physical proximity with caregivers and, thereby, presumably contributes to their safety and, ultimately, inclusive fitness (1973, 1980). Over time, Bowlby further proposed that children develop internal working models (or representations) of attachment that allow them to predict and interpret an attachment figure's behavior. Throughout the life span, these models serve as templates that guide behavior in subsequent relationships and provide a basis for interpretation of later relationship experiences (Bowlby, 1973).

Kim Bartholomew, Rebecca J. Cobb, and Jennifer A. Poole • Department of Psychology, Simon Fraser University, Burnaby, British Columbia V5A 1S6.

Sourcebook of Social Support and Personality, edited by Gregory R. Pierce, Brian Lakey, Irwin G. Sarason, and Barbara R. Sarason. Plenum Press, New York, 1997.

Hazan and Shaver (1987) were the first to extend attachment theory to the study of adult love relationships. They developed a categorical self-report measure to differentiate between three adult attachment classifications, paralleling three infant attachment patterns identified by Ainsworth and her colleagues (Ainsworth, Blehar, Waters, & Wall, 1978). *Secure* individuals were characterized by ease of trusting and getting close to others, *ambivalent* (or preoccupied) individuals by anxiety and overdependence in close relationships, and *avoidant* individuals by distrust of others and avoidance of closeness in relationships.

Bowlby (1973) identified two key features of attachment representations: whether the self is perceived to be worthy of love and attention, and whether others are viewed as warm and responsive. Building upon Hazan and Shaver's (1987) initial work, Bartholomew developed a four-category model of adult attachment in which four prototypic attachment patterns are defined in terms of the intersection of two dimensions—positivity of models of the self, and positivity of models of hypothetical others (Bartholomew, 1990; Bartholomew & Horowitz, 1991; see Figure 16.1). The self-model dimension is associated with individuals' feelings of anxiety about their worthiness of others' love, whereas the other-model dimension is associated with the degree of avoidance of proximity and intimacy in close relationships. *Secure* attachment is defined by both a positive view of self and of others (low anxiety and low avoidance); secure individuals are therefore comfortable with both closeness and autonomy. The *preoccupied* pattern is characterized by a negative view of self and positive view of others (high anxiety and low avoidance), leading to excessive dependence on others for feelings of self-worth. Two distinct forms of avoidant attachment are identified. The *fearful* pattern is characterized by both a negative self-model and other-model (high anxiety and high avoidance); fearful individuals desire social contact but are inhibited by fears of rejection. In contrast, the *dismissing* pattern is defined by a positive view of self and a negative view of others (low anxiety and high avoidance); dismissing individuals defensively deny the need or desire for intimate contact.

In previous work, Bartholomew and colleagues formally validated this model (Bartholomew & Horowitz, 1991; Griffin & Bartholomew, 1994a, 1994b), investigated stability and change in attachment representations over time (Scharfe & Bartholomew,

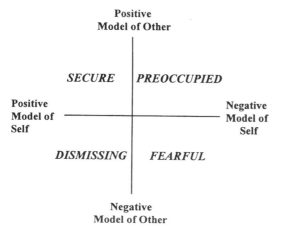

FIGURE 16.1. Four-category model of adult attachment.

1994), and applied the model to understanding relationship processes in established couples (e.g., Scharfe & Bartholomew, 1995). Various studies have also confirmed that two dimensions underlie adult attachment patterns, and that these two dimensions conform to the dimensions proposed by the four-category model (e.g., Bartholomew & Griffin, 1994a; Shaver & Hazan, 1993).

THEORETICAL LINKS BETWEEN ATTACHMENT AND SOCIAL SUPPORT

The concepts of social support and attachment are linked by some of the defining features of each construct. Social support has been defined as a sense of support, general perceptions that others are available to provide support, and, by extension, a sense of acceptance: feelings of being loved, cared for, and accepted fully by others (Sarason, Pierce, & Sarason, 1990a). Similarly, the secure attachment pattern reflects feelings of the self as worthy of love and acceptance by others, the view of others as supportive and available, and the willingness to seek help when needed (Bartholomew, 1990).

The seeking of support in adulthood is parallel to *proximity seeking* in childhood (Cotterell, 1992). One of the goals of the attachment behavior system in childhood is the regulation of a sense of felt security. Anxiety during times of stress, pain, threat, or illness can be relieved by behaviors designed to seek or maintain proximity to the caregiver, the so-called *safe haven* function of attachment relationships. Similarly, in adulthood, a sense of security may be gained through the receiving of supportive behaviors from persons within an individual's social network. Thus, the attachment behavior—support seeking—is elicited when individuals experience some threat to their feelings of personal or emotional security, and support providers fulfill the role of *safe haven* in times of stress or anxiety.

A second component of the attachment system is that of a *secure base* from which the individual may venture from the proximity of the caregiver to explore the environment while maintaining a sense of security. This may be seen as analogous to assessing the availability of support prior to attempting a task that may necessitate support from others (Pierce, Sarason, Sarason, Joseph, & Henderson, 1996). Perceptions that others are available and willing to provide support in the event such help is needed may enable the individual to attempt demanding or potentially stressful undertakings.

Pierce and colleagues (1996) describe the expectations a person has for social support as a social support schema. The schema incorporates previous experiences of receiving support into a mental model similar to the internal working models of self and other that define attachment representations. As such, the social support schema is expected to develop in much the same way as internal working models of attachment, specifically through experiences with primary caregivers throughout childhood (Pierce, Sarason, & Sarason, 1991; Sarason, Pierce, Bannerman & Sarason, 1993; Sarason et al., 1990a). Internal working models of attachment are a system of expectations and beliefs children develop about themselves and about others through relationship experiences. Likewise, a child who has support needs met will develop positive expectations of others, leading to perceptions of others as available and supportive. These expectations of the general availability of support are thought by some researchers to reflect a stable personality characteristic defined as a *sense of support*

(Sarason, Pierce, & Sarason, 1990b). In contrast, if a child does not have the experience of others as supportive and comforting, a schema of others as unavailable and rejecting in times of stress will result.

RESEARCH LINKING ATTACHMENT AND SOCIAL SUPPORT

A number of studies have demonstrated that attachment security is positively associated with perceived social support and reported willingness to seek social support. In a sample of college students, Blain, Thompson, and Whiffen (1993) examined the interaction between working models of self and other in relation to perceptions of social support. They found that both a positive model of self and a positive model of others was required for high levels of perceived support from friends and family. Having a negative model of either self or of others led to lowered perceptions of social support. Ognibene and Collins (1997), in a study of coping strategies, attachment, and social support among college students, also found that positive models of self were associated with a tendency to confront and deal with problems, to seek support when needed, and to perceive greater support from family. Wallace and Vaux (1993) found that secure college students reported more positive social support network orientations than did their insecure peers. Mikulincer, Florian, and Weller (1993) found that secure college students reported more support-seeking strategies (relative to the insecure) to deal with a specific traumatic event (Iraqi missile attacks on Israel during the Gulf War). Finally, Kobak and Sceery (1988) found that secure adolescents were able to acknowledge their distress, seek support from others, and in turn reported high levels of perceived support.

A defining feature of security of attachment is the ability to see others as dependable and available for comfort and support (Collins & Read, 1990). Such positive perceptions of the trustworthiness of others allow secure individuals to seek help when needed. To date, just one study has assessed help-seeking *behaviors* in relation to adult attachment. Simpson, Rholes, and Nelligan (1992) conducted a laboratory study in which they observed support seeking and support giving in romantic couples after the female partner had been placed in an anxiety-provoking situation. They observed that as anxiety increased, thereby activating the attachment system, support seeking by secure women also increased.

Although the links between attachment security and reports of support seeking and perceptions of support have been well established, a number of the previously cited studies could not differentiate insecure attachment patterns in terms of social support, or these distinctions were ambiguous (e.g., Blain et al., 1993; Ognibene & Collins, 1997; Wallace & Vaux, 1993). Table 16.1 presents the findings from a study of 237 college students that demonstrates this pattern. Four attachment patterns were assessed by combining prototype ratings from the Relationship Questionnaire (Bartholomew & Horowitz, 1991) and the Relationship Scales Questionnaire (Griffin & Bartholomew, 1994b); this approach yields continuous ratings of the degree to which participants fit the prototype of *each* of the four attachment patterns. Satisfaction with support and number of supportive relationships available were assessed with the Social Support Questionnaire—Short Form (SSO; Sarason, Sarason, Shearin, & Pierce,

TABLE 16.1. Correlations of Social Support
and Attachment Pattern ($N = 237$)

	Satisfaction with support	Number of supports available
Secure	.51**	.38**
Preoccupied	−.22**	−.08
Fearful	−.33**	−.24**
Dismissing	−.16*	−.18**

*$p < .05$
**$p < .01$

1987). The associations between security and support variables were moderately strong, and, with just one exception, there were low to moderate negative associations between the insecure attachment patterns and social support. However, while the secure/support correlations differed significantly from all of the insecurity/support correlations, the insecure pattern correlations do not differ from one another. Thus, these data replicate the security/perceived support findings reviewed, but fail to reliably distinguish the insecure patterns in terms of their associations with social support.

A few studies, however, do provide insight into the associations between forms of insecurity and social support. Avoidant individuals are likely to ignore their distress and restrict support-seeking behavior (Kobak & Sceery, 1988), perceive lower levels of available support (Osborne, Cooper, & Shaver, 1993), and exhibit resistance to supportive behaviors from others (Simpson et al, 1992). In contrast, those who are preoccupied or ambivalent are overly cognizant of their own distress and excessively dependent on others as sources of support, thereby limiting their autonomy and feelings of self-confidence (Kobak & Sceery, 1988).

In summary, a growing body of research has explored the association between social support and attachment, with a particular focus on the relationship between support seeking, support perceptions, and security of attachment. However, little attention has been given to the processes linking attachment and support appraisals, and there is limited information on how different forms of insecurity may impact on social support processes.

A MODEL OF SOCIAL SUPPORT PROCESS

We have adopted the model illustrated in Figure 16.2 as a heuristic to consider the processes through which individual differences in adult attachment patterns may impact upon perceived social support. This model borrows features of Pierce and colleagues' interactional model of perceived social support (Pierce, Sarason, & Sarason, 1991; 1992), Vaux and Wood's (1987) network orientation model, Eckenrode and Wethington's (1990) description of the process of social support mobilization, and Gross and McMullen's (1983) three-stage model of help seeking. For the sake of simplicity, the model focuses on the process of gaining social support within a particular attachment relationship.

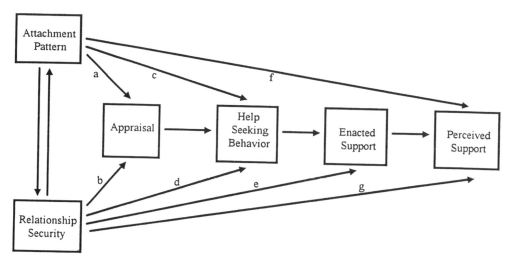

FIGURE 16.2. Proposed model of the social support process.

From the perspective of this model, a number of processes precede perceptions of support: First, individuals must feel stressed or threatened in some way (stress appraisal); then they need to communicate their need or desire for support to a relationship partner (support seeking); next their relationship partner responds (enacted support); and, finally, they perceive this response as more or less supportive and satisfying (perceived support). At each stage in the process, the attachment pattern of the support recipient and the quality of the attachment relationship with the support provider could impact upon the process.

The attachment pattern of the support recipient is conceptualized as a relatively enduring individual characteristic. As previously described, we define *attachment patterns* in terms of models of the self and of the close other that are associated with particular strategies to regulate distress in the context of close relationships. These attachment-related representations are conceptually related to Pierce and colleagues' intrapersonal context of support transactions and Vaux's network orientation. Relationship security, an aspect of network resources, refers to the qualities of the specific relationship related to the provision and receipt of support in that relationship. Security involves confidence that a particular relationship partner will be forthcoming when called upon for support, and, therefore, there is a willingness to approach the partner when in distress. In Pierce and colleagues' terms, a secure relationship would foster relationship-specific expectations of support and, more generally, is an aspect of the interpersonal context of social support.

The attachment pattern of the support recipient is expected to contribute to the security of the close relationships. A growing body of literature indicates that security is predictive of partner trust, relationship quality and satisfaction, and communication patterns (e.g., Collins & Read, 1990; Kirkpatrick & Davis, 1994; Scharfe & Bartholomew, 1995). There are many mechanisms through which individual differences in attachment may influence the quality of specific relationships, including preference in social partners, willingness and capacity for intimacy, characteristic communication patterns, and, more generally, characteristic interpersonal patterns and difficulties (Bartholomew, 1993; Shaver & Clark, 1994). Conversely, attachment models are expected to be formed from experiences in close relationships and maintained through ongoing confirmation in relationships. Although attachment models in adulthood may be less amenable to change than in childhood, at any point in life, repeated experiences that disconfirm existing models may lead to change (Kirkpatrick & Hazan, 1994; Scharfe & Bartholomew, 1994). Thus, attachment models and the quality of close relationships reciprocally influence one another over time. Of course, the attachment patterns of both members of a dyad contribute to the security of their relationship. However, to keep our model from becoming unmanageably complex, we have excluded links from the relationship partner to relationship security (and to subsequent stages in the support process).

ATTACHMENT TO STRESS APPRAISAL (A)*

Attachment models are expected to influence stress appraisals. First, the attachment systems of individuals with attachment patterns characterized by negative self-models (the preoccupied and fearful) are, by definition, more sensitive to perceptions of threat or, in attachment terms, the threshold of activation of their attachment systems is relatively low (Simpson & Rholes, 1994). Therefore, these individuals tend to experience high levels of distress and anxiety, even in response to objectively mild stressful events. In contrast, secure and dismissing individuals have an internalized sense of their ability to effectively cope with stress or, in attachment terms, the threshold of their attachment systems is relatively high. The dismissing are also expected to defensively exclude awareness of distress in order to avoid the activation of their attachment systems. Thus, the secure and dismissing are less likely than the preoccupied and fearful to perceive situations as sufficiently serious or threatening to warrant an active coping response. See Simpson and Rholes for an in-depth analysis of stress and activation of the attachment system.

RELATIONSHIP SECURITY TO STRESS APPRAISAL (B)

The presence of supportive relationship partners may assist individuals to adaptively cope by changing the appraisal of a stressful event and/or the emotional response to the event (Thoits, 1986; Wethington & Kessles, 1986). A secure relationship, characterized by confidence in the partner's good will and trustworthiness, will provide a secure base that facilitates an individual's confidence in his or her ability to cope with a perceived stressor. This stress-buffering effect would be expected to operate independent of the attachment pattern of the individual. For example, it is not uncommon for fearful individuals to develop close and trusting friendships. Although these individuals may still show fearful tendencies in the majority of their relationships and have great difficulty in forming new, close relationships, the awareness that a specific friend with whom they are securely attached is available if needed (especially if that person is in close physical proximity) may make stressful situations less threatening.

---

*The letter indicates the path in Figure 16.2.

ATTACHMENT TO HELP SEEKING (C)

Attachment patterns are expected to impact upon help-seeking behavior through the inclination or willingness to seek support, and the form that help-seeking behavior takes. Attachment patterns associated with a positive-other model (secure and preoccupied) should facilitate the willingness to use available support resources or, in the context of a specific relationship, to communicate the need for support to a relationship partner. In addition, these patterns are expected to predict relatively direct forms of help seeking, such as self-disclosure about a problem or direct requests for reassurance or help. Consistent with these expectations, security and preoccupation are positively associated with the tendency to seek out attachment figures when under stress (proximity seeking) and with self-disclosure within close relationships (Bartholomew & Horowitz, 1991). Conversely, avoidant attachment patterns (either fearful or dismissing) are associated with low levels of proximity seeking, low self-disclosure, and low emotional expressiveness (Bartholomew & Horowitz, 1991; Mikulincer & Nachshon, 1991; Simpson et al., 1992).

RELATIONSHIP SECURITY TO HELP SEEKING (D)

Individuals not only hold generalized attitudes toward help seeking, but their willingness to seek support is also expected to be influenced by their prior experiences of help seeking and receiving in specific relationships. Thus, generally secure individuals may be quite willing to openly seek support from a close friend whom they have come to trust will be responsive to their requests, but may be unwilling to seek support from a parent with whom they have a difficult and conflicted relationship.

RELATIONSHIP SECURITY TO ENACTED SUPPORT (E)

Enacted or received support represents concrete instances of helping behavior. Enacted support can come in many forms, from the communication of caring and concern to active help in dealing with a problem. Just as relationship security is expected to influence support recipients' willingness to seek support, it is also expected to influence support provider's willingness and ability to effectively provide support. In particular, more unsolicited support (Eckenrode & Wethington, 1990) may be available in closer, better functioning relationships.

ATTACHMENT TO PERCEIVED SUPPORT (F)

Perceived support refers to individuals' appraisals of how supportive, reassuring, and satisfying received support is felt to be. Perceived support may be specific to an instance of support giving, whereas generalized perceptions of support within relationships presumably arise over many instances of support seeking and receiving. Perceived support is a key aspect of social support, because it is often more strongly associated with outcome measures such as well-being than other social support variables such as enacted support or social embeddedness (Barrera, 1986). Also, perceived support may mediate the associations between social support interactions and psychological adjustment (Barrera & Baca, 1990). Consistent with Vaux and

Wood's (1987) findings that network orientation has a direct effect on support appraisals, independent of support resources and supportive behaviors, we expect that attachment will predict perceived support, independent of the intervening steps in the model. Individuals' general expectations of the availability and adequacy of social support will bias their perceptions of supportive transactions to be consistent with their expectations.

Relationship Security to Perceived Support (G)

Perceived support is dependent on a sense of security and intimacy in the relationship with the support provider, independent of support behaviors (cf. Johnson, Hobfoll, & Zalcberg-Linetzy, 1993). Aid from someone with whom the recipient has a difficult or insecure relationship may be perceived negatively, independent of the actual nature of the support offered. In such a situation, the support giver may be seen as having negative intentions, or the recipient may feel a sense of obligation to reciprocate that received help (Nadler & Fisher, 1986). Thus, Barrera and Baca (1990) found that conflictual relationships with support providers predicted dissatisfaction with support, independent of network orientation. The importance of this link between relationship security and perceived support is dramatically demonstrated in the Strange Situations paradigm used in infant attachment work. At times, a caregiver will appear to be responding to a distressed child in a sensitive appropriate way, and yet the infant does not find the support comforting. We then infer that the child is not simply responding to his or her caregiver's current behavior, but is responding based on a history of interactions in which the caregiver has not been consistently supportive.

ATTACHMENT PATTERNS AND SOCIAL SUPPORT PROCESSES

Each attachment pattern reflects a distinct strategy of coping with distress within the context of close relationships (cf. Kobak & Sceery, 1988; Simpson & Rholes, 1994). *Secure attachment* is characterized by a positive self-model and a positive model of others. Secure individuals are able to acknowledge distress and to turn to others for comfort and support, confident in the expectation that others will be responsive. At each step in the process, security of attachment is expected to facilitate the process of gaining social support. Security is associated with trusting and satisfying intimate relationships (Shaver & Hazan, 1993; Hazan & Shaver, 1994), balanced appraisals of potential stressors, the ability to seek out support as one of a range of coping responses when threatened (e.g., Mikulincer et al., 1993), and the tendency to make relatively positive attributions of the relationship partner's behaviors (Collins, 1996). Therefore, it is not surprising that security of attachment has been found to be predictive of perceived social support (e.g., Blain et al., 1993; Cobb & Bartholomew, 1995). Secure individuals are also expected to show the greatest flexibility in response to stress, drawing on a range of coping strategies, depending on the situation and availability of social supports.

In contrast, each form of insecurity is expected to be associated with a distinct pattern of difficulties in gaining and perceiving support in close relationships. Thus, we hypothesize that some previous studies have failed to differentiate between forms of insecurity in the prediction of perceived support, because they did not fully address the intermediate steps in the model between attachment and perceived support. To illustrate our hypotheses linking insecure attachment patterns and social support processes, we have included a brief description of typical individuals with each insecure pattern.

Preoccupied (or anxious–ambivalent) attachment is characterized by the combination of a negative self-model and a positive model of others. Preoccupied individuals are hypervigilant to potential sources of stress or threat: They show high general levels of distress and anxiety (Bartholomew & Horowitz, 1991; Kobak & Sceery, 1988; Mikulincer & Orbach, 1995), and intense negative reactions to external stress (Mikulincer et al., 1993). Their primary strategy for coping with distress is to seek support from attachment figures. Because past attachment figures are likely to have responded inconsistently to their expressed distress, they have learned to express their needs actively and unrelentingly in order to maximize their chances of gaining support. Thus, they often express their needs for support in a demanding, histrionic, and/or manipulative manner, overrely on potential supporters, and are indiscriminate in self-disclosure and help-seeking behaviors (Bartholomew & Horowitz, 1991; Mikulincer & Nachshon, 1991). Needless to say, these forms of help seeking are not conducive to eliciting effective support.

Like ambivalent infants who cling to their caretakers when upset but do not seem to gain comfort from that contact (Ainsworth et al., 1978), the preoccupied tend to be dissatisfied with the enacted support they receive, regardless of the objective quality of that support. Moreover, they are chronically anxious in their intimate relationships and tend to find themselves in relationships characterized by emotional extremes, jealousy, and dissatisfaction (e.g., Hazan & Shaver, 1987). Therefore, they are unlikely to enjoy the support benefits of secure relationships. The tendencies of the preoccupied to constantly seek support, to seek that support in difficult ways, and to be dissatisfied with the level and quality of support offered only serve to alienate potential support providers, thus increasing the frustration and demands of the preoccupied. Johnson et al.'s (1993) description of the "support hungry" sounds similar to the preoccupied. The following description of one of our study participants illustrates the key features of the hypothesized relations between preoccupation and social support processes.

Cindy is prototypically preoccupied. She is 33 years old, a homemaker, and a mother of two small children. She has been married for 10 years and is about to separate from her husband. Her major complaint is that her husband has not been sexually interested in her since he had brain surgery 4 weeks previously. Also, although in the past he listened to her problems and tried to comfort her when she was upset, she feels that he has become less responsive to her emotional needs. Finally, she resents the time he spends with close friends ("I should be his best friend. Why does he need them?"). She has become convinced that he no longer loves her. Cindy always has a small group of close women friends, and always one "best friend." But she has a history of falling out with friends; for instance, she cut off her most recent best friend for expressing disapproval of the way she was treating her husband.

Cindy does not deal well with stress. In her words, "I am very sensitive and emotional. My emotions control my behavior." When upset (which is often), she openly expresses her feelings and seeks support from others, preferably her husband or a close friend. She vacillates between directly asking for (and, at times, demanding) support and using manipulation to gain attention and support. When asked if she cried alone or with others, she said "I always cry with other people—why else would you cry?" When under major stress, she tends to become hysterical and inconsolable. For example, she took a family first-aid course to prepare herself for emergencies. But when her son cut his head on a chair, her response was to leave her son unattended and scream hysterically until someone arrived to help. Cindy defines her close relationships primarily in terms of support provision (e.g., "A friend is someone who will be there to accept you and support you, no matter what, who I can turn to at all times"). She prides herself on being very supportive of others, although she can be intrusive and controlling in her attempts to take care of others, and her concern for others is easily overshadowed by her own needs (as in the case of her husband's health problems). In the early stages of relationships, Cindy can feel very satisfied with the support she receives. But, over time, her support providers either fail to live up to her unreasonable expectations or they become alienated by her relentless demands. Thus, Cindy actively maintains close supportive relationships and active depends on these relationships for support. But her preoccupied pattern makes it difficult for her to consistently feel satisfied with the support she gains in these relationships.

By contrast, *avoidant attachment*, defined in terms of negative models of others, is associated with the inhibition of displays of distress and withdrawal from others when distressed. This strategy has presumably developed because of a history of relationships in which displays of distress and comfort seeking have met with no response or with rejection by attachment figures. Thus, avoidance is a defensive strategy in which the natural inclination to seek proximity to attachment figures when threatened is suppressed. This strategy is expected to be especially evident under high levels of anxiety or distress. Simpson et al. (1992) found that avoidance was only associated with suppression of support seeking under conditions of high anxiety. Similarly, Mikulincer et al. (1993) found that avoidant attachment predicted distancing as a means of coping with Iraqi missile attacks on Israel under more threatening conditions (residing in the missile-targeted area). The two avoidant patterns identified by the four-category model, fearful-avoidance and dismissing-avoidance, share the behavioral strategy of withdrawing when distressed. However, they differ in their proneness to experience distress, in their conscious reasons for avoidance, and in their investment in close relationships.

Fearful attachment is characterized by negative-other models and negative self-models. Fearful individuals, similar to the preoccupied, respond strongly to potential stressors, reporting chronically high levels of subjective distress (Bartholomew & Horowitz, 1991). However, opposite to the preoccupied pattern of actively seeking support, the fearful withdraw when under stress and only show their needs for support indirectly or, perhaps, in extreme situations, when they are unable to control their emotional display. The fearful do not seek social support, because they do not expect others to respond positively to their overtures. Fearfulness is also associated with poor quality intimate relationships (e.g., Bartholomew & Horowitz, 1991; Scharfe & Bartholomew, 1995; Carnelley, Pietromonaco, & Jaffe, 1994), which further contributes to the fearful person's difficulties in obtaining adequate support. Fearful avoidants are all too aware of their distress and their inability to effectively cope with that distress. They are also emotionally dependent on acceptance from others, and thus desire close supportive relationships. Therefore, of all the insecure patterns, they are likely to be the least satisfied with social support.

Jim is a 27-year-old letter carrier and one of the most fearful individuals we have encountered in a nonclinical sample. He has never been involved in a romantic relationship, has few acquaintances, has only one person he considers a close friend (a childhood friend, Dan), and maintains little contact with his parents. Jim is obsessed with finding someone to marry, but he is incapable of asking women out because he is afraid of rejection. The odd time he does manage to express his interest in someone, he invariably ends up feeling that she is not interested in him. He also desperately wants to make friends, but he has been similarly unsuccessful. Jim does not feel understood or appreciated by his friend Dan, and they see each other rarely. In fact, he often feels rejected and taken advantage of by Dan. However, Jim is willing to accept this treatment to maintain his one ongoing social contact.

Jim is chronically lonely and anxious. He ruminates about his inadequacies, his lack of relationships, and any other difficulties that arise in his life (such as problems at work). Sometimes he tries to distract himself with physical activities, although with little success. He does not seek support from others, because he is embarrassed to express his feelings. He also thinks that the people he does know would not be interested in listening to and supporting him. Jim has made a few indirect attempts over the years to talk with Dan about personal concerns, but each time he has ended up feeling that Dan was not sympathetic or helpful. Overall, Jim feels very frustrated and distressed with his emotional and social isolation. Not surprisingly, on the SSQ, he indicated a relatively low level of satisfaction with support available from others (3.33 on a 7-point scale, over 2 standard deviations below the sample mean). Moreover, on four of the six items assessing aspects of perceived supportiveness ("How many people can be counted on to accept you totally, to really care about you, etc."), Jim reported that there was no one he could count on.

Dismissing attachment is characterized by a positive self model and a negative model of others. Dismissing individuals downplay the importance of potential stressors, defensively avoiding acknowledgment of distress that could activate the attachment system (Bartholomew, 1990; Mikulincer & Orbach, 1995). It is very important to the dismissing to maintain a self-image as independent and not overly reliant on the support of others. Therefore, when the dismissing do experience distress, they prefer to deal with that distress on their own rather than seeking support from others. They are especially unlikely to seek support when under high levels of stress, to seek (or be willing to accept) emotional support, or to seek support for personal concerns that would make them appear emotionally vulnerable. For example, dismissing individuals may be quite comfortable discussing minor daily hassles with a romantic partner or asking a close friend for pragmatic help (such as a loan or help moving), but would be unwilling to seek support for family problems, personal doubts, or interpersonal losses. Consistent with this expectation, Bellg (1995) found that for dismissing women undergoing treatment for breast cancer, but not women with other attachment patterns, tangible support was associated with lower emotional distress. The dismissing also tend to maintain relatively superficial relationships in which the giving and receiving of emotional support is not a key component. They are, therefore, unlikely to receive much social support from others. However, because the dismissing do not expect or seek support, they are also unlikely to be strongly dissatisfied (or satisfied) with their lack of support.

Robin is a 22-year-old college student. She has a boyfriend of two-and-a-half years, a wide circle of friends, and parents that she visits very month or so. She describes herself as being committed to her education, fun-loving, and "loud and obnoxious." Most of her friends are men, because "females annoy me" and "it's easier to be one of the guys." Her friendships focus on shared activities and include minimal personal disclosure. She describes her romantic relationship as fun, stable, and predictable. Although she appears to sincerely care for and respect her partner, she insists that no love or commitment is involved in the relationship, and that she will leave "whenever someone better comes along." She feels generally satisfied with her social relationships.

Robin claims that she is rarely upset by events and has no problems in her life; rather, she describes herself as emotionally controlled, rational, well adjusted, and happy. When asked what she tends to do when she does feel upset or unhappy, she said she analyzes the situation and then either changes it or distracts herself and stops thinking about it. In her words, "I never talk to anyone about a problem. The closer things are to me, the more I keep them to myself." When asked why she would not go to others for support, she said that it would serve no purpose, and that it is inappropriate to put her problems on others. Later in the interview, when asked how responsive her romantic partner is when she would like help or support (an admittedly leading question!), Robin answered, "I don't really expect it, so I don't know how to answer that." Interestingly, she also said that she is not interested in listening to others' problems, and she expressed disdain for people who openly show their emotions.

Other aspects of Robin's story appear inconsistent with her "compulsive self-reliance." She has been in romantic relationships constantly since the age of 14, never leaving a relationship until another prospect was available. In her current relationship, she described how, when she comes home after a bad day, her partner knows just what to do without her having to say anything. And she described how sometimes she just needs to talk with a close female friend who has moved away, although not about anything personal or important. Thus, in spite of her insistence that the giving and receipt of support are not part of her close relationships, Robin appears to gain indirect support from her relationships. Moreover, Robin's failure to feel strongly supported in her relationships stems in part from her disinclination to expect or actively seek support from others.

LIMITATIONS AND FUTURE DIRECTIONS

The model of social support processes presented in Figure 16.2 focuses on aspects of the process that are of particular relevance to attachment; it is a simplification of a much more complex reality. Many other situational and individual characteristics undoubtedly also impact upon the social support process. In particular, the nature of the stressor may interact in complex ways with attachment patterns and relationship characteristics. For example, dismissing individuals may be more comfortable seeking support for noninterpersonal stressors than for interpersonal stressors that threaten their maintenance of emotional control and self-reliance. In general, we expect that attachment is most relevant to the social support process when individuals are under high levels of stress (i.e., when the attachment system is activated; Mikulincer et al., 1993; Simpson et al., 1992; Simpson & Rholes, 1994). Simpson and Rholes have also discussed how individual differences in attachment may have different implications for responses to acute and chronic stress.

The model takes as a starting point the experience of a potentially stressful event. However, attachment patterns may be associated not only with characteristic stress appraisals but also may predict the likelihood of encountering particular stressors. In the interpersonal domain, individuals with avoidant attachment strategies are expected to actively avoid interpersonal situations in which they feel vulnerable to rejection. They may, therefore, tend to encounter fewer interpersonal stressors than less avoidant individuals. In the noninterpersonal domain, it is plausible that the self-confidence associated with secure (and dismissing) attachment models and the secure base provided by secure attachment relationships may facilitate taking on potentially stressful challenges and risks. Conversely, individuals with insecure attachment representations and relationships—and preoccupied and fearful individuals in particular—may tend to constrict their life choices to avoid facing stress. However, given the multitude of unavoidable stressors that face us all (deaths, illness, accidents, job losses, etc.), regardless of attachment patterns, such avoidant strategies are unlikely to be completely successful. In addition, whereas preoccupied and fearful individuals are the most likely to feel that they lack the inner resources and social support to effectively cope with difficult or stressful situations, they are also the most likely to appraise even minor stressful events as highly stressful. Thus, we expect that individuals across the full range of attachment patterns will regularly encounter stressful situations.

The model is also limited by focusing on directional links from attachment patterns and relationship security to various stages in the social support process. In practice, there are probably bidirectional paths between most (or all) components of the model, as well as interactions among the various paths. In addition, a complete understanding of the social support process will require a parallel analysis of support giving from the perspective of the support provider. See Kunce and Shaver (1994) for a conceptual analysis and empirical demonstration of how attachment patterns predict individual differences in caregiving behavior within close relationships. Ultimately, it will be necessary to consider how each relationship partner's attachment patterns interact in predicting reciprocal caregiving and care receipt within a relationship.

DEVELOPMENTAL BASIS

One advantage of an attachment perspective on social support processes is that there is a rich and growing research base on the developmental antecedents of individual differences in adult attachment patterns (Shaver & Hazan, 1993; Shaver & Clarke, 1994). Consistent with the position of Newcomb (1990a, 1990b) and others, we see the association between individual differences in attachment patterns and social support processes as a bidirectional process. In the words of Newcomb, social support can be viewed as "an evolving transaction between the personal characteristics of an individual and those who traverse the social environment as potential resources and members of the social support network" (1990a, pp. 65–66). Thus, we expect secure attachment representations to facilitate the development and maintenance of more responsive social support networks and, conversely, experiences of supportive transactions in close relationships to facilitate the development of secure attachment relationships (e.g., Johnson et al., 1993) and representations.

Bowlby saw the formative period for the development of attachment-related internal models as extending from childhood through adolescence. However, attachment models may be updated in this reciprocal process at any point in the life span (Kirkpatrick & Hazan, 1994; Kobak & Hazan, 1991; Scharfe & Bartholomew, 1994). We offer two examples of the potential impact of support experiences on adult attachment patterns from participants who have described their relationship histories in our semistructured attachment interviews. (Of course, due to the retrospective nature of the interviews, we cannot be confident that the reports are accurate.) Luke, a relatively secure 38-year-old man with some fearful tendencies, was in a secure marital relationship when his youngest child died suddenly from a rare disease. Luke was somewhat surprised by, but deeply appreciative of, the caring and support he and his wife received from friends, co-workers, and family members following this tragedy. This support both helped Luke to deal with his loss and strengthened his confidence in the responsiveness of others and the value of his extended social network. Correspondingly, Luke became more comfortable directly expressing his feeling (e.g., he stopped worrying about crying in front of others) and directly asking for assistance and support in his close relationships. Thus, the social support Luke experienced following his loss had appeared to reconfirm and strengthen his secure attachment pattern.

Neil, a 21-year-old college student, who was coded as primarily preoccupied (with some secure tendencies), had a very different response to an interpersonal loss. Neil had been involved in a stormy 8-month romantic relationship. The relationship had involved multiple breakups and reconciliations, emotionally abusive behavior by both partners, and extreme jealousy—all the classic characteristics of the preoccupied's romances (e.g., Hazan & Shaver, 1987; Kirkpatrick & Hazan, 1994). During the positive periods, Neil had no time for his close friends. But during the more common difficult periods, Neil turned to his friends for support: He talked extensively about his relationship problems with his friends and repeatedly asked for their advice. Over time, Neil's friends became increasingly frustrated by his demands upon them, in concert with his unwillingness to leave a clearly destructive relationship. Finally, Neil's partner initiated what appeared to be a permanent split. Neil was devastated and once again turned to his friends for support and advice. After a couple of weeks of attempting to be supportive, Neil's friends became exhausted by what they saw as his hysterical overreaction, and they became less patient, telling Neil that he was better off without the romance, and that he may as well get on with his life. Neil was infuriated by their response. He felt that his friends had betrayed him. Specifically, he claimed that they had been disloyal, that they did not understand the depth of his love for his former partner, that they did not value him as an individual, and that he had been mistaken in trusting them. These conclusions further contributed to Neil's feelings of rejection and abandonment, and led him to resolve to find a new romantic relationship and a new group of friends. Thus, Neil's loss appeared to have undermined the degree of security he felt with friends and further reinforced his preoccupied tendencies.

ATTACHMENT NETWORKS

Our support model conceptualizes the process of gaining support in specific dyadic or attachment relationships. However, adults typically have multiple relationships from which they may potentially gain support. A recent project on attachment networks in adulthood indicates that most young adults have three to six attachment figures, typically including a romantic partner (where applicable), both parents, one or more siblings, and one or more friends (Trinke & Bartholomew, in press). In the childhood attachment literature, there is some evidence of benefits to be derived from multiple attachments (e.g., Howes, Rodning, Galluzo, & Meyers, 1988). Secure attachment to at least one caregiver may compensate for other insecure attachments, and it may also be advantageous to be able to turn to different attachment figures, depending on the nature of the stressful situation and/or the form of support desired. Similarly, in adulthood there may be some value of multiple attachment relationships, or at least of multiple secure attachment relationships. The findings presented in Table 16.1 suggest that avoidant individuals, in particular, may tend to have constricted networks of supportive relationships.

FUTURE RESEARCH DIRECTIONS

Our speculations regarding the links between adult attachment patterns and social support processes have limited empirical support. In general, we would advocate two complementary approaches to testing the hypotheses that we have generated: lab studies that can control elements in the social support process, and correlational studies of samples undergoing a specific stressful life experience.

Because of the inherent complexity of the social support process outlined in Figure 16.2, such as potential bidirectional and interacting influences of the various steps in the model, experimental studies will be invaluable to test specific components of the model. In a lab, it is possible to expose participants with varying attachment patterns to a common stressor. Thereby, the severity of the stressor can be varied, and the support provider can be controlled; depending on the design, other aspects of the social support process such as stress appraisals, support seeking, enacted support, and support appraisals can be assessed. Two laboratory studies in the adult attachment field are good examples of this sort of work. Simpson and colleagues (1992) observed support-seeking and support-giving behaviors in dating couples after the female partner had been led to believe she would be participating in an anxiety-provoking laboratory procedure. These behaviors were then related to participants' attachment ratings. More recently, Feeney and Kirkpatrick (1996) assessed the degree to which the presence of an attachment figure influenced stress appraisal and physiological arousal by controlling whether or not participants (with varying attachment patterns) were in the company of their romantic partners while undertaking a stressful task. In the social support field, a procedure developed by Pierce et al. (1992) could be easily adapted to testing components of our model of social support processes. In this study, enacted support was controlled by giving participants performing stressful tasks standardized notes of support from their mothers, and participants' support appraisals were assessed. Unlike the previous studies described, Pierce at al. measured both general and relationship-specific perceptions of support. Adding measures of general attachment patterns and attachment quality of the relationship between the support recipient and provider would permit testing of Paths F and G in our model (attachment pattern and relationship security to perceived stress).

Complementary correlational studies would permit examination of attachment and social support processes within the context of naturally occurring stressors. We are aware of two such studies: Bellg (1995) studied women adjusting to a recent diagnosis of breast cancer and their subsequent treatment, and Mikulincer et al. (1993) studied college students coping with Iraqi missile attacks on Israel during the Gulf War. Both studies included measures of various (although not all) components of our model, including attachment patterns, stress appraisals, and support seeking. It will be important for future studies to include additional components of the social support process and to model the intercorrelations among the various components (using path analysis or structural equation models), in addition to looking at the associations between specific pairs of variables (e.g., attachment patterns and support seeking).

We believe that an especially valuable research strategy would be to examine attachment and social support processes within a dyadic context. For example, researchers could look at married couples coping with a common stressor, such as transition to parenting, or couples in which one member is coping with a stress such as difficulties at work. It would then be possible to clearly differentiate participants' general attachment patterns (an individual difference variable) and the security or quality of the specific attachment relationship in which support is being assessed (cf. Bartholomew, 1993; Shaver & Clarke, 1994). Such an approach would also permit the use of multiple indicators of variables such as relationship security, help seeking, and enacted support. In summary, both laboratory and correlational studies offer opportunities for testing the proposed model linking attachment and social support processes.

Conclusions

The field of social support has much to offer the study of adult attachment. As convincingly argued by Simpson (Simpson et al., 1992; Simpson & Rholes, 1994), the attachment system is designed to provide security and support when individuals are threatened. Therefore, the prototypical behavioral features of each attachment pattern should be most apprent under conditions of stress. Social support research can clarify the components of the social support process that may mediate the associations between individual differences in attachment and more or less successful support receipt and provision. On the other hand, attachment theory and reserach can help provide a developmental perspective on social support, as an individual difference variable and as a social context, a perspective that has been largely lacking to date. Consideration of the various forms that insecure attachment can take may also help clarify the various paths leading to deficiencies in individuals' perceptions of support. We therefore anticipate that further examination of the links between attachment and social support processes will be a fruitful endeavor.

ACKNOWLEDGMENTS

Preparation of this paper was supported by a Social Science and Humanities Research Council of Canada research grant to the first author. We are grateful to Antonia Henderson for her helpful feedback on an earlier draft.

REFERENCES

Ainsworth, M. D. S., Blehar, M. C., Waters, E., & Wall, S. (1978). *Patterns of attachment: A psychological study of the Strange Situation*. Hillsdale, NJ: Erlbaum.

Barrera, M. Jr., & Baca, L. (1990). Recipient reactions to social support: Contributions of enacted support, conflicted support and network orientation. *Journal of Social and Personal Relationships, 7,* 541–551.

Bartholomew, K. (1990). Avoidance of intimacy: An attachment perspective. *Journal of Social and Personal Relationships, 7,* 147–178.

Bartholomew, K. (1993). From childhood to adult relationships: Attachment theory and research. In S. Duck (Ed.), *Learning about relationships: Understanding relationship processes series* (Vol. 2, pp. 30–62). Newbury Park, CA: Sage Publications.

Bartholomew, K., & Horowitz, L. (1991). Attachment styles among young adults: A test of a four-category model. *Journal of Personality and Social Psychology, 61*(2), 226–244.

Bellg, A. J. (1995). *Adult attachment and adjustment to breast cancer*. Unpublished doctoral dissertation, University of Rochester, Rochester, NY.

Blain, M. D., Whiffen, V. E., and Thompson, J. M. (1993). Attachment and perceived social support in late adolescence: The interaction between working models of self and others. *Journal of Adolescent Research, 8*(2), 226–241.

Bowlby, J. (1973). *Attachment and loss: Vol. 2.Separation*. New York: Basic Books.

Bowlby, J. (1980). *Attachment and loss: Vol. 3. Loss, sadness, and depression*. New York: Basic Books.

Bowlby, J. (1982). *Attachment and loss: Vol. 1. Attachment*, 2nd ed. New York: Basic Books. (Originally published in 1969)

Bowlby, J. (1988). Developmental psychiatry comes of age. *American Journal of Psychiatry, 145,* 1–10.

Barrera, M. J. (1986). Distinctions between social support concepts, measures, and models. *American Journal of Community Psychology, 14,* 413–445.

Carnelley, K., Pietromonaco, P., & Jaffe, K. (1994). Depression, working models of others, and relationship functioning. *Journal of Personality and Social Psychology, 66*(1), 127–140.

Cobb, R. J., & Bartholomew, K. (1995, August). *Childhood experiences and social support as predictors of attachment security*. Paper presented at the annual convention of the American Psychological Association, New York, NY.

Collins, N. L. (1996). Working models of attachmnent: Implications for explanation, emotion, and behavior. *Journal of Personality and Social Psychology, 71*(4), 810–832.

Collins, N. L., & Read, S. J. (1990). Adult attachment, working models and relationship quality in dating couples. *Journal of Personality and Social Psychology, 58,* 644–663.

Cotterell, J. L. (1992). The relation of attachments and supports to adolescent well-being and school adjustment. *Journal of Adolescent Research, 7*(1), 28–42.

Eckenrode, J. (1983). The mobilization of social supports: Some individual constraints. *American Journal of Community Psychology, 11*(5), 509–528.

Eckenrode, J., & Wethington, E. (1990) The process and outcome of mobilizing social support. In S. Duck (Ed.), *Personal relationships and social support* (pp. 83–103). Beverly Hills, CA: Sage Publications.

Feeney, B. C., & Kirkpatrick, L. A. (1996). Effects of adult attachment and presence of romantic partners on physiological responses to stress in college women. *Journal of Personality and Social Psychology, 70*(2), 255–270.

Griffin, D. W., & Bartholomew, K. (1994a). Models of the self and other: Fundamental dimensions underlying measures of adult attachment. *Journal of Personality and Social Psychology*, 67, 430–445.

Griffin, D. W., & Bartholomew, K. (1994b). The metaphysics of measurement: The case of adult attachment. In K. Bartholomew & D. Perlman (Eds.), *Advances in personal relationships: Attachment processes in adulthood* (Vol. 5, pp. 17–52). London: Jessica Kingsley.

Gross, A. E., & McMullen, P. A. (1983). Models of the help-seeking process. In B. M. DePaulo, A. Nadler, & J. D. Fisher (Eds.), *New Directions in helping* (Vol. 2, pp. 47–70). New York: Academic Press.

Hazan, C., & Shaver, P. (1987). Romantic love conceptualized as an attachment process. *Journal of Personality and Social Psychology*, 52(3), 511–524.

Hazan, C., & Shaver, P. R. (1994). Attachment as an organizational framework for research on close relationships. *Psychological Inquiry*, 5(1), 1–22.

Howes, C., Rodning, C., Galluzzo, D. C., & Myers, L. (1988). Attachment and child care: Relationships with mother and caregiver. *Early Childhood Research Quarterly*, 3, 403–416.

Johnson, R., Hobfoll, S. E., & Zalcberg-Linetzy, A. (1993). Social support knowledge and behavior and relational intimacy: A dyadic study. *Journal of Family Psychology*, 5(3), 266–277.

Kenny, M. E., & Rice, K. G. (1995). Attachment to parents and adjustment in late adolescent college students: Current status, applications and future considerations. *Counseling Psychologist*, 23(3), 433–456.

Kirkpatrick, L. A., & Davis, K. E. (1994). Attachment style, gender, and relationship stability: A longitudinal analysis. *Journal of Personality and Social Psychology*, 66, 502–512.

Kirkpatrick, L. A., & Hazan, C. (1994). Attachment styles and close relationships: A four-year prospective study. *Personal Relationships*, 1, 123–142.

Kobak, R. R., & Hazan, C. (1991). Attachment in marriage: Effects of security and accuracy of working models. *Journal of Personality and Social Psychology*, 60, 861–869.

Kobak, R. R., & Sceery, A. (1988). Attachment in late adolescence: Working models, affect regulation, and representations of self and others. *Child Development*, 59, 135–146.

Kunce, L. J., & Shaver, P. R. (1994). An attachment–theoretical approach to caregiving in romantic relationships. In K. Bartholomew & D. Perlman (Eds.), *Advances in personal relationships* (Vol. 5, pp. 205–237). London: Jessica Kingsley.

Mikulincer, M., Florian, V., & Weller, A. (1993). Attachment styles, coping strategies, and post-traumatic psychological distress: The impact of the Gulf War in Israel. *Journal of Personality and Social Psychology*, 64(5), 817–826.

Mikulincer, M., & Nachshon, O. (1991). Attachment styles and patterns of self-disclosure. *Journal of Personality and Social Psychology*, 61, 321–331.

Mikulincer, M., & Orbach, I. (1995). Attachment styles and repressive defensiveness: The accessibility and architecture of affective memories. *Journal of Personality and Social Psychology*, 68(5), 917–925.

Nadler, A., & Fisher, J. D. (1986). The role of threat to self-esteem and perceived control in recipient reaction to help: Theory development and empirical validation. In L. Berkowitz (Ed.), *Advances in experimental social psychology* (Vol. 19, pp. 81–122). Orlando, FL: Academic Press.

Newcomb, M. D. (1990a). Social support by many other names: Towards a unified conceptualization. *Journal of Social and Personal Relationships*, 7, 479–494.

Newcomb, M. D. (1990b). Social support and personal characteristics: A developmental and interactional perspective. *Journal of Social and Clinical Psychology*, 9(1), 54–68.

Ognibene, T. C., & Collins, N. L. (1997). *Attachment style differences in perceived social support and copying strategies*. Unpublished manuscript, State University of New York at Buffalo.

Osborne, J. W., Cooper, M. L., & Shaver, P. R. (1993, August). *Attachment style, social support, and psychological adjustment*. Paper presented at the annual convention of the American Psychological Association, Toronto, Ontario, Canada.

Pierce, G. R., Sarason, I. G., & Sarason, B. R. (1991). General and relationship-based perceptions of social support: Are two constructs better than one? *Journal of Personality and Social Psychology*, 61(6), 1028–1039.

Pierce, G. R., Sarason, B. R., & Sarason, I. G. (1992). General and specific support expectations and stress as predictors of perceived supportiveness: An experimental study. *Journal of Personality and Social Psychology*, 63, 297–307.

Pierce, G. R., Sarason, B. R., Sarason, I. G., Joseph, H. J., & Henderson, C. A. (1996). Conceptualizing and assessing social support in the context of the family. In G. R. Pierce, B. R. Sarason, & I. G. Sarason (Eds.), *The handbook of social support and the family* (pp. 3–23). New York: Plenum.

Sarason, B. R., Pierce, G. R., Bannerman, A., & Sarason, I. G. (1993). Investigating the antecedents of perceived social support: Parent's views of and behaviour toward their children. *Journal of Personality and Social Psychology, 65*(5), 1071-1085.

Sarason, B. R., Pierce, G. R., & Sarason, I. G. (1990a). Social support: The sense of acceptance and the role of relationships. In B. R. Sarason, I. G. Sarason, & G. R. Pierce (Eds.), *Social support: An attachment view* (pp. 97-125). New York: J Wiley.

Sarason, I. G., Pierce, G. R., & Sarason, B. R. (1990b). Social support and interaction processes: A triadic hypothesis. *Journal of Social and Personal Relationships, 7,* 485-506.

Sarason, I. G., Sarason, B. R., Shearin, E. N., & Pierce, G. R. (1987). A brief measure of social support: Practical and theoretical implications. *Journal of Social and Personal Relationships, 4,* 497-510.

Scharfe, E., & Bartholomew, K. (1994). Reliability and stability of adult attachment patterns. *Personal Relationships, 1,* 23-43.

Scharfe, E., & Bartholomew, K. (1995). Accommodation and attachment representations in young couples. *Journal of Social and Personal Relationships, 12*(3), 389-401.

Shaver, P. R., & Clarke, C. L. (1994). The psychodynamics of adult romantic attachment. In J. M. Masling & R. F. Bornstein (Eds.), *Empirical perspectives on object relations theory* (pp. 105-156). Washington, DC: American Psychological Association.

Shaver, P. R., & Hazan, C. (1993). Adult romantic attachment: Theory and evidence. In D. Perlman & W. H. Jones (Eds.), *Advances in personal relationships* (Vol. 4, pp. 29-70). London: Jessica Kingsley.

Simpson, J., & Rholes, W. S. (1994). Stress and secure base relationships in adulthood. In K. Bartholomew & D. Perlman (Eds.), *Advances in personal relationships* (Vol. 5, pp. 181-204). London: Jessica Kingsley.

Simpson, J., Rholes, W. S., & Nelligan, J. (1992). Support seeking and support giving within couples in an anxiety provoking situation: The role of attachment styles. *Journal of Personality and Social Psychology, 62*(3), 434-446.

Thoits, P. A. (1986). Social support as coping assistance. *Journal of Consulting and Clinical Psychology, 54,* 416-423.

Trinke, S. J., & Bartholomew, K. (in press). Hierarchies of attachment relationships in adulthood. *Journal of Social and Personal Relationships.*

Vaux, A., Burda, P., & Stewart, D. (1986). Orientation toward utilization of support resources. *Journal of Community Psychology, 14,* 159-170.

Vaux, A., & Wood, J. (1987). Social support resources, behaviour, and appraisals: A path analysis. *Social Behaviour and Personality: An International Journal, 15,* 107-111.

Wallace, J. L., & Vaux, A. (1993). Social support network orientation: The role of adult attachment style. *Journal of Social and Clinical Psychology, 12*(3), 354-365.

Wethington, E., & Kessler, R. C. (1986). Perceived support, received support, and adjustment to stressful life events. *Journal of Health and Social Behavior, 27,* 78-89.

CHAPTER 17

PERSONALITY AND HELP SEEKING
AUTONOMOUS VERSUS DEPENDENT
SEEKING OF HELP

ARIE NADLER

THE HELP-SEEKING DILEMMA

Consider an individual who is plagued by a constant feeling of self-doubt. He or she may be incapacitated in social relations and have difficulties concentrating on work. The person suffers and knows that a counselor, psychologist, or even a good friend could help. Yet, he or she fails to seek help. Alternatively, imagine a young engineer who has recently been hired to operate some complex machinery. He or she is unfamiliar with the task. Yet, instead of soliciting the advice of a more experienced coworker, the young engineer continues to "bang his or her head against the wall." These examples encapsulate the major topic of the present chapter and involve a common dilemma. The individual knows that he or she needs assistance to solve the problem. Yet seeking assistance may be associated with an open admission of failure and dependence on others. These anticipated psychological costs often hinder the seeking of help, which may result in the intensification of the problem (Nadler, 1991).

Research and theory in social psychology and related fields have repeatedly demonstrated the prevalence of this help-seeking dilemma between the *instrumental need* to solve the problem by seeking help, and the *psychological costs* that may decrease the willingness to seek it. This has been demonstrated in community settings (e.g., Brown, 1978), in mental health (Fischer, Weiner, & Abramowitz, 1983), and in educational (e.g., Ames & Lau, 1982) and organizational contexts (e.g., Burke, Weir, &

ARIE NADLER • Department of Psychology, Tel-Aviv University, Tel-Aviv, 69978 Israel.

Sourcebook of Social Support and Personality, edited by Gregory R. Pierce, Brian Lakey, Irwin G. Sarason, and Barbara R. Sarason. Plenum Press, New York, 1997.

Duncan, 1976). In fact, in most situations that involve coping with stress and personal difficulties, people are faced with a basic choice between "reliance on self" versus "reliance on others" in alleviating distress. The pervasiveness of this phenomenon suggests that it reflects a fundamental human conflict between the individual need to be independent and the unavoidable social necessity for help, guidance, and support. A number of major personality theorists view the resolution of this tension as the most significant task of personal development. Research indicates that whether an individual will choose to rely on the help of others to alleviate his or her distress hinges on a host of both *situational* and *personal* variables. The present chapter focuses on the relevant findings and theoretical approaches regarding the *moderating role of personality variables in determining whether an individual will seek help to resolve a distress*.

Past Research on Help Seeking

Social Psychological, Epidemiological, and Social Support Traditions of Research

The empirical and theoretical discussions of help seeking have been pursued within three broad disciplinary contexts: *social psychological* research on help seeking, *epidemiological* studies on the utilization of help, and studies within the *social support* literature on "support seeking." Each of these lines of research has applied different methodologies, investigated different problem situations, and couched the interpretation of its findings in different theoretical traditions. Much of the *social psychological* research has been experimental and is concerned with *concrete problem* situations. In a typical study, an individual performs a task, encounters difficulties on the road to successful solution, and the amount of his or her actual help-seeking behavior, or its latency, serves as dependent measure. Work in the epidemiological approach uses archival records of help seeking as its main dependent measure. Much of this research has been carried out in medical and mental health contexts and examines questions such as how actual number of visits to mental health clinics (e.g., Dew, Dunn, Bromet, & Shulberg, 1988) or university health and counseling centers (e.g., Robertson, 1988), relate to various demographic variables (e.g., socioeconomic status; Asser, 1978). It tends to focus on the seeking of professional rather than interpersonal help (e.g., seeking help from mental health professionals), and given is sociological emphasis, it highlights structural variables (e.g., socioeconomic class, level of education, age, etc.).

A third body of relevant research is constituted by the *social support* literature, which looks at coping in general and views the seeking of help as one of a number of alternative modes of coping (e.g., Folkman & Lazarus, 1980; Dunkel-Schetter, Feinstein, Taylor, & Falke, 1992; Holahan & Moos, 1987). Methodologically, this research relies heavily on individuals' self-reports concerning their intended, or past, support seeking behaviors during times of stress, and it focuses on seeking support from close others (e.g., family members) in emotionally difficult situations. However, regardless of the specific need state, methodology, or conceptual background, the social psychological, epidemiological and social support research traditions are all concerned with the same basic dilemma: What explains and predicts needy individuals' decisions to "go it alone" or "seek help" in resolving the difficulties they face?

The Role of Situational Variables: Helper and Need-State Characteristics

A help-seeking context consists of (1) a person (2) with a specific need for help who does or does not approach (3) a potential helper, or helping agency, to alleviate the distress. Past reviews of the literature on help seeking have generally followed this schematic representation and have considered characteristics of (1) the person in need, (2) the need state itself, and (3) the potential helper as affecting the help-seeking process (e.g., DePaulo, Nadler, & Fisher, 1983; Fisher, Goff, Nadler, & Chissky, 1988; Nadler, 1991). Before turning to consider the effects of the characteristics of the person in need on help seeking, and in order to acquaint the reader with the kind of situational variables used in this context, we shall begin by a brief consideration of the role of the characteristics of the helper and need state (cf. Nadler, 1991, and Wills & DePaulo, 1993, for more detailed reviews).

Regarding the *characteristics of the helper*, individuals prefer seeking help from an anonymous source, especially when the need for help reflects inadequacy on a psychologically relevant dimension (e.g., one's IQ or mental hygiene; Nadler & Porat, 1978). Social psychological research has repeatedly demonstrated that individuals are reluctant to seek and receive help from someone who is similar to them (Nadler & Fisher, 1986). This finding has been attributed to the greater "comparison stress" that one experiences when revealing inadequacy to a socially close other by seeking help from him or her. This is a major area of empirical disagreement between the social psychological and social support approaches. The social support literature maintains that we rely on similar and close others for support more than we do on more distant others. Among other things, one reason for this disagreement may lie in the fact that the two bodies of research have focused on different potential sources of help (Nadler, 1991): The social support literature has typically focused on intimate others (e.g., spouses, close friends), whereas the social psychological literature looked at nonintimate others who serve as a frame of reference for one's self-evaluations.

Ego centrality of the need for help has been singled out as an important *characteristic of the need state* that determines willingness to seek help. Due to the self-threatening information inherent in the seeking of help, individuals tend to seek help for problems they view as reflecting inadequacy on a nonego central rather than on an ego-central personal dimension (e.g., for most people, the former would include help with one's car, and the latter help to provide for one's family). This inhibitive effect of ego centrality on help seeking has been observed by numerous past studies in the social psychological (Nadler, 1991) and social support literature (e.g., Bruder-Mattson & Hovanitz, 1990). The *level of need* for help also affects the willingness to seek it. In the epidemiological literature there are common reports of linear relationships (i.e., the greater the need for help, the greater the help seeking). Thus, for example, the best predictor of the seeking of psychiatric help is severity of symptoms (e.g., Greenley & Mechanic, 1976). Yet other findings (e.g., Amato & Saunders, 1985; Karabenick & Knapp, 1988) indicate that extremely high, rather than medium, levels of felt need are associated with lower help seeking. It may be that in extremely high need states, individuals adopt a posture of helplessness in which they neither seek outside help nor help themselves.

THE MEANING OF HELP SEEKING:
AUTONOMOUS VERSUS DEPENDENT SEEKING OF HELP

The present chapter departs from other discussions in this context which have distinguished between either a behavioral or a self-report measure of seeking or not seeking help. Our emphasis will be on the role of personality characteristics as determinants of "autonomous" or "dependent" help seeking. The seeking of outside help can be an *indication of active coping*, while the decision not to seek it reflects resigning oneself to "live with the problem." Because help seeking from this perspective reflects a person's desire to use the help in order to become independent, we shall label this mode of seeking help as "autonomous help seeking." Alternatively, help seeking can mean the adoption of a *passive posture of dependence*. This is the opposite of active self-help (i.e., persisting in attempts to solve the problem on one's own). At the onset of dependent seeking, the person entertains two possibilities: investing his or her own efforts to solve the problem, or giving up by approaching a more knowledgeable or powerful helper who will solve the problem. We shall label this mode of help seeking as "dependent help seeking." Autonomous help seeking is conducive for future effective coping with the problem. Dependent help seeking is not. It is associated with relinquishing personal control and putting one's fate in the hands of the "powerful helper."

This distinction extends the help-seeking dilemma. Instead of addressing a dichotomy between seeking and not seeking help, it poses three behavioral alternatives. In these terms, if individuals' habitually depend on others, even though they can successfully solve the problem on their own, they engage in *dependent seeking* and this would be construed as the *overutilization* of help. Conversely, if individuals habitually refrain from the seeking of help, even when the consequence is failure, this is construed as a maladaptive *underutilization* of help. From this perspective, an adaptive help seeking is autonomous seeking and is construed as a behavior that is pursued when the alternative is failure and avoided when the alternative is individual achievement. The present chapter uses the distinctions between autonomous and dependent seeking, and the over- and underutilization of help as unifying themes for a review of theory and findings concerning the relation between personality and help seeking.

PERSONALITY VARIABLES AND HELP SEEKING

The previous sections have stretched the canvas on which the role of personality variables and help seeking will be drawn. The distinction between situational and personality determinants of behavior has been made in the science of psychology since its early beginnings. Although, over the years, research has moved between these two poles in a pendulum-like manner, it seems that this swing has now come to rest in the middle. The old Lewinian principle that behavior is determined by the interaction of personality and situation variables has become part of the "disciplinary matrix" of social and personality psychologists. It will also guide our present review.

The category of personality variables is a subset of the larger class of *organismic variables*, which refers to any characteristic that respondents bring with them to the situation. The major two categories of variables that are subsumed under this general category are demographic and personality characteristics. A variable that has received close attention in the epidemiological (e.g., Veroff, 1981), the social support (e.g., Greenglass, 1993a) as well as the social psychological (e.g., Nadler, Maler, & Friedman, 1984) traditions is gender. Metaphorically, gender sits on the fence between the "demographic" and "personality" sides of the "organismic field." Although gender is frequently used simply as a dichotomous distinction between men and women, social and personality psychologists have attempted to go beyond the implied "psychology of differences," and have paid close attention to the psychological meaning of such distinctions. Thus, theory and research in social psychology have considered an entire and continuous spectrum between psychological "femininity" and "masculinity." This approach can be observed in both the social psychological (e.g., Bem, 1974) and the social support (Hobfoll, Dunahoo, Ben Porath & Monnier, 1994) literature, and in it, gender can be viewed as a "bridge" between demographic and personality variables. We shall now use this bridge to cross over to the "personality side."

Differences between Men and Women: From Gender Differences to "Active Social Orientation"

Past Research and the Meaning of Gender Differences

A consistent and well-documented finding is that women seek more help than men. The robustness of this gender effect spans across a diversity of contexts. Women, for instance, seek more medical help (e.g., Verbrugge, 1981), make more visits to university counseling centers (e.g., Robertson, 1988), and are overrepresented among callers to radio counseling programs (Raviv, Raviv, & Yunovitz, 1989). Moreover, already at school age, girls seek more help than do boys (Nelson-Le Gall & Glor-Scheib, 1985). Similar effects are also reported by controlled experimental studies in social psychology (Nadler, Shapira, & Ben-Itzhak, 1982; Wallston, 1976). The explanation for this gender difference in help-seeking rests on the contents of the masculine and feminine sex roles. Research on sex role identity tells us that the feminine sex role allows, and even encourages, the display of weakness and dependence on others, while the masculine sex role puts a premium on strength, individual achievement, and independence (Meeker & Weitzel-O'Neill, 1977). Consequently, seeking help is more consistent with the feminine than the masculine sex role. In support of this rationale, studies that have used measures of "psychological gender" report that "femininity" scores were positively related to the seeking of help (Nadler et al., 1984; Wallston, 1976).

An important question is whether women's higher rates of help-seeking represent an overutilization of external resources, or if men's relatively lower willingness to seek help rather represents underutilization of help. Do women engage in dependent seeking and seek outside help even when they can solve the problem on their own (i.e., overutilize help)? The rationale of the sex-role explanation suggests a positive answer to this question. Taken to its extreme, this rationale implies that since their socialization experiences allow and even encourage dependence, women prefer to be in a dependent position. Greenglass (1993a), on the basis of her review of data on women's coping in the workplace, states that the feminine orientation towards relational behaviors and concern for the interpersonal area "have traditionally been delegated to the dependency field and thus have not been highly valued" (p. 156). She further notes that personality research assumes an implied theoretical correlation between field dependence–independence and masculinity–femininity. Accordingly, men are endowed with the qualities of the field-independent person, and women are burdened by the characteristic of the field-dependent person. All this contributes to an image of women as overutilizers of help who engage in dependent help seeking.

Yet an examination of research on women's and men's support seeking and the links of this to effective coping suggest an opposite conclusion. Women employ coping processes that involve interpersonal relations with others more than do men, and this is linked with more effective coping. Along the same lines, Burke and Belcourt (1974) found that women mention talking to one another as a way to deal with stress more often than do men. On the basis of these findings, Greenglass (1993b) suggests a modification of Lazarus and Folkman's (1984) influential distinction between "emotion-focused" coping (i.e., strategies designed to manage the emotional reactions to stress) and "problem-focused" coping (i.e., strategies that involve managing the source of stress). She suggests that women typically employ a third mechanism of *social coping*, of which active help seeking is an integral part. Hobfoll et al. (1994) have taken a similar position by proposing a "dual-axis" model of coping. The two axes in this model are (1) passive versus active coping, and (2) prosocial versus antisocial coping. Support seeking is said to be a prosocial and active form of coping, and was found by Hobfoll et al. and others (e.g., Carver, Scheier & Weintraub, 1989) to characterize women more than men. Furthermore, in agreement with the previous comments on psychological gender, Hobfoll et al. (1994) found that "[t]raditional men and women differ more distinctly in their coping strategies, whereas nontraditional men and women seem more similar in their coping approach" (p. 76).

This indicates that, compared to men, women use social coping more frequently, and this is due to women's greater emphasis on the affiliative and interpersonal dimensions. This is moreover linked with more effective coping. Greenglass (1993) found, moreover, that the active seeking of support from friends and relatives was associated with more effective coping. This link between interpersonal coping (e.g., seeking advice from others) and coping effectiveness has been documented by other studies in the context of gender differences (e.g., Long, 1988), as well as in other contexts (e.g., research on "combat stress reaction": Solomon, Mikulnicer, & Habersham, 1990; Solomon, Mikulnicer, & Hobfoll, 1986).

Thus, individuals who have an *active orientation toward the social world*—of which femininity scores are one significant correlate—tend to be more willing to actively seek others' support when they need it, which is linked to more effective coping. In the same vein, a number of studies in the social support literature have found that seeking social support is associated with better coping with stressful situations (e.g., Cronkite & Moos, 1984; Aspinwall & Taylor, 1992).

The above conceptual progression (i.e., from *sex differences*, *through psychological gender*, to *active sexual orientation*) has helped us to narrow our perspective on active social orientation, which may characterize men as well as women, and seems to be a central personal variable in the help-seeking context. Here, the term active social orientation denotes the individual's enduring tendency to see the social world as the primary reservoir of resources to draw upon during times of stress and hardship. This orientation is likely to be associated with other personality variables that indicate greater sensitivity and openness to the social world. It is moreover likely to be positively correlated with the social dimensions in the recent factorial conceptions of personality structure (e.g., the "extraversion/surgency" dimension in John's [1990] five-factor personality theory, or the "positive emotionality" dimension in Benet & Waler's [1995] seven-factor personality theory). Although people who are low on this dimension of active social orientation are not oblivious of the potentially helpful role of others, for them the primary resource for coping with difficulties is the self. Consequently, their seeking of help is likely to be less frequent and it will occur at a later stage than for those who are dispositionally more socially oriented. Furthermore, other personality characteristics underlying such an active social orientation should also be associated with increased willingness to seek assistance and result in better coping. In support of this, research has shown that high self-monitors seek more help than low self-monitors (Carver et al., 1989), and less lonely people seek more help than lonely individuals (Solomon et al., 1986; Hobfoll et al., 1994).

Another Aspect of Active Social Orientation: Resilient Children

A similar conclusion regarding the relation among "active social orientation," "help-seeking," and "better coping" emerges from research on "resilient children." These are children who, despite deprivations in their formative years, cope well with environmental stressors and are at a lesser risk of psychiatric disorders and poor scholastic achievements (Fisher, Kokes, Cole, Perkins, & Wynne, 1987; Garmezy, 1981). In a study of the psychological makeup of resilient children, Milgram and Palti (1993) compared the personality traits of high- and low-achieving children in a culturally disadvantaged community in Israel. The data indicate that the successful (i.e., resilient) children differ from their less successful counterparts in what we earlier labeled as *active social orientation*. The teachers of these children observed that they took the initiative, trusted others, were relatively less anxious or depressed, and were characteristically more likable, sociable, and helpful. Milgram and Palti characterize these children as "possessing such social support seeking and support attracting skills as being able to make friends easily with age peers, relate well to adults and help others" (p. 218). The authors cite a school nurse's description of such a resilient boy. She noted that the boy came to see her not only for routine medical examinations but also to ask her for help with psychological problems in the family "[because of] his ability to ask for help when needed, the entire family received counseling as needed" (p. 218). This illustration encapsulates the links between (1) active social orientation, (2) autonomous help seeking, and (3) enhanced coping. These data about resilient Israeli children are congruent with other findings. Parker, Cowen, Work, and Wyman (1990), who studied American inner-city children, characterized resilient children as being high in sociability, empathy, and as exhibiting high levels of both self-reliance and the ability to seek out social support. This dual emphasis on self-reliance and support-seeking skills echoes our definition of autonomous help seeking as seeking help in the service of future self-reliance.

Viewed from this perspective, autonomous help seeking is associated with higher levels of sociability. It is characteristic of individuals who are more open to the social world, are more empathic toward others, and more liked by them. From this perspective, autonomous help seeking is part of a dynamic "loop of positive feedback" in which the resilient child, for example, through being outgoing, likable, and helpful, receives from his or her social environment the message that help, in turn, will be forthcoming if he or she seeks it. This, then, encourages him or her to rely on others by seeking help from them, which results in the strengthening of trust and the active social orientation of the child. An interesting implication of this is that through training and the encouragement to seek help, individuals' active social orientation may be positively affected. Although we proposed above that active social orientation leads to the seeking of help and support when needed (i.e., autonomous seeking), and this results in enhanced coping, the causal links in this chain may be altered. In fact, it may be that by training them to seek help and support from others, less resilient children, or lonely adults, may be enabled to build a more trusting and open stance toward the social world. This would result in the activation of the positive feedback loop noted previously. This possibility remains to be assessed by future research.

Self-Esteem and the Seeking of Help

Past Research: The Vulnerability versus the Consistency Hypotheses

Much of the research in social psychology on help seeking has been guided by an assumption that the seeking and receiving of help may constitute a self-threatening experience (Nadler & Fisher, 1986). At the heart of this approach are the ideas that (1) because in Western societies, at least, positive view of self is associated with self-perceptions of self-reliance and independence, the seeking and receiving of help can be a self-threatening experience for people in need, and (2) to avoid this threat, people will often refrain from seeking help even when they need it.

That the seeking of help is self-threatening is not a "simple and sovereign" observation. It has been shown that the self-threat potential in seeking and receiving help is moderated by conceptually relevant situational and personality variables (Wills & De Paulo, 1993). In certain situations, the self-threat potential is relative high (e.g., when the task is ego-relevant), and some individuals are more sensitive than others to this threat to self-esteem. Given the important role of threat to self-esteem, it was suggested that individuals who differ in their chronic level of self-esteem will experience different levels of threat to the self associated with the seeking of help, and will therefore differ in their willingness to seek it (Nadler, 1986b). Yet, specific predictions of whether high- or low-self-esteem individuals will be more threatened by dependence and therefore seek less help are difficult to make, because two equally compelling hypotheses present themselves.

The first, the *vulnerability* hypothesis, suggests that since low-self-esteem individuals have relatively few positive self-cognitions, they are more vulnerable than high-self-esteem persons to the self-threat associated with the seeking and receiving of help. This leads to the prediction that, other things being equal, people with low self-esteem will seek less help than those with high self-esteem. The second, the *consistency* hypothesis, rests on the assumption that individuals are threatened by information that is inconsistent with their self-perceptions. For high-self-esteem individuals, dependence on others is more inconsistent with their self-perceptions or general efficacy and self-reliance than it is for low-self-esteem individuals. This leads to the suggestion that relative to low-self-esteem individuals, high-self-esteem persons will be more threatened by the prospect of interpersonal dependency, and will therefore seek less help.

Social psychological data lend greater support to the consistency than the vulnerability prediction. When situational conditions render the receipt of help potentially self-threatening, high-self-esteem individuals are more sensitive than low self-esteem individuals to this self-threat, and they seek less help. This finding was first reported by Tessler and Schwartz (1972), who observed that female undergraduates with high self-esteem sought less help from an impersonal source of help (i.e., guidelines placed conspicuously on the experimenter's desk) than did their low-self-esteem counterparts. This difference was observed only when the help-requiring task was characterized as ego-central (i.e., reflecting on intelligence and mental hygiene). Nadler, Fisher, and Streufert (1976) reported similar support for the consistency approach in the context of reactions to receiving help. In their study, high-self-esteem individuals reacted more negatively to the receipt of help than low-self-esteem individuals, when situational conditions rendered dependence self-threatening (i.e., when the helper was highly similar to the subject, and the task was described as ego-central). In a more direct examination of the moderating role of self-esteem on help seeking, Nadler (1987) reported that high-self-esteem individuals sought least help on an anagram task when the task had been defined as ego-central and the helper had been presented as interpersonally similar.

The general finding that high-self-esteem individuals are more sensitive to self-threat in interpersonal dependence is also supported by Nadler, Mayseless, Peri, and Tchemerinski (1985). They manipulated self-threat potential by the perceived opportunity (or lack of it) to reciprocate. It was expected that dependence, when the needy individual does not foresee an opportunity to reciprocate, will be more self-threatening. In line with the previous findings, Nadler et al. found that high-self-esteem children were more sensitive to this self-threat, sought less help, and took longer before seeking it than did their low-self-esteem peers. No such differences were observed when the subjects expected to be able to reciprocate.

A similar pattern of differences between high- and low-self-esteem individuals was revealed in situations outside the laboratory. In an organizational context, Burke, Weir, and Duncan (1976) found that low-self-esteem employees sought more collegial advice than did employees with high self-esteem. On the basis of a review of the psychiatric help-seeking literature, Fischer et al (1983) reported that low-self-esteem individuals sought more psychiatric treatment than did high-self-esteem individuals. Addressing the issue of dependent–compliant behaviors among alcoholics, Miller (1985) suggested that low self-esteem may increase help seeking among alcoholics. In the same vein, Nadler and Wolmer (1989) found that seeking outside help was a more common way to cope with a variety of need situations among low- than high-self-esteem subjects.

Moving closer to the social support literature, Gross, Fisher, Nadler, Stiglitz, and Craig (1979) reported that low-self-esteem women were more willing to join women's support groups than were high-self-esteem women. In a related study, Solomon (1989) compared a group of individuals who suffered from "combat stress reaction" and had sought professional help to a group of similarly affected individuals who had failed to seek such help. The findings indicate that those who had failed to seek help were characterized by a relatively high level of self-efficacy. Although self-efficacy, and not self-esteem, was the variable of interest in this study, the conceptual affinity between these two variables renders this finding as supportive of the general observation that low-self-esteem individuals seem more willing to seek help than high-self-esteem individuals. Finally, it should be noted that this higher willingness of low-self-esteem individuals to seek help was also observed when high and low levels of self-esteem were experimentally induced via false feedback on a personality test (Nadler, Altman, & Fisher, 1979), and also when social desirability was partialed out of the variance in self-esteem scores (Nadler & Fux, 1979).

This finding is explained in terms of the consistency approach by the fact that dependence is more inconsistent with the self-perception of high- than low-self-esteem individuals; the former, therefore, refrain from seeking help. Supporting this interpretation is the fact that in the social psychological experiments, the differences between high- and low-self-esteem individuals occurred only in situations that involved high self-threat (e.g., ego-central task). This bolsters the idea that threat to self-esteem is the conceptual variable that intervenes between level of self-esteem and help seeking.

Acceptance of Disability: The Role of Ego Relevance

Before considering the implications of these findings to the issues of over- or underutilization of help and dependent versus autonomous seeking, the related concept of "acceptance of inadequacy" should be considered. Nadler, Sheinberg, and Jaffe (1981) studied the link between *acceptance of disability* in male paraplegics and their willingness to seek help. In this population, acceptance of disability reflects the degree to which individuals have shifted the ability to use their legs to the periphery of their self-concept. Acceptance has occurred when individuals can say to themselves, "Although I am disabled, I am a well functioning individual." Nadler et al. (1981) indicated that paraplegics who had a relatively higher score on the acceptance-of-disability scale expressed greater willingness to seek assistance (e.g., in climbing a flight of stairs in order to enter an office) than did those who scored low on this scale. More recently, Nadler, Lewinstein, and Rahav (1991) carried out a study that focused on help-seeking preferences of parents of retarded children. Here, too, high levels of parental acceptance of retardation (e.g., an item from the scale reads, "Although we have a retarded child, our family is a healthy and normal family") was associated with greater willingness to seek outside help for problems with the retarded child.

At first glance, these findings seem at odds with the research indicating that high-self-esteem individuals are less willing to seek help than low-self-esteem individuals. Since acceptance of disability reflects a more favorable view of self as an able and well-functioning person, the consistency hypothesis would lead us to conclude that these individuals would experience dependence on others as inconsistent with their positive self-views and therefore refrain from seeking help. Yet, on closer inspection, these findings are congruent with the research on self-esteem and help seeking. As opposed to individuals who had not accepted their disability, those who did had shifted a relatively central self-attribute (e.g., being physically able or being a parent to a normal child) to the periphery of their self-concept. Thus, greater willingness of those who have accepted their disability to cope with their problems by approaching others for help is congruent with the previous discussion indicating that such readiness for assistance occurs when the state of need reflects on less ego-relevant attributes.

This described importance of the "ego implications" of dependence agrees well with the research dealing with effective coping with stress. Nicholls (1984) differentiates between task orientation and ego orientation in performance settings. The individual with an ego orientation focuses attention on the implications of performance for his or her view of self as adequate and successful. Task orientation on the other hand, is characterized by a focus on elements of the task itself, and is regarded as more adaptive to coping with stress. Building on Nicholls's distinction, Butler and Neuman (1995) have experimentally manipulated the ego versus task focus and reported that children sought more help under task orientation than under ego orientation conditions. Lazarus and Folkman's (1984) work on "emotion-focused" versus "problem-focused" coping strategies carries the same message. The problem-focused orientation is similar to Nicholls's task orientation and is characterized by efforts designed to deal with those aspects of the problem that induced stress. Emotion-focused coping strategies center on the affective consequences of stress. Seeking outside support is considered to be one manifestation of a problem-focused coping tactic. Although Nicholls centers on task performance in educational settings, Lazarus and Folkman deal with general processes of social support, and the social psychological research on ego centrality of the need for help is concerned with general processes in helping, there seems to be a convergence between these bodies of conceptual and empirical knowledge: Task-orientated, problem-focused coping, as well as the ability to view the need for help as non-ego-central are all associated with greater willingness to seek help; moreover, all these tendencies are conducive to better coping. In the terminology of the present chapter, problem-focus, task orientation, and non-ego-central need are all associated with autonomous help seeking.

Self-Esteem, Help Seeking and Coping: Autonomous versus Dependent Seeking of Help by High- and Low-Self-Esteem Individuals

The data presented in this section do not speak directly to the issue of whether high-self-esteem individuals tend to *underutilize* available help, thereby decreasing the likelihood of problem solution, or whether low-self-esteem individuals engage in dependent help seeking and *overutilize* available help, thereby decreasing the likelihood of self-achievement. A study by Weiss and Knight (1980) suggests that high-self-esteem individuals underutilize available help, and this leads, under certain conditions, to decrements in their performance. They investigated the performance of high- and low-self-esteem individuals on a task that called for frequent consulting. Because of their greater willingness to consult others, low-self-esteem individuals handed in better solutions than did high-self-esteem subjects. Weiss and Knight term this phenomenon the "utility of humility," and call our attention to the fact that in contexts which require help, high-self-esteem individuals exhibit a self-defeating tendency to underutilize existing resources of interpersonal assistance. These findings as well as data in the social support literature (e.g., Hobfoll & London, 1986), suggest that the "utility of humility" aptly describes underutilization of help by high-self-esteem individuals. This underutilization of help occurs only when the relative inadequacy and dependency associated with seeking help bears upon self-judgments. Thus, the greater willingness of low-self-esteem people to seek help should not be viewed as dependent help seeking. Because of its links with better coping, at least on tasks requiring frequent assistance and consulting, it may well reflect autonomous help-seeking. Because of their relatively more rigid adherence to self-perceptions of independence, high-self-esteem individuals, on the other hand, may often suffer from an underutilization of available help.

Highlighting Autonomous Seeking: The Partial–Instrumental Nature of Help as Moderator of Self-Esteem Help-Seeking Relationships

An important distinction that is related to the autonomous versus dependent nature of help seeking is that between partial and complete solutions. A person may approach others and ask them to provide him or her with the means (e.g., clarifying methods, hints) with which to solve the problem on his or her own. Alternatively, the individual may ask another to provide him or her with a complete solution to the problem at hand. Asser (1978) similarly distinguished between didactic and negotiating styles of help seeking (i.e., partial and full requests for help, respectively), and Nelson LeGal (1985) and Butler and Neuman (1995) referred to instrumental versus executive help seeking (i.e., partial and full requests, respectively). The psychological significance of the difference between these two styles of help seeking is great. In a partial request the individual seeks help, yet maintains a sense of independent mastery and is able to attain individual achievement. This facilitates autonomous help seeking. When one, in contrast, requests the solution to the problem, one abdicates his or her ability to attain individual achievement and opts for dependence in lieu of independent mastery.

Applying this distinction to help-seeking preferences by high- and low-self-esteem individuals suggests that since high-self-esteem individuals are more threatened by the prospects of dependence, highlighting the partial-instrumental nature of available help may allow them to adopt an autonomous perspective when seeking help. This is likely to favorably impact on their willingness to seek the needed help. In fact, under conditions that highlight the autonomous nature of help seeking (i.e., help is partial-instrumental) the vulnerability rather than the consistency prediction may prevail. On the one hand, self-threat in dependence is reduced by highlighting the instrumental nature of help, while, on the other, the valence of success, which is consistent with high self-esteem, is relatively higher for high-self-esteem individuals. This may lead high-self-esteem persons to seek more help than their low-self-esteem counterparts.

The above suggestion is congruent with Aspinwall and Taylor's (1992) findings that high self-esteem was associated with active seeking of social support from others to cope with stress. Their data indicate that the adoption of such coping strategies mediates the links between high self-esteem and higher levels of adjustment and achievement in an academic environment. This finding replicates and extends previous reports regarding positive relationships between self-esteem, optimism, and self-efficacy and effectiveness of coping with stress (e.g., Fleishman, 1984; Taylor & Brown, 1988). Relating these findings to the present discussion, an examination of the measures used in this research to assess "seeking of social support" (e.g., Folkman & Lazarus, 1984; Scheier, Weintraub & Carver, 1986) is close in its meaning to our conception of partial help seeking, which facilitates autonomous help seeking. For example, two of the items used by Aspinwall and Taylor (1992) to tap "active seeking of support" asked respondents to report how often they "talked to someone about how I was feeling," or "asked a relative or a friend I respect for advice" (p. 992). These are clear illustrations of seeking *partial help*, and reflect *autonomous help seeking*.

As noted previously, in much of the social psychological research, the person in need of help was faced with a different situation. The person could decide between *dependent seeking* (e.g., full solution, or a clear hint that leads to it), or maintaining independence by not seeking outside help. Under these conditions, where autonomous help seeking was not a viable behavior alternative, high-self-esteem individuals choose not to seek the help of others. This analysis suggests that the inconsistency between the social psychological and the social support findings in this context is due to the different nature of the helping interactions under consideration.

Drawing on the above logic, the link between self-esteem and willingness to seek help should be moderated by the *partial versus full* nature of the available help, which determines the *autonomous or dependent* nature of help seeking. In more specific terms, in situations that allow *partial request* for help (e.g., seeking advice), *autonomous seeking* is a viable alternative, and high-self-esteem individuals will seek more help than their low-self-esteem counterparts. When, however, the request for help is perceived by the person as the *seeking of full solution*, the seeking of help is *dependent seeking*, and high-self-esteem individuals will seek less help than their low-self-esteem counterparts. Thus, high self-esteem should be associated with *under-utilization* of help only when conditions where the seeking of help is viewed as dependent seeking. Moreover, viewing the above in light of help seeking as the mediator between self-esteem and adjustment and well-being suggests that high-self-esteem individuals may cope better than low-self-esteem individuals when they can engage in autonomous seeking, and low-self-esteem persons are likely to cope better than their high-self-esteem counterparts when the situation allows only for dependent seeking of help (i.e., "utility of humility"). Yet, this conceptual suggestion for the resolution of the empirical inconsistency between the social support and the social psychological findings regarding self-esteem, help seeking, and coping needs to be substantiated by future research.

DEPENDENT PERSONALITY AND HELP SEEKING

The Dependent Personality: Definition and Empirical Findings

A major personality variable that is linked to the heightened tendency to seek others' assistance is the "dependent personality" (Bornstein, 1992). As the notion implies, people who score high on a dependent personality scale would seek more help than those who score low on it. The present section reviews the research evidence pertaining to the link between dependent personality and help seeking, examines the situational conditions under which such effects are to be expected, and concludes with a discussion of the links between dependent personality, help seeking, and effective coping. This will shed light on the question of whether people characterized as having a dependent personality are dependent rather than autonomous help seekers and overutilize available helping resources.

In his recent review of the research, Bornstein (1992) refers to two relevant metatheoretical approaches to the definition of the dependent personality. The *psychodynamic* point of view sees the development of the dependent personality as related to either the frustration or the overindulgence of oral needs in early infancy. This results in an oral fixation and lifelong conflicts regarding dependenceindependence. Based on Freud's thinking, this view sees the adult dependent personality as someone who is overly dependent on others' assistance and support, and it considers this interpersonal dependency as associated with characteristic behaviors such as smoking and reliance on food as a means to cope with anxiety. The *social learning* approach to the dependent personality emphasizes the acquired nature of dependence and sees the development of the dependent personality as resulting from the degree to which passive dependent behavior was reinforced by the primary caregiver during childhood. Subsequent to this, the pleasurable experiences of dependence act as secondary reinforcers and are generalized in later life to all potential caregivers (e.g., teachers, supervisors) whose nurturance and assistance one wishes to secure.

Space limitations preclude a full review of this research (for reviews, cf. Bornstein, 1992; Masling & Schwartz, 1979), but a short methodological and empirical exposition of it will serve us in our later discussion of the moderating variables of the link between dependence and help seeking. The assessment of the dependent personality has employed both projective (e.g., Rorschach, and thematic apperception [TAT] tests) and objective measures (e.g., subscales of the Minnesota Multiphasic Personality Inventory [MMPI], or especially designed scales), and behavioral measures (e.g., peer nomination techniques).The research findings indicate that women score higher on dependent personality measures than do men (e.g., Birtchnell & Kennard, 1983), and that femininity scores are positively associated with dependency scores, while masculinity scores correlate negatively with them. A number of studies has examined the interpersonal correlates of the dependent personality and found that high scorers yielded more than low scorers to social influence on tasks using the autokinetic phenomenon (Jakubczak & Walters, 1959), or Asch-type conformity tasks (Kagan & Mussen, 1956). Importantly, this greater yielding occurred when the other was a high-status other or a figure of authority. Also, highly dependent subjects were more influenced by the experimenter's statement that "college students like yourself over/underestimate the number of dots" in a dot estimation task, which suggests that they were more sensitive to social comparison information. Highly dependent individuals are also more interpersonally sensitive than people who have a low dependency score (Pincus & Gurtman, 1995). They experienced greater discomfort in a solitary experimental condition (i.e., sitting alone for 40 minutes) than did their less dependent counterparts (Masling, Price, Goldband, & Katkin, 1981). In an interesting field demonstration of this effect, Keinan and Hobfoll (1989) report that highly dependent mothers were more anxious when they gave birth alone than when their husbands were present in the delivery room.

Dependence and Help Seeking

Regarding the link between dependence and help seeking, Bornstein (1992) states that "because dependent people are hypothesized to feel helpless and in need of guidance and support from others, they should show an elevated rate of help-seeking behaviors in a variety of settings" (p. 11). This predicted link between dependence and help seeking has been consistently supported by past research. In an early study, Bernardin and Jessor (1957) found that highly dependent men sought more help in a laboratory problem-solving situation than men characterized as low in dependence. More recently, Shilkret and Masling (1981) have studied help-seeking behavior of men and women who were designated as high or low on oral dependency and found overall support for the proposition that highly dependent individuals seek more help on the road to problem solution than do individuals with lower dependency scores. Regarding the effects of subject–experimenter gender composition, highly dependent men sought more help from both male and female experimenters, while highly dependent women sought relatively more help from a female experimenter than their low dependency counterparts. Yet, somewhat surprisingly, highly dependent women sought less help from a male experimenter than did less dependent women.

This last finding resembles De Paulo et al.'s (1983) report regarding help-seeking behavior of shy and nonshy men and women. Relative to nonshy women, shy women were the least successful in soliciting the help of male respondents. De Paulo et al. suggest that the fear to impose on the other played a significantly large role when a shy woman was to solicit the help of a man. In a similar fashion, the fear to impose may have been particularly high when the highly dependent woman in Shilkret and Masling (1981) was to solicit the help of a male authority figure (i.e., the male experimenter), and this can explain the unexpected low rates of help seeking by dependent females from a male experimenter. This interpretation is congruent with the finding that subjects characterized as oral-dependents experience greater levels of evaluation apprehension when presenting themselves to authority figures than to peers (Bornstein, Masling, & Poynton, 1987).

This general positive link between dependence and help seeking was also substantiated in studies that examined help-seeking behavior in naturalistic settings (e.g., in the classroom; Sroufe, Fox, & Pancake, 1983). Studying medical help seeking, Bornstein, Krukonis, Manning, Mastrosimone, and Rossner (1993) prescreened 181 respondents for level of dependence and subsequently monitored the level of "medical help seeking" of 100 subjects randomly selected from the total sample, for a period of 3 months. The results clearly indicate that level of interpersonal dependency was positively related to healthcare utilization in both male and female subjects. Bornstein et al. (1993) conclude their discussion by noting that "the results ... strongly support the hypotheses than an oral character is related to a help-seeking approach to the world" (p. 35).

Over- or Underutilization? The Role of the Helper's Identity

The findings in the preceding section indicate that highly dependent individuals seek more help than subjects with low dependence. Yet, the psychological processes that propel the highly dependent person indicate that this general statement is contingent on the identity of the helper. As noted, dependent individuals are motivated to maintain nurturant, helping, and supportive relations with authority figures. This usually results in greater willingness to seek the help and assistance of others who are higher in status. This suggests that the presence of a figure of authority as a source of assistance will cause the dependent personality to overutilize help. In fact, relative to low-dependent people, the highly dependent person is likely to prefer fulfillment of his or her higher needs for nurturant relations with higher status others to personal mastery and individual achievement.

In this vein, Bornstein (1992) noted that the research which examined the links between dependence and help seeking was limited to interactions with high-status others (e.g., experimenters). Whether similar processes will occur with peers remains an open question. The conceptual emphasis on the dependent individual's wish to be dependent on high-status others, and their lesser concern with pleasing peers (Bornstein et al., 1987), indicate a different relationship between dependence and help seeking when the helpers are peers. It may well be that highly dependent individuals would experience more comparison stress with a peer helper and seek relatively less help than their less dependent counterparts. Yet, the interaction between status of helper, the evaluative meaning of seeking help, and dependency needs of the helpee is left for the scrutiny of future research.

Dependency and Help Seeking: Autonomous or Dependent Help Seeking?

The term *dependent personality* itself evokes images of weakness and lack of control. This generally negative image of the dependent personality returns in the writings about the "orally dependent personality." Fromm's (1947) statements in this regard are illuminating. In describing the oral personality's stance toward the world, Fromm presents these individuals as overly concerned about others' evaluation of them, and notes that "they are always in search of a magic helper. They show a particular kind of loyalty, at the bottom of which is the gratitude for the hand that feeds them and the fear of ever losing it" (pp. 62–63). The picture is an unflattering one, likening the dependent person to a pet on a leash. It suggests that highly dependent people relinquish control over their personal fate and engage in "dependent" help-seeking.

Yet, in their study of medical-help utilization by high- and low-dependency individuals, Bornstein et al. (1993) remind us that "it is important to note that frequent utilization of health services actually represents active—rather than passive—behavior on the part of the dependent person" (p. 274). Moreover, relative to non-dependent persons, dependent individuals are endowed with positive qualities of greater interpersonal sensitivity, more cooperativeness and greater willingness to help others (Bornstein et al., 1993). In line with our previous assertion that people with an active social orientation are better able to cope with stress through seeking others' assistance, highly dependent individuals may be autonomous seekers of help. In a context in which overcoming difficulty requires assistance, highly dependent individuals may cope better than individuals who have low dependency needs. We do not know whether the dependent people who sought more medical help in Bornstein et al.'s study were actually in better health than their low-dependency counterparts who avoided the seeking of help. Available data do not provide us with empirical evidence to answer this issue. To be able to address it, data linking together dependency, help seeking, and effectiveness of coping would need to be collected.

This discussion suggests that dependence is not necessarily equated with dependent help seeking. The active social orientation that is presumably linked to more effective coping is more characteristic of high- than low-dependency individuals. We are reminded here that the research tended to view the greater willingness of low-self-esteem individuals in general, and women in particular, as the epitome of dependent help seeking, showing a preference for relinquishing control to place oneself in the hands of the "magic helper." Yet, the links between active social orientation, help seeking, and enhanced coping highlight the autonomous element of active coping which is associated with help seeking, and the weaker and less effective elements, which are associated with rigid adherence to the norms of self-reliance resulting in underutilization of help. Although the logic behind the theory of the dependent personality indicates that under certain conditions (i.e., help of higher-status others) this individual will display dependent help-seeking and overutilize help, the notion of "the utility of humility" may be used here to refer to the autonomous element, which is also associated with this willingness of the highly dependent individual to seek help.

Multifaceted Conception of Dependence: Implications for Help Seeking

In their recent reconceptualization of dependence, Pincus and Gurtman (1995) empirically validated three distinct facets of interpersonal dependence: (1) "Love Dependency," which taps the component of enhanced interpersonal sensitivity and affiliative behaviors characteristic of the dependent person; (2) "Exploitable Dependency," which reflects the strong evaluation apprehension characteristic of the highly dependent personality; and (3) "Submissive Dependency," which captures the dependent person's tendency to yield to high authority. Although their study did not address the issue of help seeking directly, Pincus and Gurtman seem to hold the view that help seeking is a manifestation of submissiveness, and that it reflects a weak dependence. In fact, they note that the "yielding, compliance and *guidance seeking*" (emphasis added) behaviors characteristic of the dependent person are part of the submissive dependency facet (p. 753, emphasis added). In the present context, this suggests that high-submissive dependency will be reflected in dependent help seeking. Yet, a dependent person who is characterized by relatively high scores on love dependency (i.e., high affiliative tendencies and interpersonal sensitivity) and low scores on submissive dependency is dependent on the social world but not submissive to it. In line with our earlier emphasis on the beneficial aspects of active social orientation, such an individual is more likely to exhibit autonomous rather than dependent help seeking.

In summary, it seems that the links between dependent personality and help seeking have been portrayed in a one-sided manner. In descriptions of the dependent personality, the dependent persons' greater reliance on others for help has tended to be equated with submissiveness and willingness to relinquish control over their fate, in order to obtain nurturant relationships with powerful figures (Bornstein, 1992; Pincus & Gurtman, 1995). Our distinction between autonomous and dependent help seeking suggests that, although this may be the case, it is not necessarily so. If one considers the dependent person's greater affiliative tendencies, then dependent personality may be associated with higher levels of autonomous help seeking. The preceding sections suggest that both the situational characteristic of the helping encounter (e.g., the status of the helper) and the exact makeup of dependence (e.g., emphasis on submissiveness or love dependency) will together determine whether the greater willingness of the dependent person to seek help should be seen as either autonomous or dependent help seeking.

ATTACHMENT STYLES AND HELP SEEKING

Attachment Styles: Secure, Avoidant, and Anxious–Ambivalent

The concept of dependent personality is theoretically close to that of "attachment styles." In fact, the two conceptualizations are embedded within one psychodynamic meta-theoretical approach. Whereas the theorizing on the dependent oral personality has its origins in Freud's writings, the theory about attachment styles hails from more recent psychodynamic developments. It is grounded in Bowlby's (1973) attachment theory and Ainsworth, Blehar, Waters and Wall's (1978) empirical research on the quality of attachment between the child and his or her caregivers.

Hazan and Shaver (1987) pioneered the adaptation of the tripartite definition of children's attachment behaviors to the study of social relationships in adulthood. On the basis of Bowlby's theorization, they distinguished between three attachment styles: secure, avoidant, and anxious–ambivalent. The manifestation of these three behavioral styles is most salient during times of stress. Secure individuals have developed a secure scheme of interpersonal relations and believe that attachment figures (e.g., a spouse) will be there for them when they need them. Insecure individuals have not developed this outlook: They view attachment figures more suspiciously and have doubts about the extent to which significant others will be available when they need them. The two insecure types (i.e., the anxious–ambivalent and the avoidant) deal with this insecurity in different ways. While the anxious–ambivalent individual displays oversensitivity to the distress and deals with it by adopting a watchful and guarded stance, the avoidant individual uses denial and inhibition of emotions as a way of coping. Much recent research has documented how these three different attachment styles are related to a wide range of social phenomena. Secure individuals were shown to be less lonely (Hazan & Shaver, 1987) and have fewer physical symptoms (Hazan & Shaver, 1990), as well as being less anxious and hostile (Kobak & Sceery, 1988) than were their less secure counterparts.

Attachment and Help Seeking

Attachment theory suggests that a major area of interpersonal behavior in which secure, avoidant and anxious–ambivalent personalities would differ is the willingness to seek others' assistance in times of need. In fact, the availability of significant others as sources of support and help is a key element in Bowlby's theorizing and is associated with early attachment experience. Capitalizing on this, Simpson, Rholes, and Nelligan (1992) studied support seeking and support giving among dating heterosexual couples as affected by their attachment styles. Subjects were instructed to come to the laboratory with an intimate other of the opposite sex. First, attachment styles of both the men and women were assessed. Subsequently, the experimenter asked the woman to accompany him, while the man was to wait in an adjoining room. The woman was told by the experimenter that she would be exposed to a stressful and noxious stimulus (i.e., electric shock), and was asked to return to the waiting room to join her male partner. The ensuring interaction between the man and the woman was videotaped and analyzed to assess degree of support seeking by the anxious woman, and support giving by the nonanxious man. In their analyses, Simpson et al. focused on examining support-seeking behaviors of securely attached and avoidant women.

The results indicate that, as their anxiety increased, secure women sought more support from their partners. An opposite pattern was observed for avoidant women. As their anxiety increased, they sought less support from their partner and coped with the stressful situation by withdrawing into themselves. These findings support the basic premise of attachment theory in showing that securely attached persons seek more support than avoidant individuals. From this, however, we cannot conclude that avoidant persons are *generally* more unwilling to seek help than secure individuals. These findings are dependent on the level of anxiety experienced by the person in need. In accordance with attachment theory, the attachment system is activated only under conditions of high anxiety.

In another application of attachment theory to the context of help and support seeking, Mikulnicer and Florian (1995) examined self-reports of coping among young Israeli soldiers during the intensive 4 months of basic training. In line with attachment theory, securely attached persons reported seeking more support from their peers to cope with the stress of basic training than did avoidant individuals. This finding replicates those of an earlier study (Mikulnicer, Florian, & Weller, 1993) which showed that, compared to avoidant persons, securely attached individuals reported seeking more support to cope with the stress experienced during the Iraqi missile attacks on Israeli cities during the 1991 Gulf War.

The help-seeking behavior of anxious–ambivalent persons seems less stable across situations. In Mikulnicer and Florian's 1995 study, level of support seeking reported by the anxious–ambivalent soldiers was high and similar to that of securely attached persons. In the Gulf War study, however, anxious–ambivalent individuals reported a significantly lower level of support seeking than did their securely attached counterparts. Mikulnicer and Florian suggest that this variance in the ambivalent individuals' support-seeking behavior may originate in the different kinds of support providers in the two studies. In the Gulf War setting, interactions were confined, for the most part, to close family members, and a similarly high level of stress was experienced by all. In the basic training situation, interactions occurred with peers, who may or may not have been similarly affected by the hardships of army basic training. This suggests that ambivalent individuals behave like secure individuals and seek needed help when stress is shared with others (i.e., the Gulf War study), while they behave like avoidant individuals by refraining from seeking help when the stress is a more private experience (i.e., the basic training study). This, or any alternative interpretation, needs to be substantiated by future research. Regardless, however, the overall pattern of the data suggests that as level of stress increases, securely attached individuals turn to others for help and support. Avoidant persons refrain from help seeking even when the level of stress is high, and ambivalently attached people are more unpredictable in their help-seeking preferences. Their willingness to seek help is affected by situational variables that are unrelated to the degree of stress (e.g., the degree to which stress is shared or not).

In our present terms, securely attached individuals engage in autonomous help seeking. They seem to be better able to walk the tightrope between self-reliance and dependence. They seek help only when objective–instrumental conditions render reliance on self counterproductive for coping. Avoidant people seem locked into a posture of self-reliance, even when situational conditions render the refusal to seek help counterproductive for effective coping. They display a rigid underutilization of help. Ambivalently attached individuals are more volatile in their behavior. Depending on nonproblem relevant conditions (e.g., identity of the helper, the degree to which stress is shared, etc.), they may exhibit either over- or underutilization behavior.

Similarities between Attachment Styles and Autonomous versus Dependent Seeking

The tripartite distinction of attachment styles closely resembles our identification of autonomous help seeking (i.e., the securely attached person), dependent help seeking (i.e., the ambivalently attached person under certain conditions), and the phenomenon of rigid underutilization of help (i.e., the avoidant person). This continuity between attachment styles and our conceptualization of help-seeking behaviors suggests that securely attached people will seek help only when this is instrumental for problem solution. The two insecure types should be relatively unaffected by situational variations in the instrumentality of help. Avoidant individuals will refrain from seeking help even when help is clearly instrumental for problem solution, and ambivalently attached individuals will be affected by non-problem relevant variables.

In an effort to examine these hypotheses, Tzafrir, Nadler, and Friedland (1996) looked at help seeking as it is affected by the instrumentality of help and by the person's attachment style. Prior to the experiment, subjects' scores on the secure, avoidant, and anxious–ambivalent scales were obtained. Subsequently, respondents were presented with a cognitive task that was described in ego-central terms (i.e., an anagram task). Subjects could obtain help in solving the task although some of the items on this task were in fact insoluble. In the highly instrumental help conditions, subjects were told that in past administrations of this task people who had sought help had generally been able to solve the problem. In the noninstrumental conditions, subjects were told that only a small proportion of people in past administrations had found the assistance they obtained helpful. The analysis revealed that highly avoidant people were unaffected by the instrumentality of help manipulation. They maintained a relatively low level of help-seeking across all situations. Highly ambivalent individuals were also unaffected by the situational variation of instrumentality. They exhibited relatively high levels of help seeking in all conditions. Securely attached individuals varied in their help seeking in line with the perceived instrumentality of help. They sought significantly more help when help had been presented as instrumental than either the control or the noninstrumental help conditions.

These findings support earlier research regarding the links between attachment styles and help seeking. Moreover, they add an important dimension to these earlier empirical discussions. In earlier studies, the help-seeking setting involved an intense emotional need (i.e., waiting for a "scary" experiment, experiencing the traumas of missile attacks or the hardships of basic military training), and the help was provided by another person. In this study, subjects sought instrumental help to complete an emotionally neutral task, and help was impersonal (i.e., they were to scratch a spot on the page to reveal guiding information). The fact that under these circumstances, too, attachment predicted help seeking in a conceptually consistent manner, suggests that attachment schemas also exert their influence in instrumental-achievement settings. The patterns of reliance on close others in times of stress seem to generalize to more general help-seeking tendencies.

OTHER PERSONALITY DETERMINANTS OF HELP SEEKING: NEED FOR ACHIEVEMENT, SHYNESS, AND SELF-CONSCIOUSNESS

Beyond the aforementioned personality determinants and their effects on help seeking, other personality characteristics that were also identified in past research will be briefly reviewed before concluding this chapter.

Achievement Motivation and Help Seeking

A consideration of the relationship between the need for achievement and help seeking suggests a relatively complex picture. On the one hand, the valence of success for high achievers is higher than it is for low achievers, and this should propel the former to seek more help to further successful task completion. Yet, since need for achievement is associated with a desire for individual achievement rather than achievement per se, high achievers should also tend to avoid seeking help. Nadler (1986a) reports data that touch upon these two facets of the achievement help seeking relationship. When achievement was defined in individualistic terms, a negative correlation indicated that high-need achievers sought less help than low-need achievers. This finding is also supported by Tessler and Schwartz (1972). Yet, when achievement was defined in group terms a positive relationship between need for achievement and help seeking was obtained. The magnitude of this relationship was especially high when group success was important for respondents (i.e., members of a communally oriented Kibbutz culture). Supporting the idea that the need for individual achievement inhibits help seeking, Newman (1990) found that among elementary-school children, strivings for independent mastery were negatively correlated with willingness to seek help. Although there are no empirical data to tell us whether this reluctance of high achievers to seek help is linked to lower coping, thereby representing a underutilization of help, the dynamics that caused high-self-esteem individuals to underutilize help seems relevant here too. In trying to fulfill an ego-relevant goal (i.e., individual achievement), high achievers may in fact enter the trap of underutilization of help.

Ames's (1983) analysis of help seeking sheds light on the psychological determinants that may reverse the above trend. In line with our previous discussions, which highlight the facilitative effects of task-orientation rather than ego-orientation on help seeking, Ames specifies an attributional pattern that facilitates help seeking. He suggests that (1) attributing the need for help to a specific rather than a global lack of ability, and (2) maintaining perceptions of control by viewing effort as a major causal factor in task performance will facilitate the seeking of help. In support of this analysis, Ames and Lau (1982) observed that students who were characterized by such an attitude were most willing to attend helping sessions before a test. It is also of importance to note that this enhanced willingness to seek help occurred when the help offered was "partial-instrumental" (i.e., the helping sessions were aimed to accomplish future success on subsequent individual test performance). Supporting the role of partial-instrumental help in this context, Newman (1990) reports that students who scored high on strivings for independent mastery showed a marked preference for hints rather than full solutions. Phrased differently, the attributional pattern described by Ames is conducive to autonomous help seeking, and this is facilitated by the availability of partial-instrumental help. Given the greater motivation for success of high achievers, we would expect them to seek more help under these conditions.

Shyness and Help Seeking

Zimbardo (1977) notes that unwillingness to seek help or advice is the shy person's major behavioral characteristic. Empirical research has supported this suggestion. Shy individuals indicate that seeking help is hard for them; they report a smaller number of people in their social network to whom they can turn for help and see others as offering less support than do nonshy individuals (Jones & Carpenter, 1986). Other research indicates that shy people are reluctant to seek help in educational contexts and are also quite unwilling to seek help in coping with their shyness (Wills & De Paulo, 1993). As might be expected, this reluctance to seek help is enhanced by evaluation apprehension in interpersonal encounters. In fact, De Paulo et al. (1983) indicated that shy individuals were particularly less successful in actually obtaining help when the other was an opposite-sex other. Relative to requesting help from a same-sex other, this situation is presumed to be more laden with evaluation apprehension.

Thus, it seems that the shy person is an underutilizer of helping resources. This underutilization is likely to result in lower coping, especially in circumstances requiring reliance on others who are a potential source of negative evaluation of oneself. Since fears of negative social evaluation seem to block shy people's help seeking, it is likely that when the source of help is impersonal (e.g., a computer), these individuals will not shrink from seeking assistance. Thus, tailoring the appropriate helping source (i.e., offering an impersonal source) may allow the shy person to move away from underutilization of help to more autonomous help seeking.

Self-Consciousness and Help Seeking

Self-aware individuals are said to be more self-critical than non-self-aware people (Carver, 1981). Given the inhibitive role of self-threat in the willingness to seek help, self-aware individuals should also be less willing to seek help than individuals who are not self-aware. Since self-consciousness is the personality analog of self-awareness (Fenigstein, Scheier, & Buss, 1975), individuals who score high on self-consciousness should be more critical of themselves and therefore less wiling to seek help. For them, the negative self-evaluative elements of dependence on others should be more salient and inhibit the seeking of assistance. This analysis has received empirical support from La Morto-Corse and Carver (1980), who found that individuals high in self-consciousness sought help less than those characterized as low in self-consciousness. In terms of our previous discussion of ego versus task orientation, highly self-conscious individuals adopt an ego-relevant perspective when faced with difficulty and this inhibits their willingness to seek help. This finding is supportive of our earlier suggestion that individuals will be more autonomous in their help seeking when adopting a task orientation (Nicholls, 1984), choosing problem-focused coping mechanisms (Lazarus & Folkman, 1980) and considers the need for help as nonego-central (Nadler, 1986b).

SUMMARY AND CONCLUSIONS

In the previous sections we reviewed the available data regarding the role of personality variables as determinants of help seeking. This review began with gender differences, which led us to the consideration of active social orientation as a major determinant of help seeking. We continued by considering the role of self-esteem in this context. Subsequently, our view shifted to a consideration of the variables of dependence and attachment styles, and we concluded our review by referring to additional conceptually relevant variables (i.e., need for achievement, shyness, and self-consciousness).

Much of past research on the personal determinants of help seeking has been marked by two characteristics: (1) it has focused on a dichotomy between seeking and not seeking help, and (2) it adopted the view that the seeking of help represents dependence on others and lack of persistence. In fact, whether discussing the greater willingness to seek help of low-self-esteem or highly dependent individuals in general or of women in particular, the spirit of the discussion was that seeking help epitomizes weakness, the opposite of which is strong self-reliance. This widespread trend may be attributable to the centrality of the values of self-reliance and independence in Western society (e.g., Markus & Kitayama, 1991).

In contrast, the present review has drawn attention to the more complex nature of help seeking and focused on the subtler meanings of this behavior. Throughout, we have considered the links between help seeking and effective coping. This has led to the distinction between (1) autonomous help seeking, which results in future independence; (2) dependent help seeking (i.e., overutilization of help), which results in future dependence; and (3) underutilization of help, which may end in the prolongation of hardship or suffering. This has led us to view effective help seeking as autonomous help seeking, in which the individuals succeed in walking the tightrope between not seeking help when they can attain individual achievement, and seeking help when the alternative is failure and continued difficulties.

We began by considering gender differences in help seeking. Past research tended to view women's greater willingness to seek help as representing weakness and dependence, which agrees well with the contents of the traditional feminine sex role. By considering the links between gender, affiliative behaviors, and coping with stress, we shifted attention to the concept of active social orientation. This resulted in the suggestion that people with an active social orientation find it easier to rely on others during stress, leading to better coping. People who do not have such an orientation (e.g., high scorers on masculinity scales) display rigid adherence to the norm of self-reliance and underutilize available help. The findings about resilient children lended further support to this analysis.

Self-esteem and the dependent personality are conceptually relevant to the prediction and explanation of help-seeking behavior. The data indicate that relative to high-self-esteem individuals, low-self-esteem persons are more willing to seek help on their way to solving a problem or completing a task. The interpretation that this is due to the greater consistency between dependence and low feelings of esteem assumes that the low-self-esteem person is a dependent seeker (i.e., overutilization of help). Yet, we proposed that, at least when frequent consulting is needed, low-self-esteem persons seem to cope better because of their willingness to seek help. Under these circumstances, at least, low-self-esteem individuals emerge as autonomous seekers, whereas high-self-esteem individuals underutilize help.

Traditionally, individuals who have a high score on the dependent personality scale are viewed as dependent seekers, that is, individuals for whom the psychological benefits of being dependent on powerful others outweigh the rewards gained by personal achievement. Thus, they are motivated to be overutilizers of help and seek it even if they can do without it. Here too we have questioned the accuracy of this view of dependency. It has been noted that unless the links between dependency, help-seeking and coping, are examined, it cannot be ascertained whether the highly dependent person's greater readiness to seek help is always representative of dependent help seeking. Furthermore, we have noted that recent empirical and conceptual developments (Pincus & Guntmar, 1995) suggest that highly dependent persons are not all made of the same stuff, and that some definitions of dependence (i.e., high scores on love dependency and low ones on submissive dependence) are likely to be associated with autonomous seeking.

Attachment styles have also been related to help seeking, suggesting that securely attached individuals seek help when it is likely to foster the solution of the problem, and avoid seeking it when it is not instrumental for problem solution. Avoidant individuals habitually refrain from seeking help, and ambivalent–anxious persons fluctuate between over- and underutilization depending on non-problem-related variables (e.g., the identity of the helper). This has led us to view these three attachment styles as analogous to autonomous help seeking (i.e., the securely attached person), underutilization of help (i.e., the avoidant person), and dependent help seeking as expressed in overutilization of help (i.e., the ambivalent–anxious individual, in certain situations). We concluded our review by noting the relationships between need for achievement, shyness, and self-consciousness and help seeking.

But personality variables do not tell the whole story. Our review has touched upon a number of situational variables that interact in a conceptually consistent manner with a particular personality characteristic to determine the occurrence of autonomous help seeking, dependent help seeking, or underutilization of help. Thus, for example, the helper's status determines the desirability of help seeking for the highly dependent person, and evaluation apprehension potential affects the help seeking of the shy person. Two situational characteristics seem to stand out in this context, and deserve special mention: ego versus task orientation at the onset of help seeking, and the partial-instrumental versus complete-full nature of the help available.

Diverse bodies of research and theoretical approaches tell us that attending to task-relevant information facilitates autonomous help seeking and decreases the tendency to underutilize help, which is associated with an ego perspective at the onset of seeking help. This has been noted in educational contexts (i.e., Nicholls, 1984), social support processes (i.e., Lazarus & Folkman, 1984) and experimental social psychological research (i.e., Nadler & Fisher, 1986). Furthermore, the availability of partial-instrumental help allows one to be assisted by others, while retaining a sense of personal control and individual achievement. Such help encourages autonomous help seeking. Help that constitutes a complete solution to the problem, on the other hand, discourages autonomous help seeking and allows only dependent help seeking. In conclusion, the distinction between *autonomous* seeking, *dependent* seeking, and *underutilization* of help has allowed us to shift the focus from viewing dependence on others as wholly synonymous with weakness, to considering help seeking as, at times, a way of active coping.

REFERENCES

Ainsworth, M., Blehar, M., Waters, E., & Wall, S. (1978). *Patterns of Attachment*. Hillsdale, NJ: Erlbaum.

Amato, P. R., & Saunders, J. (1985). The perceived dimensions of help-seeking episodes. *Social Psychology Quarterly, 48*, 130-138.

Ames, R. (1983). Help-seeking and achievement orientation: Perspectives from attribution theory. In B. M. DePaulo, A. Nadler, & J. D. Fisher (Eds.), *New Directions in helping (Vol. 2). Help-Seeking* (pp. 165-186). New York: Academic Press.

Ames, R., & Lau, S. (1982). An attributional analysis of help-seeking in academic settings. *Journal of Educational Psychology, 74*, 414-423.

Aspinwall, L. G., & Taylor, S. E. (1992). Modeling cognitive adaptation: A longitudinal investigation of the impact of individual differences and coping on college adjustment and performance. *Journal of Personality and Social Psychology, 63*, 989-1003.

Asser, E. S. (1978). Social class and help-seeking behavior. *American Journal of Community Psychology, 6*, 465-474.

Belle, D., Burr., R., & Conney, J. (1987). Boys and girls as social support theorists. *Sex Roles, 17*, 657-665.

Bem, S. L. (1974). The measurement of psychological androgeny. *Journal of Consulting and Clinical Psychology, 42*, 155-162.

Bernardin, A., & Jessor, R. (1957). A construct validation of the Edwards Personal Preference Schedule with respect to dependency. *Journal of Consulting Psychology, 21*, 63-67.

Birtchnell, J., & Kennard, J. (1983). What does the MMPI dependency really measure. *Journal of Clinical Psychology, 39*, 532-543.

Bornstein, R. F. (1992). The dependent personality: Developmental, social and clinical perspectives. *Psychological Bulletin, 112*, 3-23.

Bornstein, R. F., Krukonis, A. B., Manning, K. A., Mastrosimone, C., & Rossner, S. C. (1993). Interpersonal dependency and health service utilization in college student sample. *Journal of Social and Clinical Psychology, 12*, 262-279.

Bornstein, R. F., Masling, J. M., & Poynton, F. G. (1987). Orality as a factor in interpersonal yielding. *Psychoanalytic Psychology, 4*, 161-170.

Bowlby, J. (1973). *Attachment and loss: Separation, anxiety and anger*. New York: Basic Books.

Brown, B. B. (1978). Social and psychological correlates of help-seeking behavior among urban adults. *American Journal of Community Psychology, 6*, 425-439.

Bruder-Mattson, S. F., & Hovanitz, C. A. (1990). Coping and attributional styles as predictors of depression. *Journal of Clinical Psychology*, *46*, 557-565.

Burke, R. J., & Belcourt, M. L. (1974). Managerial role stress and coping responses. *Journal of Business Administration*, *5*, 55-68.

Burke, R. J., Weir, T., & Duncan, G. (1976). Informal helping relationships in work organizations. *Academy of Management Journal*, *19*, 370-377.

Butler, R., & Neuman, O. (1995). Effects of task and ego achievement goals on help-seeking behaviors and attitudes. *Journal of Educational Psychology*, *87*, 261-271.

Carver, C. S. (1981). *Attention and self-regulation: A control theory approach to human behavior*. New York: Springer-Verlag.

Carver, C. S., Scheier, M. F., & Weintraub, J. K. (1989). Assessing coping strategies: A theoretically based approach. *Journal of Personality and Social Psychology*, *56*, 267-283.

Cronkite, R. C., & Moos, R. H. (1984). The role of predisposing and moderating factors in the stress-illness relationship. *Journal of Health and Social Behavior*, *25*, 372-393.

DePaulo, B. M., Nadler, A., & Fisher, J. D. (Eds.) (1983). *New directions in helping (Vol. 2). Help-Seeking*. New York: Academic Press.

Dew, M. A., Dunn, L. O., Bromet, E. J., & Schulberg, H. C. (1988). Factors affecting help-seeking during depression in a community sample. *Journal of Affective Disorders*, *14*, 233-234.

Dunkel-Schetter, C., Feinstein, L., Taylor, S. E., & Falke, R. (1992). Patterns of coping with cancer and their correlates. *Health Psychology*, *11*, 79-87.

Fenigstein, A., Scheier, M. F., & Buss, A. H. (1975). Public and private self-consciousness: Assessment and theory. *Journal of Consulting and Clinical Psychology*, *43*, 522-527.

Fischer, E. H., Weiner, D., & Abramowitz, S. I. (1983). Seeking professional help for psychological problems. In A. Nadler, J. D. Fisher, & B. M. DePaulo (Eds.), *New Directions in Helping* (Vol. 3). New York: Academic Press.

Fisher, J. D., Goff, B. A., Nadler, A., & Chinsky, J. M. (1988). When will people seek social support? Implications for interventions. In B. H. Gottlieb (Ed.), *Marshalling social support: Formats, processes and effects* (pp. 265-305). Beverly Hills, CA: Sage.

Fisher, L., Kokes, R. F., Cole, R. E., Perkins, P. M., & Wynne, L. C. (1987). Competent children at risk: A study of well-functioning offspring of disturbed parents. In E. J. Anthony & B. J. Cohler (Eds.), *The Invulnerable Child* (pp. 211-228). New York: Guilford.

Fisher, J. D., Goff, B. A., Nadler, A., & Chinsky, J. M. (1988). Social psychological influences on help seeking and support from peers. In B. H. Gottlieb (Ed.), *Marshalling social support: Formats, processes, and affects* (pp. 267-304). Newburg Park, CA: Sage.

Fleishman, J. A. (1984). Personality characteristics and coping patterns. *Journal of Health and Social Behavior*, *25*, 229-244.

Folkman, S., & Lazarus, R. S. (1980). An analysis of coping in middle aged community sample. *Journal of Health and Social Support*, *21*, 219-239.

Garmezy, N. (1981). Children under stress: Perspectives on antecedents and correlates of vulnerability and resistance to psychopathology. In A. I. Rabin, J. Aronoff, A. M. Barclay, & R. A. Zucker (Eds.), *Further explorations in personality* (pp. 196-269). New York: Wiley.

Greenglass, E. R. (1993a). Social support and coping of employed women. In B. C. Long & S. E. Kahn (Eds.), *Women, work and coping* (pp. 154-169). Montreal: McGill-Queens.

Greenglass, E. R. (1993b). The contribution of social support to coping strategies. *Applied Psychology: An International Review*, *42*, 323-340.

Greenley, J. R., & Mechanic, D. (1976). Social selection in seeking help for psychological problems. *Journal of Health and Social Behavior*, *17*, 249.

Gross, A. E., Fisher, J. D., Nadler, A., Stiglitz, E., & Craig, C. (1979). Correlates of help utilization at a women's counseling service. *Journal of Community Psychology*, *7*, 42-49.

Hazan, C., & Shaver, P. (1987). Romantic love conceptualized as an attachment process. *Journal of Personality and Social Psychology*, *52*, 511-524.

Hazan, C., & Shaver, P. (1990). Love at work: An attachment-theoretical perspective. *Journal of Personality and Social Psychology*, *59*, 270-280.

Hobfoll, S. E., Dunahoo, C. L., Ben-Porath, Y., & Monnier, J. (1994). Gender and coping: The dual axis model of coping. *American Journal of Community Psychology*, *22*, 49-82.

Hobfoll, S. E., & London, P. (1986). The relationship of self-concept and social support to emotional distress among women during war. *Journal of Social and Clinical Psychology, 12*, 87-100.

Holahan, C. J., & Moos, R. H. (1987). Personality and contextual determinants of coping strategies. *Journal of Personality and Social Psychology, 51*, 389-395.

Jakubczak, L. F., & Walters, R. H. (1959). Suggestibility as dependency behavior. *Journal of Abnormal and Social Psychology, 59*, 102-107.

Jones, W. H., & Carpenter, B. N. (1986). Shyness, social behavior and relationships. In W. H. Jones, J. M. Cheek & S. R. Briggs (Eds.), *Shyness: Perspectives and research on treatment*, (pp. 227-238). New York: Plenum.

Kagan, J., & Mussen, P. (1956). Dependency themes on the TAT and group conformity. *Journal of Consulting Psychology, 20*, 29-32.

Karabenick, S. A., & Knapp, J. R. (1988). Help-seeking and the need for assistance. *Journal of Educational Psychology, 80*, 406-408.

Keinan, G., & Hobfoll, S. E. (1989). Stress, dependency and social support: Who benefits from husband's presence in delivery? *Journal of Social and Clinical Psychology, 8*, 32-44.

Kobak, R. R., & Sceery, A. (1988). Attachment in late adolescence: Working models, affect regulation, and representations of self and others. *Child Development, 59*, 145-146.

LaMorto-Corse, A. M., & Carver, C. S. (1980). Recipient reactions to aid: Effects of locus of initiation attributions and individual differences. *Bulletin of the Psychonomic Society, 16*, 265-268.

Lazarus, R. S., & Folkman, S. (1984). *Stress, appraisal and coping*. New York: Springer.

Long, B. D. (1988). Work-related stress and coping strategies of professional women. *Journal of Employment Counseling, 25*, 37-44.

Markus, H. R., & Kitayama, S. (1991). Culture and the self: Implications for cognition, emotion, and motivation. *Psychological Review, 98*, 224-253.

Masling, J. M., Price, J., Goldband, S., & Katkin, E. S. (1981). Oral imagery and autonomic arousal in social isolation. *Journal of Personality and Social Psychology, 40*, 395-400.

Masling, J. M., & Schwartz, M. A. (1979). A critique of research in psychoanalytic theory. *Genetic Psychology Monographs, 100*, 257-307.

Meeker, B. F., & Weitzel-O'Neill, P. A. (1977). Sex roles and interpersonal behavior in task-oriented groups. *American Sociological Review, 42*, 91-105.

Mikulnicer, M., & Florian, V. (1995). Appraisal and coping with a real life stressful situation: The contribution of attachment styles. *Personality and Social Psychology Bulletin, 21*, 406-414.

Mikulnicer, M., Florian, V., & Weller, A. (1993). Attachment styles, coping strategies, and posttraumatic psychological distress: The impact of the Gulf War in Israel. *Journal of Personality and Social Psychology, 64*, 817-826.

Milgram, N. A., & Palti, G. (1993). Psychosocial characteristics of resilient children. *Journal of Research in Personality, 27*, 207-221.

Miller, W. R. (1985). Motivation for treatment: A review with a special emphasis on alcoholism. *Psychological Bulletin, 98*, 84-107.

Nadler, A. (1986a). Self-esteem and the seeking and receiving of help: Theoretical and empirical perspectives. In B. Maher & W. Maher (Eds.), *Progress in experimental personality research*, (Vol. 14, pp. 115-163). New York: Academic Press.

Nadler, A. (1986b). Help-seeking as a cultural phenomenon: Differences between city and Kibbutz individuals. *Journal of Personality and Social Psychology, 57*, 976-983.

Nadler, A. (1987). Determinants of help-seeking behavior: The effects of helper's similarity, task centrality and recipient's self-esteem. *European Journal of Social Psychology, 17*, 57-67.

Nadler, A. (1991). Help-seeking behavior: Psychological costs and instrumental benefits. In M. S. Clark (Ed.), *Review of personality and social psychology*, (Vol. 12, pp. 290-312). New York: Sage.

Nadler, A., & Fisher, J. D. (1986). The role of threat to self-esteem and perceived control in recipient reactions to aid: Theory development and empirical validation. In L. Berkowitz (Ed.), *Advances in Experimental Social Psychology*, (Vol. 19, pp. 81-123). New York: Academic Press.

Nadler, A., Fisher, J. D., & Streufert, S. (1976). When helping hurts: The effects of donor-recipient similarity and recipient self-esteem on reactions to aid. *Journal of Personality, 44*, 310-321.

Nadler, A., & Fux, B. (1979). Self-esteem, social desirability and the seeking of help. Unpublished manuscript, Tel Aviv Univesity, Israel.

Nadler, A., Lewinstein, E., & Rahav, G. (1991). Acceptance of retardation and help-seeking: Correlates of help-seeking preferences of mothers and fathers of retarded children. *Mental Retardation, 29.*

Nadler, A., Maler, S., & Friedman, A. (1984). Effects of helper's sex, subject's sex, subject's androgyny and self-evaluation on males' and females' willingness to seek and receive help. *Sex Roles, 10,* 327–339.

Nadler, A., Mayseless, O., Peri, N., & Tchemerinski, A. (1985). Effects of self-esteem and ability to reciprocate on help-seeking behavior. *Journal of Personality, 53,* 23–36.

Nadler, A., & Porat, I. (1978). When names do not help: Effects of anonymity and locus of need attributions on help-seeking behavior. *Personality and Social Psychology Bulletin, 4,* 624–628.

Nadler, A., Shapira, R., & Ben-Itzhak, S. (1982). Good looks may help: Effects of helper's physical attractiveness and sex of helper on males' and females' help-seeking behavior. *Journal of Personality and Social Psychology, 42,* 90–99.

Nadler, A., Sheinberg, L., & Jaffe, Y. (1981). Coping with stress by help seeking: Help seeking and receiving behaviors in male paraplegics. In C. Spielberger, I. Sarason & N. Milgram (Eds.), *Stress and Anxiety* (Vol. 8, pp. 375–386). Washington, DC: Hemisphere.

Nadler, A., & Wolmer, L. (1989). Motivation to change and motivation to receive help: Two related and distinct psychological constructs. Unpublished manuscript, Tel Aviv University, Israel.

Nelson-Le Gall, S. (1985). Help-seeking behavior in learning. In E. W. Gordon (Ed.), *Review of research in education,* (Vol. 12, pp. 55–90). Washington, DC: American Educational Research Association.

Nelson-Le Gall, S., & Glor-Scheib, S. (1985). Academic help seeking and peer relations in school. *Contemporary Educational Psychology, 11,* 187–193.

Newman, R. S. (1990). Children's help-seeking in the classroom: The role of motivational factors and attitudes. *Journal of Educational Psychology, 82,* 71–80.

Nicholls, J. G. (1984). Achievement motivation: Conceptions of ability, subjective experience, task choice and performance. *Psychological Review, 91,* 328–346.

O'Neill, R. M., & Bornstein, R. F. (1990). Oral dependence and gender: Factors in help-seeking response set and self-reported psychopathology in psychiatric inpatients. *Journal of Personality Assessment, 55,* 28–40.

Parker, G. R., Cowen, E. L., Work, W. C., & Wyman, P. A. (1990). Test correlates of stress resilience among urban school children. *Journal of Primary Prevention, 11,* 19–35.

Pincus, A. L., & Gurtman, M. B. (1995). The three faces of interpersonal dependency: Structural analyses of self-report dependency measures. *Journal of Personality and Social Psychology, 69,* 744–758.

Raviv, A., Raviv, A., & Yunovitz, R. (1989). Radio psychology and psychotherapy: A comparison of client attitudes and expectations. *Professional Psychology: Research and Practice, 20,* 1–7.

Robertson, M. F. (1988). Differential use by male and female students of the counseling services design and counseling models. *International Journal for the Advancement of Counseling, 11,* 231–240.

Scheier, M. F., Weintraub, J. K., & Carver, C. S. (1986). Coping with stress: Divergent strategies of optimists and pessimists. *Journal of Personality and Social Psychology, 51,* 1257–1264.

Shilkret, C. J., & Masling, J. M. (1981). Oral dependence and dependent behavior. *Journal of Personality Assessment, 45,* 125–129.

Simpson, J. A., Rholes, W. S., & Nelligan, J. S. (1992). Support seeking and support giving within couples in an anxiety provoking situation: The role of attachment styles. *Journal of Personality and Social Psychology, 62,* 434–446.

Solomon, Z. (1989). Untreated combat-related PTSD: Why some Israeli veterans do not seek help. *Israeli Journal of Psychiatry and Related Sciences, 26,* 111–123.

Solomon, Z., Mikulnicer, M., & Habershaim, N. (1990). Life events, coping strategies, social resources and somatic complaints among combat stress reaction casualties. *British Journal of Medical Psychology, 63,* 137–148.

Solomon, Z., Mikulnicer, M., & Hobfoll, S. E. (1986). Effects of social support and battle intensity on loneliness and breakdown during combat. *Journal of Personality and Social Psychology, 51,* 1269–1276.

Sroufe, L.A., Fox, N. E., & Pancake, V. R. (1983). Attachment and dependency in developmental perspective. *Child Development, 54,* 1615–1627.

Taylor, S. E., & Brown, J. D. (1988). Illusion and well-being: A social-psychological perspective on mental health. *Psychological Bulletin, 103,* 193–210.

Tessler, R. C., & Schwartz, S. H. (1972). Help-seeking, self-esteem, and achievement motivation: An attributional analysis. *Journal of Personality and Social Psychology, 21,* 318–326.

Tzafrir, A., Nadler, A., & Friedland, N. (1996). *Attachment styles, self-esteem and help-seeking as a function of help's instrumentality.* Unpublished manuscript, Tel Aviv University, Israel.

Veroff, J. B. (1981). The dynamics of help-seeking in men and women. *Psychiatry, 44,* 189–200.

Verbrugge, L. M. (1981). Sex differentials in health and mortality. In A. H. Stomberg (Ed.), *Women, health and medicine.* Palo Alto, CA: Mayfield.

Wallston, B. S. (1976). The effects of sex role ideology, self-esteem, and expected future interactions with an audience on male help-seeking. *Sex Roles, 2,* 353–365.

Weiss, H. M., & Knight, P. A. (1980). The utility of humility: Self-esteem, information search and problem-solving efficiency. *Organizational Behavior and Human Performance, 25,* 216–223.

Wills, T. A., & DePaulo, B. M. (1991). Interpersonal analysis of the help-seeking process. In C. R. Snyder & D. R. Forsyth (Eds.), *Handbook of social and clinical psychology,* pp. 350–375). New York: Pergamon.

Zimbardo, P. G. (1977). *Shyness: What it is, What to do about it.* Reading, MA: Addison-Wesley.

Chapter 18

SOCIAL SUPPORT, STRESS, AND PERSONALITY

DO ALL WOMEN BENEFIT FROM THEIR HUSBAND'S PRESENCE DURING CHILDBIRTH?

Giora Keinan

When Sarah was in the seventh month of her pregnancy, her husband Isaac proposed that he attend the birth of their second child. "I want to share the experience with you," declared Isaac, "to help coach you through the delivery." Sarah was not enthusiastic about the idea. "There are some moments in life when a woman needs to be alone," she thought to herself. She also admitted to herself that since she was not especially anxious about the upcoming delivery, she did not feel she needed support. She decided, nevertheless, to take up Isaac's offer of help; it was common practice these days and she did not want to hurt his feelings.

When Sarah went into labor two months later, Isaac rushed her to the hospital. Overwhelmed with emotion, he muttered under his breath that at moments like these it is vital to remain calm. Sarah was admitted to the hospital, examined by a gynecologist, and led into the delivery room. Isaac remained at her side throughout, holding her hand in his trembling hand.

The delivery took about an hour. Isaac sat tensely by his wife's side; from time to time he stood up and reprimanded the midwife for not being able to do anything to alleviate Sarah's suffering and for not speeding up the delivery. Sarah tried unsuccessfully to silence him a few times, but gave up in the end. Once Jacob finally came into the world, Sarah asked her husband to leave her alone with her son.

Giora Keinan • Department of Psychology, Tel-Aviv University, Tel-Aviv, Israel 69978.

Sourcebook of Social Support and Personality, edited by Gregory R. Pierce, Brian Lakey, Irwin G. Sarason, and Barbara R. Sarason. Plenum Press, New York, 1997.

This real-life story gives rise to a number of interesting questions related to the field of social support. Are attempts to provide social support beneficial to all people under all circumstances? Is social support liable to harm as well as benefit the supportee? What factors might influence the efficacy of supportive behavior? This chapter is devoted to an examination of the above questions. It presents a theoretical model that depicts the relationship between supportive behavior offered by the supporter, the supportee's appraisal of this behavior, and the outcomes of such support. Also included in the model are moderating variables likely to have an influence on the efficacy of support. The two studies presented thereafter, conducted in conjunction with colleagues, examine certain elements of this model. In these studies, the hospital delivery room served as a research laboratory.

CHANGING ATTITUDES REGARDING
THE EFFICACY OF SOCIAL SUPPORT

Early studies investigating the effects of social support concluded that it is directly related to lower levels of mental and physical symptomatology and a higher ability to cope with various types of environmental stress (e.g., Berkman & Syme, 1979; Cobb, 1976; Nuckolls, Cassel, & Kaplan, 1972). Later studies indicated that these unequivocal conclusions may have been too hasty and oversimplified. Social support was found not to benefit all individuals in all interactions and under all conditions (e.g., Coyne & DeLongis, 1986; Coyne & Smith, 1991; Dakof & Taylor, 1990; Sandler & Lakey, 1982). Coyne and Smith (1991), for example, found that the efficacy of the support given by wives to husbands who had undergone a myocardial infarction was dependent on the type of infarct, the nature of the couple's interaction with the medical staff, and the quality of their marital relationship. Similarly, Sandler and Lakey (1982) found that the negative affectivity arising in the wake of a stressful event was "mellowed" by social support in individuals displaying internal locus of control, an effect not found in subjects characterized by external locus of control. Furthermore, over the years, it has become obvious that in certain cases, well-intended social support might in fact bring about an increase in recipients' stress and even poorer adjustment (e.g., Hobfoll & London, 1986; Pierce, Sarason, & Sarason, 1990; Rook, 1984; Swann & Predmore, 1985). Hobfoll and London (1986), for example, found that there is a direct relationship between the extent of support received by women whose loved ones had been mobilized at time of war and the degree of psychological distress experienced.

It appears that the pioneers in the field of social support tended to ignore relevant theories dealing with the complexity of the possible outcomes arising from interpersonal interactions. Hobfoll (1988) writes:

> In the rush and excitement over social support, researchers and theorists side-stepped information from social exchange models (Blau, 1964; Homans, 1961), clearly suggesting that social interactions involve both benefits and costs for the provider and recipient of support. A blind eye was also turned to family systems theory, which illustrates how close personal ties may provide destructive kinds of support even with the most positive intent (Minuchin, 1974). (p. 147)

The theoretical model presented here is founded on the current, widely accepted notion that supportive behavior does not necessarily lead to a beneficial outcome for the supportee. Offers of support might improve well-being and health under certain conditions but can lack a positive impact, or even lead to a negative outcome under a different set of conditions.

THE EFFICACY OF SOCIAL SUPPORT: A THEORETICAL MODEL

The proposed model focuses on conditions and factors that might influence the efficacy of social support after it has been offered, without going into the reasons and factors that potentially influence the proffering of such support. It puts forward a cognitive and interactive viewpoint largely influenced by the theoretical works of House (1981), Hobfoll and Vaux (1993), and Sarason, Pierce, and Sarason (1994). The model (see Figure 18.1) incorporates three basic concepts: *supportive behavior*, *appraisal of support*, and *support outcomes*.

Supportive behavior, originating with the supporter, has been defined, following Shumaker and Brownell (1984), as an exchange of resources between individuals, perceived by the provider as aimed at improving the well-being, the functioning, or the health of the recipient. Such supportive behavior might be founded on tangible resources extended by the provider (as manifested in the giving of a loan or a present), on emotional resources (as manifested in the giving of encouragement or showing affection), or on informational resources (as manifested in the giving of advice or feedback).

The concept of *appraisal of support* refers to subjective interpretation or evaluative assessment by the recipient with regard to supportive behavior and his or her relationship to the provider (see also Vaux, 1988).

The *support outcomes* are related to the degree of efficacy of the supportive behavior. These results are likely to be measurable both psychologically (the level of functioning or adjustment of the supportee, the level of stress experienced or the level of the supportee's morale) and physically (the degree of physiological arousal and health indices).

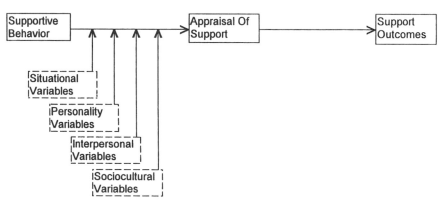

FIGURE 1. The efficacy of social support: a theoretical model.

According to the present model, supportive behavior does not influence the outcomes of support directly, but, rather, undergoes cognitive mediation based on appraisal. Accordingly, the subjective interpretation by the supportee for objective events has a considerable influence on the extent of the efficacy of the support (e.g., Antonucci & Israel, 1986; Pierc et al., 1990; Wethington & Kessler, 1986).

Once the process of appraisal has been completed, the extent to which the supportive behavior is perceived by the recipient as positive or as compatible with the needs is determined. The more positive or compatible with the supportee's needs the perception of the supportive behavior, the greater the chances that the support outcomes will be positive, and vice versa. Thus, for example, in the introductory story about Sarah and Isaac, there is evidence that the supportive behavior offered by Isaac was not perceived by Sarah as compatible with her needs. Her reactions intimate that Isaac's well-meaning intentions did not have the desired effective outcome.

Figure 18.1 shows that a number of moderating variables, outlined here, might influence the appraisal of the support.

SITUATIONAL VARIABLES

A *situational variable* that exerts a critical influence on the appraisal of support and, consequently, over its outcome, is the degree to which the reaction-producing event is stressful (a run-in with the boss at work vs. open-heart surgery).

According to the stress-buffering hypothesis, the positive effects of social support are apparent only or primarily under stressful conditions (e.g., Cassel, 1974; Gore, 1981; Wilcox, 1981). This hypothesis has received extensive empirical confirmation (e.g., Cohen & Hoberman, 1983; Henderson, 1981; Norbeck & Tilden, 1983), and is adopted in the present model with the following rationale: Since stress increases the need for support, the intensity of stress to which the supportee is exposed is directly related to the recipient's appraisal of the supportive behavior regarding its compatibility with his or her needs. Hence, a more positive outcome is expected under high-stress conditions than under low-stress conditions.

Additional situational variables that are likely to influence the appraisal of support are related to the interpersonal setting. The degree of physical closeness between a supporter and supportee is one example of this class of variables. Thus, support transmitted via the telephone might, because of the physical distance, be perceived as less compatible with the supportee's needs than face-to-face support incorporating tactile or tangible aid. The presence of potential providers of support in the supportee's environment is another interpersonal factor that is likely to influence the appraisal of support. If the supportee accepts support when there are no other supporters in his or her immediate surroundings, the help given might be appraised differently than would be help volunteered when there are other individuals around who might also be able to help (sometimes with more efficacy).

PERSONALITY VARIABLES

Personality traits of both the provider and the recipient play an important role in the appraisal of support, and, consequently, on the degree of the support efficacy (cf., Cutrona, 1989; Elliot & Grambling, 1990; Sarason, Pierce, Shearin, Sarason, Waltz, &

Poppe, 1991). Among the personality traits of the recipient that significantly influence the appraisal of support are self-esteem and self-confidence. Several studies reported that individuals with high self-esteem and self-confidence derive greater benefit from social support than do individuals low on these traits (Hansson, Jones, & Carpenter, 1984; Hobfoll & Lerman, 1989; Holahan & Moos, 1991). It may be assumed that a person who is confident in his or her own capabilities, and who is endowed with a high level of self-esteem, would tend to interpret the supportive behavior as positive, since he or she would feel capable of deriving more advantage from it. Another relevant trait is the level of depression. Because of the dysphoric affect that characterizes depressive people, and because of their negative self-image, such people might minimize the value of support offered to them and perceive it as ineffective and unhelpful. Coyne, Aldwin, and Lazarus (1981) found, for instance, that depressed women are not well served by social support, even though they get more support than nondepressed women. Additional personality traits of the supportee that might influence the efficacy of the support are hardiness, locus of control, hostility, suspiciousness, level of chronic anxiety, and dependence.

Some of the personality traits of the provider that might influence the appraisal and efficacy of support include sensitivity to others, bossiness, self-confidence, degree of introversion, as well as the level of anxiety and depression. Thus, for instance, the supportive behavior of a person who is insensitive to others is likely to be appraised negatively by the supportee, since it would not meet his or her needs; the efficacy of this support would consequently be significantly reduced. Furthermore, supportive behavior that does not take into consideration the needs of the supportee could arouse anger and provoke outright rejection. Similarly, an anxious supporter could intimidate the supportee and make it difficult for him or her to accept the proffered support. An anxious supporter might arouse the supportee's suspicion regarding his or her ability to be of help ("He cannot help himself, so how could he possibly help me?"), ability to reason ("With such anxiety, how can I depend on this person's reasoning?"), and the ability to be consistent in giving help. These doubts might become part of the appraisal of support and reduce its efficacy.

Interpersonal Variables

Additional variables that could have an influence on the efficacy of support are those related to the nature of the relationship between the supportee and the supporter, and the manner in which the support is given (see Barrera & Beca, 1990; Dunkel-Schetter & Skokan, 1990; Leatham & Duck, 1990). The variables that seem to be the most relevant in this context are the degree of intimacy that characterizes the relationship between the provider and recipient, the degree of conflict that exists between the two individuals, and the extent to which the support is unsolicited.

Numerous empirical findings indicate that intimate ties make a special contribution to stress resistance and well-being (e.g., Habif & Lahey, 1980; Hobfoll & Leiberman, 1987; Kessler & Essex, 1982). Hobfoll and Leiberman (1987), for example, found intimacy with a spouse to be related to better stress resistance among women after childbirth. It appears that intimate relations might induce a more positive appraisal of support than distant ties, since intimacy should direct the supporter toward a more exact perception of the needs of the supportee. In addition, the more intimate the ties, the greater the trust that the supportee feels toward the supporter, which in turn makes it easier for the former to accept the support and take advantage of it.

In contrast, conflictual ties between the provider and the recipient might very well lead to a negative perception of support, resulting in a reduction of the efficacy, and there is empirical evidence supporting this possibility (e.g., Coyne & DeLongis, 1986; Stephens, Kinney, Norris, & Ritchie, 1987; Zavislak & Sarason, 1991). When a conflict is involved in the relationship, the recipient might find it difficult to trust the supporter's intentions. Also, the anger that frequently accompanies a problematic relationship could lead to an outright rejection of support. Finally, a conflictual relationship could make the receiver feel indebtedness and, accordingly, produce a negative outcome (Pierce et al., 1990).

Despite the fact that unsolicited support might at times be intrusive and un-welcome (e.g., Wortman & Dunkel-Schetter, 1979), it appears that its advantages could quite often be more significant for the supportee (e.g., Bolger, DeLongis, Kessler, & Shilling, 1989). Unsolicited support could lead to a positive appraisal of the support, since it constitutes less of a threat to the self-esteem and competence of the supportee. Furthermore, the giving of unsolicited support might induce the recipient to perceive the supporter as sensitive and considerate. Such appraisal could ease the acceptance of the support and increase its efficacy.

SOCIOCULTURAL VARIABLES

Other moderating variables that might be related to the efficacy of support include *sociocultural variables* (see House, 1981). Although there are only few empirical results in this field (Dressler, 1985; Jackson, Antonucci, & Gibson, 1990), it is reasonable to assume that social norms and cultural values might have a significant influence on the appraisal of support.

Thus, for example, the prevalent norm among men from "patriarchal" cultures that dictates that weaknesses should not be exhibited outwardly, could influence appraisal of support, since acceptance of support presupposes an admission of diffi-culty. Likewise, the common social norm, found in some Western countries, that assigns great importance to protecting the privacy of others might have bearing on the appraisal of support. In these countries, support, especially when it is unsolicited, might be sometimes perceived as intrusive or inappropriate.

Finally, it should be emphasized that the model presented here maintains that interactions also exist among the moderating variables themselves, besides inter-actions among each of the moderating variables and the supportive behavior. For instance, it would be expected that under high stress, certain personality traits would have a stronger effect on the outcome of support than under low-stress conditions (e.g., Lefcourt, Martin, & Selah, 1984).

THE EFFICACY OF SOCIAL SUPPORT DURING CHILDBIRTH

The fact that childbirth is a stressful event involving a threat to the physical and psychological integrity of the mother (e.g., Gjerdingen, Froberg, & Fontaine, 1991), along with the relatively new practice of often having a companion present during delivery, represents an intriguing opportunity and challenge for researchers of social support. Indeed, in the past two decades, several studies have investigated the effects of the presence of a husband or a companion on the degree of stress and pain experienced by the woman, the incidence of complications, and the duration of delivery (e.g., Block & Block, 1975; Henneborn & Cogan, 1975; Kennell, Klaus, McGrath, Robertson, & Hinkley, 1991; Klaus, Kennell, Robertson, & Sosa, 1986; Wente & Crockenberg, 1976).

Studies on the effect of the presence of a supportive woman (*doula*)* during childbirth were conducted in Guatemala and the United States (Kennell et al., 1991; Klaus et al., 1986; Sosa, Kennel, Klaus, Robertson, & Urrutia, 1980). In these studies, the expectant mother was introduced before the birth to a woman previously unknown to her, whose task was to provide information, reassurance, contact, and comfort. Sosa et al. (1980), the first to investigate the effect of the *doula*'s support, found that mothers who were paired with these women had significantly fewer complications during delivery (e.g., cesarean section, fetal distress) than did those who had no supportive companion. Moreover, when only those subjects who experienced no complications during childbirth were examined, a significant difference was found between the two groups for duration of labor and delivery. The process required slightly more than 19 hours for unsupported women and somewhat less than 10 hours for women assigned to a supportive companion.

In the study conducted by Kennell et al. (1991), women giving birth for the first time were divided into three groups: a supported group, an observed group, and a control group. Women in the supported group were comforted, stroked, encouraged, and coached by a *doula*, who stayed by their side throughout the birth, from the moment they were admitted to the hospital. Women in the observed group were monitored by an inconspicuous observer. Here the *doula* merely kept a record of staff contacts, interactions, and procedures, without establishing any interaction with the mother herself. Women in the control group were neither supported nor observed.

Results showed a relationship between the degree of support and the percentage of complications during delivery (e.g., cesarean sections were performed on 8% of the supported group, 13% of the observed group, and 18% of the control group). The groups also differed in the degree of use of anesthetics (an epidural was administered to 7.8% of the supported group, 22.6% of the observed group, and 55.3% of the control group). Duration of labor, prolonged infant hospitalization, and maternal fever exhibited a similar pattern.

Whereas studies conducted on female companions produced unequivocal results, those investigating the effect of the husband's presence during childbirth are far from definitive. Several studies indicate that the husband's presence has a positive impact on the wife. Tanzer (1968), for example, found that women whose husbands were present during delivery reported less pain and expressed more positive attitudes toward birth and pregnancy than those whose husbands were absent from the delivery room. Similarly, Henneborn and Cogan (1975) found that women whose husbands were

*The word comes from the Greek and refers to a woman who helps the mother in her infant-care tasks.

present during labor and delivery reported less pain and required less medication than those whose husbands were present only during labor.

Other studies, however, have failed to find a positive contribution of husband's presence during childbirth. Nettelbladt, Fagerstrom, and Uddenberg (1976) and Wente and Crockenberg (1976), for example, found no significant differences in the level of reported pain between women whose husbands were present during delivery and those whose husbands were absent. These contradictory results might point to the involvement of moderating variables that determine whether the presence of the husband in the delivery room is beneficial to his wife.

We conducted two studies that sought to test this possibility (see Keinan, Ezer, & Feigin, 1992; Keinan & Hobfoll 1989). In these studies we chose to examine the influence of two types of moderating variables that appear in the theoretical model presented earlier: personality and situational variables.

STUDY 1

The aim of this study (Keinan & Hobfoll, 1989) was to investigate the effect of the wife's degree of dependence and stress level on the benefit she derived from the presence of her husband during childbirth.

Our first hypothesis was that women who experienced a high level of stress during birth would benefit more from the presence of their husbands in the delivery room than would women experiencing a lower level of stress. This prediction was based on the idea that the need for support increases under stress that disrupts the individual's equilibrium. Thus, it might be expected that social support would be more relevant and effective under high-stress conditions than under low-stress conditions (see also Caplan, 1974; Cobb, 1976; Rook, 1987).

Our second hypothesis was that women high on dependence would benefit more from the presence of their husbands during delivery than would women low on this trait. This was based on the notion that individuals high on dependence display, by definition, a strong need for social support (cf. Bornstein, 1992, 1993); therefore, such support is likely to be more significant and effective for them than for low-dependence individuals.

A further rationale for this hypothesis stems from the study of Nadler and Mayse-less (1983), who noted that people who perceive assistance as consistent with their view of self are less threatened by the negative messages inherent in it than those who see themselves as self-sufficient. It therefore follows that people who view themselves as dependent would be less threatened by receiving help, and therefore more likely than more independent individuals to benefit from social support.

The husband's presence versus absence during childbirth was used as an objective measure of social support offered to the mother. We considered it a valid measure of social support, since it reflects the degree of the husband's concern, affection, and esteem for his wife, and his willingness to share her difficulties. The variable of ordinal number of delivery was chosen as an index of women's stress level, as numerous studies have found that primiparous women report a higher degree of stress and pain than do multiparas (e.g., Cogan, 1975; Leifer, 1980; Melzack, Taenzer, Feldman, & Kinch, 1981). State anxiety and state anger, both stress-related emotions, were chosen as key outcome measures. Together, they compose the classic fight-or-flight reaction to stress. Furthermore, the experience of these emotions during childbirth may impact on the woman's physiological responses (e.g., by causing a rise in blood pressure or increased muscle tonus), thereby incurring a higher degree of complications during delivery, with ramifications for the health of the infant.

METHOD

Subjects

Sixty-seven women who gave birth in a regional hospital in Israel participated in the study. Their ages ranged from 20 to 36 ($M = 27$) and all were married. For 31 of the subjects, this was their first birth, whereas for the other 36, it was the second or subsequent birth. Only Hebrew-speaking women whose deliveries were spontaneous were sampled.

Instruments

Dependency Scale. The level of the women's dependence was measured by the Passive Dependency Scale (Kessler, 1953). Only those items assessing the trait of dependence (26 items) were extracted from the questionnaire for purposes of this study. Possible scores ranged between 0 and 26, with a higher score indicating greater dependence. Women who scored higher than the median (12) were defined as "high" on dependence, whereas those who scored lower than the median were defined as "low" on dependence. The internal consistency of the questionnaire was found to be quite high (Cronbach's alpha = .86).

Anxiety and Anger Scales. The State–Trait Personality Inventory (Spielberger, 1979) was used to examine the women's level of negative affectivity during childbirth. We employed only those subscales that assess the level of state anxiety and state anger. Each of these subscales consists of 10 items. The possible scores on each subscale range from 10 to 40, with higher scores indicating higher levels of state anxiety or state anger. The internal consistency coefficients (Cronbach's alpha) in this study were found to be high (.84 for State Anxiety subscale and .95 for State Anger subscale).

Procedure

The researchers obtained from the medical staff the names of women who had had spontaneous deliveries and approached them 12–24 hours after they had given birth. After congratulating the mothers, the interviewers introduced themselves as university researchers who were conducting a study of women's feelings during childbirth. The women were asked to complete the questionnaires, and were assured that their responses would be used for research purposes alone. While they completed the questionnaires, the interviewer sat beside the respondents in order to answer any questions, and to guarantee that they were performing the task on their own.

Experimental Design

A 2 × 2 × 2 factorial design was employed. The three independent variables and their levels were as follows:

1. Husband's Presence during childbirth (husband present or absent)
2. Ordinal Number of Birth (first or later delivery)
3. Level of Trait Dependency ("high" or "low")

The dependent variables were the amount of state anxiety and state anger experienced by the woman during the delivery.

RESULTS

The study hypotheses were first examined using state anxiety as the dependent variable. A three-way analysis of variance (ANOVA) was performed, with Husband's Presence, Ordinal Number of Birth, and Level of Trait Dependency serving as independent variables. This analysis yielded two significant main effects, one for Dependency, $F(1,59) = 5.39; p < .05$, and the other for Husband's Presence, $F(1,59) = 10.61, p < .05$. These results were qualified by two interaction effects supporting the hypotheses: Husband's Presence × Ordinal Number of Delivery, $F(1,59) = 18.94, p < .05$; and Husband's Presence × Dependency, $F(1,59) = 11.02, p < .05$.

In order to test the first interaction, analyses of simple main effects were carried out. These revealed that primiparous women whose husbands were present during the birth experienced significantly less state anxiety during delivery that those whose husbands were not present, $F(1,59) = 22.29; p < .001$. However, in the case of subsequent deliveries, there was no significant difference in the amount of anxiety experienced by women whose husbands were present as opposed to those whose husbands were absent.

The second interaction referred to the relationship between husband's presence and woman's level of dependence. Post hoc analyses of the data revealed that dependent women whose husbands were present during delivery experienced significantly less state anxiety than those whose husbands were absent, $F(1,59) = 11.04; p < .01$. Among low dependency women, however, no significant difference in state anxiety was found as a result of husband's presence or absence.

The study hypotheses were then examined using State Anger as the dependent variable, again by means of a three-way ANOVA. This analysis yielded only one significant finding, the interaction between Husband's Presence and Ordinal Number of Delivery, $F(1,59) = 5.66; p < .05$.

Analyses of simple main effects performed on the data revealed that for first deliveries, women whose husbands were absent during the birth experienced significantly more anger than those whose husbands were beside them in the delivery room, $F(1,59) = 4.75; p < .05$. However, for muliparous women, no significant difference was found due to husband's presence.

STUDY 2

The second study (Keinan et al., 1992) sought to further investigate the efficacy of social support in the experimental context of childbirth. As in our previous study, the husband's presence or absence during delivery was used as an objective measure of social support, and the ordinal number of delivery served as the measure of woman's stress level. However, here trait anxiety was chosen as the personality variable that might explain the differential effect of social support.

The possibility that social support may differentially affect individuals who vary in their level of trait anxiety has received little attention. Nevertheless, the stress-buffering hypothesis would predict that this personality variable should be highly relevant for the recruitment and exploitation of support. More specifically, since individuals characterized by a high level of trait anxiety constantly experience stress, tension, and apprehension, and are more in need of aid, they may be expected to derive greater benefit from social support. This notion led us to predict that women high on trait anxiety would benefit more from the presence of their husband during delivery than women low on this trait.

The second hypothesis of this study was also based on the stress-buffering hypothesis and was identical to that examined in the previous study: primiparas would benefit more from the presence of their husbands in the delivery room than would multiparous women.

In an attempt to extend the generalizability of the results, the outcome variables in this study were examined in different ways. Thus, the woman's stress level was not determined solely by self-report of her level of anxiety and anger during delivery (as was the case in the previous study), but also by self-reports of pain, along with physiological and behavioral measures.

METHOD

Subjects

One hundred and twenty women who gave birth in a regional hospital in Israel participated in the study. Their ages ranged from 20 to 41 (M = 29), and all were married. Approximately one-third of the women (38) were primiparas, and the rest (82) were multiparas. All were Hebrew speakers who had had spontaneous deliveries without complications.

Instruments and Measures

Trait Anxiety Scale.   The trait anxiety of the women was measured by the State–Trait Anxiety Inventory (Spielberger, Gorsuch, & Lushene, 1970). The inventory relating to trait anxiety consists of 20 items. Possible scores range from a low of 20 to a high of 80, the latter indicating high, chronic anxiety. Women who scored higher than the median (34 or above) were defined as "high" on anxiety, whereas those scoring lower than the median were defined as "low" on this trait. The Hebrew version of the questionnaire, which is widely used in Israel (cf. Freidland & Keinan, 1991; Keinan,

1987), has been found to have high internal consistency (Cronbach's alpha = .90), as well as significant correlation with other anxiety scales (Teichman & Melnick, 1978).

State Anxiety and Anger Scales.   The State–Trait Personality Inventory employed in the first study was used here as well.

Feelings and Sensations Ratings (FSR).   This questionnaire was developed especially for the present study. The inventory consists of four questions related to the subject's feelings and sensations. The first and second items ask the woman to rate the level of pain and tension she experienced during childbirth. The third focuses on the degree of her desire to have her husband present in the delivery room (regardless of whether he was actually there). The final question asks the woman to note which of her deliveries was the most stressful (addressed only to multiparous women).

Blood Pressure.   Each woman's blood pressure was measured when she entered the delivery room and again a day after she had given birth. The two measurements enabled us to examine the degree of change in blood pressure, with the latter (24 hours after delivery) serving as the baseline.

Use of Tranquilizers.   The amount (in milligrams) of two tranquilizing medications administered to the women was examined. The two drugs, Fenergan and pethidin, are generally given together by means of injection.

Procedure

The procedure employed here was identical to that of the first study.

Experimental Design

A $2 \times 2 \times 2$ factorial design was again used, as in the previous study. The three independent variables were Husbands's Presence, Ordinal Number of Delivery, and level of Trait Anxiety. The dependent variables were level of State Anxiety and State Anger, level of Tension and Pain experienced during birth, changes in Blood Pressure, and amount of Tranquilizing Medication administered.

RESULTS

Stress and Ordinal Number of Delivery

In order to see whether women experience more stress during their first delivery than during subsequent births, the responses of the multiparous women to the question: "Which of your deliveries was the most stressful?" were examined. Sixty-three percent of all respondents stated that their first delivery was the most stressful. It is interesting to note that this response was given by the majority of subjects, despite the fact that the question was presented only a few hours after they had given birth. In addition, it was found that the use of tranquilizing medication was significantly higher among women giving birth for the first time than among those for whom this was not their first delivery, $t(118) = 2.89$, $p < .01$.

Examination of Research Hypotheses

In order to test our hypotheses, a three-way analyses of covariance (ANCOVA) was performed, with Husband's Presence, Ordinal Number of Delivery, and level of Trait Anxiety serving as the independent variables, and level of Education as the covariate. In the first stage, the hypotheses were examined using the self-report measures as dependent variables. ANCOVA performed on the state anxiety scores revealed a significant main effect for Trait Anxiety, $F(1,110) = 13.07, p < .001$. These results were qualified by two significant interaction effects: Husband's Presence × Ordinal Number of Delivery, $F(1,110) = 3.86, p = .05$, and Husband's Presence × Trait Anxiety, $F(1,110) = 5.18, p < .05$.

Analyses of simple main effect, performed to examine the nature of the first interaction, revealed that women giving birth for the first time, whose husbands were present in the delivery room, experienced significantly less state anxiety than primiparous women whose husbands were not present, $F(1,110) = 5.26, p < .05$. In contrast, for multiparous women, no difference was found for the level of state anxiety between those whose husbands were present and those whose husbands were not in the delivery room.

In the case of the second interaction (Husband's Presence × Trait Anxiety), post hoc analyses revealed that women "high" on trait anxiety experienced significantly less state anxiety if their husbands were present during the birth than if they were absent, $F(1,110) = 8.6, p < .01$. However, among women "low" on trait anxiety, the presence of the husband during birth produced no significant effect on the level of state anxiety.

ANCOVA performed with State Anger as the dependent variable revealed a significant main effect for Trait Anxiety, $F(1,110) = 7.56, p < .01$, and a close-to-significant main effect for Ordinal Number of Delivery, $F(1,110) = 2.62, p < .06$. These results were qualified by an interaction of Husband's Presence × Trait Anxiety, $F(1,110) = 4.09, p < .05$. Post hoc analyses on this interaction revealed that women high on Trait Anxiety whose husbands were present in the delivery room experienced significantly less anger than those whose husbands were absent, $F(1,110) = 4.87, p < .05$. On the other hand, for women "low" on Trait Anxiety, there was no effect of husband's presence on the level of the subjects' anger.

Additional significant results were produced by analysis of the tension scores on the FSR questionnaire. ANCOVA performed on this dependent variable yielded a main effect for Husband's Presence, $F(1,110) = 4.7, p < .05$. This effect was qualified by a two-way interaction of Husband's Presence × Ordinal Number of Delivery, $F(1,110) = 10.09, p < .01$, as well as a three-way interaction, $F(1,110) = 4.54, p < .05$. Analysis of the two-way interaction produced results similar to those found when State Anxiety and State Anger were employed as dependent variables. However, post hoc analysis of the three-way interaction revealed a more complex picture.

Let us first consider the self-reports of women "high" on Trait Anxiety. Subjects of this type, for whom this was a first delivery, and whose husbands were present during the birth, reported less tension than primiparous women whose husbands were not present, $F(1,110) = 3.92, p < 0.5$, whereas Husband's Presence was not found to have an effect in the case of subsequent deliveries. Different results were obtained for women "low" on Trait Anxiety. Women of this type, for whom this was a first delivery, benefited more from the presence of their husbands during the birth than primiparas whose husbands were absent from the delivery room, $F(1,110) = 8.98$, $p < .01$, but the opposite was found for subsequent deliveries: Multiparous women whose husbands were present during delivery reported more tension than those whose husbands were absent, $F(1,110) = 5.91$, $p < .05$.

ANCOVA performed on a further dependent variable derived from the FSR—the level of reported pain—yielded no significant results.

In the case of blood pressure, significant findings emerged only when changes in diastolic pressure were examined. ANCOVA performed on these scores produced a significant interaction effect of the variables of Husband's Presence and Ordinal Number of Delivery, $F(1,110) = 3.71$, $p = .05$. *Post hoc* analysis on this interaction yielded results consistent with our hypothesis. Specifically, it was found that for primiparous women, the diastolic blood pressure scores of women whose husbands were not present in the delivery room, were higher than those of women whose husbands were present, $F(1,110) = 3.86$, $p < .05$. No significant effect of Husband's Presence on blood pressure scores was found for multiparous women. Finally, ANCOVA performed on the amount of tranquilizers administered revealed a main effect only for Ordinal Number of Delivery, $F(1,110) = 5.39$, $p < .05$. No other findings were produced in support of our hypothesis regarding this variable.

CONCLUSIONS AND DISCUSSION

These two studies examined whether situational and personality variables can moderate the efficacy of social support. More specifically, it was hypothesized that primiparous women and those high on dependency and trait anxiety would benefit more from the presence of the husband in the delivery room than multiparous women and those low on these traits. The results of both studies indicate that when self-report measures of negative affectivity (State Anxiety, State Anger, and Tension) were examined, our hypotheses were almost fully confirmed. In this context, the three-way interaction found for tension scores in the second study is particularly illuminating. For multiparas low on trait anxiety, the presence of the husband during childbirth produced a higher level of tension than did his absence. This implies that when social support is not consistent with situational and personal requirements, not only is it of no help, but also it may even be detrimental. This finding is in line with earlier results indicating that under certain circumstances, social support may actually increase stress (Hobfoll & London, 1986; Rook, 1984).

In regard to physiological measures (employed only in the second study), our hypotheses were confirmed only by results of the diastolic blood pressure, and only for the situational factor. However, the fact that blood pressure is an objective measure, and is related to the mother's physical health, lends special significance to this finding. It concurs with other research evidence suggesting that social support may reduce physiological arousal, including blood pressure level (e.g., Kamarck, Manuck, & Jennings, 1990).

Our hypotheses were not confirmed when tested on pain scores and amount of tranquilizers administered. The failure of the pain measure to yield significant results could indicate that stress and pain do not reflect common underlying mechanisms. However, a more likely explanation may be related to problems in the measurement of the pain variable. Examination of the women's pain scores reveals that the majority of subjects rated the level of pain during delivery as high (a mean of 7.68 on a 9-point scale). Thus, a ceiling effect may have been produced, preventing the other predicted effects from emerging. The amount of tranquilizing medication administered likewise proved to be a problematic measure. It was learned after the fact that although physicians in the department are instructed to administer tranquilizers only to women who expressly request them, medication was, in practice, often also offered to women who did not voice such a request. Consequently, the amount of tranquilizing medication administered may not faithfully reflect the level of stress and pain experienced by the mothers and their need to alleviate it.

Both studies revealed that husband's presence in the delivery room was more effective during a first experience of childbirth than in later births. This result lends support to the stress-buffering hypothesis: When women are under greater stress, their husbands' support has more of a positive impact than when they are experiencing stress of a lesser magnitude. Cohen and Wills (1985) suggested that the buffering hypothesis should be supported primarily when subjective measures are used, since the buffering qualities of social support are, at least to some extent, cognitively mediated. The results of our studies demonstrate that confirmation of this hypothesis may also be obtained with objective measures of support. It is possible that the most fundamental factor affecting the confirmation or rejection of the hypothesis is not the degree of objectivity of the measure, but rather the relevance of the support function to the stressors with which the individual must cope. The greater the correspondence between the specific need elicited by a stressful event and the support provided, the greater the buffering effect that can be expected (see also Cohen & McKay, 1984; Cutrona, 1990).

The findings regarding the effect of personal resources (dependency and trait anxiety) on the degree of benefit derived from social support also deserve consideration and explanation. By definition, more dependent individuals have a greater need for the presence and support of others (see Bornstein, 1993). This need grows stronger in times of stress, and it is therefore understandable why the presence of the husband during childbirth—a particularly stressful event—answers the needs of dependent women and brings them comfort. Since more independent women have less of a need for support, it is less relevant and, therefore, of less benefit to them. These findings of a moderating effect of dependency on the benefit derived from social support are in line with other findings that social support can ameliorate the negative effects of stress on dependent subjects' health status (Bornstein, 1995).

In regard to the possible effect of chronic anxiety on the efficacy of support, it might be claimed that anxious people are preoccupied with themselves and have limited energy resources, and may, therefore, find it more difficult than low-anxiety individuals to derive benefit from social support. Our finding that high-anxiety women benefited more from social support than their low-anxiety counterparts is inconsistent with such a possibility. One reason for this pattern of results may stem from the fact that the women in our study did not have to actively recruit support. Were it necessary for them to do so under stress, it is possible that the anxious women would have more difficulty recruiting support because of their limited energy resources. In such a case, the potential social support might have less of an effect on them. This suggests that the extent of active involvement in recruiting support may be an important parameter in determining the influence of personality attributes on the efficacy of social support.

Proponents of the stress-buffering hypothesis have referred primarily to acute or episodic stress (e.g., Gore, 1981; Wilcox, 1981). Our findings regarding the moderating effect of trait anxiety on the efficacy of social support provide a first indication that the hypothesis can be expanded to include conditions of chronic stress.

In our research, we used an objective measure of social support, but we did not examine how the expectant mother appraised the offered support. The theoretical model presented at the beginning of the chapter emphasized the centrality of the appraisal of support and its effect on the outcome variables. Given this, it is suggested that future research examine the appraisal and interpretations given by the expectant mother of a companion's supportive behavior. In this way, it would be possible to examine whether, and to what degree, this measure improves the prediction of the outcomes of support.

The theoretical model presented here notes four types of moderating variables that might influence the efficacy of support: situational, personality, interpersonal, and sociocultural variables. The first two have been included in the research presented above. It is recommended that future research examine the influence of the latter two on the outcomes of support as well. In the context of support carried out under high-stress conditions, it would be particularly intriguing to examine the mediating influence of the couple's relationship. The couple's degree of intimacy, or alternately, the intensity of any conflict in their relationship, would appear to be variables that are likely to be very significant in predicting the extent of the benefit a prospective mother might get from the support.

To conclude, our studies seem to confirm the notion that social support is not a panacea for everyone in all conditions. Rather, our findings indicate that the benefit derived from such support depends both on situational factors and on the personal resources of the supported individual. The delivery room appears to offer wide-ranging opportunities for the study of social support and the conditions in which it may be effective. Future studies should be conducted in the same arena in order to expand our knowledge of this intriguing issue.

REFERENCES

Antonucci, T. C., & Israel, B. A. (1986). Veridicality of social support: A comparison of principal and network members' responses. *Journal of Consulting and Clinical Psychology*, 54, 432–437.

Barrera, M. Jr., & Beca, L. M. (1990). Recipient reactions to social support: Contributions of enacted support, conflicted support, and network orientation. *Journal of Social and Personal Relations*, 7, 541–551.

Berkman, L. F., & Syme, S. L. (1979). Social networks, host resistance, and mortality: A nine-year follow-up study of Alameda County residents. *American Journal of Epidemiology*, 109, 186–204.

Blau, P. M. (1964). *Exchange and power in social life*. New York: Wiley.

Block, C., & Block, R. (1975). Effect of support of the husband and obstetrician on pain perception and control in childbirth. *Birth and Family Journal*, 2, 43–50.

Bolger, N., DeLongis, A., Kessler, R. C., & Schilling, E. A. (1989). Effects of daily stress on negative mood. *Journal of Personality and Social Psychology*, 57, 808–818.

Bornstein, R. F. (1992). The dependent personality: Developmental, social and clinical perspectives. *Psychological Bulletin, 112*, 3-23.

Bornstein, R. F. (1993). *The dependent personality*. New York: Guilford.

Bornstein, R. F. (1995). Interpersonal dependency and physical illness: The mediating roles of stress and social support. *Journal of Social and Clinical Psychology, 14*, 225-243.

Caplan, G. (1974). *Social support and community mental health: Lectures on concept development*. New York: Behavioral Publications.

Cassel, J. (1974). Social science in epidemiology: Psychosocial processes and "stress," theoretical formulation. *International Journal of Health Sciences, 4*, 537-549.

Cobb, S. (1976). Social support as a moderator of life stress. *Psychosomatic Medicine, 38*, 300-314.

Cogan, R. (1975). Comfort during prepared childbirth as a function of parity, reported by four classes of participant observers. *Journal of Psychosomatic Research, 19*, 33-37.

Cohen, S., & Hoberman, H. M. (1983). Positive events and social supports as buffers of life change stress. *Journal of Applied Social Psychology, 13*, 99-125.

Cohen, S., & McKay, G. (1984). Social support, stress and the buffering hypothesis: A theoretical analysis. In A. Baum, J. E. Singer, & S. E. Taylor (Eds.), *Handbook of psychology and health* (pp. 253-267). Hillsdale, NJ: Erlbaum.

Cohen, S., & Wills, T. A. (1985). Stress, social support, and the buffering hypothesis. *Psychological Bulletin, 98*, 310-357.

Coyne, J. C., Aldwin, C., & Lazarus, R. S. (1981). Depression and coping in stressful episodes. *Journal of Abnormal Psychology, 90*, 439-447.

Coyne, J. C., & DeLongis, A. M. (1986). Going beyond social support: The role of social relationships in adaptation. *Journal of Consulting and Clinical Psychology, 54*, 454-460.

Coyne, J. C., & Smith, D. A. F. (1991). Couples coping with a myocardial infarction: A contextual perspective on wives' distress. *Journal of Personality and Social Psychology, 61*, 404-412.

Cutrona, C. E. (1989). Ratings of social support by adolescents and adult informants: Degree of correspondence and prediction of depressive symptoms. *Journal of Personality and Social Psychology, 57*, 723-730.

Cutrona, C. E. (1990). Stress and social support: In search of optimal matching. *Journal of Social and Clinical Psychology, 9*, 3-14.

Dakof, G. A., & Taylor, S. E. (1990). Victims' perceptions of social support: What is helpful from whom? *Journal of Personality and Social Psychology, 58*, 80-89.

Dressler, W. W. (1985). Extended family relationships, social support and mental health in a southern black community. *Journal of Health and Social Behavior, 26*, 39-48.

Dunkel-Schetter, C., & Skokan, L. A. (1990). Determinants of social support provision in personal relationships. *Journal of Social and Personal Relationships, 7*, 437-450.

Elliott, T. R., & Gramling, S. E. (1990). Personal assertiveness and the effects of social support among college students. *Journal of Counseling Psychology, 37*, 427-436.

Friedland, N., & Keinan, G. (1991). The effects of stress, ambiguity tolerance, and trait anxiety on the formation of causal relationships. *Journal of Research in Personality, 25*, 88-107.

Gjerdingen, D. K., Froberg, D. G., & Fontaine, P. (1991). The effects of social support on women's health during pregnancy, labor and delivery, and postpartum period. *Family Medicine, 23*, 370-375.

Gore, S. (1981). Stress-buffering functions of social supports: An appraisal and clarification of research models. In B. S. Dohrenwend & B. F. Dohrenwend (Eds.), *Stressful life events and their contexts* (pp. 202-222). New York: Prodist.

Habif, V. L., & Lahey, B. B. (1980). Assessment of the life stress-depression relationship: The use of social support as a moderator variable. *Journal of Behavioral Assessment, 2*, 167-173.

Hansson, R. D., Jones, W. H., & Carpenter, B. N. (1984). Relational competence and social support. In P. Shaver (Ed.), *Review of personality and social psychology* (Vol. 5, pp. 265-284). Beverly Hills, CA: Sage.

Henderson, S. (1981). Social relationships, adversity and neurosis: An analysis of projective observations. *British Journal of Psychiatry, 138*, 391-398.

Henneborn, W. J., & Cogan, R. (1975). The effect of husband participation on the reported pain and probability of medication during labor and birth. *Journal of Psychosomatic Research, 19*, 215-222.

Hobfoll, S. E. (1988). *The ecology of stress*. New York: Hemisphere.

Hobfoll, S. E., & Leiberman, Y. (1987). Personality and social resources in immediate and continued stress resistance among women. *Journal of Personality and Social Psychology, 52*, 18-26.

Hobfoll, S. E., & Lerman, M. (1989). Predicting receipt of social support: A longitudinal study of parents' reactions to their child's illness. *Health Psychology, 8*, 61–77.

Hobfoll, S. E., & London, P. (1986). The relationship of self-concept and social support to emotional distress among women during war. *Journal of Social and Clinical Psychology, 4*, 189–203.

Hobfoll, S. E., & Vaux, A. (1993). Social support: Social resources and social context. In L. Goldberger & S. Breznitz (Eds.), *Handbook of stress* (pp. 685–705). New York: Free Press.

Holahan, C. J., & Moos, R. H. (1991). Life stressors, personal and social resources, and depression: A 4-year structural model. *Journal of Abnormal Psychology, 100*, 31–38.

Homans, G. C. (1961). *Social behavior: Its elementary forms*. New York: Harcourt, Brace & World.

House, J. S. (1981). *Work stress and social support*. Reading, MA: Addison-Wesley.

Jackson, J. S., Antonucci, T. C., & Gibson, R. C. (1990). Social relations, productive activities, and coping with stress in late life. In M. A. P. Stephens, J. H. Crowther, S. E. Hobfoll, & D. L. Tennenbaum (Eds.), *Stress and coping in later-life families* (pp. 193–212). New York: Hemisphere.

Kamarck, T. W., Manuck, S. B., & Jennings, J. R. (1990). Social support reduces cardiovascular reactivity to psychological challenge: A laboratory model. *Psychosomatic Medicine, 52*, 42–58.

Keinan, G. (1987). Decision-making under stress: Scanning of alternatives under controllable and uncontrollable threats. *Journal of Personality and Social Psychology, 52*, 639–644.

Keinan, G., Ezer, A., & Feigin, M. (1992). The influence of situational and personal variables on the effectiveness of social support during childbirth. *Anxiety Research, 4*, 325–337.

Keinan, G., & Hobfoll, S. E. (1989). Stress, dependency, and social support: Who benefits from husband's presence in delivery? *Journal of Social and Clinical Psychology, 8*, 32–49.

Kennell, J., Klaus, M., McGrath, S., Robertson, S., & Hinkley, C. (1991). Continuous emotional support during labor in a U.S. hospital. *Journal of American Medical Association, 265*, 2197–2201.

Kessler, R. C., & Essex, M. (1982). Marital status and depression: The importance of coping resources. *Social Forces, 61*, 484–507.

Kessler, S. (1953). An experimental comparison of EEG patterns of normal and passive dependent individuals. *Speech Monograph, 20*, 124.

Klaus, M. H., Kennell, J. H., Robertson, S. S., & Sosa, R. (1986). Effects of social support during participation on maternal and infant morbidity. *British Medical Journal, 293*, 585–587.

Leatham, G., & Duck, S. (1990). Conversations with friends and the dynamics of social support. In S. Duck (Ed.), *Personal relationships and social support*. Beverly Hills, CA: Sage.

Lefcourt, H. M., Martin, R. A., & Selah, W. E. (1984). Locus of control and social support: Interactive moderators of stress. *Journal of Personality and Social Psychology, 47*, 378–389.

Leifer, M. (1980). *Psychological effects of motherhood: A study of first pregnancy*. New York: Praeger.

Melzack, R., Taenzer, P., Feldman, P., & Kinch, R. A. (1981). Labor is still painful after prepared childbirth training. *Canadian Medical Association Journal, 125*, 357–363.

Minuchin, S. (1974). *Families and family therapy*. Cambridge, MA: Harvard University Press.

Nadler, A., Mayseless, O. (1983). Recipient self-esteem and reactions to help. In J. D. Fisher, A. Nadler, & B. M. Depaulo (Eds.), *New directions in helping: Recipient reactions to aid* (pp. 167–189). New York: Academic Press.

Nettelbladt, P., Fagerstrom, C. F., & Uddenberg, N. (1976). The significance of reported childbirth pain. *Journal of Psychosomatic Research, 20*, 215–221.

Norbeck, T., & Tilden, V. (1983). Life stress, social support and emotional disequilibrium in complications of pregnancy: A prospective multivariate study. *Journal of Health and Social Behavior, 24*, 30–46.

Nuckolls, K. G., Cassel, J., & Kaplan, B. H. (1972). Psychosocial assets, life crisis and the prognosis of pregnancy. *American Journal of Epidemiology, 95*, 431–441.

Pierce, G. R., Sarason, B. R., & Sarason, I. G. (1990). Integrating social support perspectives: Working models, personal relationships, and situational factors. In S. Duck (Ed.), *Personal relationships and social support* (pp. 173–189). Newbury Park, CA: Sage.

Rook, K. S. (1984). The negative side of social interaction: Impact on psychological well-being. *Journal of Personality and Social Psychology, 52*, 1132–1147.

Rook, K. S. (1987). Social support versus companionship: Effects on life stress, loneliness, and evaluations by others. *Journal of Personality and Social Psychology, 52*, 1132–1147.

Sandler, I., & Lakey, B. (1982). Locus of control as a stress moderator: The role of control perceptions and social support. *American Journal of Community Psychology, 8*, 41–52.

Sarason, B. R., Pierce, G. R., Shearin, E. N., Sarason, I. G., Waltz, J. A., & Poppe, L. (1991). Perceived social support and working models of self and actual others. *Journal of Personality and Social Psychology*, 60, 273–283.

Sarason, I. G., Pierce, G. R., & Sarason, B. R. (1994). General and specific perceptions of social support. In W. R. Avison & I. H. Gotlib (Eds.), *Stress and mental health* (pp. 151–177). New York: Plenum.

Shumaker, S. A., & Brownell, A. (1984). Toward a theory of social support: Closing the conceptual gaps. *Journal of Social Issues*, 40, 11–36.

Sosa, R., Kennell, J., Klaus, M., Robertson, S., & Urrutia, J. (1980). The effect of supportive companion in perinatal problems, length of labor and mother–infant interacting. *New England Journal of Medicine*, 303, 597–600.

Spielberger, C. D. (1979). *Preliminary manual for the State-Trait Personality Inventory (STPI)*. Tampa: University of South Florida Resources Institute.

Spielberger, C. D., Gorsuch, R. L., & Lushene, R. E. (1970). *Test manual for the State-Trait Anxiety Inventory*. Palo Alto, CA: Consulting Psychologists Press.

Stephens, M. A. P., Kinney, J. M., Norris, V. K., & Ritchie, S. W. (1987). Social networks as assets and liabilities in recovery from stroke by geriatric patients. *Psychology and Aging*, 2, 125–129.

Swann, W. B., & Predmore, S. C. (1985). Intimates as agents of social support: Sources of consolation or despair. *Journal of Personality and Social Psychology*, 49, 1609–1627.

Tanzer, D. (1968). Natural childbirth: Pain or peak experience? Psychology Today, 2, 17–21.

Teichman, Y., & Melnick, C. (1978). *Manual for the Hebrew State-Trait Anxiety Inventory*. Tel Aviv, Israel: Tel Aviv University.

Vaux, A. (1988). *Social support: Theory, research, and intervention*. New York: Praeger.

Wente, A. S., & Crockenberg, S. B. (1976, October). Transition to fatherhood: Lamaze preparation, adjustment, difficulty and husband–wife relationship. *Family Coordinator*, pp. 351–357.

Wethington, E., & Kessler, R. C. (1986). Perceived support, received support, and adjustment to stressful life events. *Journal of Health and Social Behavior*, 27, 78–84.

Wilcox, B. (1981). Social support, life stress and psychological adjustment: A test of the buffering hypothesis. *American Journal of Community Psychology*, 9, 371–387.

Wortman, C. B., & Dunkel-Schetter, C. A. (1979). Interpersonal relationships and cancer: A theoretical analysis. *Journal of Social Issues*, 35, 120–155.

Zavislak, N., & Sarason, B. R. (1991, August). *Predicting parent-child relationships: Influence of marital conflict and family behavior*. Paper presented at the annual meeting of the American Psychological Association, Washington, DC.

CHAPTER 19

PERSONALITY AND THE PROVISION OF SUPPORT

EMOTIONS FELT AND SIGNALED

REBECCA L. COLLINS AND ADAM DI PAULA

SOCIAL SUPPORT AND CARING: A PROCESS APPROACH

After decades spent establishing a link between social support and well-being, researchers have turned their attention to important related issues: determination of the processes through which support exerts its effects, and the prediction of support receipt. Our work (e.g., Collins, 1994; Trobst, Collins, & Embree, 1994) has addressed the latter question, but with the assumption that the two research agendas are related: Since they are part of the same process, factors that promote supportive behavior and the function that support serves should be linked in a meaningful way. By approaching the prediction of support from a process perspective, we have been able to formulate hypotheses that link specific attributes of providers and recipients to a specific support function. This may be critical to the development of support interventions (Thoits, 1985). Currently, the applied value of support research has been limited by what Heller, Price, and Hogg (1990) describe as "implicit assumptions of homogeneity concerning the support process, how it is delivered, and who benefits from its administration" (p. 482).

In pursuing this strategy, we have focused on social support's effect of making one feel loved or cared for (Cobb, 1976). A substantial body of evidence suggests that feeling cared for is not only part of why people benefit from support, but also is

REBECCA L. COLLINS • RAND, 1700 Main Street, P.O. Box 2138, Santa Monica, California 90407-2138.
ADAM DI PAULA • Department of Psychology, University of British Columbia, Vancouver, British Columbia,
Canada V6T 1Z4.

Sourcebook of Social Support and Personality, edited by Gregory R. Pierce, Brian Lakey, Irwin G. Sarason,
and Barbara R. Sarason. Plenum Press, New York, 1997.

probably central to its effects on well-being. Perceived emotional support predicts mental and physical health better than network measures, tangible , and other forms of support (Cohen & Hoberman, 1983; House, Landis, & Umberson, 1988; Lin, Woelfel, & Light, 1985). Indeed, although the type of support that is *most* helpful to recipients may vary according to stressor (Cutrona & Russell, 1990; Martin, Davis, Baron, Suls, & Blanchard, 1994), provider (Dakof & Taylor, 1990), or stage of illness (Helgeson, 1993), perceived emotional support is more *consistently* beneficial than support of other types. The mechanism responsible for this robust effect has yet to be identified, but it is conjectured that feeling cared about fosters a sense of security and a reappraisal of threat (Cobb, 1976). We may be biologically programmed to react to care in this manner, or we may learn it in infancy (Bowlby, 1969, 1973). Regardless of this, a feeling that others are concerned for one's well-being appears to facilitate health and adjustment.

Thus, we have targeted our efforts at predicting this outcome. Figure 19.1 depicts central aspects of the process that determines perceived caring. By *caring*, we mean a range of feelings including empathy, concern, affection, and love. We define the concept broadly, because those who are the objects of these emotions should find them supportive for similar reasons. Each implies an emotional bond between provider and recipient that forms the basis of felt security. Note from the figure that we view providers' true feelings as a central contributor to recipients' perceptions. There is not a perfect correlation between one person's feelings and another's perceptions of these feelings, since it is possible for someone to feel cared for in the absence of real

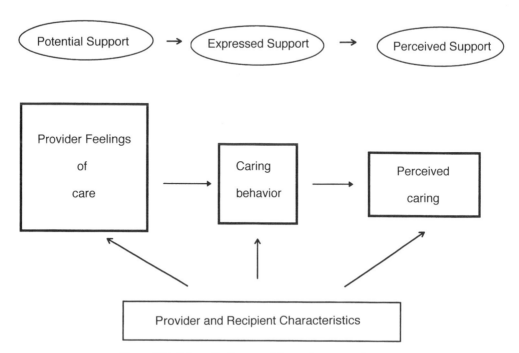

Figure 19.1 Schematic diagram of the caring support process.

sentiment, or to misinterpret a gesture of caring. However, it is reasonable to assume that when someone *is* cared for, he or she is more likely to *feel* cared for. Provider feelings not only predict support but also are a form of social support, as is each of the variables in Figure 19.1. However, they are known only to the provider at this point in our model and cannot affect the recipient unless communicated in some way, so we have labeled this variable *potential support*.

This highlights the importance of the next variable in the model. A provider's behavior is the window through which his or her emotions can be viewed by a potential support recipient. Our model shows caring as influencing behavior, consistent with research indicating that people are more likely to assist others when they feel empathic concern for them (e.g., Batson, 1991; Eisenberg & Strayer, 1987). There are, however, some notable differences between our ideas and the association documented in the empathy literature. Our concept of caring encompasses more than empathy, as we have noted. In addition, we believe that caring does not simply catalyze a provider into instrumental, problem-solving action, but, rather, that supportive behaviors are demonstrations of caring. Unintentionally or by design, when a person acts to alleviate another's distress, he or she is saying, "I care about your well-being."*

We have obtained some preliminary evidence of this in our laboratory. We asked college students to vividly imagine that a particular one of their close friends had a serious drinking problem (Trobst et al., 1994, Study 1). They were provided with details of the situation likely to develop, and when they had the scenario firmly in mind, they were to indicate the probability that they would perform each of 34 supportive actions in an attempt to help. The list of actions was derived from cancer patients' reports of the most helpful and unhelpful things that a variety of persons (e.g., doctor, acquaintance, spouse) had done since their diagnosis (Dakof & Taylor, 1990).† We edited the diverse set of behaviors produced in that study, revising or eliminating cancer-specific items to fit our alcoholism scenario.

Students' responses to this Supportive Actions Scale (SAS) were then subjected to principal components analysis. The solution we obtained had three factors with eigenvalues greater than 1, but a single factor accounted for most of the explained variance and was the only factor whose items formed a cohesive scale. The highest loading item (.77) was "Reassure my friend that I will stick with him/her through all of this," characterizing this factor as a measure of caring. Significantly, clear instances of tangible support ("Help my friend complete assignments") and informational support ("Pass knowledge on to my friend") also loaded strongly on this factor (.48 and .59, respectively). A single caring-like factor has also been obtained in an analysis of Barrera, Sandler, and Ramsay's (1981) Inventory of Socially Supportive Behaviors (ISSB) scale,

---

*Of course, not all supportive actions must stem from or convey caring. Providers may give support because they feel obligated to (Amato, 1990), and recipients may be aware of this. Indeed, we would expect that perceptions of a given support attempt as stemming from concern versus obligation will moderate its impact, a hypothesis we are currently testing. However, we believe that many supportive behaviors stem from and convey a message of caring, although some actions may be more caring than others.

†We chose to include the unhelpful behaviors as well, because we used the list to assess support from the provider's perspective, and the behaviors were probably intended to be helpful (Lehman & Hemphill, 1990).

which measures supportive behavior from the recipient's perspective (Stokes & Wilson, 1984).

Both findings suggest that emotional support is expressed and perceived through a diverse array of behaviors, including instrumental action, as well as direct expressions of concern. Given their shared underpinnings, we would include all such behaviors in the Caring Behavior variable in Figure 19.1. Since these actions communicate providers' emotions to the support recipient, we have labeled this variable Expressed Support in Figure 19.1. Although this label is nonspecific, it should be kept in mind that we refer only to that subset of enacted support that expresses caring. Supportive behavior may in many cases stem from, or be seen as indicating, other motives (see footnote 1).

The final variable in Figure 19.1 is the perception of being cared for by another person (Perceived Caring). Although each component of the figure is, in a different sense, social support, it is ultimately this perception that we wish to predict. According to the figure, a very limited set of variables contributes to perceived concern. We caution the reader that this is a drastically reductionist portrayal of the caring process. The figure was developed to illustrate the factors that are most central to caring support, their interrelationship, and how they are influenced by personality. In particular, it elucidates our view of the relationship between expressed and perceived caring. Often, differences between enacted and perceived support are emphasized in the literature, and they are viewed as having distinct predictors (Dunkel-Schetter & Bennett, 1990). We do see them as separate constructs, but as highly related to one another. Behaviors affect perceptions, as the figure indicates. In addition, both are influenced by similar personality factors. We will identify some of these in the following pages. Given the purpose of this volume, we will focus mostly on personality characteristics of providers and recipients.

CHARACTERISTICS THAT ELICIT SOCIAL SUPPORT: EXPRESSED DISTRESS

The amount of distress displayed by potential support recipients is particularly important to caring and its demonstration. This is suggested by two separate lines of research. One, the aforementioned empathy literature, shows that distress displays elicit feelings of concern in potential support providers (Eisenberg & Strayer, 1987), thus influencing the first variable in Figure 19.1. The second, attachment theory, links the distress displayed by infants to supportive behavior on the part of their caregivers (Bowlby, 1973). Thus, expressed distress might improve one's likelihood of feeling cared about by affecting both providers' behaviors *and* their feelings. We have looked at each of these routes.

Our initial investigation was reported in Trobst et al. (1994, Study 2). In that study, we showed a group of college students a videotape of a peer purportedly undergoing significant stress as the result of a relationship breakup. Eight versions of the tape were created, varying the sex of the student in need of support and using multiple actors to enhance generalizability. In addition, the level of distress indicated by the actors' nonverbal behavior was systematically varied to examined its influence on empathic concern and support provision. In one set of tapes, the actors appeared unhappy but fairly calm; in the other, they described their difficulties with teary eyes, stuttering speech, and tissue in hand. The tapes were identical in their verbal content; both versions made it clear that the student was experiencing significant problems with sleeping, eating, social life, and schoolwork, but was attempting to cope with them. The high- and low-distress versions were rated as equally realistic by participants.

After viewing a tape, participants were provided with a slightly revised version of the Supportive Actions Scale (SAS) we described earlier. They were asked to indicate the likelihood that they would perform each action to help the student in the tape, and we scored their responses on the Caring subscale. The students were also to rate their overall desire to support the student, on a single-item scale. We found that participants felt more generally supportive of the student who cried and looked upset, and had a stronger intention of helping him or her through caring-related action. In short, more distress led to more social support. We also found that expressed distress influenced potential providers' feelings in response to the tapes: Scores on a 6-item measure of empathy were positively affected by distress display. Additional tests indicated that empathy mediated the distress–support relationship, supporting the causal sequence that we hypothesize.*

Our subsequent tests of the distress hypothesis were quite different from this one. In them, we examined emotional expression using correlationship methods. This change in approach allowed us to broaden the generalizability of our findings to circumstances involving repeated contact with distress, as well as exposure to the distress of loved ones. Both may be considerably more aversive than a stranger's one-time distress display, and may elicit qualitatively different reactions from potential providers. In addition, we examined distress display as an individual difference variable. Although the expression of distress can be situationally evoked, there are also significant individual differences in emotional expression (Hatfield, Cacioppo, & Rapson, 1994; King & Emmons, 1990) that may result in chronic differences in support receipt.

The data were collected as part of a larger interview study of 92 HIV-infected, symptomatic, gay men (see Collins, 1994, for details). During the interview, respondents identified members of their intimate social network and completed a measure of perceived support (a version of the Social Support Questionnaire—Short Form (SSQ-S); Sarason, Sarason, & Pierce, 1987) in regard to each of these persons (up to five total). The scale included items such as "To what extent can you count on (the identified other) to care about you, no matter what is happening to you?" Thus, it captured perceived caring extremely well. We scored the scale in two ways, calculating the average amount of support across respondents' networks, as well as the amount of support available from the most supportive individual. The latter reflects the availability of at least one individual in times of need, whereas the former indicates how intimates typically respond to the participant. We used both measures because, although availability of support from any one person has been established to be of central

*Although we did obtain evidence of mediation, empathic reactions did not account for as much of the variance shared by expressed distress and support as might be expected, given our model. However, the measure of empathy was a combination of items assessing concern, egocentric distress, and attempts to take the distressed individual's perspective. This is a broader construct than that addressed by the present model, and its use may have attenuated our ability to observe mediation.

importance to well-being, a cumulative measure is more likely to show the impact of personality variables.

Individual differences in the display of distress were assessed using an instrument administered as a subscale of the Ways of Coping Inventory (WOC; Folkman, Lazarus, Dunkel-Schetter, DeLongis, & Gruen, 1986). The scale, which we have labeled the Self-Presentational Coping Index (SPC), is made up of 14 items generated to reflect a variety of self-presentational strategies for dealing with stress. Sample SPC items include "I tried to put up a happy front when around others," "I tried to avoid letting others know how bad my situation was," and "I manipulated conversations to avoid discussion of my problem." In pretests with a group of undergraduates, SPC scores correlated moderately with other WOC subscales and with the Marlowe–Crowne Social Desirability Scale (Crowne & Marlow, 1964), suggesting its validity as a measure of self-presentation specific to situations involving stress. Because of its length, the SPC (and the rest of the WOC scale) was left with respondents at the end of the interview, completed within a day or two, and returned to the experimenter by mail (response rate was 84%). SPC scores demonstrated high internal consistency (alpha = .85) and moderate overlap with other WOC subscales (r's ranged from .01 to .57).

The distress hypothesis predicts that SPC scores should be inversely related to social support receipt, since they indicate *lack* of distress expression. When we looked at support available from one's best provider, we found a negative, but nonsignificant, relationship with the SPC ($r = -.16$, $p > .15$). Using the measure of average level of support receipt, the relationship was stronger, but only marginally significant ($r = -.21$, $p = .07$). However, when we controlled for physical health in a final analysis (a measure of self-reported HIV-symptoms was included in the interview), the relationship between distress suppression and perceived support reached standard levels of statistical significance ($r = -.24$, $p < .05$).

Although this finding supports our hypothesis, a competing interpretation of the result remained: Persons who expend more effort hiding distress may *be* more distressed than others. We were able to test this possibility, since we collected two measures of distress as part of the larger study. Respondents had completed the Symptom Checklist 90 (SCL-90; Derogatis, 1977), which includes a measure of state anxiety, and had also rated their HIV-specific distress on a 5-point scale. When we examined these variables, we found that neither was significantly correlated with perceived support, even after controlling for level of illness. Thus, our findings concerning distress display are not the result of experienced distress, but of the way distress is manifest to others.

Based on these studies, we feel fairly sure that expressed distress elicits support by influencing providers' feelings and the actions that demonstrate them. However, we believe that the relationship between distress and support can also take some more complex forms. First, it seems likely that the relationship between displays of distress and social support is reciprocal. People are more likely to reveal their anxiety to those whom they see as caring. The correlation between expressed distress and support that was obtained in our HIV study may at least partially reflect a reciprocal relationship. Second, the effect of distress on support may depend on the way in which distress is displayed. The depression literature indicates that people sometimes avoid contact with the chronically depressed, and that depressed individuals often develop interpersonal problems (Coyne, 1976). Thus, the display of some negative emotions may reduce support receipt.

The effect of emotional displays may also depend on how the potential support recipient is coping with his or her feelings. Silver and colleagues found that a supposed victim of cancer who described her experience in negative terms elicited a less supportive reaction than one who spoke of her situation more positively (Silver, Wortman, & Crofton, 1990). In contrast to our laboratory study, in which all portrayals showed a student actively coping with her problems, the amount of coping effort displayed by Silver et al.'s cancer patient varied across conditions. This may, in itself, explain their findings, since no coping attempts were described in the negative condition, and people may help only those who make an effort to help themselves. Alternatively, distress display may elicit support *in conjunction* with displays of active coping (i.e., the effect may be interactive).

Finally, we note that distress may influence some potential support providers more than others. The relationship between distress expression and support from one's most supportive provider was weak in our HIV study. This may be a byproduct of our methods. The range on the "most supportive" measure was somewhat restricted, and that may have attenuated the correlation. Alternatively, self-presentation strategies may be employed inconsistently, so that their impact would be most evident using aggregate measures. There may also be more substantive reasons for our findings. People may not self-present to their closest confidant, or such confidants may be hard to fool. These possibilities are of both theoretical and practical interest, and warrant additional study.

INDIVIDUAL DIFFERENCES IN THE PERCEPTION OF BEING CARED FOR: SELF-ESTEEM AND ATTACHMENT STYLES

In our two studies of the distress hypothesis, we used very different measures of support. Both focused on caring and concern, but they included tangible, emotional, perceived, and received support. The parallel results for these measures are of particular significance, because a distinction between perceived and enacted support has been well established (Dunkel-Schetter & Bennett, 1990; Lakey & Cassady, 1990; Wethington & Kessler, 1986). Perceptions such as those measured with the SSQ-S tend to be stable over time and are often regarded as a cognitive-personality variable, more so than a reflection of recent support experiences (Sarason, Sarason, & Shearin, 1986; Lakey & Cassady, 1990). Our earlier comments on this issue make it clear that we regard circumstance to be at least as important to support perceptions as personality, but we do not discount personality's role entirely. To predict the perception of caring, any model must recognize that traits guide the cognitive processing of support-related experiences.

Personality also influences the relationship between perceived support and other variables. In an article that has had an important impact on the conceptualization of social support, Lakey and Cassady (1990) demonstrated that perceived support is correlated with adjustment partly because both variables are a function of self-esteem. In their study, the correlation between perceived support and dysphoria was reduced from $-.45$ to $-.20$ when self-esteem level was statistically controlled. Thus, personality not only contributes to support perceptions, but it also provides an important "third variable" interpretation of correlations between perceived support and other constructs.

Lakey and Cassady used a broad measure of perceived support in their study, one likely to encompass more than just perceived caring. However, self-esteem probably contributes to the specific class of support perceptions that involve caring as well. Indeed, some theories of esteem-development posit that self-esteem is a product of perceived caring (Rosenberg, 1979). Self-esteem may also account for a portion of the caring–distress relationship. Low self-esteem is known to covary with anxiety (Watson & Clark, 1984), and may also correlate with its display.

A second personality characteristic offers these same interpretative possibilities. Theories of adult attachment (e.g., Bartholomew & Horowitz, 1991) have identified individuals who chronically expect and perceive others to be supportive of them, and persons who chronically feel rejected or unloved. Attachment styles are not entirely redundant with measures of perceived emotional support, but they do influence the perception of being cared for. Attachment styles can also account for the correlation between perceived support and distress. Among the various styles of attachment is one labeled *avoidant*. Persons in this group see other people as uncaring and unsupportive. Interestingly, avoidant individuals tend to hide their negative emotions. In contrast, the group that displays the highest levels of distress, sometimes crying during the interviews used to assess attachment styles, sees others as most supportive (the *preoccupied* group; Bartholomew & Horowitz, 1991). Thus, individual differences in attachment style may account for some of the variance shared by expressed distress and perceived emotional support.

We have conducted some secondary analyses of our HIV data to investigate the role of personality in perceived caring. Our first test capitalized on the unique structure of our data set. As we have noted, our respondents provided us with measures of perceived support separately in regard to several members of their social network. To the extent that these individuals were perceived similarly, this suggests that respondents' personalities influenced their reports (although there may be some genuine similarity in the supportiveness of a given individual's providers, we minimized this in our study by asking respondents to describe both their most and least supportive relationships during the interview). To test for intranetwork homogeneity, we subjected provider support scores to an analysis of variance (ANOVA), using the interview respondent associated with each provider as the independent variable (i.e., provider was the unit of analysis). This revealed a significant and strong respondent effect, F $(76,99) = 1.97$, $p < .001$, indicating that the extent of support "provided" was highly dependent upon who did the reporting, as a personality analysis of perceived caring would predict.

We then examined whether this effect was attributable to the respondent's self-esteem (we did not assess attachment styles, and so were unable to test this variable). Our measure of participants' self-esteem was the Rosenberg (1979) inventory, which had been included in the questionnaire left with participants at the end of the interview. The correlation between Rosenberg scores and the average level of perceived emotional support across an individual's providers was significant, $r(75) = .24$,

$p < .05$, indicating that self-esteem contributes to perceptions of being cared for. Self-esteem did not, however, contribute to the distress–support relationship. When we calculated the correlation between SPC and Rosenberg scores, we found that they were unrelated ($p > .50$).

In summary, chronic personality traits are responsible, to some extent, for people's perceptions that they care cared for by others. Self-esteem, and perhaps attachment style, explains a significant portion of the variance in SSQ-S scores calculated across an individual's social support network. This finding adds to the body of work linking self-esteem to perceived support, since our version of the SSQ-S was somewhat different in nature from that used in previously published work. It is possible that personality also accounts for some of the relationship between expressed distress and support. Self-esteem did not do so in our HIV sample, but attachment styles may still play such a role and should be included in future work examining expressed distress and perceived emotional support.

INDIVIDUAL DIFFERENCES IN CARING FOR AND ABOUT OTHERS: ATTRIBUTIONS AND EMPATHY

We have contended throughout this chapter that providers' feelings of care and concern underlie supportive behavior. Situational factors, such as recipient expressed distress, are partially responsible for these feelings. Next, we argue that characteristics of providers should also be influential in determining their concern for others. Two factors that have been shown to predict emotional reactions to persons in distress are dispositional empathy and causal attributions.

When people witness an unexpected or negative event, they usually make an inference about its cause. When the event in question is another individual's misfortune, these causal attributions have a strong impact on whether observers feel concern (Weiner, 1986). Studies indicate that attributions also predict the provision of emergency and charitable aid (Piliavin, Rodin, & Piliavin, 1969; Weiner, 1986), and it has been suggested that this work should generalize to the social support realm (Dunkel-Schetter & Skokan, 1990).

Although causal attributions are usually examined as products of situational factors (e.g., Kelley, 1971), there is much evidence that they also depend on the personality of those who make them. For example, individual differences in self-esteem have been linked to distinct patterns of causal attribution following success or failure (Tennen & Herzberger, 1987). High-self-esteem individuals typically attribute failure to external factors, shifting blame away from themselves. In contrast, internal attributions are common among low-self-esteem individuals. Individual differences have also been observed in people's attributions concerning others. Of particular interest to us are the attributional conclusions drawn by persons with "authoritarian personalities" (Altemeyer, 1988).

Authoritarianism is a conglomerate of attributes, including submission to established authorities, conventionalism, and a tendency to aggress against those who violate traditional norms. Authoritarians believe in rigid adherence to established social hierarchies, and they tend to view the misfortunes of those low in the hierarchy or nontraditional in their behavior as deserved. According to theories of attribution and emotion (Weiner, 1986), as causal explanations for others' victimization shift from external (nonblaming) to internal (blaming) loci, emotions shift from caring and concern to anger and neglect. Thus, authoritarianism should be negatively correlated with caring about and providing caring support to groups who violate social norms, or who are low in the social hierarchy.

We examined this possibility in the HIV study (Collins, 1994) by looking at the effects of prejudice toward homosexuals (homophobia) on support provision. Homophobia is a subset of authoritarian attitudes (Hayes & Oziel, 1976) directly relevant to that study's gay sample. As we have so far described the HIV study, participants were a group of seropositive gay men. The design also included their support providers as participants—a subsample of up to three network members for whom support scores had been reported during the interviews. These individuals were mailed questionnaires containing a homophobia scale, a scale that measured the extent to which they blamed the interview participant for his contraction of HIV infection, and a set of measures for a separate study (Collins, in press).

Because we were interested in the impact of specific providers' level of prejudice on their support provision, providers were the unit of analysis for our statistical tests. However, since one individual was the source of the social support data for several providers, a standard analysis would violate the statistical assumption of independent observations. To eliminate this problem, we used the interview respondent as a covariate in our analyses. Our findings were fairly straightforward. Heterosexual support providers who scored higher on the homophobia scale were more blaming than those with lower scores, $F(1,55) = 7.20, p < .05$.* Blame was, in turn, associated with lower levels of support, $F(1,142) = 9.86, p < .01$. Ancillary analyses confirmed that this was a mediated effect; that is, prejudice reduced support *because* it led to blame.

We should note that, as a byproduct of controlling for respondent-based variance, the personality effects on support perceptions that we reported earlier were also statistically controlled. Our results therefore reflect some combination of perceived and enacted support—perceptions, but perceptions unique to particular providers. Thus, our findings link the chronic attributional style of a prejudice-prone personality to both forms of social support. Our test was of a specific prejudice, but we believe the finding is more broadly applicable. Whenever a trait influences attributions of blame, it should also influence emotional reactions to victims and, consequently, the support provided to them. Authoritarianism, specific prejudices, indeed, *any* belief systems that emphasize blame (e.g., see Lerner, 1970) are all likely influences on the caring process.

A second characteristic that we believe influences emotions and the provision of caring support is dispositional empathy (Batson, 1991; Eisenberg & Strayer, 1987). This trait has been variously defined, sometimes as an emotional capacity, and other times as both cognitive and emotional. The specific emotions experienced by empathic individ-

*The relationship between homophobia and support was nonsignificant among homosexual providers. This is consistent with our perspective, in that authoritarianism is reduced or eliminated by contact with low-status groups (Altemeyer, 1988). Thus, internalized homophobia probably represents a qualitatively different form of prejudice from that exhibited by heterosexuals.

uals are also a matter of debate. Nonetheless, nearly all definitions of empathy include the tendency to experience concern or sympathy in regard to another's circumstances (see Davis, 1994, for a comprehensive review). Thus, by definition, empathy has an impact on feelings of care and concern.* Trait empathy also has an effect on helping behavior, according to a great deal of research (see Eisenberg & Miller, 1987; Davis, 1994, for reviews). For example, several experiments have shown that when offered an easy escape from the observation of distress, individuals high in dispositional empathy prefer to aid the distressed individual, whereas those low in empathy choose to exit (Eisenberg et al., 1989).

It has been argued that empathy should also influence support provision (Dunkel-Schetter & Skokan, 1990). Our examination of this question was incorporated in the two studies of undergraduates reported at this chapter's outset (Trobst et al., 1994). Students' scores on a measure of dispositional empathy, the Interpersonal Reactivity Index (Davis, 1980), were collected at the beginning of these experiments and used to predict both caring and caring support. The reader will recall that in one study the students were imagining their behavior toward an alcoholic friend, and in the other, their reaction was in response to a heartbroken peer. In both cases, those high in dispositional empathy indicated greater feelings of concern and stronger intent to act in a caring manner (r's from .33 to .44, p's < .0001).

CONCLUSIONS

Few would argue with the idea that there is a fundamental human need to be loved and cared for, to feel that we are not alone. When laypeople talk and think about social support, it is to this need that they refer. To some extent, such feelings are illusory, so predicting perceived emotional support partly relies on understanding "recipient" characteristics. But reality also plays a major role in people's perceptions. Thus, it is critical to establish who actually feels concern for others (because they will give support), and who is able to evoke these feelings in other people (because they will get support). Of course, in order to provide a sense of security to their object, feelings must be communicated. The actions of support providers are therefore also of central interest. Sometimes, caring is expressed directly, through declarations of sympathy or affection, or promises to "be there." However, caring can also be manifest in offers of concrete assistance. For example, when the Republican-led Congress sought to cut funding to the Medicare program, it was suggested that GOP stands for "Get Old People," and furthermore, that Republican Newt Gingrich did not *care* about the elderly. The action was not considered an indication of budgetary restraint and tough economic times, but evidence of an individual's feelings, or lack of them. Our actions toward those in need signal our sentiments.

Caring may be felt and demonstrated in the course of a brief transaction, or shared

*In fact, the results reported vary when other operationalizations of empathy are considerd. Dispositional tendencies toward egocentric distress and cognitive, perspective-taking capacities are not related to caring behavior in the same way as the capacity for concern (see Trobst et al., 1994). This is consistent with, and provides some justification for, the process-specific approach that we have taken to the study of social support.

among providers and recipients in a communicative exchange that lasts over the years of their relationship. Actions that do not appear particularly caring to an observer may mean more to someone who is part of the relationship (Kelley, 1979). In fact, we believe that emotions can be signaled so subtly that neither provider nor recipient may be able to explain *how* they were communicated, only that it happened. Feelings can be shared through cues such as the use of particular facial muscles (Hatfield et al., 1994), a process so subtle that it has been labeled *emotional contagion*. Thus, behavioral measures of support need to be extremely sensitive in order to capture caring, and may sometimes need to assess behavior over long periods of time.

Much of the work we have presented is an extension of the empathy–altruism model. This model argues that people aid other people when they witness their distress, share in it, and feel sympathetic concern (Batson, 1991). The data we have presented suggest the same, but we have added to this work the prediction of a variety of types of support, including support perceptions, feelings, and actions. We also build on this work by operationalizing distress display and empathy in terms of personality characteristics: self-presentational coping, attachment style, trait empathy, and attributional style. We should note that these personality constructs are not entirely unrelated. For example, trait empathy may be as strongly related to causal attributions as is authoritarianism. Several studies have induced empathic reactions in participants and found that their attributions for others' problems were less blaming as a result (reviewed in Davis, 1994). We also suspect that self-presentational coping is related to attachment style, as we indicated earlier, although we have not yet had an opportunity to test this.

We began this chapter by noting the importance of taking a process approach to the study of social support. Whereas our perspective is broader than previous work, in that it considers many predictor and outcome variables to be related, it is also more specific, in that we focus only on caring support. This approach is important to making accurate predictions regarding the effects of support. Those factors most directly related to felt, expressed, and perceived caring are most likely to result in felt security and (we believe) adjustment to stress. This mapping of variables onto particular outcomes is critical in the design of interventions, where one must know who will benefit from a particular change and in what way.

In regard to intervention, Helgeson and Cohen (1996) have recently noted that support group participation (a common support intervention) does not seem to influence adjustment to cancer in the same way that perceived support from friends and family does. We believe this is because the two kinds of support involve different processes. Most support groups are structured and formal environments that do not involved the development of intimacy at a dyadic level. People may feel accepted by the group, may feel that the group understands their situation and even cares about their well-being, but the caring in this instance is abstract. Typically, there is no indication that the individual's relationship with the other participants holds in contexts outside the group, or that any feelings are specific to the individual, rather than the problem he or she shares with the other participants. Perhaps most importantly, group-level interaction does not force the provider to bare his or her concern for the recipient, and thus to have those feelings accepted or rejected, a central part of intimacy formation. We see caring as requiring this personal form of interaction.

This argument is as yet untested, as is our central claim that the effects of certain person characteristics are process specific. At present, our findings are potentially more broadly applicable than we intend. It may be that all of the factors we have looked at influence support other than caring support and have diverse effects. Our next step will be to identify the boundaries of our model by demonstrating that this is not the case. One way we plan to do so will be to look at the impact of caring variables on "uncaring" support—support that is given out of obligation. We expect that distress, empathy, and attributions will have little effect on it. We also expect that this form of support will have very different psychological effects on recipients from those of caring. For example, whereas we believe caring support increases feelings of mastery, we expect that obligatory support will undercut personal efficacy. The obligation to assist implies that the recipient could not get along without the provider's help.

Given the purpose of this volume, we concentrated this chapter on personality factors in caring support. This may seem incongruent with the interest in developing support interventions that we have claimed. Personality is, after all, considered to be rather stable. However, at least some person characteristics are malleable (Heatherton & Weinberger, 1994), and it may be possible to influence support provision by trying to change people. Prejudice, for example, is fairly stable, but it is nonetheless a trait that stems from, and is open to influence by, societal factors (Devine, 1989). Thus, interventions to reduce relevant forms of prejudice might be implemented at a societal level to increase caring support to particular groups. In other cases, personality tests may be used to determine where intervention is needed, rather than trying to change personality *through* our interventions.

In conclusion, we point out that our analysis of the support process colors it with emotion, something that is particularly lacking in the current literature. With a few notable exceptions (e.g., Reis, 1989), the focus has been on specific behaviors, or on the cognitions of providers and recipients. For us, emotion is central to support at every stage. Recipients' emotions influence providers, providers' emotions influence their behavior, and the feeling of being cared for (which we believe is emotional as well as cognitive), all play a part in explaining why social relationships influence our health and well-being.

ACKNOWLEDGMENTS

The research reported was supported by grants from the Social Services and Humanities Research Council of Canada and the Canadian National Health Research and Development Program—AIDS.

REFERENCES

Altemeyer, B. (1988). Enemies of freedom: Understanding right-wing authoritarianism. San Francisco: Jossey-Bass.

Amato, P. (1990). Personality and social network involvement as predictors of helping behavior in everyday life. *Social Psychology Quarterly, 53*, 31–43.

Barrera, M., Jr., Sandler, I. N., & Ramsay, T. B. (1981). Preliminary development of a scale of social support: Studies on college students. *American Journal of Community Psychology, 9*, 435–447.

Bartholomew, K. & Horowitz, L. (1991). Attachment styles among young adults: A test of a four-category model. *Journal of Personality and Social Psychology, 61,* 226-244.

Batson, C. D. (1991). *The altruism question: Toward a social-psychological answer.* Hillsdale, NJ: Erlbaum.

Bowlby, J. (1969). *Attachment and loss: Vol. I. Attachment.* New York: Random House.

Bowlby, J. (1973). *Attachment and loss: Vol. 2. Separation: Anxiety and anger.* New York: Basic Books.

Cobb, S. (1976). Social support as a moderator of life stress. *Psychosomatic Medicine, 38,* 300-314.

Cohen, S., & Hoberman, H. M. (1983). Positive events and social supports as buffers of life change stress. *Journal of Applied Social Psychology, 13,* 99-125.

Collins, R. L. (1994). Social support provision to HIV-infected gay men. *Journal of Applied Social Psychology, 24,* 1848-1869.

Collins, R. L. (In press). Social identity and HIV infection: The experiences of gay men living with HIV. In V. J. Derlega & A. P. Barbee (Eds.), *HIV infection and social interactions.* Thousand Oaks, CA: Sage.

Coyne, J. (1976). Depression and the response of others. *Journal of Abnormal Psychology, 85,* 186-193.

Crowne, D. P., & Marlowe, D. (1964). *The Approval Motive.* New York: Wiley.

Cutrona, C., & Russell, D. (1990). Type of social support and specific stress: Toward a theory of optimal matching. In G. Sarason, B. R. Sarason, & G. R. Pierce (Eds.), *Social support: An interactional view* (pp. 319-366). New York: Wiley.

Dakof, G. A., & Taylor, S. E. (1990). Victims' perception of social support: What is helpful from whom? *Journal of Personality and Social Psychology, 58,* 80-89.

Davis, M. H., (1980). A multidimensional approach to individual differences in empathy. *JSAS Catalog of Selected Documents in Psychology, 10,* 85.

Davis, M. H. (1994). Empathy: A social psychological approach. Madison, WI: Brown & Benchmark.

Derogatis, L. (1977). *SCL-90 manual.* Baltimore, MD: Clinical Psychometric Research.

Devine, P. G. (1989). Stereotypes and prejudice: Their automatic and controlled components. *Journal of Personality and Social Psychology, 56,* 5-18.

Dunkel-Schetter, C., & Bennett, T. (1990). Differentiating the cognitive and behavioral aspects of social support. In B. R. Sarason, I. G. Sarason, & G. R. Pierce (Eds.), *Social support: An interactional view* (pp. 267-296). New York: Wiley.

Dunkel-Schetter, C., & Skokan, L.A. (1990). Determinants of social support provision in personal relationships. *Journal of Personal and Social Relationships, 7,* 437-450.

Eisenberg, N., & Miller, P. A. (1987). Empathy and prosocial behavior. *Psychological Bulletin, 101,* 91-119.

Eisenberg, N., Miller, P. A., Schaller, M., Fabes, R. A., Fultz, J., Shell, R., & Shea, C. L. (1989). The role of sympathy and altruistic personality traits in helping: A reexamination. *Journal of Personality, 57,* 41-67.

Eisenberg, N., & Strayer, J. (1987). Critical issues in the study of empathy. In N. Eisenberg & J. Strayer (Eds.), *Empathy and its development* (pp. 3-13). Cambridge, UK: Cambridge University Press.

Folkman, S., Lazarus, R., Dunkel-Schetter, C., DeLongis, A., & Gruen R. (1986). Dynamics of a stressful encounter: Cognitive appraisal, coping, and encounter outcomes. *Journal of Personality and Social Psychology, 50,* 992-1003.

Hatfield, E., Cacioppo, J., & Rapson, R. (1994). *Emotional contagion.* New York: Cambridge University Press.

Hayes, S. N., & Oziel, L. J. (1976). Homosexuality: Behaviors and attitudes. *Archives of Sexual Behavior, 5,* 283-289.

Heatherton, T. F., & Weinberger, J. L. (1994). Can personality change? Washington, DC: American Psychological Association.

Helgeson, V. (1993). Two important distinctions in social support: Kind of support and perceived versus received. *Journal of Applied Social Psychology, 23,* 825-845.

Helgeson, V., & Cohen, S. (1996). Social support and adjustment to cancer: Reconciling descriptive, correlational, and intervention research. *Health Psychology, 15,* 135-148.

Heller, K., Price, R. H., & Hogg, J. R. (1990). The role of social support in community and clinical intervention. In B. R. Sarason, I. G. Sarason, & G. R. Pierce (Eds.), *Social support: An interactional view* (pp. 482-507). New York: Wiley.

House, J. S., Landis, K. R., & Umberson, D. (1988). Social relationships and health. *Science, 241,* 540-545.

Kelley, H. H. (1971). *Attributions in social interactions.* Morristown, NJ: General Learning Press.

Kelley, H. H. (1979). *Personal relationships: Their structures and processes.* Hillsdale, NJ: Erlbaum.

King, L. A., & Emmons, R. A. (1990). Conflict over emotional expression: Psychological and physical correlates. *Journal of Personality and Social Psychology, 58*, 864–877.

Lakey, B., & Cassady, P. B. (1990). Cognitive processes in perceived social support. *Journal of Personality and Social Psychology, 59*, 337–343.

Lehman, D. R., & Hemphill, K. J. (1990). Recipients' perception of support attempts and attributions for support attempts that fail. *Journal of Social and Personal Relationships, 7*, 563–564.

Lerner, M. J. (1970). The desire for justice and reactions to victims. In J. McCauley & L. Berkowitz (Eds.), *Altruism and helping behavior* (pp. 205–229). New York: Academic Press.

Lin, N., Woelfel, M. W., & Light, S. C. (1985). The buffering effect of social support subsequent to an important life event. *Journal of Health and Social Behavior, 26*, 247–263.

Martin, R., Davis, G., Baron, R., Suls, J., & Blanchard, E. (1994). Specificity in social support: Perceptions of helpful and unhelpful provider behaviors among irritable bowel syndrome, headache, and cancer patients. *Health Psychology, 13*, 432–439.

Piliavin, I., Rodin, J., & Piliavin, J. (1969). Good Samaritanism: An underground phenomenon? *Journal of Personality and Social Psychology, 13*, 289–299.

Reis, H. (1989). The role of intimacy in interpersonal relations. *Journal of Social and Clinical Psychology, 9*, 15–30.

Rosenberg, M. (1979). *Conceiving the Self.* New York: Basic Books.

Sarason, I. G., Sarason, B. R., & Shearin, E. N. (1986). Social support as an individual difference variable: Its stability, origins, and relational aspects. *Journal of Personality and Social Psychology, 50*, 845–855.

Sarason, I. G., Sarason, B. R., Shearin, E. N., & Pierce, G. R. (1987). A brief measure of social support: Practical and theoretical implications. *Journal of Social and Personal Relationship, 4*, 497–510.

Silver, R. C., Wortman, C. B., & Crofton, C. (1990). The role of coping is support provision: The self-presentational dilemma of victims of life crises. In B. R. Sarason, I. G. Sarason, & G. R. Pierce (Eds.), *Social support: An interactional view* (pp. 397–426). New York: Wiley.

Stokes, J. P., & Wilson, D. G. (1984). The inventory of socially supportive behaviors: Dimensionality, prediction, and gender differences. *American Journal of Community Psychology, 12*, 53–70.

Tennen, H., & Herzberger, S. (1987). Depression, self-esteem, and the absence of self-protective attributional biases. *Journal of Personality and Social Psychology, 52*, 72–80.

Thoits, P. A. (1985). Social support and psychological well-being: Theoretical possibilities. In I. Sarason & B. Sarason (Eds.), *Social support: Theory, research, and application* (pp. 51–72). Dordrecht, The Netherlands: Martinus Nijhoff.

Trobst, K. K., Collins, R. L., & Embree, J. M. (1994). The role of emotion in social support provision: Gender, empathy, and expressions of distress. *Journal of Social and Personal Relationships, 11*, 45–62.

Watson, D., & Clark, L. A. (1984). Negative affectivity: The predisposition to experience aversive emotional states. *Psychological Bulletin, 96*, 465–490.

Wethington, E., & Kessler, R. C. (1986). Perceived support, received support, and adjustment to stressful life events. *Journal of Health and Social Behavior, 27*, 78–89.

Weiner, B. (1986). *An attributional theory of motivation and emotion.* New York: Springer-Verlag.

Chapter 20

OPENNESS TO EMOTION AS PREDICTOR OF PERCEIVED, REQUESTED, AND OBSERVER REPORTS OF SOCIAL SUPPORT

Patricia M. Colby and Robert A. Emmons

It is through emotional communication that personal relationships are created and cemented.

—R. Buck (1989)

In this chapter, we propose to demonstrate that emotion-management strategies are fundamental for understanding individual differences in social support. Our basic assumption is that social interactions are, for the most part, transactions of affect; that is, social interchanges generate and are mediated by the affect of their participants. Manstead (1991b) has argued that there is a bidirectional relation between affect and social transactions. For example, affect has an impact on social perception and, in turn, the social context has an impact on the expression and experience of emotion.

Manstead (1991a) maintains that emotions are an integral part of the quality of social relationships; that is, emotions play a role in the creation, maintenance, and dissolution of social relationships. Thus, understanding the link between affect and social support may provide clues about the availability, use, and satisfaction with support. To the extent that a person's affective life impacts social relationships, individual differences in how affect is managed may provide important clues for understanding differences in the use and satisfaction with social support. In the empirical section of this chapter, we compare reports of perceived availability, daily

Patricia M. Colby • Department of Psychology, Skidmore College, Saratoga Springs, New York 12866-1632.
Robert A. Emmons • Department of Psychology, University of California at Davis, Davis, California 95616.

Sourcebook of Social Support and Personality, edited by Gregory R. Pierce, Brian Lakey, Irwin G. Sarason, and Barbara R. Sarason. Plenum Press, New York, 1997.

use, and observer reports of support provided and requested in individuals with differing styles.

INDIVIDUAL DIFFERENCES IN EMOTIONAL STYLES

The experience, management, and expression of emotions constitute fundamental differences between people that have important consequences for adjustment (Greenberg, 1993). Persons approach the experience of emotion in different ways: Some seek out emotional experiences, focus on and monitor their moods closely, process emotion more deeply, engage in conscious strategies to regulate mood, and generally have a rich emotional life. Others tend to avoid emotion, especially negative emotion, tend to monitor their emotions less carefully, tend to believe that emotion is less prone to regulation, and generally tend to have more impoverished emotional lives.

Interest in these broad emotional styles has recently emerged in various theoretical perspectives that emphasize people's (in)ability to use emotion effectively in solving important life problems. These include theory and research on emotional education (Buck, 1984, 1989), emotional competence (Saarni, 1984), emotional intelligence (Goleman, 1995; Salovey & Mayer, 1990), and emotional creativity (Averill & Nunley, 1992). A major focus within these theoretical frameworks is individual differences in the ways in which emotion-inducing situations are approached or avoided and in how emotions are experienced. Examples of these differences include repressiveness–defensiveness (Weinberger, 1990), levels of emotional awareness (Lane & Schwartz, 1987), meta-mood monitoring (Salovey, Hsee, & Mayer, 1993), affect intensity (Larsen & Diener, 1987), and ambivalence over expressing emotion (King & Emmons, 1990).

At a general level, emotional styles can be grouped into regulatory strategies designed to alter cognitive, physiological, or behavioral components of an emotional experience. Individual differences in emotional regulation may be observed in the degree to which persons may alter each of these components. These regulatory processes need not be deliberate or conscious, but may be automatic or unconscious. At their most basic level, emotional styles may be differentiated by whether an emotional experience is approached or avoided. This basic distinction, the excitation or inhibition of emotion, has been defined as a fundamental dichotomy in coping with emotional stress (Roth & Cohen, 1986), and in regulating the behavioral components of emotion (Frijda, 1986). Frijda has argued that what is ultimately felt or expressed depends upon how competing approach or avoidance tendencies are balanced.

At a more advanced level, emotional styles can be conceptualized as differences in the ability to create novel emotional experiences, and to utilize these experiences for personal growth. For example, emotionally creative persons, in part, are described by Averill and Thomas-Knowles (1991, p. 291) as considering their emotions important and valuable, using the knowledge acquired through previous emotional experiences to cope with new situations, enjoying situations that elicit uncommon emotions, communicating their emotions well, and as having emotions that reflect who they really are.

In this study, we conceptualized emotional styles as characteristics that facilitate or inhibit emotional experience; that is, whether the individual reports approaching or avoiding emotion-inducing situations, whether emotions are attended to or ignored, and differences in emotion-regulation strategies. We do not deny that general approach or avoidance tendencies may also affect the behavioral and physiological components of emotion. However, our present goal is to understand how stable individual differences in the subjective experience of emotion affect perceptions and use of social support.

EMOTIONAL STYLE CONSTRUCTS

Emotional Intelligence

This construct refers to a related set of emotional skills that contribute to the recognition of emotion in oneself and others, and to the ability to effectively communicate one's emotional states (Salovey & Mayer, 1990). Salovey et al. (1993) developed the Trait Meta-Mood Scale to assess three components of emotional intelligence: attention to feelings, clarity of mood and emotions, and beliefs about the desire to maintain or repair moods. Trait meta-moods are dispositional orientations toward emotion management and regulation. These traits are considered *metatraits*; that is, they capture how an individual feels about her or his feelings.

Emotional Regulation

The expectancy that affective states are prone to regulation varies among persons. Some people believe that their emotional states are more controllable than others. Based on social learning theory, Catanzaro and Mearns (1990) stipulate that believing that one's moods can be altered may lead to mood enhancement. This mood-regulating effect is expected to take place even if the actual coping strategies employed do not have inherent mood-altering properties. The Generalized Expectancy for Negative Mood Regulation Scale (NMR; Catanzaro & Mearns, 1990) measures coping strategies believed to be effective in regulating negative moods.

Openness to Experience

The tendency of individuals to be open to emotion-eliciting stimuli is captured by this construct. Individuals high on openness to experience are described as curious, creative, willing to entertain novel ideas, having unconventional values, and experiencing both positive and negative emotions strongly (Costa & McCrae, 1985). Men and women scoring low on openness, on the other hand, are conventional in behavior and conservative in outlook, with muted emotional reactions.

Emotional Inhibition

Several constructs have been suggested to play a role in the attenuation or inhibition of emotional experience. These include defensiveness (Crowne & Marlowe, 1960), emotional inhibition (Rogers & Nesshoever, 1987), self-deception (Sackeim & Gur, 1979), and repressive–defensiveness (Weinberger, 1990). People scoring high on these constructs may be considered emotionally avoidant. These individuals tend to describe themselves as rational, self-controlled, and not easily provoked by emotional stimuli. Three of the more widely used measures of emotional avoidance are the Marlowe-Crowne Social Desirability Scale (Crowne & Marlowe, 1960), the Weinberger Adjustment Inventory (Weinberger & Schwartz, 1990), and the Self-Deception Questionnaire (Sackeim & Gur, 1979). These three measures correlate modestly with each other (King, Emmons, & Woodley, 1992).

Emotional Intensity/Reactivity

The magnitude with which emotions are typically felt is another aspect of emotional experience that differs across individuals. Emotional reactivity is a stable characteristic of individuals (Larsen & Diener, 1987) and is independent of the valence of the emotion; that is, individuals high on affect intensity demonstrate not only a preference for experiencing strong emotions, but also lead emotional lives characterized by swings between strong positive and strong negative emotions. Affect intensity can be assessed via the Affect Intensity Measure (AIM; Larsen & Diener, 1987), which assesses the characteristic magnitude or intensity with which a person reports experiencing his or her emotions.

Emotional Conflict/Ambivalence

People not only differ in their tendencies to approach or avoid different emotions, but also in their tendencies to experience ambivalence or conflict over the experience and expression of emotion. The Ambivalence over Emotional Expressiveness Questionnaire (AEQ; King & Emmons, 1990) measures the experience of conflict over emotional expression. This questionnaire distinguishes two types of emotional ambivalence: inhibition, which refers to wanting to express and not being able to; and rumination, which entails expressing emotion and later regretting it. King and Emmons demonstrated that scores on the AEQ are relatively independent of measures of self-reported emotional expressiveness.

Emotional Expression

People differ in their beliefs or attitudes regarding the desirability of expressing emotion. The Emotional Expressiveness Attitudes Questionnaire (EEAQ; King & Emmons, 1990) assesses an individual's tendency to hold favorable or unfavorable attitudes toward expressing both positive and negative emotions.

It should be pointed out that emotional styles are independent of valence; that is, these styles describe strategies aimed at managing both positive and negative affect. Individuals high on emotional intelligence not only seek to savor positive emotions, but they also attend to negative, emotion-eliciting experiences. These individuals seek out both types of encounters in the service of personal growth (Salovey & Mayer, 1990). Moreover, people who experience intense emotions do so for both positive and negative emotions (Larsen & Diener, 1987). Similarly, *emotional regulation* refers to the ability to manage both positive and negative emotions, and those who are ambivalent over expressing emotion tend to be conflicted over expressing both positive and negative emotions (King & Emmons, 1990). Thus, differences in emotional styles reflect abilities to manage affective experiences in general, and are not simply compensatory mechanisms for overcoming negative emotions.

Differences in emotional style are related to the accuracy of recall of emotions experienced over extended periods of time. Colby and Emmons (1994) found that individuals who believe that negative moods are prone to regulation, and who approach emotion-inducing situations, overestimated the frequency of their positive mood and tended to underestimate the frequency of their negative moods over the prior month. Individuals who attend to and discriminate among their feelings, on the other hand, are fairly accurate in recalling the actual mood experienced. These results suggest that individual differences in emotion-management style are systematically related to both concurrent and long-term recall of affect.

EMOTIONAL STYLE AND SOCIAL SUPPORT

In their seminal work on personality and mood, Wessman and Ricks (1966) contrasted individuals open to experiencing a wide variety of affect from those who avoided emotional experiences. They found that the tendency to experience emotions openly leads individuals to have more positive social interactions when compared to the relationships of individuals who are less open to emotion; that is, differences in emotion regulation were reflected in how individuals engaged with their social world. More recently, Isen (1987) summarized the results of numerous studies linking affect, cognitive processes, and social behavior, and argued that affect has both "stimulus properties and meaning properties and that both of these aspects of feelings can serve to organize material for encoding, memory storage, and retrieval of information" (p. 245). That is important because, for example, positive affect increases flexibility in thinking and problem solving, and results in the use of more integrative problem-solving strategies in interpersonal disputes. Moreover, when in a positive mood, individuals tend to use fewer manipulative or self-centered strategies for solving social problems (Isen, 1987). Clark and Isen (1982) reviewed a series of studies suggesting that affective experiences shape several cognitive processes that may be related to social support. Specifically, being in a positive mood is correlated positively with liking others and having more positive conceptions of people. In addition, being in a positive mood increases individuals' willingness to strike up a conversation or to approach strangers for information.

There are at least three possible ways in which feeling states may influence social behavior (Moore & Isen, 1990, pp. 12–13): (1) Feelings may be used as sources of information by individuals in judgments of themselves and others; (2) feelings may also direct attention to specific aspects of the environment; and (3) feelings may facilitate retrieval of memories that are congruent with the current emotional state. These links between feelings states and social behavior are likely to be mediated by the person's characteristic emotional style.

Persons who typically seek out and pay attention to emotional experiences may be more likely to rely on affective cues to judge their social environment. On the other hand, persons who tend to chronically inhibit emotion, or who are emotionally ambivalent, may be less likely to voluntarily pay attention to and explore their emotional experiences when evaluating or engaging with their social environment.

Individual differences in emotional style have been shown to distinguish the type of affect experienced and recalled by individuals (Colby & Emmons, 1994). If one considers affect or emotion to act as a screen through which incoming stimuli are filtered, as suggested by Moore and Isen (1990), then persons exhibiting those styles related to the experience of positive emotion may make positive evaluations of the social environment. In addition, according to Buck's (1989) developmental–interactionist view of emotional education, individuals who are open to the experience of emotion and attend to it are also more likely to have developed in a social environment that is responsive to their emotional needs. As a result, these individuals are more likely to perceive their social environment as supportive.

Individual differences in emotional style may also have an impact on enacted social support. For example, in managing emotion, people may regulate their affective states through their social relationships. Given that most emotions are aroused in interpersonal exchanges (Lazarus, 1991b), the existence of individual differences in the experience, management, and recall of emotion implies that people may actively avoid, engage in, or seek certain social transactions as vehicles for experiencing emotion. Individuals who avoid social interactions are likely to suffer from diminished social support. The consideration of measures of emotional styles may provide a unique opportunity to sample differences in underlying tendencies to approach others when in need of support.

Larsen and Diener (1987) presented research suggesting that individuals who score high on the AIM tend to seek out emotionally arousing experiences on a day-to-day basis as a way of experiencing intense positive and negative emotions. In relation to social support, high AIM scores correlated with less-dense social networks (people who do not know one another) when controlling for number of acquaintances. This finding was interpreted as suggesting that individuals with high AIM scores use their social network as a source of emotional arousal (Jolly, 1987). These results support the notion that individual differences in affect management have important implications for social support processes.

Our research has demonstrated that feeling ambivalent about expressing emotion, and fearing intimate exchanges, are related negatively to indices of perceived support and positively to coping strategies related to not seeking support on a daily basis (Emmons & Colby, 1995). The perceptions of low available support mediated the relation between these emotional styles and well-being; that is, perceptions of low or no social support available aggravated the negative link between emotional inexpressiveness and conflict with well-being. These results linked personality characteristics related to poor emotion understanding and management to detrimental interpersonal support strategies. In this chapter, we report the results of a study that explores how differences in people's ability to use emotion effectively to cope with everyday problems are linked to social support. The chapter starts with an overview of three broad dimensions that summarize individual differences in emotional styles. Following this preliminary analysis, the social support correlates of being open to the experience and expression of emotion are presented in detail.

The following hypotheses were tested. First, persons with an emotional style characterized by seeking out, paying attention to, and regulating their affective experiences would be more likely to perceive that they have social support available than persons with low scores on this style. Second, emotionally open individuals were hypothesized to actively seek out their social network to cope with important problems. Third, we predicted that the social network members of emotionally-open individuals would report being solicited to provide social support. Finally, perceptions of social support were believed to mediate the relation between having an open emotional style and well-being.

METHOD

Procedure

One hundred and five undergraduate psychology students completed a package of questionnaires that contained the social support, emotional styles, and well-being measures. Participants were instructed to complete the package at home and return it 2 days later, during the next regularly scheduled class period. Participants also completed diary reports for 21 consecutive days, in which they recorded each day's most important problem and whether they approached their social network to cope with the problem. In addition, five observers who knew the participant well reported the amount of support they provided to, and the amount of support requested by, the study participant.

Participants

The sample consisted of 89 women and 16 men (mean age = 21) enrolled in an upper division Psychology course at the University of California, Davis. Students were awarded extra credit points in the class for participating in the study.

Measures of Emotional Styles

The Trait–Meta-Mood Scale (TMMS; Salovey et al. (1993). This scale assesses strategies of evaluating, monitoring, and regulating feelings. The 48 items of the TMMS are rated on a 5-point scale ranging from strongly disagree (1) to strongly agree (5). The TMMS is composed of the following subscales: Attention to Feelings ("I don't pay attention to my feelings," "When I am happy, I realize how foolish most of my worries are"), Clarity of Feelings ("I am rarely confused about how I feel," "I usually don't have too much energy when I'm sad"), and Mood Maintenance/Repair ("If I'm in too good a mood, I remind myself of reality to bring myself down," "I try to think good thoughts no matter how badly I feel"). When exposed to a distressing film, research participants who scored high on the three subscales of the TMM had fewer distressing ruminations and recovered faster from the emotionally distressing event (Salovey, Hsee, & Mayer, 1993).

The Generalized Expectancy for Negative Mood Regulation Scale (NMR; Catanzaro & Mearns, 1990). This 30-item scale measures generalized expectancies regarding the ability to regulate one's negative moods. Items are answered, based on the stem "When I'm upset I believe that …," with a five-point Likert-type scale ranging from Strong Disagreement (1) to Strong Agreement (5). The scale contains items tapping five distinct domains, ranging from generalized beliefs about the possibility of regulating negative moods ("I can usually find a way to cheer myself up") to actual cognitive and behavioral strategies for alleviating negative moods ("I can feel better by doing something creative"). High scores on the NMR scale correlate moderately and negatively with having an internal locus of control for women, but not for men. In addition, NMR scores are negatively correlated with reports of depression and experiencing sadness. On the other hand, scores on the NMR scale are not correlated to other negative affects such as guilt, anxiety, or fear (Catanzaro & Mearns, 1990). Mearns (1991) demonstrated that individuals with favorable expectancies for mood regulation were less depressed following the breakup of a romantic relationship.

The NEO Openness to Experience Scale (NEO; Costa & McCrae, 1985).   This scale assesses proactive seeking and appreciation of experience for its own sake and toleration for, and exploration of, the unfamiliar. The Openness to Experience scale measures six facets. Individuals who score high on the Fantasy subscale have an active imagination and fantasy life. High scores on the Aesthetic scale indicate a deep appreciation for art and beauty. Individuals who score high on the Feelings scale have a deeper range of emotional experiences of both positive and negative affect. High scores on the Action scale represent a tendency to try new activities. Individuals who score high on the Ideas subscale demonstrate a tendency to consider new ideas. The Openness to Values subscale measures a readiness to consider new social, political, and religious values. Individuals scoring on the Openness factor of the NEO are described as "having a strong interest in experience for its own sake. They seek out novelty and variety, and have a marked preference for complexity. They have a heightened awareness of their own feelings and are perceptive in recognizing the emotions of others" (McCrae, 1993, pp. 49–50).

In this study we calculated an overall openness score by summing across all items of the subscales. This overall scale score was used in the preliminary factor analysis. In subsequent analyses, results are presented for the Feelings and Fantasy facets only. Sample items include "I have a very active imagination," and "Without strong emotions, life would be uninteresting to me," for the Fantasy and Feelings facets, respectively.

The Marlowe-Crowne Social Desirability Scale (MCSD; Crowne & Marlowe, 1960).   This 33-item true–false scale contains items that tap a tendency to deny negative qualities. Although originally designed as a gauge of extraneous effects of impression management in self-report responses, this scale has been proven to tap the more psychologically meaningful concepts of self-deception and other-deception (Millham & Kellog, 1980; Paulhus, 1987). Sample items include "I never take a long trip without checking the safety of my car" and "I never hesitate to go out of my way to help someone in trouble." High scores on the MCSD are related to low self-reported anxiety, coupled with physiological indices that indicate high levels of arousal. In addition, peers report that individuals with high scores on the MCSD tend to conform to high standards of self-control (Weinberger, 1990).

The Self-Deception Questionnaire (SDQ; Sackeim & Gur, 1979).   This scale consists of 20 items rated on a "Yes" or "No" scale. This scale, like the MCSD, taps universally true but psychologically threatening behavior tendencies. Sample items include "Do you ever feel guilty?" and "Have you ever felt like you wanted to kill someone?". High scores on the SDQ are negatively correlated with psychopathology (e.g., depression, neuroticism, and manifest symptoms questionnaires).

The Weinberger Adjustment Inventory Repressive-Defensiveness scale (WAI-RD; Weinberger & Schwartz, 1990).   This 11-item scale assesses the denial of negative ideation and behavior, especially if aggressive, and the denial of not measuring up to very high standards of conduct. Items are rated on a 5-point scale ranging from *False* (1) to *True* (5). Sample items include "I am never unkind to people I don't like" and "I never act like I know more about something than I really do." High scores on the WAI-RD scale are judged by observers as being high in self-control and low in the expression of negative affect, without being particularly high in positive affect (Weinberger, 1990, p. 371).

The Affect Intensity Measure (AIM; Larsen & Diener, 1987).   This 40-item scale assesses the typical strength or intensity with which one experiences a variety of positive and negative emotions. Items are rated on a 6-point scale ranging from *Never* (1) to *Always* (6). Test–retest reliability for the AIM averages around .80. Sample items include "When I'm happy I bubble over with energy" and "I can remain calm even in the most trying days." Alphas for the AIM range from .90 to .94. Scores on the AIM are strongly correlated with the variability of affect reported by experience sampling and diary methods. In addition, high scores on the AIM are positively correlated with the General Behavior Inventory (GBI; Depue et al., 1981). Scores on the GBI are indicative of a mild form of bipolar disorder (cyclothymia).

The Ambivalence over Emotional Expressiveness Questionnaire (AEQ; King & Emmons, 1990).   The AEQ assesses conflict over one's emotional expressiveness style. Items on the AEQ pertain to wanting to express emotion and being unable to do so, as well as to expressing emotion and later regretting it. The scale consists of 28 items rated on a 5-point scale ranging from *I Never Feel Like This* (1) to *I Frequently Feel Like This* (5). Sample items include "I would like to express my affection more physically, but I am afraid others will get the wrong impression" and "I try to avoid sulking, even when I feel like it." Alpha for the AEQ equals .89, and 6-week test–retest reliability is reported to equal .78. High scores on the AEQ are negatively correlated to self-reported and peer-related expressiveness. In addition, high AEQ scores are positively related to measures of psychological ill-being (e.g., depression, anxiety, guilt, and obsessive–compulsive tendencies).

The Emotional Expression Attitudes Questionnaire (EEAQ; King & Emmons, 1991).   This 30-item scale measures beliefs about the usefulness versus harmfulness of expressing emotion in a variety of contexts. Items are answered based on a 7-point scale ranging from *Strongly Agree* (1) to *Strongly Disagree* (7). Sample items include "Showing emotion in public is embarrassing" and "I love a good fight."

The Emotional Expressiveness Questionnaire (EEQ; King & Emmons, 1990). This questionnaire assesses the expression of both positive and negative emotions. The EEQ's 16 items are rated on a 7-point scale ranging from *Strongly Disagree* (1) to *Strongly Agree* (7). Sample items for the EEQ include "Watching television or reading a book can make me laugh out loud," and "Whenever people do nice things for me, I feel 'put on the spot' and have trouble expressing my gratitude." The authors of the scale report an alpha of .78 for the EEQ. High scores on the EEQ are positively correlated to peer ratings of expressiveness, positive affect, and global measures of psychological well-being.

Social Support Measures

The Interpersonal Support Evaluation List (ISEL; Cohen, Mermelstein, Kamarck, & Hoberman, 1985). This 40-item scale consists of a list of statements concerning the perceived availability of four separate functions of social support (Tangible, Appraisal, Self-Esteem, and Belonging). The overall score can also be used as an overall functional support measure of perceived social support. The Tangible subscale assesses the perceived availability of material aid. The Appraisal subscale measures the perceived availability of someone to talk with about one's problems. The Self-Esteem subscale measures the availability of a positive comparison when judging one's self with others. The Belonging subscale assesses the perceived availability of people with whom to do things. Respondents are asked to indicate whether each statement is *Probably True* or *Probably False* about themselves. Two sample items include "I don't get invited to do things with others" and "When I need suggestions for how to deal with a personal problem, I know there is someone I can turn to."

The Network Orientation Scale (NOS; Vaux, Burda, & Stewart, 1986). The NOS is a 20-item scale that assesses the extent to which an individual believes that it is inadvisable, impossible, useless, or potentially dangerous to draw on network resources. Items on the NOS are rated on a 4-point scale ranging from *Strongly Agree* (1) to *Strongly Disagree* (4). Sample items include "If you confide in other people, they will take advantage of you" and "If you can't figure out your problems then nobody can."

The Inventory of Socially Supportive Behaviors (ISSB; Barrera, Sandler, & Ramsey, 1981). The ISSB is a 40-item scale assessing the type and frequency of receipt of socially supportive behaviors during the past month. Items on the ISSB are rated on a 5-point scale ranging from *Not at All* (1) to *About Every Day* (5). The authors of the ISSB report internal consistency coefficients ranging from .92 to .94. Two sample items in the ISSB are "Gave you some information on how to do something" and "Expressed interest and concern in your well-being."

Diary Reports. Participants were asked to complete a diary report for 21 consecutive days. They were instructed to complete the form at the end of each day and return them every 3–4 days to an envelope provided in class. Participants were asked to describe a specific issue or problem they were concerned with each day, and to answer a small questionnaire based on the described problem. This 8-item questionnaire, based on the Folkman and Lazarus (1980) Ways of Coping Checklist, examined both efforts at seeking social support (5 items, alpha = .95) and avoidant coping strategies (3 items, alpha = .94) as ways of coping with the daily problem. Items assessing daily efforts at seeking support included "I talked to someone to find out more about the situation," "I talked to someone who could do something concrete about the problem," "I talked to someone about how I was feeling," "I accepted sympathy and understanding from someone," "I got professional help." Daily avoidant coping strategies were assessed with the following items: "I made light of it; refused to get too serious about it," "I tried not to think about it," and "I went on as if nothing had happened." The avoidant coping items were included to provide an alternate strategy to seeking social support as a direct form of coping. These daily report items were rated on a "Yes"/"No" scale. Ninety-nine participants completed 21 daily reports.

Observer Reports. Participants were provided with five envelopes containing the observer measures of social support. Participants were instructed to give each envelope to an individual who knew them well. The observer reports were distributed after the conclusion of the 21-day diary entry period. Observers were instructed to rate the extent to which they had provided support to the participant during the past month, the same time period as the diary reports of the participants. Most entries were mailed back to us within 3 weeks of being handed out. Observers included relatives (9%), same-sex and opposite-sex friends (55%), partners/spouse/boyfriend/girlfriend (6%), and parents (11%). The observers were instructed to mail the questionnaire back directly to the principal investigator in a prestamped and addressed envelope. A total of 390 reports were returned (79% return rate), consisting of an average of four reports back per subject. In general, the observers sampled seemed to be well acquainted with the participants. Only 1% of the observers reported seeing the participants once a month or less, and 30% of the observers reported seeing the subject every day. The mean length of relationship reported was 8 years, with a range from 2 months to 30 years. In addition, 79% of the observers reported getting along with the subject about the same or better than usual.

The observer questionnaire consisted of a 6-item social support measure based on the daily report questionnaire. Each questionnaire was modified to include "her" for female participants and "him" for male participants. Social support items sampled both social support provided to (3 items, alpha = .70) and requested by (3 items, alpha = .76) the participant. Support-provided items consisted of "I loaned or gave her money or other material goods," "I gave her advice regarding a personal problem," and "I provided emotional support (sympathy, comfort, understanding)." Conversely, support requested was assessed with the three following items: "She asked me for financial assistance or other material good," "She expressed feelings about a personal problem of hers to me," and "She asked me for advice." The social support scale was rated on a 6-point scale ranging from *Once a Month or Less* (1) to *Every Day* (6).

Subjective Well-Being Measures

The Satisfaction with Life Scale (SWLS; Diener, Emmons, Larsen, & Griffin, 1985). This scale consists of five items designed to assess life satisfaction as a cognitive-judgmental process. Items are rated on a 7-point scale ranging from *Strongly Disagree* (1) to *Strongly Agree* (7). Items include "In most ways my life is close to my ideal" and "If I could live my life over, I would change almost nothing."

The Happiness Measure (HM; Fordyce, 1988).   This 3-item inventory asks respondents to estimate on the average the percentage of time they are happy, unhappy, and neutral. This scale has demonstrated adequate reliability and validity (Sandvik, Diener, & Seidlitz, 1993).

The Brief Symptom Inventory (BSI; Derogatis & Spence, 1982).   This scale consists of 53 items that are rated on a 5-point scale ranging from *Not at All* (0) to *Extremely* (4). Only the Anxiety (6 items) and Depression (6 items) scales of the BSI were utilized in this study. Items in the Anxiety scale describe symptoms characteristic of high levels of manifest anxiety, in addition to including cognitive and somatic correlates of anxiety. The Depression scale consists of items that are characteristic of clinical depression, including negative moods, low motivation, and social isolation. Sample items include "Feeling tense and keyed up" for the Anxiety scale and "Feeling lonely when you are with people" for the Depression scale.

Positive and Negative Affect.   Based on Diener and Emmons (1984), participants rated the extent to which they had experienced a series of emotions during the past month. The emotions listed were rated on a 6-point scale ranging from *Not at All* (1) to *Extremely Much* (6). Positive mood adjectives included *happy, pleased, joyful,* and *enjoyment/fun.* Negative mood adjectives included *angry, unhappy, frustrated, anxious,* and *depressed/blue.* These composite scales have been used in earlier studies and their temporal stability and internal consistency approach .90 (see Diener, 1984, for a review).

Rating of Overall Health.   This well-being index consists of one item that asks participants to rate their physical health in general. The rating is based on a 5-point scale ranging from *Poor* (1) to *Excellent* (5).

RESULTS

Analyses of participant attrition, gender, and differences in type and number of observer reports returned are presented in detail in Emmons and Colby (1995). In general, no gender differences were observed in any of the measures reported in this study, with the exception of social support provided. Observers reported providing more social support to women (t (88) = − 2.67, p < .01). However, in our sample, women outnumbered men by approximately 5 to 1. Therefore, no conclusive remarks can be made regarding gender differences in this study.

Factors Underlying Emotional Style

To determine the factorial structure of the emotional style construct, we conducted exploratory factor analyses. A correlation matrix was computed between the emotional style measures described earlier. The correlation matrix was entered into an exploratory principal components analysis. This analysis will help us determine if the emotional style scales tap similar aspects of self-reported emotional experience, which scales come together under a particular component, and how much of the variance of a broader emotional style construct is accounted for by these scales.

The appropriateness of the data for performing a factor analysis was first tested. The case to variable ratio was considered acceptable (105 participants completed 9 measures), as it met the suggested minimum of 10 participants per 1 measure. In addition, the correlation matrix was not an identity matrix (Bartlett test of sphericity = 225.63, $p < .001$). The variables as a set were adequately intercorrelated (Kaiser–Meyer–Olkin measure of sampling adequacy = .69). These results led us to believe that sufficient common variance existed between the measures of emotional styles to proceed with a principal components analysis.

The measures included in this study are believed to sample different aspects of a global emotional style; therefore, we decided to explore factor structures that allowed the underlying factors to interrelate. After evaluating the results of several analyses, the preferred solution resulted from a principal components analysis with oblimin rotation. This factor solution is presented in Table 20.1.

TABLE 20.1. Factor Loadings of Emotional Style Measures from a Principal Components Analysis with Oblimin Rotation

Emotional styles	Factor 1 Open	Factor 2 Closed	Factor 3 Conflicted
NEO-Open ($\alpha = .80$)	.74		
TMM-Attention ($\alpha = .81$)	.73		
EEAQ ($\alpha = .81$)	.73		
TMM-Repair ($\alpha = .81$)	.68		
AIM ($\alpha = .86$)	.69		
NMR ($\alpha = .88$)	.61		
MCSD ($\alpha = .65$)		.85	
RD ($\alpha = .73$)		.73	
SDQ ($\alpha = .68$)		.73	
AEQ ($\alpha = .88$)			.90
EEQ ($\alpha = .84$)	.56		−.67
TMM-Clarity ($\alpha = .90$)			−.82
Eigen Value	4.09	2.03	1.22
Pct. Expl. Var.	34.1	16.9	10.2

Note. $N = 105$. Total variance explained = 61.2. Only loadings greater than .40 are represented. NEO-Open = NEO—Openness to Experience Scale; TMMs = Trait–MetaMood Scale (Attention, Repair and Clarity Subscales); EEAQ = Emotional Expression Attitudes Questionnaire; AIM = Affect Intensity Measure; NMR = Negative Mood Regulation Scale; MCSD = Marlowe–Crowne Social Desirability Scale; RD = Weinberger Adjustment Inventory Repressive Defensiveness Scale; SDQ = Self-Deception Questionnaire; AEQ = Ambivalence over Emotional Expressiveness Questionnaire; EEQ = Emotional Expressiveness Questionnaire; α = internal consistency coefficient for this sample.

The number of components retained was based on eigenvalues greater than 1 and confirmed by examination of the Scree plot. This solution indicated that 61.2% of the variance could be accounted for by three factors. The first factor (eigenvalue = 4.09) was composed of the NEO–Openness to Experience Scale, the Trait–Meta-Mood Attention and Repair scales, the Emotional Expression Attitudes Questionnaire (EEAQ), the Affect Intensity Measure (AIM), and the Negative Mood Regulation scale (NMR). These scales assess different aspects of being open to the experience of emotion. In particular, these scales tap preferences for seeking out and expressing emotions, being attentive to feelings, and believing that emotions are prone to regulation. This factor accounted for 34.1% of the variance of the broader construct of emotional style and will be referred to as an "Open" emotional style in the remainder of this chapter.

The second factor (eigenvalue = 2.03) contains the three repressive defensiveness measures (Marlowe–Crowne Social Desirability, Self-Deception Questionnaire, and Repressive–Defensiveness), and explains 16.9% of the total variance. Individuals who score high on these questionnaires are characterized by not acknowledging emotions in themselves and avoiding situations that might arouse strong feelings. Therefore, we will refer to this factor as a "Closed" emotional style throughout the rest of this chapter.

The third factor accounted for 10.2% of the total variance and had an eigenvalue of 1.22. The highest loading scale in this factor was the Ambivalence over Emotional Expressiveness Questionnaire (AEQ), followed by the Emotional Expressiveness Questionnaire (EEQ, negative load) and the Trait–Metamood Clarity subscale (negative load). As a result, this factor represents self-reported, emotion-management strategies characterized by conflict over the expression of emotion, lack of expression, and lack of clarity about feelings. This factor will be labeled as a "Conflicted" emotional style in the rest of this chapter.

These results indicate that emotional style may be represented by three fundamental strategies: being open, closed, and conflicted about the experience and expression of emotion. The following factor correlations were observed among the three factors. The Open emotional style was not correlated with the Closed style, but was negatively correlated with the Conflicted style ($r = -.31$). Similarly, the Closed style was negatively correlated with the conflicted style ($r = -.23$). In general, it appears that individuals who report being open to the experience and expression of emotion are less likely to report conflict about expressing and being unclear about what they are feeling. Emotional defensiveness or being closed to emotion is not related to self-reports of expression and strategies used to regulate those expressions.

Factor Structure Replication

The reliability of the factor structure obtained was examined in an equivalent second sample. This sample consisted of 93 students (70 females and 23 males) who were awarded extra credit for participating in the study. The mean age of this sample was 22 years. This sample was administered all the scales except for the Negative Mood Regulation Scale (NMR) and the NEO–Openness to Experience scale. Therefore, for replication purposes, a principal component analyses of the first sample was recalculated excluding the NMR and the NEO–Openness scales. Deleting these scales did not alter the three-factor structure already presented.

The data from the replication sample also met all the assumptions for conducting a factor analysis. As in the analyses previously presented, only components with an eigenvalue greater than 1 were retained. This resulted in a three-factor solution that explained 62.9% of the variance. The three factors obtained were consistent with the factor solution previously reported. Pearson product moment correlations were computed to test the equivalence of the resulting factor structures between the two samples. Correlations were calculated among the three factors obtained from each sample. The Open style correlated .85 between the two samples. The Closed style correlated .97 between the two samples. The conflicted style correlated .99 between the two samples.

Overall, the high correlations obtained between the factors from these two samples led us to believe that the construct of emotional style is multifaceted. Based on the two solutions from two independent samples, the construct of emotional style could be broadly described as consisting of the following three components: The first component (Open) consists of strategies designed to approach, attend to, and regulate emotions; the second component (Closed) incorporates strategies aimed at distancing oneself from the experience of emotions; the third component (Conflicted) consists of strategies that describe conflict, lack of emotional expression, and a lack of clarity of feelings.

In this chapter we will describe the social support correlates of the emotional style scales included in the Open factor. The social support correlates of the Closed and Conflicted factors are described in Emmons and Colby (1995). To further enhance our understanding of the relation between social support and individual differences related to being open to emotion, we decided to explore which facets of the NEO–Openness to Experience scale related to social support. The results of an exploratory principal components analysis revealed that the subscales of the NEO could adequately be represented by two factors.* The first factor was formed by the Ideas, Actions, Values, and Aesthetics facets of the NEO-Openness scale (eigenvalue = 2.34). The second factor, on the other hand, was formed by the Feelings and Fantasy facets (eigenvalue = 1.11). These two factors explained 57.6% of the total variance. The scales in the first factor of the NEO-Openness scale did not demonstrate any significant correlations with the measures of social support used in this study. Therefore, only the correlates of the second factor (composed of the Feelings and Fantasy facets of the NEO-Openness scale) will be described in the remainder of this chapter (labeled *Feeling* in the tables).

Emotional Style and Self-Reports of Social Support

To explore the relations between an individual's Open emotional style and perceptions of social support availability, Pearson correlations were computed. These correlations are presented in Table 20.2. As predicted, high scores on all the scales included in

*An exploratory factor analysis was conducted including all six facets of the NEO-Openness scale with the rest of the emotional style factors. These results are not reported in a table because of the likely instability of the findings; that is, including all six facets of the NEO-Openness scale increased the number of variables from 12 to 17. This increase resulted in a violation of the recommended case to variable ratio of 10 to 1. With this caveat in mind, the results revealed that the factor composition did not vary from that presented in Table 20.1. Instead, a fourth factor was added that included the Ideas, Action, Values, and Aesthetics facets of the NEO. As was anticipated, the Feelings and Fantasy facets loaded on the "Open" factor as it is reported in Table 20.1. The four-factor solution explained 60% of the total variance.

TABLE 20.2. Pearson Product–Moment Correlations between the Open Emotional
Style Scales and Self-Reported Social Support

	Open	Feeling	Attention	EEAQ	Repair	Aim	NMR
Social support							
ISEL	.51**	.36***	.31***	.32***	.40***	.34***	.39***
Appraisal	.41**	.43**	.32***	.35***	.25**	.34***	.28**
Belonging	.53**	.38***	.31***	.32***	.34***	.44***	.41***
Tangible	.13	.15	.06	.09	.19	.10	.14
Esteem	.39**	.22*	.26**	.25**	.47***	.22*	.40***
NOS	−.59**	−.54***	−.51***	−.52***	−.61***	−.40**	−.41**
ISSB	.43**	.27**	.20*	.26**	.31***	.35***	.24**

Note. $N = 105$ except for NOS, where $N = 49$. ISEL = Interpersonal Support Evaluation List; NOS = Network Orientation Scale; ISSB = Inventory of Socially Supportive Behaviors; Open = Open Emotional Style Factor score, Feeling = NEO-Openness to Experience factor (Feelings and Fantasy facets); Attention = TMMs-Attention to Feelings scale; EEAQ = Emotional Expression Attitudes Questionnaire; Repair = TMMs-Repair scale; NMR = Negative Mood Regulation.
*$p < .05$ (2-tailed)
**$p < .01$
***$p < .001$

the Open emotional style factor were correlated with perceiving high levels of social support.

The subscales of the ISEL showed different patterns of correlations with the Open emotional style scales. In particular, the Tangible subscale was not correlated with any measure of emotional style. Apparently, the emotional style of an individual is not related to whether that person believes there are others who can provide material aid. However, emotional style is significantly related to whether an individual perceives there are others available to talk or provide information ($r = .41$, $p < .01$), with the sense of belonging in a social group ($r = .53$, $p < .01$), and with positive comparisons between self and others ($r = .39$, $p < .01$).

Overall, these results indicate that how individuals report managing their emotions is related to perceptions of social support. Specifically, individuals open to the experience of emotion tend to score high on measures of available social support. This relationship holds across a variety of different measures of emotional openness (e.g., paying attention to feelings, believing emotions can be regulated, feeling intense emotions, and having a positive attitude toward the expression of emotion).

Emotional Style and Diary Measures of Social Support

The relations between the scales that comprised the Open emotional style and the diary measures of social support were examined using partial correlations. From each correlation between the emotional style scales and the daily records of seeking social support, we partialed out the effects of the composite measure of avoidant coping. Likewise, we partialed the composite measure of approaching social support from the correlations between the emotional style scales and the daily records of avoidant coping. The calculation of partial correlations was necessary to separate each type of strategy (approaching social support to deal with a problem vs. avoiding dealing with the problem) from total coping effort.

Diary Records of Approaching Social Support.   In general, the Open emotional style factor score was moderately correlated with daily efforts at seeking social support (composite approach $r = .23$, $p < .05$). The only daily report strategy used to elicit social support that was not related to the Open emotional style was talking to somebody who could do something concrete about the problem. However, examination of the correlates of each individual scale with the daily reports of seeking social support revealed that the positive correlations observed between the Open factor score and daily efforts at seeking support were due to a few scales. In particular, The TMM-Attention to feelings scale was positively related to reports of talking to somebody about feelings ($r = .21$, $p < .05$). The EEAQ was positively related to seeking professional help ($r = .20$, $p < .05$). Scores on the TMM-Repair scale were positively correlated to the composite measure of approaching social support ($r = .20$, $p < .05$), and to talking about feelings ($r = .22$, $p < .05$). The AIM showed the most consistent patterns of correlations with the daily support items. In particular, scores on the AIM correlated positively with the composite approach measure ($r = .25$, $p < .05$), the "Find out More about the Situation" item ($r = .26$, $p < .05$), the "get professional help" item ($r = .25$, $p < .05$), and the "Talk about how I was Feeling" item ($r = .22$, $p < .05$). Last, scores on the NMR scale correlated positively with the composite approach measure ($r = .22$, $p < .05$), the "Find out More about the Situation" item ($r = .25$, $p < .05$), and the "Talk about how I was feeling item" ($r = .22$, $p < .05$).

Diary Records of Avoidant Coping.   The results of partial correlation analyses revealed that, in general, scores on the Open emotional style factor were not related to the daily records of avoidant coping. Only two of the scales comprising the Open emotional style had significant correlations with the Avoidant coping items. Scores on the TMM-Attention scale were negatively correlated with the Tried Not to Think about It item ($r = -.21$, $p < .05$). EEAQ scores were negatively related to the composite measure of Avoidant coping and the Made Light of the Situation item ($r = -.23$, $p < .05$, for both).

Apparently then, having an Open emotional style is related to the use of social support to cope with a daily problem. This style, however, is not related to avoiding dealing with the problem altogether (with the exception of the few negative correlations reported earlier). The Avoidant coping items do not address whether the individual actually avoided social contact. To the extent that individuals can "mask" their internal experience, it is likely that the social network could be used as a distraction and not just as a problem-solving aid.

Emotional Style and Observer Reports of Social Support

Each observer rated the extent to which the participant had asked for and was provided with support. Therefore, it is not surprising that observer reports of providing social support and being asked for social support were highly and positively correlated ($r = .87$, $p < .001$). This high correlation led us to create a single index of observer-reported social support; that is, a single index of observer-reported social support was computed by averaging both support requested and provided from each observer. Pearson correlations were computed between the observer-reported social support index and the scales that comprised the Open emotional style factor. These correlations are presented in Table 20.3. The only significant correlation observed was between observer-reported social support and the Feeling factor of the NEO-Openness. Apparently, observers reported providing more social support to individuals characterized as being "more emotionally responsive, sensitive, empathic, valuing feelings (Feeling facet), and being imaginative" (Fantasy facet; Costa & McCrae, 1985).

Observer-Rated Expressiveness and Observer Reports of Social Support

The surprising lack of correlations obtained between the Open emotional style scales and the observer reports of support requested/provided (except for those observed with the Feeling factor of the NEO-Openness), led us to explore other variables that may differentiate to whom observers report providing support. Pearson correlations were computed between the observer's ratings of knowing the participant (casually to intimately), frequency of contact (seeing or talking to the participant), emotional expressiveness, and support provided. The results of these correlations are presented in Table 20.3.

Observer reports of knowing the subject intimately were positively correlated with having an Open emotional style ($r = .25, p < .05$). In particular, ratings of how well the observer knew the participant were related to high scores on the Feelings and

TABLE 20.3. Pearson Product–Moment Correlations between Observer Reports of Emotionality, Quality of the Relationship, and Open Emotional Style Factor Scales

	Observer reports			
	Well	Contact	Express	Social support
Observer reports				
Well				
Contact	−.01			
Expressiveness	.53**	.01		
Social support	.36	.40***	.38***	
Tangible	.18	.39***	.06	
Information	.35***	.33**	.34***	
Emotional	.34***	.32**	.44***	
Open emotional style	.25*	.07	.52**	.23*
Feeling	.30**	.16	.49***	.30**
Attention	.16	.05	.46***	.12
EEAQ	.29**	.05	.35***	.19
Repair	.15	−.04	.34***	.08
Aim	.18	.13	.46***	.19
NMR	.02	−.04	.22*	.00

Note. $N = 90$. Well = How well do you know …?; Contact = How often do you see and/or talk to …?; Express = Emotional expressiveness; Social Support = Mean of Support requested and Support provided. See Table 20.1 for a description of the scales included in the Open emotional style.
*$p < .05$ **$p < .01$ ***$p < .001$ (2-tailed).

Fantasy facets of the NEO-Openness ($r = .30$, $p < .01$), and to high scores on the EEAQ ($r = .29$, $p < .01$). Relatedly, observers tended to rate as more expressive individuals who scored high on the Open emotional style ($r = .52$, $p < .01$). Correlations between all the scales of the Open emotional style and observer ratings of expressiveness ranged from .22 ($p < .05$) to .49 ($p < .001$).

An examination of the correlations between the observer measures of expressiveness, knowledge of the participant, frequency of contact, and social support revealed that observers reported knowing more intimately those individuals they rated as being more emotionally expressive ($r = .53$, $p < .001$). In addition, observer-reported expressiveness was positively correlated with observer-reported social support ($r = .38$, $p < .001$). Last, and not surprising, observers reported being in contact more often with those individuals to whom they provided social support ($r = .40$, $p < .001$).

Previous studies have documented that emotional support is the most potent predictor of reduced ill-being (Cohen & McKay, 1983; Heller, 1979; House, 1981; Thoits, 1985; Turner, 1981). We conducted a multiple regression analysis to determine the most potent predictor of observer-provided emotional support (controlling for support requested). The results revealed that when entered as a block, only observer-reported expressiveness ($\beta = .20$, $t = 2.74$, $p < .05$) and not observer ratings of how well they know the person ($\beta = .02$, $t = .21$, $p = $ ns), significantly contributes to ratings of emotional support provided ($R^2 = .55$, $p < .001$); that is, being rated as emotionally expressive is a stronger predictor of being provided with support than is intimacy or familiarity *per se*. It is highly likely that emotionally expressive individuals unambiguously communicate signals of need to others. In this manner, expressive people are more likely to elicit sympathy and understanding from observers.

Relation between Emotional Style, Social Support, and Well-Being

Table 20.4 shows the Pearson correlations between emotional style, self-reported measures of social support, and well-being indices. In general, having an Open emotional style is related to high well-being (average $r = .39$). As expected, perceptions of available social support (ISEL) are related to psychological well-being (average $r = .46$). And, having a negative attitude toward support (NOS) is related to ill-being (average $r = .37$). The perception of support available during the past month (ISSB) was only significantly correlated with the SWLS ($r = .20$, $p < .05$) and with positive affect ($r = .39$, $p < .001$). Only the Esteem subscale of the ISEL was significantly correlated with the physical health item ($r = .40$, $p < .001$).

Do Perceptions of Social Support Mediate the Relation between Having an Open Emotional Style and Well-Being?

Total scores on the eight well-being scales were standardized (transformed to z scores) and combined to create a composite measure of emotional well-being (i.e., zSWLS + zHappy + zPa + zHealth − zUnhappy − zAnx − zDep − zNa, $\alpha = .84$). This composite measure of well-being was used as a dependent variable in the analysis testing for mediational effects. Correlations among the well-being measures, the emotional styles, and the self-reported social support questionnaires are reported in Table

TABLE 20.4. Pearson Product-Moment Correlations between the Open Emotional Style Scales, Social Support, and Well-Being Measures

				Well-being					
	SWLS	%Happy	%Unhappy	Anx	Dep	PA (N = 80)	NA (N = 80)	Health (N = 72)	WB
Open emotional style									
Feeling	.32**	.39**	-.44**	-.12	-.45***	.48***	-.25*	.35***	.47***
Attention	.14	.22*	-.19*	.08	-.19	.25**	-.16	.14	.21
EEAQ	.29**	.33***	-.39***	-.05	-.34**	.27**	-.21*	.22*	.38***
Repair	.18	.36***	-.29**	-.01	-.29**	.11	-.15	.29*	.35**
Aim	.44***	.40***	-.55***	-.36***	-.63***	.44***	-.34***	.30**	.62***
NMR	.15	.22*	-.12	.09	-.20*	.36***	-.01	.14	.20
	.44***	.36***	-.49***	-.36***	-.61***	.47***	-.30**	.35***	.60***
Social support									
ISEL (α = .84)	.50**	.40**	-.41**	-.22*	-.47***	.47***	-.26*	.02	.52***
Appraisal	.24*	.30**	-.27**	-.02	-.18	.24*	-.15	.18	.33**
Belonging	.35**	.25**	-.31**	-.19	-.36**	.41***	-.24*	.20*	.40***
Tangible	.22*	.21*	-.19	.00	.14	.24*	-.13	.07	.18
Esteem	.56**	.37**	-.39**	-.35**	-.55***	.51***	-.26*	.40***	.55***
NOS (N = 49, α = .80)	-.40**	-.29*	.38**	.16	.45***	-.40***	-.47***	.02	-.59***
ISSB (α = .80)	.20*	.15	-.19	.00	-.08	.39***	-.08	-.18	.17
Well-being									
SWLS (α = .88)									
%Happy (1 item)	.36***								
%Unhappy (1 item)	-.42***	-.64***							
Anx (α = .85)	-.51***	-.23*	.42***						
Dep (α = .86)	-.60***	-.37***	.56***	.64***					
PA (α = .89)	.60***	.24*	-.51***	-.54***	-.57***				
NA (α = .86)	-.31**	-.10	.23*	.44***	.44***	-.47***			
Health (1 item)	.41***	.27**	-.20	.08	-.34***	.29*	-.06		

Note. $N = 105$ except where indicated in parentheses. SWLS = Satisfaction with Life Scale; %Happy and %Unhappy = items from the Happiness Measure; Anx = Anxiety Scale of the Brief Symptom Inventory; Dep = Depression Scale of the Brief Symptom Inventory; PA = positive affect; NA = negative affect; Health = rating of physical health; WB = Composite measure of well-being; α = internal consistency coefficient for this sample.
*$p < .05$ **$p < .01$ ***$p < .001$ (2-tailed).

20.4. The Open emotional style was used as the independent variable, and perception of social support (as assessed by the ISEL) was used as the mediator in the mediation analysis.

Baron and Kenny (1986) stipulated a series of guidelines for determining mediation effects. Following these authors' suggestions, social support can be considered to mediate the relation between the Open emotional style (the predictor) and well-being (the criterion) under the following conditions:

1. Emotional style (the independent variable) is related to social support (the mediator).
2. Emotional style is related to well-being (the dependent variable).
3. Social support is related to well-being.
4. Finally, we can claim perfect mediation if the Open emotional style has no effect on well-being after controlling for perceived social support.

As shown in Table 20.5, the result of the regression analysis indicate that perceptions of social support mediate the relation between having an Open emotional style and well-being; that is, when both perceived social support and Open emotional style are included in the analysis, they explain 28% of the variance. Most importantly, however, the standardized beta coefficient for the Open emotional style dropped from .47 to .32 ($p < .05$) when perceived social support is controlled, satisfying Baron and Kenny's fourth condition. It is not surprising that perfect mediation was not observed (i.e., complete elimination of the link between an Open emotional style and well-being) when controlling for perceptions of social support. It is highly probable that other variables contribute to the positive link between emotional openness and well-

TABLE 20.5. Stepwise Regression Analysis:
Test of the Mediating Effects of Social Support
on the Relation between Open Emotional Style and Well-Being

Mediation conditions[a]	Independent Variable = Open Emotional Style Mediator = Perceived Social Support (ISEL) Dependent Variable = Well-Being Composite				
	R^2	Standardized β	SE β	t	p
1	.23	.48	.12	5.5	.001
2	.22	.47	.51	4.4	.001
3	.20	.45	.33	4.2	.001
4	.28	.32	.36	2.5	.01[b]

Note. N = 105. Well-Being Composite = Scores on the Happiness Measure (HM)—%Happy and %Unhappy items; PA and NA, Anxiety and Depression scales of the Brief Symptom Inventory and General Rating of Health (α = .84, 8 items). ISEL = Interpersonal Support Evaluation List; Open Emotional Factor includes the NEO—Openness to Experience Scale (Feelings and Fantasy facets), the TMMs Attention and Repair subscales, the EEAQ, AIM, and NMR scales.
[a]Baron and Kenny's (1986) conditions to establish mediation effects. See text for a description of mediation conditions 1–4.
[b]Mediation is present, yet not both a necessary and sufficient condition for the effect to occur.

being. However, the results show that perceived social support is a potent, yet not necessary and sufficient, condition to explain the relation between an Open emotional style and higher well-being.

DISCUSSION

The role of individual differences in affect-management strategies in social support processes has been largely ignored. In fact, most studies of personality and social support have focused on cognitive variables. For example, negative views of self and other have been proposed to underlie perceptions of available support (see Lakey & Cassady, 1990; Mankowski & Wyer, 1993; Sarason et al., 1991). These individual differences in schemas have proven to be important in understanding the cognitive processes that give rise to perceptions of available support. However, other aspects of an individual's personality, such as motives (Colby, Rabin, & Emmons, 1994) and emotional styles, may provide additional insight into how individuals shape their social resources (see Sarason, Sarason, & Shearin, 1986).

In this chapter, we presented the results of research linking individual differences in self-reported emotional style to three indices of social support. Through factor analyses, several measures of emotion management were reduced to three underlying factors. These factors were labeled emotionally Open, Closed, and Conflicted, and are believed to represent fundamental differences in how emotions are managed, or emotional style.

Individuals scoring high on the emotionally Open factor are characterized by approaching emotionally arousing situations, paying attention to their feelings, having an open attitude toward expressing emotion, reporting the experience of strong emotions, and, believing that negative moods can be regulated. The Conflicted emotional style, on the other hand, was represented by high scores on the ambivalence over expressing emotion questionnaire, low scores on emotional expressiveness, and being unclear about affective experiences. The emotionally Closed, or inhibited, factor was composed of the Marlowe–Crowne Social Desirability Scale, the Weinberger Repressiveness–Defensiveness questionnaire, and the Self-Deception Questionnaire. These three scales tap an individual's tendency to avoid emotion-inducing situations, and a tendency to deny experiencing both positive and negative affect. Correlations between the emotion inhibition and conflict factor scales with social support indices were reported in Emmons and Colby (1995) and were not presented in this chapter.

Emotional Styles and Perceptions of Social Support

We explored how individual differences related to being open to the experience of emotion correlated with several measures of social support and well-being. The results showed that being open to the experience of emotion is related to experiencing positive mood, happiness, and perceptions that social support is available.

Emotional style appears to underlie the type of affect likely to be experienced by an individual, and how that affect is recalled (Colby & Emmons, 1994), and as a result, the retrieval of memories congruent with that affective state (Isen, 1987). In this study, individuals with an Open emotional style were more likely to evaluate the availability of social support positively. These results suggest that emotional styles may provide another avenue by which affect influences social behavior; that is, affect-regulation strategies, and not just type of affect (i.e., positive or negative) have an impact on social behavior. Moore and Isen (1990) summarized research relating affect to social judgments. These authors conclude that "results seem to indicate that people in positive affective states tend to have positive information more accessible in memory, are optimistic about future performances, make more favorable judgments, are more friendly, open, and giving to others" (p. 16). Relatedly, negative moods decrease attraction to others, increases negative conceptions of others, and, lead to perceptions of negative affect in other's facial expressions (Clark & Isen, 1982).

This study was not designed to answer whether the evaluations of social support sampled are the result of a biasing effect of current mood on recall. It is likely, however, that individuals who are characterized by an emotionally Open style use their feelings to evaluate their social network. Or, as described by Schwarz (1990), individuals open to the experience of emotion may be more prone to use the "How do I feel about it" heuristic in evaluating their social support network.

Future studies should examine the link between individual differences in physiological measures of affect regulation and social behavior. For example, are individuals who regulate their negative affective reactions (e.g., by lowering their blood pressure after an anger-eliciting situation) better able to handle a frustration-inducing social task? The answer to this question awaits further investigation.

The relation between emotional styles and cognitive personality variables associated to perceptions of social support should also be investigated. Buck's (1989) theory of emotional development predicts that an Open emotional style would develop from being surrounded by an emotionally receptive social environment; that is, each person learns to label and understand his or her inner affective experiences through a social–biofeedback process. Individuals exposed to a social environment that is responsive to their emotional needs are not only likely to be emotionally, open, but also to have developed a positive image of themselves and others. According to Buck (1989, p. 154), the quality of the emotional education received by a person determines much of the quality of that person's social relationships. The links between emotional style and self–other schemas remain open to investigation.

Emotional Styles and Diary Reports of Social Support

Individuals who approached their social network to deal with a daily problem by talking to others to find out more about the situation, getting professional help, talking about their feelings, and accepting sympathy or understanding were more likely to be emotionally Open. The emotionally Open style was not related to the use of avoidant coping strategies on a daily basis. Clearly, seeking out the help of others to cope with a problem is likely to involve retelling the emotionally inducing event, and most likely, the reliving of the affective experience. If an individual is not comfortable with emotional experiences, it is unlikely that he or she would actively seek to reexperience the emotions originally induced by a troubling event.

These results have important implications for social support theory and research. Individual differences in emotion management should be included in studies aimed at understanding enacted social support. The results suggest that an important mediator of the impact of support groups on well-being may be the individual's comfort with emotional experience and expression. Rime, Mesquita, Philoppot, and Boca (1991, p. 439) hypothesized that "through the social sharing of emotion, the person finds opportunities to clarify ambiguous emotional sensations, to cognitively articulate the emotion, to redefine their self-concept, to get coping assistance, and to preserve their cultural integration." Unfortunately, as a result, the lack of sharing of emotional experiences is likely to intensify the emotionally conflicted individual's affect-management style (e.g., ambivalence and lack of clarity; see Emmons & Colby, 1995, for elaboration on emotional conflict and social support).

Emotional Styles and Observer Reports of Support Requested/Provided

With one exception, the scales that comprised the Open emotional style were not related to the observer reports of social support. However, observer reports of the emotional expressiveness of the participant were related to ratings of knowing the participant more intimately. In addition, observers rated participants with an Open emotional style as being more emotionally expressive. Apparently, the self-reported emotional style measures discriminate individuals who are rated by observers as differing in emotional expressiveness.

Observers reported providing more emotional support to those participants they rated as being more expressive. Moreover, observer ratings of knowing the participant more intimately were positively correlated with ratings of emotional expressiveness. However, the results of a multiple-regression analysis revealed that being rated as emotionally expressive, and not how well the observer knew the participant (intimately to casually), predicted being provided with emotional support.

The relation observed between observer-reported emotional expression and the provision of emotional support contributes further evidence for the impact on social support processes of individual differences in affect management. Individuals who are emotionally expressive are more likely to convey clear signals of their need for support to their social network members. Moreover, individuals with a self-reported Open emotional style were rated as being more expressive by observers. These individuals also scored high on the measures of well-being included in this study. As indicated by Manstead (1991a), talking to others about how we feel is generally considered to be beneficial, because it helps to build and maintain relationships, it is a way of seeking support, or it allows the expression of feelings that may otherwise be repressed.

METHODOLOGICAL ISSUES

In this study, we included several indices of social support (self-report, observer report, and diary entries). The results revealed differing patterns of relations between these three indices of support and the emotional styles. This study highlights the importance of sampling social support as a multidimensional construct and, moreover, of recognizing that findings in one aspect of social support may not generalize to others.

The results of this study are limited by several factors. First, individuals were classified into the different emotional styles based only on self-report measures. Future studies should incorporate behavioral indices of the emotional styles. Second, the daily reports did not include a direct measure of avoiding social support. The daily, avoidant coping items only sampled not dealing with the problem directly. As was mentioned earlier, the social network could be used as a distraction and not necessarily as a problem-solving aid. Third, we did not include any measure of the emotional style of the support provider. Sampling the style of the provider may help elucidate social compensatory mechanisms in the use of support networks. Perhaps it is the provider's style that is the more important determinant of support, and not the style of the person in need (aside from expressing the need for support). Last, the support observers were selected by the research participants. Therefore, the relationships sampled can be considered an average of the support available to each participant. Different results may be obtained if the observer reports were divided by type of relationship (e.g., spouses vs. roommates).

The interdependence of affect and social life has been recognized by researchers interested in understanding emotion and mood (Averill, 1980; Buck, 1984, 1989; Lazarus, 1991b; Manstead, 1991a; Moore and Isen, 1990). This close link is well represented by Zajonc (1980, p. 753), who states that "affect dominates social interaction, and it is the major currency in which social interaction is transacted." Given the acknowledged symbiosis between social life and affect, the shortage of research in understanding emotion management and its repercussions for social support is surprising. Emotional experiences require social outlets for their satisfactory completion (Rime et al., 1991). Likewise, understanding social support processes requires considering emotional styles.

REFERENCES

Averill, J. R. (1980). A constructivist view of emotion. In R. Plutchik & H. Kellerman (Eds.), *Emotion: Theory, research and experience: Vol. 1. Theories of emotion* (pp. 305–339). New York: Academic Press.

Averill, J. R., & Thomas-Knowles, C. (1991). Emotional creativity. In K. T. Strongman (Ed.), *International review of studies on emotion* (pp. 269–299). Chichester, UK: Wiley.

Averill, J. R., & Nunley, E. P. (1992). *Voyages of the heart: Living an emotionally creative life*. New York: Free Press.

Baron, R. M., & Kenny, D. A. (1986). The moderator–mediator variable distinction in social psychological research: Conceptual, strategic, and statistical considerations. *Journal of Personality and Social Psychology*, *51*, 1173–1182.

Barrera, M. Jr., Sandler, I. N., & Ramsey, T. B. (1981). Preliminary development of a scale of social support: Studies on college students. *American Journal of Consulting Psychology*, *9*, 435–447.

Buck, R. (1984). *The communication of emotion*. New York: Guilford.

Buck, R. (1989). Emotional communication in personal relationships: A developmental–interactionist view. In C. Hendrick (Ed.), *Review of personality and social psychology: Vol. 10. Close relationships.* (pp. 144–163). Beverly Hills, CA: Sage Publications.

Catanzaro, S. J., & Mearns, J. (1990). Measuring generalized expectancies for negative mood regulation: Initial scale development and implications. *Journal of Personality Assessment*, *54*, 546–563.

Clark, M. S., & Isen, A. (1982). Toward understanding the relationship between feeling states and social behavior. In A. H. Hastorf & A. M. Isen (Eds.), *Cognitive social psychology* (pp. 73–108). New York: Elsevier/North-Holland.

Cohen, S., & McKay, G. (1983). Social support, stress and the buffering hypothesis: A theoretical analysis. In A. Baum, E. Singer, & S. E. Taylor (Eds.), *Handbook of psychology and health* (Vol. 4, pp. 253–267). Hillsdale, NJ: Erlbaum.

Cohen, S., Mermelstein, R., Kamarck, T., & Hoberman, H. M. (1985). Measuring the functional components of social support. In I. G. Sarason & B. Sarason (Eds.), *Social support: Theory, research and applications* (pp. 73–94). The Hague, The Netherlands: Martinus Nijhoff.

Colby, P. M., & Emmons, R. A. (1994). *Emotional styles, mood accuracy and the experience of daily mood.* Poster presented at the 74th Annual Convention of the Western Psychological Association, Kona, HI.

Colby, P. M., Rabin, N., & Emmons, R. A. (1994). *Intimacy strivings and well-being: The role of social support.* Poster presented at the 102nd Annual Convention of the American Psychological Association, Los Angeles, CA.

Costa, P. T., & McCrae, R. R. (1985). *Manual for the NEO Personality Inventory,* Odessa, FL: Psychological Assessment Resources.

Crowne, D. P., & Marlowe D. (1960). A new scale of social desirability independent of psychopathology. *Journal of Consulting Psychology, 24,* 349–354.

Depue, R. A., Slater, J. F., Wolfstetter-Kausch, H., Klein, D., Goplerud, E., & Farr, D. (1981). A behavioral paradigm for identifying persons at risk for bipolar affective disorder: A conceptual framework and five validational studies. *Journal of Abnormal Psychology Monographs, 90,* 381–437.

Derogatis, L. R., & Spence, P. M. (1982). *The Brief Symptom Inventory (BSI).* Baltimore: Clinical Psychometric Research.

Diener, E. (1984). Subjective well-being. *Psychological Bulletin, 95,* 542–575.

Diener, E., & Emmons, R. (1984). The independence of positive and negative affect. *Journal of Personality and Social Psychology, 47,* 1105–1117.

Diener, E., Emmons, R. A., Larsen, R., & Griffin, S. (1985). The Satisfaction with Life Scale. *Journal of Personality Assessment, 49,* 71–75.

Emmons, R. A., & Colby, P. M. (1995). Emotional conflict and well-being: Relation to pereceived availability, daily utilization and observer reports of social support. *Journal of Personality and Social Psychology, 68,* 947–959.

Folkman, S., & Lazarus, R. S. (1980). An analysis of coping in a middle-aged community sample. *Journal of Health and Social Behavior, 21,* 219–239.

Fordyce, M. W. (1988). A review of research on the happiness measure: A sixty second index of happiness and mental health. *Social Indicators Research, 20,* 355–381.

Frijda, N. H. (1986). *The emotions.* New York: Cambridge University Press.

Goleman, D. (1995). *Emotional intelligence.* New York: Bantam Books.

Greenberg, L. S. (1993). Emotion and change processes in psychotherapy. In M. Lewis & J. Haviland (Eds.), *Handbook of emotions* (pp. 499–508). New York: Guilford.

Heller, K. (1979). The effects of social support: Prevention and treatment implications. In A. P. Goldstein & F. H. Kanfer (Eds.), *Maximizing treatment gains: Transfer enhancement in psychotherapy* (pp. 353–382). New York: Academic Press.

House, J. S. (1981). *Work, stress and social support.* Reading, MA: Addison-Wesley.

Isen, A. M. (1987). Positive affect, cognitive processes, and social behavior. In L. Berkowitz (Ed.), *Advances in experimental social psychology* (Vol. 20, pp. 203–253). New York: Academic Press.

Jolly, E. A. (1987, August). Social structure effects on emotional experience. *Dissertation Abstracts International,* V48(n2-B), 597.

King, L. A., & Emmons, R. A. (1990). Conflict over emotional expression: Psychological and physical correlates. *Journal of Personality and Social Psychology, 58,* 864–877.

King, L. A., & Emmons, R. A. (1991). Psychological, physical, and interpersonal correlates of emotional expressiveness, conflict, and control. *European Journal of Personality, 5,* 131–150.

King, L. A., Emmons, R. A., & Woodley, S. (1992). The structure of inhibition. *Journal of Research in Personality, 26,* 85–102.

Lakey, B., & Cassady, P. B. (1990). Cognitive processes in perceived social support. *Journal of Personality and Social Psychology, 59,* 337–343.

Lane, R. D., Quinlan, D. M., Schwartz, G. E., Walker, P. A., & Zeitlin, S. B. (1990). The Levels of Emotional

Awareness Scale: A cognitive-developmental measure of emotion. *Journal of Personality Assessment*, *55*, 124-134.

Lane, R. D., & Schwartz, G. E. (1987). Levels of emotional awareness: A cognitive-developmental theory and its application to psychopathology. *American Journal of Psychiatry*, *48*, 84-91.

Larsen, R. J., & Diener, E. (1987). Affect intensity as an individual difference characteristic: A review. *Journal of Research in Personality*, *21*, 1-39.

Lazarus, R. S. (1991a). Progress on a cognitive-motivational-relational theory of emotion. *American Psychologist*, *46*, 819-834.

Lazarus, R. S. (1991b). *Emotion and adaptation*. New York: Oxford University Press.

Mankoski, R., & Wyer, R. S., Jr. (1993). *Perceived social support and the processing of hypothetical social interactions: The effect of relationship perspective*. Paper presented at the annual meeting of the Midwestern Psychological Association, Chicago, IL.

Manstead, A. S. (1991a). Emotion in social life. *Cognition and Emotion*, *5*, 353-362.

Manstead, A. S. (1991b). Expressiveness as an individual difference. In R. S. Feldman & B. Rime (Eds.), *Fundamentals of non-verbal behavior* (pp. 285-328). New York: Cambridge University Press.

McCrae, R. R. (1993). Openness to experience as a basic dimension of personality. *Imagination, Cognition, and Personality*, *13*, 39-55.

McCrae, R. R., & Costa, P. T. (1985). Openness to experience. In R. Hogan & W. H. Jones (Eds.), *Perspectives in personality* (Vol. 1, pp. 145-172). Greenwich, CT: JAI Press.

Mearns, J. (1991). Coping with a breakup. Negative mood regulation expectancies and depression following the end of a romantic relationship. *Journal of Personality and Social Psychology*, *60*, 327-334.

Millham, J., & Kellog, R. W. (1980). Need for social approval: Impression management or self-deception? *Journal of Research in Personality*, *14*, 445-457.

Moore, B. S., & Isen, A. M. (1990). Affect and social behavior. In B. S. Moore & A. M. Isen (Eds.), *Affect and social behavior* (pp. 1-21). Cambridge, UK: Cambridge University Press.

Paulhus, D. L. (1987). Self-deception and impression management in test responses. In A. Angleitner & J. S. Wiggins (Eds.), *Personality assessment via questionnaires* (pp. 145-165). New York: Springer-Verlag.

Rime, B., Mesquita, B., Philoppot, P., & Boca, S. (1991). Beyond the emotional event: Six studies on the social sharing of emotion. *Cognition and Emotion*, *5*, 435-465.

Rogers, D., & Nesshoever, W. (1987). The construction and preliminary validation of a scale for measuring emotional control. *Personality and Individual Differences*, *8*, 527-534.

Roth, S., & Cohen, L. J. (1986). Approach, avoidance, and coping with stress. *American Psychologist*, *41*, 813-819.

Saarni, C. (1984). Observing children's use of display rules: Age and sex differences. *Child Development*, *55*, 1504-1513.

Sackeim, H. A., & Gur, R. C. (1979). Self-deception, other-deception, and self-reported psychopathology. *Journal of Consulting and Clinical Psychology*, *47*, 213-215.

Salovey, P., Hsee, C. K., & Mayer, J. D. (1993). Emotional intelligence and the self-regulation of affect. In D. M. Wegner & J. W. Pennebaker (Eds.), *Handbook of mental control* (pp. 259-277). Englewood Cliffs, NJ: Prentice-Hall.

Salovey, P., & Mayer, J. D. (1990). Emotional intelligence. *Imagination, Cognition, and Personality*, *9*, 185-211.

Sandvick, E., Diener, E., & Siedlitz, L. (1993). Subjective well-being: The convergence and stability of self-report and non self-report measures. *Journal of Personality*, *61*, 317-342.

Sarason, B. R., Pierce, G. R., Shearin, E. N., Sarason, I. G., Waltz, J. A., & Poppe, L. (1991). Perceived social support and working models of the self and actual others. *Journal of Personality and Social Psychology*, *60*, 273-287.

Sarason, I. G., Sarason, B. R., & Shearin, E. N. (1986). Social support as an individual differnce variable: Its stability, origins, and relational aspects. *Journal of Personality and Social Psychology*, *50*, 845-855.

Schwarz, N. (1990). Feelings as information: Informational and motivational functions of affective states. In E. T. Higgins & R. M. Sorrentino (Eds.), *Handbook of motivation and cognition* (Vol. 2, pp. 527-561). New York: Guilford.

Schwarz, N., & Clore, G. L. (1988). How do I feel about it? Informative functions of affective states. In K. Fiedler & J. Forgas (Eds.), *Affect, cognition and social behavior* (pp. 44-62). Toronto: Hogrefe International.

Thoits, P. A. (1985). Social support processes and psychological well-being: Theoretical possibilities. In I. G. Sarason & B. Sarason (Eds.), *Social support:Theory, research, and applications* (pp. 51-72). The Hague, The Netherlands: Martinus Nijhoff.

Turner, R. J. (1981). Social support as a contingency in psychological well-being. *Journal of Health and Social Behavior, 23,* 145-159.

Vaux, A.C., Burda, P. C., & Stewart, D. (1986). Orientation toward utilization of support resources. *Journal of Community Psychology, 14,* 159-170.

Weinberger, D. A. (1990). The construct validity of the repressive-defensive coping style. In J. L. Singer (Ed.), *Repression and dissociation: Defense mechanisms and personality styles* (pp. 337-386). Chicago: University of Chicago Press.

Weinberger, D. A., & Schwartz, G. E. (1990). Distress and restraint as superordinate dimensions of self-reported adjustment: A typological approach. *Journal of Personality, 58,* 381-417.

Wessman, A. E., & Ricks, D. F. (1966). *Mood and personality.* New York: Holt, Rinehart & Winston.

Zajonc, R. B. (1980). Feeling and thinking: Preferences need no inferences. *American Psychologist, 35,* 151-175.

AUTHOR INDEX

SUBJECT INDEX

489